THE CANADIAN
BED &
BREAKFAST
GUIDE

18TH EDITION

MARYBETH MOYER

Fitzhenry & Whiteside

This issue of **The Canadian Bed and Breakfast Guide** *is dedicated to my husband Jay, who has laughed with me at the funny things and listened to my raving at the frustrating things. His assistance with host contact, his work on the maps, "Sources of Information for the Traveller" and various other portions of the project is invaluable. He is truly "The wind beneath my wings."*

The Canadian Bed & Breakfast Guide, 18th Edition
Copyright © 2007 Marybeth Moyer

Fitzhenry and Whiteside Limited
195 Allstate Parkway
Markham, Ontario L3R 4T8

In the United States:
311 Washington Street,
Brighton, Massachusetts 02135

www.fitzhenry.ca   godwit@fitzhenry.ca

Fitzhenry & Whiteside acknowledges with thanks the Canada Council for the Arts, and the Ontario Arts Council for their support of our publishing program.
We acknowledge the financial support of the Government of Canada through the Book Publishing Industry Development Program (BPIDP) for our publishing activities.

Library and Archives Canada has catalogued this publication as follows:

The Canadian bed and breakfast guide.
Annual (irregular).   Began with 1983 ed.
Imprint varies.
Includes some text in French.
Some issues have title: Canadian bed & breakfast guide. ISSN 0836-5717
ISBN 1-55041-368-6 (18th edition)

1. Bed and breakfast accommodations – Canada – Directories. ?I.
Title: Canadian bed & breakfast guide.?
TX910.C2P35   647'.9471   C88-039020-4 rev?
United States Cataloguing-in-Publication Data

Moyer, Marybeth.
The Canadian bed and breakfast guide / Marybeth Moyer
18th ed.
[420] p. : ill., photos., maps ; cm.
Includes index.   Included a birdwatching section.
ISBN: 1-55041-368-6 (pbk.)
1 Bed and breakfast accommodations – Canada – Directories. I. Title.
647.9471/03/05 dc22   TX907.5.C2C36 2006

Cover design by Kerry Plumley
Interior design by Darrell McCalla
Printed and bound in Canada

1 3 5 7 9 10 8 6 4 2

CONTENTS

UNDERSTANDING THE
BED AND BREAKFAST LISTINGS

The actual town in which the B&B is located is given in the address, but each B&B may choose to be listed under a nearby town that may be better known to the traveller. The maps give you the relative location of towns in which listed B&Bs are located.

All means of contacting the B&B are provided and the B&B web site, when one is available, is provided as a source for additional information on the B&B. Host names are, normally provided.

The Canadian Bed and Breakfast Guide includes a descriptive section in each listing in which the host in his or her own words provides information on his B&B that he believes will be useful to the traveller in making a decision on choosing accommodations. This space is limited so some are more inventive than others in the way they compress information. Some are more lyrical in their narrative, others more limited in expression. Whatever the presentation, it is the host talking, the person directly responsible for your pleasure and satisfaction. We chose this approach as it supports the B&B reality. At a B&B the quality of the experience for the traveller is irrevocably tied to the personality and character of the host. The ability of the host to make you feel welcome, to provide genuine hospitality at an appropriate level of involvement is key. While facilities are important, the host's persona is paramount. In an hotel, facilities, services and professional staff are everything. The host is a concept not a real person.

Hence the Marita Dreger quote concerning The Guide

> *"it beautifully reflects the people and places that make Canada special."*

The factual description of the B&B its features, attributes and items of general interest such as local activities are listed at the bottom of each description. It is always a good idea to phone for more details on the B&B you have selected if you have any concerns about any of its features. This applies in particular to accessibility, if a guest has any special physical needs, or to pets either in the B&B or if you travel with your pet. You should also mention dietary needs, so that the host can prepare to accommodate these. You will find some categories in the feature list have no entries, i.e. AIR, with no following information indicates that no air conditioning is provided. This is often not necessary in some climates. Other categories may not have following material because changes were being planned at the time that the listing was made or that the host prefers to discuss these items with the prospective guest.

Pictures are supplied by the host in the best form available. Most hosts choose to show the exterior view of their property, but in some cases rooms or other features will be shown. A few hosts did not supply photos. This should not be viewed as indication of a problem with the B&B but rather a difficulty in obtaining a suitable photo. A frequent challenge for the host in getting a suitable photo is tree coverage. That often makes for an attractive B&B but an impossible photo opportunity.

Occasionally an additional phone number may be listed in the description.

What is a Bed and Breakfast

Bed and Breakfast is the quintessential cottage business. The cottage is the business. It is the least commercial form of accommodation service available, with most hosts going out of their way to provide an ambiance that is free from the commercial nature of hotels, resorts and motels or inns. The distinguishing feature of the B&B from other forms of accommodation services is hospitality. The host of the fine B&B establishes an ambience of warmth, friendliness and welcome beyond what is possible for more commercially oriented establishments.

There are variations of this fast growing accommodations service but the version generally considered to be the standard form is the home that has been put to use for the purpose of providing accommodations for travellers, and in which the hosts make their full time residence.

Homes put to use in this manner vary from those in which no special decorative changes were made or renovations undertaken, to those designed to be operated as bed and breakfast homes.

In most cases the B&B residence would fall somewhere between the two extremes with décor carefully chosen, bathrooms added and furnishings especially selected to give the home a distinctive character.

As the name implies breakfast is a standard offering of the B&B home. The actual meal varies from host to host with continental, home-baked, full breakfast and self-catered breakfasts in which the host will provide food and facilities for preparation. The continental breakfast will vary from the standard hot beverage, juice and a pastry to that plus a selection of pastries and cereal and fruit. Home-baked emphasizes the hosts efforts in putting quality home prepared food on the table.

One of the special pleasures of using B&B service is to experience the unique attractiveness of many of the B&B homes available to the guest. Many are of heritage quality, restored and furnished with period antiques. Many offer architectural features of interest or are unique in other ways. The variations are numerous and provide for an ongoing experience of pleasant surprises reflecting the character and life style of the hosts who reside in these homes.

There are many reasons for a couple or a person to turn their home into a B&B. The financial motive is only a part of what makes a person interested in becoming a provider of accommodations for travellers. It can be an interesting alternative way to provide a second income for the family. It gives hosts a chance to show their unique property to others. It brings new relationships, which frequently develop into friendship. Many hosts simply find it an enjoyable seasonal occupation to bring some fresh faces into their lives.

The above qualities of the B&B have made it one of the fastest, possibly the fastest growing form of accommodation services in Canada.

Why Choose
Bed and Breakfast Accommodation

• **To connect to the area.**

B&B hosts are well known for their local knowledge and share that knowledge with their guests. Selecting B&B accommodation in an area that you will visit on more than one occasion will give you a place to which you can return, where you know you will be welcome and where you will be greeted by familiar people who will be pleased to see you back as much for who you are as for the income you provide.

• **To have your accommodations in non-commercial areas.**

In the main B&Bs will be away from the busy commercial centres of town, located in quiet residential areas, often with fine gardens, tree lined streets, pleasant neighbourhoods.

• **For the social benefit from establishing new relationships with both hosts and guests.**

Hosts and guests often establish a relationship beyond the commercial nature of its origin and become friends. With the usual common breakfast table, conversing with other guests is the norm and here too relationships can develop. Interchange of local information between guests often leads to maximizing the enjoyment of the visit.

• **To enjoy the hospitality of the well hosted B&B.**

The primary quality of the fine B&B is hospitality that goes beyond what is necessary for commercial success. You will feel truly welcome in a good B&B.

• **To avoid crowds and lines and inconvenience.**

There will be no crowded lobbies, no line-ups for breakfast; no rush to make sure you get the next cab at the curb at a B&B. You will find them far more relaxing and easy going than other types of accommodation. You will not find yourself parking in an underground or remote parking lot. Parking will be on premise or very close.

• For a variety of experiences.

B&Bs are as varied as their hosts because of the individual personalities of the hosts. From historic homes to contemporary homes, to farm homes, to homes of architectural uniqueness, plus others you will find new experiences. The hosts themselves have a variety of backgrounds that keeps the B&B experience free from the boredom of sameness.

• For value

While you may chose a B&B for its price. You are more likely to choose B&B accommodation for value. Often they are not the cheapest form of accommodation in any given area but you can normally expect that what you receive for what you pay will provide the best value available.

• Breakfasts

In the B&B serving a "full breakfast" as it is generally termed, the dining experience is usually excellent in quality and quantity to a point where lunch may not be wanted. When selecting your B&B check out the breakfast service it varies from full to continental to self-catered.

GUEST SUGGESTIONS FOR MAXIMIZING B&B ENJOYMENT

My husband and I have had the pleasure of providing the first opportunity for many to enjoy bed and breakfast accommodations. We have often been asked questions about using B&Bs. There are differences from other forms of accommodation but they present no serious challenge. To assist the uninitiated, we provide these common sense suggestions. You will find they closely resemble what the thoughtful guest will practice when visiting family or friends.

1. While drop in guests are often welcomed by the B&B, phoning ahead when you can is recommended. (Some B&Bs will only take guests that have an advance reservation.) In addition to giving the host notice of a guest and of course making sure that space is available it also gives you a chance to get some feeling for the reception you will receive and the opportunity to assess to some degree, the desirability of your choice. It also gives the host the opportunity to get some advance knowledge of the person to be welcomed. In some locations, advance booking of several months is necessary, to be assured of the time desired.

2. Try to avoid phoning your prospective hosts prior to 11:00 am. Remember they will very likely be busy with the breakfast and other needs of guests in residence or checking out. Phoning after 10:00 pm can also be a problem for hosts depending on their life styles. Remember a true B&B has no front desk and the host performs all service functions. That includes early rising for breakfast preparation.

3. Do your best to provide your host with an arrival time and phone to advise of significant change in that time. The host has a variety of responsibilities such as shopping for your breakfast needs, etc. that may require being away from the B&B. Occasionally, a host may find it necessary to leave a note to welcome the guest. Do not be offended by this, time away from the B&B may be unavoidable.

4. While late night arrivals are some times unavoidable, remember that your host carries all the responsibilities including early mornings to get guest breakfasts prepared. Hosts recognize that not all guests can arrange their time to the advantage of all and will do their best to accommodate the late arrival.

5. Remember that a B&B is a small accommodation facility and a cancellation of a reservation can make a major dent in the hosts income. Cancellations cannot, of course, always be avoided. Be prepared for a cancellation charge. Ask about cancellation policy when you make your booking.

6. Most B&Bs will not have separate guest phone lines. So remember that when using a hosts phone you are tying up the hosts line for other reservations and personal use and keep the call as short as you can.

7. Advise your host of special needs such as dietary needs in advance. B&Bs are very flexible but cannot stock all special needs.

8. Most B&Bs serve breakfast at a communal table, at a fixed time and their breakfast preparation is geared to that. If that time is not suitable to you, ask in advance to see if a change can be arranged; usually it can. Remember too, that unless you advise your host otherwise, breakfast will be prepared for you and failure to show at the sitting is a costly inconvenience to the host.

9. Check in advance on methods of payment, many B&Bs do take credit or debit cards, personal or travellers cheques but many do not. If you are travelling from another country remember that you will get your best rates of exchange at banks. Most B&Bs will be fair in the exchange but may not know the current rate and will also face a service charge when depositing foreign currency at their bank. A rate within 5% of the official rate should be considered fair.

10. Hospitality is the dominant feature of the good B&B. Service is the dominant feature of the good hotel. If it is important to you, to have room service, valet service, etc. the B&B may not be the best accommodation for you. On the other hand you will not be constantly tipping for each service you receive.

11. Most B&B homes will have some means of notifying guests about certain aspects of their stay. If these are not readily apparent or made known by the host on your arrival, it will pay to ask the host for guidelines on house use while you are in residence.

12. With the hosts acting as staff, preparing guest rooms between the departure of one guest and the arrival of the next, can be challenging. This can make observation of check out time more important in the B&B than in the hotel or motel. Many hosts just want full access to the room at the stated time to make it ready for the next guest's arrival, and will allow guests to use other facilities as available, until they depart. Do not assume that this is the case. Always have a clear understanding with your host on check out policy.

13. Many B&Bs are adult oriented. It pays to check with your intended hosts on the suitability of their home for children. Frequently, host pets or such location factors as unprotected waterfronts make the home a risk for children.

14. If you travel with your pet be sure that you pick a B&B that accepts pets or can arrange local pet accommodation. Never arrive at a B&B with a pet without first checking with the host on arrangements they make for the pet and on the suitability of any particular pet.

In reading the foregoing remember that there is a considerable amount of generalization and that exceptions can be expected.

Acknowledgements
and Credits

While compiling the information for the 18th edition of *The Canadian Bed and Breakfast Guide*, my husband and I have been privileged to speak with many B&B owners across our great country. We have also, over the past several years, been able to stay at many of the B&B homes listed in The Guide. What a great experience! The hosts become our friends and we never cease to marvel at the unique ambience and warm hospitality of each one.

I would like to express my appreciation to the many people who have assisted in the preparation of the 18th edition. It would not have been possible without them. Following is our key group:

My children, who always express their interest in my activities, and my husband Jay, who plays a most vital role in the preparation of this work.

To them I extend sincere thanks and love.

Bill Janzen, of Future Access, who does the programming for the website and fields all manner of panic calls in his usual calm manner.

Laurie Green for her excellent skills in web design and site promotion.

Annie Burkitt who took our rough ideas on turning the cover into a presentation of the broader B&B experience for the guest, and who works so skillfully and industriously on the maps.

Yvan Bureau, who has given beyond the call of duty in assisting with host translations and the development of the French portion of the project.

The B&B hosts, who have been with us in the book and on the website for many years, as well as the new B&B hosts who have joined us this year.

To my publishers, Fitzhenry and Whiteside, who are willing to share their experience and enthusiasm for The Guide, as well as listen to our new ideas, I express my sincere thanks. We are proud to be associated with such a fine Canadian house.

Listings of Bed and Breakfasts by Province, Territory and Towns

BRITISH COLUMBIA
AND VANCOUVER ISLAND

CANADIAN BED AND BREAKFAST GUIDE

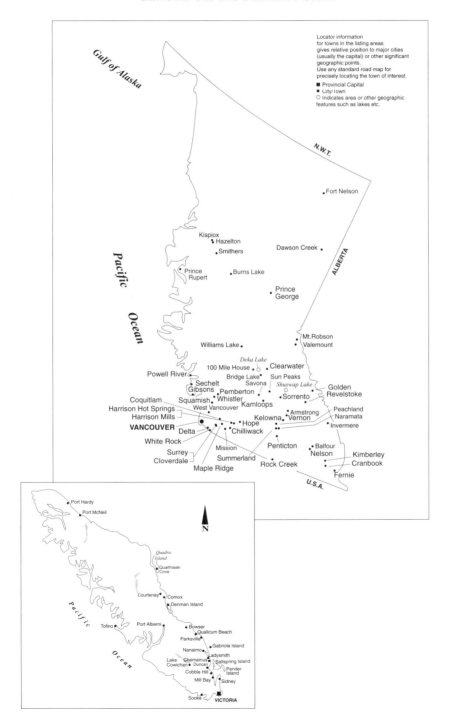

Locator information
for towns in the listing areas
gives relative position to major cities
(usually the capital) or other significant
geographic points.
Use any standard road map for
precisely locating the town of interest.

■ Provincial Capital
● City/Town
○ Indicates area or other geographic
features such as lakes etc.

Gulf of Alaska

N.W.T.

● Fort Nelson

Kispiox
↘ Hazelton
● Smithers

Dawson Creek ●

ALBERTA

Pacific

● Prince
Rupert

● Burns Lake

● Prince
George

Ocean

Williams Lake ●

● Mt.Robson
● Valemount

Deka Lake
100 Mile House ○ ● Clearwater
Powell River ● Bridge Lake ● Sun Peaks
● Sechelt   Savona ● *Shuswap Lake* ○ Golden
Gibsons ● Pemberton ●   ● Sorrento ● Revelstoke
Coquitlam ● ● Whistler Kamloops
Squamish ● ● Kelowna ● ● Armstrong Peachland ●
Harrison Hot Springs West Vancouver ● Vernon ● Naramata
Harrison Mills   ● ● Hope ● Invermere
VANCOUVER ● ● Chilliwack
Delta
White Rock ●   ● Balfour
Surrey ● Mission ● Penticton ● ● Nelson ● Kimberley
Cloverdale Summerland ●   ● Cranbook
Maple Ridge ● Rock Creek ●   ● Fernie

U.S.A.

N

Port Hardy ●
Port McNeil ●

*Quadra
Island*
● Quaithiaski
/Cove

Courtenay ● ● Comox
● Denman Island

Pacific

Tofino ● Port Alberni ● ● Bowser
● Qualicum Beach
Parksville ●
Nanaimo ● ● Gabriola Island
Lake Chemainus ● ● Ladysmith
Cowichan ● ● Duncan ● Saltspring Island
Cobble Hill ● ● Pender
Mill Bay ● Island
● Sidney
Ocean
Sooke ● **VICTORIA** ■

1

100 MILE HOUSE *(south-central BC)*

Attwood Creek Ranch Bale, Bed & Breakfast

(Christine Maeder)

7244 Watch Lake Rd, PO Box 39, Lone Butte, BC, V0K 1X0
www.attwoodcreekranch.com
E-mail cmaeder@bcinternet.net

250-395-1159

Welcome to the Attwood Creek Ranch in beautiful South Cariboo. Sleep in one of the guest rooms or in the beautiful heritage homestead and enjoy a delicious, full "cowboy" breakfast. There are numerous activities in the area, including, canoeing, white-water rafting, hiking, birdwatching, golfing and mountain biking. We are located just 20 minutes from 100 Mile House, between Lone Butte on Hwy 24 and Watch Lake/Green Lake. The perfect place for a family holiday.

ROOMS Upper floor, **Baths** Private, Shared with guest, **Beds** Queen, Pullout sofa, **Smoking** Outside, **OTHERS** Open all year, Pets in residence, Pets welcome, **PAYMENT** Cash, Trvl's cheques, **BREAKFASTS** Full, Continental, **AMENITIES** Barbecue, Kitchen, Fridge, **THINGS TO DO** Trail nearby, Golf, Fishing, Museums, Art, Attractions, Cross-country skiing, Downhill skiing, Swimming, Horseback riding, Beach, Birdwatching, **LANGUAGE** Eng., Ger., **PRICE** (2 persons) 75–80 **(check with hosts for pricing details)**

100 MILE HOUSE

Maverick Moose B&B

(John and Kay Buck)

87 Blaine Rd, RR #1, Lone Butte, BC, V0K 1X0
www.bbcanada.com/mavmoose
E-mail mavmoose@telus.net

250-593-0173
Fax 250-593-4259

A true Cariboo Country setting on Deka Lake shore. Enjoy the comfort of our traditional log home. Watch sunsets from the deck, fire pit or hot tub. Great fly-fishing area, walking trails, cross-country skiing, ice fishing or just sit and watch Mother Nature. A stress-free experience, be it one night or more. From Hwy 24, take Horse Lake Rd 4.5 km. Right on Mahood 4.6 km. Right on Burgess 2.7 km. Right on Womack 2.1 km. Left on Sangster .2 km on Beazley. Follow signs.

ROOMS Upper floor, **Baths** Shared with guest, **Beds** Double, **Smoking** Outside, **OTHERS** Rural, Open all year, Pets in residence, Pets welcome, **PAYMENT** Cheques accepted, Cash, Trvl's cheques, **BREAKFASTS** Full, **AMENITIES** Central TV, Central phone, Whirlpool, Fridge, Lounge, Patio, **THINGS TO DO** Trail nearby, Rental canoe or boat, Golf, Fishing, Cross-country skiing, Swimming, Horseback riding, Birdwatching, **LANGUAGE** Eng., **PRICE** (2 persons) 75–85 **(check with hosts for pricing details)**

ARMSTRONG *(southeastern BC)*

A Country Haven Bed & Breakfast

(Betty Anne and Ron Neufeld)

1796 Rashdale Rd, Armstrong, BC, V0E 1B3
www.acountryhavenbb.com
E-mail relax@acountryhavenbb.com

250-546-2921
TFr 1-866-751-8175

A gorgeous, peaceful 80-acre working farm which offers beautiful views, decks, organic menu choices, country walks, amazing beds and luxurious rooms with handcrafted quilts. Watch for wildlife from the garden bench. Poolside Room: King, sofabed, satellite TV, ensuite, patio door. Raspberry Room: King/twins, sat.TV, private bath/entrance. Mountain View Room: Queen, DVD TV, private bath. Box stalls/paddocks. Take McCleery off Hwy 97A between Armstrong and Enderby. Stay right and take Rashdale up the hill.

ROOMS Ground floor, Private entrance, **Baths** Private, Ensuite, **Beds** King, Queen, Twin, Pullout sofa, **Air** Central, **Smoking** Outside, **In Room** TV, **OTHERS** Rural, Open all year, **PAYMENT** Visa, MC, Cash, Trvl's cheques, **BREAKFASTS** Full, Home-baked, **AMENITIES** Central TV, Central phone, Swimming pool, Fridge, Hot bev. bar, Lounge, Patio, Central VCR/DVD, **THINGS TO DO** Trail nearby, Rental canoe or boat, Golf, Fishing, Museums, Art, Theatre, Entertainment, Attractions, Wineries/Breweries, Shopping, Cross-country skiing, Downhill skiing, Swimming, Beach, Birdwatching, Antiquing, **LANGUAGE** Eng., **PRICE** (2 persons) 75–99 **(check with hosts for pricing details)**

BALFOUR *(southeastern BC)*

Murray Pond B&B

(Janet McCulloch)

Box 34, 552 Glady Rd, Balfour, BC, V0G 1C0
www.murraypond.com
E-mail info@murraypond.com

250-229-5204

Murray Pond Bed & Breakfast is a quiet retreat of relaxation and tranquility, moments from the heart of Balfour. Private entrance, king bed and twin sofabed, both with premium mattresses and fine linens. Huge ensuite bath with antique tub and shower. Private patio with lily pond. Full breakfast with home baking. A short walk to beach, pubs, fast food, fine dining, grocery and liquor store, coffee shop and bakery. A short drive to hot springs, trails, parks, skiing, boating and mountain climbing.

ROOMS Ground floor, Private entrance, **Baths** Private, Ensuite, **Beds** King, Double, Twin, **Smoking** Outside, **In Room** Thermostat, TV, Internet , VCR/DVD, **OTHERS** Rural, Adult, Open all year, Pets in residence, **PAYMENT** Cheques accepted, Cash, Trvl's cheques, **BREAKFASTS** Full, Continental, Home-baked, **AMENITIES** Barbecue, Fridge, Hot bev. bar, Patio, **THINGS TO DO** Trail nearby, Rental canoe or boat, Golf, Fishing, Museums, Art, Theatre, Entertainment, Attractions, Shopping, Cross-country skiing, Downhill skiing, Tennis, Swimming, Beach, **LANGUAGE** Eng., **PRICE** (2 persons) 95–120 **(check with hosts for pricing details)**

BOWSER
(north of Nanaimo, Vancouver Island)

Shoreline Bed and Breakfast

(Dave and Audrie Sands)

4969 Shoreline Dr, Bowser, BC, V0R 1G0
www.shorelinebnb.ca
E-mail info@shorelinebnb.ca

250-757-9807
Fax 250-757-9807

We offer you a waterfront bedroom with private bathroom, and a walk-on beach on Baynes Sound with a lighthouse on an island in front of your windows. On sunny days, breakfast is on the oceanfront deck or in our new waterfront gazebo, and always includes a fruit bowl, our own entree features like smoked salmon omelets, scrambled egg torte or smoked salmon quiche, lots of hash browns and back bacon and fresh tea, coffee and juices. Find us at Deep Bay, off Hwy 19A, on the east coast of Vancouver Island.

ROOMS Lower floor, Private entrance, **Baths** Private, **Beds** Queen, **Smoking** Outside, **In Room** Thermostat, TV, **OTHERS** Rural, Adult, Open all year, Pets in residence, Pets welcome, **PAYMENT** Visa, MC, Cash, Trvl's cheques, **BREAKFASTS** Full, **AMENITIES** Patio, **THINGS TO DO** Trail nearby, Rental canoe or boat, Golf, Fishing, Museums, Art, Theatre, Attractions, Shopping, Swimming, Beach, Birdwatching, **LANGUAGE** Eng., **PRICE** (2 persons) 90–90 **(check with hosts for pricing details)**

BRIDGE LAKE *(south-central BC)*

Hawthorn Acres Bed & Breakfast

(Lorraine and Frank Jerema)

6847 Judson Rd, Bridge Lake, BC, V0K 1E0
www.bbcanada.com/7026.html
E-mail hawthorn@telus.net

250-593-2384
Fax 250-593-2347

Peaceful farm setting; well-appointed, bright rooms in spacious modern country home. Large comfortable sitting lounge w/TV, fridge/coffeemaker. Walking trails, excellent bird and wildlife viewing, close to many lakes, resident animals. Cash/personal cheques only. Pets welcome. Single, $50, Double, $60, Queen, $70. We're 61 km west of Little Fort Hwy 24, turn on Judson Rd 8 km; 45 km from Jct 97 and 24. Call for directions. Mailing address: C16 Crossroads, RR #1, Lone Butte, BC, V0K 1X0.

ROOMS Ground floor, Private entrance, **Baths** Private, Shared with guest, **Beds** Queen, Double, Single or cots, Pullout sofa, **Smoking** Outside, **OTHERS** Rural, Seasonal, Additional meals, Pets in residence, Pets welcome, **PAYMENT** Cheques accepted, Cash, **BREAKFASTS** Full, Continental, Home-baked, **AMENITIES** Central TV, Central phone, Fridge, Lounge, Patio, Central VCR/DVD, **THINGS TO DO** Trail nearby, Golf, Fishing, Attractions, Cross-country skiing, Downhill skiing, Swimming, Horseback riding, Birdwatching, Antiquing, **LANGUAGE** Eng., **PRICE** (2 persons) 50–70 **(check with hosts for pricing details)**

BURNS LAKE *(north-central BC, between Smithers and Prince George)*

Ninth Ave Guest House

(Jack and Marg Nickel)

530 – 9th Ave, Burns Lake, BC, V0J 1E0
www.angelfire.com/bc3/ninthavguesthouse
E-mail nickel99@telus.net

250-692-3618
Fax 250-692-3634

Ninth Ave Guest House "bed & breakfast" is along Hwy 16, 226 km west of Prince George on route to Alaska or Prince Rupert, BC. We are just minutes from downtown Burns Lake restaurants and shopping. Our guest house has a private entrance suite and a driveway that will accommodate many guests or tenant parking. Beautiful rooms on every floor (some hardwood), 5 1/2 bathrooms, a spacious working kitchen and an eloquent dining room to the side. The living room is very cozy with the warmth of a fireplace.

ROOMS Family suite, Upper floor, Lower floor, Private entrance, **Baths** Private, Ensuite, Shared with guest, **Beds** Queen, Twin, Single or cots, Pullout sofa, **Smoking** Outside, **In Room** Thermostat, Phone, TV, Fireplace, Internet access, **OTHERS** Urban, Handicapped access, Additional meals, **PAYMENT** Cheques accepted, Cash, Trvl's cheques, **BREAKFASTS** Full, Home-baked, **AMENITIES** Central TV, Central phone, Barbecue, Kitchen, Fridge, Lounge, Central VCR/DVD, **THINGS TO DO** Trail nearby, Golf, Fishing, Museums, Art, Shopping, Swimming, Beach, **LANGUAGE** Eng., Ger., **PRICE** (2 persons) 65–65 **(check with hosts for pricing details)**

BURNS LAKE

Nobody's Inn

(Ann and P.J. Lenhard)

25720 East End Rd, Burns Lake, BC, V0J 1E3
www.nobodys-inn.com
E-mail pjmal1194@telus.net

250-692-0034
Fax 250-692-0064
TFr 1-866-692-0034

A large home with spacious rooms, cozy, friendly people and laid back atmosphere. Lots of wildlife to watch and many trails to hike and cross-country ski. If you love the outdoors, this is the place for you. We are right off Hwy 16, so if you are passing through, stop in and see us.

ROOMS Upper floor, Ground floor, **Baths** Private, Ensuite, Shared with guest, **Beds** King, Queen, Double, **Smoking** Outside, **OTHERS** Babysitting, Rural, Open all year, Pets in residence, **PAYMENT** Cheques accepted, Cash, Trvl's cheques, **BREAKFASTS** Full, Home-baked, **AMENITIES** Central TV, Central phone, Whirlpool, Hot bev. bar, Central VCR/DVD, **THINGS TO DO** Trail nearby, Fishing, Cross-country skiing, Horseback riding, Birdwatching, **LANGUAGE** Eng., **PRICE** (2 persons) 65–125 **(check with hosts for pricing details)**

CHEMAINUS
(north of Victoria)

Be Delighted B&B

(Jane Riley)

3784 Panorama Cres, Chemainus, BC, V0R 1K4
www.BeDelighted.ca
E-mail bedelighted@xplornet.com

250-246-4560
Fax 250-246-4560
TFr 1-800-803-1279

Luxurious bed & breakfast with ocean
and mountain vista on Vancouver Island.
Your hosts, Dan and Jane, are well travelled, personable and health-oriented and
offer gracious hospitality to their guests.
Directions provided when booking. Be
Delighted is on Panorama Ridge just off
the Trans-Canada Hwy (Hwy 1) between
Chemainus and Ladysmith.

ROOMS Ground floor, **Baths** Private, Ensuite, Shared
with guest, **Beds** Queen, **Air** Ceiling fans, **In Room**
Internet access, **OTHERS** Rural, Adult, Open all year,
Handicapped access, **PAYMENT** Visa, MC, Amex, Direct
debit, Cheques accepted, Cash, Trvl's cheques, **BREAK-
FASTS** Full, Home-baked, **AMENITIES** Central TV,
Central phone, Whirlpool, Laundry, Fridge, Hot bev.
bar, Lounge, Patio, Central Internet access, Central
VCR/DVD, **THINGS TO DO** Trail nearby, Golf, Fishing,
Museums, Art, Theatre, Entertainment, Attractions,
Wineries/Breweries, Shopping, Tennis, Swimming,
Beach, Birdwatching, Antiquing, **LANGUAGE** Eng.,
PRICE (2 persons) 85–115 **(check with hosts for pric-
ing details)**

CHEMAINUS

Island Haven B&B

(Donna and Dave Smeed)

9959 Panorama Ridge Rd, Chemainus, BC, V0R 1L4
www.islandhaven.ca
E-mail dsmeed@island.net

250-246-2781
Fax 250-246-2720

Come to Island Haven for a romantic getaway in our Sunrise Room. Enjoy a full private breakfast served in your room or on
any of our decks. A country setting with
a panoramic view of the Gulf Islands,
just 5 minutes from the little town of
Chemainus. Our Rose Suite has one or
two bedrooms, great for families, full
kitchen, hot tub and BBQ available. Great
base for seeing the island. One hour to
Victoria for day trips. Kayaking, golf, wine
tours, antiquing or live theatre to enjoy
are all nearby.

ROOMS Family suite, Ground floor, **Baths** Private,
Ensuite, **Beds** Queen, **Air** Central, **Smoking** Outside, **In
Room** TV, Fireplace, **OTHERS** Rural, Adult, Open all
year, Handicapped access, Pets in residence, **PAYMENT**
Visa, MC, Cash, Trvl's cheques, **BREAKFASTS** Full, Self-
catered, **AMENITIES** Central TV, Central phone,
Whirlpool, Barbecue, Kitchen, Fridge, Hot bev. bar,
Patio, Central VCR/DVD, **THINGS TO DO** Trail nearby,
Rental canoe or boat, Golf, Fishing, Museums, Art,
Theatre, Entertainment, Wineries/Breweries,
Shopping, Horseback riding, Birdwatching, Antiquing,
LANGUAGE Eng., **PRICE** (2 persons) 130–160 **(check
with hosts for pricing details)**

CHEMAINUS

Ladysmith Bed and Breakfast
(Celeste Bonnet)

515 Louise Rd, Ladysmith, BC, V9G 1W7
www.LadysmithBandB.com
E-mail Book@LadysmithBandB.com

250-245-0633
TFr 1-866-568-4060

Book today to ensure your warm, comfy visit in our new oceanview home. Feast your senses with stunning ocean views, forest, yummy continental breakfast and luxury rooms with private baths. Relax in our casual atmosphere. We cater to groups, families, grandparents, couples – guests who value privacy, convenience and beauty. Short, 10-minute drive to downtown Chemainus or Historic Ladysmith, off Island Hwy onto South Davis Rd, then Louise Rd. (Small children in home.)

ROOMS Family suite, Upper floor, Ground floor, Private entrance, **Baths** Private, Shared with guest, **Beds** Queen, Single or cots, **Air** Ceiling fans, **Smoking** Outside, **In Room** TV, **OTHERS** Babysitting, Urban, Adult, Open all year, Pets in residence, **PAYMENT** Visa, MC, Cash, Trvl's cheques, **BREAKFASTS** Continental, Home-baked, **AMENITIES** Central phone, Fridge, Hot bev. bar, Lounge, Patio, Central Internet access, **THINGS TO DO** Trail nearby, Rental canoe or boat, Golf, Fishing, Museums, Art, Theatre, Entertainment, Attractions, Wineries/Breweries, Shopping, Tennis, Swimming, Horseback riding, Beach, Birdwatching, Antiquing, **LANGUAGE** Eng., **PRICE** (2 persons) 95–95 **(check with hosts for pricing details)**

CHILLIWACK *(east of Vancouver)*

Cedar Grove Bed and Breakfast
(Fred and Audrey Kraubner)

9911 Parkwood Dr S, Rosedale, BC, V0X 1X0
www.cedargrovebedandbreakfast.ca
E-mail cedargrovebnb@shaw.ca

604-794-9988
Fax 604-794-9988

Located in a new subdivision of fine new homes in the shadow of Mount Cheam near Minter Gardens and Bridal Falls. There is hiking, golf and hang gliding at Bridal Falls. Harrison Hot Springs with its pool and beach, and the village of Agassiz nearby with their quaint shops and restaurants. Your hosts offer you a complete suite for families as well as a bedroom with private bath. To find us, just take Exit 135 from Hwy 1, turn left onto Yale Rd for two blocks and then left again to Parkwood Dr.

ROOMS Family suite, Ground floor, Private entrance, **Baths** Private, **Beds** Queen, Single or cots, Pullout sofa, **Air** Central, **In Room** Thermostat, TV, Fireplace, Internet access, VCR/DVD, **OTHERS** Rural, Open all year, Pets in residence, **PAYMENT** Visa, MC, Cash, Trvl's cheques, **BREAKFASTS** Full, Continental, **AMENITIES** Central phone, Whirlpool, Laundry, Kitchen, Fridge, Hot bev. bar, Lounge, Patio, **THINGS TO DO** Trail nearby, Golf, Fishing, Museums, Theatre, Attractions, Shopping, Cross-country skiing, Downhill skiing, Swimming, Horseback riding, Beach, Birdwatching, **LANGUAGE** Eng., Ger., **PRICE** (2 persons) 65–105 **(check with hosts for pricing details)**

CLEARWATER
(northeast of Kamloops)

Tanglewood

(Kirsten and Michael Allchin)

1048 Clearwater Valley Rd, Clearwater, BC, V0E 1N0
www.tanglewoodlodge.net
E-mail info@tanglewoodlodge.net

250-674-3537

Tanglewood is set just 3 km from the village of Clearwater, on the upper slopes of the Clearwater Valley, and on the road into the wilds of Wells Gray Park. It offers a private apartment comprising two bedrooms, a sitting room, full bathroom and kitchen, which will sleep as many as eight people (one queen bed, three twins, one double futon, one foldout). We'll be happy to help you to get the most from your visit to this beautiful area – from hiking, biking and paddling, to cross-country and back-country skiing.

ROOMS Family suite, Lower floor, Private entrance, **Baths** Private, **Beds** Queen, Twin, Single or cots, Pullout sofa, **In Room** TV, **OTHERS** Babysitting, Rural, Open all year, **PAYMENT** Visa, MC, Direct debit, Cheques accepted, Cash, Trvl's cheques, **BREAKFASTS** Continental, Home-baked, Self-catered, **THINGS TO DO** Rental bikes, Trail nearby, Rental canoe or boat, Golf, Cross-country skiing, Horseback riding, Birdwatching, **LANGUAGE** Eng., Fr., Ger., **PRICE** (2 persons) 70–95 **(check with hosts for pricing details)**

CLEARWATER

Trophy Mountain Buffalo Ranch

(Joe Fischer and Jamie Blackmore)

4373 Clearwater Valley Rd, Clearwater, BC, V0E 1N0
www.buffaloranch.ca
E-mail buffranch@hotmail.com

250-674-3095
Fax 250-674-3131

Trophy Mountain Buffalo Ranch is located 20 minutes from Wells Gray Park. The ranch has a quiet, country setting with bison grazing in the front field. There is Horseback riding and hiking from the ranch. We offer a variety of bison meat in our restaurant for guests to try.

ROOMS Upper floor, Ground floor, Private entrance, **Baths** Private, Ensuite, Shared with guest, **Beds** Queen, Double, Single or cots, **Smoking** Outside, **OTHERS** Rural, Seasonal, **PAYMENT** Visa, MC, Direct debit, Cash, Trvl's cheques, **BREAKFASTS** Full, **AMENITIES** Central TV, Barbecue, Fridge, Hot bev. bar, Patio, **THINGS TO DO** Trail nearby, Rental canoe or boat, Golf, Fishing, Cross-country skiing, Tennis, Swimming, Horseback riding, **LANGUAGE** Eng., Ger., **PRICE** (2 persons) 40–65 **(check with hosts for pricing details)**

COBBLE HILL [VICTORIA] *(north of Victoria)*

Country Treasures B and B Guest Cottage

(Dolly and Cordell Sandquist)

1133 Fisher Rd, Cobble Hill, BC, V0R 1L0
www.countrytreasuresbandbguestcottage.com
E-mail csandquist@telus.net

250-743-4374
Fax 250-743-4364
TFr 1-888-824-2879

Come to the country for a peaceful, quiet stay in our quaint country cottage. Nestled in the trees on our 7-acre property, the cottage is separate from the main house. Privacy is yours! Enjoy your choice of breakfast served to you at the cottage. You will find total peace and quiet and a chance to get away from it all!
The cottage is tastefully decorated with antiques and collectibles. A small kitchenette is available for your use. The perfect spot for two to spend some quiet time!

ROOMS Family suite, **Baths** Private, **Beds** Queen, **In Room** Fireplace, **OTHERS** Rural, Adult, Open all year, Additional meals, Pets in residence, **PAYMENT** Visa, MC, Cash, Trvl's cheques, **BREAKFASTS** Full, Continental, Home-baked, Self-catered, **AMENITIES** Barbecue, Kitchen, Fridge, Patio, **THINGS TO DO** Trail nearby, Fishing, Museums, Art, Theatre, Entertainment, Attractions, Wineries/Breweries, Shopping, Tennis, Swimming, Horseback riding, Beach, Birdwatching, Antiquing, **LANGUAGE** Eng., **PRICE** (2 persons) 95–95 **(check with hosts for pricing details)**

COMOX
(north of Nanaimo, Vancouver Island)

Alpine House B&B

(Marie and Earl Rogers)

263 Alpine St, Comox, BC, V9M 1G1
www.alpinehousebb.com
E-mail alpinehouse@telus.net

250-339-6181
Fax 250-339-4892
TFr 1-877-339-6181

Tourism BC approved. *Canada Select* 3 1/2-stars. A charming home in central Comox set among beautifully landscaped gardens. Within walking distance of restaurants, marina and shopping. Two rooms with queen beds, private and ensuite baths. Guest sitting room with TV and VCR. Full breakfasts. Adult-oriented. Open year round. Guest entrance. Smoke and pet free. Seasonal rates available.

ROOMS Upper floor, **Baths** Private, Ensuite, **Beds** Queen, **Smoking** Outside, **In Room** Thermostat, **OTHERS** Adult, Open all year, Seasonal, **PAYMENT** Visa, MC, Amex, Cheques accepted, Cash, Trvl's cheques, **BREAKFASTS** Full, Continental, Home-baked, **AMENITIES** Central TV, Central phone, Laundry, Lounge, Central VCR/DVD, **THINGS TO DO** Rental bikes, Trail nearby, Rental canoe or boat, Golf, Fishing, Museums, Art, Theatre, Entertainment, Shopping, Cross-country skiing, Tennis, Swimming, Horseback riding, Beach, Birdwatching, Antiquing, **LANGUAGE** Eng., Fr., **PRICE** (2 persons) 60–90 **(check with hosts for pricing details)**

Comox

Copes Islander
Oceanfront B&B
(Mike and Patti Copes)

1484 Wilkinson Rd, Comox, BC, V9M 4B3
www.bbvancouverisland-bc.com
E-mail mike@bbvancouverisland-bc.com

250-339-1038
TFr 1-888-339-1038

Experience the spectacular view, tranquil setting and unforgettable breakfasts at our beachfront B&B and vacation rental accommodations in the Comox Valley, Vancouver Island, BC. Our two spacious rooms and self-contained suite all have private entrances with the beach just a few steps away. Each room has a superb view of Georgia Strait and the Coast Mountain Range. There are miles of shoreline to explore and virtually every kind of outdoor activity can be enjoyed nearby.

ROOMS Family suite, Upper floor, Ground floor, Private entrance, **Baths** Private, Shared with guest, **Beds** Queen, Double, **Smoking** Outside, **In Room** TV, Internet access, **OTHERS** Open all year, Pets in residence, Pets welcome, **PAYMENT** Visa, MC, Amex, Cash, Trvl's cheques, **BREAKFASTS** Full, **THINGS TO DO** Trail nearby, Golf, Fishing, Museums, Art, Theatre, Entertainment, Shopping, Cross-country skiing, Downhill skiing, Tennis, Swimming, Horseback riding, Beach, Birdwatching, Antiquing, **LANGUAGE** Eng., **PRICE** (2 persons) 75–115 **(check with hosts for pricing details)**

Comox

Singing Sands
Bed & Breakfast
(Gail and Mark Hill)

1951 Singing Sands Rd, Comox, BC, V9M 3X9
www.singingsandsbb.com
E-mail info@singingsandsbb.com

250-339-3552
Fax 250-339-3552
TFr 1-866-339-3551

Located just steps from a beautiful beach with ocean and mountain views. Close to the towns of Comox and Courtenay in the beautiful Comox Valley. We offer two queen rooms with their own ensuite bathrooms, guest lounge and large deck area. Guests can enjoy our hot tub situated in our flower garden. We are close and convenient for Powell River Ferry and Comox Airport. Directions from ferry: Take first left turning onto Wilkinson Rd, first left again into Singing Sands Rd. We are at the end by the ocean.

ROOMS Upper floor, Private entrance, **Baths** Ensuite, **Beds** Queen, **Air** Ceiling fans, **Smoking** Outside, **OTHERS** Adult, Open all year, **PAYMENT** Visa, Cash, Trvl's cheques, **BREAKFASTS** Full, Home-baked, **AMENITIES** Central phone, Whirlpool, Barbecue, Fridge, Hot bev. bar, Lounge, **THINGS TO DO** Golf, Fishing, Museums, Theatre, Attractions, Shopping, Cross-country skiing, Downhill skiing, Swimming, Horseback riding, Beach, Birdwatching, **LANGUAGE** Eng., **PRICE** (2 persons) 70––85 **(check with hosts for pricing details)**

COQUITLAM *(east of Vancouver)*

Fig Tree B&B

(Gerry and Angela Parfeniuk)

413 Mariner Way, Coquitlam, BC, V3C 5A4
www.figtreebandb.com
E-mail gerry@caresmarketing.com

604-464-3441
Fax 604-464-8996

Our spacious suite is at ground level and located far from traffic noises for you to enjoy a peaceful stay. It has one large bedroom, queen-sized bed and private bath. A separate dining area and living room with gas fireplace are yours to enjoy. Enjoy freshness, cleanliness, great views, comfort and our homestyle hospitality. Your stay will be memorable and satisfying. Our breakfasts include cereals, fruit, pastries, juice and a hot beverage. Alternate telephone numbers are 604-464-4024 and 604-644-6698.

ROOMS Family suite, Lower floor, **Baths** Private, **Beds** Queen, Pullout sofa, **Smoking** Outside, **In Room** TV, Fireplace, OTHERS Urban, Open all year, PAYMENT Cheques accepted, Cash, Trvl's cheques, **BREAKFASTS** Self-catered, **AMENITIES** Central phone, Laundry, Kitchen, Fridge, Central Internet access, THINGS **TO DO** Trail nearby, Golf, Entertainment, Tennis, **LANGUAGE** Eng., **PRICE** (2 persons) 70–90 **(check with hosts for pricing details)**

COURTENAY
(north of Nanaimo, Vancouver Island)

Gramar B&B

(Grant and Marie Atchison)

3754 Dove Creek Rd, Courtenay, BC, V9J 1R9
www.gramar-bb-courtenay.com
E-mail gatchi@island.net

250-334-1591
Fax 250-334-1551
TFr 1-866-334-1591

Welcome to Gramar Farm Bed and Breakfast, our delightfully comfortable, hospitable country bed and breakfast home. Gramar Farm B&B is an adult-oriented accommodation located on a hobby farm in the beautiful Comox Valley, just six minutes from Courtenay and only a 30-minute drive from Mount Washington ski resort. Relax in the evening sitting on the huge deck, enjoying the mountain and pastoral views. Then retire at your leisure to a tastefully decorated one-bedroom suite complete with private bathroom and sitting room with satellite TV.

ROOMS Upper floor, **Baths** Private, Ensuite, **Beds** Double, Pullout sofa, **Air** Ceiling fans, **In Room** TV, OTHERS Rural, Adult, Open all year, Pets in residence, Pets welcome, **PAYMENT** Cheques accepted, Cash, **BREAKFASTS** Full, Home-baked, **AMENITIES** Barbecue, Laundry, Kitchen, **THINGS TO DO** Comp. bikes, Trail nearby, Golf, Fishing, Museums, Art, Theatre, Entertainment, Attractions, Shopping, Cross-country skiing, Downhill skiing, Swimming, Horseback riding, Beach, **LANGUAGE** Eng., **PRICE** (2 persons) 75–95 **(check with hosts for pricing details)**

CRANBROOK *(southeast BC)*

Singing Pines
Bed and Breakfast
(Robert and Sandy Dirom)

5180 Kennedy Rd, Cranbrook, BC, V1C 7C1
www.singingpines.ca
E-mail info@singingpines.ca

250-426-5959
Fax 250-426-5959
TFr 1-800-863-4969

Singing Pines Bed and Breakfast would like to welcome you to our quiet forested country retreat located in a broad valley surrounded by spectacular mountain views of the Rocky and Purcell mountains. Wildlife and birdwatching opportunities. One-level living, private baths, guest lounges, large deck, patios, outdoor hot tub, picnic tables, BBQ, fire pit, paved lighted parking and much more. Hearty country-style breakfast. Relaxed western hospitality. We are a *Canada Select* 4 1/2-star property.

ROOMS Family suite, Ground floor, Private entrance, **Baths** Private, Ensuite, **Beds** Queen, Double, Twin, Pullout sofa, **Air** Central, **Smoking** Outside, **In Room** Thermostat, Phone, TV, **OTHERS** Rural, Adult, Seasonal, Pets in residence, **PAYMENT** Visa, MC, Diners, Amex, Cheques accepted, Cash, **BREAKFASTS** Full, Home-baked, **AMENITIES** Central TV, Central phone, Whirlpool, Barbecue, Laundry, Fridge, Hot bev. bar, Lounge, Patio, **THINGS TO DO** Trail nearby, Golf, Fishing, Museums, Art, Theatre, Entertainment, Attractions, Shopping, Cross-country skiing, Tennis, Swimming, Horseback riding, Beach, **LANGUAGE** Eng., **PRICE** (2 persons) 100–120 **(check with hosts for pricing details)**

DAWSON CREEK *(northeastern BC)*

Meadow Vale House
(Dieter and Brigitte Schwetz)

6879 217 Rd, PO Box 2662, Dawson Creek, BC, V1G 5A1
www.meadowvalehouse.bc.ca
E-mail schwetz@meadowvalehouse.bc.ca

250-784-0161
Fax 250-784-0100
TFr 1-888-784-0161

Paradise found. A spectacular 1,047 sq.ft., three-room suite with an air-conditioned 250 sq.ft. bedroom, studio kitchen and 700 sq.ft. living room awaits you in this magnificent home, surrounded by rolling hills and pastoral meadows. Within the Agricultural Land Reserve, yet only 7 km from downtown Dawson Creek and the world famous "Mile 0" post. This 5,000 sq.ft. home is owned by Dieter Schwetz, retired 5-star global hotelier and offers a "near town" location with the serenity of a country retreat.

ROOMS Ground floor, Private entrance, **Baths** Ensuite, **Beds** King, **Air** Central, **In Room** Thermostat, Phone, TV, Fireplace, **OTHERS** Rural, Adult, Seasonal, Pets in residence, **PAYMENT** Visa, MC, Amex, Cash, Trvl's cheques, **BREAKFASTS** Full, **AMENITIES** Barbecue, Laundry, Kitchen, Fridge, Patio, **THINGS TO DO** Art, **LANGUAGE** Eng., Ger., **PRICE** (2 persons) 95–115 **(check with hosts for pricing details)**

DELTA *(southeast of Vancouver)*

Canoe Pass Inn B&B

(Jackie and Colin Smith)

3383 River Rd W, Ladner, BC, V4K 3N2
www.canoepassinn.com
E-mail canoepassinn@dccnet.com

604-946-6780
Fax 604-946-6750

Located at the mouth of the Fraser River in historic Ladner, a quaint fishing/farming village. Private serene romantic rooms in a floating home with spectacular views of the river and abundant bird and wildlife. Very close to world famous Reifel Bird Sanctuary, and centrally located 20 minutes from Vancouver International Airport and 35 minutes to downtown Vancouver. Only 15 minutes to the Vancouver Islands Ferry.

ROOMS Family suite, Ground floor, Private entrance, **Baths** Private, Ensuite, **Beds** Queen, Single or cots, Pullout sofa, **Smoking** Outside, **In Room** Thermostat, Phone, TV, Fireplace, **OTHERS** Rural, Open all year, **PAYMENT** Cheques accepted, Cash, **BREAKFASTS** Full, Home-baked, **AMENITIES** Central phone, Whirlpool, Barbecue, Laundry, Kitchen, Fridge, Lounge, Patio, **THINGS TO DO** Comp. bikes, Trail nearby, Golf, Fishing, Museums, Attractions, Wineries/Breweries, Shopping, Tennis, Swimming, Beach, **LANGUAGE** Eng., **PRICE** (2 persons) 130–150 **(check with hosts for pricing details)**

DENMAN ISLAND *(east-central Vancouver Island)*

Hawthorn House B&B

(Tim Hicks and Barbara Kane)

3375 Kirk Rd, Denman Island, BC, V0R 1T0
www.hawthornhouse.ca
E-mail hhouse@island.net

250-335-0905
Fax 250-335-1656
TFr 1-877-335-0905

Hawthorn House offers comfortable and attractive rooms and great breakfasts in a relaxed setting. All rooms have satellite TV, feather comforters, patchwork quilts and private bathrooms. The view is across the water of Baynes Sound and up to the mountains on Vancouver Island. Enjoy our gardens, sit around the large pond or soak in the hot tub. We're within a short walk of "downtown" Denman. Our "cottage room" is in a separate cottage beside the house and has a small fridge and microwave.

ROOMS Upper floor, Ground floor, Private entrance, **Baths** Private, Ensuite, **Beds** Queen, Double, Twin, **Air** Central, **Smoking** Outside, **In Room** Thermostat, TV, **OTHERS** Rural, Open all year, Pets in residence, **PAYMENT** Visa, MC, Amex, Cash, Trvl's cheques, **BREAKFASTS** Full, Home-baked, **AMENITIES** Central phone, Whirlpool, Laundry, Fridge, Patio, Central Internet access, **THINGS TO DO** Rental bikes, Trail nearby, Rental canoe or boat, Fishing, Art, Entertainment, Attractions, Cross-country skiing, Downhill skiing, Tennis, Swimming, Beach, Birdwatching, **LANGUAGE** Eng., Fr., **PRICE** (2 persons) 85–105 **(check with hosts for pricing details)**

DUNCAN *(north of Victoria)*

Sunflower Inn Bed & Breakfast

(Rob Rensing and Joy Larson)

3415 Glenora Rd, Duncan, BC, V9L 6S2
www.sunflowerinn.ca
E-mail sunflowerinn@telus.net

250-748-7920
Fax 250-748-7941
TFr 1-800-953-6572

Located in the heart of the Cowichan Valley wine country, Zanatta's vineyards and gourmet restaurant is just a five-minute walk down the road. Come hike the Cowichan River Trail (with wonderful swimming holes) or bike the nearby Trans-Canada Trail. Visit the Forestry Discovery Centre and the Native Heritage Centre. And the downtown Duncan Farmer's Market is a must or relax in a hammock with wide views of the mountains and forest. Reading a book with your eyes closed is highly recommended here!

ROOMS Upper floor, **Baths** Shared with guest, **Beds** Queen, Twin, **Smoking** Outside, **In Room** Thermostat, **OTHERS** Rural, Adult, Open all year, Pets in residence, **PAYMENT** Visa, Cash, Trvl's cheques, **BREAKFASTS** Full, Home-baked, **AMENITIES** Barbecue, Lounge, Patio, **THINGS TO DO** Trail nearby, Golf, Fishing, Museums, Art, Theatre, Entertainment, Attractions, Wineries/ Breweries, Shopping, Cross-country skiing, Tennis, Swimming, Horseback riding, Birdwatching, **LANGUAGE** Eng., Dutch, **PRICE** (2 persons) 65–75 **(check with hosts for pricing details)**

FERNIE *(southeastern BC)*

Barbara Lynn's Country Inn

(Barbara Bowles and Knud Larsen)

691 – 7th Ave Box 1077, Fernie, BC, V0B 1M0
www.BLCI.ca
E-mail info@BLCI.ca

250-423-6027
Fax 250-423-6024
TFr 1-888-288-2148

Warm and friendly welcome awaits you in this traditional inn with the comforts of home and spectacular mountain views! Four season destination in the Canadian Rockies. Walk to dine or shop. Guest TV room/kitchen, wireless Internet. We are environmentally friendly and use products without harsh chemicals, artificial fragrances, colour, or synthetic preservatives. Fly fishing/kayaking/hiking/biking/wildlife/ski and golf packages. Shuttle to Fernie Alpine Resort/winter. Relax in the hot tub (winter). CP 10 days.

ROOMS Family suite, Upper floor, Ground floor, Private entrance, **Baths** Ensuite, Shared with guest, **Beds** Queen, Double, Twin, Pullout sofa, **Smoking** Outside, **In Room** Thermostat, **OTHERS** Rural, Open all year, **PAYMENT** Visa, MC, Amex, Direct debit, Cash, Trvl's cheques, **BREAKFASTS** Continental, Home-baked, **AMENITIES** Central TV, Central phone, Whirlpool, Barbecue, Kitchen, Fridge, Hot bev. bar, Lounge, Patio, Central Internet access, Central VCR/DVD, **THINGS TO DO** Rental bikes, Trail nearby, Rental canoe or boat, Golf, Fishing, Museums, Art, Theatre, Entertainment, Attractions, Wineries/ Breweries, Shopping, Cross-country skiing, Downhill skiing, Tennis, Swimming, Horseback riding, Beach, Birdwatching, **LANGUAGE** Eng., Danish, **PRICE** (2 persons) 46–92 **(check with hosts for pricing details)**

FORT NELSON *(northeastern BC)*

Ardendale Wilderness Experience

(Frank and Gail Parker)

RR #1, Box 5, Mile 305, Old Alaska Hwy, Fort Nelson, BC, V0C 1R0
www.canadianbandbguide.ca/bb.asp?ID=2333

250-774-2433
Fax 250-774-2436

Huge country log home. Three rooms, private baths. Hot tub and sitting room. Hearty Canadian breakfast. No pets or smoking. Gateway to Northern Rockies and Muskwa Kechika. Plan your vacation at our lodge. Wilderness pack horse trips and trail rides, stagecoach, covered wagon and buggy rides. Reasonable rates. We help you arrange riverboat, rafting, aircraft and helicopter viewing and fishing trips with other local operators. Your best vacation ever. See you soon.

ROOMS Upper floor, **Baths** Private, Ensuite, **Beds** Queen, **Smoking** Outside, **OTHERS** Rural, Open all year, PAYMENT Visa, Cheques accepted, Cash, Trvl's cheques, **BREAKFASTS** Full, **AMENITIES** Central TV, Central phone, Whirlpool, Barbecue, Lounge, **THINGS TO DO** Comp. canoe or boat, Golf, Fishing, Museums, Attractions, Swimming, Horseback riding, **LANGUAGE** Eng., **PRICE** (2 persons) 70–70 **(check with hosts for pricing details)**

GABRIOLA ISLAND
(north of Salt Spring Island)

Island Bed & Breakfast

(Linda Olsen)

1024 Dirksen Rd, Gabriola Island, BC, V0R 1X2
www.gabriolaislandbandb.com
E-mail islandbandb@uniserve.com

250-247-9058

Enjoy the gracious country charm of our West Coast home, nestled among tall evergreen trees and not far from ferry and shopping village. Turn off South Rd to end of Dirksen Rd. Our spacious guest room with access to a sheltered verandah has a queen bed plus single sofa bed, cable TV and large ensuite bath. Complimentary coffee, tea and juice. We serve a varied menu of delicious breakfasts and can accommodate special dietary needs. Wheelchair access. No smoking, no pets. Cash or cheque only.

ROOMS Ground floor, Private entrance, **Baths** Ensuite, **Beds** Queen, Pullout sofa, **Air** Ceiling fans, **Smoking** Outside, **In Room** Thermostat, TV, VCR/DVD, **OTHERS** Rural, Open all year, Handicapped access, **PAYMENT** Cheques accepted, Cash, **BREAKFASTS** Full, Home-baked, **AMENITIES** Central TV, Fridge, Lounge, Patio, Central VCR/DVD, **THINGS TO DO** Rental bikes, Trail nearby, Rental canoe or boat, Golf, Fishing, Museums, Art, Entertainment, Attractions, Shopping, Tennis, Swimming, Beach, Birdwatching, **LANGUAGE** Eng., **PRICE** (2 persons) 80–80 **(check with hosts for pricing details)**

Gibsons *(north of Vancouver)*

A Waterfront Hideaway

(Nezam Zeineddin)

354 Avalon Dr, Gibsons, BC, V0N 1V8
www.waterfronthideaway.com
E-mail info@waterfronthideaway.com

604-886-2912
Fax 604-886-2995

Luxury waterfront B&B located in prestigious bluff in Gibsons, Sunshine Coast.
Magnificent views of How Sound, coastal
mountains and surrounding island.
Private beach, three spacious and tastefully appointed suites, with separate
entrance, kitchen, bedroom, private sitting room, ensuite bathrooms, fireplace,
TV/DVD, etc. In addition to the hospitality
and comfort, Waterfront Hideaway has a
full-size Jacuzzi, in a separate glass-front-
ed annex that affords the same magnificent views.

ROOMS Family suite, Private entrance, **Baths** Ensuite,
Beds King, Queen, Twin, **In Room** Thermostat, Phone,
TV, Fireplace, Internet access, VCR/DVD, **OTHERS** Open
all year, **PAYMENT** Visa, MC, Direct debit, Cheques
accepted, Cash, **BREAKFASTS** Self-catered, **AMENITIES**
Central TV, Central phone, Whirlpool, Barbecue,
Laundry, Kitchen, Fridge, Lounge, Patio, Central
Internet access, Central VCR/DVD, **THINGS TO DO**
Rental bikes, Trail nearby, Rental canoe or boat, Golf,
Fishing, Museums, Art, Theatre, Entertainment,
Attractions, Shopping, Cross-country skiing, Tennis,
Swimming, Beach, Birdwatching, Antiquing, **LAN-
GUAGE** Eng., Swedish, Persian, **PRICE** (2 persons)
135–155 **(check with hosts for pricing details)**

Gibsons

Caprice Bed and Breakfast

(Lois Choksy and Jeanette Panagapka)

Box 315, 1111 Gower Point Rd, Gibsons, BC, V0N 1V0
www.capricebb.com
E-mail caprice@dccnet.com

604-886-4270
TFr 1-866-886-4270

Situated on an acre of oceanview land,
Caprice Bed and Breakfast is a quiet,
romantic retreat with luxurious rooms,
ensuite bathrooms, kichenettes and private entrances. Swimming pool and hot
tub. Whether you choose to hike the scenic Sunshine Coast trails, kayak on the
beautiful waters of the Strait of Georgia,
golf or simply relax and unwind on the
Caprice terrace you will experience a holiday to remember – a 40-minute ferry ride
from Vancouver. Pets welcome.

ROOMS Ground floor, Lower floor, Private entrance,
Baths Ensuite, **Beds** Queen, **In Room** Thermostat, TV,
Internet access, **OTHERS** Rural, Adult, Open all year,
Pets welcome, **PAYMENT** Visa, MC, Trvl's cheques,
BREAKFASTS Full, Home-baked, **AMENITIES** Central
TV, Central phone, Swimming pool, Whirlpool, Fridge,
Hot bev. bar, Patio, Central Internet access, **THINGS TO
DO** Trail nearby, Golf, Fishing, Museums, Art,
Attractions, Shopping, Cross-country skiing,
Swimming, Horseback riding, Beach, Antiquing, **LAN-
GUAGE** Eng., **PRICE** (2 persons) 90–130 **(check with
hosts for pricing details)**

GIBSONS

Ocean Breezes Bed & Breakfast

(Donna and Ralph Schilling)

1243 Gower Point Rd, Gibsons, BC, V0N 1V3
www.oceanbreezes.ca
E-mail info@oceanbreezes.ca

604-886-7105
Fax 604-886-7932
TFr 1-877-886-7104

Elegant new waterfront suites in tranquil setting with panoramic ocean views from private balconies and window walls. Private entrances, gourmet breakfast served to rooms, fireplace, entertainment and hospitality centres, deluxe queen pillowtop bed, designer bath with ceramic and glass plus soaker tub or sofa bed option. Beautiful 45-minute ferry ride from West Vancouver and 5 to 10 minutes from local ferry, trails, golf, beaches, restaurants and shopping. Featured in the *Vancouver Sun* and BC Approved.

ROOMS Family suite, Upper floor, Lower floor, Private entrance, **Baths** Ensuite, **Beds** Queen, Pullout sofa, **Smoking** Outside, **In Room** Thermostat, TV, Fireplace, VCR/DVD, **OTHERS** Adult, Open all year, **PAYMENT** Visa, MC, Amex, Cash, Trvl's cheques, **BREAKFASTS** Full, Continental, Home-baked, **AMENITIES** Central phone, Fridge, Central Internet access, **THINGS TO DO** Comp. bikes, Trail nearby, Golf, Fishing, Museums, Art, Theatre, Entertainment, Attractions, Shopping, Cross-country skiing, Tennis, Swimming, Horseback riding, Beach, Birdwatching, Antiquing, **LANGUAGE** Eng., **PRICE** (2 persons) 120–180 **(check with hosts for pricing details)**

GIBSONS

Rosewood Country House

(Susan Berryman/Frank Tonne)

575 Pine St, Gibsons, BC, V0N 1V5
www.rosewoodcountryhouse.com
E-mail rosewood@uniserve.com

604-886-4714
Fax 604-886-8119
TFr 1-888-409-1486

Rosewood is located on three acres on the beautiful Sunshine Coast. Cosy romantic guest suites with private entrance afford one an opportunity to feel pampered, inside a large 1910 crafts-man-style home. There are two suites: Sunset Suite overlooks the ocean and Vancouver Island, and the Garden Suite overlooks the east garden. Both suites have private bath, soaker tubs, fireplace, wet bar, TV/VCR and CD player. A games room, complete with antique snooker table, is available to guests.

ROOMS Ground floor, Private entrance, **Baths** Private, Ensuite, **Beds** Queen, **Smoking** Outside, **In Room** Thermostat, TV, Fireplace, Internet access, VCR/DVD, **OTHERS** Rural, Adult, Seasonal, **PAYMENT** Visa, Cheques accepted, Cash, Trvl's cheques, **BREAKFASTS** Full, **AMENITIES** Fridge, Lounge, Patio, **THINGS TO DO** Trail nearby, Rental canoe or boat, Golf, Fishing, Art, Entertainment, Tennis, Beach, Birdwatching, Antiquing, **LANGUAGE** Eng., **PRICE** (2 persons) 220–220 **(check with hosts for pricing details)**

GIBSONS

The Maritimer Cottage and Suites

(Stu and Wendy Iglesias)

521 South Fletcher Rd, Gibsons, BC, V0N 1V0
www.maritimerbb.com
E-mail wendy@maritimerbb.com

604-886-0664
Fax 604-886-0696
TFr 1-877-886-0664

Our house is a traditional home set among our magnificent gardens. We overlook Gibsons Harbor with a panoramic view of the Strait of Georgia, Howe Sound and the Coast Mountains. An "active" view allows us to watch the local boat traffic from the spacious deck, where breakfast is served. Adult-oriented, luxurious and spacious suites, private entrance and sundeck, cozy beds and luxury linens. From The Maritimer you can take an easy walk through the harbour and explore this quaint village.

ROOMS Family suite, Upper floor, Ground floor, Lower floor, Private entrance, **Baths** Ensuite, **Beds** King, Queen, Double, Pullout sofa, **Smoking** Outside, **In Room** Thermostat, Phone, TV, Fireplace, Internet access, **OTHERS** Rural, Adult, Open all year, **PAYMENT** Visa, MC, Cash, **BREAKFASTS** Full, Home-baked, **AMENITIES** Barbecue, Laundry, Kitchen, Fridge, Hot bev. bar, Patio, **THINGS TO DO** Trail nearby, Golf, Fishing, Museums, Art, Theatre, Entertainment, Attractions, Shopping, Tennis, Swimming, Beach, Birdwatching, Antiquing, **LANGUAGE** Eng., Fr., Sp., **PRICE** (2 persons) 129–189 **(check with hosts for pricing details)**

GOLDEN *(southeastern BC)*

A Quiet Corner Bed & Breakfast

(Sharon Kriese)

607 14th St S, Golden, BC, V0A 1H0
www.aquietcorner.com
E-mail sharon@aquietcorner.com

250-344-7869
Fax 250-344-7868
TFr 1-877-344-7869

A lovely open beam home, combining comfort and elegance, situated in a treed residential area of Golden, BC, conveniently located within an hour's drive of five national parks, and only 13 km from Kicking Horse Mountain Resort. Whether you choose skiing, golfing, white-water rafting, hiking, sightseeing, horseback riding, birdwatching, reading or a romantic, quiet getaway, you will find A Quiet Corner the perfect place to stay. I offer a smoke- and pet-free home and healthy nutritious breakfasts.

ROOMS Family suite, Upper floor, Ground floor, Private entrance, **Baths** Private, Shared with guest, **Beds** King, Queen, Twin, Pullout sofa, **Smoking** Outside, **In Room** Thermostat, TV, Fireplace, **OTHERS** Urban, Adult, Open all year, **PAYMENT** Visa, MC, Amex, Cash, Trvl's cheques, **BREAKFASTS** Full, **AMENITIES** Central TV, Central phone, Whirlpool, Hot bev. bar, Lounge, Patio, **THINGS TO DO** Trail nearby, Golf, Fishing, Museums, Attractions, Shopping, Cross-country skiing, Downhill skiing, Tennis, Swimming, Horseback riding, **LANGUAGE** Eng., **PRICE** (2 persons) 85–140 **(check with hosts for pricing details)**

GOLDEN

Blaeberry Mountain Lodge
(Rainer Grund and Renate Polzer)

1680 Moberly School Rd, Golden, BC, V0A 1H1
www.blaeberrymountainlodge.bc.ca
E-mail info@blaeberrymountainlodge.bc.ca

250-344-5296
Fax 250-344-5296

Be one with nature ...
Experience nature in our beautiful log
lodge or cozy cabins on 64 hectares of
private land, 15 km northwest of Golden.
Summer and winter activities are available, as well as German-style breakfast
and dining. The peace and tranquility you
will experience in our accommodations
(lodge, cabins or cottage) will stand out in
your memories forever.

ROOMS Family suite, Upper floor, Ground floor, Private
entrance, **Baths** Private, Shared with guest, **Beds**
Queen, Twin, Single or cots, Pullout sofa, **Air** Ceiling
fans, **Smoking** Outside, **In Room** Fireplace, **OTHERS**
Rural, Open all year, Pets in residence, Pets welcome,
PAYMENT Visa, MC, Direct debit, Cash, Trvl's cheques,
BREAKFASTS Home-baked, Self-catered, **AMENITIES**
Kitchen, Fridge, **THINGS TO DO** Rental bikes, Trail
nearby, Rental canoe or boat, Golf, Fishing, Attractions,
Cross-country skiing, Downhill skiing, Horseback rid-
ing, Birdwatching, **LANGUAGE** Eng., Ger., **PRICE** (2 per-
sons) 99–169 **(check with hosts for pricing details)**

GOLDEN

Columbia Valley Lodge, B&B
(Erwin Perzinger)

2304 Hwy 95 S, Golden, BC, V0A 1H0
www.columbiavalleylodge.com
E-mail info@columbiavalleylodge.com

250-348-2508
Fax 250-348-2505
TFr 1-800-311-5008

European-style B&B, unique touch, friendly atmosphere. Located 23 km south of
Golden on Hwy 95; surrounded by the
Columbia Valley Wetlands, of major
importance in bird migratory routes, and
six national parks. Austrian chef (owner)
prepares Canadian and European dishes.
Licensed, air-conditioned dining room; its
style allows great relaxation and discus-
sion; full breakfast and selected dinner
menu. Nature walks, birdwatching, canoeing, ski packages, golf course, Kicking
Horse Mountain Resort – short distance.

ROOMS Family suite, Upper floor, Ground floor, Private
entrance, **Baths** Private, **Beds** Queen, Double, Twin,
Single or cots, **Air** Central, **Smoking** Outside, **In Room**
Thermostat, TV, **OTHERS** Rural, Open all year, Seasonal,
Additional meals, Pets in residence, **PAYMENT** Visa,
MC, Direct debit, Cash, Trvl's cheques, **BREAKFASTS**
Full, Home-baked, **AMENITIES** Central TV, Central
phone, Barbecue, Kitchen, Fridge, Lounge, Patio,
Central Internet access, Central VCR/DVD, **THINGS TO
DO** Trail nearby, Rental canoe or boat, Comp. canoe or
boat, Cross-country skiing, Downhill skiing, Horseback
riding, Birdwatching, **LANGUAGE** Eng., Ger., **PRICE** (2
persons) 85–115 **(check with hosts for pricing
details)**

GOLDEN

Farview Bed and Breakfast

(Stan and Olive Stobbe)

2186 Campbell Rd, Golden, BC, V0A 1H7
www.farvieweather.com/bandb
E-mail bandb@farvieweather.com

250-348-2272
Fax 250-348-2279
TFr 1-866-349-2272

Farview B&B is set on 13 acres of picturesque young forest with stunning views
of the Rocky and Purcell Mountains. We
offer two lovely bedrooms in the newly
constructed mountain chalet-style home.
Each room has an adjoining sitting room
with a futon or hideabed that can open
into a double bed. A guest lounge is available with satellite TV, VCR, microwave and
small fridge. A BBQ is available for guest
use. A short walk or drive leads to the
secluded Hideaway Cabin which has full
facilities for cooking and sleeping. Hike or
Nordic ski from the house or cabin along
trails on our property and nearby. We
offer our guests a comprehensive breakfast menu to select from. Our B&B is 20
minutes south of historic Golden.

ROOMS Upper floor, Lower floor, **Baths** Private,
Ensuite, **Beds** Queen, Pullout sofa, **OTHERS** Rural,
Open all year, Pets welcome, **PAYMENT** Visa, MC,
Amex, Cash, Trvl's cheques, **BREAKFASTS** Full, Home-
baked, **AMENITIES** Central TV, Central phone, Kitchen,
Fridge, Lounge, **THINGS TO DO** Rental bikes, Trail
nearby, Rental canoe or boat, Golf, Fishing, Museums,
Art, Attractions, Cross-country skiing, Downhill skiing,
Horseback riding, Birdwatching, **LANGUAGE** Eng.,
PRICE (2 persons) 60–80 **(check with hosts for pricing
details)**

GOLDEN

Historic HG Parson House B&B

(Susan Ambler and Jeff Harris)

815 – 12 St S, Golden, BC, V0A 1H0
www.hgparsonhousebb.com
E-mail hgparsonhousebb@redshift.bc.ca

250-344-5001
Fax 250-344-5181
TFr 1-866-333-5001

Historical 1890s heritage home. Guest
rooms are furnished with elegant
antiques, family heirlooms and sophisti-
cated modern furniture and artwork.
Quiet location. Located one block from
main street; close to restaurants, shopping, walking trails and park. Private
baths, Jacuzzi tubs, outdoor hot tub and
cable TV. Full breakfast available. Central
location for skiing at four major ski
resorts and day trips to Banff, Glacier or
Yoho National Park. Cancellation policy is
7 days 30%, 48 hours 50%.

ROOMS Upper floor, **Baths** Private, Ensuite, **Beds** King,
Queen, Twin, **Smoking** Outside, **In Room** Thermostat,
TV, VCR/DVD, **OTHERS** Urban, Adult, Open all year, Pets
in residence, **PAYMENT** Visa, MC, Amex, Cash, Trvl's
cheques, **BREAKFASTS** Full, **AMENITIES** Whirlpool,
Fridge, Lounge, Patio, **THINGS TO DO** Rental bikes,
Trail nearby, Rental canoe or boat, Golf, Fishing,
Museums, Attractions, Shopping, Cross-country skiing,
Downhill skiing, Horseback riding, Birdwatching,
LANGUAGE Eng., **PRICE** (2 persons) 80–105 **(check
with hosts for pricing details)**

GOLDEN

Moberly Mountain Lodge

(Dave and Corinne Rimstad)

1402 Adolf Johnson Rd, Golden, BC, V0A 1H0
www.moberlymountainlodge.com
E-mail info@moberlymountainlodge.com

250-344-5544
Fax 250-344-5593
TFr 1-866-240-4814

Moberly Mountain Lodge Bed and Breakfast offers seven guest rooms with private ensuites, jetted tubs or showers and a scrumptious breakfast. Enjoy a game of pool, sit by the roaring fireplace, then soak in our outdoor hot tub. Or enjoy the privacy of your own log cabin complete with full kitchen, fireplace and jetted tubs. Take advantage of the "Four Season" Adventures Golden, BC, has to offer. Situated 12 minutes from Golden, this pristine wilderness setting provides the perfect getaway!

ROOMS Upper floor, Ground floor, Private entrance, **Baths** Private, Ensuite, **Beds** King, Queen, Twin, Pullout sofa, **Smoking** Outside, **In Room** Thermostat, **OTHERS** Pets in residence, **PAYMENT** Visa, MC, Amex, Cash, Trvl's cheques, **BREAKFASTS** Full, Continental, Home-baked, **AMENITIES** Central TV, Central phone, Whirlpool, Barbecue, Kitchen, Fridge, Hot bev. bar, Lounge, Patio, **THINGS TO DO** Trail nearby, Golf, Fishing, Museums, Downhill skiing, Tennis, Swimming, Horseback riding, **LANGUAGE** Eng., **PRICE** (2 persons) 79–140 **(check with hosts for pricing details)**

HARRISON HOT SPRINGS *(east of Vancouver)*

Harrison Heritage House & Kottages

(Sonja and Robert Reyerse)

312 Lillooet Ave, Box 475, Harrison Hot Springs, BC, V0M 1K0
www.bbharrison.com
E-mail rreyerse@bbharrison.com

604-796-9552
TFr 1-800-331-8099

Newly restored heritage house surrounded by mountains, lakes and rivers. We offer you unequalled natural beauty. Our B&B offers a place for you to explore and be touched by the wonder of nature. Relax and recharge in this tranquil one-acre setting along the peaceful banks of the Miami River. All rooms feature private entrance, private bathroom, sitting area, TV/VCR, coffeemaker, queen bed with down duvet. B&B rooms with double Jacuzzi and fireplace. Self-contained luxury riverside cottages also available.

ROOMS Family suite, Ground floor, Private entrance, **Baths** Private, Ensuite, **Beds** Queen, Twin, **Smoking** Outside, **In Room** Thermostat, TV, Fireplace, VCR/DVD, **OTHERS** Open all year, Handicapped access, **PAYMENT** Visa, MC, Direct debit, Cash, Trvl's cheques, **BREAKFASTS** Continental, Home-baked, **AMENITIES** Kitchen, Fridge, Lounge, Patio, **THINGS TO DO** Rental bikes, Trail nearby, Rental canoe or boat, Comp. Canoe or boat, Golf, Fishing, Attractions, Shopping, Cross-country skiing, Downhill skiing, Tennis, Swimming, Horseback riding, Beach, Birdwatching, **LANGUAGE** Eng., Dutch, **PRICE** (2 persons) 105–165 **(check with hosts for pricing details)**

Harrison Hot Springs

South Garden Bed and Breakfast

(Jacquie and John Zuidhof)

3048 Hot Springs Rd, Agassiz, BC, V0M 1A1
www.southgardenbandb.com
E-mail zuidhof@shaw.ca

604-796-3048
TFr 1-866-796-3048

Welcome to the "country comfort" of South Garden Bed and Breakfast, just 4 km from Harrison Hot Springs. We are situated at the foot of Green Mountain on a lush grassy yard, surrounded by a mature forest. For your comfort we offer three suites, each with a four-piece private ensuite. Included is a basket of treats and a full continental breakfast brought to your suite at your designated time. Soothe your senses in the outdoor hot tub tucked into the edge of the forest. Come, relax and enjoy.

ROOMS Ground floor, Private entrance, **Baths** Private, Ensuite, **Beds** Queen, Single or cots, Pullout sofa, **Air** In rooms, **Smoking** Outside, **In Room** Thermostat, TV, Fireplace, **OTHERS** Rural, Open all year, **PAYMENT** Visa, MC, Direct debit, Cash, Trvl's cheques, **BREAKFASTS** Continental, Home-baked, **AMENITIES** Central phone, Whirlpool, Fridge, Patio, **THINGS TO DO** Trail nearby, Rental canoe or boat, Golf, Fishing, Museums, Art, Entertainment, Attractions, Shopping, Cross-country skiing, Tennis, Swimming, Horseback riding, Beach, **LANGUAGE** Eng., **PRICE** (2 persons) 90–105 **(check with hosts for pricing details)**

Harrison Mills *(east of Vancouver)*

Rowena's Inn on the River

(Betty Anne Faulkner)

14282 Morris Valley Rd, Harrison Mills, BC, V0M 1L0
www.rowenasinn.com
E-mail info@rowenasinn.com

604-796-0234
TFr 1-800-661-5108

At Rowena's, enjoy a comfortable night's sleep in one of five luxurious guest rooms, with an overstuffed bed, soft pillows, antique furnishings and private bathroom. Each room has a unique charm and beautiful view. For a truly romantic escape, seclude yourself in one of the cozy guest cottages, complete with Jacuzzi tubs and fireplaces for two. The inn is surrounded by the spectacular Sandpiper Golf Course, an 18-hole, par 72 set along the beautiful waters of the Harrison River. River's Edge Restaurant on property.

ROOMS Upper floor, Ground floor, **Baths** Private, Ensuite, **Beds** King, Queen, Twin, **Smoking** Outside, **In Room** Thermostat, Fireplace, **OTHERS** Rural, Adult, Open all year, Handicapped access, Additional meals, **PAYMENT** Visa, MC, Amex, Cheques accepted, Cash, Trvl's cheques, **BREAKFASTS** Full, **AMENITIES** Central TV, Central phone, Swimming pool, Fridge, Hot bev. bar, Lounge, Patio, **THINGS TO DO** Trail nearby, Golf, Fishing, Museums, Art, Attractions, Cross-country skiing, Swimming, Beach, **LANGUAGE** Eng., **PRICE** (2 persons) 175–325 **(check with hosts for pricing details)**

HAZELTON (KISPIOX RIVER) *(northwestern BC)*

Poplar Park Farm & B&B

(David and Kathy Larson)

Box 23, Site M, RR #1, Hazelton, BC, V0J 1Y0
www.kispiox.com/poplarpark
E-mail ppf@bulkley.net

250-842-6406
Fax 250-842-6412

Poplar Park Farm & B&B is a certified organic working farm on the banks of the world-famous Kispiox River. Salmon fishing in July/August and steelhead fishing in Sept/October. We have four guest rooms with three guest bathrooms and can accommodate up to eight guests. Our master suite has a Jacuzzi tub, fireplace and private balcony with a view of the river. We offer all meals, laundry service, airport shuttles and sell fishing licenses and rent boats. We also have miles of cross-country ski trails.

ROOMS Upper floor, Lower floor, Private entrance, **Baths** Private, Ensuite, Shared with guest, **Beds** King, Queen, Double, **Air** Ceiling fans, **Smoking** Outside, **In Room** Thermostat, Phone, Fireplace, **OTHERS** Rural, Open all year, Additional meals, Pets in residence, **PAYMENT** Visa, MC, Amex, Cheques accepted, Cash, Trvl's cheques, **BREAKFASTS** Full, Home-baked, **AMENITIES** Central TV, Central phone, Barbecue, Laundry, Lounge, Patio, Central Internet access, Central VCR/DVD, **THINGS TO DO** Trail nearby, Rental canoe or boat, Fishing, Cross-country skiing, **LANGUAGE** Eng., **PRICE** (2 persons) 60–150 **(check with hosts for pricing details)**

HOPE *(east of Vancouver)*

Evergreen B&B & Spa

(Paul and Corinna Yorke)

1208 Ryder St, Hope, BC, V0X 1L4
www.evergreen-bb.com
E-mail evergreenbb@telus.net

604-869-9918
Fax 604-869-9918
TFr 1-800-810-7829

Canada Select 4-star accommodation and Tourism BC Approved. Custom-built for a B&B with separate entrances to three suites, each with full private ensuite bathrooms, 6-foot soaker tubs and blowdryers. Suites feature balconies with majestic mountain views, patio furniture, TV/VCR/movies/CD players, A/C, bar fridges, fireplaces, coffee, tea. Relax in the hot tub or book a spa service, massage, facials, etc. Complimentary canoe or bikes with two-day stay. Close to many tourist sites. A perfect destination!

ROOMS Family suite, Upper floor, Ground floor, Private entrance, **Baths** Private, Ensuite, **Beds** Queen, Double, Pullout sofa, **Air** In rooms, **Smoking** Outside, **In Room** Thermostat, Phone, TV, Fireplace, Internet access, VCR/DVD, **OTHERS** Open all year, **PAYMENT** Visa, MC, Amex, Direct debit, Cash, Trvl's cheques, **BREAKFASTS** Full, **AMENITIES** Whirlpool, Barbecue, Laundry, Fridge, Hot bev. bar, Lounge, Patio, **THINGS TO DO** Comp. bikes, Comp. canoe or boat, Golf, Fishing, Museums, Art, Entertainment, Attractions, Tennis, Swimming, Horseback riding, Birdwatching, Antiquing, **LANGUAGE** Eng., **PRICE** (2 persons) 99–129 **(check with hosts for pricing details)**

Hope

Mountainview
Bed and Breakfast
(Tony and Joyce Jongedijk)

71712 Cone Ct, Hope, BC, V0X 1L5
www.mountainviewbnb.com
E-mail mountainviewbb@uniserve.com

604-869-5022
TFr 1-866-869-5022

A peaceful, quiet bed and breakfast in the Canadian Cascade Mountains near Hope, BC. New home with modern spacious rooms. Easy connections to Hwy 1, Hwy 3 and Hwy 5, only minutes from Manning Provincial Park and Fraser Canyon sightseeing. If you are new to our area, or plan to stay one or more days, we'll gladly assist you with trip planning and things to do. We are longtime residents of Sunshine Valley, and we want you to have a memorable stay in our B&B.

ROOMS Upper floor, **Baths** Private, Ensuite, **Beds** King, Queen, Twin, **Smoking** Outside, **In Room** Thermostat, Internet access, VCR/DVD, **OTHERS** Seasonal, **PAYMENT** Cash, Trvl's cheques, **BREAKFASTS** Full, Home-baked, **AMENITIES** Central phone, Whirlpool, Barbecue, Kitchen, Patio, Central Internet access, Central VCR/DVD, **THINGS TO DO** Rental bikes, Trail nearby, Rental canoe or boat, Fishing, Attractions, Cross-country skiing, Downhill skiing, Horseback riding, Birdwatching, **LANGUAGE** Eng., Dutch, **PRICE** (2 persons) 85–99 **(check with hosts for pricing details)**

Invermere *(southeastern BC)*

Harmington House
(Buzz and Norma Harmsworth)

2411 Westside Rd, Invermere, BC, V0A 1K4
www.harmingtonhouse.com
E-mail harmingtonhouse@cyberlink.bc.ca

250-342-6773
TFr 1-877-342-6773

Serene country acreage with wonderful mountain views and fresh air. Comfortable beds that you won't want to get out of. Chipping green, fireside circle, BBQs on patios, hot tub under the stars. Three-bedroom suite, fireplace, full kitchen, private entrances (master bedroom ensuite washroom), air-conditioned. Buzzards Roost apartment, kitchen, washroom with shower, sitting room, gas fireplace. Walking and biking trails very close by. Nearby public beaches. Golf, tennis, arts and culture.

ROOMS Family suite, Lower floor, Private entrance, **Baths** Ensuite, **Beds** King, Queen, Twin, **Air** Central, Ceiling fans, **In Room** Thermostat, **OTHERS** Urban, Open all year, Handicapped access, Seasonal, Additional meals, Pets in residence, Pets welcome, **PAYMENT** Cheques accepted, Cash, Trvl's cheques, **BREAKFASTS** Full, Continental, Self-catered, **AMENITIES** Central TV, Central phone, Whirlpool, Barbecue, Laundry, Kitchen, Fridge, Hot bev. bar, Lounge, Patio, Central VCR/DVD, **THINGS TO DO** Rental bikes, Trail nearby, Rental canoe or boat, Golf, Fishing, Museums, Art, Entertainment, Shopping, Cross-country skiing, Downhill skiing, Tennis, Swimming, Horseback riding, Beach, Birdwatching, Antiquing, **LANGUAGE** Eng., **PRICE** (2 persons) 85–225 **(check with hosts for pricing details)**

KAMLOOPS *(south-central BC)*

Matter House

(Kitty Matter)

225 McGill Rd, Kamloops, BC, V2C 1M2
www.bbcanada.com/1063.htmml

250-374-8011
TFr 1-800-586-0666

Clean, quiet comfortable home. Beautiful view of city, river and mountains. Within walking distance of restaurants and malls. Full homemade breakfast, good beds, queen and twins, private bathrooms, patio and a beautiful flower garden terrace. In the host's own words: "I treat people the way I would like to be treated." *Ich spreche Deutsch.* BC Tourism Approved. Nominated by Chamber of Commerce for excellence award.

ROOMS Upper floor, Ground floor, **Baths** Private, Ensuite, **Beds** Queen, Twin, Single or cots, **Air** Central, **Smoking** Outside, **OTHERS** Urban, Open all year, **PAYMENT** Cash, Trvl's cheques, **BREAKFASTS** Full, Homebaked, **AMENITIES** Central TV, Central phone, Hot bev. bar, Lounge, Patio, **THINGS TO DO** Rental bikes, Trail nearby, Golf, Fishing, Museums, Art, Theatre, Shopping, Cross-country skiing, Downhill skiing, Tennis, Swimming, Horseback riding, **LANGUAGE** Eng., Ger., **PRICE** (2 persons) 65–80 **(check with hosts for pricing details)**

KAMLOOPS

Riverside Mansion Bed and Breakfast

(Rachael and Gerald Van Yerxa)

2736 Thompson Dr, Kamloops, BC, V2C 4L6
www.riversidemansion.com
E-mail riversidemansion@shaw.ca

250-374-9355
Fax 250-374-9354
TFr 1-866-925-9367

Welcome to spectacular Riverside Mansion, a wonderful supernatural British Columbia waterfront B&B set picture-perfect minutes from downtown Kamloops on the waters of the Thompson River. It is one of the most beautiful rivers on earth... dotted with soft sandy beaches and waterfront residences. Be sure to see our original Web site!

ROOMS Family suite, Ground floor, Private entrance, **Baths** Private, Ensuite, **Beds** King, **Air** Central, In rooms, **Smoking** Outside, **In Room** Phone, TV, Fireplace, **PAYMENT** Visa, MC, Amex, Cash, Trvl's cheques, **BREAKFASTS** Full, **AMENITIES** Central TV, Central phone, Swimming pool, Whirlpool, Barbecue, Laundry, Fridge, Lounge, Patio, Central Internet access, Central VCR/DVD, **THINGS TO DO** Rental bikes, Trail nearby, Rental canoe or boat, Golf, Fishing, Museums, Art, Theatre, Entertainment, Attractions, Wineries/Breweries, Shopping, Cross-country skiing, Tennis, Swimming, Horseback riding, Beach, **LANGUAGE** Eng., **PRICE** (2 persons) 149–199 **(check with hosts for pricing details)**

KAMLOOPS

Sunshine Mountain Bed and Breakfast

(Carlos and Danielle Alburquenque)

1417 Sunshine Ct, Kamloops, BC, V2E 2M3
www.sunshinemountainbnb.ca
E-mail bookasuite@sunshinemountainbnb.ca

250-377-0713

This is true comfort in style. Come, relax in our large exclusive two-bedroom suite. One queen bed and one double bed await you, dressed with fine linens. This 1,200-sq. ft. suite contains A/C, private entrance, kitchen with fridge and microwave, living room with TV, VCR and phone, plus a luxurious bathroom with a large jetted tub. We are situated just a few minutes from the info centre, mall, theatres, golf courses and restaurants. Massage therapist available. Large continental breakfast is included.

ROOMS Family suite, Lower floor, Private entrance, **Baths** Private, **Beds** Queen, Double, Pullout sofa, **Air** Central, **In Room** Phone, TV, VCR/DVD, **OTHERS** Urban, Open all year, Pets in residence, **PAYMENT** Visa, Amex, Cash, Trvl's cheques, **BREAKFASTS** Continental, **AMENITIES** Central TV, Central phone, Whirlpool, Kitchen, Fridge, Patio, Central VCR/DVD, **THINGS TO DO** Trail nearby, Golf, Theatre, Shopping, Tennis, **LANGUAGE** Eng., Sp., **PRICE** (2 persons) 75–140 **(check with hosts for pricing details)**

KELOWNA *(south-central BC)*

A Lakeview Heights Bed & Breakfast

(Anne and Mike Murphy)

3626 Royal Gala Dr, Kelowna, BC, V4T 2N9
www.mountainsideaccommodations.com
E-mail info@mountainsideaccommodations.com

250-707-1234
Fax 250-768-3972
TFr 1-800-967-1319

Conveniently located on the Okanagan Winery, Golf & Tourist Route is A Lakeview Heights B&B – a *Canada Select* 4-star property. Enjoy panoramic lake and mountain views from the deck, lounge and most guest rooms. Guest rooms/ensuite bathrooms have been carefully designed for relaxation, comfort and convenience. We offer an extensive, well-presented gourmet breakfast with an international atmosphere and interesting conversation. We look forward to meeting you and helping make your trip truly memorable.

ROOMS Ground floor, Lower floor, **Baths** Private, Ensuite, **Beds** King, Queen, Single or cots, **Air** Central, **Smoking** Outside, **In Room** TV, Internet access, VCR/DVD, **OTHERS** Urban, Rural, Open all year, Handicapped access, **PAYMENT** Visa, MC, Cash, Trvl's cheques, **BREAKFASTS** Full, Home-baked, **AMENITIES** Central phone, Laundry, Fridge, Hot bev. bar, Lounge, Patio, Central Internet access, **THINGS TO DO** Rental bikes, Trail nearby, Rental canoe or boat, Golf, Fishing, Museums, Art, Theatre, Entertainment, Attractions, Wineries/Breweries, Shopping, Cross-country skiing, Downhill skiing, Tennis, Swimming, Horseback riding, Beach, Birdwatching, Antiquing, **LANGUAGE** Eng., Fr., some German and Italian, **PRICE** (2 persons) 70–125 **(check with hosts for pricing details)**

A View To Remember B&B

(Sue and Dann Willis)

1090 Trevor Dr, Kelowna, BC, V1Z 2J8
www.KelownaBandB.com
E-mail Info@KelownaBandB.com

250-769-4028
Fax 250-769-6168
TFr 1-888-311-9555

Established in 1982 this is Kelowna's original bed and breakfast. Located in Lakeview Heights on Kelowna's west side among the wineries, our B&B boasts a panoramic view of Lake Okanagan, mountains, apple orchards and lush vineyards. Our very spacious, beautifully detailed queen bed suites with private entrance not only offer a restful stay for any traveller, but have all of the amenities and comforts of home for those wishing to stay and enjoy their getaway in the heart of the Okanagan Valley.

ROOMS Ground floor, Private entrance, **Baths** Ensuite, **Beds** Queen, Pullout sofa, **Air** Central, **Smoking** Outside, **In Room** TV, Fireplace, Internet access, VCR/DVD, **OTHERS** Rural, Open all year, Pets in residence, Pets welcome, **PAYMENT** Visa, MC, Diners, Amex, Cash, Trvl's cheques, **BREAKFASTS** Full, Home-baked, **AMENITIES** Central phone, Fridge, Hot bev. bar, Patio, **THINGS TO DO** Rental bikes, Trail nearby, Rental canoe or boat, Golf, Fishing, Museums, Art, Theatre, Entertainment, Attractions, Wineries/Breweries, Shopping, Cross-country skiing, Downhill skiing, Tennis, Swimming, Horseback riding, Beach, Birdwatching, **LANGUAGE** Eng., **PRICE** (2 persons) 89–110 **(check with hosts for pricing details)**

Accounting for Taste Bed and Breakfast

(Rosemary and Michael Botner)

1108 Menu Rd, Kelowna, BC, V1Z 2J5
www.accountingfortaste.ca
E-mail rosemary@accountingfortaste.ca

250-769-2836
Fax 250-769-2865
TFr 1-866-769-2836

Minutes from downtown Kelowna, on Mount Boucherie with panoramic view of Lake Okanagan and local vineyards. BC Tourism Approved Accommodation with Superhost accreditation. We are located in British Columbia's Wine Country surrounded by world-class wineries. Your host, Michael Botner, wine writer and educator, can provide custom wine tours. Relax on the deck or in our hot tub with a spectacular view of the lake. Golf courses, beaches, parks and trails are nearby. Packages and gift certificates are available.

ROOMS Lower floor, Private entrance, **Baths** Private, Ensuite, **Beds** Queen, **Air** Central, **In Room** TV, Fireplace, **OTHERS** Adult, Open all year, Pets in residence, **PAYMENT** Visa, MC, Amex, Cash, Trvl's cheques, **BREAKFASTS** Full, Continental, Home-baked, **AMENITIES** Central phone, Whirlpool, Fridge, Hot bev. bar, Lounge, Patio, Central Internet access, Central VCR/DVD, **THINGS TO DO** Golf, Museums, Art, Theatre, Entertainment, Attractions, Wineries/Breweries, Shopping, Cross-country skiing, Swimming, Horseback riding, Beach, **LANGUAGE** Eng., Fr., **PRICE** (2 persons) 75–105 **(check with hosts for pricing details)**

Kelowna

Alto Vista B&B

(Lillian Mouillierat)

1257 Menu Rd, Kelowna, BC, V1Z 3K3
www.altovista.ca
E-mail altovistab&b@telus.net

250-769-7316

Unique, custom-designed home, air-conditioned, panoramic view overlooking Okanagan Lake, Mission Hill and Quails Gate Winery, vineyards. King, queen beds: private ensuites, decks, sitting lounge, big-screen TV; near beaches, marina, golfing, fine dining, gourmet breakfast. CP 7 days.

ROOMS Lower floor, Private entrance, **Baths** Private, **Beds** King, Queen, Double, Twin, Pullout sofa, **Air** Central, **PAYMENT** Visa, MC, Cash, Trvl's cheques, **BREAKFASTS** Full, **AMENITIES** Central TV, Central phone, Laundry, Fridge, Central Internet access, **THINGS TO DO** Golf, Fishing, Wineries/Breweries, Beach, **LANGUAGE** Eng., Fr., **PRICE** (2 persons) 99–150 **(check with hosts for pricing details)**

Kelowna

A Mykonos

(Beryl Rackow and Eric Moller)

318 Poplar Point Dr, Kelowna, BC, V1Y 1Y1
www.amykonos.com
E-mail berylsmarketing@yahoo.ca

250-763-8929
Fax 250-763-2817

This lakefront bed & breakfast and retreat is for those who prize luxury. Minutes away from the heart of Kelowna, this bed & breakfast and retreat exudes luxury. When considering a vacation in beautiful Okanagan, think A Mykonos! Poplar Point Dr is located at base of Knox Mountain and runs along the lake to the left.

ROOMS Family suite, Lower floor, Private entrance, **Baths** Private, Ensuite, **Beds** Queen, Pullout sofa, **Air** Ceiling fans, **Smoking** Outside, **In Room** Thermostat, Phone, TV, Fireplace, Internet access, VCR/DVD, **OTHERS** Open all year, **PAYMENT** Visa, MC, Cash, **BREAKFASTS** Continental, Self-catered, **AMENITIES** Central TV, Central phone, Barbecue, Laundry, Kitchen, Fridge, Hot bev. bar, Lounge, Patio, Central Internet access, Central VCR/DVD, **THINGS TO DO** Golf, Fishing, Museums, Art, Theatre, Entertainment, Attractions, Wineries/Breweries, Shopping, Cross-country skiing, Downhill skiing, Tennis, Swimming, Horseback riding, Beach, Birdwatching, Antiquing, **LANGUAGE** Eng., **PRICE** (2 persons) 99–150 **(check with hosts for pricing details)**

KELOWNA

An English Rose Garden

(Mina Muench)

305 Stellar Dr, Kelowna, BC, V1W 4K5
www.anenglishrosegarden.com
E-mail arosegarden@shaw.ca

250-764-5231
Fax 250-717-0272
TFr 1-877-604-6259

Elegance inside and out, lake view, award-winning garden featuring large pond, waterfalls, streams and over 175 rose bushes, close to wineries, fine dining, beaches, golf. Cotswold Ensuite: queen bed, lake view, ensuite has bath framed with Corinthian columns, separate shower stall. Wicker Ensuite: garden view, features either king or twin beds, wicker furniture, Murphy wallbed in this area. Ensuites have gold faucets, marble counters and fully tiled walls. Full breakfast of your choice with a varied menu.

ROOMS Family suite, Ground floor, Private entrance, **Baths** Ensuite, **Beds** King, Queen, Double, Twin, Single or cots, **Air** Central, **Smoking** Outside, **OTHERS** Urban, Open all year, **PAYMENT** Visa, MC, Diners, Amex, Cheques accepted, Cash, Trvl's cheques, **BREAKFASTS** Full, Home-baked, **AMENITIES** Central TV, Central phone, Fridge, Patio, Central Internet access, Central VCR/DVD, **THINGS TO DO** Rental bikes, Trail nearby, Rental canoe or boat, Golf, Fishing, Museums, Art, Theatre, Entertainment, Attractions, Wineries/Breweries, Shopping, Cross-country skiing, Tennis, Swimming, Horseback riding, Beach, **LANGUAGE** Eng., **PRICE** (2 persons) 75–95 **(check with hosts for pricing details)**

KELOWNA

Cozy Corner Guesthouse B&B

(Myrna White)

4304 Lakeshore Rd, Kelowna, BC, V1W 1W3
www.cozycornerbedandbreakfast.com
E-mail cozyguest@shaw.ca

250-878-2851
Fax 250-764-8862

Cozy two-bedroom guesthouse suited for four-plus. Queen bed in one, double in other. Single cot, baby bed available. Full kitchen and bath. A good variety of breakfast foods included in price for you to prepare. Quiet, clean and very relaxing. BBQ. Porch and patio. Private. Fenced. Also available: in main home (private entrance); bedsitting room (Nautical Suite) queen bed. Has microwave, toaster, grill, coffee pot. Use of spare fridge. Own BBQ. Bath with shower. Near beach. Only 7 km from downtown.

ROOMS Family suite, Ground floor, Private entrance, **Baths** Private, Ensuite, **Beds** Queen, Double, Single or cots, **Air** Central, Ceiling fans, **Smoking** Outside, **In Room** Thermostat, Phone, TV, VCR/DVD, **OTHERS** Urban, Open all year, Pets welcome, **PAYMENT** Cheques accepted, Cash, Trvl's cheques, **BREAKFASTS** Self-catered, **AMENITIES** Central TV, Central phone, Swimming pool, Barbecue, Laundry, Fridge, Patio, Central VCR/DVD, **THINGS TO DO** Rental bikes, Trail nearby, Rental canoe or boat, Golf, Museums, Art, Theatre, Entertainment, Attractions, Wineries/Breweries, Shopping, Swimming, Beach, Birdwatching, Antiquing, **LANGUAGE** Eng., **PRICE** (2 persons) 65–120 **(check with hosts for pricing details)**

Kelowna

Joyce House Bed & Breakfast
(Keith and Judy Standing)

455 Park Ave, Kelowna, BC, V1Y 5R3
www.members.shaw.ca/joycehouse
E-mail joycehouse@shaw.ca

250-717-1912
TFr 1-866-799-1912

A 1905 heritage home within easy walking distance of beaches, parks and Kelowna's downtown with its casino and many excellent restaurants. An award-winning restoration has resulted in a beautiful home with comfortable air-conditioned accommodations. A full breakfast is served in our formal dining room or on our lovely front verandah. Allergies, diabetic, low-cholesterol or vegetarian breakfasts are available on prior request. Enjoy the private hot tub. High-speed Internet access is available.

ROOMS Upper floor, **Baths** Private, Ensuite, **Beds** Queen, Twin, Single or cots, Pullout sofa, **Air** Central, **Smoking** Outside, **In Room** TV, VCR/DVD, **OTHERS** Urban, Open all year, **PAYMENT** Visa, MC, Diners, Amex, Cheques accepted, Cash, Trvl's cheques, **BREAKFASTS** Full, Home-baked, **AMENITIES** Central phone, Whirlpool, Barbecue, Laundry, Fridge, Hot bev. bar, Lounge, Patio, **THINGS TO DO** Comp. bikes, Trail nearby, Golf, Fishing, Museums, Art, Theatre, Entertainment, Attractions, Wineries/Breweries, Shopping, Cross-country skiing, Downhill skiing, Tennis, Swimming, Horseback riding, Beach, Birdwatching, Antiquing, **LANGUAGE** Eng., **PRICE** (2 persons) 100–120 **(check with hosts for pricing details)**

Kelowna

Lakeshore Bed & Breakfast
(Louise and Andy Griffin)

4186 Lakeshore Rd, Kelowna, BC, V1W 1V9
www.hometown.aol.com/lakeshorebandb
E-mail lakeshorebandb@aol.com

250-764-4375
Fax 250-763-6663
TFr 1-866-806-5890

Located just 6 km from downtown Kelowna on the shore of beautiful Okanagan Lake, we offer first-class luxury for the tasteful traveller. We have two spacious guest rooms with queen-size beds, private ensuite baths, satellite TV, central air-conditioning and Ceiling fans. We serve a full breakfast in our dining room featuring seasonal Okanagan delights. We would invite you to enjoy the hot tub overlooking the gardens, or swimming and kayaks on the beach, or just relax with a book in the gardens.

ROOMS Upper floor, **Baths** Private, Ensuite, **Beds** Queen, **Air** Central, **Smoking** Outside, **In Room** TV, **OTHERS** Adult, Open all year, **PAYMENT** Visa, MC, Cash, Trvl's cheques, **BREAKFASTS** Full, Home-baked, **AMENITIES** Central TV, Whirlpool, Fridge, Central Internet access, **THINGS TO DO** Trail nearby, Comp. Canoe or boat, Golf, Wineries/Breweries, Cross-country skiing, Downhill skiing, Swimming, Beach, **LANGUAGE** Eng., **PRICE** (2 persons) 85–135 **(check with hosts for pricing details)**

KELOWNA

Love's Lakeview Bed & Breakfast

(Donna and Ed Love)

2800 Lakeview Rd, Kelowna, BC, V1Z 1Y4
www.bbcanada.com/6021.html
E-mail love7@telus.net

250-769-6307

Guests say, "This is like a 5-star resort!" Our 5, 000 sq.ft. home is on a half-acre and has an outstanding view of the lake and city. Relax by our large in-ground pool and hot tub and enjoy the beautifully landscaped gardens surrounding the property. Indulge in Chef Ed's (retired teacher) gourmet breakfasts and Donna's homemade jams and syrups. Have breakfast on our large deck overlooking the fantastic view. We welcome guests from all over the world. Come and stay at our little piece of paradise!

ROOMS Upper floor, Ground floor, **Baths** Private, Ensuite, **Beds** Queen, Double, Twin, Single or cots, **Air** Central, **Smoking** Outside, **In Room** TV, **OTHERS** Open all year, **PAYMENT** Cash, Trvl's cheques, **BREAKFASTS** Full, Home-baked, **AMENITIES** Central TV, Central phone, Swimming pool, Barbecue, Kitchen, Fridge, Hot bev. bar, Lounge, Patio, **THINGS TO DO** Trail nearby, Golf, Fishing, Museums, Art, Theatre, Entertainment, Wineries/Breweries, Shopping, Cross-country skiing, Downhill skiing, Tennis, Swimming, Horseback riding, Beach, Birdwatching, **LANGUAGE** Eng., **PRICE** (2 persons) 60–90 **(check with hosts for pricing details)**

KELOWNA

Magical Bliss Bed & Breakfast

(Sylvia Lange and Heinz Boshart)

167 Wizard Ct, Kelowna, BC, V1V 1N2
www.magicalbliss.info
E-mail stay@magicalbliss.info

250-717-0616
Fax 250-717-0616

Breathtaking and stunning lakeview! Luxurious and totally private! Your German/Canadian hosts extend a warm invitation to you to share their spacious, award-winning custom built home. Magical Bliss is situated in a tranquil and peaceful cul-de-sac of executive homes where you will have an unobstructed view of Okanagan Lake and the surrounding mountains. This is a gorgeous wilderness setting bordering onto parkland. Especially ideal for those seeking peace and quiet, yet close to all tourist amenities.

ROOMS Family suite, Lower floor, Private entrance, **Baths** Private, Ensuite, **Beds** Queen, **Air** Central, **Smoking** Outside, **In Room** Thermostat, TV, Internet access, VCR/DVD, **OTHERS** Adult, Open all year, **PAYMENT** Cash, Trvl's cheques, **BREAKFASTS** Full, Continental, Home-baked, Self-catered, **AMENITIES** Central TV, Central phone, Laundry, Kitchen, Fridge, Hot bev. bar, Lounge, Patio, Central Internet access, Central VCR/DVD, **THINGS TO DO** Trail nearby, Golf, Fishing, Museums, Art, Theatre, Entertainment, Attractions, Wineries/Breweries, Shopping, Cross-country skiing, Downhill skiing, Tennis, Swimming, Horseback riding, Beach, Birdwatching, **LANGUAGE** Eng., Ger., **PRICE** (2 persons) 100–150 **(check with hosts for pricing details)**

Mission Hills Vacation Suite
(Ed and Linda Schupsky)

472 Curlew Dr, Kelowna, BC, V1W 4L1
www.rentalo.com/21152/missionhills.html
E-mail schupsky@shaw.ca

250-764-2915
Fax 250-764-8407

Suite (900 sq. ft.) – Fully self-contained, sleeps five, very roomy and bright. Unit has vaulted ceilings, private bathroom, kitchenette, dinette and laundry room. Our home is situated in a prestigious residential area among the pines, overlooking the lake and mountains. Suite is tastefully furnished and decorated and features the luxury of privacy and independence in a home-like environment, with your own private front yard, patio, parking and private entry at grade level. Downtown Kelowna drive is 14 minutes.

ROOMS Family suite, Ground floor, Private entrance, **Baths** Private, **Beds** Queen, Single or cots, Pullout sofa, **Air** Central, **Smoking** Outside, **In Room** Thermostat, Phone, TV, Internet access, VCR/DVD, **OTHERS** Urban, Adult, Open all year, Handicapped access, **PAYMENT** Cheques accepted, Cash, Trvl's cheques, **BREAKFASTS** Continental, Home-baked, Self-catered, **AMENITIES** Barbecue, Laundry, Kitchen, Fridge, Patio, **THINGS TO DO** Rental bikes, Trail nearby, Rental canoe or boat, Golf, Fishing, Museums, Art, Theatre, Entertainment, Attractions, Wineries/Breweries, Shopping, Cross-country skiing, Downhill skiing, Tennis, Swimming, Horseback riding, Beach, Birdwatching, Antiquing, **LANGUAGE** Eng., Ger., **PRICE** (2 persons) 70–155 **(check with hosts for pricing details)**

The Grapevine Bed & Breakfast
(Brian and Margaret Arnold)

2621 Longhill Rd, Kelowna, BC, V1V 2G5
www.grapevineokanagan.com
E-mail info@grapevineokanagan.com

250-860-5580
TFr 1-800-956-5580

Come and join us in the tranquil charm of our Cape Cod-style bed and breakfast, centrally located in the beautiful Okanagan Valley in BC. We are near to all Kelowna attractions, including world-class wineries, golfing, skiing and hiking. Enjoy our hot tub, pool and gourmet cuisine.

ROOMS Upper floor, **Baths** Private, Ensuite, **Beds** King, Queen, **Air** Central, **Smoking** Outside, **In Room** Phone, TV, **OTHERS** Adult, Open all year, **PAYMENT** Visa, MC, Cash, **BREAKFASTS** Full, Home-baked, **AMENITIES** Central phone, Swimming pool, Whirlpool, Fridge, Lounge, Patio, Central Internet access, **THINGS TO DO** Rental bikes, Trail nearby, Golf, Museums, Attractions, Wineries/Breweries, Cross-country skiing, Swimming, Horseback riding, Beach, **LANGUAGE** Eng., **PRICE** (2 persons) 140–150 **(check with hosts for pricing details)**

KELOWNA

WatersEdge
Bed and Breakfast

(Marcia, Caroline and Douglas)

1404 Green Bay Rd, Westbank, BC, V4T 2B8
www.kelownawatersedge.com
E-mail westsidewatersedge@shaw.ca

250-768-8650
Fax 250-768-8650
TFr 1-866-768-8650

Air-conditioned rooms with queen-size beds. Located on the water with docking for your boat. Full breakfast by the lake, varied menu. Minutes away from golf courses, wineries, fine dining and downtown Kelowna. Waterskiing, wakeboarding, kayaking available. Inviting guest lounge with TV, movies, CDs, games.

ROOMS Upper floor, **Baths** Ensuite, Shared with guest, **Beds** Queen, Single or cots, **Air** Central, In rooms, **In Room** Thermostat, **OTHERS** Open all year, **PAYMENT** Visa, MC, Cash, Trvl's cheques, **BREAKFASTS** Full, **AMENITIES** Central TV, Central phone, Lounge, Patio, **THINGS TO DO** Rental bikes, Trail nearby, Rental canoe or boat, Golf, Fishing, Museums, Theatre, Entertainment, Attractions, Wineries/Breweries, Shopping, Cross-country skiing, Tennis, Swimming, Horseback riding, Beach, **LANGUAGE** Eng., **PRICE** (2 persons) 80–140 **(check with hosts for pricing details)**

KELOWNA

Wine Country Suites
Bed and Breakfast

(Beverley Forbes and Lynn Raby)

2785 Thacker Dr, Kelowna, BC, V1Z 1W5
www.winecountrysuitesbb.com
E-mail winecountrybb@shaw.ca

250-769-7995
Fax 250-769-7945
TFr 1-877-769-7995

Nestled among vineyards, three luxurious air-conditioned suites with private entrances overlooking beautiful Lake Okanagan. Both suites are beautifully decorated to reflect the wine industry of the region, and have large sitting rooms, bedrooms with queen-size beds, and full baths. Full multi-course breakfasts of your choice are served on private balconies. Snack baskets are provided upon arrival. Amenities include a large heated pool, atrium Jacuzzi and steam room. Barbecue/Internet available.

ROOMS Family suite, Upper floor, Ground floor, Private entrance, **Baths** Ensuite, **Beds** Queen, Pullout sofa, **Air** Central, **Smoking** Outside, **In Room** Thermostat, Phone, TV, Internet access, VCR/DVD, **OTHERS** Urban, Adult, Open all year, **PAYMENT** Visa, MC, Cash, **BREAK-FASTS** Full, Home-baked, **AMENITIES** Swimming pool, Sauna, Whirlpool, Barbecue, Laundry, Fridge, Hot bev. bar, Lounge, Patio, Central Internet access, **THINGS TO DO** Comp. bikes, Trail nearby, Golf, Fishing, Museums, Art, Theatre, Entertainment, Attractions, Wineries/Breweries, Shopping, Tennis, Swimming, Beach, Birdwatching, **LANGUAGE** Eng., Sp., **PRICE** (2 persons) 100–150 **(check with hosts for pricing details)**

Kelowna

Yellow Rose
Bed and Breakfast

(Paul and Lynda Durose)

504 Curlew Dr, Kelowna, BC, V1W 4K9
www.bctravel.com/okanagan/yellowrose/
E-mail lynda@yellowrose.ca

250-764-5257
Fax 250-764-5257

Beautiful romantic modern executive home in an exclusive residential area. Well-appointed central air-conditioned rooms. Robes and slippers provided. Each guest room is equipped with cable TV, high-speed Internet and bar fridge. Delicious hot and cold breakfasts served on antique Yellow Rose china. Close to wineries, golf courses, restaurants and other amenities. Expert advice available regarding day trips and events: sports, sightseeing, etc. Courteous, pampered service is our specialty.

ROOMS Upper floor, Ground floor, Private entrance, **Baths** Private, Ensuite, **Beds** King, Queen, Single or cots, **Air** Central, **Smoking** Outside, **In Room** TV, Internet access, **OTHERS** Urban, Adult, Open all year, **PAYMENT** Cash, Trvl's cheques, **BREAKFASTS** Full, Home-baked, **AMENITIES** Central phone, Whirlpool, Fridge, Patio, **THINGS TO DO** Rental bikes, Trail nearby, Rental canoe or boat, Golf, Fishing, Museums, Art, Theatre, Entertainment, Attractions, Wineries/Breweries, Shopping, Cross-country skiing, Downhill skiing, Tennis, Swimming, Horseback riding, Beach, Birdwatching, Antiquing, **LANGUAGE** Eng., **PRICE** (2 persons) 90–125 **(check with hosts for pricing details)**

Kimberley *(southeastern BC)*

Wasa Lakeside B&B Resort

(James and Mary Swansburg)

4704 Spruce Rd, Box 122, Wasa, BC, V0B 2K0
www.wasalakeresort.com
E-mail info@wasalakeresort.com

250-422-3636
Fax 250-422-3551
TFr 1-888-422-3636

Our lakefront B&B is an escape from the ordinary. A truly unique experience, combining comforts with adventure. Our B&B has lush green lawns, tall shade trees and our own private beach. All rooms have lake and mountain views, queen beds, private entrances and private baths. Swimming, waterskiing and sailing are waiting just outside your door. Bicycling, hiking and tennis are right next door, and 11 golf courses are close by. South of Banff and Lake Louise, AB, near Kimberley and Cranbrook, BC.

ROOMS Private entrance, **Baths** Private, Ensuite, **Beds** Queen, Single or cots, Pullout sofa, **Air** In rooms, Ceiling fans, **Smoking** Outside, **In Room** Thermostat, Fireplace, **OTHERS** Babysitting, Rural, Seasonal, Pets in residence, **PAYMENT** Visa, MC, Cash, Trvl's cheques, **BREAKFASTS** Full, **AMENITIES** Whirlpool, Barbecue, Kitchen, Fridge, Lounge, Patio, **THINGS TO DO** Comp. bikes, Trail nearby, Comp. canoe or boat, Golf, Fishing, Museums, Theatre, Entertainment, Attractions, Shopping, Tennis, Swimming, Horseback riding, Beach, Birdwatching, **LANGUAGE** Eng., **PRICE** (2 persons) 125–150 **(check with hosts for pricing details)**

LADYSMITH *(north of Victoria)*

Hansen House Vacation Suite
(Kim Hansen)

4901 Brenton Page Rd, Ladysmith, BC, V9G 1J6
www.hansenhouse.ca
E-mail hansenhousebandb@shaw.ca

250-245-2373

Fully self-contained 900 sq. ft. suite. Choice of king or twin with extra bedding available. Soaker tub/shower. Internet access, phone, cable TV. Private entrances/parking and patio. Beautifully decorated and tastefully designed. Nestled on two parklike acres. Close to Nanaimo Airport, BC Ferries and all amenities. Wonderful outdoor activities abound; beaches, kayaking, hiking and more. Perfect for vacation base or business travellers. Short drive to Nanaimo and 1 hour to Victoria.

ROOMS Ground floor, Private entrance, **Baths** Private, **Beds** King, Twin, Pullout sofa, **Smoking** Outside, **In Room** Thermostat, Phone, TV, Internet access, VCR/DVD, **OTHERS** Rural, Adult, Open all year, Handicapped access, Pets in residence, **PAYMENT** Visa, MC, Amex, Cheques accepted, Cash, **BREAK-FASTS** Continental, Self-catered, **AMENITIES** Central TV, Central phone, Whirlpool, Laundry, Kitchen, Fridge, Lounge, Patio, Central Internet access, Central VCR/DVD, **THINGS TO DO** Trail nearby, Golf, Fishing, Museums, Art, Theatre, Entertainment, Attractions, Wineries/Breweries, Shopping, Cross-country skiing, Downhill skiing, Tennis, Swimming, Horseback riding, Beach, Birdwatching, Antiquing, **LANGUAGE** Eng., **PRICE** (2 persons) 125–125 **(check with hosts for pricing details)**

LAKE COWICHAN *(north of Victoria)*

Kidd's B&B
(David and Beth Kidd)

518 Point Ideal Dr (Box 1152), Lake Cowichan, BC, V0R 2G0
www.bbcanada.com/kiddsbb
E-mail kiddde@shaw.ca

250-749-7790
Fax 250-749-4229
TFr 1-866-749-7790

Visit with flexible and courteous hosts in a large new home with lake views and an easy walk to beach, marina and town. We offer the one-bedroom suite with queen and hide-a-bed; the purple room with queen and twin beds; and the murphy room with queen bed and wheelchair access. All have ensuite bathrooms and TV/DVD. We serve a full breakfast. Scenic Lake Cowichan has boating, kayaking, swimming, hiking, biking. It is centrally located near Duncan, 90 km from Victoria and 80 km from Nanaimo.

ROOMS Family suite, Upper floor, Ground floor, Private entrance, **Baths** Ensuite, **Beds** Queen, Twin, Pullout sofa, **Air** Central, **Smoking** Outside, **In Room** TV, VCR/DVD, **OTHERS** Rural, Open all year, Handicapped access, **PAYMENT** Visa, MC, Amex, Cash, Trvl's cheques, **BREAKFASTS** Full, **AMENITIES** Central phone, Barbecue, Laundry, Fridge, Patio, **THINGS TO DO** Comp. bikes, Trail nearby, Comp. canoe or boat, Golf, Fishing, Museums, Art, Attractions, Swimming, Beach, Birdwatching, **LANGUAGE** Eng., **PRICE** (2 persons) 60–120 **(check with hosts for pricing details)**

MAPLE RIDGE *(east of Vancouver)*

Bob's B&B

(Maria and Jorge Santana)

21089 Dewdney Trunk Rd, Maple Ridge, BC, V2X 3G1
www.bobsbb.com
E-mail stay@bobsbb.com

604-463-5052
Fax 604-463-3505

Come and visit, you will feel at home at Bob's. Located near Vancouver. Friendly and courteous service, with three large, comfortable, bright suites with queen beds and full ensuite bathrooms. Cable TV. Friendly service and great conversations in our dining room. Our resident cat is very friendly. Very quiet area close to nice lakes, good fishing and good trails. We will do our best to make your stay enjoyable. Your choice of hearty traditional or special breakfast will be carefully prepared and tastefully presented in your private dining area or in the central salon. Wireless high-speed Internet.

ROOMS Family suite, Ground floor, Private entrance, **Baths** Private, Ensuite, **Beds** King, Queen, Single or cots, **Smoking** Outside, **In Room** TV, **OTHERS** Babysitting, Rural, Open all year, Pets in residence, Pets welcome, **PAYMENT** Visa, MC, Diners, Direct debit, Cash, Trvl's cheques, **BREAKFASTS** Full, Home-baked, **AMENITIES** Central TV, Central phone, Barbecue, Laundry, Kitchen, Fridge, Hot bev. bar, Lounge, Patio, Central VCR/DVD, **THINGS TO DO** Comp. bikes, Trail nearby, Rental canoe or boat, Golf, Fishing, Museums, Art, Theatre, Entertainment, Wineries/Breweries, Shopping, Cross-country skiing, Tennis, Swimming, Horseback riding, Birdwatching, Antiquing, **LANGUAGE** Eng., Portuguese, **PRICE** (2 persons) 65–85 **(check with hosts for pricing details)**

MILL BAY *(north of Victoria)*

Bluemoon Bed and Breakfast

(Jean and Dale Davis)

2458 Millbay Rd, Mill Bay, BC, V0R 2P4
www.bluemoonbedandbreakfast.com
E-mail stay@bluemoonbedandbreakfast.com

250-743-3565
TFr 1-866-379-2023

Located on beautiful South Vancouver Island. Enjoy ocean views or walk to village, college or beaches. The Victoria Suite offers a separate bedroom with queen bed and tiled spa-type bathroom, a well-equipped kitchenette area and living room with satellite TV, VCR and pull-out sofa. The Brentwood Suite has a separate bedroom with queen bed, four-piece bath, kitchenette, satellite TV, VCR and pullout sofa. Enjoy garden and ocean views from each suite. BC Tourism Approved.

ROOMS Ground floor, Private entrance, **Baths** Ensuite, **Beds** Queen, Pullout sofa, **Smoking** Outside, **In Room** Thermostat, Phone, TV, Fireplace, Internet access, VCR/DVD, **OTHERS** Rural, Open all year, **PAYMENT** Cheques accepted, Cash, Trvl's cheques, **BREAKFASTS** Continental, Self-catered, **AMENITIES** Central phone, Barbecue, Laundry, Kitchen, Fridge, Hot bev. bar, Patio, Central Internet access, Central VCR/DVD, **THINGS TO DO** Trail nearby, Golf, Fishing, Museums, Art, Theatre, Entertainment, Attractions, Wineries/Breweries, Shopping, Tennis, Beach, Birdwatching, Antiquing, **LANGUAGE** Eng., **PRICE** (2 persons) 85–85 **(check with hosts for pricing details)**

MILL BAY

Ocean Breeze Bed & Breakfast

(Beryl and David Allen)

2585 Sea View Rd, RR #1, Mill Bay, BC, V0R 2P1
www.oceanbreeze.bc.ca
E-mail stay@oceanbreeze.bc.ca

250-743-0608
Fax 250-743-0603
TFr 1-877-743-0654

Perched on the hillside overlooking scenic Mill Bay, this 80-year-old character home provides our guests with privacy, ambience and warm and friendly hospitality. There are three tastefully decorated, air-conditioned guest rooms, all with private bathrooms. Our guests are treated each morning to a delectable three-course breakfast. Mill Bay is in the heart of Vancouver Island's Wine Country as well as being the gateway to the rest of Vancouver Island. Come and pamper yourself in this relaxing setting.

ROOMS Upper floor, Ground floor, **Baths** Ensuite, **Beds** King, Queen, Twin, **Air** Central, **In Room** Thermostat, TV, **OTHERS** Rural, Adult, Open all year, **PAYMENT** Visa, MC, Amex, Cash, Trvl's cheques, **BREAKFASTS** Full, **AMENITIES** Central TV, Central phone, Fridge, Hot bev. bar, Lounge, Patio, **THINGS TO DO** Comp. bikes, Trail nearby, Rental canoe or boat, Golf, Fishing, Museums, Art, Theatre, Attractions, Wineries/Breweries, Shopping, Swimming, Horseback riding, Beach, **LANGUAGE** Eng., **PRICE** (2 persons) 85–125 **(check with hosts for pricing details)**

MISSION *(east of Vancouver)*

Cascade Falls Bed and Breakfast

(Jack and Shirley Van Alphen)

14077 Sylvester Rd, RR #3, Mission, BC, V2V 4J1
www.cascadefallsbb.com
E-mail info@cascadefallsbb.com

604-820-0486
Fax 604-814-2503
TFr 1-800-820-0486

Cascade Falls Bed and Breakfast offers you a romantic getaway 12 miles from the quaint town of Mission and only 11/2 hours from Vancouver. Our home offers you two beautiful suites from which to choose. Each suite features a queen-size Spring Air pillowtop bed, private bath, complimentary soaps, shampoos, conditioners and hairdryer. Each suite has a private entrance, sitting area with fireplace. Satellite TV, VCR, DVD. The oak kitchenettes have fridge, stove and microwave and a private covered patio.

ROOMS Ground floor, Private entrance, **Baths** Private, **Beds** Queen, **Smoking** Outside, **In Room** Phone, TV, Fireplace, VCR/DVD, **OTHERS** Open all year, **PAYMENT** Visa, MC, Cash, **BREAKFASTS** Full, Continental, **AMENITIES** Swimming pool, Whirlpool, Barbecue, Laundry, Kitchen, Fridge, Patio, Central VCR/DVD, **THINGS TO DO** Trail nearby, Golf, Fishing, Museums, Theatre, Attractions, Shopping, Downhill skiing, Swimming, Horseback riding, Birdwatching, Antiquing, **LANGUAGE** Eng., Netherlands, **PRICE** (2 persons) 100–125 **(check with hosts for pricing details)**

MISSION
Fleur de Sel French Country Bed and Breakfast
(Bonnie and Pierre Dubrulle)

8720 Goundrey St, Mission, BC, V2V 6Y5
www.fleurdesel.ca
E-mail bnb@fleurdesel.ca

604-814-2646
Fax 604-814-2646
TFr 1-866-800-2646

Fleur de Sel is surrounded by an award-winning 1-acre perennial garden that has been featured in *Garden West Magazine* and on the TV show *Garden Architecture*. The B&B is comfortably furnished with many antiques and collectables, while both guest rooms are beautifully appointed with cozy pillowtop mattresses and quality linens. Delicious breakfasts include homemade breads and jams. Pierre was the founder of the Pierre Dubrulle Culinary School. Good food in glorious surroundings await.

ROOMS Upper floor, **Baths** Ensuite, **Beds** Queen, **Air** Ceiling fans, **PAYMENT** Visa, MC, Cash, **BREAKFASTS** Full, Continental, Home-baked, **AMENITIES** Lounge, **THINGS TO DO** Trail nearby, Golf, Fishing, Museums, Art, Theatre, Entertainment, Attractions, Wineries/Breweries, Shopping, Downhill skiing, Birdwatching, Antiquing, **LANGUAGE** Eng., Fr., **PRICE** (2 persons) 110–120 **(check with hosts for pricing details)**

NANAIMO *(north of Victoria)*
A-Mays-Inn Lakeside B&B
(Kevin and Wendy May)

2662 Lambert Rd, Ladysmith, BC, V9G 1E1
www.a-mays-inn.com
E-mail info@a-mays-inn.com

250-722-4627
Fax 250-722-4627

Luxury country home (6,200 sq. ft.) on 7 peaceful lakefront acres. Large private suites, king and queen beds with duvets, romantic soaker tubs, stone fireplace. Gourmet breakfasts out on the deck overlooking the lake. TV, lounge, kitchen. Hot tub. Swing and hammock for two. Great bass and trout fishing, hiking, birdwatching, biking. Dock, canoe, fishing boat, swimming. Sand volleyball court, table tennis and exercise equipment. Complimentary bottle of wine and pick-up from ferries and airport.

ROOMS Upper floor, Private entrance, **Baths** Private, **Beds** King, Queen, **Air** In rooms, **In Room** Fireplace, **OTHERS** Rural, Adult, Open all year, Pets in residence, **PAYMENT** Visa, MC, Diners, Amex, Cash, **BREAKFASTS** Full, Continental, Home-baked, **AMENITIES** Central TV, Central phone, Whirlpool, Barbecue, Laundry, Kitchen, Fridge, Hot bev. bar, Lounge, Patio, **THINGS TO DO** Comp. bikes, Trail nearby, Comp. canoe or boat, Fishing, Museums, Art, Theatre, Swimming, **LANGUAGE** Eng., **PRICE** (2 persons) 75–150 **(check with hosts for pricing details)**

NANAIMO

Island View B&B

(Darlene Dillon)

5391 Entwhistle Dr, Nanaimo, BC, V9V 1H2
www.bbcanada.com/1017.html
E-mail islandviewbb@shaw.ca

250-758-5536
TFr 1-888-475-3399

Warm and friendly atmosphere in two-storey, entry-level home in quiet area on half-acre garden paradise. Relax on the deck with a view of the Sunshine Coastline and beautiful sunsets. Breakfast is served in the main floor dining room at guest's convenience. Free pickup and delivery in Nanaimo. One-bedroom apartment with full kitchen.

ROOMS Family suite, Ground floor, Private entrance, **Baths** Private, **Beds** King, Queen, Double, Twin, Single or cots, Pullout sofa, **Air** Ceiling fans, **Smoking** Outside, **In Room** Phone, TV, Fireplace, VCR/DVD, **OTHERS** Urban, Open all year, **PAYMENT** Cheques accepted, Cash, Trvl's cheques, **BREAKFASTS** Full, Home-baked, **AMENITIES** Central TV, Central phone, Laundry, Kitchen, Fridge, Hot bev. bar, Lounge, Patio, Central VCR/DVD, **THINGS TO DO** Trail nearby, Rental canoe or boat, Golf, Fishing, Museums, Art, Theatre, Entertainment, Attractions, Wineries/Breweries, Shopping, Tennis, Swimming, Horseback riding, Beach, Bird-watching, Antiquing, **LANGUAGE** Eng., **PRICE** (2 persons) 50–100 **(check with hosts for pricing details)**

NANAIMO

Pacific Terrace
Bed & Breakfast

(Josie and Wilf Heine)

168 Pacific Terrace, Nanaimo, BC, V9S 3G2
www.canadianbandbguide.ca/bb.asp?ID=3330
E-mail wjheine42@hotmail.com

250-751-2474

Central location, 5 minutes from Departure Bay Ferry Terminal. Enjoy your abundant home-cooked breakfast as you take in the beautiful ocean view of Departure Bay and the Coastal Mountains. We specialize in lox and hot smoked salmon. Complimentary home-baked goods and refreshments on arrival. Our guest area is spacious and has all the comforts of home: TV, fireplace, phone, e-mail, kitchen, laundry. Short walk to the beach and shopping. Courtesy pickup on request. Minutes from downtown, theatre, restaurants, harbour, trails, beach and shopping.

ROOMS Family suite, Lower floor, Private entrance, **Baths** Shared with guest, **Beds** King, Double, Pullout sofa, **Smoking** Outside, **OTHERS** Urban, Seasonal, Additional meals, **PAYMENT** Cash, Trvl's cheques, **BREAKFASTS** Full, Home-baked, **AMENITIES** Central TV, Central phone, Laundry, Kitchen, Fridge, Hot bev. bar, Lounge, Patio, Central VCR/DVD, **THINGS TO DO** Comp. bikes, Trail nearby, Golf, Fishing, Museums, Art, Theatre, Entertainment, Attractions, Wineries/Breweries, Shopping, Cross-country skiing, Tennis, Swimming, Horseback riding, Beach, Birdwatching, **LANGUAGE** Eng., Ger., **PRICE** (2 persons) 55–70 **(check with hosts for pricing details)**

NARAMATA *(south-central BC)*

Majestic Hills Bed & Breakfast Guesthouse

(Joy and Mel Harris)

2815 Arawana Rd, RR #1, Site 9, Comp 24, Naramata, BC, V0H 1N0
www.majestichillsbb.com/
E-mail reservations@majestichillsbb.com

250-496-5525
TFr 1-866-412-5500

Majestic Hills has been created to serve those who enjoy the finer things in life, and who truly like to be pampered. Our B&B is an adult-oriented establishment and we have tried to provide our guests with all the little finer touches that some-times have been missed, from the fine linens to the complimentary bottle of wine and the bathrobes. Pamper your-selves with a stay at Majestic Hills B&B Guesthouse.

ROOMS Family suite, Upper floor, Private entrance, **Baths** Private, **Beds** King, Queen, **Air** In rooms, **In Room** Thermostat, TV, **OTHERS** Open all year, Pets in residence, **PAYMENT** Visa, MC, Direct debit, Cheques accepted, Cash, **BREAKFASTS** Self-catered, **AMENITIES** Central TV, Swimming pool, Whirlpool, Barbecue, Kitchen, Fridge, Lounge, Patio, Central VCR/DVD, **THINGS TO DO** Trail nearby, Golf, Fishing, Museums, Art, Theatre, Entertainment, Attractions, Wineries/Breweries, Shopping, Cross-country skiing, Tennis, Swimming, Horseback riding, Beach, **LAN-GUAGE** Eng., **PRICE** (2 persons) 190–235 **(check with hosts for pricing details)**

NELSON *(southeastern BC)*

Inn the Garden B&B and Guest House

(Lynda Stevens and Jerry VanVeen)

408 Victoria St, Nelson, BC, V1L 4K5
www.innthegarden.com
E-mail info@innthegarden.com

250-352-3226
Fax 250-352-3284
TFr 1-800-596-2337

This beautifully restored Victorian home and the charming private guest house are comfortably decorated with plants, wick-er and antiques. Conveniently located in Nelson's historic downtown, the Inn is only one block from shopping, restau-rants and galleries. Breakfasts are varied and generous and special diets can be accommodated. Golf and ski packages are available. Recommended by most major travel guides including *Northwest Best Places*.

ROOMS Family suite, Upper floor, Ground floor, Private entrance, **Baths** Private, Ensuite, Shared with guest, **Beds** Queen, Double, Twin, Single or cots, **Air** In rooms, **Smoking** Outside, **In Room** Phone, TV, Fireplace, **OTHERS** Urban, Adult, Open all year, Pets in residence, **PAYMENT** Visa, MC, Amex, Cash, Trvl's cheques, **BREAKFASTS** Full, Home-baked, Self-catered, **AMENITIES** Central phone, Kitchen, Fridge, Hot bev. bar, Lounge, Patio, **THINGS TO DO** Rental bikes, Trail nearby, Rental canoe or boat, Golf, Fishing, Museums, Art, Theatre, Entertainment, Attractions, Shopping, Cross-country skiing, Tennis, Swimming, Horseback riding, Beach, **LANGUAGE** Eng., Dutch, **PRICE** (2 per-sons) 85–190 **(check with hosts for pricing details)**

PARKSVILLE *(north of Victoria)*

Arrowsmith Bed and Breakfast (House on the Corner)

(Ed and Kathryn Collins)

701 Arrowsmith Way, Parksville, BC, V9P 2N9
www.canadianbandbguide.ca/bb.asp?ID=3794
E-mail ed_kathryncollins@telus.net

250-752-8746
Fax 250-752-8746

We are in French Creek between Parksville and Qualicum, and centrally located on the eastern coast of Vancouver Island. This area enjoys Canada's mildest year-round climate. The Arrowsmith Bed and Breakfast is just one block away from the Morningstar Golf Course and 10 minutes from Eaglecrest Golf Course. We are just a 5-minute drive to the famous Coombs Market where there are actually goats on the roof. Other points of interest are the French Creek Marina and the beautiful Milner Gardens.

ROOMS Ground floor, Private entrance, **Baths** Private, Ensuite, Shared with hosts, **Beds** Queen, Single or cots, **Air** Central, **Smoking** Outside, **In Room** Phone, TV, Internet access, VCR/DVD, **OTHERS** Open all year, Handicapped access, Pets in residence, **PAYMENT** Cash, Trvl's cheques, **BREAKFASTS** Full, Continental, Home-baked, **AMENITIES** Laundry, Kitchen, Fridge, Hot bev. bar, Lounge, Patio, Central Internet access, Central VCR/DVD, **THINGS TO DO** Comp. bikes, Trail nearby, Rental canoe or boat, Golf, Fishing, Museums, Art, Theatre, Entertainment, Attractions, Shopping, Cross-country skiing, Downhill skiing, Tennis, Swimming, Horseback riding, Beach, Birdwatching, Antiquing, **LANGUAGE** Eng., Fr., Ger., **PRICE** (2 persons) 90–125 **(check with hosts for pricing details)**

PEACHLAND *(south-central BC)*

Casa Serene

(Monica Gruber)

5811 Vicary Rd, Peachland, BC, V0H 1X4
www.canadianbandbguide.ca/bb.asp?ID=3821
E-mail casaserene@telus.net

250-767-2909

A panoramic view from a Mediterranean-style casa overlooking Okanagan Lake to Kelowna. Very quiet and serene, 5 minutes from the lake and surrounded by beautiful garden. There are two suites with a large living room and ensuite with outside terrace. Gourmet breakfasts and fresh fruit from the garden of Casa Serene with catered dinners available upon request. From the intersection of Hwy 97 and Princeton Ave (the only traffic light in Peachland) take Princeton up the hill away from the lake to Columbia and turn right on Columbia. Take Columbia to Vicary and turn right.

ROOMS Family suite, Upper floor, Lower floor, Private entrance, **Baths** Private, Ensuite, **Beds** Queen, **Air** Central, Ceiling fans, **In Room** Thermostat, Phone, TV, VCR/DVD, **OTHERS** Babysitting, Urban, Adult, Open all year, Additional meals, **PAYMENT** Cash, Trvl's cheques, **BREAKFASTS** Full, Home-baked, **AMENITIES** Central TV, Central phone, Barbecue, Laundry, Kitchen, Fridge, Hot bev. bar, Lounge, Patio, Central VCR/DVD, **THINGS TO DO** Rental bikes, Trail nearby, Rental canoe or boat, Golf, Fishing, Museums, Art, Theatre, Entertainment, Attractions, Wineries/ Breweries, Shopping, Cross-country skiing, Downhill skiing, Tennis, Swimming, Horseback riding, Beach, Birdwatching, Antiquing, **LANGUAGE** Eng., Ger., **PRICE** (2 persons) 105–135 **(check with hosts for pricing details)**

PEMBERTON *(north of Vancouver)*

Country Meadows Bed & Breakfast

(Brenda Williams and Heribert Anhofer)

1431 Collins Rd, Pemberton, BC, V0N 2L0
www.bbcanada.com/countrymeadows
E-mail countrymeadows@look.ca

604-894-6605
Fax 604-894-6605

A European-style abode with outdoor hot tub. Located on 6 acres in Pemberton Meadows. Beautiful views of snow-capped Mount Currie. Near two golf courses and the airport at Pemberton. Hearty country breakfasts. To find us turn off Hwy 99 at the traffic light and drive to the round-about. Go straight through and follow the road (by the high school) to Urdal Rd. Turn left, drive until the road turns into Collins Rd (at the corner). We are the second house on the right. There is a sign in the driveway. No tax.

ROOMS Family suite, Upper floor, Ground floor, Private entrance, **Baths** Private, Ensuite, **Beds** King, Queen, Twin, Single or cots, Pullout sofa, **Smoking** Outside, **In Room** Thermostat, TV, Internet access, **OTHERS** Rural, Adult, Open all year, Pets in residence, **PAYMENT** Cheques accepted, Cash, Trvl's cheques, **BREAKFASTS** Full, Continental, Home-baked, Self-catered, **AMENITIES** Central TV, Central phone, Whirlpool, Kitchen, Fridge, Hot bev. bar, Lounge, Patio, **THINGS TO DO** Comp. bikes, Trail nearby, Golf, Fishing, Museums, Wineries/Breweries, Shopping, Cross-country skiing, Horseback riding, Birdwatching, **LANGUAGE** Eng., Ger., **PRICE** (2 persons) 75–120 **(check with hosts for pricing details)**

PENDER ISLAND *(north of Victoria)*

Gnome's Hollow Bed & Breakfast

(Dave and Tania Schissler)

4844 Cutlass Ct, Pender Island, BC, V0N 2M2
www.gnomeshollow.com
E-mail info@gnomeshollow.com

250-629-3844

Log home nestled in a secluded tranquil and unique, magical woodlands setting. For the nostalgic, Bapcha's Room: antique furniture and old photos. Seafaring rogues will like the Captain's Room with its nautical flare. Garden Room: nature lovers will enjoy watching birds by our waterfall. Pre-breakfast beverage delivered to your room. In the evening soak in our romantic outdoor hot tub at the edge of the 15-foot waterfall, or relax in our guests lounge with a warm inviting fireplace, cable TV and stereo.

ROOMS Upper floor, Lower floor, Private entrance, **Baths** Private, Ensuite, **Beds** Queen, Double, **Smoking** Outside, **In Room** Thermostat, **OTHERS** Rural, Adult, Open all year, Pets in residence, Pets welcome, **PAYMENT** Cheques accepted, Cash, Trvl's cheques, **BREAKFASTS** Full, Home-baked, **AMENITIES** Central TV, Whirlpool, Fridge, Lounge, Patio, **THINGS TO DO** Trail nearby, Rental canoe or boat, Golf, Fishing, Museums, Art, Wineries/Breweries, Shopping, Tennis, Swimming, Horseback riding, Beach, Birdwatching, Antiquing, **LANGUAGE** Eng., Ukrianian, **PRICE** (2 persons) 90–110 **(check with hosts for pricing details)**

PENTICTON *(south of Kelowna)*

Inn Paradise Bed & Breakfast

(Haley and Gary McCune)

1050 Churchill Ave, Penticton, BC, V2A 1E4
www.members.shaw.ca/InnParadise
E-mail InnParadise@shaw.ca

250-486-0400

Our guests tell us we have the best location in Penticton! Inn Paradise is located
on a quiet street around the corner from
the sandy beaches of Okanagan Lake, the
restaurants of Sunset Strip, the River
Channel for walking or floating from lake
to lake, as well as many other attractions.
A short walk to convention centre, casino,
downtown, pubs. In the heart of Wine
Country! You name it; we're close to it! Our
four rooms each have a private entrance,
small fridge, queen bed, TV and A/C.

ROOMS Upper floor, Ground floor, Private entrance,
Baths Ensuite, **Beds** Queen, **Air** In rooms, Ceiling fans,
Smoking Outside, **In Room** Thermostat, TV, Internet
access, **OTHERS** Adult, Open all year, **PAYMENT** Visa,
MC, Cash, Trvl's cheques, **BREAKFASTS** Continental,
Self-catered, **AMENITIES** Central phone, Whirlpool,
Barbecue, Kitchen, Fridge, Lounge, Patio, **THINGS TO
DO** Rental bikes, Trail nearby, Rental canoe or boat,
Golf, Fishing, Museums, Art, Theatre, Entertainment,
Attractions, Wineries/Breweries, Shopping, Cross-
country skiing, Downhill skiing, Tennis, Swimming,
Horseback riding, Beach, Birdwatching, Antiquing,
LANGUAGE Eng., **PRICE** (2 persons) 95–135 **(check
with hosts for pricing details)**

PENTICTON

Pinetree Bed and Breakfast

(Linda and Peter Tremblay)

2501 Pinetree Place, Penticton, BC, V2A 9B2
www.bbcanada.com/pinetree
E-mail pinetreeplace@shaw.ca

250-492-0076

Lovely air-conditioned, smoke-free home
with a hot tub and patio where you can
enjoy a breathtaking view of lakes, the
City of Penticton and the mountains.
Quiet rural setting within 3 minutes of
Penticton and less than 10 minutes to
golf courses, Skaha climbing bluffs,
beaches, casino, bike and walking paths
on the Kettle Valley Railway trail, wineries
and orchards. Apex Ski Hill, a hidden
jewel, is within 30 km. We are open all
year and it would be our pleasure to
serve you our homemade full gourmet
breakfast!

ROOMS Upper floor, **Baths** Ensuite, Shared with
guest, **Beds** King, Queen, Double, **Air** Central,
Smoking Outside, **In Room** TV, VCR/DVD, **OTHERS**
Rural, Open all year, **PAYMENT** Cash, Trvl's cheques,
BREAKFASTS Full, Home-baked, **AMENITIES** Central
TV, Central phone, Whirlpool, Patio, Central Internet
access, Central VCR/DVD, **THINGS TO DO** Trail nearby,
Golf, Fishing, Museums, Art, Theatre, Entertainment,
Attractions, Wineries/Breweries, Shopping, Cross-
country skiing, Downhill skiing, Tennis, Swimming,
Horseback riding, Beach, Birdwatching, Antiquing,
LANGUAGE Eng., **PRICE** (2 persons) 69–110 **(check
with hosts for pricing details)**

Penticton

Royal Bed and Breakfast
(Barb and Rick Aoki)

1929 Sandstone Dr, Penticton, BC, V2A 8Y6
www.PentictonBB.com E-mail
RoyalBedAndBreakfast@PentictonBB.com

250-490-3336
TFr 1-866-490-3336

Enjoy the peace and tranquility of the Okanagan Valley in a quiet suburb just 5 minutes from downtown Penticton, the beach, convention centre and restaurants. Just 25 minutes to Apex Ski Resort; and centrally located to the Okanagan's finest wineries and champion golf courses. Our large bedrooms have king-size beds. The Family Suite will accommodate up to four people. Enjoy a panoramic view of the city and lakes below. Ask about our couples getaway packages. Come visit us and pamper yourself with a deep muscle massage from our onsite masseuse, feast on our gourmet breakfasts and enjoy the view!

ROOMS Family suite, Ground floor, **Baths** Private, Ensuite, **Beds** King, Twin, **Air** Central, **Smoking** Outside, **In Room** TV, Fireplace, Internet access, VCR/DVD, **OTHERS** Urban, Open all year, **PAYMENT** Visa, MC, Amex, **BREAKFASTS** Full, Continental, **AMENITIES** Central TV, Central phone, Whirlpool, Fridge, Hot bev. bar, Lounge, Patio, Central Internet access, **THINGS TO DO** Rental bikes, Trail nearby, Rental canoe or boat, Golf, Fishing, Museums, Art, Entertainment, Attractions, Wineries/ Breweries, Shopping, Cross-country skiing, Downhill skiing, Tennis, Swimming, Horseback riding, Beach, Birdwatching, Antiquing, **LANGUAGE** Eng., **PRICE** (2 persons) 125–170 **(check with hosts for pricing details)**

Port Alberni *(northwest of Nanaimo)*

Alpine Springs Farm and B&B
(Jacinthe Deschambault and Elmar Langle)

6860, Desmond Rd, Port Alberni, BC, V9Y 8T5
www.alpinespringsfarm.ca
E-mail info@alpinespringsfarm.ca

250-724-6841
Fax 250-724-6840

Unique working hobby farm including fresh spring water, several waterfalls, waterwheels and water cannon. Peaceful country setting (your home away from home), adjacent to the famous 'Log Train Trail' and many other hiking trails. Queen beds, down quilts, ensuite bathrooms, private entrance and full homemade breakfast menu. We can serve you in English, French and *wir sprechen Deutsch*. Smoke-free environment. Our guests are welcome to use our picnic table, hammock and benches for resting and relaxing.

ROOMS Family suite, Ground floor, Private entrance, **Baths** Ensuite, **Beds** Queen, **Smoking** Outside, **In Room** Thermostat, **OTHERS** Rural, Open all year, **PAYMENT** Visa, MC, Trvl's cheques, **BREAKFASTS** Full, Home-baked, **AMENITIES** Central TV, Central phone, Barbecue, Fridge, Central Internet access, **THINGS TO DO** Rental bikes, Trail nearby, Rental canoe or boat, Golf, Fishing, Museums, Attractions, Wineries/Breweries, Shopping, Swimming, Beach, Birdwatching, **LANGUAGE** Eng., Fr., Ger., **PRICE** (2 persons) 70–90 **(check with hosts for pricing details)**

PORT HARDY *(northern Vancouver Island)*

Hamilton Bed and Breakfast
(Lorne and Betty Hamilton)

9415 Mayor's Way, Box 1926, Port Hardy, BC, V0N 2P0
www.bbcanada.com/hamiltonbb

250-949-6638

Modern home in residential area. Twin, double, queen beds; shared baths: robes provided: complimentary tea, coffee, hot chocolate; ferry shuttle arranged. Near town, fishing, hiking, diving. Travel up Hwy 19 to the four-way stop, turn left on Granville St (Hospital sign), and continue to Mayor's Way. Turn left to the first house on the left. We are government inspected. Have food-safe course. Rates: Single $50, Double $65, Twin or Queen $70.

ROOMS Upper floor, Ground floor, **Baths** Shared with guest, **Beds** Queen, Double, Twin, Single or cots, **Air** Central, **Smoking** Outside, **OTHERS** Urban, Open all year, **PAYMENT** Cash, Trvl's cheques, **BREAKFASTS** Home-baked, **AMENITIES** Central phone, Lounge, **THINGS TO DO** Trail nearby, Rental canoe or boat, Golf, Fishing, Museums, Art, Attractions, Shopping, Tennis, Swimming, Beach, Birdwatching, **LANGUAGE** Eng., **PRICE** (2 persons) 65–70 **(check with hosts for pricing details)**

PORT MCNEILL *(northern Vancouver Island)*

C-Shasta Bed & Breakfast
(Caroline Westrum)

2511 Cassiar Place, Port McNeill, BC, V0N 2R0
www.cshasta.com
E-mail cshasta@island.net

250-956-4610
Fax 250-956-4610

Nestled on the hilltop in the picturesque coastal community of Port McNeill, BC, on Northern Vancouver Island, C-Shasta Bed & Breakfast with its wonderful ocean and coastal mountain views offers private and tranquil guest accommodations in a charming and cozy home. Warmly furnished and charmingly elegant guest rooms are a haven of comfort and relaxing ambience. Quiet residential neighbourhood and within short walking distance to marina, shops, restaurants and town centre. Hospitality from the heart!

ROOMS Family suite, Upper floor, Ground floor, Private entrance, **Baths** Private, Ensuite, **Beds** Queen, Pullout sofa, **Smoking** Outside, **In Room** Phone, TV, Internet access, **OTHERS** Rural, Open all year, Pets in residence, **PAYMENT** Cash, Trvl's cheques, **BREAKFASTS** Full, **AMENITIES** Central TV, Central phone, Barbecue, Fridge, Hot bev. bar, Lounge, Patio, Central Internet access, Central VCR/DVD, **THINGS TO DO** Golf, Fishing, Museums, Art, Attractions, Shopping, Cross-country skiing, Downhill skiing, Beach, Birdwatching, **LANGUAGE** Eng., **PRICE** (2 persons) 75–85 **(check with hosts for pricing details)**

POWELL RIVER *(northwest of Vancouver)*

Adventure B&B

(Owen Gaskell and Daphne Wilson)

7439 Nootka St, Powell River, BC, V8A 1K5
www.adventureb-b.com
E-mail info@adventureb-b.com

604-485-7097

Adventure B&B is in quiet setting on 5 acres. All rooms have queen-size beds. Suite has private entrance and deck and bathroom and a double sofa/futon. Two upstairs rooms have additional sleeping lofts. Full gourmet breakfast with home baking. Vegetarian and organic meals on request. Guest sunroom overlooking garden. Picnic, campfire area and sauna. Smoke-free home. Pets are restricted to outdoors. Families with children are welcome. Hosts are environmentally- and health-conscious. Spanish spoken.

ROOMS Family suite, Upper floor, Ground floor, Lower floor, Private entrance, **Baths** Private, Ensuite, Shared with guest, **Beds** Queen, Double, Pullout sofa, **Air** Central, In rooms, **Smoking** Outside, **In Room** Thermostat, **OTHERS** Babysitting, Rural, Open all year, Additional meals, **PAYMENT** Visa, MC, Cash, Trvl's cheques, **BREAKFASTS** Full, Home-baked, **AMENITIES** Central phone, Sauna, Barbecue, Laundry, Kitchen, Fridge, Lounge, Patio, **THINGS TO DO** Trail nearby, Rental canoe or boat, Golf, Fishing, Museums, Art, Theatre, Attractions, Shopping, Cross-country skiing, Tennis, Swimming, Horseback riding, Beach, Birdwatching, Antiquing, **LANGUAGE** Eng., Sp., **PRICE** (2 persons) 70–90 **(check with hosts for pricing details)**

POWELL RIVER

Beacon B&B and Spa

(Roger and Shirley Randall)

3750 Marine Ave, Powell River, BC, V8A 2H8
www.beaconbb.com
E-mail stay@beaconbb.com

604-485-5563
Fax 604-485-9450
TFr 1-877-485-5563

Feel the sea breeze in our centrally located, waterfront, smoke-free adult-oriented home. We offer two cozy rooms, private baths plus a luxurious, wheelchair accessable, two-bedroom, self-contained suite overlooking the Strait of Georgia (sleeps five). Marvel at our everchanging ocean vista, awesome sunsets and soaring eagles. Relax with onsite massage and soak in our hot tub. Awake to a full gourmet breakfast! We are business and tourist friendly. Wireless available. We look forward to meeting you all!

ROOMS Family suite, Upper floor, Lower floor, Private entrance, **Baths** Private, Ensuite, **Beds** Queen, Twin, **Smoking** Outside, **In Room** Thermostat, Phone, TV, Internet access, VCR/DVD, **OTHERS** Adult, Open all year, Handicapped access, Pets welcome, **PAYMENT** Visa, MC, Cash, Trvl's cheques, **BREAKFASTS** Full, Home-baked, **AMENITIES** Central TV, Laundry, Kitchen, Fridge, Hot bev. bar, Lounge, Patio, Central Internet access, Central VCR/DVD, **THINGS TO DO** Trail nearby, Golf, Fishing, Museums, Art, Theatre, Shopping, Tennis, Swimming, Horseback riding, Beach, Birdwatching, **LANGUAGE** Eng., **PRICE** (2 persons) 85–155 **(check with hosts for pricing details)**

POWELL RIVER

Cedar Lodge
(Andy and Mary Payne)

C-8/9825 Malaspina Rd, RR #2, Powell River, BC, V8A 4Z3
www.prcn.org/cedar
E-mail andymaryp@yahoo.ca

604-483-4414
Fax 604-483-4414

Cedar Lodge Bed and Breakfast is your gateway to the Sunshine Coast Trail and Desolation Sound Marine Park. An area of incredible beauty and unlimited wilderness recreation. Kayak and boat rental as well as organized tours all available nearby. Our self-catering suite is ideal for families. Guests are welcome to use the barbecue facilities. Come and enjoy Cedar Lodge with its comfortable rooms, excellent breakfasts and warm and friendly hospitality. We look forward to welcoming you to our home!

ROOMS Family suite, Lower floor, Private entrance, **Baths** Private, Ensuite, Shared with guest, Beds Queen, Single or cots, Pullout sofa, **Air** In rooms, **Smoking** Outside, **In Room** Thermostat, TV, VCR/DVD, **OTHERS** Rural, Open all year, **PAYMENT** Visa, MC, Amex, Direct debit, Cash, Trvl's cheques, **BREAKFASTS** Full, Home-baked, **AMENITIES** Barbecue, Laundry, Kitchen, Fridge, **THINGS TO DO** Trail nearby, Rental canoe or boat, Golf, Fishing, Attractions, Shopping, Beach, **LANGUAGE** Eng., Malay, **PRICE** (2 persons) 70–120 **(check with hosts for pricing details)**

POWELL RIVER

Hummingbird Bed & Breakfast
(James and Anita Silvestrini)

7139 Ladner St, Powell River, BC, V8A 5G1
www.hummingbirdbandb.com
E-mail stay@hummingbirdbandb.com

604-485-5658
Fax 604-485-5658
TFr 1-877-362-6989

Bright spacious home. Large sundecks, panoramic view, quiet neighbourhood, centrally located. Self-contained suite, private entrance, sleeps four (weekly, monthly rates available). Oceanview Room with ensuite, private sundeck. Garden Room: queen bed, private bathroom. Gourmet breakfast, A/C. No smoking or pets. Major credit cards accepted. CP 7 days.

ROOMS Family suite, Ground floor, Private entrance, **Baths** Private, Ensuite, **Beds** Queen, Single or cots, **Air** Central, **Smoking** Outside, **In Room** TV, **OTHERS** Open all year, **PAYMENT** Visa, MC, Amex, Cash, Trvl's cheques, **BREAKFASTS** Full, **AMENITIES** Central TV, Central phone, Laundry, Kitchen, Fridge, Lounge, Patio, **THINGS TO DO** Rental bikes, Trail nearby, Rental canoe or boat, Golf, Fishing, Museums, Art, Theatre, Entertainment, Attractions, Shopping, Tennis, Swimming, Beach, **LANGUAGE** Eng., Italian, **PRICE** (2 persons) 85–125 **(check with hosts for pricing details)**

PRINCE GEORGE *(northern BC)*

A Prince George Bed and Breakfast Hotline

Prince George, BC, V2K 5Y7
www.PrinceGeorgeBnB.com
E-mail bbhotline@princegeorge.com

250-562-2222
TFr 1-877-562-2626

Prince George B&B Hotline hosts invite you to experience our "Northern Hospitality." Select from a variety of quality, inspected, comfortable accommodations complete with experienced, friendly, knowledgeable hosts. For availability and reservations call our toll-free number.

PRINCE GEORGE

Chalet Sans Souci B&B
(Lutz and Jacqueline Klaar)

10350 Pooley Rd, Prince George, BC, V2N 5V7
www.pgonline.com/bnb/chalet.html
E-mail chalet@mag-net.com

250-963-7202
Fax 250-963-5634
TFr 1-866-963-7202

Experience our unique host-built and decorated "Gingerbread House" minutes from town on 16 wooded hectares with beaver pond in quiet country setting. Area offers hiking, birdwatching, horseback riding, golfing, fishing. Frequent wildlife sightings, cross-country and downhill skiing in the winter. Choice of full, continental or vegetarian breakfast. Horse corral available. Laundry facilities, access to Internet and fax machine. Three rooms. Family rates available. Approved by Tourism BC.

ROOMS Upper floor, Ground floor, **Baths** Private, **Beds** Queen, Twin, **Air** Central, **Smoking** Outside, **In Room** Thermostat, TV, **OTHERS** Babysitting, Rural, Open all year, **PAYMENT** Visa, MC, Amex, Cash, Trvl's cheques, **BREAKFASTS** Full, Continental, Home-baked, **AMENITIES** Central TV, Central phone, Barbecue, Laundry, Kitchen, Fridge, Hot bev. bar, Lounge, Patio, Central Internet access, Central VCR/DVD, **THINGS TO DO** Comp. bikes, Trail nearby, Rental canoe or boat, Golf, Fishing, Museums, Art, Theatre, Entertainment, Attractions, Wineries/Breweries, Shopping, Cross-country skiing, Swimming, Horseback riding, Birdwatching, **LANGUAGE** Eng., Fr., Ger., **PRICE** (2 persons) 65–75 **(check with hosts for pricing details)**

PRINCE GEORGE

Fox Hollow B&B
(Kathy and Bob Weston)

3600 Emile Crest, Prince George, BC, V2K 5Y7
www.foxhollowbnb.com
E-mail foxhollow@foxhollowbnb.com

250-962-4982
TFr 1-866-809-8249

Come and enjoy our peaceful, wooded acreage north of the city off Hwy 97(follow the blue B&B signs). Spacious queen, and queen with single, private baths, guest robes and private entrance. Guest lounge provides a satellite TV/VCR, pool table, fireplace and guest fridge. Enjoy a delicious home-cooked full or continental breakfast in our country kitchen while you watch for wildlife (resident foxes, rabbit, grouse and the odd moose). Smoke/pet-free environment. Shuttle service to VIA Rail. Families welcome!

ROOMS Upper floor, Ground floor, Private entrance, **Baths** Private, **Beds** Queen, Twin, Pullout sofa, **Smoking** Outside, **OTHERS** Rural, Open all year, **PAYMENT** Visa, MC, Diners, Amex, Cash, Trvl's cheques, **BREAKFASTS** Full, Continental, Home-baked, **AMENITIES** Central TV, Fridge, Lounge, Patio, Central VCR/DVD, **THINGS TO DO** Golf, Fishing, Museums, Art, Theatre, Wineries/Breweries, Shopping, Cross-country skiing, Swimming, **LANGUAGE** Eng., **PRICE** (2 persons) 70–85 **(check with hosts for pricing details)**

PRINCE GEORGE

Griffiths on Gilbert Bed and Breakfast
(Julie and Peter Griffiths)

3913 Gilbert Dr, Prince George, BC, V2K 4Z6
www.griffithsbnb.com
E-mail julie@griffithsbnb.com

250-612-0273
Fax 250-612-0215
TFr 1-877-612-1144

Experience northern BC at its best! Our bed and breakfast suite is private and perfect for families and small groups. Our beautifully landscaped B&B is located in a quiet wooded area adjacent to over 100 km of hiking trails, yet only a scenic 10-minute drive to Prince George amenities.

ROOMS Family suite, Lower floor, Private entrance, **Baths** Private, **Beds** Queen, Ceiling fans, Twin, Single or cots, Pullout sofa, **Air** Ceiling fans, **Smoking** Outside, **OTHERS** Urban, Rural, Open all year, Pets in residence, Pets welcome, **PAYMENT** Visa, MC, Diners, Amex, Cash, Trvl's cheques, **BREAKFASTS** Full, Continental, Home-baked, **AMENITIES** Central TV, Central phone, Whirlpool, Barbecue, Laundry, Kitchen, Fridge, Hot bev. bar, Lounge, Patio, Central Internet access, Central VCR/DVD, **THINGS TO DO** Comp. bikes, Trail nearby, Golf, Fishing, Museums, Art, Theatre, Entertainment, Attractions, Wineries/Breweries, Shopping, Cross-country skiing, Downhill skiing, Tennis, Swimming, **LANGUAGE** Eng., **PRICE** (2 persons) 70–75 **(check with hosts for pricing details)**

Prince George
Mead Manor B&B
(Bob and Laura Mead)

4127 Baker Rd, Prince George, BC, V2N 5K2
www.pgonline.com/bnb/mead.html
E-mail meadmanor@shaw.ca

250-964-8496
Fax 250-964-8449
TFr 1-866-215-4679

Relax in a cozy, casual environment. Four-level split home that has welcomed many guests with the same charm and warmth that will make you feel right at home. This is a place to get away and relax from the everyday pressures. Stop off while en-route to wherever you're headed. Two large rooms are tastefully decorated, with a private bath and queen bed in each. Breakfast is served in our sunroom overlooking the garden-like setting with a choice from our gourmet menu. Something to please every palette.

ROOMS Upper floor, Ground floor, Private entrance, **Baths** Private, Ensuite, **Beds** Queen, Twin, Single or cots, **Air** Central, In rooms, Ceiling fans, **Smoking** Outside, **In Room** Thermostat, Phone, TV, **OTHERS** Urban, Open all year, **PAYMENT** Visa, MC, Diners, Amex, Cheques accepted, Cash, Trvl's cheques, **BREAKFASTS** Full, Home-baked, **AMENITIES** Central TV, Central phone, Laundry, Fridge, Lounge, Patio, Central VCR/DVD, **THINGS TO DO** Golf, Museums, Art, Theatre, Entertainment, Attractions, Shopping, Cross-country skiing, Swimming, **LANGUAGE** Eng., **PRICE** (2 persons) 60–75 **(check with hosts for pricing details)**

Prince George
Pine Ridge Bed and Breakfast
(John and Gwen Reimer)

3869 Brentwood Pl, Prince George, BC, V2K 3Y1
www.pineridgebb.com
E-mail jreimer@mag-net.com

250-962-8469
Fax 250-962-8467
TFr 1-866-307-6440

Large, comfortable home on quiet cul-de-sac and green belt. Off-street parking. No stairs. Host John enjoys taking guests fishing. Hostess Gwen provides full breakfast and evening snacks with home baking served in the dining room or bright sunroom. Families welcome. Warm, caring Christian hospitality. Smoke-free and pet-free environment. Access to e-mail and fax. Just 5 minutes from Aberdeen Glen, a world-class golf course. We live 7 km north of town. Free bus, train shuttle. Come watch the squirrels play tag.

ROOMS Ground floor, **Baths** Ensuite, Shared with guest, **Beds** Queen, Twin, **Smoking** Outside, **OTHERS** Urban, **PAYMENT** Cheques accepted, Cash, Trvl's cheques, **BREAKFASTS** Full, Home-baked, **AMENITIES** Central phone, Laundry, Patio, **THINGS TO DO** Trail nearby, Golf, Fishing, Museums, Art, Theatre, Entertainment, Attractions, Wineries/Breweries, Shopping, Cross-country skiing, Swimming, **LANGUAGE** Eng., **PRICE** (2 persons) 55–75 **(check with hosts for pricing details)**

PRINCE GEORGE

Rosels Bed and Breakfast
(Wilf and Rosel Vogt)

2959 Sullivan Cres, Prince George, BC, V2N 5H6
www.roselsbnb.com
E-mail roselsbnb@telus.net

250-964-4608
Fax 250-964-9702
TFr 1-888-964-4608

Award-winning hospitality. The 780-sq. ft. suite offers king-size bed, ensuite bath, private sitting-room with fireplace, TV, VCR, full kitchen, private deck with garden access. Second room has queen-size bed, TV, VCR, private bath. Continental to full breakfast served. Complimentary pickup at all terminals. Close to restaurants, shopping, university, entertainment and sports facilities. Whether you visit Prince George for business or pleasure, stay with us. We would love to pamper you. *Wir sprechen Deutsch.*

ROOMS Family suite, Upper floor, Ground floor, **Baths** Private, Ensuite, **Beds** King, Queen, **Air** Central, **Smoking** Outside, **In Room** Phone, TV, Fireplace, Internet access, VCR/DVD, **OTHERS** Open all year, Handicapped access, **PAYMENT** Visa, MC, Diners, Amex, Cash, Trvl's cheques, **BREAKFASTS** Full, **AMENITIES** Central phone, Laundry, Kitchen, Fridge, Patio, **THINGS TO DO** Trail nearby, Golf, Museums, Art, Theatre, Entertainment, Attractions, Wineries/ Breweries, Shopping, Cross-country skiing, Tennis, Swimming, Birdwatching, **LANGUAGE** Eng., Ger., **PRICE** (2 persons) 70–115 **(check with hosts for pricing details)**

PRINCE GEORGE

Water's Edge
(Stuart and Marie Willmot)

4374 Stevens Dr, Prince George, BC, V2K 1E3
www.watersedgebnb.ca
E-mail wilmostuart@yahoo.ca

250-563-1905
Fax 250-563-1905
TFr 1-888-567-3311

Welcome to Water's Edge, one of Prince George's premier B&Bs. Nestled on the banks of the beautiful Nechako River, Water's Edge occupies an idyllic spot. We invite you to share our home, hospitality, captivating views and the peace and tranquility that is the essence of Water's Edge. Directions: Turn off Hwy 97 at John Hart Bridge over Nechako, onto North Nechako Rd. Head northwest towards Foothills Bridge for 2 km. Turn onto Churchill Rd, then left onto Stevens Dr. Go to the end of road.

ROOMS Family suite, Upper floor, **Baths** Private, **Beds** Double, **Smoking** Outside, **In Room** Thermostat, Phone, TV, Fireplace, Internet access, VCR/DVD, **OTHERS** Open all year, **PAYMENT** Visa, Cash, Trvl's cheques, **BREAKFASTS** Full, **AMENITIES** Central TV, Central phone, Fridge, Lounge, Patio, Central Internet access, Central VCR/DVD, **THINGS TO DO** Comp. bikes, Trail nearby, Comp. canoe or boat, Golf, Fishing, Museums, Art, Theatre, Entertainment, Attractions, Wineries/Breweries, Shopping, Cross-country skiing, Tennis, Swimming, Horseback riding, **LANGUAGE** Eng., **PRICE** (2 persons) 70–75 **(check with hosts for pricing details)**

Prince Rupert *(northwestern BC)*

Eagle Bluff B&B

(Mary Allen and Bryan Cox)

201 Cow Bay Rd, Prince Rupert, BC, V8J 1A2
www.citytel.net/eaglebluff
E-mail eaglebed@citytel.net

250-627-4955
Fax 250-627-7945
TFr 1-800-833-1550

Next to Cow Bay Wharf and Atlin Terminal Visitor Centre on Cow Bay Rd, four blocks from Hwy 16 and Third Ave light. Renovated fishing home in unique harbour setting in historic area. See freighters, pleasure craft and commercial fishing boats delivering and gearing up. See soaring eagles, sunsets from the deck. Near gourmet cafes, specialty shops, attractions. Short walk to downtown. Next to airport pickup and visitor info, short ride to train, ferry terminals, historic district. Families welcome. Winter/weekly rates.

ROOMS Family suite, Upper floor, Ground floor, Lower floor, Private entrance, **Baths** Ensuite, Shared with guest, **Beds** King, Queen, Twin, **Air** In rooms, **Smoking** Outside, **In Room** Thermostat, Phone, TV, Fireplace, VCR/DVD, **OTHERS** Urban, Open all year, Handicapped access, **PAYMENT** Visa, MC, Cash, Trvl's cheques, **BREAKFASTS** Full, Home-baked, **AMENITIES** Laundry, Kitchen, Fridge, Lounge, Patio, Central Internet access, Central VCR/DVD, **THINGS TO DO** Trail nearby, Golf, Fishing, Museums, Art, Theatre, Entertainment, Attractions, Shopping, Beach, Birdwatching, **LANGUAGE** Eng., **PRICE** (2 persons) 55–99 **(check with hosts for pricing details)**

Prince Rupert

Studio 1735 Bed & Breakfast & Art Retreat

(Diana Hoffman)

1735 Graham Ave, Prince Rupert, BC, V8J 1C7
www.canadianbandbguide.ca/bb.asp?ID=1908
E-mail studio1735@hotmail.com

250-622-2787
Fax 250-622-2787
TFr 1-877-922-2787

A B&B with an art studio and views of the harbour and mountains. Guests can use the art studio, which has a fireplace, art instruction sessions, art therapy sessions and art supplies for a fee. One guest room has an ensuite bathroom with Jacuzzi and skylight. There are two other rooms each with a double bed. Guests are served breakfast in the dining room with a view of the harbour, and may relax in the living room with fireplace, TV and balcony and porch with views of the ocean. Walking distance to downtown.

ROOMS Upper floor, **Baths** Ensuite, Shared with guest, **Beds** Double, **Smoking** Outside, **In Room** Phone, **OTHERS** Urban, Open all year, Pets in residence, **PAYMENT** Cheques accepted, Cash, Trvl's cheques, **BREAKFASTS** Full, **AMENITIES** Central TV, Sauna, Laundry, Kitchen, Fridge, Hot bev. bar, Lounge, Patio, Central Internet access, Central VCR/DVD, **THINGS TO DO** Trail nearby, Golf, Fishing, Museums, Art, Theatre, Entertainment, Attractions, Shopping, Tennis, Swimming, Beach, **LANGUAGE** Eng., **PRICE** (2 persons) 40–60 **(check with hosts for pricing details)**

QUADRA ISLAND *(east-central Vancouver Island)*

Firesign Art & Design Studio and B&B

(Nanci Cook and Tracy Tomlinson)

730 Smiths Rd, PO Box 265, Quathiaski Cove, BC, V0P 1N0
www.firesignartanddesign.com
E-mail info@firesignartanddesign.com

250-285-3390

Firesign B&B is a cozy, comfortable, friendly and quiet home-away-from-home on private wooded acreage near hiking, beaches and wilderness adventure. Firesign Studio has original art, reproductions, art cards and other gift items by Nanci Cook. Firesign also hosts painting and mixed media workshops with visiting artists. Check-in 4 p.m., check-out 11 a.m. Directions: On Vancouver Island take Hwy 19 north to downtown, Campbell River to Quadra Island ferry. Drive up hill on Quadra, turn right at stop sign, drive up to end of road, turn left on Heriot Bay Rd follow to Smiths Rd on right to first driveway on left past Cedar Dr.

ROOMS Family suite, Ground floor, Private entrance, **Baths** Private, Ensuite, Shared with guest, **Beds** Queen, Twin, **Smoking** Outside, **In Room** Thermostat, **OTHERS** Rural, Open all year, Handicapped access, Pets welcome, **PAYMENT** Visa, MC, Amex, Cheques accepted, Cash, Trvl's cheques, **BREAKFASTS** Full, Home-baked, **AMENITIES** Central TV, Central phone, Barbecue, Kitchen, Fridge, Hot bev. bar, Lounge, Patio, Central Internet access, Central VCR/DVD, **THINGS TO DO** Rental bikes, Trail nearby, Rental canoe or boat, Fishing, Museums, Art, Theatre, Entertainment, Attractions, Wineries/ Breweries, Shopping, Cross-country skiing, Tennis, Swimming, Beach, **LANGUAGE** Eng., **PRICE** (2 persons) 65–85 **(check with hosts for pricing details)**

QUADRA ISLAND

Moonlight Shadows B&B

(Richard and Madlyn Andres)

672 Macklin Rd, PO Box 219, Heriot Bay, BC, V0P 1H0
www.moonlightshadowsbandb.com
E-mail moonlightshadows@gicable.com

250-285-2422
Fax 250-285-2422

Large cedar home on an acre of peaceful quiet setting. Five rooms, all with private baths. King continental breakfast. Just 2 1/2 blocks from Heriot Bay Inn and all the amenities. We are a 5-minute walk from Cortes Island ferry terminal, only 4 km from Rebecca Spit, a wonderful walk on the ocean. Come rest your mind, body and spirit in this peaceful home and let us pamper you.

ROOMS Upper floor, **Baths** Private, **Beds** Queen, **Smoking** Outside, **In Room** Thermostat, **OTHERS** Seasonal, **PAYMENT** Cash, Trvl's cheques, **BREAKFASTS** Continental, **AMENITIES** Patio, **THINGS TO DO** Rental bikes, Trail nearby, Rental canoe or boat, Fishing, Art, Entertainment, Attractions, Wineries/ Breweries, Swimming, Beach, **LANGUAGE** Eng., **PRICE** (2 persons) 75–150 **(check with hosts for pricing details)**

QUALICUM BEACH *(north of Victoria)*

A & K Oceanside Retreat
(Al and Kathy Heinrich)

3188 Island Hwy W, Qualicum Beach, BC, V9K 2C5
www.OceansideRetreat.ca
E-mail agh@shaw.ca

250-738-0192
Fax 250-738-0193

The house is situated across from the ocean surrounded by beautiful shrubbery, flowers, a pond, a creek and an estuary. Whether you choose to hike through the lush, green forest, kayak on the beautiful waters of the Strait of Georgia, golf on one of six scenic golf courses, partake in the oceanfront activity or simply relax in the gazebo in the backyard, you will experience a holiday to remember. Cell numbers: 250-927-5777 or 250-927-6777. B&B is 2 km north of Qualicum Beach Info Centre.

ROOMS Family suite, Upper floor, Ground floor, Private entrance, **Baths** Private, Ensuite, **Beds** Queen, Single or cots, **Air** Central, **Smoking** Outside, **OTHERS** Urban, Adult, Open all year, **PAYMENT** Visa, Cash, Trvl's cheques, **BREAKFASTS** Continental, Home-baked, **AMENITIES** Central phone, Kitchen, Fridge, Hot bev. bar, Patio, Central Internet access, **THINGS TO DO** Rental bikes, Trail nearby, Rental canoe or boat, Golf, Fishing, Museums, Art, Theatre, Entertainment, Attractions, Shopping, Swimming, Beach, Birdwatching, **LANGUAGE** Eng., Fr., **PRICE** (2 persons) 80–125
(check with hosts for pricing details)

REVELSTOKE *(southeastern BC)*

Alpenrose Bed and Breakfast
(Christa and Richard Krisman)

1524 Nichol Rd, Revelstoke, BC, V0E 2S1
www.bnbsincanada.com/alpenrose
E-mail rkrisman@rctvonline.net

250-837-6165

Cozy B&B, close to the ski hill and Williamson Lake. Breakfast of your choice. Hot tub. Senior/children/low-season discounts. German management. Much to see and do around town. To find us: Exit Hwy 1, follow hospital sign up to Airport Way – DO NOT turn right into Newland Rd, but turn left at the next intersection onto Nichol Rd.

ROOMS Family suite, Upper floor, **Baths** Ensuite, Shared with guest, **Beds** Queen, **Smoking** Outside, **In Room** Thermostat, TV, **OTHERS** Urban, Open all year, Pets in residence, **PAYMENT** Visa, Cash, Trvl's cheques, **BREAKFASTS** Full, **AMENITIES** Central TV, Whirlpool, Fridge, Patio, Central Internet access, **THINGS TO DO** Trail nearby, Golf, Fishing, Museums, Art, Attractions, Wineries/Breweries, Cross-country skiing, Swimming, **LANGUAGE** Eng., Sp., Ger., **PRICE** (2 persons) 80–95
(check with hosts for pricing details)

ROCK CREEK *(south-central BC)*

Kettle Country B&B
(Karen and Hakon Nielsen)

3245 Hwy 3, Rock Creek, BC, V0H 1Y0
www.kettlecountrybb.com
E-mail info@kettlecountrybb.com

250-446-2512

Kettle Country B&B has 10 acres on the Kettle River, halfway between Midway and Rock Creek. The Kettle Valley Golf Course is across the highway and the Trans-Canada Trail is across the river. Come for a round of golf, tube, canoe or fish the river, bike/hike the Trans-Canada Trail or just relax and enjoy the scenery. Our one-bedroom cabin is self-contained with a full kitchen, large bathroom and a covered deck. We also have two bedrooms in the main house. We are close to three ski hills – Big White, Mount Baldy and Phoenix.

ROOMS Family suite, Upper floor, Private entrance, **Baths** Private, Ensuite, Shared with guest, **Beds** Queen, Double, **Smoking** Outside, **In Room** Thermostat, TV, Fireplace, **OTHERS** Babysitting, Rural, Open all year, Pets welcome, **PAYMENT** Cash, Trvl's cheques, **BREAKFASTS** Full, Continental, Home-baked, Self-catered, **AMENITIES** Central TV, Whirlpool, Barbecue, Kitchen, Fridge, Lounge, Patio, **THINGS TO DO** Rental bikes, Trail nearby, Rental canoe or boat, Golf, Fishing, Museums, Attractions, Wineries/Breweries, Shopping, Cross-country skiing, Swimming, Horseback riding, Beach, **LANGUAGE** Eng., Danish, **PRICE** (2 persons) 90–115 **(check with hosts for pricing details)**

SALT SPRING ISLAND *(north of Victoria)*

Belvedere Place
(Ann and Hubert King)

151 Devine Dr, Salt Spring Island, BC, V8K 2H5
www.belvedereplace.ca
E-mail annking@island.net

250-537-2615
Fax 250-537-2655

Comfortable self-contained 800-sq. ft. suite in the lower level of our home. Located on a quiet hillside with beautiful views over Ganges Inlet of the coastal mountains and Mount Baker. Breakfast foods provided for self-catering in the fully equipped kitchen. Sleeps up to six. Local phone, satellite TV/VCR and library, games and puzzles. Ideal for families. Weekly rates $450 – $550 for two people.

ROOMS Family suite, Ground floor, Private entrance, **Baths** Private, **Beds** Queen, Twin, Single or cots, Pullout sofa, **Smoking** Outside, **In Room** Thermostat, Phone, TV, VCR/DVD, **OTHERS** Rural, Open all year, **PAYMENT** Visa, MC, Cash, **BREAKFASTS** Self-catered, **AMENITIES** Barbecue, Laundry, Kitchen, Fridge, Lounge, **THINGS TO DO** Rental canoe or boat, Fishing, Art, Theatre, Entertainment, Wineries/ Breweries, Shopping, Tennis, Swimming, Beach, Birdwatching, **LANGUAGE** Eng., **PRICE** (2 persons) 75–95 **(check with hosts for pricing details)**

Salt Spring Island

Blue Heron
(Elizabeth Anne Turner)

131 Westcott Rd, Salt Spring Island, BC, V8K 1C2
www.BlueHeronBB.ca
E-mail ETurner@BlueHeronBB.ca

250-537-1373
Fax 250-537-1365

Embrace the dream of a French country cottage by the sea! If you cannot visit France this year, coming here gives you a taste of Provence. Peaceful seaview retreat with abundant birdlife. All suites have luxuriously comfortable beds and kitchenettes. Breakfast food supplied and fresh baking delivered daily by host. French doors open onto patio with tables and chairs for lounging or dining. Walk oceanside for 8 km. Excellent cafe at dock (4-minute walk). Ganges Village with galleries, shops, restaurants 7 km.

ROOMS Ground floor, Private entrance, **Baths** Ensuite, **Beds** King, Queen, Twin, **In Room** Thermostat, Phone, **OTHERS** Rural, Adult, Open all year, **PAYMENT** Visa, MC, Cheques accepted, Cash, Trvl's cheques, **BREAKFASTS** Continental, Home-baked, Self-catered, **AMENITIES** Central TV, Central phone, Barbecue, Kitchen, Fridge, Lounge, Patio, **THINGS TO DO** Trail nearby, Golf, Fishing, Museums, Art, Theatre, Entertainment, Attractions, Wineries/Breweries, Shopping, Tennis, Swimming, Horseback riding, Beach, Birdwatching, Antiquing, **LANGUAGE** Eng., **PRICE** (2 persons) 150–175 **(check with hosts for pricing details)**

Salt Spring Island

Cedar Lane Bed & Breakfast
(Greta and John Graham)

190 Holmes Rd, Salt Spring Island, BC, V8K 1T6
www.cedarlanebb.ca
E-mail cedarlane@uniserve.com

250-653-4012
Fax 250-653-2401
TFr 1-866-485-3440

This beautifully designed waterfront cedar home is located approximately 6 km from the Fulford Harbour Ferry Terminal on Isabella Point Rd. You can enjoy the peace and tranquility of this beautiful setting. Luxury, spacious rooms with sunrise views from your private balcony while enjoying your early morning coffee, private bath, full delicious breakfast, afternoon tea. Come and experience our warm hospitality, capture the sunrises and enjoy the beauty of nature around us.

ROOMS Upper floor, **Baths** Ensuite, **Beds** Queen, Twin, **In Room** Thermostat, **OTHERS** Rural, Adult, Open all year, **PAYMENT** Visa, MC, Cheques accepted, Cash, Trvl's cheques, **BREAKFASTS** Full, Home-baked, **AMENITIES** Central TV, Central phone, Fridge, Lounge, **THINGS TO DO** Rental bikes, Trail nearby, Rental canoe or boat, Golf, Fishing, Museums, Art, Theatre, Entertainment, Attractions, Wineries/Breweries, Shopping, Tennis, Swimming, Horseback riding, Birdwatching, **LANGUAGE** Eng., **PRICE** (2 persons) 95–110 **(check with hosts for pricing details)**

SALT SPRING ISLAND

Ocean Spray Bed & Breakfast By The Sea

(Ilse Leader)

1241 Isabella Point Rd, Salt Spring Island, BC, V8K 1T5
www.pixsell.bc.ca/bb/146.htm

250-653-4273
Fax 250-653-4273

A roomy cedar home (built by architect of Frank Lloyd Wright School). Located on Satellite Channel with panoramic view of the Gulf Islands and Mount Baker. On five acres of forested waterfront with the sea a stone's throw away from the bedroom deck, offering an everchanging scene of marine life. Ferry to Salt Spring Island from Tsawwassen via Swartz Bay on Vanvouver Island, or direct to Long Harbour on SS1. Go through Ganges to Fulford Harbour. Turn off to Isabella Point Rd.

ROOMS Family suite, Lower floor, Private entrance, **Baths** Private, **Beds** Twin, Pullout sofa, **Smoking** Outside, **In Room** Thermostat, **OTHERS** Rural, Open all year, Pets in residence, Pets welcome, **PAYMENT** Visa, MC, Cheques accepted, Cash, Trvl's cheques, **BREAKFASTS** Self-catered, **AMENITIES** Central phone, Kitchen, Fridge, Patio, **THINGS TO DO** Rental bikes, Trail nearby, Rental canoe or boat, Golf, Fishing, Art, Theatre, Entertainment, Attractions, Wineries/Breweries, Shopping, Tennis, Swimming, Horseback riding, Beach, Birdwatching, **LANGUAGE** Eng., Ger., **PRICE** (2 persons) 95–95 **(check with hosts for pricing details)**

SALT SPRING ISLAND

Quarrystone House

(Kelly & Barry Kazakoff)

1340 Sunset Dr, Salt Spring Island, BC, V8K 1E2
www.quarrystone.com
E-mail quarrystone@uniserve.com

250-537-5980
Fax 250-537-5937
TFr 1-866-537-5980

Situated on 5 country acres with stunning ocean and sunset views. All rooms are in a separate building from the main house, ensuring complete privacy. Each of the four rooms has an ocean view, private entrance, Jacuzzi tub, fireplace, TV/VCR, fridge, microwave, private ensuites and private patios/balconies. Children are welcome. A full three-course breakfast is included.

ROOMS Upper floor, Ground floor, Private entrance, **Baths** Private, Ensuite, **Beds** King, Queen, Twin, Single or cots, Pullout sofa, **Air** In rooms, **Smoking** Outside, **In Room** Thermostat, TV, Fireplace, VCR/DVD, **OTHERS** Babysitting, Rural, Open all year, Handicapped access, Pets in residence, Pets welcome, **PAYMENT** Visa, MC, Cash, Trvl's cheques, **BREAKFASTS** Full, **AMENITIES** Central phone, Barbecue, Laundry, Fridge, Central Internet access, **THINGS TO DO** Trail nearby, Golf, Fishing, Art, Theatre, Entertainment, Attractions, Wineries/Breweries, Shopping, Tennis, Swimming, Horseback riding, Beach, Birdwatching, Antiquing, **LANGUAGE** Eng., **PRICE** (2 persons) 110–195 **(check with hosts for pricing details)**

SECHELT *(north of Vancouver)*

A Place by the Sea Bed and Breakfast & Spa

(Nancy and Shay Moudahi)

5810 Marine Way, Sechelt, BC, V0N 3A6
www.aplacebythesea.com
E-mail info@aplacebythesea.com

604-885-2745
Fax 604-885-2726
TFr 1-866-885-2746

A Place by the Sea is a deluxe waterfront B&B and spa, a spectacular waterfront retreat offering luxurious accommodations, outdoor adventure in scenic beauty, privacy and warm hospitality. Featuring theme suites, our rooms are waterfront and boast private entrances, stunning ocean views, fireplaces, Jacuzzi tubs, king-size beds, kitchenettes, TV, DVD players, CD players, robes, internet and more! Enjoy oceanview, hot tub, sauna, private beach, spa services, kayaking and boat cruises.

ROOMS Private entrance, **Baths** Private, Ensuite, **Beds** King, Queen, **Smoking** Outside, **In Room** Thermostat, Phone, TV, Fireplace, Internet access, VCR/DVD, **OTHERS** Adult, Open all year, **PAYMENT** Visa, MC, Direct debit, Cash, **BREAKFASTS** Full, **AMENITIES** Sauna, Whirlpool, Barbecue, Laundry, Kitchen, Fridge, **THINGS TO DO** Rental bikes, Rental canoe or boat, Golf, Fishing, Art, Shopping, Tennis, Swimming, Horseback riding, Beach, Birdwatching, Antiquing, **LANGUAGE** Eng., **PRICE** (2 persons) 179–199 **(check with hosts for pricing details)**

SECHELT

Country Haven B&B, formerly Rocky Rd B&B

(Clarissa Tufts and Billy Hume)

4196 Rocky Rd, Sechelt, BC, V0N 3A1
www.user.dccnet.com/rockyroadbb
E-mail countryhaven@dccnet.com

604-885-4542
TFr 1-866-885-4542

Visit our quiet country acreage located halfway between Gibsons and Sechelt on the Sunshine Coast. We are 5 minutes from the beach at Davis Bay and 5 minutes from golfing. We have plenty of mountain biking and walking trails, or just enjoy our hot tub, smell the flowers and relax. We serve a full breakfast with fresh free range eggs and whatever is available in our garden.

ROOMS Family suite, Ground floor, Lower floor, **Baths** Private, **Beds** Queen, Twin, **In Room** Thermostat, **OTHERS** Rural, Open all year, Pets in residence, **PAYMENT** Visa, MC, Cash, **BREAKFASTS** Full, Home-baked, **AMENITIES** Central TV, Central phone, Whirlpool, Fridge, Lounge, Patio, **THINGS TO DO** Trail nearby, **LANGUAGE** Eng., **PRICE** (2 persons) 70–90 **(check with hosts for pricing details)**

SIDNEY *(north of Victoria)*

Honeysuckle Cottage Bed & Breakfast

(Andrew Truman and Brenda LaPrairie)

1030 Clayton Rd, North Saanich, BC, V8L 5P6
www.honeysucklecottagebb.com
E-mail honeysuckle_cottage@shaw.ca

250-655-6474

Self-catered, bright, secluded, 650-sq. ft. self-contained cottage, located on a tranquil country acreage. Perfect for romantic getaways and family holidays. Year-round use of ozonated hot tub in fully enclosed gazebo. Bedroom with cozy duvets and robes, bathroom and separate comfortable living room with cozy gas fireplace, TV and DVD. Separate dining area, full kitchen, laundry room and private deck with barbecue. Broadband Internet access and free local calls. Complimentary tea and coffee. Smoking is not permitted.

ROOMS Family suite, Ground floor, Private entrance, **Baths** Private, Ensuite, **Beds** Queen, Single or cots, Pullout sofa, **Air** In rooms, **Smoking** Outside, **In Room** Thermostat, Phone, TV, Fireplace, Internet access, VCR/DVD, **OTHERS** Rural, Open all year, Handicapped access, **PAYMENT** Cheques accepted, Cash, Trvl's cheques, **BREAKFASTS** Continental, Home-baked, Self-catered, **AMENITIES** Central TV, Central phone, Whirlpool, Barbecue, Laundry, Kitchen, Fridge, Patio, Central Internet access, Central VCR/DVD, **THINGS TO DO** Rental bikes, Trail nearby, Rental canoe or boat, Golf, Fishing, Museums, Art, Theatre, Entertainment, Attractions, Wineries/Breweries, Shopping, Cross-country skiing, Downhill skiing, Tennis, Swimming, Horseback riding, Beach, Birdwatching, Antiquing, **LANGUAGE** Eng., **PRICE** (2 persons) 100–140 (**check with hosts for pricing details)**

SIDNEY

Inlet Beach House B&B

(Ken and Linda Wigbers)

10830 Madrona Dr, North Saanich, BC, V8L 5P1
www.inletbeachhousebandb.com
E-mail kwigbers@shaw.ca

250-656-3239

Located on the beautiful Saanich Inlet, this sunny 760-sq. ft. oceanfront B&B is a queen bedroom unit with private entrance, four-piece bath, living rooom, 32-inch TV and DVD; also fridge, microwave, toaster, etc., and double pullout bed. Twenty easy steps to Lowbank Beach with great swimming, snorkeling, canoeing and hiking. Three levels of deck and a BBQ on the ocean! Warm from the oven breakfast tray with fresh fruit to be enjoyed at your leisure in the comfort and privacy of your own home-away-from-home.

ROOMS Family suite, Ground floor, Private entrance, **Baths** Private, **Beds** Queen, Pullout sofa, **Smoking** Outside, **In Room** Thermostat, Phone, TV, Fireplace, Internet access, VCR/DVD, **OTHERS** Rural, Open all year, Pets welcome, **PAYMENT** Visa, Cheques accepted, Cash, Trvl's cheques, **BREAKFASTS** Continental, Home-baked, Self-catered, **AMENITIES** Barbecue, Laundry, Kitchen, Fridge, Hot bev. bar, Lounge, Patio, **THINGS TO DO** Comp. bikes, Trail nearby, Comp. Canoe or boat, Golf, Fishing, Museums, Art, Theatre, Entertainment, Attractions, Wineries/Breweries, Shopping, Tennis, Swimming, Horseback riding, Beach, Birdwatching, Antiquing, **LANGUAGE** Eng., **PRICE** (2 persons) 95–120 (**check with hosts for pricing details)**

Sidney
Lovat House B&B
(Fran and Chris Atkinson)

9625 – 2nd St, Sidney, BC, V8L 3C3
www3.telus.net/freestyle
E-mail sailingfor2@telus.net

250-656-3188
Fax 250-656-3188

Located across from Washington State Ferry and walking distance to Sidney, close to shops and restaurants. Nice sea-view from patio and room. We provide a full breakfast: Bacon or ham, eggs, juice, toast, tea or coffee. For those not wishing a large breakfast, cereal, fruit and muffins or toast may be substituted. Served between 8:00 a.m. and 9:30 a.m. Dining room breakfast is served during the summer season only.

ROOMS Upper floor, **Baths** Private, Ensuite, **Beds** Queen, Double, Single or cots, **Smoking** Outside, **In Room** Thermostat, TV, **PAYMENT** Cash, Trvl's cheques, **BREAKFASTS** Continental, Self-catered, **AMENITIES** Central TV, Kitchen, Fridge, Hot bev. bar, Patio, **THINGS TO DO** Golf, Museums, Art, Entertainment, Wineries/Breweries, Shopping, Birdwatching, **LANGUAGE** Eng., **PRICE** (2 persons) 75–90 **(check with hosts for pricing details)**

Sidney
Seventh Haven
(Mrs Valerie Freeman)

9617– 7th St, Sidney, BC, V8L 2V4
www.canadianbandbguide.ca/bb.asp?ID=3173

250-655-4197

A cozy cottage-style home in the heart of Sidney By The Sea. Minutes to airport and ferries, 20 to 30 minutes to Buchart Gardens and Victoria. Walk to beach, town centre with many shops and restaurants, marina and seaside activities. A quiet home in a quiet location of a beautiful little town. Travel east on Beacon Ave, south at 5th St, west at Orchard Ave, south at 7th St.

ROOMS Ground floor, **Baths** Ensuite, **Beds** Queen, **Air** Central, **Smoking** Outside, **In Room** Phone, TV, **OTHERS** Urban, Open all year, **PAYMENT** Cheques accepted, Cash, Trvl's cheques, **BREAKFASTS** Full, Home-baked, **AMENITIES** Central TV, Central phone, Patio, **THINGS TO DO** Rental bikes, Rental canoe or boat, Golf, Fishing, Museums, Art, Theatre, Entertainment, Attractions, Wineries/Breweries, Shopping, Tennis, Swimming, Horseback riding, Beach, Birdwatching, Antiquing, **LANGUAGE** Eng., **PRICE** (2 persons) 70–70 **(check with hosts for pricing details)**

SMITHERS *(northwestern BC)*

Bulkley Valley Guesthouse
(Helga and Gunter Zweifler)

Box 2636, Gelly Rd, Smithers, BC, V0J 2N0
www.fishtourcanada.bc.ca
E-mail bandb@fishtourcanada.bc.ca

250-847-9233
Fax 250-847-9233

New B&B located only a couple of minutes west of Smithers near Hwy 16, on Lake Kathlyn. Quiet, private setting on 5 acres overlooking the lake and mountains. Two units are available with private bathroom and private entrance, each accommodating up to four people. We offer 24-hour pickup service from airport, bus or train. Free use of canoes to explore the lake. Guiding service for outdoor adventure, sightseeing and fishing is also available. Call regarding rates.

ROOMS Family suite, Private entrance, **Baths** Private, **Beds** Queen, Twin, Pullout sofa, **Air** Ceiling fans, **Smoking** Outside, **In Room** Thermostat, Phone, TV, Fireplace, VCR/DVD, **OTHERS** Open all year, Pets welcome, **PAYMENT** Visa, MC, Cash, **BREAKFASTS** Full, **AMENITIES** Central TV, Kitchen, Fridge, Patio, Central Internet access, **THINGS TO DO** Rental bikes, Trail nearby, Comp. canoe or boat, Golf, Fishing, Theatre, Attractions, Shopping, Cross-country skiing, Tennis, Swimming, Horseback riding, Beach, Birdwatching, **LANGUAGE** Eng., Ger., **PRICE** (2 persons) 90–90 **(check with hosts for pricing details)**

SMITHERS

Glacier View
(Jensen and Carla Goltz)

8335 Kroeker Rd, Smithers, BC, V0J 2N2
www.bedsandbreakfasts.ca/smithers-bed-breakfast.htm
E-mail gletscherblick@bulkley.net

250-847-6045
Fax 250-847-6045

Welcome to Glacier View Bed and Breakfast. We're located in Smithers, nestled in the heart of Bulkley Valley in northern British Columbia. Our cozy log B&B home features beautiful views in a delightful natural setting. Glacier View B&B is surrounded by dazzling snow-capped mountains and spectacular natural vistas at every turn. It is no wonder that Smithers is referred to as "Little Switzerland". Your hosts are experts on the Smithers area and would be pleased to assist you.

ROOMS Ground floor, **Baths** Private, Shared with guest, **Beds** Queen, Twin, **Smoking** Outside, **OTHERS** Open all year, **PAYMENT** Cheques accepted, Cash, Trvl's cheques, **BREAKFASTS** Full, **AMENITIES** Barbecue, Fridge, **THINGS TO DO** Rental bikes, Trail nearby, Rental canoe or boat, Golf, Fishing, Museums, Art, Shopping, Cross-country skiing, Downhill skiing, Tennis, Swimming, Horseback riding, Birdwatching, **LANGUAGE** Eng., Ger., **PRICE** (2 persons) 80–100 **(check with hosts for pricing details)**

Sooke *(west of Victoria)*

A Secluded Romantic Retreat at Sooke River Estuary

(Linda and Hugh Audet)

2056 Glenidle Rd, Sooke, BC, V0S 1N0
www.sookeriver.com
E-mail info@sookeriver.com

250-642-4655
Fax 250-642-4621
TFr 1-888-681-4677

Secluded, romantic, oceanfront cottage, hot tub and home. Enjoy the spectacular views of Sooke Harbour, our warm hospitality and delicious full, hot breakfasts delivered to your room. The Harbourside Cottage is one of three options, designed around a two-person jetted tub. At night, dim the lights, turn on the Vermont Castings fireplace, sit in the bubbles and enjoy a bottle of wine while looking out onto the water. Follow Hwy 14 till the 6000 block of Sooke Rd, turn left on Idlemore Rd, then right on Glenidle Rd.

ROOMS Ground floor, Private entrance, **Baths** Ensuite, **Beds** Queen, Single or cots, Pullout sofa, **Air** In rooms, Ceiling fans, **Smoking** Outside, **In Room** Thermostat, Phone, TV, Fireplace, VCR/DVD, **OTHERS** Rural, Open all year, **PAYMENT** Visa, MC, Direct debit, Cash, Trvl's cheques, **BREAKFASTS** Full, **AMENITIES** Central TV, Central phone, Sauna, Whirlpool, Barbecue, Laundry, Kitchen, Fridge, Hot bev. bar, Lounge, Patio, **THINGS TO DO** Rental bikes, Trail nearby, Comp. canoe or boat, Golf, Fishing, Museums, Art, Theatre, Attractions, Shopping, Swimming, Beach, Birdwatching, Antiquing, **LANGUAGE** Eng., **PRICE** (2 persons) 149–189 **(check with hosts for pricing details)**

Sooke

Barking Crow

(Pernell and Sue-Lin Tarnowski)

7798 West Coast Rd, Sooke, BC, V0S 1N0
www.barkingcrow.ca
E-mail info@barkingcrow.ca

250-642-1876
TFr 1-866-642-1876

Located on a magnificent acreage with beach access to a small pebbly beach, the Barking Crow offer guests a double room and a self-contained two-bedroom suite. Both units have private entrances and private full bathrooms. Complimentary snacks, bottled water and tea and coffee are standard offerings which add to the comfort of your stay. The Beatrice Room is equipped with microwave, coffeemaker, kettle and fridge. The Benedick Suite is an apartment-style two-bedroom suite which can accommodate up to six. It offers a master bedroom with a king bed, a second bedroom with a bunk bed, full kitchen, sofabed in the sitting area and a dining area. High chair and portable crib are available.

ROOMS Family suite, Upper floor, Lower floor, Private entrance, **Baths** Private, Ensuite, **Beds** King, Twin, Pullout sofa, **Smoking** Outside, **In Room** Thermostat, Internet access, **OTHERS** Rural, Adult, Open all year, Handicapped access, **PAYMENT** Visa, MC, Amex, Cash, Trvl's cheques, **BREAKFASTS** Full, Home-baked, **AMENITIES** Central phone, Barbecue, Kitchen, Fridge, Patio, **THINGS TO DO** Rental bikes, Trail nearby, Golf, Fishing, Museums, Art, Attractions, Shopping, Tennis, Swimming, Horseback riding, Beach, **LANGUAGE** Eng., Chinese, **PRICE** (2 persons) 75–130 **(check with hosts for pricing details)**

Sooke

Blue Waters Bed and Breakfast

(Michael and Margaret Wood)

1010 Seaside Dr, Sooke, BC, V0S 1N0
www.bluewatersbb.com
E-mail info@bluewatersbb.com

250-646-2624

This is a romantic, private and tranquil oceanside property looking out over the Juan De Fuca Strait to the snow-capped montains of the Olympic Range. Sit in our hot tub and enjoy the everchanging view of the sea and the beautiful British Columbia sunsets. We are a few minutes walk from French Beach Provincial Park and within easy distance from the Juan De Fuca Marine Trail and much much more. Our full English breakfast is served in the solarium dining room and delights all who partake.

ROOMS Ground floor, Private entrance, **Baths** Ensuite, **Beds** King, Queen, Twin, **Smoking** Outside, **In Room** Thermostat, TV, Fireplace, VCR/DVD, **OTHERS** Rural, Open all year, **PAYMENT** Visa, MC, Cheques accepted, Cash, **BREAKFASTS** Full, Home-baked, **AMENITIES** Barbecue, Fridge, **THINGS TO DO** Trail nearby, Beach, Birdwatching, Antiquing, **LANGUAGE** Eng., **PRICE** (2 persons) 110–145 **(check with hosts for pricing details)**

Sooke

Lilac House B&B & Wisteria Honeymoon Cottage

(Gail Harris)

1910 Connie Rd, Victoria, BC, V9C 4C2
www.lilachousecountrybandb.com
E-mail info@lilachousecountrybandb.com

250-642-2809
Fax 250-642-2809
TFr 1-866-225-4522

Experience Vancouver Island's natural wonders while enjoying all the comforts of our Heritage-style inn. Furnished with antiques, quilts and featherbeds, our charming guest rooms invite you to rest and rejuvenate. Delectable breakfasts, hot tub under the stars, 5 acres to explore, historic pub close by. If you prefer seclusion, enjoy our romantic Wisteria Honeymoon Cottage with four-poster queen bed, gas river rock fireplace, Victorian soaker tub and self-catering kitchenette. Honeymoon packages.

ROOMS Upper floor, Ground floor, Private entrance, **Baths** Ensuite, Shared with hosts, **Beds** Queen, Double, Single or cots, Pullout sofa, **Smoking** Outside, **In Room** Thermostat, TV, Fireplace, VCR/DVD, **OTHERS** Rural, Adult, Open all year, Pets in residence, **PAYMENT** Cash, Trvl's cheques, **BREAKFASTS** Full, Continental, Home-baked, Self-catered, **AMENITIES** Central TV, Central phone, Whirlpool, Barbecue, Laundry, Kitchen, Fridge, Hot bev. bar, Lounge, Patio, Central Internet access, Central VCR/DVD, **THINGS TO DO** Rental bikes, Trail nearby, Rental canoe or boat, Golf, Fishing, Museums, Entertainment, Attractions, Tennis, Swimming, Horseback riding, Beach, Bird-watching, **LANGUAGE** Eng., **PRICE** (2 persons) 70–150 **(check with hosts for pricing details)**

SOOKE

Ocean Wilderness Inn and Spa

(Marion Rolston)

9171 West Coast Rd, Sooke, BC, V0S 1N0
www.oceanwildernessinn.com
E-mail info@oceanwildernessinn.com

250-646-2116
Fax 250-646-2317
TFr 1-800-323-2116

A log building on 5 forested oceanfront
acres. Elegant comfortable rooms,
canopied beds. Wander the gardens, trails
or take a luxurious soak in the hot tub
overlooking the ocean and Olympic
mountains. Explore our beach where
seals, otters and bald eagles live. A full
country breakfast is included in the rates.
Treat yourself to the spa services here
onsite. Massages, clay facials and full body
wraps of mud or seaweed are some of the
offerings. Gift certificates available. Weddings, reunions, etc., can be arranged.

ROOMS Upper floor, Ground floor, Private entrance,
Baths Private, Ensuite, **Beds** King, Queen, Twin, Single
or cots, Pullout sofa, **Smoking** Outside, **In Room**
Thermostat, **OTHERS** Urban, Rural, Open all year,
Handicapped access, Pets in residence, Pets welcome,
PAYMENT Visa, MC, Amex, Cheques accepted, Cash,
Trvl's cheques, **BREAKFASTS** Full, **AMENITIES** Central
phone, Laundry, Fridge, **THINGS TO DO** Rental bikes,
Trail nearby, Rental canoe or boat, Golf, Fishing,
Museums, Art, Attractions, Shopping, Horseback rid-
ing, Beach, **LANGUAGE** Eng., **PRICE** (2 persons)
99–175 **(check with hosts for pricing details)**

SORRENTO (SHUSWAP LAKE)
(northeast of Vancouver)

A Rover's Rest Bed & Breakfast

(Kimberly and David May)

2660 Balmoral Rd, Blind Bay, BC, V0E 1H1
www.aroversrest.com
E-mail info@aroversrest.com

250-675-4405   Fax 250-675-3070
TFr 1-866-768-3722

Secluded log home overlooking Shuswap
Lake in the heart of BC. Three suites, each
with unique decor, ensuite bathroom with
shower. Romantic hideaway for getaways,
weddings, anniversaries, a special night.
Honeymoon suite with heart-shaped tub,
king bed and fireplace. Easy access to
beach/marina, minutes to golf, tennis,
shopping and fine/casual dining. Hearty
breakfast. Guest lounge with snack/bever-
age centre, book/video libraries and fireplace. Eight-person hot tub. Tourism BC
Approved, *Canada Select* 4-star rating.

ROOMS Family suite, Ground floor, Private entrance,
Baths Ensuite, **Beds** King, Queen, Double, Twin, Single
or cots, **Smoking** Outside, **In Room** Thermostat, Fire-
place, Internet access, **OTHERS** Rural, Adult, Open all
year, Pets in residence, **PAYMENT** Visa, MC, Amex, Cash,
Trvl's cheques, **BREAKFASTS** Full, Continental, **AMENI-
TIES** Central TV, Central phone, Whirlpool, Barbecue,
Fridge, Hot bev. bar, Lounge, Patio, Central Internet
access, Central VCR/DVD, **THINGS TO DO** Trail nearby,
Rental canoe or boat, Golf, Fishing, Museums, Art,
Theatre, Entertainment, Attractions, Wineries/Breweries,
Shopping, Cross-country skiing, Downhill skiing, Tennis,
Swimming, Horseback riding, Beach, Birdwatching,
Antiquing, **LANGUAGE** Eng., **PRICE** (2 persons) 90–120
(check with hosts for pricing details)

SORRENTO (SHUSWAP LAKE)

The Maples Waterfront Inn

(Sonja and Herb Heide)

1283 Dieppe Rd, Sorrento, BC, V0E 2W0
www.ShuswapMaples.com
E-mail sonja@shuswapmaples.com

250-675-2433
Fax 250-675-4837
TFr 1-877-611-4251

The historic Waterfront Inn includes four elegant suites with modern private baths. Its waterside deck provides a spectacular view of Shuswap Lake, our spacious lawn and gardens, giant maples, sandy beach and outdoor activities. The cosy living/dining room includes a river rock fireplace and kitchenette. The Maples Suite overlooking the lake features a king bed, fireplace and Jacuzzi tub, making this a great setting for special occassions. A one-minute drive from the Trans-Canada Hwy ensures the absence of highway noise.

ROOMS Upper floor, Ground floor, **Baths** Ensuite, **Beds** King, Queen, Double, **Smoking** Outside, **In Room** Fireplace, **OTHERS** Rural, Adult, Open all year, **PAYMENT** Visa, MC, Direct debit, Cash, **BREAKFASTS** Full, Continental, **AMENITIES** Barbecue, Fridge, Hot bev. bar, Lounge, Patio, **THINGS TO DO** Comp. canoe or boat, Golf, Fishing, Museums, Art, Theatre, Entertainment, Wineries/Breweries, Cross-country skiing, Swimming, Beach, **LANGUAGE** Eng., Ger., **PRICE** (2 persons) 59–156 **(check with hosts for pricing details)**

SORRENTO (SHUSWAP LAKE)

The Roost Bed and Breakfast

(Sherran King)

5170 Eagle Bay Rd, Eagle Bay, BC, V0E 1T0
www.bbcanada.com/theroost
E-mail theroost@jetstream.net

250-675-3711
Fax 250-675-3716

Stunning lake and mountain views from this charming chalet with floor-to-ceiling windows, on 10 acres, overlooking Shuswap Lake. Two tastefully appointed suites. Private Loft nest for romantics is awesome. Fabulous food and fun hosts, massive decks, guest lounge, wiener roast pit, etc. Beach, boat launch, spa, golf and many area attractions nearby. Wildlife abounds so bring your camera and enjoy a piece of natural paradise at Eagle Bay. (Near Sorrento, BC, halfway between Calgary and Vancouver).

ROOMS Family suite, Upper floor, Ground floor, Private entrance, **Baths** Private, Ensuite, **Beds** Queen, Twin, Single or cots, Pullout sofa, **Air** Central, **Smoking** Outside, **In Room** Phone, Fireplace, **OTHERS** Rural, Open all year, Additional meals, **PAYMENT** Visa, Cash, Trvl's cheques, **BREAKFASTS** Full, Continental, Home-baked, **AMENITIES** Central TV, Central phone, Barbecue, Kitchen, Fridge, Lounge, Patio, Central VCR/DVD, **THINGS TO DO** Trail nearby, Rental canoe or boat, Golf, Fishing, Museums, Art, Attractions, Wineries/Breweries, Shopping, Cross-country skiing, Swimming, Horseback riding, Beach, Birdwatching, Antiquing, **LANGUAGE** Eng., **PRICE** (2 persons) 55–105 **(check with hosts for pricing details)**

Sorrento (Shuswap Lake)

Thimbleberry Cottage B&B
(Rae and Marv Jury)

2902 Coates Rd, Sorrento, BC, V0E 2W0
www.thimbleberrycottage.com
E-mail info@thimbleberrycottage.com

250-675-2278

Seasonal B&B, located on the waterfront just west of Sorrento town centre on Shuswap Lake. Thimbleberry Cottage is an adult-oriented B&B located on a large waterfront property near Sorrento, on Shuswap Lake. The location is private with 1,000 feet of shoreline, free boat moorage and a dock. We also have space to park your boat trailer during your stay if required. A full breakfast is offered and is normally served in the dining room or, weather-permitting, on the sundeck, both overlooking the lake.

ROOMS Upper floor, **Baths** Ensuite, **Beds** King, Queen, **Air** Ceiling fans, **Smoking** Outside, **OTHERS** Rural, Adult, Seasonal, **PAYMENT** Visa, MC, Cash, **BREAKFASTS** Full, **AMENITIES** Central TV, Central phone, Fridge, Lounge, Patio, Central VCR/DVD, **THINGS TO DO** Trail nearby, Golf, Fishing, Wineries/Breweries, Swimming, Beach, **LANGUAGE** Eng., **PRICE** (2 persons) 94–99 **(check with hosts for pricing details)**

Squamish *(North of Vancouver)*

Coneybeare Lodge
(Jim and Claire Harvey)

40549 Ayr Dr, Garibaldi Highlands, BC, V0N 1T0
www.coneybearelodge.com
E-mail info@coneybearelodge.com

604-898-9299
Fax 604-898-3092
TFr 1-866-815-9299

Canada Select 4-star rated, affordable, luxury accommodation in the outdoor recreation Capital of Canada – Squamish, BC. Only 35 minutes from Whistler and 50 minutes from Vancouver. Beautiful private rooms with spectacular views. Each room has a balcony, fireplace, soaker tub, TV, VCR, bar fridge, phone, etc. Close to world class skiing, golf, mountain biking, climbing, hiking, windsurfing, rafting, birdwatching and much more. Located within 30 km of six provincial parks.

ROOMS Family suite, Upper floor, Ground floor, Private entrance, **Baths** Ensuite, **Beds** Queen, Double, **Air** In rooms, **Smoking** Outside, **In Room** Thermostat, Phone, TV, Fireplace, Internet access, VCR/DVD, **OTHERS** Babysitting, Open all year, **PAYMENT** Visa, MC, Cash, Trvl's cheques, **BREAKFASTS** Full, **AMENITIES** Swimming pool, Sauna, Laundry, Kitchen, Fridge, Patio, **THINGS TO DO** Rental bikes, Trail nearby, Rental canoe or boat, Golf, Fishing, Museums, Art, Theatre, Entertainment, Cross-country skiing, Downhill skiing, Tennis, Swimming, Horseback riding, Beach, Birdwatching, **LANGUAGE** Eng., Fr., Sp., **PRICE** (2 persons) 105–180 **(check with hosts for pricing details)**

SQUAMISH

True North Bed and Breakfast
(Tony and Deanna Edmonds)

1037 Glacier View Dr, Garibaldi Highlands, BC, V0N 1T0
www.truenorthbedandbreakfast.com
E-mail info@truenorthbedandbreakfast.com

604-898-4155
Fax 604-898-4154
TFr 1-800-898-8816

Experience panoramic mountain and ocean views from your private, spacious, self-contained two-bedroom B&B suite in this new mountain-architectural home. Featuring a private entrance, fully equipped kitchen, two queen beds, one sofabed, gas fireplace, satelite TV, tub/shower, washer/dryer and a full continental breakfast included. Conveniently located 45 minutes from Vancouver and 35 minutes from Whistler ski resort, making it the perfect destination for business or pleasure.

ROOMS Family suite, Lower floor, Private entrance, **Baths** Private, **Beds** Queen, Single or cots, Pullout sofa, **Smoking** Outside, **In Room** Thermostat, Phone, TV, Fireplace, VCR/DVD, **OTHERS** Rural, Open all year, **PAYMENT** Visa, MC, Cash, Trvl's cheques, **BREAKFASTS** Continental, **AMENITIES** Laundry, Kitchen, Central Internet access, **THINGS TO DO** Rental bikes, Trail nearby, Rental canoe or boat, Golf, Fishing, Museums, Art, Theatre, Entertainment, Attractions, Wineries/Breweries, Shopping, Cross-country skiing, Tennis, Swimming, Horseback riding, Beach, Birdwatching, Antiquing, **LANGUAGE** Eng., **PRICE** (2 persons) 90–145 **(check with hosts for pricing details)**

SUMMERLAND *(south central BC)*

A Touch of English Bed and Breakfast
(Clare and Kelly Sucloy)

6111 Tavender Ct, Summerland, BC, V0H 1Z7
www.touchofenglish.com
E-mail clare@touchofenglish.com

250-494-0212
TFr 1-866-492-0212

A Traditional English bed and breakfast in the heart of Okanagan's wine country. Magnificient views, gourmet breakfasts overlooking the english gardens, afternoon tea, featherbeds, king, queen, two singles. Air-conditioned home. Minutes to beaches, fine dining and scenic walks. Approved Accommodations, Western Innkeepers Association, Super Host Member. Credit cards accepted, children 8 and over welcome. Hosts have a wonderful sense of humour. Come as guests and leave as friends.

ROOMS Family suite, Upper floor, Private entrance, **Baths** Private, Ensuite, **Beds** King, Queen, Twin, Single or cots, **Air** Central, In rooms, Ceiling fans, **Smoking** Outside, **In Room** Phone, TV, Fireplace, Internet access, VCR/DVD, **OTHERS** Babysitting, Urban, Rural, Adult, Open all year, Handicapped access, Pets in residence, Pets welcome, **PAYMENT** Visa, MC, Cash, Trvl's cheques, **BREAKFASTS** Full, Home-baked, **AMENITIES** Central TV, Central phone, Fridge, Lounge, Patio, **THINGS TO DO** Trail nearby, Rental canoe or boat, Golf, Fishing, Museums, Art, Theatre, Entertainment, Attractions, Wineries/Breweries, Shopping, Cross-country skiing, Downhill skiing, Tennis, Swimming, Horseback riding, Beach, Birdwatching, **LANGUAGE** Eng., **PRICE** (2 persons) 85–125 **(check with hosts for pricing details)**

Grape Escape Guest House

(Gerri Davis and George Lerchs)

28411 Garnet Valley Rd, Summerland, BC, V0H 1Z3
www.grapeescape.ca
E-mail bajoreef@telus.net

250-404-4281
Fax 250-404-4281

Located on a 4-acre working vineyard, property features large pergola, waterfall, hot tub and fabulous views in quiet country setting. Georgous room with queen, four-poster bed overlooks vineyard. Room has satellite TV, small fridge, sitting area and ensuite bathroom. Suite: Tastefully appointed suite with private entrance, private bath and fully equipped kitchen, large living room area, also includes comfy queen-size bed and double Murphy bed. Suite opens onto huge deck.

ROOMS Family suite, Upper floor, Ground floor, Private entrance, **Baths** Private, Ensuite, **Beds** Queen, Double, **Air** Central, **Smoking** Outside, **In Room** Phone, TV, VCR/DVD, **OTHERS** Babysitting, Rural, Adult, Seasonal, Additional meals, Pets welcome, **PAYMENT** Cash, **BREAKFASTS** Full, **AMENITIES** Whirlpool, Barbecue, Kitchen, Fridge, Lounge, Patio, **THINGS TO DO** Rental bikes, Trail nearby, Golf, Fishing, Museums, Art, Theatre, Entertainment, Attractions, Wineries/Breweries, Shopping, Swimming, Horseback riding, Beach, Birdwatching, **LANGUAGE** Eng., Fr., Latvian, **PRICE** (2 persons) 75–95 **(check with hosts for pricing details)**

Sun Valley Bed & Breakfast

(Ian McArthur)

7305 Cahilty Cres, Whitecroft Village, BC, V0E 1Z0
www.sunvalleybandb.com
E-mail info@sunvalleybandb.com

250-578-8595
Fax 250-578-8402
TFr 1-877-839-2060

Privacy, comfort and great food too! Located just six minutes from Sun Peaks Resort, this family-oriented pet-friendly 3 1/2 star *Canada Select* rated holiday accommodation is perfect for family vacations or reunions. Each of our beautiful mountainview suites sleeps up to six adults and includes a television, VCR, three queen-size beds and a private four-piece ensuite bathroom. Relax in our huge eight man hot tub and drink in the views of the forested slopes of our valley. Full breakfast served daily.

ROOMS Family suite, Upper floor, Ground floor, **Baths** Private, Shared with guest, **Beds** Queen, **Smoking** Outside, **In Room** TV, VCR/DVD, **OTHERS** Rural, Open all year, Additional meals, Pets welcome, **PAYMENT** Visa, MC, Amex, Direct debit, Cash, Trvl's cheques, **BREAKFASTS** Full, Home-baked, **AMENITIES** Central TV, Central phone, Fridge, Hot bev. bar, Lounge, Patio, **THINGS TO DO** Rental bikes, Trail nearby, Rental canoe or boat, Golf, Fishing, Museums, Art, Entertainment, Shopping, Cross-country skiing, Downhill skiing, Tennis, Swimming, Horseback riding, Beach, Birdwatching, Antiquing, **LANGUAGE** Eng., **PRICE** (2 persons) 69–164 **(check with hosts for pricing details)**

SURREY (CLOVERDALE) *(east of Vancouver)*

Cloverdale Manor
Bed & Breakfast

(Menno and Vi Janzen)

18656 53A Ave, Surrey, BC, V3S 9H3
www.bbcanada.com/5268.html
E-mail mennojanzen@telus.net

604-576-5060
TFr 1-866-576-5060

Welcome to Cloverdale Manor Bed & Breakfast, located in the heart of Surrey. Custom-built home in year 2000 for our guest's enjoyment and relaxation, bordering a quiet country setting with beautiful gardens and many plants surrounding a pond with a waterfall. Spacious bedrooms with private bathrooms. Enjoy homemade gourmet breakfasts. Something special for the men, Menno is always working on old cars. Easy access to ferry, Vancouver, US border and airports. Come as guests and leave as friends.

ROOMS Family suite, Upper floor, Lower floor, **Baths** Private, Ensuite, **Beds** Queen, Double, Single or cots, **Smoking** Outside, **In Room** Internet access, VCR/DVD, **OTHERS** Rural, Open all year, Pets in residence, **PAYMENT** Cash, Trvl's cheques, **BREAKFASTS** Full, Continental, Home-baked, **AMENITIES** Central TV, Central phone, Kitchen, Fridge, Central VCR/DVD, **THINGS TO DO** Golf, Fishing, Museums, Art, Theatre, Attractions, Wineries/Breweries, Shopping, Swimming, Beach, Antiquing, **LANGUAGE** Eng., low German, **PRICE** (2 persons) 50–90 **(check with hosts for pricing details)**

TOFINO
(west-central Vancouver Island)

Cable Cove Inn

(Phil Van Bourgondien)

201 Main St, Tofino, BC, V0R 2Z0
www.cablecoveinn.com
E-mail cablecin@island.net

250-725-4236
Fax 250-725-2857
TFr 1-800-663-6449

Cable Cove Inn offers you seven romantic oceanfront rooms all with either a large Jacuzzi tub inside or a private hot tub outside on your deck. All rooms have a fireplace, one queen-size bed with down duvets and a private oceanfront deck with some nice cedar furniture. Tofino is famous for whale watching and surfing as well as long beach walks. Cable Cove Inn is located in the heart of the action but is on a small point that juts out into the ocean, so it is always nice and quiet. Adults only. No pets please.

ROOMS Upper floor, Ground floor, **Baths** Private, **Beds** Queen, **Smoking** Outside, **In Room** Thermostat, Fireplace, **OTHERS** Rural, Adult, Open all year, Handicapped access, **PAYMENT** Visa, MC, Amex, Cash, Trvl's cheques, **BREAKFASTS** Continental, **AMENITIES** Whirlpool, Laundry, Kitchen, Fridge, Hot bev. bar, Lounge, Patio, **THINGS TO DO** Rental bikes, Trail nearby, Rental canoe or boat, Golf, Fishing, Museums, Art, Theatre, Attractions, Shopping, Tennis, Swimming, Beach, Birdwatching, **LANGUAGE** Eng., **PRICE** (2 persons) 110–275 **(check with hosts for pricing details)**

TOFINO

Clayoquot Retreat

(Lynn and Robert Barton)

Box 292, 120 Arnet Rd, Tofino, BC, V0R 2Z0
www.clayoquotretreat.com
E-mail lbarton@seaviewcable.net

250-725-3305
Fax 250-725-3300

Clayoquot Retreat is on 3/4 acre of quiet waterfront. Each room has ocean views of Clayoquot Sound, private full bathroom, private entrance, TV, and small fridge, tables and chairs. Our sumptuous full home-baked breakfasts are yours to enjoy in the privacy of your room. Just a short walk to town and Tonquin Beach. Our outdoor hot tub overlooks the sea, which often includes whale sightings, boats, loons and nesting eagles. Rooms have patio and picnic table. Hosts are long-term residents of Tofino. Extra person: $30.

ROOMS Ground floor, Lower floor, Private entrance, **Baths** Ensuite, **Beds** Queen, **Smoking** Outside, **In Room** Thermostat, TV, VCR/DVD, **OTHERS** Open all year, Pets in residence, Pets welcome, **PAYMENT** Visa, MC, Cash, **BREAKFASTS** Full, Home-baked, **AMENITIES** Whirlpool, Fridge, Patio, **THINGS TO DO** Shopping, Beach, Birdwatching, **LANGUAGE** Eng., **PRICE** (2 persons) 85–120 **(check with hosts for pricing details)**

TOFINO

Gull Cottage Bed & Breakfast

(Robin Pearce)

1254 Lynn Rd, Tofino, BC, V0R 2Z0
www.gullcottagetofino.com
E-mail gullcott@island.net

250-725-3177

Country-style B&B and only a short walk to Chesterman Beach. Gull Cottage Bed & Breakfast is nestled among the ancient rainforest on the West Coast of Vancouver Island, just outside the village of Tofino. A scenic 65-m (200-ft.) trail leads to beautiful Chesterman Beach with over 2 km of open Pacific Ocean to stroll. Available to our guests are a den with TV/VCR, and living room. Complete with fireplace – perfect for reading or enjoying soft music. Common space offers a fridge for your use and complimentary tea and coffee.

ROOMS Upper floor, **Baths** Private, Ensuite, Shared with guest, **Beds** King, Queen, Twin, Single or cots, **Air** Central, **Smoking** Outside, **In Room** Thermostat, **PAYMENT** Visa, Cash, **BREAKFASTS** Full, **AMENITIES** Central TV, Whirlpool, Fridge, Hot bev. bar, Lounge, Central VCR/DVD, **THINGS TO DO** Rental bikes, Trail nearby, Rental canoe or boat, Golf, Fishing, Beach, Birdwatching, **LANGUAGE** Eng., **PRICE** (2 persons) 135–165 **(check with hosts for pricing details)**

TOFINO

Seafarers B&B

(Siegrun Meszaros (Ziggy)

1212 Lynn Rd, Tofino, BC, V0R 2Z0
www.seafarersbb.com
E-mail seafarer@island.net

250-725-1267
Fax 250-725-1268

Seafarer's B&B is a 4 1/2-star rated *Canada Select* establishment located at beautiful Chesterman Beach, nestled among tall evergreens. The open Pacific Ocean is a 250-foot stroll away. We offer two large rooms each with private sitting area, fireplace, TV, VCR, private bathroom with jetted tub. Our Portside Room has a king size bed and our Santa Fe Room a queen and a single bed. We serve a full breakfast. We also have a hot tub. Older children are welcome.

ROOMS Family suite, Upper floor, **Baths** Private, **Beds** King, Queen, Single or cots, **Smoking** Outside, **In Room** Thermostat, TV, **OTHERS** Open all year, Pets welcome, **PAYMENT** Visa, MC, Amex, Cash, Trvl's cheques, **BREAKFASTS** Full, Home-baked, Self-catered, **AMENITIES** Central TV, Whirlpool, Laundry, Kitchen, Fridge, Hot bev. bar, Lounge, Patio, **THINGS TO DO** Rental bikes, Trail nearby, Golf, Fishing, Art, Shopping, Beach, **LANGUAGE** Eng., Ger., Hungarian, **PRICE** (2 persons) 140–160 **(check with hosts for pricing details)**

TOFINO

Solwood

(Janine Wood)

1298 Lynn Rd, Box 468, Tofino, BC, V0R 2Z0
www.solwood.ca
E-mail solwood@island.net

250-725-2112
TFr 1-866-725-2112

Our unique West Coast home is nestled in our forest gardens of Chesterman Beach. Stay in the main house and enjoy a full delicious breakfast prepared for you and your loved ones with an emphasis on flavour, fullfilment and nutrition. Or rent one of our cozy cottages and prepare meals in your own kitchenette. Enhance your vacation by enjoying our wide range of spa therapy treatments with a 5% discount offered to our guests. End your day with a sunset stroll at the beach, a minute's walk from your door.

ROOMS Family suite, Upper floor, Ground floor, Private entrance, **Baths** Private, Ensuite, Shared with guest, **Beds** King, Queen, Double, Twin, Pullout sofa, **Smoking** Outside, **In Room** Thermostat, Fireplace, **OTHERS** Babysitting, Rural, Open all year, Pets in residence, Pets welcome, **PAYMENT** Visa, MC, Cheques accepted, Cash, Trvl's cheques, **BREAKFASTS** Full, Self-catered, **AMENITIES** Central phone, Kitchen, Fridge, Lounge, Patio, **THINGS TO DO** Trail nearby, Golf, Fishing, Art, Attractions, Shopping, Tennis, Swimming, Beach, **LANGUAGE** Eng., Sp., **PRICE** (2 persons) 85–225 **(check with hosts for pricing details)**

TOFINO
Summerhill Guest House
(Melody Sadler)

Box 512, 1101 Fellowship Dr, Tofino, BC, V0R 2Z0
www.alberni.net/summerhill
E-mail summerhill@alberni.net

250-725-2447
Fax 250-725-2447

Your friendly hosts offer private, comfortable accommodation in a quiet setting surrounded by old-growth rainforest. We are located minutes from the sandy beaches of the Pacific Ocean and the town of Tofino. We offer self-contained, private kitchenette suites for families and couples looking to explore Pacific Rim National Park. Both suites include private entrances, bathrooms and soundproofing. Activities in the area include hiking, whale, bear- and bird-watching, surfing, hot springs, kayaking and diving tours.

ROOMS Family suite, Ground floor, Private entrance, **Baths** Private, Ensuite, **Beds** Queen, Double, Twin, Single or cots, Pullout sofa, **In Room** Thermostat, Phone, TV, VCR/DVD, **OTHERS** Rural, Open all year, **PAYMENT** Cheques accepted, Cash, Trvl's cheques, **BREAKFASTS** Continental, Home-baked, Self-catered, **AMENITIES** Kitchen, Fridge, Hot bev. bar, Patio, **THINGS TO DO** Rental bikes, Trail nearby, Rental canoe or boat, Golf, Fishing, Museums, Art, Attractions, Shopping, Tennis, Swimming, Beach, Birdwatching, **LANGUAGE** Eng., **PRICE** (2 persons) 90–120 **(check with hosts for pricing details)**

VALEMOUNT *(east-central BC)*
Dream Catcher Inn
(Doreen VanAsten)

310 Hwy 5 N, Valemount, BC, V0E 2Z0
www.dreamcatcherinn.ca
E-mail dreaminn@telus.net

250-566-4226
Fax 250-566-9128
TFr 1-800-566-9128

The Dream Catcher's 10-acre site has all the country comforts. Walk through the park-like area into the village just 800 metres away or simply enjoy the garden setting. Reasonable rates, quality accommodation. The lodge has six bedrooms, all with mountain views. Our two-room log chalets include a bedroom, sitting area, full bathroom and large decks with a beautiful view of the Rocky Mountains. We welcome groups. Our facility is Tourism British Columbia Approved, Certified Super Hosts.

ROOMS Family suite, Upper floor, Ground floor, **Baths** Private, **Beds** Queen, Twin, **Smoking** Outside, **OTHERS** Rural, Open all year, **PAYMENT** Visa, MC, Amex, Direct debit, Cash, Trvl's cheques, **BREAKFASTS** Continental, **AMENITIES** Central TV, Central phone, Fridge, **THINGS TO DO** Trail nearby, Rental canoe or boat, Golf, Fishing, Attractions, Cross-country skiing, Horseback riding, **LANGUAGE** Dutch, **PRICE** (2 persons) 79–119 **(check with hosts for pricing details)**

VALEMOUNT

Summit River Lodge, Cabins and campsites

(Bill and Connie Achterberg)

19345 Hwy 5, Valemount, BC, V0E 2Z0
www.bbcanada.com/summitriver
E-mail summitriver@telus.com

250-566-9936
Fax 250-566-9934

Unique Log Home on 16 private ha, with a breath-taking view of the Albreda Glacier and surrounding mountains. Five comfortable guestrooms, with private bathrooms. Large sitting areas, suitable for groups, up to 22 people. Located in the heart of a great snowmobile area. Two furnished cabins, the large cabin has a full kitchen and livingroom, 2 bedrooms. The smaller cabin has two rooms, each with 2 single beds and a kitchentte. Both have running water and indoor bathrooms. Thirty RV sites.

ROOMS Upper floor, Ground floor, **Baths** Private, Ensuite, **Beds** Double, Twin, **Smoking** Outside, **In Room** Thermostat, Internet access, **OTHERS** Rural, Open all year, Pets in residence, **PAYMENT** Visa, MC, Cash, Trvl's cheques, **BREAKFASTS** Full, **AMENITIES** Central TV, Central phone, Whirlpool, Fridge, Lounge, Central Internet access, **THINGS TO DO** Trail nearby, Golf, Fishing, Cross-country skiing, Horseback riding, Birdwatching, **LANGUAGE** Eng., Dutch, **PRICE** (2 persons) 75–120 **(check with hosts for pricing details)**

VANCOUVER *(southwestern BC)*

A Harbourview Retreat B&B

(Wayman and Penny Crosby)

4675 West 4th Ave, Vancouver BC, BC, V6R 1R6
www.ahvr.com
E-mail penny@ahvr.com

604-221-7273
Fax 604-224-0954
TFr 1-866-221-7273

Experience ... an oasis in the heart of the city. Whether you're traveling for work or pleasure, make yourself at home in Vancouver's premier 1912 Bed & Breakfast in one of Vancouver's most exclusive neighbourhoods. Harbourview combines the amenities of a boutique hotel with the genuine care of the world's finest B&Bs. Close to everywhere you want to be ...
• steps from unspoiled beaches, nature trails and University Golf Course;
• minutes from UBC, Granville Island, Downtown and Stanley Park.

ROOMS Upper floor, **Baths** Private, Ensuite, **Beds** Queen, Single or cots, **Air** Ceiling fans, **Smoking** Outside, **In Room** Thermostat, Phone, Internet access, **OTHERS** Adult, Open all year, Pets in residence, **PAYMENT** Visa, MC, Direct debit, **BREAKFASTS** Full, **AMENITIES** Central TV, Central phone, Whirlpool, Kitchen, Fridge, Hot bev. bar, Lounge, Patio, Central Internet access, Central VCR/DVD, **THINGS TO DO** Trail nearby, Museums, Theatre, Entertainment, Shopping, **PRICE** (2 persons) 139-199 **(check with hosts for pricing details)**

VANCOUVER
A Suite @ Kitsilano Cottage
(Christopher de H.- Wirth)

3449 West 7th Ave, Vancouver, BC, V6R 1W2
www.ASuiteAtKitsilanoCottage.com
E-mail pamperedinluxury@asuiteatkitsilanocottage.com

604-434-7470
Fax 604-434-7470

Upscale, self-contained, garden-level two-bedroom suite, 825 sq. ft. King, queen bed and double sofabed. Private entry, patio, phone, TV/VCR/DVD, broadband, internet, CD, bathroom (tub/shower), full kitchen facilities, in suite laundry. Guests staying more than a week are provided weekly linen and cleaning service. Breakfast is not served. Fresh fruit, baking, coffee and tea are provided for a complimentary, self-catered continental breakfast for the first morning. Please note, no provision for pets and a non-smoking facility.

ROOMS Family suite, Ground floor, Private entrance, **Baths** Private, **Beds** King, Queen, Pullout sofa, **Smoking** Outside, **In Room** Thermostat, Phone, TV, Internet access, VCR/DVD, **OTHERS** Urban, Pets in residence, **PAYMENT** Visa, MC, Diners, Amex, Cash, **BREAKFASTS** Continental, Self-catered, **AMENITIES** Barbecue, Laundry, Kitchen, Fridge, Patio, **THINGS TO DO** Comp. bikes, Rental bikes, Trail nearby, Rental canoe or boat, Golf, Fishing, Museums, Art, Theatre, Entertainment, Attractions, Wineries/Breweries, Shopping, Cross-country skiing, Downhill skiing, Tennis, Swimming, Horseback riding, Beach, Birdwatching, Antiquing, **LANGUAGE** Eng., some Hungarian, **PRICE** (2 persons) 165–400 **(check with hosts for pricing details)**

VANCOUVER
A Tree House B&B
(Barb and Bob Selvage)

check it out

2490 W49 Ave, Vancouver, BC, V6M 2V3
www.treehousebb.com
E-mail bb@treehousebb.com

604-266-2962
Fax 604-266-2960
TFr 1-877-266-2960

Gourmet breakfasts in a friendly, modern B&B. Recommended by *Lonely Planet*, *Best Places To Kiss*, *Romantic BC* and *BC Tourism*. Located in the safe, prestigious neighbourhood of Kerrisdale near UBC, airport, major sightseeing attractions. Steps to public transit. All the amenities you deserve in a serene, urban setting. *Sunset Magazine* says, "Barb Selvage cooks a four-course gourmet breakfast fit for a Mountie". A tree house provides a unique experience. Discover why our guests return year after year!

ROOMS Family suite, Upper floor, Ground floor, **Baths** Private, Ensuite, **Beds** Queen, Single or cots, Pullout sofa, **Air** In rooms, **Smoking** Outside, **In Room** Thermostat, Phone, TV, VCR/DVD, **OTHERS** Urban, Adult, Open all year, **PAYMENT** Visa, MC, Amex, Cheques accepted, Cash, Trvl's cheques, **BREAKFASTS** Full, Continental, Home-baked, **AMENITIES** Whirlpool, Fridge, Hot bev. bar, Lounge, Patio, **THINGS TO DO** Trail nearby, Golf, Museums, Art, Theatre, Entertainment, Attractions, Shopping, Tennis, Swimming, Horseback riding, Beach, **LANGUAGE** Eng., **PRICE** (2 persons) 115–175 **(check with hosts for pricing details)**

VANCOUVER
Alida's Twin Hollies Bed & Breakfast
(Alida Kulash)

604 East 23rd Ave, Vancouver, BC, V5V 1X8
www.twinhollies.com
E-mail info@twinhollies.com

604-876-1017
Fax 604-876-1029

1912 Heritage home, centrally located in Vancouver. We have a great view of Vancouver and the mountains, as well as huge trees on our property that make it fun for birdwatching. One block from Antique Row as well as 28 ethnic restaurants Close to Queen Elizabeth Gardens and Granville Island. Our rooms have king-size and queen-size beds and the lounge area provides coffee bar, wet bar and Internet access. Voted "The Best Kept Secret" in Vancouver. Close to Olympic events.

ROOMS Family suite, Upper floor, **Baths** Private, Shared with guest, **Beds** King, Queen, **Air** Ceiling fans, **OTHERS** Adult, Open all year, **PAYMENT** Visa, MC, Amex, Cheques accepted, Trvl's cheques, **BREAKFASTS** Full, Home-baked, Self-catered, **AMENITIES** Central phone, Barbecue, Fridge, Lounge, Patio, Central Internet access, Central VCR/DVD, **THINGS TO DO** Entertainment, Attractions, Birdwatching, Antiquing, **LANGUAGE** Eng., Ger., Dutch, Flemmish, Croatian, Russian, **PRICE** (2 persons) 75–110 **(check with hosts for pricing details)**

VANCOUVER
Alma Beach B&B Manor & Spa
(Manfred Schultz and Carol McDermott)

3756 West 2nd Ave, Vancouver, BC, V6R 1J9
www.almabeachvancouver.com
E-mail stay@almabeachvancouver.com

604-221-1950
Fax 604-221-7869
TFr 1-866-221-1950

Canada Select 4-star B&B "By the sea – in the heart of the city." Vancouver's best location, just steps from the beach, 6 minutes to downtown. Luxurious Thai inspired rooms with private baths, Jacuzzi tub, heated towel racks, 400-count-thread sheets in very comfortable top-of-the-line beds. Enjoy a decadent three-course hot gourmet breakfast. If you want to be on your own, stay in our Heritage Manor – fully furnished self-catered suites: studio to three bedrooms. Come to our full-service spa and receive special VIP pricing – myspa.ca.

ROOMS Family suite, Upper floor, Private entrance, **Baths** Private, Ensuite, **Beds** King, Queen, Twin, **In Room** Thermostat, **OTHERS** Urban, Adult, Open all year, **PAYMENT** Visa, MC, Cheques accepted, Cash, Trvl's cheques, **BREAKFASTS** Full, Home-baked, Self-catered, **AMENITIES** Central TV, Central phone, Laundry, Kitchen, Lounge, Patio, Central Internet access, Central VCR/DVD, **THINGS TO DO** Rental bikes, Trail nearby, Art, Theatre, Entertainment, Attractions, Shopping, Tennis, Swimming, Beach, **LANGUAGE** Eng., Fr., Ger., **PRICE** (2 persons) 125–179 **(check with hosts for pricing details)**

Vancouver

AnnSarah Camilla House Bed and Breakfast

(Sarah Ma)

2538 West 13th Ave, Vancouver, BC, V6K 2T1
www.vancouver-bb.com
E-mail info@vancouver-bb.com

604-737-2687
Fax 604-739-3328
TFr 1-866-563-0051

Welcome! Luxury and comfort await you at AnnSarah's Camilla House Bed and Breakfast, located on a tree-lined street in the heart of Vancouver, BC, Canada. At Camilla House, we offer the finest accommodations. Our focus is on comfort and cleanliness within elegant presentations. Warm, friendly hospitality and luxurious surroundings await you in this elegant, traditional Vancouver B&B located within a close distance to a variety of shops, restaurants, beaches and other sight-seeing activities.

ROOMS Family suite, Upper floor, Ground floor, Lower floor, **Baths** Private, Ensuite, Shared with guest, **Beds** King, Queen, Double, Twin, **In Room** Thermostat, Phone, TV, Fireplace, Internet access, **OTHERS** Open all year, **PAYMENT** Visa, MC, Cash, Trvl's cheques, **BREAKFASTS** Full, **AMENITIES** Central TV, Central phone, Barbecue, Laundry, Kitchen, Fridge, Hot bev. bar, Lounge, Central Internet access, **THINGS TO DO** Theatre, Attractions, Shopping, Beach, **LANGUAGE** Eng., Chinese, **PRICE** (2 persons) 65–155 **(check with hosts for pricing details)**

Vancouver

Arbutus House Bed & Breakfast

(Joan and Claes Fredriksson)

2913 West 28th Ave, Vancouver, BC, V6L 1X3
www.arbutushouse.com
E-mail stay@arbutushouse.com

604-678-5665
TFr 1-800-636-8509

Relax in casual elegance in the beautiful tree-lined MacKenzie Heights area just minutes from the downtown core and most major attractions. Arbutus House offers two elegant, modern and self-contained garden suites suitable for visitors as well as business travellers. Only minutes from the downtown core, major attractions, the University of British Columbia, beaches and shopping.

ROOMS Family suite, Ground floor, Private entrance, **Baths** Private, Ensuite, **Beds** Queen, Pullout sofa, **Smoking** Outside, **In Room** Thermostat, Phone, TV, Internet access, VCR/DVD, **OTHERS** Open all year, Pets in residence, **PAYMENT** Visa, MC, Cash, Trvl's cheques, **BREAKFASTS** Continental, Self-catered, **AMENITIES** Kitchen, Fridge, Hot bev. bar, Patio, **THINGS TO DO** Trail nearby, Golf, Horseback riding, **LANGUAGE** Eng., Swedish, Cantonese, Mandarin, **PRICE** (2 persons) 110–165 **(check with hosts for pricing details)**

VANCOUVER

Beachside Vancouver Bed & Breakfast

(Gibbs Family)

1180 Renton Pl, West Vancouver, BC, V7S 2K7
www.beach.bc.ca
E-mail info@beach.bc.ca

604-922-7773
Fax 604-926-8073
TFr 1-800-563-3311

Enjoy exclusive, luxury rooms with privacy just minutes from city centre. Quiet, spectacular city and ocean views. Sit on our balcony and see Alaska Cruise ships sail by. A favourite retreat of celebrities, recording artists and honeymooners. Great for a getaway. Enjoy quiet breakfast on the patio. TV/VCR, free movies, private bath, fridge, microwave, coffee, Jacuzzi tub. Free parking. Non-smoking. Warm hospitality, fragrant garden, flowers. Don't miss it! Enjoy our brand new luxury home just 10 minutes from downtown, 5 minutes to Stanley Park.

ROOMS Family suite, Upper floor, Private entrance, **Baths** Ensuite, **Beds** King, Queen, Twin, Single or cots, **Smoking** Outside, **In Room** Thermostat, Phone, TV, Internet access, VCR/DVD, **OTHERS** Urban, Open all year, Pets in residence, **PAYMENT** Visa, MC, Cheques accepted, Cash, Trvl's cheques, **BREAKFASTS** Full, **AMENITIES** Swimming pool, Whirlpool, Barbecue, Laundry, Fridge, Lounge, Patio, Central Internet access, **THINGS TO DO** Trail nearby, Golf, Fishing, Museums, Art, Theatre, Attractions, Shopping, Cross-country skiing, Downhill skiing, Tennis, Swimming, Antiquing, **LANGUAGE** Eng., **PRICE** (2 persons) 100–300 **(check with hosts for pricing details)**

VANCOUVER

Camelot Inn

(Inara and Juris Austrins)

2212 Larch St, Vancouver, BC, V6K 3P7
www.camelotinnvancouver.com
E-mail stay@camelotinnvancouver.com

604-739-6941
Fax 604-739-6937

Heritage award-winning home located in the heart of Vancouver's prestigious and quiet Kitsilano area. We are right beside shopping and fine dinning. Steps from transportation and Kits Beach. Minutes to Grandville Island Public Market, Stanley Park, downtown, and UBC, etc. All rooms have large private bathrooms, king, queen or twin featherbeds, TV/VCR, phone jacks, Persian carpets and fine furnishing. We serve a three-course homemade breakfast and provide onsite parking. You will love this place.

ROOMS Family suite, Upper floor, Ground floor, Lower floor, Private entrance, **Baths** Private, Ensuite, **Beds** King, Queen, Twin, **Smoking** Outside, **In Room** Phone, TV, **OTHERS** Urban, Open all year, Handicapped access, Seasonal, **PAYMENT** Visa, Cheques accepted, Cash, Trvl's cheques, **BREAKFASTS** Full, Home-baked, **AMENITIES** Central TV, Central phone, Kitchen, Fridge, Lounge, **THINGS TO DO** Trail nearby, Rental canoe or boat, Golf, Fishing, Museums, Art, Theatre, Entertainment, Attractions, Wineries/Breweries, Shopping, Cross-country skiing, Tennis, Swimming, Horseback riding, Beach, **LANGUAGE** Eng., Latvian, **PRICE** (2 persons) 109–179 **(check with hosts for pricing details)**

Vancouver

Casa Mora

(Mariette and Neville West)

4538 West 12th Ave, Vancouver, BC, V6R 2R5
www.casamora.com
E-mail info@casamora.com

604-228-8079
TFr 1-800-294-9984

Ideally located in West Point Grey above
Locarno and Jericho Beaches, very close
to UBC and express bus to downtown
(three stops to Granville St); 2 blocks to
excellent shopping/fine dining on 10th
Ave. Traditional B&B rooms or independ-
ent, self-catering suites with views, decks
or garden patio, kitchens, baths, phone,
high-speed Internet access, private
entrances. B&B room with phone, high-
speed Internet access, 3 piece ensuite.
Discounts after Thanksgiving. Breakfast
included with B&B rooms. Hot tub in garden for all.

ROOMS Family suite, Upper floor, Ground floor, Lower
floor, Private entrance, **Baths** Private, Ensuite, **Beds**
King, Queen, Twin, Pullout sofa, **Air** In rooms, **In Room**
Thermostat, Phone, TV, Fireplace, **OTHERS** Urban,
Open all year, Seasonal, **PAYMENT** Visa, MC, Diners,
Amex, Cash, Trvl's cheques, **BREAKFASTS** Full,
Continental, Home-baked, Self-catered, **AMENITIES**
Central TV, Central phone, Whirlpool, Barbecue,
Laundry, Kitchen, Fridge, Lounge, Patio, **THINGS TO
DO** Rental bikes, Trail nearby, Rental canoe or boat,
Golf, Fishing, Museums, Art, Theatre, Entertainment,
Attractions, Wineries/Breweries, Shopping, Cross-
country skiing, Tennis, Swimming, Horseback riding,
Beach, **LANGUAGE** Eng., Fr., some Spanish, **PRICE**
(2 persons) 110–215 **(check with hosts for pricing
details)**

Vancouver

Cassiar Figs Bed and Breakfast

(Beverly Kingston)

504 Cassiar St, Vancouver, BC, V5K 4M9
www.cassiarfigsbb.com
E-mail info@cassiarfigsbb.com

604-299-4039
TFr 1-877-299-4090

Affordable character home, close to
downtown core and the North Shore
Mountains, with quick access to Hwy 1,
Horseshoe Bay ferry terminal and
Whistler. A vegetarian breakfast with
dairy products and free-range eggs is
served.

Baths Shared with guest, **Beds** King, Queen, Twin,
Smoking Outside, **PAYMENT** Cash, Trvl's cheques,
BREAKFASTS Full, **AMENITIES** Central TV, Central
phone, Laundry, Patio, Central Internet access, **THINGS
TO DO** Trail nearby, Museums, Art, Theatre, Entertain-
ment, Attractions, Shopping, Cross-country skiing,
Downhill skiing, **LANGUAGE** Eng., **PRICE** (2 persons)
70–85 **(check with hosts for pricing details)**

VANCOUVER

Chocolate Lily

(Karen Erickson and Rob Grant)

1353 Maple St, Vancouver, BC, V6J 3S1
www.chocolatelily.com
E-mail choclily@telus.net

604-731-9363
Fax 604-731-9363

Stylish, self-catering suites with private garden patios. Excellent location close to Kitsilano Beach, Stanley Park, downtown, Granville Island, UBC and public transit. Fully equipped kitchenettes with microwave, fridge, kettle, coffeemaker, toaster and sink. Wireless high-speed Internet, TV, stereo. Beautifully tiled bathrooms. Covered off-street parking. Close proximity to a wide selection of fine cafes, bakeries and delicatessens. Comfortable queen-size beds with down duvets. A great place to stay.

ROOMS Private entrance, **Baths** Private, **Beds** Queen, **Smoking** In rooms, **In Room** Thermostat, Phone, TV, Fireplace, Internet access, **OTHERS** Urban, Open all year, **PAYMENT** Visa, MC, Cheques accepted, Cash, Trvl's cheques, **BREAKFASTS** Self-catered, **THINGS TO DO** Rental bikes, Trail nearby, Rental canoe or boat, Museums, Art, Theatre, Entertainment, Attractions, Shopping, Tennis, Swimming, Beach, **LANGUAGE** Eng., **PRICE** (2 persons) 95–165 **(check with hosts for pricing details)**

VANCOUVER

Corkscrew Inn

(Marnie DiGiandomenico and Wayne Meadows)

2735 West 2nd Ave, Vancouver, BC, V6K 1K2
www.corkscrewinn.com
E-mail info@corkscrewinn.com

604-733-7276
Fax 604-733-7371
TFr 1-877-737-7276

Our bed and breakfast is a restored 1912 Craftsman-style heritage home on a quiet, tree-lined residential street in the popular Kitsilano neighbourhood with easy access to the major attractions of Vancouver. Within a very short walk, our guests will find a sandy ocean beach, tennis courts, a park, shops and some of Vancouver's best restaurants. Downtown Vancouver, Granville Island, Stanley Park, the University of British Columbia and the cruise ship terminals are only minutes away via transit.

ROOMS Upper floor, Lower floor, **Baths** Private, Ensuite, **Beds** Queen, **Air** Central, **Smoking** Outside, **In Room** Thermostat, Phone, TV, Fireplace, Internet access, VCR/DVD, **OTHERS** Urban, Adult, Open all year, **PAYMENT** Visa, MC, Diners, Amex, Cheques accepted, Cash, **BREAKFASTS** Full, Continental, Home-baked, Self-catered, **AMENITIES** Central phone, Fridge, Hot bev. bar, Lounge, Patio, **THINGS TO DO** Rental bikes, Trail nearby, Rental canoe or boat, Golf, Fishing, Museums, Art, Theatre, Entertainment, Attractions, Wineries/Breweries, Shopping, Cross-country skiing, Tennis, Swimming, Horseback riding, Beach, Antiquing, **LANGUAGE** Eng., Sp., **PRICE** (2 persons) 130–210 **(check with hosts for pricing details)**

Vancouver
Duck Inn Riverfront Cottages
(Jill and Allen York)

4349 River Rd, W, Ladner, BC, V4K 1R9
www.duckinn.net
E-mail duckinn@dccnet.com

604-946-7521
Fax 604-946-7521

Two romantic waterfront cottages, featured in *Best Places To Kiss*, perched on pilings on the Fraser River in the historic fishing village of Ladner just south of Vancouver. Fireplaces, hot tubs, king featherbeds; living rooms with TV/VCR/CD, phone, high-speed Internet; kitchens with gourmet breakfast treats; large balconies; wonderful water views. Explore the river in our canoe, bike country roads, barbecue under our riverside willow, relax in hammocks, feed the ducks and swans from private dock.

ROOMS Family suite, Upper floor, Ground floor, Private entrance, **Baths** Private, Ensuite, **Beds** King, Twin, Pullout sofa, **Smoking** Outside, **In Room** Thermostat, Phone, TV, Fireplace, Internet access, VCR/DVD, **OTHERS** Urban, Rural, Open all year, Pets in residence, Pets welcome, **PAYMENT** Visa, MC, Amex, Cash, Trvl's cheques, **BREAKFASTS** Full, Self-catered, **AMENITIES** Whirlpool, Barbecue, Laundry, Kitchen, Fridge, Patio, **THINGS TO DO** Comp. bikes, Trail nearby, Comp. canoe or boat, Golf, Fishing, Museums, Art, Theatre, Entertainment, Attractions, Wineries/Breweries, Shopping, Tennis, Swimming, Beach, Birdwatching, **LANGUAGE** Eng., **PRICE** (2 persons) 130–200 **(check with hosts for pricing details)**

Vancouver
Ellison House
(Ellison Massey)

542 East 1st St, North Vancouver, BC, V7L 1B9
www.b-b.com/ellisonhouse
E-mail ellison@b-b.com

604-990-6730
Fax 604-990-5876
TFr 1-800-561-3223

A bright sunny, comfortable home centrally located in a quiet residential neighbourhood. Close to Lonsdale Quay and seabus service to downtown Vancouver. Close to Grouse Mountain Skyride, Capilano Suspension Bridge, Stanley Park. Long-term rates are available. Hostess operates Canada-West Accommodations Reservation Service. From Second Narrows Bridge to Lonsdale Exit to East 1st St.

ROOMS Ground floor, **Baths** Shared with guest, **Beds** Queen, Double, **OTHERS** Urban, Adult, Open all year, Pets in residence, **PAYMENT** Visa, MC, Cash, Trvl's cheques, **AMENITIES** Central TV, Central phone, Kitchen, **THINGS TO DO** Trail nearby, Golf, Fishing, Museums, Art, Theatre, Entertainment, Attractions, Shopping, Cross-country skiing, Tennis, Swimming, Beach, Birdwatching, **LANGUAGE** Eng., **PRICE** (2 persons) 60–80 **(check with hosts for pricing details)**

Greystone Bed and Breakfast

(Graham and Lee Laxton)

2006 West 14th Ave, Vancouver, BC, V6J 2K4
www.greystonebb.com
E-mail stay@greystonebb.com

604-732-1375
Fax 604-731-1015
TFr 1-866-518-1000

Welcome to our charming 1910 heritage
Craftsman-style home. Situated 10 minutes from the downtown core in the
quiet and safe Kitsilano area. All rooms
and our two-bedroom suite (sleeps six)
are tastefully decorated, have private
bathrooms, queen-size beds and TV/VCR.
Delicious full breakfasts included in rates.
Complimentary high-speed wireless
Internet access. Good Times + Good Value
= Greystone B&B.

ROOMS Private entrance, **Baths** Ensuite, **Beds** Queen,
Air Ceiling fans, **Smoking** Outside, **In Room** TV,
VCR/DVD, **OTHERS** Urban, Adult, Open all year, Pets in
residence, **PAYMENT** Visa, MC, Cash, Trvl's cheques,
BREAKFASTS Full, Home-baked, **AMENITIES** Central
phone, Whirlpool, Kitchen, Lounge, Patio, Central
Internet access, **THINGS TO DO** Trail nearby, Museums,
Art, Theatre, Entertainment, Attractions, Shopping,
Cross-country skiing, **LANGUAGE** Eng., **PRICE** (2 per-
sons) 90–140 **(check with hosts for pricing details)**

Hycroft Bed and Breakfast

(Pam and Randy Vogel)

1248 West 15th Ave, Vancouver, BC, V6H 1R8
www.hycroft.com
E-mail stay@hycroft.com

604-307-2300
Fax 604-733-2963

Private accommodation, choice of two
beautiful suites. In prestigious South
Granville/Shaughnessy area, only two
blocks from a long strip of the city's finest
shopping, restaurants, boutiques, art galleries, coffee shops, live theatre and transit. The suites are spacious, with your own
private lounge areas, fireplaces, sofas,
kitchenettes, all slate floors heated by in-
floor hot water heat. Full ensuite bathrooms with all the amenties, private
entrances, free off-street parking, full
homecooked breakfasts, warm welcome.

ROOMS Ground floor, Private entrance, **Baths** Ensuite,
Beds Queen, Twin, Single or cots, Pullout sofa,
Smoking Outside, **In Room** Thermostat, Phone, TV,
Fireplace, **OTHERS** Urban, Open all year, Pets in resi-
dence, **PAYMENT** Visa, MC, Diners, Amex, Direct debit,
Cash, **BREAKFASTS** Full, Home-baked, **AMENITIES**
Central TV, Central phone, Kitchen, Fridge, Hot bev.
bar, Patio, **THINGS TO DO** Rental bikes, Trail nearby,
Rental canoe or boat, Golf, Fishing, Museums, Art,
Theatre, Entertainment, Attractions, Wineries/
Breweries, Shopping, Cross-country skiing, Tennis,
Swimming, Horseback riding, Beach, **LANGUAGE** Eng.,
PRICE (2 persons) 115–200 **(check with hosts for
pricing details)**

VANCOUVER

Kenya Court Oceanfront Guest House

(Dr. and Mrs Hugh Williams)

2230 Cornwall Ave, Vancouver, BC, V6K 1B5
www.bbcanada.com/822.html
E-mail h&dwilliams@telus.net

604-738-7085

Large 1,000 sq.ft. deluxe oceanview suites in downtown Vancouver on Kitsilano Bay, all with spectacular views of the oceans, beaches, North Shore Mountains and the city of Vancouver. A car is not necessary but garages are available. Buffet breakfast is served in a rooftop solarium with stunning water and city views. An Olympic-size heated salt water swimming pool and tennis courts are across the street. Close to major attractions, first-class restaurants, and shops of 4th Ave.

ROOMS Family suite, Upper floor, Ground floor, Lower floor, Private entrance, **Baths** Private, Ensuite, **Beds** King, Queen, Twin, **Air** Central, **Smoking** Outside, **In Room** Phone, TV, Fireplace, **OTHERS** Urban, Adult, Open all year, **PAYMENT** Cheques accepted, Cash, Trvl's cheques, **BREAKFASTS** Full, Home-baked, **AMENITIES** Central TV, Central phone, Swimming pool, Kitchen, Fridge, **THINGS TO DO** Rental bikes, Trail nearby, Rental canoe or boat, Golf, Fishing, Museums, Art, Theatre, Entertainment, Attractions, Wineries/Breweries, Shopping, Cross-country skiing, Tennis, Swimming, Horseback riding, Beach, **LANGUAGE** Eng., Fr., Ger., Italian, **PRICE** (2 persons) 145–165 **(check with hosts for pricing details)**

VANCOUVER

Kitsilano Cottage By The Sea

(Judith Milliken and Trevor Todd)

1350 Walnut St, Vancouver, BC, V6J 3R3
www.kitsilanocottagebythesea.com
E-mail judithmilliken@telus.net

604-261-4951
Fax 604-264-8490

Elegant three-bedroom tourist suite in ideal location by downtown, beach, parks and Granville Island. Family, child and pet friendly, we offer a quiet garden suite in a heritage home in a safe and trendy neighbourhood a five minute walk from the spectacular ocean-front Kitsilano Beach. Tastefully decorated, it includes three bedrooms, two bathrooms, living room, fully equipped kitchen, laundry, cable television and high-speed Internet, parking, telephone and separate entrance to private back garden and hot tub.

ROOMS Family suite, Ground floor, Private entrance, **Baths** Private, Ensuite, **Beds** Queen, Double, **Smoking** Outside, **In Room** Thermostat, Phone, TV, Internet access, VCR/DVD, **OTHERS** Babysitting, Urban, Open all year, Pets in residence, Pets welcome, **PAYMENT** Cheques accepted, Cash, Trvl's cheques, **BREAKFASTS** Self-catered, **AMENITIES** Central TV, Central phone, Whirlpool, Barbecue, Laundry, Kitchen, Fridge, Patio, **THINGS TO DO** Rental bikes, Trail nearby, Rental canoe or boat, Golf, Museums, Art, Theatre, Entertainment, Attractions, Shopping, Cross-country skiing, Tennis, Swimming, Beach, Birdwatching, Antiquing, **LANGUAGE** Eng., Fr., Sp., **PRICE** (2 persons) 100–100 **(check with hosts for pricing details)**

VANCOUVER

Kitsilano Point B&B

(Larry and Jennifer Barr)

1936 McNicoll Ave, Vancouver, BC, V6J 1A6
www.canadianbandbguide.ca/bb.asp?ID=1971
E-mail barr@telus.net

604-738-9576
Fax 604-738-9576

A Craftsman-style house located north end of Cypress St, one block west of Burrard St near Kitsilano Beaches with parks, pool, museums and planetarium. Shortcut to downtown restaurants, stores and English Bay by foot-ferry (small boat which holds about 12) near house. Short drive to Stanley Park Science Centre, Grouse Mountain, airport and UBC. Quiet friendly hospitality in 1911 house with shaded garden in convenient location. Not suitable for preschool children.

ROOMS Upper floor, **Baths** Ensuite, Shared with guest, **Beds** Double, Twin, **Smoking** Outside, **In Room** Fireplace, **OTHERS** Open all year, **PAYMENT** Cash, Trvl's cheques, **BREAKFASTS** Full, **THINGS TO DO** Museums, Theatre, Entertainment, Attractions, Tennis, Swimming, Beach, **LANGUAGE** Eng., Fr., **PRICE** (2 persons) 85–110 **(check with hosts for pricing details)**

VANCOUVER

Mickeys Kits Beach Chalet

(John Dewart)

2146 West 1st Ave, Vancouver, BC, V6K 1E8
www.mickeysbandb.com
E-mail info@mickeysbandb.com

604-739-3342
Fax 604-739-3342
TFr 1-888-739-3342

Welcome to the charm and comfort of a cozy bed and breakfast two blocks from the beach in beautiful Kitsilano right in the heart of Vancouver. With this unbeatable location you'll find all the major attractions at your fingertips. Continental breakfast, a serene garden, privacy and convenience are the trademarks of this delightful B&B. Whether on business or pleasure we can provide all your needs year round with great service in an intimate home atmosphere.

ROOMS Upper floor, Ground floor, Private entrance, **Baths** Private, Ensuite, Shared with guest, **Beds** King, Queen, Single or cots, Pullout sofa, **Smoking** Outside, **In Room** Thermostat, Phone, TV, Fireplace, Internet access, **OTHERS** Babysitting, Urban, Open all year, **PAYMENT** Visa, MC, Amex, Direct debit, Cheques accepted, Cash, Trvl's cheques, **BREAKFASTS** Continental, Self-catered, **AMENITIES** Fridge, Patio, **THINGS TO DO** Rental bikes, Trail nearby, Rental canoe or boat, Golf, Fishing, Museums, Art, Theatre, Enter-tainment, Attractions, Wineries/Breweries, Shopping, Cross-country skiing, Tennis, Swimming, Beach, **LANGUAGE** Eng., **PRICE** (2 persons) 85–155 **(check with hosts for pricing details)**

Vancouver

'O Canada' House B&B

(Helene Barton)

1114 Barclay St, Vancouver, BC, V6E 1H1
www.ocanadahouse.com
E-mail info@ocanadahouse.com

604-688-0555
Fax 604-488-0556
TFr 1-877-688-1114

Vancouver's foremost B&B located on a quiet residential street within easy walking to Stanley Park, Robson St shops and restaurants, English Bay Beach, Granville Island, theatres and downtown core. This award-winning heritage home was restored in 1995 and is where the first English version of our national anthem was penned. Gourmet breakfasts, complimentary sherry and a 24-hour guest pantry is provided.

ROOMS Family suite, Upper floor, Ground floor, Private entrance, **Baths** Ensuite, **Beds** King, Queen, **Air** Ceiling fans, **Smoking** Outside, **In Room** Phone, TV, Fireplace, Internet access, VCR/DVD, **OTHERS** Urban, Adult, Open all year, **PAYMENT** Visa, MC, Direct debit, Cash, Trvl's cheques, **BREAKFASTS** Full, **AMENITIES** Central TV, Central phone, Fridge, Hot bev. bar, Lounge, Central Internet access, Central VCR/DVD, **THINGS TO DO** Rental bikes, Trail nearby, Rental canoe or boat, Golf, Museums, Art, Theatre, Entertainment, Shopping, Tennis, Swimming, Beach, Antiquing, **LANGUAGE** Eng., Fr., **PRICE** (2 persons) 135–265 **(check with hosts for pricing details)**

Vancouver

Ocean Breeze B&B and Furnished Apartments

(Margaret Gradowska)

462 E 1st St, Vancouver, BC, V7L 1B7
www.oceanbreezevancouver.com
E-mail info@oceanbreezevancouver.com

604-988-0546
Fax 604-988-7002
TFr 1-800-567-5171

Ocean Breeze Executive B&B is centrally located to all major tourist attractions, with fantastic views of Vancouver Harbour and Alaskan cruise ships, and within walking distance to waterfront restaurants, pubs, shops. Only 10 minutes to busy downtown core by famous water bus – Seabus. Rooms are well appointed with diplomat fridges, coffee/tea makers, TVs and wireless Internet. Children and small dogs are welcome in one of our Family suites on the side of the main building. Babysitting service is available (inquire).

ROOMS Family suite, Upper floor, Ground floor, Private entrance, **Baths** Private, Ensuite, **Beds** King, Queen, Double, Twin, **Smoking** Outside, **In Room** Thermostat, Phone, TV, Fireplace, Internet access, VCR/DVD, **OTHERS** Babysitting, Open all year, Pets welcome, **PAYMENT** Visa, MC, Amex, Cheques accepted, Cash, Trvl's cheques, **BREAKFASTS** Full, Self-catered, **AMENITIES** Barbecue, Laundry, Kitchen, Fridge, Hot bev. bar, Patio, Central Internet access, **THINGS TO DO** Rental bikes, Trail nearby, Rental canoe or boat, Golf, Fishing, Museums, Art, Theatre, Entertainment, Attractions, Shopping, Cross-country skiing, Downhill skiing, Tennis, Swimming, Beach, Birdwatching, **LANGUAGE** Eng., Ger., Polish, Italian **PRICE** (2 persons) 110–169 **(check with hosts for pricing details)**

VANCOUVER
Peloquin's Pacific Pad
(Janet Peloquin)

426 West 22 Ave, Vancouver, BC, V5Y 2G5
www.vancouver-bc.com/peloquin/
E-mail peloquin@vancouver-bc.com

604-874-4529
Fax 604-874-6229

We are here to greet you year round. Situated in a quiet, residential tree-lined neighbourhood, minutes to downtown, hospital, UBC, Granville Island, Q.E.Park, Science World and bus pickup to Victoria. Walk to restaurants, cafes, shops, parks, cinema and buses. Easy access to airport, ferries, bus, train and Hwy 99 from US and Hwy 1. From Hwy 1, use Grandview Exit to Cambie St, go left on 22 Ave. Hosting since 1986. We enjoy sharing helpful info about our 2010 Olympic City. Children and non-smokers welcome. No pets please.

ROOMS Lower floor, Private entrance, **Baths** Private, **Beds** Double, Single or cots, Pullout sofa, **Air** Central, **Smoking** Outside, **In Room** TV, **OTHERS** Urban, Open all year, **PAYMENT** Cash, Trvl's cheques, **BREAKFASTS** Full, Home-baked, **AMENITIES** Central phone, Kitchen, Fridge, Hot bev. bar, **THINGS TO DO** Rental bikes, Trail nearby, Rental canoe or boat, Golf, Fishing, Museums, Art, Theatre, Entertainment, Attractions, Wineries/ Breweries, Shopping, Cross-country skiing, Tennis, Swimming, Horseback riding, Beach, **LANGUAGE** Eng., Fr., Ukrainian, **PRICE** (2 persons) 69-110 **(check with hosts for pricing details)**

VANCOUVER
Pendrell Suites
(Rosemary and Boyd McConnell)

1419 Pendrell St, Vancouver, BC, V6G 1S3
www.pendrellsuites.com
E-mail rosemary@pendrellsuites.com

604-609-2770
Fax 604-685-8675
TFr 1-888-250-7211

English Bay, Stanley Park, Robson St, Denman and downtown are all close when you enjoy a first-class stay in one of our six, exclusive "homes" while in Vancouver for business or pleasure – short or long-term. There are only two grand suites per floor in this brick heritage building built in 1910 and refurbished completely in 1996. Spacious residence in a quiet residential area.

ROOMS Family suite, Upper floor, Ground floor, Lower floor, Private entrance, **Baths** Private, Ensuite, Shared with guest, **Beds** Queen, Double, Twin, Single or cots, Pullout sofa, **Smoking** Outside, **In Room** Thermostat, Phone, TV, Fireplace, Internet access, VCR/DVD, **OTHERS** Urban, Open all year, Pets in residence, Pets welcome, **PAYMENT** Visa, MC, Amex, Direct debit, Cash, Trvl's cheques, **BREAKFASTS** Self-catered, **AMENITIES** Central TV, Whirlpool, Barbecue, Laundry, Kitchen, Fridge, Lounge, Patio, **THINGS TO DO** Rental bikes, Trail nearby, Rental canoe or boat, Golf, Fishing, Museums, Art, Theatre, Entertainment, Attractions, Wineries/Breweries, Shopping, Cross-country skiing, Downhill skiing, Tennis, Swimming, Beach, Birdwatching, Antiquing, **LANGUAGE** Eng., **PRICE** (2 persons) 99–750 **(check with hosts for pricing details)**

Vancouver

The Doorknocker Bed and Breakfast

(Jeanette Jarville)

13211 Steveston Hwy, Richmond, BC, V6W 1A5
www.thedoorknocker.com
E-mail thedoorknocker@shaw.ca

604-277-8714
TFr 1-866-877-8714

Central Vancouver location, minutes to downtown, YVR Airport, Victoria/Gulf Island Ferry Terminals, Riverrock Casino and Historic Steveston Village. The Doorknocker B&B is a 9,200 sq. ft. Tudor home on 1 acre of beautiful gardens. It boasts many amenities – large luxury rooms, king, queen and twin beds, wireless Internet, library, indoor heated pool, hot tub and much more! Close to shops, restaurants and entertainment complex! Your hostess is a professional artist and her art is showcased throughtout the home.

ROOMS Upper floor, **Baths** Private, Ensuite, Shared with guest, **Beds** King, Queen, Twin, **Air** Ceiling fans, **Smoking** Outside, **In Room** TV, Internet access, VCR/DVD, **OTHERS** Rural, Adult, Open all year, Pets in residence, **PAYMENT** Visa, MC, Amex, Cash, Trvl's cheques, **BREAKFASTS** Full, **AMENITIES** Central TV, Central phone, Swimming pool, Sauna, Whirlpool, Fridge, Hot bev. bar, Lounge, Patio, Central Internet access, **THINGS TO DO** Trail nearby, Golf, Fishing, Museums, Art, Theatre, Entertainment, Attractions, Shopping, Swimming, Birdwatching, **LANGUAGE** Eng., Ger., **PRICE** (2 persons) 89–165 **(check with hosts for pricing details)**

Vancouver

ThistleDown House

(Ruth Crameri and Rex Davidson)

3910 Capilano Rd, North Vancouver, BC, V7R 4J2
www.thistle-down.com
E-mail info@thistle-down.com

604-986-7173
Fax 604-980-2939
TFr 1-888-633-7173

Highly acclaimed *Canada Select* 4 1/2-star 1920 heritage-listed Craftsman-style property filled with fine antiques and works of art from around the world. Five rooms, all ensuite, are beautifully finished and furnished and equipped with many amenities. Afternoon tea is served and breakfast is deliciously creative and multi-course. Recipient of the prestigious Turner Award for Hospitality in 2004. Just 15 minutes from the core of the city, ThistleDown House is situated on Vancouver's spectacular north shore.

ROOMS Upper floor, Ground floor, **Baths** Ensuite, **Beds** King, Queen, Twin, **Air** Central, **Smoking** Outside, **In Room** Thermostat, TV, Fireplace, **OTHERS** Urban, Adult, Open all year, Pets in residence, **PAYMENT** Visa, MC, Cash, Trvl's cheques, **BREAKFASTS** Full, **AMENITIES** Central phone, Fridge, Hot bev. bar, Lounge, Patio, Central Internet access, **THINGS TO DO** Rental bikes, Trail nearby, Rental canoe or boat, Golf, Fishing, Museums, Art, Theatre, Entertainment, Attractions, Shopping, Cross-country skiing, Downhill skiing, Tennis, Swimming, Birdwatching, Antiquing, **LANGUAGE** Eng., Ger., **PRICE** (2 persons) 110–275 **(check with hosts for pricing details)**

Vancouver (S Delta)

Our House Bed and Breakfast

(Carol Dillman and Irene Scarth)

4837 – 44A Ave, Delta (Ladner), BC, V4K 1E3
www.ourhouse.bc.ca
E-mail info@ourhouse.bc.ca

604-946-2628
Fax 604-946-6869
TFr 1-866-946-2628

Enjoy a stay at our clean, comfortable, residential B&B. Or ask about our fully furnished and equiped condos for your longer stays. Located in picturesque Ladner, close to Vancouver Airport and the ferries to Vancouver and the Gulf Islands. Chilren are welcome. Call regarding pets.

ROOMS Upper floor, **Baths** Private, Ensuite, Shared with guest, **Beds** Queen, Single or cots, **Smoking** Outside, **OTHERS** Urban, Open all year, Pets welcome, **PAYMENT** Visa, MC, Amex, Cheques accepted, Cash, Trvl's cheques, **BREAKFASTS** Full, **AMENITIES** Central TV, Central phone, Fridge, Lounge, Patio, Central Internet access, Central VCR/DVD, **THINGS TO DO** Golf, Fishing, Museums, Theatre, Attractions, Wineries/Breweries, Shopping, Tennis, Swimming, Horseback riding, Beach, Birdwatching, **LANGUAGE** Eng., **PRICE** (2 persons) 60–85 **(check with hosts for pricing details)**

Vancouver (Surrey)

Bed & Breakfast "On the Ridge"

(Dale and Mary Fennell)

5741 – 146th St, Surrey, BC, V3S 2Z5
www.bbridgesurrey.com
E-mail stay@bbridgesurrey.com

604-591-6065
Fax 604-591-6059
TFr 1-888-697-4111

A delightful B&B with a quiet, country ambience but surrounded by hours of playful enjoyment. By car within 10 minutes your choice of nine top rated golf courses, Crescent or White Rock ocean beaches, Skytrain to Vancouver highlights, shopping malls, antique malls, YMCA, hiking trails, two casinos, two large aquatic centres. Three tastefully decorated bedrooms with private bathrooms, hair dryers, TV/VCR. Guest sitting lounge, guest use of enormous sundeck. Gourmet breakfast. Twenty five minutes to airports/ferries to Victoria

ROOMS Upper floor, **Baths** Private, Ensuite, **Beds** Queen, Twin, Single or cots, **Air** In rooms, **Smoking** Outside, **In Room** TV, VCR/DVD, **OTHERS** Urban, Rural, Open all year, **PAYMENT** Cash, Trvl's cheques, **BREAKFASTS** Full, **AMENITIES** Central phone, Fridge, Lounge, Patio, Central Internet access, Central VCR/DVD, **THINGS TO DO** Golf, Fishing, Museums, Attractions, Wineries/Breweries, Shopping, Swimming, Horseback riding, Beach, Birdwatching, Antiquing, **LANGUAGE** Eng., Hungarian, **PRICE** (2 persons) 60–110 **(check with hosts for pricing details)**

Vancouver Island

Island Treasures B&B, Vacation Rental

(Maggie Glenn)

2397 Granville Rd, Nanoose Bay, BC, V9P 9K8
www.islandtreasuresbb.com
E-mail islandtreasuresbb@shaw.ca

250-468-0190
Fax 250-468-0190
TFr 1-866-468-0190

This lovely suite is detached from the main house for complete privacy with its own keyless entrance. Private patio with hot tub, queen-size bed with down duvet, four-piece bath, wall-mount TV with cable and movie channels, DVD, fridge, coffee-maker, microwave. Island Treasures vacation rental provides a calming, peaceful atmosphere to unwind, reconnect and recharge. Indulge yourself, surrounded by natural beauty in our new West Coast Home in Nanoose Bay on beautiful Vancouver Island, BC.

ROOMS Ground floor, Private entrance, **Baths** Private, Ensuite, **Beds** Queen, **Air** Central, In rooms, **Smoking** Outside, **In Room** Thermostat, TV, Fireplace, Internet access, VCR/DVD, **OTHERS** Urban, Rural, Adult, Open all year, Additional meals, Pets welcome, **PAYMENT** Visa, MC, Direct debit, Cash, Trvl's cheques, **BREAKFASTS** Full, Continental, Home-baked, Self-catered, **AMENITIES** Central TV, Whirlpool, Barbecue, Laundry, Kitchen, Fridge, Hot bev. bar, Patio, **THINGS TO DO** Trail nearby, Rental canoe or boat, Golf, Fishing, Museums, Art, Theatre, Entertainment, Attractions, Wineries/Breweries, Shopping, Cross-country skiing, Tennis, Swimming, Horseback riding, Beach, **LANGUAGE** Eng., **PRICE** (2 persons) 115–125 **(check with hosts for pricing details)**

Vernon *(south-central BC)*

Alpineflowers Bed and Breakfast

(Jack and Aileen Benzie)

8245 Rogers Rd, Vernon, BC, V1B 3M7
www.bbcanada.com/alpineflowers
E-mail alpineflowers@telus.net

250-542-8553

Ours is a charming Cape Cod-style home surrounded by majestic trees on six acres on the slopes of Silver Star Mountain. A full breakfast is served in our family dining room overlooking tranquil woods. Convenient location halfway between Vernon and Silver Star Ski Village. We offer a private guest lounge with TV as well as laundry facilities for your use. You can walk to many beautiful trails.

ROOMS Family suite, Upper floor, **Baths** Private, Shared with guest, **Beds** Queen, Double, Single or cots, **Air** Ceiling fans, **Smoking** Outside, **OTHERS** Rural, Adult, Open all year, Pets in residence, **PAYMENT** Cheques accepted, Cash, Trvl's cheques, **BREAKFASTS** Full, Home-baked, **AMENITIES** Central TV, Laundry, Lounge, Central VCR/DVD, **THINGS TO DO** Trail nearby, Golf, Fishing, Museums, Art, Theatre, Entertainment, Attractions, Wineries/Breweries, Shopping, Cross-country skiing, Downhill skiing, Horseback riding, Beach, Birdwatching, **LANGUAGE** Eng., **PRICE** (2 persons) 70–85 **(check with hosts for pricing details)**

VERNON

Castle On The Mountain

(Eskil and Sharon Larson)

8227 Silver Star Rd, Vernon, BC, V1B 3M8
www.castleonthemountain.com
E-mail castle@airspeedwireless.ca

250-542-4593 Fax 250-542-2206
TFr 1-800-667-2229

Luxury Tudor mountainside estate designed and built by artist/hosts. Ten km east of
Hwy 97 on 48 Ave. Panoramic view of city
and lakes. Guest sitting area, kitchen for
light snacks, outdoor hot tub, walking
paths, covered parking. High-quality
rooms, family apartment, luxury suites for
that special occasion. "Stargazer tower"and
"Sailaway" have two person Jacuzzi, gas
fireplace, balconies and breakfast to the
door. Luxury cottage. All Canadian spoiler
breakfast. Enjoy the Eskila Gallery. Year-
round Paradise.

ROOMS Family suite, Upper floor, Ground floor, Lower
floor, Private entrance, **Baths** Private, Ensuite, **Beds**
King, Queen, Twin, Single or cots, Pullout sofa, **Air**
Central, In rooms, **Smoking** Outside, **In Room**
Thermostat, Phone, TV, Fireplace, VCR/DVD, **OTHERS**
Rural, Adult, Open all year, **PAYMENT** Visa, MC, Amex,
Cheques accepted, Cash, Trvl's cheques, **BREAKFASTS**
Full, Home-baked, Self-catered, **AMENITIES** Central TV,
Central phone, Whirlpool, Barbecue, Laundry, Kitchen,
Fridge, Hot bev. bar, Lounge, Patio, Central VCR/DVD,
THINGS TO DO Trail nearby, Golf, Museums, Art,
Theatre, Entertainment, Attractions, Wineries/
Breweries, Shopping, Cross-country skiing, Downhill
skiing, Tennis, Swimming, Horseback riding, Beach,
Birdwatching, Antiquing, **LANGUAGE** Eng., **PRICE**
(2 persons) 85–250 **(check with hosts for pricing
details)**

VERNON

Cedar Grove B&B

(Eileen and Ian Kilpatrick)

303 Kildare Way, Killiney Beach, BC, V1T 7Z3
www.cedargrovebedandbreakfast.com
E-mail ianfk@telus.net

250-542-2497
Fax 250-542-2497

(April–October) Westside Rd 7 km north
of Fintry Park. A quiet taste of the
Okanagan, overlooking lake. Queen beds.
Private entrance, patio, TV lounge, three
units, family-oriented. Full breakfast.
Cabin with full amenites. Pyramid Suite –
one bedroom, full bath, kitchenette/
livingroom, hide-a-bed, barbecue, deck.
Emerald Suite – two bedrooms, TV
lounge, barbecue and limited cooking
facilities, patio. Weekly rentals available
for all units.

ROOMS Family suite, Ground floor, Lower floor, Private
entrance, **Baths** Private, Shared with guest, **Beds**
Queen, **Air** In rooms, Ceiling fans, **Smoking** Outside, **In
Room** Thermostat, Phone, TV, VCR/DVD, **OTHERS**
Rural, Seasonal, Pets welcome, **PAYMENT** Cheques
accepted, Cash, Trvl's cheques, **BREAKFASTS** Full,
AMENITIES Barbecue, Kitchen, Fridge, Lounge, Patio,
Central Internet access, **THINGS TO DO** Trail nearby,
Golf, Fishing, Wineries/Breweries, Shopping,
Swimming, Horseback riding, Beach, Birdwatching,
LANGUAGE Eng., **PRICE** (2 persons) 75–85 **(check
with hosts for pricing details)**

Vernon
Harbour Lights B&B
(Joyce and Doug Stewart)

135 Joharon Rd, Vernon, BC, V1H 1C1
www.harbourlights.ca
E-mail harbourlights@telus.net

250-549-5117
Fax 250-549-5162

Custom-built B&B on 2 quiet hillside acres. Three large guest rooms, each with queen-size bed, ensuite bath and picture windows that offer a panoramic view of Lake Okanagan and the mountains. Enjoy a hearty breakfast featuring juice, fresh fruit, homemade bread, scones/muffins, preserves and hot entree. Hosts have a background of business, agriculture and marketing. Their interests include travel, wine, sailing, cooking, reading. They'd love to share their home with you. BC Tourism Approved.

ROOMS Ground floor, Lower floor, **Baths** Ensuite, **Beds** Queen, **Air** Central, **OTHERS** Urban, Adult, Open all year, **PAYMENT** Visa, Cash, Trvl's cheques, **BREAKFASTS** Full, Home-baked, **AMENITIES** Central TV, Central phone, Fridge, Lounge, Patio, Central Internet access, Central VCR/DVD, **THINGS TO DO** Trail nearby, Rental canoe or boat, Golf, Fishing, Museums, Art, Theatre, Entertainment, Attractions, Wineries/Breweries, Shopping, Cross-country skiing, Downhill skiing, Tennis, Swimming, Horseback riding, Beach, Birdwatching, Antiquing, **LANGUAGE** Eng., **PRICE** (2 persons) 80–90 **(check with hosts for pricing details)**

Vernon
High View Bed & Breakfast
(Derek and Marjorie Allen)

618 Mt Thor Dr, Vernon, BC, V1B 3A3
www.highviewbandb.com
E-mail highview@shaw.ca

250-542-5367
Fax 250-542-5317
TFr 1-866-482-2632

A modern air-conditioned home overlooking world-famous Kalamalka Lake and picturesque Coldstream Valley. One room with twin beds, one room with queen bed, private entrance, guest lounge with TV/VCR; gas fireplace. Delicious breakfasts. Close to beaches, golf courses, hiking, shopping and dining. Only 30 minutes to skiing at world-famous, Silver Star Mountain. Adult-oriented, smoking outside, no pets. Major credit cards, CP 7 days.

ROOMS Lower floor, Private entrance, **Baths** Shared with guest, **Beds** Queen, Twin, **Air** Central, **Smoking** Outside, **In Room** Thermostat, **OTHERS** Adult, Open all year, **PAYMENT** Visa, MC, Diners, Amex, Cheques accepted, Cash, **BREAKFASTS** Full, **AMENITIES** Central TV, Central phone, Lounge, Patio, **THINGS TO DO** Golf, Fishing, Museums, Art, Theatre, Entertainment, Wineries/Breweries, Shopping, Cross-country skiing, Tennis, Horseback riding, Beach, **LANGUAGE** Eng., **PRICE** (2 persons) 50–80 **(check with hosts for pricing details)**

VERNON

The Maples

(Owen and Martha Cloudesley)

1990 Otter Lake Cross Rd, Armstrong, BC, V0E 1B6
www.bbcanada.com/8465.html
E-mail ocloud@telus.net

250-546-2540
Fax 250-546-2570

Situated in rural Spallumcheen, surrounded by farmland. Enjoy our flower and veggie gardens, guest lounge and rooms in our Cape Cod home. Fifty maple trees line the perimeter. There is a working artist onsite. Guided fly-fishing and scenic deluxe 4X4 tours. We're 15 minutes north of Vernon, 5 minutes south of Armstrong. Call for detailed driving instructions. BC Tourism Approved.

ROOMS Upper floor, **Baths** Shared with guest, **Beds** Queen, Twin, **Air** Ceiling fans, **Smoking** Outside, **OTHERS** Rural, Seasonal, **PAYMENT** Visa, MC, Cash, **BREAKFASTS** Continental, **AMENITIES** Fridge, Hot bev. bar, Lounge, Patio, **THINGS TO DO** Trail nearby, Golf, Fishing, Museums, Art, Theatre, Cross-country skiing, Downhill skiing, Horseback riding, Birdwatching, Antiquing, **LANGUAGE** Eng., Dutch (little), **PRICE** (2 persons) 75 **(check with hosts for pricing details)**

VICTORIA *(south Vancouver Island)*

A View to Sea

(Russ and Evelyne Lacey)

626 Fernhill Rd, Victoria, BC, V9A 4Y9
www.aviewtosea.com
E-mail info@aviewtosea.com

250-388-6669
Fax 250-382-5108
TFr 1-888-424-9911

A lovely California-style home located on a high bluff overlooking the city. Spectacular views of the ocean and Olympic Mountains. Noted for sumptuous breakfasts and its romantic setting, the balconies, gardens hot tub and fireplaces offer relaxation and privacy. Cozy rooms with private bath and reading lofts. Bright cheerful guest lounge with bar-fridge, complimentary snacks and beverages. Located about a 5-minute drive to downtown with excellent bus service. Parks and scenic walkways nearby.

ROOMS Family suite, Private entrance, **Baths** Private, **Beds** King, Queen, **Smoking** Outside, **In Room** Thermostat, Fireplace, VCR/DVD, **OTHERS** Urban, Open all year, **PAYMENT** Visa, MC, Direct debit, Cash, **BREAKFASTS** Full, **AMENITIES** Central TV, Sauna, Laundry, Fridge, Lounge, Patio, Central Internet access, **THINGS TO DO** Trail nearby, Golf, Fishing, Museums, Art, Theatre, Entertainment, Attractions, Wineries/Breweries, Shopping, Tennis, Beach, Antiquing, **LANGUAGE** Eng., Fr., **PRICE** (2 persons) 89–185 **(check with hosts for pricing details)**

VICTORIA

Across the Harbour Bed & Breakfast Inn

(Barbara and Lorne McDougall)

485 Head St, Victoria, BC, V9A 5S1
www.acrosstheharbour.com
E-mail relax@acrosstheharbour.com

250-474-7497
Fax 250-474-7397
TFr 1-866-474-7497

Oceanfront on Victoria's Inner Harbour, 5 minutes from downtown by car. Walk downtown via the West Bay seaside boardwalk (30-minute walk) which starts four doors away. Or take the water taxi – it comes every 15 minutes. Deep air-jetted tubs (42 jets) and showers, fireplaces; high-speed Internet, cable TV/VCR, private ensuite baths, down duvets, beautiful garden, pond and birdbaths, free onsite parking. Hot delicious breakfasts served on the veranda overlooking the garden and harbour. *Canada Select* 4 1/2 stars.

ROOMS Upper floor, Ground floor, Private entrance, **Baths** Private, Ensuite, **Beds** King, Queen, **Air** In rooms, **Smoking** Outside, **In Room** Thermostat, TV, Fireplace, **OTHERS** Urban, Open all year, **PAYMENT** Visa, MC, Amex, Direct debit, Cash, Trvl's cheques, **BREAKFASTS** Full, **AMENITIES** Fridge, Hot bev. bar, Lounge, Patio, **THINGS TO DO** Rental bikes, Trail nearby, Rental canoe or boat, Golf, Fishing, Museums, Art, Theatre, Entertainment, Attractions, Wineries/Breweries, Shopping, Tennis, Swimming, Horseback riding, Beach, **LANGUAGE** Eng., **PRICE** (2 persons) 145–225 **(check with hosts for pricing details)**

VICTORIA

Amethyst Inn at Regents Park

(Karl and Grace Sands)

1501 Fort St, Victoria, BC, V8S 1Z6
www.Amethyst-Inn.com
E-mail innkeeper@amethyst-inn.com

250-595-2053
TFr 1-888-265-6499

Experience an award-winning 5 Star bed and breakfast inn. Casually elegant accommodations for guests celebrating special occasions and cozy retreats. Amethyst Inn's comfortable rooms and suites have sitting areas, king or queen beds and private baths, many with double hydrotherapy spa tubs. Most rooms have fireplaces. Enjoy gracious hospitality and delicious breakfasts. Surrounded by mansions, tree-lined streets and gardens, the Inn is convenient to Victoria attractions. Concierge services. Free parking.

ROOMS Upper floor, Ground floor, Private entrance, **Baths** Ensuite, **Beds** King, Queen, Pullout sofa, **Smoking** Outside, **In Room** Thermostat, Fireplace, Internet access, **OTHERS** Adult, Open all year, **PAYMENT** Visa, MC, Cash, Trvl's cheques, **BREAKFASTS** Full, Home-baked, **AMENITIES** Central phone, Lounge, Patio, **THINGS TO DO** Rental bikes, Trail nearby, Rental canoe or boat, Golf, Fishing, Museums, Art, Theatre, Entertainment, Attractions, Wineries/Breweries, Shopping, Tennis, Swimming, Horseback riding, Beach, Birdwatching, Antiquing, **LANGUAGE** Eng., **PRICE** (2 persons) 129–399 **(check with hosts for pricing details)**

VICTORIA

Amore by the Sea B&B & Seaside Spa

(D. Spence)

246 Delgada Rd, Victoria, BC, V9C 3W2
www.AmoreByTheSea.com
E-mail Romance@AmoreByTheSea.com

250-474-5505
Fax 250-474-5957
TFr 1-888-828-4397

Voted 2004 "Best for Honeymoon and Anniversary!" Oceanfront B&B and spa offers seaside luxury. All rooms have unobstructed ocean views, fireplaces, jetted tubs and much more. Our Seaside Spa is famous for our romantic couples side-by-side massages! Visit our photo-filled Web site.

ROOMS Upper floor, **Baths** Private, **Beds** Queen, **In Room** Thermostat, TV, Fireplace, **OTHERS** Open all year, **PAYMENT** Visa, MC, Cash, Trvl's cheques, **BREAKFASTS** Full, **AMENITIES** Central phone, Swimming pool, Whirlpool, Fridge, Hot bev. bar, Lounge, Patio, **THINGS TO DO** Rental bikes, Trail nearby, Rental canoe or boat, Golf, Fishing, Theatre, Entertainment, Attractions, Wineries/Breweries, Shopping, Tennis, Horseback riding, **PRICE** (2 persons) 195–265 **(check with hosts for pricing details)**

VICTORIA

Arbutus Hill Bed and Breakfast

(Jos and Donna Lindenberg)

356 Cyril Owen Pl, Victoria, BC, V9E 2B6
www.arbutushillbedandbreakfast.com
E-mail relax@arbutushillbedandbreakfast.com

250-727-6400
Fax 250-479-3836
TFr 1-866-727-6401

Arbutus Hill Bed and Breakfast is located on a 5-acre lot atop a wooded hill on the outskirts of urban Victoria. It is a quiet refuge from the bustle of traffic, yet only 20 minutes from downtown and 15 minutes from Butchart Gardens. Our goal is to provide clean, modern accommodation at a reasonable rate, a healthy and hearty breakfast and warm, helpful hospitality. We cater to special diets – vegetarian, vegan, gluten-free, for example.

ROOMS Upper floor, Ground floor, **Baths** Ensuite, Shared with guest, **Beds** Queen, Pullout sofa, **Smoking** Outside, **In Room** Thermostat, **OTHERS** Rural, Open all year, **PAYMENT** Visa, MC, Diners, Amex, Cash, Trvl's cheques, **BREAKFASTS** Full, Home-baked, **AMENITIES** Central TV, Central phone, Laundry, Central Internet access, Central VCR/DVD, **THINGS TO DO** Birdwatching, **LANGUAGE** Eng., Dutch, **PRICE** (2 persons) 70–80 **(check with hosts for pricing details)**

Victoria

Beacon Inn at Sidney
(Denise Peat)

9724 Third St, Sidney, BC, V8L 3A2
www.beaconinns.com
E-mail info@beaconinns.com

250-655-3288
TFr 1-877-420-5499

Well known for being the only *Canada Select* 5-star property in the area, providing elegant, yet very reasonably priced accommodation. A complimentary full gourmet breakfast awaits guests each morning. Our nine designer-created guest rooms each have a private ensuite bathroom, bathrobes, hairdryer, queen feather bed, gas fireplace (all but one room), air-conditioning, CD/clock/radio, WI-FI Internet access. Walking distance to shops, restaurants and the waterfront. Just a short drive to Victoria and Butchart Gardens.

ROOMS Upper floor, Ground floor, **Baths** Ensuite, **Beds** Queen, Pullout sofa, **Air** In rooms, **Smoking** Outside, **In Room** Thermostat, TV, Fireplace, Internet access, **OTHERS** Urban, Adult, Open all year, **PAYMENT** Visa, MC, Direct debit, Cash, Trvl's cheques, **BREAKFASTS** Full, **AMENITIES** Central phone, Hot bev. bar, Lounge, Patio, Central Internet access, **THINGS TO DO** Rental bikes, Trail nearby, Rental canoe or boat, Golf, Fishing, Museums, Art, Theatre, Entertainment, Attractions, Wineries/Breweries, Shopping, Swimming, Horseback riding, Beach, Birdwatching, Antiquing, **LANGUAGE** Eng., Fr., **PRICE** (2 persons) 119–259 **(check with hosts for pricing details)**

Victoria

Bender's Bed & Breakfast
(Glenda Bender)

4254 Thornhill Cres, Victoria, BC, V8N 3G7
www.members.shaw.ca/ggbender
E-mail ggbender@shaw.ca

250-472-8993
Fax 250-472-8995

Modern home in quiet residential area. Double and queen beds, private and shared bathrooms. Full breakfast. TV in lounge. Near shopping centre and University of Victoria. On city bus route. No smoking, no credit cards – cash or cheque only. No pets please. Parks and beach are close by.

ROOMS Ground floor, **Baths** Private, Ensuite, Shared with guest, **Beds** Queen, Double, Twin, **Air** Central, **In Room** TV, Fireplace, **OTHERS** Open all year, **PAYMENT** Cheques accepted, Cash, **BREAKFASTS** Full, **AMENITIES** Central TV, Central Internet access, Central VCR/DVD, **THINGS TO DO** Trail nearby, Museums, Art, Theatre, Entertainment, Attractions, Wineries/Breweries, Shopping, Swimming, Beach, Birdwatching, Antiquing, **LANGUAGE** Eng., **PRICE** (2 persons) 50–65 **(check with hosts for pricing details)**

VICTORIA

Birds of a Feather Victoria Oceanfront B&B

(Annette Moen and Dieter Gerhard)

206 Portsmouth Dr, Victoria, BC, V9C 1R9
www.victorialodging.com/
E-mail frontdesk@victorialodging.com

250-391-8889
Fax 250-391-8883
TFr 1-800-730-4790

Victoria Waterfront (with plenty of free parking): Our backyard is a 120-acre lagoon, connected to, but sheltered from, the Pacific Ocean. The lagoon is designated a Migratory Bird Sanctuary and is ideal for safe canoeing, row-boating and kayaking; boats and mountain bikes supplied free of charge. We are surrounded by the Historic Fort Rodd Hill, the 1860 Fisgard Lighthouse and the Hatley Castle and Gardens. All of this is nestled amidst 600 acres of accessible old-growth forest.

ROOMS Family suite, Upper floor, Ground floor, Private entrance, **Baths** Private, Ensuite, **Beds** King, Queen, Double, Twin, **Smoking** Outside, **In Room** Thermostat, Phone, TV, Fireplace, Internet access, VCR/DVD, **OTHERS** Open all year, **PAYMENT** Visa, MC, Cheques accepted, Cash, Trvl's cheques, **BREAKFASTS** Full, **AMENITIES** Central TV, Central phone, Laundry, Kitchen, Fridge, Hot bev. bar, Patio, Central Internet access, **THINGS TO DO** Comp. bikes, Rental bikes, Trail nearby, Rental canoe or boat, Comp. canoe or boat, Golf, Fishing, Museums, Art, Theatre, Entertainment, Attractions, Wineries/Breweries, Shopping, Tennis, Swimming, Horseback riding, Beach, Birdwatching, **LANGUAGE** Eng., Ger., **PRICE** (2 persons) 85–225 **(check with hosts for pricing details)**

VICTORIA

Bonavista B and B

(Debbie and Kevin Dunn)

5187 Patricia Bay Hwy, Victoria, BC, V8Y 1S8
www.bonavistabandb.com
E-mail info@bonavistabandb.com

250-658-1517
Fax 250-658-1572

Make us a part of your Island experience. New home built with your comfort and privacy in mind. Centrally located on the peninsula across from Elk Lake. Private entrances and ensuite bathrooms. TV and coffee in each room. Close to airport and ferries. Lots to do in the immediate area and only 15 minutes in all directions from all the main attractions Victoria has to offer. We offer room only rates for those that don't eat breakfast. Friendly hosts. Babysitting available. Very comfortable.

ROOMS Ground floor, Private entrance, **Baths** Private, Ensuite, **Beds** King, Queen, **Smoking** Outside, **In Room** Thermostat, TV, VCR/DVD, **OTHERS** Babysitting, Open all year, Pets in residence, Pets welcome, **PAYMENT** Visa, MC, Cash, Trvl's cheques, **BREAKFASTS** Full, Continental, Self-catered, **AMENITIES** Central TV, Central phone, Fridge, Central Internet access, **THINGS TO DO** Trail nearby, Rental canoe or boat, Golf, Fishing, Museums, Art, Attractions, Wineries/Breweries, Shopping, Swimming, Beach, **LANGUAGE** Eng., **PRICE** (2 persons) 65–90 **(check with hosts for pricing details)**

VICTORIA

Celtic House B&B
(Mary Fay)

8626 Lochside Dr, Sidney, BC, V8L 1M7
www.celticbandb.com
E-mail celtichousebb@shaw.ca

250-656-1304

Celtic House B&B is conveniently located close to ferries and Victoria International Airport. Twenty minutes to Victoria and 15 minutes to the world-renowned Butchart Gardens. Enjoy beautiful views of Bazan Bay and Mount Baker. A warm, friendly welcome awaits you, a gourmet breakfast is served in the dining room. Whether you stay a night or a month, we will do our best to make your stay as comfortable as possible. Minutes from Sidney by the Sea, a book town and great for gifts.

ROOMS Upper floor, **Baths** Ensuite, **Beds** Queen, Twin, Single or cots, Pullout sofa, **Smoking** Outside, **In Room** TV, VCR/DVD, **PAYMENT** Visa, Cheques accepted, Cash, Trvl's cheques, **BREAKFASTS** Full, **AMENITIES** Lounge, **THINGS TO DO** Rental bikes, Trail nearby, Rental canoe or boat, Golf, Fishing, Museums, Wineries/Breweries, Shopping, Beach, **LANGUAGE** Eng., **PRICE** (2 persons) 60–90 **(check with hosts for pricing details)**

VICTORIA

Cordova Bay Vacations
(Terri and Doug Steele)

5302 Sayward Hill Cres, Victoria, BC, V8Y 3H8
www.cordovabayvacationsvictoria.com
E-mail cordovabayvacations@shaw.ca

250-478-0035

Enjoy your stay in our brand new 1,000 sq. ft. self-contained suite with private bedroom, bathroom, fully equipped kitchenette and eating bar. Sitting area with television, DVD, VCR, Internet, with two fold-down double sofa beds. Private entrance, patio and parking on 1/3 acre of beautifully landscaped property. Located next to world class Cordova Bay golf courses, beach, biking/walking trails, unique gift shops, market, coffee bar and restaurants. Linens and welcome food items supplied.

ROOMS Family suite, Ground floor, Private entrance, **Baths** Private, **Beds** Queen, Double, Pullout sofa, **Air** Central, **Smoking** Outside, **In Room** Thermostat, TV, Internet access, VCR/DVD, **OTHERS** Urban, Open all year, Handicapped access, **PAYMENT** Cheques accepted, Cash, Trvl's cheques, **BREAKFASTS** Continental, Self-catered, **AMENITIES** Central TV, Kitchen, Fridge, Hot bev. bar, Lounge, Patio, Central Internet access, Central VCR/DVD, **THINGS TO DO** Comp. bikes, Trail nearby, Rental canoe or boat, Golf, Fishing, Museums, Art, Theatre, Entertainment, Attractions, Wineries/ Breweries, Shopping, Tennis, Swimming, Horseback riding, Beach, Birdwatching, **LANGUAGE** Eng., **PRICE** (2 persons) 115–140 **(check with hosts for pricing details)**

VICTORIA

Cordova Ridge B&B
(Dennis and Zandra Johnston)

4963 Dustin Ct, Victoria, BC, V8Y 3B5
www.cordovaridge.ca
E-mail relax@cordovaridge.ca

250-658-4800
TFr 1-888-834-1155

Large, ultra-clean rooms with queen beds
and private or ensuite baths. Full country
breakfasts. TV room with premium La-Z-
Boy recliners. Covered sundeck with
peaceful view. Situated on a small quiet
street with easy access to and from the
highway. Central location 15 minutes
from downtown, airport or Butchart
Gardens. Excellent restaurants nearby.
Hostess is a quilter. We enjoy meeting
people and will ensure your stay is memorable and enjoyable.

ROOMS Family suite, Upper floor, Ground floor, Lower
floor, Private entrance, **Baths** Private, Ensuite, **Beds**
Queen, Single or cots, Pullout sofa, **Smoking** Outside,
OTHERS Urban, Adult, Open all year, Pets in residence,
PAYMENT Visa, MC, Diners, Amex, Cheques accepted,
Cash, **BREAKFASTS** Full, Continental, Home-baked,
Self-catered, **AMENITIES** Central TV, Central phone,
Kitchen, Fridge, Lounge, Patio, **THINGS TO DO** Trail
nearby, Rental canoe or boat, Golf, Fishing, Museums,
Art, Theatre, Entertainment, Attractions, Wineries/
Breweries, Shopping, Tennis, Swimming, Horseback
riding, Beach, **LANGUAGE** Eng., **PRICE** (2 persons)
85–125 **(check with hosts for pricing details)**

VICTORIA

Cougar's Crag Extreme B&B
(Steve Schweighofer and Michel Wagner)

1155 Woodley Ghyll Dr, Victoria, BC, V9C 4H9
www.cougarscrag.com
E-mail info@cougarscrag.com

250-478-8993
Fax 250-478-8993
TFr 1-888-808-2724

The Crag is a spectacular Arts and Crafts-
style lodge featuring split-level living
spaces with full amenities, situated on a
ridge surrounded by our 15 wilderness
acres, 30 minutes from downtown
Victoria. We're near some of the most
beautiful parks on Vancouver Island, are
pet-friendly, can provide a variety of
special services for guests (such as ferry
pickups). We're available for weddings,
receptions and retreats – and make the
perfect honeymoon getaway. Visit our
Web site for full details.

ROOMS Family suite, Private entrance, **Baths** Private,
Beds Queen, Pullout sofa, **Air** Central, **Smoking**
Outside, **In Room** Thermostat, TV, Fireplace, VCR/DVD,
OTHERS Rural, Open all year, Additional meals, Pets in
residence, Pets welcome, **PAYMENT** Visa, MC, Cheques
accepted, Cash, Trvl's cheques, **BREAKFASTS** Full,
Continental, Home-baked, **AMENITIES** Central TV,
Barbecue, Laundry, Kitchen, Fridge, Patio, Central
Internet access, **THINGS TO DO** Rental bikes, Trail
nearby, Rental canoe or boat, Golf, Fishing, Museums,
Art, Attractions, Wineries/Breweries, Swimming,
Horseback riding, Beach, Birdwatching, Antiquing,
LANGUAGE Eng., Fr., **PRICE** (2 persons) 160–300
(check with hosts for pricing details)

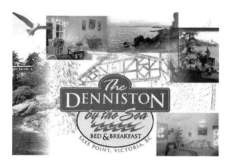

VICTORIA

Denniston By The Sea

(Rosemary Denniston)

430 Grafton St, Victoria, BC, V9A 6S3
www.dennistonbythesea.com
E-mail info@dennistonbythesea.com

250-385-1962
Fax 250-385-5100
TFr 1-888-796-2699

Victorian Tudor-style 1928 waterfront "Hawaii of Canada." Beautiful guest room views of the water and snow-capped mountain. A short drive to Victoria's Inner Harbour activity and romance. Surrounded by bird and sea life and ocean ferries and ships. Former hideaway of concert pianist Madam Huntley Green. Waterfront walkway, picnic tables, parks; near CFB Esquimalt. A short distance to shopping and restaurants, museums etc. Gift certificates available; we welcome "winter escapees."

ROOMS Family suite, Upper floor, Ground floor, **Baths** Private, Ensuite, **Beds** King, Queen, Double, Twin, Single or cots, Pullout sofa, **Smoking** Outside, **In Room** Thermostat, TV, **OTHERS** Babysitting, Urban, Open all year, **PAYMENT** Visa, MC, Cheques accepted, Cash, Trvl's cheques, **BREAKFASTS** Full, **AMENITIES** Central TV, Central phone, Hot bev. bar, Lounge, **THINGS TO DO** Rental bikes, Trail nearby, Rental canoe or boat, Golf, Fishing, Museums, Art, Theatre, Entertainment, Attractions, Wineries/Breweries, Shopping, Tennis, Swimming, Horseback riding, Beach, **LANGUAGE** Eng., **PRICE** (2 persons) 95–125 **(check with hosts for pricing details)**

VICTORIA

Forgett-Me-Nott B&B

(Monica and Andy Reekie)

4388 Northridge Cres, Victoria, BC, V8Z 4Z3
www3.telus.net/forgettmenott
E-mail khyllah@telus.net

250-744-2047
Fax 250-744-2047
TFr 1-877-736-7438

Come and be yourself for a while! Ideally located for exploring the Saanich Peninsula. A short drive to downtown Victoria, Butchart Gardens, wineries, Elk Lake/Beaver Lake park, restaurants, shopping, golf, Commonwealth Pool or stroll the trails along Colquitz Creek. Enjoy hearty homemade breakfasts served in the formal dining room. Well behaved, friendly dogs and cats welcome (two dogs live here). $25 administration fee applied to all cancellations. CP 7 days. May friends always meet!

ROOMS Upper floor, **Baths** Private, Ensuite, **Beds** Queen, Double, Single or cots, **Smoking** Outside, **In Room** Thermostat, Internet access, **OTHERS** Urban, Adult, Open all year, Pets in residence, Pets welcome, **PAYMENT** Visa, MC, Cash, **BREAKFASTS** Full, Home-baked, **AMENITIES** Central TV, Central phone, Fridge, **THINGS TO DO** Trail nearby, Golf, Fishing, Museums, Art, Theatre, Entertainment, Attractions, Wineries/Breweries, Shopping, Tennis, Swimming, Horseback riding, Beach, **LANGUAGE** Eng., **PRICE** (2 persons) 75–95 **(check with hosts for pricing details)**

VICTORIA

Hillside House

(Carol and Jim Clarke)

1216 Montrose Ave, Victoria, BC, V8T 2K4
www.tourismmall.victoria.bc.ca/hillsideB&B
E-mail hillsidehouse@shaw.ca

250-384-2811
Fax 250-384-7686

Enjoy the ambience from the front porch of this gracious 1919 character home overlooking Victoria and Olympic Mountains. Two large, cheery, ensuite rooms sleep up to four guests and take up the entire second floor. Minutes from major attractions, the Inner Harbour and UVic. Hearty breakfasts feature fresh fruit salad, juice, homemade jams/muffins, Jim's choice of the day, bottomless coffee and friendly conversation. Families welcome. We have a great view but we're on a hill and there are steps up to the house.

ROOMS Upper floor, **Baths** Private, **Beds** Queen, Double, Twin, Pullout sofa, **Smoking** Outside, **In Room** Thermostat, Phone, **OTHERS** Babysitting, **PAYMENT** Cash, Trvl's cheques, **BREAKFASTS** Full, **AMENITIES** Central TV, Fridge, **THINGS TO DO** Rental bikes, Trail nearby, Rental canoe or boat, Golf, Museums, Art, Theatre, Entertainment, Attractions, Wineries/ Breweries, Shopping, Tennis, Swimming, Horseback riding, Beach, **LANGUAGE** Eng., a bit of French, **PRICE** (2 persons) 85–110 **(check with hosts for pricing details)**

VICTORIA

Humboldt House

(David Booth)

867 Humboldt St, Victoria, BC, V8V 2Z6
www.humboldthouse.com
E-mail rooms@humboldthouse.com

250-383-0152
Fax 250-383-6402
TFr 1-888-383-0327

Escape to the romantic luxury of the Humboldt House Bed and Breakfast Inn, just two blocks from Victoria's beautiful inner harbour. Elegant guest rooms feature wood-burning fireplaces and large Jacuzzi tubs. Enjoy a gourmet breakfast in the privacy of your room, and homemade chocolate truffles with champagne on arrival. Inquire about our romantic getaway packages and low season discounts. Voted best of Victoria.

ROOMS Family suite, Upper floor, Ground floor, Lower floor, Private entrance, **Baths** Private, Ensuite, **Beds** King, Queen, Single or cots, **Smoking** Outside, **In Room** Thermostat, Fireplace, **OTHERS** Urban, Adult, Open all year, **PAYMENT** Visa, MC, Amex, Direct debit, Cash, Trvl's cheques, **BREAKFASTS** Full, **AMENITIES** Central phone, Laundry, Fridge, Lounge, **THINGS TO DO** Rental bikes, Museums, Art, Theatre, Entertainment, Attractions, Wineries/Breweries, Shopping, Tennis, Swimming, Horseback riding, Beach, **LANGUAGE** Eng., Fr., Ger., Czech., **PRICE** (2 persons) 147–315 **(check with hosts for pricing details)**

Victoria

Millstream Llama Farm Bed & Breakfast

(Lavinia and Alan Stevens)

355 Atkins Rd, Victoria, BC, V9B 3A1
www.millstreamllamas.com
E-mail mail@millstreamllamas.com

250-478-9969
TFr 1-866-849-3938

A unique country lifestyle only 6 miles from downtown Victoria. Come and visit our 6-acre llama farm on the banks of historic Millstream Creek. Total privacy in our secluded hideaway, with only llamas and herons for company. Our spacious and luxurious suites overlook the peaceful grazing llamas. We are only 15 minutes from all the attractions of Victoria, the capital city of British Columbia. Enjoy fresh flowers in your room. Complimentary tea or coffee and cookies on arrival, as well as sherry in your room.

ROOMS Ground floor, Private entrance, **Baths** Private, Ensuite, **Beds** Queen, **Smoking** Outside, **In Room** Thermostat, TV, Fireplace, VCR/DVD, **OTHERS** Rural, **PAYMENT** Visa, MC, Direct debit, Cash, **BREAKFASTS** Full, Home-baked, **AMENITIES** Whirlpool, Fridge, Patio, **THINGS TO DO** Trail nearby, Rental canoe or boat, Golf, Fishing, Museums, Art, Theatre, Entertainment, Attractions, Wineries/Breweries, Shopping, Tennis, Swimming, Horseback riding, Beach, Birdwatching, Antiquing, **LANGUAGE** Eng., **PRICE** (2 persons) 90–125 **(check with hosts for pricing details)**

Victoria

Morningside Bed and Breakfast

(Kjerstin Redden and Erik Wang)

512 Linden Ave, Victoria, BC, V8V 4G5
www.morningsidebedandbreakfast.ca
E-mail kj.erik@shaw.ca

250-519-0019

Featuring a private second floor entrance with views of the Olympic Mountains, and a short stroll to the ocean and the heart of downtown Victoria. You can always reach us on our cell, (250-661-7019). From the ferry or airport, follow the Pat Bay Hwy into downtown Victoria (Blanshard St) until you reach Fairfield Rd. Turn left and follow Fairfield past Cook St to Linden Ave. Turn left on Linden, we are the second house on the left side.

ROOMS Family suite, Upper floor, Private entrance, **Baths** Private, **Beds** Queen, Single or cots, **Smoking** Outside, **In Room** TV, Internet access, VCR/DVD, **OTHERS** Open all year, Pets in residence, **PAYMENT** MC, Cash, Trvl's cheques, **BREAKFASTS** Continental, Home-baked, **AMENITIES** Fridge, Hot bev. bar, **THINGS TO DO** Golf, Fishing, Museums, Art, Theatre, Entertainment, Attractions, Wineries/Breweries, Shopping, Swimming, Beach, Antiquing, **LANGUAGE** Eng., Swedish, **PRICE** (2 persons) 95–150 **(check with hosts for pricing details)**

VICTORIA

Oceanside Gardens Retreat
(Diane and John Lum)

5653 Sooke Rd, Sooke, BC, V0S 1N0
www.oceansidegardens.com
E-mail frontdesk@oceansidegardens.com

250-642-0244
Fax 250-384-4736
TFr 1-877-647-5500

Oceanfront accommodations and Fishing Charters. Close to hiking and biking trails, amazing beaches and fresh water swimming holes and lakes. Ivy Cottage – open plan styling, wraparound deck with oceanview. Magnolia House – Old English-style with large bay windows to enjoy views. Heated outdoor pool and cedar sauna. Private mature acreage, perfect for quiet getaways or small weddings. Book our affiliate service Devonian Charters for saltwater fishing. "Winter specials available".

ROOMS Family suite, Upper floor, Ground floor, Private entrance, **Baths** Private, Ensuite, **Beds** King, Queen, Double, Single or cots, Pullout sofa, **Smoking** Outside, **OTHERS** Babysitting, Rural, Open all year, **PAYMENT** Visa, MC, Cash, Trvl's cheques, **BREAKFASTS** Self-catered, **AMENITIES** Central TV, Central phone, Swimming pool, Sauna, Whirlpool, Barbecue, Laundry, Kitchen, Central VCR/DVD, **THINGS TO DO** Rental bikes, Trail nearby, Rental canoe or boat, Golf, Fishing, Museums, Art, Theatre, Entertainment, Attractions, Wineries/Breweries, Shopping, Tennis, Swimming, Horseback riding, Beach, Birdwatching, Antiquing, **LANGUAGE** Eng., Chinese, **PRICE** (2 persons) 150–425 **(check with hosts for pricing details)**

VICTORIA

Prior House B&B Inn
(C. Cooperrider)

620 St Charles St, Victoria, BC, V8S 3N7
www.priorhouse.com
E-mail innkeeper@priorhouse.com

250-592-8847
Fax 250-592-8223
TFr 1-877-924-3300

In Rockland, one of the most charming and historic of Victoria's neighbourhoods. Walking distance to Government House and gardens, Craigdaroch Castle and antique row, 5 minutes drive to inner harbour, old Victoria and Oak Bay Village. Built by King George V, this Inn exudes wonderfully elegant old-world charm with white oak panelling, boxed ceilings, hardwood floors, sunny terraces, surrounding estate gardens, 12 fireplaces and an inviting warm, hospitable ambience. Afternoon tea in the parlour with fresh-baked scones. Breakfast in your room or formal dining room.

ROOMS Family suite, Upper floor, Ground floor, Private entrance, **Baths** Private, Ensuite, **Beds** King, Queen, Pullout sofa, **Smoking** Outside, **In Room** Thermostat, Phone, TV, Fireplace, Internet access, VCR/DVD, **OTHERS** Urban, Pets welcome, **PAYMENT** Visa, MC, Cash, Trvl's cheques, **BREAKFASTS** Full, Home-baked, **AMENITIES** Whirlpool, Laundry, Fridge, Hot bev. bar, Lounge, Patio, Central Internet access, **THINGS TO DO** Rental bikes, Trail nearby, Golf, Museums, Art, Theatre, Entertainment, Attractions, Wineries/Breweries, Shopping, Tennis, Swimming, Beach, Birdwatching, Antiquing, **LANGUAGE** Eng., **PRICE** (2 persons) 125–295 **(check with hosts for pricing details)**

VICTORIA

Wintercott Country House

(Peter and Diana Caleb)

1950 Nicholas Rd, Saanichton, BC, V8M 1X8
www.wintercott.com
E-mail wintercott@shaw.ca

250-652-2117
Fax 250-652-8884
TFr 1-800-708-4344

An English-style country home 5 minutes from Butchart Gardens, 15 minutes from Victoria. Located on quiet, garden acreage. Guest rooms have four-poster beds and all the amenities for a comfortable stay. Garden gazebo and patio for summer relaxation. Children and well-behaved dogs welcome. *Canada Select* 4-stars. From Hwy 17 (coming from either direction) turn west onto Sayward Rd, right on Brookleigh, turn right on Oldfield then left on Nicholas.

ROOMS Ground floor, **Baths** Ensuite, **Beds** Queen, Twin, **Smoking** Outside, **In Room** TV, Internet access, VCR/DVD, **OTHERS** Rural, Open all year, Pets welcome, **PAYMENT** Visa, Cheques accepted, Cash, Trvl's cheques, **BREAKFASTS** Full, Home-baked, **AMENITIES** Central phone, Whirlpool, Laundry, Fridge, Hot bev. bar, Lounge, Patio, **THINGS TO DO** Rental bikes, Trail nearby, Rental canoe or boat, Golf, Fishing, Museums, Art, Theatre, Entertainment, Attractions, Wineries/Breweries, Shopping, Tennis, Swimming, Horseback riding, Birdwatching, Antiquing, **LANGUAGE** Eng., **PRICE** (2 persons) 95–105 **(check with hosts for pricing details)**

WEST VANCOUVER *(north of Vancouver)*

The Tree House Bed & Breakfast

(Penny Nelson-Abbott and Neville Abbott)

125 Sunset Dr, Lions Bay, BC, V0N 2E0
www.thetreehousebnb.com
E-mail stay@thetreehousebnb.com

604-921-5991
Fax 604-922-5290

High in the forest with spectacular ocean views, The Tree House is perfect for both summer and winter getaways. Enjoy the many outdoor activities (including golf and hiking) close by in summer. Come ski/ride the 2010 Olympic slopes of Cypress Mountain and Whistler in winter, or book a massage and just come to relax. We're 15 minutes from Horseshoe Bay Ferry Terminal, 25 minutes from Downtown Vancouver and 1 hour from Whistler. Take Lions Bay exit off the Sea to Sky Hwy (Hwy 99) to Sunset Dr. See Web site for details.

ROOMS Upper floor, **Baths** Ensuite, **Beds** Queen, Twin, **In Room** Thermostat, TV, Internet access, VCR/DVD, **OTHERS** Rural, Open all year, Additional meals, Pets in residence, **PAYMENT** Visa, MC, Direct debit, Cash, Trvl's cheques, **BREAKFASTS** Home-baked, **AMENITIES** Central TV, Central phone, Whirlpool, Barbecue, Fridge, Hot bev. bar, Lounge, Patio, Central Internet access, Central VCR/DVD, **THINGS TO DO** Rental bikes, Trail nearby, Rental canoe or boat, Golf, Fishing, Museums, Art, Theatre, Attractions, Cross-country skiing, Downhill skiing, Swimming, Horseback riding, Beach, Birdwatching, **LANGUAGE** Eng., **PRICE** (2 persons) 135–165 **(check with hosts for pricing details)**

WHISTLER *(north of Vancouver)*

Auberge du Pre
Bed & Breakfast

(Michel Thibodeau/Joan Swain)

7705 Pemberton Meadows, Pemberton, BC, V0N 2L0
www.pemberton-bc-bb-whistler.com
E-mail aubergedupre@mycoast.net

604-894-1471
Fax 604-894-1199
TFr 1-866-894-1471

Stylish Craftsman home in the sunny Pemberton Meadows, just a short distance from Whistler, offering pampering accommodations and warm BC hospitality in a rural setting with modern conveniences. The guest wing includes separate living area with fireplace, TV/DVD, wireless Internet and outdoor hot tub. All guest rooms offer mountain views, air-conditioning, room-controlled heat, quality linens, comfy duvets and thoughtful amenities for your comfort. Outdoor swimming pool and fire pit in summer.

ROOMS Upper floor, Ground floor, **Baths** Ensuite, **Beds** King, Queen, Twin, **Air** In rooms, **Smoking** Outside, **In Room** Thermostat, **OTHERS** Rural, Adult, Open all year, Additional meals, **PAYMENT** Visa, MC, Trvl's cheques, **BREAKFASTS** Full, Home baked, **AMENITIES** Central TV, Central phone, Swimming pool, Whirlpool, Lounge, Patio, **THINGS TO DO** Rental bikes, Trail nearby, Rental canoe or boat, Golf, Fishing, Attractions, Cross-country skiing, Swimming, Horseback riding, **LANGUAGE** Eng., Fr., **PRICE** (2 persons) 95–125 **(check with hosts for pricing details)**

WHISTLER

Chalet Bambi
Bed and Breakfast

(Cora and Abraham Inniger)

6182 Eagle Dr, Whistler, BC, V0N 1B6
www.chaletbambi.com
E-mail abraham@whooshnet.com

604-938-3292
Fax 604-932-4493

Chalet Bambi Bed and Breakfast is a traditional Swiss chalet located within a short 10-minute walk to Whistler village and ski lifts. Enjoy a 180 degree view of the surrounding mountains from the chalet, nestled in an exclusive residential area amidst beautiful log homes. We offer nice, comfortable and clean accommodations, complimentary delicious breakfasts and shuttle sevice for those with no transportation. Discounted lift tickets are provided with accommodation.

ROOMS Family suite, Ground floor, Private entrance, **Baths** Private, Ensuite, **Beds** King, Queen, Twin, **In Room** Thermostat, TV, Fireplace, **OTHERS** Open all year, Pets in residence, **PAYMENT** Visa, MC, Cheques accepted, Cash, Trvl's cheques, **BREAKFASTS** Full, Home-baked, **AMENITIES** Central TV, Central phone, Whirlpool, Barbecue, Laundry, Kitchen, Fridge, Hot bev. bar, Lounge, Patio, **THINGS TO DO** Comp. bikes, Rental bikes, Trail nearby, Rental canoe or boat, Golf, Fishing, Museums, Art, Theatre, Entertainment, Attractions, Shopping, Cross-country skiing, Tennis, Swimming, Horseback riding, Beach, **LANGUAGE** Eng., Ger., Swiss and Tagalog, **PRICE** (2 persons) 90–160 **(check with hosts for pricing details)**

Whistler

Farmhouse Bed and Breakfast
(Carol and Peter Shore)

7611 Pemberton Meadows Rd, Box 121, Pemberton, BC, V0N 2L0
www.bbcanada.com/farmhouse
E-mail farmhouse@uniserve.com

604-894-6205
Fax 604-894-6205
TFr 1-888-394-6205

Our 1928 farmhouse, nestled in beautiful gardens with mature trees, offers character with elegance, serenity with amazing mountain views. Three cozy, spacious rooms offer fine art on all walls. Quality beds and thoughtful accoutrements ensure a lovely private, peaceful night in the countryside. Abundant books, a library-style livingroom, friendly, tolerant hosts and Jade, the cat greet weary guests. Pemberton Valley, near Whistler, offers year-round outdoor pleasures beyond our 170 acres of serenity. Serious coffee.

ROOMS Upper floor, Ground floor, **Baths** Private, Ensuite, Shared with guest, Shared with hosts, **Beds** Queen, Double, Twin, Single or cots, **Smoking** Outside, **In Room** TV, **OTHERS** Rural, Pets in residence, Pets welcome, **PAYMENT** Cheques accepted, Cash, Trvl's cheques, **BREAKFASTS** Full, Continental, Home-baked, **AMENITIES** Central TV, Central phone, Whirlpool, Fridge, Lounge, Patio, Central Internet access, **THINGS TO DO** Rental bikes, Trail nearby, Rental canoe or boat, Golf, Fishing, Museums, Art, Wineries/Breweries, Shopping, Cross-country skiing, Downhill skiing, Tennis, Swimming, Horseback riding, Birdwatching, **LANGUAGE** Eng., **PRICE** (2 persons) 85–115 **(check with hosts for pricing details)**

Whistler

Golden Dreams Bed and Breakfast
(Ann and Terry Spence)

6412 Easy St, Whistler, BC, V0N 1B6
www.goldendreamswhistler.com
E-mail ann@goldendreamswhistler.com

604-932-2667
Fax 604-932-7055
TFr 1-800-668-7055

True West Coast Hospitality since 1987! Be surrounded by nature's beauty, relax in the outdoor hot tub, sleep on a cozy featherbed and awake to a nutritious breakfast. Just 1 mile to ski lifts/restaurants! Unique Aztec, Victorian, Wild West "theme" rooms offering velour robes, sherry decanter. Luxurious heated slate floors in bathrooms/entrance! West Coast fireside livingroom, "Elmira" country kitchen, BBQ sundeck. On bus route and trail system. Discount ski passes! Bike rentals/maps/info onsite.

ROOMS Upper floor, Ground floor, Private entrance, **Baths** Private, Shared with guest, **Beds** Queen, Double, Twin, **Smoking** Outside, **In Room** Thermostat, **OTHERS** Urban, Open all year, Pets in residence, Pets welcome, **PAYMENT** Visa, MC, Cheques accepted, Cash, Trvl's cheques, **BREAKFASTS** Full, Home-baked, **AMENITIES** Central TV, Central phone, Whirlpool, Barbecue, Kitchen, Fridge, Lounge, Patio, **THINGS TO DO** Rental bikes, Trail nearby, Rental canoe or boat, Golf, Fishing, Museums, Art, Entertainment, Attractions, Shopping, Cross-country skiing, Tennis, Swimming, Horseback riding, Beach, **LANGUAGE** Eng., Fr., Ger., **PRICE** (2 persons) 85–155 **(check with hosts for pricing details)**

WHISTLER

Inn at Clifftop Lane

(Alan and Sulee Sailer)

2828 Clifftop Lane, Whistler, BC, V0N 1B2
www.innatclifftop.com
E-mail info@innatclifftop.com

604-938-1229
Fax 604-938-9880
TFr 1-888-281-2929

A warm, charming Whistler B&B Inn rated
4 1/2-stars *Canada Select*. A fine decor of
antiques and original artworks. All guest
suites equipped with satelliteTV/VCR and
each has ensuite complete with Jacuzzi
tub, hair dryer and cozy bathrobes. A
varying gourmet full breakfast is included
and served each morning. Guest lounge
with library, guest dining area with separate table seating; two fireplaces. High-
speed Internet connection. Located in a
lovely neighbourhood close to ski lifts,
trails, lakes, shops and restaurants.

ROOMS Upper floor, Private entrance, **Baths** Ensuite,
Beds King, Queen, Twin, **Air** Central, **In Room** TV,
VCR/DVD, **OTHERS** Rural, Open all year, Pets in resi-
dence, **PAYMENT** Visa, MC, Cash, Trvl's cheques,
BREAKFASTS Full, **AMENITIES** Central phone, Fridge,
Hot bev. bar, Lounge, Patio, Central Internet access,
THINGS TO DO Rental bikes, Trail nearby, Rental canoe
or boat, Golf, Fishing, Art, Shopping, Cross-country ski-
ing, Downhill skiing, Tennis, Swimming, Horseback rid-
ing, Beach, Birdwatching, **LANGUAGE** Eng., Fr., Thai,
PRICE (2 persons) 109–189 **(check with hosts for pricing details)**

WHITE ROCK *(south of Vancouver)*

"A Beach House B&B ...
on the Beach ... Naturally! "

(Marke and June Barens)

15241 Marine Dr, White Rock, BC, V4B 1C7
www.WhiteRockBedBreakfast.ca
E-mail ABeachHouse@Telus.net

604-536-5200 Fax 604-536-1948

Waterfront location and views unmatch-
ed. West Coast living! A beach house, casual with oceanfront decks, roof-top terrace,
spa showers, Guest kitchen, with dishwasher. A private, quiet retreat for personal or
business. Featherbeds, fine linens, fluffy
robes. Five minutes to US border, 30 minutes to downtown Vancouver. Two minutes
beachfront stroll to the pier, museum,
promenade, restaurants, shops, cafes, day
spas, art galleries, artists. Hunt seashells
barefoot in the sand! Voted #1 B&B
Accommodation 2004/2005 *Trip Advisors*.

ROOMS Family suite, Upper floor, Ground floor, **Baths**
Ensuite, Shared with guest, **Beds** King, Queen, Double,
Twin, Pullout sofa, **Smoking** Outside, **In Room**
Thermostat, TV, Fireplace, Internet access, VCR/DVD,
OTHERS Babysitting, Urban, Adult, Open all year, Pets
in residence, **PAYMENT** Visa, MC, Amex, Direct debit,
Cash, **BREAKFASTS** Full, Continental, Self-catered,
AMENITIES Central phone, Barbecue, Laundry,
Kitchen, Fridge, Lounge, Patio, Central Internet access,
THINGS TO DO Trail nearby, Rental canoe or boat,
Golf, Fishing, Museums, Art, Theatre, Entertainment,
Attractions, Wineries/Breweries, Shopping, Cross-
country skiing, Downhill skiing, Tennis, Swimming,
Horseback riding, Beach, Birdwatching, Antiquing,
LANGUAGE Eng., **PRICE** (2 persons) 75–150 **(check
with hosts for pricing details)**

WHITE ROCK

Abbey Lane B&B

(Ken and Roslyn Ehmann)

14778 Thrift Ave, White Rock, BC, V4B 2J5
www.abbeylanebandb.ca
E-mail stay@abbeylanebandb.ca

604-535-1225

Warm and friendly hospitality in a bright, comfortable, spacious home. We have an ocean view in a quiet residential area. Close to ocean and beach with promenade, shopping centres, arena, curling rink, on bus route to downtown. Vancouver and surrounding areas. Close to Vancouver Island ferries, Peace Arch Park and US border.

ROOMS Family suite, Upper floor, Ground floor, Private entrance, **Baths** Private, Ensuite, **Beds** Queen, **Smoking** Outside, **In Room** TV, Fireplace, **OTHERS** Urban, Adult, Open all year, Handicapped access, Pets in residence, **PAYMENT** Cash, Trvl's cheques, **BREAKFASTS** Full, **AMENITIES** Central TV, Central phone, Fridge, Lounge, Patio, **THINGS TO DO** Trail nearby, Rental canoe or boat, Golf, Fishing, Museums, Art, Theatre, Entertainment, Attractions, Wineries/ Breweries, Shopping, Tennis, Swimming, Horseback riding, Beach, **LANGUAGE** Eng., **PRICE** (2 persons) 60–110 **(check with hosts for pricing details)**

WHITE ROCK

Bellevue House Bed and Breakfast

(Silvia and Bruce Kleeberger)

14635 Bellevue Cres, White Rock, BC, V4B 2V1
www.bellevuehouse.ca
E-mail silviak@telus.net

604-536-7324
Fax 604-536-7324
TFr 1-888-880-7324

A premier B&B located 10 minutes from the Peace Arch, the Canada/US border. Well-appointed rooms with private entrance and private baths. Enjoy lavish breakfasts while overlooking White Rock's pier, promenade and Semiahmoo Bay. We are conveniently located two blocks from the beach, shopping and many restaurants. Enjoy the panoramic view or enjoy nearby attractions including golfing, cycling, kayaking, birdwatching, art galleries to name a few. Easy access to BC Ferries (30 minutes) and Vancouver (45 minutes).

ROOMS Lower floor, Private entrance, **Baths** Private, **Beds** Queen, **Smoking** Outside, **In Room** Thermostat, TV, Fireplace, VCR/DVD, **OTHERS** Urban, Adult, Open all year, Pets in residence, **PAYMENT** Visa, MC, Amex, Cash, Trvl's cheques, **BREAKFASTS** Full, Continental, Home-baked, Self-catered, **AMENITIES** Central phone, Whirlpool, Barbecue, Fridge, Hot bev. bar, Patio, Central Internet access, **THINGS TO DO** Trail nearby, Rental canoe or boat, Golf, Fishing, Museums, Art, Theatre, Entertainment, Attractions, Wineries/ Breweries, Shopping, Cross-country skiing, Downhill skiing, Tennis, Swimming, Horseback riding, Beach, Birdwatching, **LANGUAGE** Eng., Ger., **PRICE** (2 persons) 90–135 **(check with hosts for pricing details)**

Kent Manor Guest House B&B

(Richard and Lorna Christie)

835 Kent St, White Rock, BC, V4B 4S7
www.kentmanor.ca
E-mail info@kentmanor.ca

604-535-9835
Fax 604-535-9853

Kent Manor is a beautiful new Victorian-style Guest House located steps from the beach and promenade. Private and peaceful, clean and cozy. Kent Manor offers you a 'home away from home' where you can relax in comfort. We are close to the US border and within walking distance of all the amenities that White Rock has to offer. We are a loving Christian couple who enjoy meeting new people. We offer special rates (one week or more). You may arrive as strangers, but we are sure you will leave as friends.

ROOMS Upper floor, **Baths** Private, **Beds** Queen, **Air** Central, **Smoking** Outside, **OTHERS** Urban, Adult, Open all year, Pets in residence, **PAYMENT** Visa, MC, Cash, Trvl's cheques, **BREAKFASTS** Home-baked, **AMENITIES** Central TV, Central phone, Fridge, Lounge, Patio, **THINGS TO DO** Trail nearby, Rental canoe or boat, Golf, Fishing, Museums, Art, Theatre, Entertainment, Attractions, Wineries/Breweries, Shopping, Cross-country skiing, Downhill skiing, Tennis, Swimming, Horseback riding, Beach, Birdwatching, Antiquing, **LANGUAGE** Eng., **PRICE** (2 persons) 75–85 **(check with hosts for pricing details)**

Sand & Sea B&B Guest Suites

(Ken and Helen Hesp)

15671 Columbia Ave, White Rock, BC, V4B 1L2
www.canadianbandbguide.ca/bb.asp?ID=3784
E-mail sandandsea@shaw.ca

604-535-0034

Two exceptional self-contained suites located two blocks from the beautiful Semiahmoo Beach, promenade and restaurants. Suite #1: bedroom, living-room, fireplace, hide-a-bed, kitchen, TV, phone and lovely garden patio. Suite #2: bedroom, livingroom, hide-a-bed, kitch-enette, TV, phone, optional second bed-room. Children and pets welcome in this suite. Both suites have a private entrance and are furnished with a decorative touch, very clean, quiet and reasonably priced. Fantastic breakfast! Cell phone 604-306-1121.

ROOMS Family suite, Ground floor, Private entrance, **Baths** Private, **Beds** Queen, Twin, Pullout sofa, **Smoking** Outside, **In Room** Phone, TV, Fireplace, VCR/DVD, **OTHERS** Urban, Open all year, Handicapped access, Pets in residence, Pets welcome, **PAYMENT** Cheques accepted, Cash, Trvl's cheques, **BREAKFASTS** Full, Continental, Self-catered, **AMENITIES** Barbecue, Kitchen, Fridge, Patio, Central Internet access, **THINGS TO DO** Rental bikes, Trail nearby, Rental canoe or boat, Golf, Fishing, Museums, Art, Theatre, Entertainment, Attractions, Wineries/Breweries, Shopping, Cross-country skiing, Downhill skiing, Tennis, Swimming, Horseback riding, Beach, Birdwatching, Antiquing, **LANGUAGE** Eng., **PRICE** (2 persons) 65–110 **(check with hosts for pricing details)**

WHITE ROCK

The Daly Bed and Bread Guest House

(Susan and John Howard)

13152 Marine Dr, Surrey, BC, V4A 1E7
www.dalybedandbread.com
E-mail reservations@dalybedandbread.com

604-531-2531
Fax 604-531-2531
TFr 1-877-523-1399

Our suites offer fantastic ocean and mountain views with balconies and private entrances. Suites come equipped with frig/microwave, for coffee and tea making, phone, security alarm, high-speed Internet and satellite TV and are suitable for long-term stay. Breakfasts are served in our oceanview dining room. Easy access to Freeways and US border, Vancouver and airport. Minutes from White Rock Beach, pier and promenade, or quiet charm of Crescent Beach and Blackie Spit's World Heritage Wildlife Site.

ROOMS Family suite, Ground floor, Lower floor, Private entrance, **Baths** Private, Ensuite, **Beds** Queen, Single or cots, Pullout sofa, **Air** Ceiling fans, **Smoking** Outside, **In Room** Thermostat, Phone, TV, Fireplace, Internet access, VCR/DVD, **OTHERS** Urban, Open all year, Additional meals, Pets welcome, **PAYMENT** Visa, MC, Diners, Amex, Cheques accepted, Cash, Trvl's cheques, **BREAKFASTS** Full, Continental, Home-baked, Self-catered, **AMENITIES** Barbecue, Laundry, Kitchen, Fridge, Hot bev. bar, Lounge, Patio, **THINGS TO DO** Comp. bikes, Trail nearby, Rental canoe or boat, Golf, Fishing, Museums, Art, Theatre, Entertainment, Attractions, Wineries/Breweries, Shopping, Tennis, Swimming, Horseback riding, Beach, Birdwatching, Antiquing, **LANGUAGE** Eng., Fr., Ger., **PRICE** (2 persons) 90–150 **(check with hosts for pricing details)**

WILLIAMS LAKE *(central BC)*

Rowat's Waterside Bed & Breakfast

(Helmut and Marilyn Strohschein)

1397 Borland Rd, Williams Lake, BC, V2G 5K5
www.wlakebb.com
E-mail rowatswatersidebb@shaw.ca

250-392-7395
Fax 250-392-7395
TFr 1-866-392-7395

Walk to downtown Williams Lake, our famous Stampede Grounds, mini-golf, stroll to Scout Island, browse the Nature House, or drive out to Farwell Canyon for some breathtaking sights and hike the sand dunes. Try your skill at mountain climbing or biking, plenty of trails from which to choose! Park and ride, whether it be horseback riding or jet boating down the Fraser River. Enjoy the privacy of our home. Sit back, relax and enjoy the view from our deck. Treat yourself to the best in Cariboo hospitality.

ROOMS Family suite, Upper floor, Private entrance, **Baths** Private, **Beds** King, Queen, Double, Twin, Single or cots, **Air** In rooms, **Smoking** Outside, **OTHERS** Urban, Open all year, Additional meals, **PAYMENT** Visa, MC, Diners, Direct debit, Cheques accepted, **BREAKFASTS** Full, **AMENITIES** Central TV, Central phone, Laundry, Fridge, Lounge, Patio, Central Internet access, Central VCR/DVD, **THINGS TO DO** Rental bikes, Trail nearby, Golf, Fishing, Museums, Art, Theatre, Entertainment, Attractions, Shopping, Cross-country skiing, Tennis, Swimming, Horseback riding, Beach, Birdwatching, Antiquing, **LANGUAGE** Eng., Ger., **PRICE** (2 persons) 72–80 **(check with hosts for pricing details)**

Northwest Territories and Yukon

CANADIAN BED AND BREAKFAST GUIDE

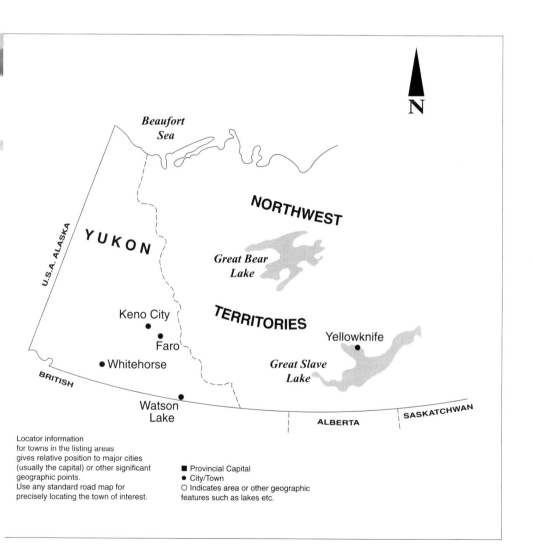

Locator information
for towns in the listing areas
gives relative position to major cities
(usually the capital) or other significant
geographic points.
Use any standard road map for
precisely locating the town of interest.

■ Provincial Capital
● City/Town
○ Indicates area or other geographic
features such as lakes etc.

Yellowknife
(south NWT on Great Slave Lake)

Gill-Power Bed & Breakfast

(James Gill and Rosalie Power)

4206 – 49A Ave Box 2491, Yellowknife,
NWT, X1A 2P8
www.canadianbandbguide.ca/bb.asp?ID=2520
E-mail rpower@internorth.com

867-873-5735
Fax 867-669-0761

We are 10 minute's walking distance from
downtown and "old town" which is the
tourist area of Yellowknife. We provide
pickup and dropoff service when we are
available. We have two guests rooms, one
double bedroom and one single bedroom,
double room has TV/VCR with private
entrance. Telephone in both rooms with
shared bathroom. We serve a continental
breakfast with some use of the kitchen
facilities and laundry.

ROOMS Ground floor, Private entrance, **Baths** Shared
with guest, **Beds** Double, Twin, **In Room** Phone, TV,
Internet access, VCR/DVD, **OTHERS** Open all year,
Handicapped access, Pets in residence, **PAYMENT**
Cash, Trvl's cheques, **BREAKFASTS** Continental,
AMENITIES Barbecue, Laundry, Kitchen, Patio, **THINGS
TO DO** Comp. bikes, Trail nearby, Golf, Fishing,
Museums, Art, Theatre, Entertainment, Attractions,
Shopping, Cross-country skiing, Tennis, Swimming,
Horseback riding, Beach, Birdwatching, Antiquing,
Aurora viewing, dog sled rides **LANGUAGE** Eng.,
PRICE (2 persons) 60–70 **(check with hosts for pricing
details)**

Faro *(southeastern Yukon)*

Blue B&B (Nature Friends)

(Michael Cerutti)

Campbell, 440, Faro, YT, Y0B 1K0
www.nfyukon.com/e_b&b.htm
E-mail naturefriends-bb@yknet.ca

867-994-2106
Fax 867-994-2106

Our B&B is located in the friendly full-
service community of Faro in Central
Yukon, accessible off the Campbell Hwy.
We welcome you in our cosy, clean and
elegant bed & breakfast which features a
fantastic view over the Tintina Valley and
the Pelly River. Our guests can enjoy their
own living room, the kitchen, the sunny
deck and the garden. We serve a generous breakfast. It is a perfect place to relax
at a few minutes' walk from all commodi-
ties. We offer summer activities and we
rent canoes.

ROOMS Upper floor, Lower floor, **Baths** Ensuite,
Shared with guest, **Beds** Queen, Twin, **PAYMENT** Visa,
MC, Cash, **BREAKFASTS** Full, **AMENITIES** Laundry,
Kitchen, Fridge, Hot bev. bar, **THINGS TO DO** Trail near-
by, Rental canoe or boat, Golf, Fishing, Swimming,
Birdwatching, **LANGUAGE** Eng., Fr., Ger., **PRICE** (2 per-
sons) 80–100 **(check with hosts for pricing details)**

The Bear's Den B&B & ATV Tours

(Ray and Tina Henderson and Family)

#517 Ladue Dr, Faro, YT, Y0B 1K0
www.bctravel.com/yukon/bearsden/
E-mail the_bears_den_faro_yukon@hotmail.com

867-994-2103
Fax 867-994-2104

Two large bedrooms with queen-size beds, common kitchen and dining room, shared bathroom with other guest(s), parquet hardwood floors, pet-and smoke-free, satellite TV, all for only $80 plus GST. Also there are guided ATV tours available. Custom packages available to suit every adventurer and skill level. The possibilities are endless! So, give us a call! We believe "A good night's rest makes for a great day's adventure!"

ROOMS Upper floor, **Baths** Shared with guest, **Beds** Queen, Single or cots, **Smoking** Outside, **OTHERS** Open all year, Pets in residence, **PAYMENT** Visa, Cash, Trvl's cheques, **BREAKFASTS** Continental, **AMENITIES** Central TV, Central phone, Kitchen, **THINGS TO DO** Trail nearby, Rental canoe or boat, Golf, Fishing, Art, **LANGUAGE** Eng., **PRICE** (2 persons) 85 **(check with hosts for pricing details)**

Keno Cabins B&B

(Insa Schultenkotter)

Site 1, Box 7 (1st house on left), Keno City, YT, Y0B 1J0
www.kenocity.info/cabins.htm
E-mail insa@polarcom.com

867-995-2892
Fax 867-995-2892

Relax in a cozy, self-contained cabin and experience the simple life in a small frontier community of 20. Explore the great back country. Ideal for outdoor activities: hiking, fishing, rock-hunting, gold panning, photography, skiing, etc. Also an ideal refuge for people with artistic interests, i.e., quiet and unhurried. A vacation for people who would like to experience the wilderness while still enjoying the comforts of civilization. Our guest cabins are fully equipped, breakfast is served upon request.

ROOMS Family suite, Ground floor, Private entrance, **Baths** Private, Shared with guest, **Beds** Twin, Single or cots, Pullout sofa, **Smoking** In rooms, **In Room** TV, Fireplace, **OTHERS** Rural, Open all year, Pets welcome, **PAYMENT** Visa, MC, Cheques accepted, Cash, Trvl's cheques, **BREAKFASTS** Full, Continental, Self-catered, **AMENITIES** Central TV, Sauna, Barbecue, Kitchen, Fridge, Patio, **THINGS TO DO** Trail nearby, Fishing, Museums, Art, Attractions, Cross-country skiing, **LANGUAGE** Eng., Ger., **PRICE** (2 persons) 74–115 **(check with hosts for pricing details)**

WATSON LAKE *(southeastern Yukon)*

Cozy Nest Hideaway B&B

(Cindy and Gord Sundby)

1175 Robert Campbell Hwy, Box 335, Watson Lake,
YT, Y0A 1C0
www.cozynestbandb.com
E-mail cozynest@northwestel.net

867-536-2204

Cozy Nest is situated on the shores of
Watson Lake 7 km/5 m from town, north
on the Robert Campbell Hwy. We offer
warm hospitality and beautiful views.
Rest and relax looking out at our pristine
lake. Go fishing, swimming or canoeing.
Visit the Northern Lights Centre, world
famous Signpost Forest and Wye Lake
Park. In the winter, go skiing or sledding
from our door. See the northern lights
with your own eyes. Cozy Nest is a hideaway. Quiet and cozy. So come to rest and
relax at Cindy's B&B.

ROOMS Ground floor, Private entrance, **Baths** Shared
with guest, **Beds** Queen, Double, **Smoking** Outside,
OTHERS Rural, Open all year, **PAYMENT** Visa, MC,
Amex, Cash, Trvl's cheques, **BREAKFASTS** Continental,
AMENITIES Central TV, Central phone, Sauna, Fridge,
Hot bev. bar, Lounge, Patio, **THINGS TO DO** Comp.
bikes, Comp. canoe or boat, Golf, Fishing, Theatre,
Shopping, Cross-country skiing, Tennis, Swimming,
Beach, **LANGUAGE** Eng., **PRICE** (2 persons) 80 **(check
with hosts for pricing details)**

WHITEHORSE *(south-central Yukon)*

Midnight Sun Bed & Breakfast

(Farshid Amirtabar)

6188 – 6th Ave, Whitehorse, YT, Y1A 1N8
www.midnightsunbb.com
E-mail midnightsunbb@northwestel.net

867-667-2255
Fax 867-668-4376
TFr 1-866-284-4448

Luxury, spacious, bright, comfortable and
affordable. Newest and largest accommodation in downtown Whitehorse, Yukon.
Four theme rooms with private bathroom, hairdryer, cable TV, phone. Free e-
mail, high-speed Internet access service.
Guest full kitchen/lounge, microwave 32-
inch TV/VCR, video and magazines.
Laundry and barbecue facilities. Walking
distance to tourism site/shopping cen-
tre/movie theatre. Continental or full
breakfast/evening snacks. Approved by
CAA/AAA as 3 Diamond.

ROOMS Upper floor, **Baths** Private, Ensuite, **Beds** King,
Queen, Twin, Pullout sofa, **Air** Central, In rooms,
Smoking Outside, **In Room** Thermostat, Phone, TV,
OTHERS Open all year, **PAYMENT** Visa, MC, Amex,
Direct debit, Cash, Trvl's cheques, **BREAKFASTS** Full,
Continental, **AMENITIES** Central TV, Central phone,
Barbecue, Laundry, Kitchen, Fridge, **THINGS TO DO**
Comp. bikes, Rental bikes, Trail nearby, Rental canoe or
boat, Comp. canoe or boat, Golf, Fishing, Museums,
Art, Theatre, Entertainment, Attractions,
Wineries/Breweries, Shopping, Cross-country skiing,
Tennis, Swimming, Horseback riding, Beach, **LAN-
GUAGE** Eng., **PRICE** (2 persons) 85–130 **(check with
hosts for pricing details)**

WHITEHORSE

Muktuk Guest Ranch

(Frank and Anne Turner)

Km 1442.5 Alaska Hwy, Whitehorse, YT, Y1A 7A2
www.muktuk.com
E-mail muktuk@northwestel.net

867-668-3647
Fax 867-633-4200
TFr 1-866-968-3647

Secluded guest ranch on the shores of
the Takhini River in the Ibex Valley, just 20
minutes from downtown Whitehorse.
Guest cabins located near the river in a
beautiful, peaceful setting, surrounded by
magnificent mountain landscapes.
Unique setting, with working sled-dog
ranch. Kennel tours daily, and great trails
nearby. Close to Takhini Hotsprings and
the Wildlife Preserve. RVs, families and
pets welcome.

ROOMS Family suite, Lower floor, **Beds** King, Queen,
Double, Twin, Single or cots, Pullout sofa, **Smoking**
Outside, **OTHERS** Rural, Open all year, Handicapped
access, Additional meals, Pets in residence, Pets wel-
come, **PAYMENT** Visa, MC, Direct debit, Cash, Trvl's
cheques, **BREAKFASTS** Full, Home-baked, **AMENITIES**
Sauna, Fridge, Central Internet access, **THINGS TO DO**
Trail nearby, Rental canoe or boat, Comp. canoe or
boat, Golf, Fishing, Museums, Art, Theatre, Entertain-
ment, Attractions, Wineries/Breweries, Shopping,
Cross-country skiing, Downhill skiing, Tennis,
Swimming, Horseback riding, Beach, Birdwatching,
LANGUAGE Eng., Ger., **PRICE** (2 persons) 81–101
(check with hosts for pricing details)

WHITEHORSE

Red Door Bed & Breakfast

(Jacques and Mary Anne Boily)

61 Teslin Rd, Whitehorse, YT, Y1A 3M5
www.bbcanada.com/reddooryukon
E-mail boily@northwestel.net

867-633-4615
Fax 867-456-4677

Red Door B&B adjoins our home and
offers a touch of yesteryear. Our red doors
are welcoming and bright. The large
guest common room offers a dining and
lounging area and laundry. The bedrooms
have brass beds and some antique
wardrobes and dressers. All rooms are
tastefully decorated. Our home is situated
in Riverdale, a 20 to 30 minute stroll from
downtown; less than 5 minutes by vehicle. The transit stops just two doors away
and there are hiking trails nearby. We are
45 plus year residents of Yukon!

ROOMS Ground floor, Private entrance, **Baths** Ensuite,
Shared with guest, **Beds** Queen, Twin, Single or cots,
Air Central, **Smoking** Outside, **OTHERS** Urban, Open
all year, **PAYMENT** Visa, MC, Amex, Cash, Trvl's
cheques, **BREAKFASTS** Full, **AMENITIES** Central TV,
Central phone, Laundry, Fridge, Hot bev. bar, Lounge,
Patio, **THINGS TO DO** Rental bikes, Trail nearby, Rental
canoe or boat, Golf, Fishing, Museums, Art, Theatre,
Entertainment, Attractions, Wineries/Breweries,
Shopping, Cross-country skiing, Swimming, Horseback
riding, **LANGUAGE** Eng., Fr., **PRICE** (2 persons) 70–110
(check with hosts for pricing details)

ALBERTA

CANADIAN BED AND BREAKFAST GUIDE

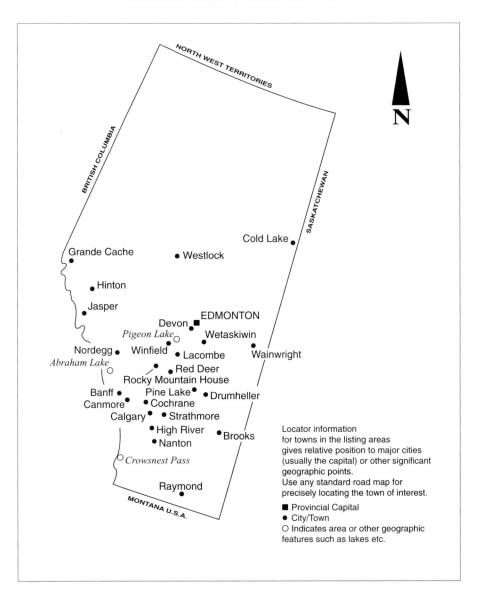

Locator information
for towns in the listing areas
gives relative position to major cities
(usually the capital) or other significant
geographic points.
Use any standard road map for
precisely locating the town of interest.

■ Provincial Capital
● City/Town
○ Indicates area or other geographic
features such as lakes etc.

ABRAHAM LAKE *(northwest of Calgary)*

Aurum Lodge
(Madeleine and Alan Ernst)

Abraham Lake, Nordegg, AB, T0M 2H0
www.aurumlodge.com
E-mail info@aurumlodge.com

403-721-2117
Fax 403-721-2118

Alberta's unique and award-winning all-season eco-tourism country inn in Bighorn Country, adjacent to Banff National Park. Explore the central Canadian Rockies from the comfort and seclusion of our lodge or self-contained cottage units. This adult-oriented retreat is located off the beaten path but close to the parks; an ideal destination for individuals, couples or small special-interest groups (nature, low-impact activities, visual arts, etc.). Many low-impact activities available year round.

ROOMS Upper floor, Ground floor, **Baths** Ensuite, **Beds** King, Single or cots, **In Room** Thermostat, **OTHERS** Adult, Open all year, Handicapped access, Additional meals, Pets in residence, **PAYMENT** Visa, MC, Diners, Cash, Trvl's cheques, **BREAKFASTS** Full, **AMENITIES** Central TV, Central phone, Lounge, Patio, **THINGS TO DO** Comp. bikes, Trail nearby, Fishing, Horseback ridingriding, **LANGUAGE** Eng., Fr., Ger., **PRICE** (2 persons) 110–200 **(check with hosts for pricing details)**

BANFF *(west of Calgary)*

A Homestead Bed & Breakfast
(Colline and Ron Seabrook)

168 Carey, Canmore, AB, T1W 2R4
www.bbexpo.com/homestead
E-mail bed@telusplanet.net

403-678-1886
Fax 403-678-3684

Spectacular mountain views await you! Built in 1996 with B&B area. Licensed and inspected. Very clean, quiet and spacious rooms each with TV, phone, sofa, one room with fireplace. Guest entrance. Hearty Canadian "brekkie" served with a mountain view from 8:00–9:30a.m., near the fireplace or on the deck overlooking park. In-room complimentary coffee and tea. Games room with views, fireplace, deck. Forest setting on quiet side of the valley. Discount for multiple night stays. Homey!

ROOMS Ground floor, Private entrance, **Baths** Private, Ensuite, **Beds** Queen, Double, Twin, Pullout sofa, **Air** Ceiling fans, **Smoking** Outside, **In Room** Phone, TV, Fireplace, **OTHERS** Urban, Open all year, **PAYMENT** Cash, Trvl's cheques, **BREAKFASTS** Full, Continental, Home-baked, **AMENITIES** Fridge, Lounge, Patio, **THINGS TO DO** Rental bikes, Trail nearby, Rental canoe or boat, Golf, Fishing, Museums, Art, Theatre, Entertainment, Attractions, Shopping, Cross-country Skiing, Tennis, Swimming, Horseback ridingriding, Birdwatching, Antiquing, **LANGUAGE** Eng., **PRICE** (2 persons) 75–115 **(check with hosts for pricing details)**

Pension Tannenhof

(Herbert and Fannye Riedinger)

121 Cave Ave, Banff, AB, T1L 1B7
www.pensiontannenhof.com
E-mail riedinger@hotmail.com

403-762-4636
Fax 403-762-5660
TFr 1-877-999-5011

Tannenhof ... meaning "Lodge in the Pine Trees" is a beautiful English-style mansion built in 1942 with an elegant yet homey atmosphere. The surroundings let you enjoy the beauty of nature at your own pace, i.e., mountain biking, fishing, rafting, horseback riding, golfing, tennis, etc. The history of Banff will unfold at the Cave and Basin Hot Springs only a short walk from the Pension Tannenhof. Prepare your own supper on the world's oldest barbecue – it is made from petrified dinosaur bone.

ROOMS Family suite, Upper floor, Ground floor, **Baths** Private, Ensuite, **Beds** King, Queen, Twin, Pullout sofa, **Smoking** Outside, **In Room** TV, Fireplace, **OTHERS** Urban, Open all year, **PAYMENT** Visa, MC, Amex, Cheques accepted, Cash, **BREAKFASTS** Full, **AMENITIES** Sauna, Barbecue, Laundry, Fridge, Lounge, Patio, Central Internet access, **THINGS TO DO** Trail nearby, Rental canoe or boat, Golf, Fishing, Museums, Theatre, Attractions, Shopping, Cross-country skiing, Tennis, Swimming, Horseback riding, **LANGUAGE** Eng., Fr., Sp., **PRICE** (2 persons) 75–185 **(check with hosts for pricing details)**

Creekside Country Inn

(Kirsty Hughes and Jen Racicot)

709 Benchlands Trail, Canmore, AB, T1W 3G9
www.creeksidecountryinn.com
E-mail info@creeksidecountryinn.com

403-609-5522
Fax 403-609-5599
TFr 1-866-609-5522

Creekside Country Inn is a beautiful 12-room B&B-style Inn nestled in the sunny, quiet neighborhood of Eagle Terrace. Away from train and highway this picturesque inn features timberframe and slate styling in a majestic mountain setting. Perfect for individual travellers, family gatherings, weddings, conferences or any kind of private function, Creekside can accommodate from 2 to 46 people overnight and up to 85 for a catered meal in our Sunview Room. See our Web site for more!

ROOMS Family suite, Upper floor, Ground floor, Lower floor, **Baths** Private, **Beds** King, Queen, Pullout sofa, **Air** In rooms, Ceiling fans, **OTHERS** Babysitting, Urban, Open all year, Pets welcome, **PAYMENT** Visa, MC, Amex, Cash, Trvl's chequescheques, **BREAKFASTS** Continental, Home-baked, **AMENITIES** Central TV, Central phone, Sauna, Barbecue, Kitchen, Fridge, Hot bev. bar, Lounge, Patio, Central Internet access, Central VCR/DVD, **THINGS TO DO** Rental bikes, Golf, Fishing, Museums, Art, Entertainment, Attractions, Wineries/Breweries, Shopping, Cross-country skiing, Downhill skiingskiing, Swimming, Horseback ridingriding, Birdwatching, Antiquing, **LANGUAGE** Eng., Fr., **PRICE** (2 persons) 89–199 **(check with hosts for pricing details)**

BROOKS

A Lake Shore B&B

(Richard and Kathy Gette)

Box 1664, #1 White Pelican Way, Lake Newell Resort, Brooks, AB, T1R 1C7
www.alakeshorebb.com E-mail info@alakeshorebb.com

403-363-8080
Fax 403-501-5868
TFr 1-866-501-5275

"Luxury at the Lake" for business or pleasure. Our 4-star *Canada Select* B&B was built with our guest's comfort in mind. Our home is nestled beside a park and overlooks beautiful Lake Newell. We have three distinctly decorated suites, two of which have ultra-masseur tubs and private lakefront entrances. We are located only minutes from the World Heritage Site Dinosaur Provincial Park and five golf courses. Ask about spa packages including Stone Therapy Massage, Salt Glows, Body Talk and more.

ROOMS Ground floor, Private entrance, **Baths** Private, Ensuite, **Beds** Queen, Pullout sofa, **Air** Central, **Smoking** Outside, **In Room** Thermostat, **OTHERS** Rural, Open all year, **PAYMENT** Visa, MC, Direct debit-debit, Cheques accepted, Cash, **BREAKFASTS** Full, **AMENITIES** Central TV, Central phone, Whirlpool, Barbecue, Laundry, Fridge, Hot bev. bar, Lounge, Patio, Central Internet access, Central VCR/DVD, **THINGS TO DO** Trail nearby, Comp. canoe or boat, Golf, Fishing, Museums, Theatre, Attractions, Tennis, Swimming, Beach, Birdwatching, Antiquing, **LANGUAGE** Eng., **PRICE** (2 persons) 89–129 **(check with hosts for pricing details)**

CALGARY *(southern Alberta)*

18 Ave Uptown Mount Royal Bed and Breakfast

(Michael Stuart)

809 – 18th Ave SW, Calgary, AB, T2T 0G9
www.mountroyalbb.com
E-mail mdstuart@shaw.ca

403-245-9371
TFr 1-800-556-1436

Charming 1912 built Edwardian house in fashionable Mount Royal area, in Calgary's trendiest downtown neighbourhood: Uptown 17th Ave. This area features Thompkins Park, a multitude of superb restaurants, coffee houses, boutiques, gifts, antique & clothing shops, nightclubs, numerous art galleries, etc. Centrally located – business travellers can easily walk downtown in 10 minutes. Garden-side room has lovely private deck. Fireside room has its own cozy fireplace. Very clean, quiet accomodation with antique decor and offering full, gourmet breakfasts. Special rates for business travellers on longer stays.

ROOMS Ground floor, **Baths** Private, Ensuite, Shared with guest, **Beds** Queen, Twin, **Air** Central, **Smoking** Outside, **In Room** Thermostat, Phone, Fireplace, **OTHERS** Adult, Open all year, **PAYMENT** Visa, MC, Amex, Cheques accepted, Cash, Trvl's cheques, **BREAKFASTS** Full, Home-baked, **AMENITIES** Central TV, Central phone, Barbecue, Hot bev. bar, Patio, **THINGS TO DO** Comp. bikes, Museums, Art, Theatre, Entertainment, Attractions, Shopping, **LANGUAGE** Eng., Fr., **PRICE** (2 persons) 58–123 **(check with hosts for pricing details)**

CALGARY

1910 Elbow River Manor Bed & Breakfast

(Roger Wiewel)

2511 – 5th St SW, Calgary, AB, T2S 2C2
www.elbowrivermanor.com
E-mail reservations@elbowrivermanor.com

403-802-0799 Fax 403-547-9151
TFr 1-866-802-0798

Built in 1910, Elbow River Manor is a fully restored 3,500-sq. ft. heritage B&B situated across from the scenic Elbow River and park pathway system. Elbow River Manor is a *Canada Select* 4-star bed and breakfast which offers the perfect getaway for business travellers, tourists and urban romantics. This luxurious, centrally located B&B is a short walk from downtown and the famous Calgary Stampede Grounds. Our oversized suites are all unique and offer total comfort and privacy.

ROOMS Family suite, Upper floor, **Baths** Private, Ensuite, **Beds** Queen, Double, Single or cots, Pullout sofa, **Air** Central, **Smoking** Outside, **In Room** Thermostat, Phone, TV, Fireplace, Internet accessaccess, VCR/DVD, **OTHERS** Urban, Open all year, Additional meals, Pets in residence, **PAYMENT** Visa, MC, Amex, Direct debit, Cheques accepted, Cash, Trvl's cheques, **BREAKFASTS** Full, Home-baked, **AMENITIES** Central TV, Central phone, Whirlpool, Barbecue, Laundry, Fridge, Hot bev. bar, Lounge, Patio, Central Internet access, Central VCR/DVD, **THINGS TO DO** Rental bikes, Trail nearby, Golf, Fishing, Museums, Art, Theatre, Entertainment, Attractions, Wineries/ Breweries, Shopping, Cross-country skiing, Tennis, Swimming, Horseback riding, Birdwatching, **LANGUAGE** Eng., **PRICE** (2 persons) 100–165 **(check with hosts for pricing details)**

CALGARY

1919@Along River Ridge Bed & Breakfast

(Dianne Haskell)

1919 – 52nd St NW, Calgary, AB, T3B 1C3
www.alongriverridgebb.com
E-mail haskell@alongriverridgebb.com

403-247-1330
Fax 403-247-1328
TFr 1-888-434-9555

An all seasons retreat on the Bow River; 9 minutes to downtown. Two charming bedrooms with ensuites, TV, VCR, telephone. A lovely guest lounge with fireplace, billiards, microwave, fridge, beverage bar and solarium with Jacuzzi. CDs, videos, books, games, magazines, flowers, robes, candles. Excellent attention to details. A marvellous breakfast! A backyard haven and a garden of delights. Fifty-foot river deck with fire pit. Walking and bike trails nearby. A touch of country in the city! Private parking and entrance. Fax, e-mail and Internet.

ROOMS Private entrance, **Baths** Ensuite, **Beds** Queen, **Smoking** Outside, **In Room** Phone, TV, **OTHERS** Urban, Adult, Open all year, Additional meals, **PAYMENT** Visa, MC, Amex, Cash, Trvl's cheques, **BREAKFASTS** Full, Home-baked, **AMENITIES** Central TV, Central phone, Whirlpool, Barbecue, Laundry, Fridge, Hot bev. bar, Lounge, Patio, Central Internet access, **THINGS TO DO** Rental bikes, Trail nearby, Rental canoe or boat, Golf, Fishing, Museums, Theatre, Entertainment, Attractions, Shopping, Cross-country skiing, Downhill skiing, Tennis, Swimming, Horseback riding, Birdwatching, **LANGUAGE** Eng., **PRICE** (2 persons) 75–99 **(check with hosts for pricing details)**

CALGARY

60 Harvest Lake Bed & Breakfast

(Kathi and David Hamilton)

60 Harvest Lake Cres NE, Calgary, AB, T3K 3Y7
www.members.shaw.ca/harvestlakebandb
E-mail harvestlakebandb@shaw.ca

403-226-3025
Fax 403-226-4993
TFr 1-877-226-3025

Just a 10-minute drive from the airport
and 15 minutes to downtown. We are
conveniently located to satisfy vacation
and/or business needs. Quickly unwind in
the peace and tranquility of this lakeside
setting. Experience our warm, friendly and
relaxing atmosphere. Relax in the garden,
enjoy a leisurely walk around the lake or
read in the screened-in sunroom or in the
lounge by a cozy fire. Close to restaurants,
movie theatres, shopping, golf courses,
leisure centre and public transportation.

ROOMS Ground floor, Private entrance, **Baths** Private,
Beds Queen, Twin, Single or cots, **Air** Central,
Smoking Outside, In Room, **OTHERS** Urban, Open all
year, Pets in residence, **PAYMENT** Visa, MC, Cash, Trvl's
cheques, **BREAKFASTS** Full, Continental, Home-baked,
Self-catered, **AMENITIES** Central TV, Central phone,
Laundry, Fridge, Hot bev. bar, Lounge, Patio, Central
Internet access, **THINGS TO DO**
Rental bikes, Trail nearby, Rental canoe or boat, Golf,
Fishing, Museums, Art, Theatre, Entertainment,
Attractions, Wineries/Breweries, Shopping, Cross-
country skiing, Swimming, **LANGUAGE** Eng., Fr.,
PRICE (2 persons) 85–95 **(check with hosts for
pricing details)**

CALGARY

A B&B at Calgary Lions Park

(Dori Wood)

1331 – 15th St NW, Calgary, AB, T2N 2B7
www.lionsparkbb.com
E-mail info@lionsparkbb.com

403-282-2728
Fax 403-289-3485
TFr 1-800-475-7262

Central Calgary – 1911 historic home of
Calgary's first Chief Librarian. Walking dis-
tance to downtown and the University of
Calgary. Five-minute walk to Southern
Alberta Institute of Technology, Jubilee
Auditorium, Alberta College of Art and
Design. Kensington Area. Twenty-minute
ride from the airport. Two blocks south of
Trans-Canada Hwy. Nutritious breakfasts.
Ideal home for business or vacation trav-
ellers to relax and have conversations
with guests from around the world. Spa
therapy/salt water pool.

ROOMS Family suitesuite, Upper floor, Private
entrance, **Baths** Private, Ensuite, **Beds** King, Queen,
Twin, **Air** Central, In rooms, **In Room** Phone, TV,
Internet , **OTHERS** Urban, Open all year, **PAYMENT**
Visa, MC, Amex, Direct debit, Cash, Trvl's cheques,
BREAKFASTS Full, Home-baked, **AMENITIES** Central
TV, Central phone, Swimming pool, Laundry, Fridge,
Hot bev. bar, Lounge, Patio, Central Internet access,
Central VCR/DVD, **THINGS TO DO** Comp. bikes, Rental
bikes, Trail nearby, Golf, Fishing, Museums, Art, Theatre,
Entertainment, Attractions, Wineries/Breweries,
Shopping, Cross-country skiing, Tennis, Swimming,
Horseback riding, Antiquing, **LANGUAGE** Eng., Fr.,
PRICE (2 persons) 85–150 **(check with hosts for
pricing details)**

CALGARY

A Good Knight B&B
(Kathryn and Ken Knight)

1728 – 7th Ave NW, Calgary, AB, T2N 0Z4
www.agoodknight.com
E-mail stay@agoodknight.com

403-270-7628
TFr 1-800-261-4954

Victorian-styled home in quiet, central location. Gorgeous upstairs rooms decorated in local themes, each with queen bed, private bath, cable TV and coffee service. Pamper yourself in our luxury suite with cozy pine sleigh bed, balcony, Jacuzzi and shower-for-two – perfect for honeymooners. Apartment with full kitchen for long-term stays. You'll love our extensive teapot and teddy bear collection. Wonderful breakfasts! Close to everything – walk to restaurants and shops. Hosts are lifelong Calgarians.

ROOMS Upper floor, Ground floor, **Baths** Private, Ensuite, **Beds** Queen, Pullout sofa, **In Room** Phone, TV, **OTHERS** Urban, Adult, Open all year, **PAYMENT** Visa, MC, Amex, Cash, Trvl's cheques, **BREAKFASTS** Full, Home-baked, **AMENITIES** Central phone, Kitchen, Fridge, Hot bev. bar, Lounge, Patio, Central Internet access, **THINGS TO DO** Trail nearby, Golf, Fishing, Museums, Art, Theatre, Entertainment, Attractions, Shopping, Swimming, **LANGUAGE** Eng., **PRICE** (2 persons) 79–150 **(check with hosts for pricing details)**

CALGARY

A Hilltop Ranch B&B
(Gary and Barbara Zorn)

Box 54, Priddis, AB, T0L 1W0
www.hilltopranch.net
E-mail gary@hilltopranch.net

403-931-2639
Fax 403-931-3426
TFr 1-800-801-0451

Fifteen minutes Southwest of Calgary. Beautiful spot! All rooms have private bathrooms. Safe. Easy to find. Ranch breakfast served each morning. Morgan Horses. Room for the travelling horse. Mountain views. "If you are coming to Calgary you should have a Western Bed and Breakfast Experience."

ROOMS Family suite, Ground floor, **Baths** Private, Ensuite, **Beds** Queen, Double, Twin, **Smoking** Outside, **In Room** Thermostat, **OTHERS** Rural, Open all year, Pets in residence, Pets welcome, **PAYMENT** Visa, MC, Cash, Trvl's cheques, **BREAKFASTS** Full, Home-baked, **AMENITIES** Central TV, Central phone, Kitchen, Fridge, Lounge, Patio, Central Internet access, Central VCR/DVD, **THINGS TO DO** Trail nearby, Fishing, Horseback riding, Birdwatching, Antiquing, **LANGUAGE** Eng., **PRICE** (2 persons) 90–140 **(check with hosts for pricing details)**

CALGARY

Big Springs Estate B and B Inn
(Earle and Carol Whittaker)

RR #1, Airdrie, AB, T4B 2A3
www.bigsprings-bb.com
E-mail bigsprings@bigsprings-bb.com

403-948-5264
Fax 403-948-5851
TFr 1-888-948-5851

Elegance in the Wild West! *Canada Select* 4-stars. Exclusive countryside Inn 20 minutes northwest of Calgary in foothills of Canadian Rockies. Easy driving distance to exciting adventures and some of our nearby scenic wonders including the Rocky Mountains, Banff and Lake Louise, and 25 minutes to Calgary Intl. Airport. Spacious suites, fireplaces, ultra masseur tubs, superb cuisine, attentive service. Guest lounge, TV lounge, hot tub, gardens, nature trail. Self-guide driving tours. Romantic/Rocky Mountain Adventure Packages.

ROOMS Upper floor, Ground floor, **Baths** Private, Ensuite, **Beds** King, Queen, **Air** Central, In rooms, **Smoking** Outside, **In Room** Thermostat, Phone, Fireplace, **OTHERS** Rural, Adult, Open all year, **PAYMENT** Visa, MC, Amex, Cash, Trvl's cheques, **BREAKFASTS** Full, **AMENITIES** Central TV, Central phone, Whirlpool, Laundry, Fridge, Hot bev. bar, Lounge, Patio, **THINGS TO DO** Trail nearby, Golf, Fishing, Museums, Art, Theatre, Entertainment, Attractions, Shopping, Horseback riding, **LANGUAGE** Eng., **PRICE** (2 persons) 119–250 **(check with hosts for pricing details)**

CALGARY

Bow River House B&B
(Geri and Bill Brennan)

3208 Parkdale Blvd NW, Calgary, AB, T2N 3T3
www.bowriverhousebb.com
E-mail bowrivbb@shaw.ca

403-270-0576
Fax 403-270-7025
TFr 1-866-770-0576

Built in 1914 and lovingly restored, Bow River House offers comfort and convenience to its guests. It is located across from the Bow River, known for its fishing as well as the hiking and biking trails. We are also close to the Foothills Hospital and to Kensington shopping area. Bus service goes past the door with downtown only 10 minutes away. We offer full or continental breakfasts with homemade bread and muffins. Beds are cosy with feather duvets. Guest lounge, wireless Internet. Off-street park.

ROOMS Upper floor, **Baths** Private, Ensuite, Shared with guest, **Beds** Queen, Double, Single or cots, **Air** In rooms, **Smoking** Outside, **In Room** TV, Internet access, **OTHERS** Urban, Adult, Open all year, **PAYMENT** Visa, MC, Diners, Amex, Cash, Trvl's cheques, **BREAKFASTS** Full, Continental, Home-baked, **AMENITIES** Central TV, Central phone, Whirlpool, Fridge, Hot bev. bar, Lounge, Patio, Central Internet access, Central VCR/DVD, **THINGS TO DO** Rental bikes, Trail nearby, Fishing, Museums, Art, Theatre, Entertainment, Attractions, Shopping, **LANGUAGE** Eng., **PRICE** (2 persons) 75–100 **(check with hosts for pricing details)**

CALGARY

Calgary Historic Bed and Breakfast at Twin Gables

(Deirdre Brost)

611– 25th Ave SW, Calgary, AB, T2S 0L7
www.twingables.ca
E-mail twingables@shaw.ca

403-271-7754
TFr 1-866-271-7754

Canada Select 4 1/2-star luxury accomodations in downtown Calgary. This 1910 Arts and Crafts home is one block away from trendy 4th St with many shops and restaurants and 1 block from the Elbow River with miles of jogging and walking paths. Each suite has its own in-room private 4-piece bathroom. Complete with TV/VCR, city views from all suites, computers in rooms linked to high-speed Internet. Relax in our solarium or just lounge in the parlour among the antiques and ambience of past days.

ROOMS Family suite, Upper floor, Ground floor, Private entrance, **Baths** Ensuite, **Beds** King, Queen, Double, Twin, **Air** In rooms, **Smoking** Outside, **In Room** Phone, TV, Fireplace, **OTHERS** Urban, Open all year, **PAYMENT** Visa, MC, Amex, Cash, Trvl's cheques, **BREAKFASTS** Full, Home-baked, **AMENITIES** Central TV, Central phone, Barbecue, Fridge, Hot bev. bar, Lounge, Patio, **THINGS TO DO** Trail nearby, Golf, Fishing, Museums, Art, Theatre, Entertainment, Attractions, Wineries/Breweries, Shopping, **LANGUAGE** Eng., Fr., **PRICE** (2 persons) 99–165 **(check with hosts for pricing details)**

CALGARY

Calgary Westways Guest House

(Jonathon Lloyd and Graham McKay)

216 – 25th Ave SW, Calgary, AB, T2S 0L1
www.westways.ab.ca
E-mail calgary@westways.ab.ca

403-229-1758
TFr 1-866-846-7038

Experience our 1912 Arts and Crafts heritage home with its English ambience. Relax, be comfortable and be you, say Jonathon and Graham. Located in the Mission district (voted the most desirable community in Calgary). Downtown is a 20-minute walk and the Calgary Stampede Park entrance is 10 minutes away. We are the only CAA/AAA 3-Diamond B&B in Calgary. Stay with us and share our experiences of Calgary and enjoy our hospitality, hearty breakfasts prepared by your award-winning chef/ host Jonathon. *Canada Select* 4 stars.

ROOMS Upper floor, **Baths** Ensuite, **Beds** King, Queen, Single or cots, **Air** Central, In rooms, Ceiling fans, **Smoking** Outside, **In Room** Thermostat, Phone, TV, Fireplace, Internet access, VCR/DVD, **OTHERS** Urban, Adult, Pets in residence, Pets welcome, **PAYMENT** Visa, MC, Amex, Direct debit, Cash, Trvl's cheques, **BREAKFASTS** Full, **AMENITIES** Central TV, Central phone, Whirlpool, Laundry, Fridge, Hot bev. bar, Lounge, Patio, Central Internet access, Central VCR/DVD, **THINGS TO DO** Comp. bikes, Trail nearby, Golf, Fishing, Museums, Art, Theatre, Entertainment, Attractions, Shopping, Cross-country skiing, Tennis, Swimming, Birdwatching, Antiquing, **LANGUAGE** Eng., **PRICE** (2 persons) 69–149 **(check with hosts for pricing details)**

CALGARY

Hartwood House B&B

(Veronica and Michael Marsden)

1727 – 47th Ave SW, Calgary, AB, T2T 2S3
www.hartwoodhouse.ca
E-mail info@hartwoodhouse.ca

403-287-0551
Fax 403-287-8143

Hartwood House offers a special kind of comfort in a charming and delightful environment full of warm hospitality and genuine friendship. Located in the inner city, with close and easy access to all tourist attractions and public transportation. Great hike and bike trails and a lovely river park 3 minutes from the door. We are on the direct route to the Rockies and all highways going west. A library with a computer is available to our guests. Complimentary beverages are offered on arrival.

ROOMS Family suitesuite, Upper floor, Private entrance, **Baths** Private, Ensuite, **Beds** Queen, Twin, **Air** In rooms, **Smoking** Outside, **In Room** Thermostat, TV, **OTHERS** Urban, Open all year, Additional meals, **PAYMENT** Visa, MC, Amex, Cash, Trvl's cheques, **BREAKFASTS** Full, **AMENITIES** Central TV, Lounge, Patio, **THINGS TO DO** Comp. bikes, Trail nearby, Golf, Fishing, Museums, Art, Theatre, Entertainment, Attractions, Shopping, Cross-country skiing, Tennis, Swimming, Horseback riding, **LANGUAGE** Eng., **PRICE** (2 persons) 70–110 **(check with hosts for pricing details)**

CALGARY

Home Away From Home

(Helen and George Carsted)

135 Mt Reliant Place SE, Calgary, AB, T2Z 2G2
www.canadianbandbguide.ca/bb.asp?ID=1811
E-mail gruenrock@shaw.ca

403-257-0425

Large home near the banks of the Bow River with a terraced backyard and flower garden. Relax on the front porch and enjoy the lovely evening and the view of the Rockies. Your hosts, both retired, a nurse and teacher/soldier respectively, are interested in health issues, history, politics and military affairs. Enjoy evening tea in congenial company. Double is $55 and single is $30.

ROOMS Upper floor, **Baths** Shared with guest, **Beds** Double, **Air** Central, **Smoking** Outside, **OTHERS** Urban, Adult, Open all year, Additional meals, **PAYMENT** Cheques accepted, Cash, **BREAKFASTS** Full, **AMENITIES** Central TV, Central phone, **THINGS TO DO** Trail nearby, Golf, Museums, Art, Theatre, Entertainment, Attractions, Shopping, **LANGUAGE** Eng., Ger., Polish, **PRICE** (2 persons) 30–55 **(check with hosts for pricing details)**

CALGARY

Inglewood Bed and Breakfast

(Valinda Larson and Helmut Schoderbock)

1006 – 8th Ave SE, Calgary, AB, T2G 0M4
www.inglewoodbedandbreakfast.com
E-mail info@inglewoodbedandbreakfast.com

403-262-6570
Fax 403-262-6570

Convenient, quiet location in city centre, close to attractions. Built in 1993 with B&B in mind, it offers comfortable rooms, tasty meals and helpful hosts. Free off-street parking, free Internet access. Please check our Web site for directions and other information.

ROOMS Upper floor, Ground floor, Private entrance, **Baths** Ensuite, **Beds** Queen, **Smoking** Outside, **OTHERS** Urban, Open all year, **PAYMENT** Visa, MC, Cash, Trvl's cheques, **BREAKFASTS** Full, **AMENITIES** Central TV, Central phone, Fridge, **THINGS TO DO** Trail nearby, Fishing, Museums, Art, Theatre, Entertainment, Attractions, Shopping, Tennis, Horseback riding, **LANGUAGE** Eng., Ger., **PRICE** (2 persons) 90–135 **(check with hosts for pricing details)**

CALGARY

Knobhill "Room With A View" Bed & Breakfast

(Kory Ireland)

2105 – 19th St SW, Calgary, AB, T2T 4W8
www.knobhillbb.com
E-mail knobhill@knobhillbb.com

403-244-7672
Fax 403-244-7629

City view! Victorian executive-style home! Located in the city centre. Easy access to all sights, attractions. Restaurants and shopping are close by. Spacious and unique rooms come with queen-size bed, private bath and sitting area. Enjoy a scrumptious breakfast while taking in the view of downtown Calgary and the Bow River Valley. Calgary's friendly hospitality and accommodation at its best.

ROOMS Upper floor, Lower floor, **Baths** Private, Ensuite, **Beds** Queen, **PAYMENT** Visa, MC, Direct debit, Cheques accepted, Cash, Trvl's cheques, **BREAKFASTS** Full, Continental, **AMENITIES** Central TV, Central phone, **THINGS TO DO** Golf, Museums, Art, Theatre, Entertainment, Attractions, Shopping, **LANGUAGE** Eng., **PRICE** (2 persons) 70–95 **(check with hosts for pricing details)**

CALGARY

Pathway Cottage
Bed and Breakfast

(Dave and Trish Bruce)

111 Sun Canyon Park SE, Calgary, AB, T2X 2W4
www.pathwaycottage.com
E-mail pathwaycottage@shaw.ca

403-256-1995
Fax 403-201-1995
TFr 1-866-356-1995

This executive home backing onto a
3,000-acre provincial park offers relaxing,
quiet accommodation for business and
leisure travellers. Two comfortable guest
rooms plus a spacious suite are available.
High-speed, Wi-Fi Internet access is available. A full hot breakfast is served in the
formal dining room. Relax in the garden
by the waterfall and pond. This cozy
Calgary B&B is not just accommodations,
it's a refreshing and peacefull experience!
Families welcome.

ROOMS Family suitesuite, Upper floor, Ground floor,
Lower floor, **Baths** Ensuite, Shared with guest, **Beds**
King, Queen, Double, Twin, Single or cots, **Smoking**
Outside, **In Room** Thermostat, TV, Internet access,
OTHERS Urban, Rural, Open all year, **PAYMENT** Visa,
MC, Diners, Amex, Cheques accepted, Cash, Trvl's
cheques, **BREAKFASTS** Full, Home-baked, **AMENITIES**
Central TV, Central phone, Fridge, Hot bev. bar,
Lounge, Patio, Central Internet access, **THINGS TO DO**
Comp. bikes, Trail nearby, Golf, Fishing, Museums, Art,
Theatre, Entertainment, Attractions, Shopping, Cross-
country skiing, Swimming, Horseback riding, Beach,
Birdwatching, **LANGUAGE** Eng., **PRICE** (2 persons)
90–110 **(check with hosts for pricing details)**

CALGARY

Riverview Bed and Breakfast

(Brian and Jennifer McNeill)

PO Box 787, Okotoks, AB, T1S 1A9
www.riverviewbnb.ca
E-mail jmcneill@ciphersoftinc.com

403-938-5862
Fax 403-995-0019
TFr 1-866-938-2069

Beautiful 10,000 sq. ft. bed and breakfast
located directly overlooking the Sheep
River. This B&B is beautifully appointed
with a large indoor swimming pool and
Jacuzzi, steam room, sauna and large
games room. A big-screen theatre and
many large central rooms allow guests to
enjoy the views of the mountains and the
river. The property is located on 80 acres
with many hiking trails and great fishing.

ROOMS Upper floor, Ground floor, Private entrance,
Baths Private, Ensuite, **Beds** Queen, Ceiling fans, **Air**
Ceiling fans, **Smoking** Outside, **In Room** Phone, TV,
Fireplace, Internet access, VCR/DVD, **OTHERS**
Babysitting, Rural, Open all year, Handicapped access,
Pets in residence, **PAYMENT** Visa, MC, Amex, Cash,
Trvl's cheques, **BREAKFASTS** Full, Continental, Home-
baked, Self-catered, **AMENITIES** Central TV, Central
phone, Swimming pool, Sauna, Whirlpool, Barbecue,
Laundry, Kitchen, Fridge, Hot bev. bar, Lounge, Patio,
Central Internet access, Central VCR/DVD, **THINGS
TO DO** Trail nearby, Golf, Fishing, Entertainment,
Shopping, Cross-country skiing, Swimming, Bird-
watching, Antiquing, **LANGUAGE** Eng., **PRICE** (2 per-
sons) 110–200 **(check with hosts for pricing details)**

Calgary

Shangarry Bed and Breakfast

(Josephine Davy-Seetal)

432 Wilderness Dr SE, Calgary, AB, T2J 1Z2
www.shangarry.com
E-mail stay@shangarry.com

403-271-5704

Elegant home in a quiet neighbourhood.
Enjoy the garden with it's "borrowed
view" of a private golf course. Wonderful
breakfasts served on fine china and
Waterford crystal. After breakfast feel free
to relax on the patio overlooking the golf
course, or if you feel inspired to tinkle the
ivories there's a grand piano in the living
room. Located in the southeast of Calgary,
close to numerous amenities, as well as
public transit. Spruce Meadows, Stampede
Park, fly fishing. "Irish Hospility."

ROOMS Ground floor, Lower floor, **Baths** Ensuite,
Shared with guest, **Beds** Queen, Double, Twin, **Air**
Central, **OTHERS** Adult, Open all year, Pets in residence, **PAYMENT** Visa, MC, Diners, Amex, Cash, Trvl's
cheques, **BREAKFASTS** Full, Home-baked, **AMENITIES**
Central TV, Laundry, Fridge, Lounge, Central Internet
access, **THINGS TO DO** Fishing, Shopping, **LANGUAGE**
Eng., **PRICE** (2 persons) 85–95 **(check with hosts for
pricing details)**

Calgary

Sweet Dreams and Scones

(Karen McLeod)

2443 Uxbridge Dr NW, Calgary, AB, T2N 3Z8
www.sweetdreamsandscones.com
E-mail karenbandb@hotmail.com

403-289-7004
Fax 403-289-7004

Imaginative food, inspiring decor, congenial hostess and reasonable rates make this
unique B&B a popular spot. Dine by candlelight and music in the antique-filled
dining room as you watch the birds in the
exquisite gardens. Two bedrooms with
queen beds plus huge two-room suite
available, all with private or ensuite baths
and comfy beds. Located in a quiet setting just 4 blocks off Hwy 1, close to
University and foothills, Hospital, 10 minutes drive to downtown. Enjoy a unique
experience and sweet dreams!

ROOMS Family suite, Upper floor, **Baths** Private,
Ensuite, **Beds** King, Queen, Double, Twin, **Smoking**
Outside, **OTHERS** Urban, Open all year, **PAYMENT** Visa,
MC, Cash, Trvl's cheques, **BREAKFASTS** Full, Continen-
tal, Home-baked, **AMENITIES** Central TV, Central
phone, Hot bev. bar, Lounge, Patio, Central Internet
access, Central VCR/DVD, **THINGS TO DO** Museums,
Art, Theatre, Entertainment, Shopping, **LANGUAGE**
Eng., **PRICE** (2 persons) 85–130 **(check with hosts for
pricing details)**

CALGARY/STRATHMORE

Sproule Heritage B&B

(Winston and Vera Sproule)

Box 43, Site 12, RR #1, Strathmore, AB, T1P 1J6
www.canadianbandbguide.ca/bb.asp?ID=3203

403-934-3219

On Trans-Canada Hwy 1, 30 minutes east of Calgary, 10 minutes east of Strathmore. Authentically restored, and declared a Registered Alberta Historic Farmsite (Est. 1909). Bright upstairs bedroom with quality beds and bedding have been accommodating guests for 17 years. Appreciate the casual elegance, original wood, antique furniture (restored or replicas) handmade by host who welcomes guests to his woodworking shop. Inquire re children. No pets please. Cosy cottage (no stairs) also available. Near Rocky Mountains, Banff and more.

ROOMS Upper floor, **Baths** Private, Shared with guest, **Beds** Queen, **OTHERS** Rural, Adult, Open all year, **PAYMENT** Cheques accepted, Cash, Trvl's cheques, **BREAKFASTS** Full, Home-baked, **THINGS TO DO** Golf, Museums, Theatre, Attractions, **LANGUAGE** Eng., Russian, **PRICE** (2 persons) 75–95 **(check with hosts for pricing details)**

CANMORE *(west of Calgary)*

Avens ReNaissance B&B

(Marie-Joëlle Driard)

252 Lady MacDonald Dr, Canmore, AB, T1W 1H8
www.bbcanmore.com/renaissance
E-mail renaisbb@telusplanet.net

403-678-1875
Fax 403-678-1875

Close to Banff and other national and provincial parks. Bright and charming home nestled in the foothills of the spectacular Canadian Rockies. Sunny and quiet residential area near Cougar Creek and Canyon trails. Luxurious suite will seduce your soul and steal your heart. Private walkout entrance from garden patio. Delicious hearty breakfast. Hostess is an artist, ski/telemark instructor originally from Quebec. Enjoy exclusive and friendly service. Discount on extended stay. No taxes. You certainly deserve it!

ROOMS Family suitesuite, Ground floor, Private entrance, **Baths** Ensuite, **Beds** Queen, Pullout sofa, **Air** Central, **Smoking** Outside, **In Room** TV, Fireplace, Internet access, VCR/DVD, **OTHERS** Babysitting, Rural, Open all year, Additional meals, **PAYMENT** Cheques accepted, Cash, Trvl's cheques, **BREAKFASTS** Full, Home-baked, **AMENITIES** Central phone, Barbecue, Laundry, Fridge, Patio, **THINGS TO DO** Rental bikes, Trail nearby, Golf, Fishing, Museums, Art, Theatre, Entertainment, Attractions, Wineries/Breweries, Shopping, Cross-country skiing, Downhill skiing, Tennis, Swimming, Horseback riding, Beach, Birdwatching, Antiquing, **LANGUAGE** Eng., Fr., **PRICE** (2 persons) 150–170 **(check with hosts for pricing details)**

CANMORE

Elli's Bed and Breakfast

(Elli and Lou Stabile)

295 Three Sisters Dr, Canmore, AB, T1W 2M5
www.bbexpo.com/ab/ellis.htm
E-mail louiss@telusplanet.net

403-678-5436
Fax 403-609-2267

Quiet area, large decks with breathtaking views of majestic mountains. Rooms with ensuite bathrooms, robes and slippers, teas, cocoa, etc. Homemade biscotti, TV/VCR, fridge in each room. Choose your breakfast from our 16-item gourmet menu. End your day of outdoor activities in our private sauna. Bike and ski storage available. Your hosts Elli and Lou have 31 years of knowledge in the area about hiking, walking, skiing, cycling, etc. Located just a 5-minute drive from Banff Park gates.

ROOMS Ground floor, Lower floor, **Baths** Ensuite, **Beds** Queen, Pullout sofa, **Smoking** Outside, **In Room** TV, Fireplace, **OTHERS** Rural, Open all year, **PAYMENT** Visa, MC, Cash, Trvl's cheques, **BREAKFASTS** Full, Home-baked, **AMENITIES** Central phone, Sauna, Barbecue, Laundry, Fridge, Patio, **THINGS TO DO** Rental bikes, Trail nearby, Golf, Fishing, Museums, Art, Theatre, Shopping, Cross-country skiing, Tennis, Swimming, Horseback riding, **LANGUAGE** Eng., Italian, **PRICE** (2 persons) 75–105 **(check with hosts for pricing details)**

CANMORE

Riverview & Main B&B

(Wayne and Wynn Schneider)

918 – 8th (Main) St, Canmore, AB, T1W 2B8
www.riverviewandmain.com
E-mail mrfreeze@agt.net

403-678-9777

Conveniently situated in downtown Canmore, surrounded by the spectacular Canadian Rockies, our B&B features bright, sunny rooms with beautiful mountain views from every window. One block from the glacier-fed Bow River and extensive walking trails, we are within walking distance of all amenities. A 10-minute drive to Banff National Park or Alberta's Kananaskis Country.

ROOMS Family suitesuite, Upper floor, Ground floor, Private entrance, **Baths** Private, Ensuite, **Beds** Queen, Twin, **Smoking** Outside, **OTHERS** Urban, Adult, Open all year, Pets in residence, **PAYMENT** Visa, MC, Cash, Trvl's cheques, **BREAKFASTS** Self-catered, **AMENITIES** Central TV, Central phone, Fridge, Hot bev. bar, Lounge, Patio, Central Internet access, Central VCR/DVD, **THINGS TO DO** Trail nearby, Golf, Fishing, Museums, Art, Theatre, Entertainment, Attractions, Shopping, Cross-country skiing, Downhill skiing, Tennis, Swimming, Horseback riding, Birdwatching, **LANGUAGE** Eng., **PRICE** (2 persons) 85–120 **(check with hosts for pricing details)**

COCHRANE

Mountview Cottage B&B

(Neil and Marilyn Degraw)

27 Mount View E, Cochrane, AB, T4C 2B2
www.bbcanada.com/3681.html
E-mail degraw@nucleus.com

403-932-4586
Fax 403-932-1095
TFr 1-877-433-8193

Valley view with Rocky mountains 180-degrees on the horizon. From the top of the ridge you can view the valley, filled with prairie-wool, grazing cattle, deer and bald eagles. Beautiful English gardens with trees, waterfall and benches to relax. Our hillside bungalow features a walkout basement with a recreation room and patio doors open onto the deck. This room has a large sitting area for our guests to relax and enjoy a wood fire, TV, wet bar, microwave, billiard table and library.

ROOMS Upper floor, Ground floor, Private entrance, **Baths** Ensuite, **Beds** Queen, **In Room** Thermostat, Phone, Internet access, **OTHERS** Rural, Adult, Open all year, Handicapped access, **PAYMENT** Visa, Cheques accepted, Cash, Trvl's cheques, **BREAKFASTS** Full, Home-baked, **AMENITIES** Central TV, Central phone, Sauna, Whirlpool, Barbecue, Laundry, Fridge, Hot bev. bar, Lounge, Patio, Central Internet access, Central VCR/DVD, **THINGS TO DO** Comp. bikes, Trail nearby, Golf, Fishing, Art, Attractions, Shopping, Cross-country skiing, Downhill skiing, Horseback riding, Birdwatching, Antiquing, **LANGUAGE** Eng., **PRICE** (2 persons) 75–125 **(check with hosts for pricing details)**

COLD LAKE *(northeast of Edmonton)*

Hamilton House Bed and Breakfast Inn

(Debbie and Brian Hamilton)

Box 136, Cherry Grove, AB, T0A 0T0
www.hamiltonhouse.com
E-mail hamhouse@worldpost.ca

780-594-7257
Fax 780-594-0778

Hamilton House is in a tranquil setting within the Northern Boreal Forest, 14 km southeast of the City of Cold Lake. We have 5 acres of lawns, gardens, a large pond and countless acres adjacent to us for hiking, biking and cross-country skiing on groomed trails, with a small lake for canoeing and wildlife viewing. We are 3 km south of Cold Lake on Hwy 28 and 10.5 km east on Hwy 55. See our Web site with a printable map and/or call Debbie's cell phone 780-812-6525 if you cannot reach the number above.

ROOMS Family suitesuite, Upper floor, Ground floor, Lower floor, Private entrance, **Baths** Ensuite, **Beds** Queen, Double, Single or cots, **Smoking** Outside, **In Room** Thermostat, Phone, Fireplace, Internet access, **OTHERS** Rural, Open all year, Additional meals, **PAYMENT** Visa, MC, Amex, Direct debit, Cash, Trvl's cheques, **BREAKFASTS** Full, Home-baked, **AMENITIES** Central TV, Central phone, Whirlpool, Barbecue, Laundry, Fridge, Lounge, Patio, Central Internet access, Central VCR/DVD, **THINGS TO DO** Trail nearby, Comp. canoe or boat, Golf, Fishing, Museums, Art, Theatre, Entertainment, Attractions, Shopping, Cross-country skiing, Downhill skiing, Tennis, Swimming, Horseback riding, Beach, Birdwatching, **LANGUAGE** Eng., **PRICE** (2 persons) 75–100 **(check with hosts for pricing details)**

CROWSNEST PASS *(southwest of Calgary)*

Blairmore Heritage House B&B, Tea & Gift Shop

(Lois Green)

Box 1517, 13319 – 20th Ave, Blairmore, AB, T0K 0E0
www.members.shaw.ca/logreen/index.html
E-mail logreen@shaw.ca

403-562-2660
Fax 403-562-2660
TFr 1-877-562-2660

Need to get away? Have we got a bed for you! We offer two queen rooms and two twins that are delightful. There is lovely Widows Walk that has an awesome view of the surrounding mountains and countryside. The beds, well I've been told they send you directly to dreamland. Fluffy robes are available for your convenience. Your breakfast: ham and eggs served on a toasted english muffin smothered with hollandaise, fruit, cheese, OJ and coffee/tea. Paradise in the mountains!

ROOMS Upper floor, Ground floor, **Baths** Shared with guest, **Beds** Queen, Twin, **Air** In rooms, **OTHERS** Open all year, Additional meals, **PAYMENT** Visa, Cheques accepted, Cash, Trvl's cheques, **BREAKFASTS** Full, Home-baked, **AMENITIES** Central TV, Central phone, Whirlpool, Laundry, Kitchen, Central Internet access, Central VCR/DVD, **THINGS TO DO** Trail nearby, Rental canoe or boat, Golf, Fishing, Museums, Art, Theatre, Entertainment, Attractions, Shopping, Cross-country skiing, Downhill skiing, Tennis, Swimming, Horseback riding, Birdwatching, **LANGUAGE** Eng., French available by request, **PRICE** (2 persons) 75–75 **(check with hosts for pricing details)**

DRUMHELLER *(east of Calgary)*

Pearl's Country Cottages

(The Lucas Family)

Box 1558, Drumheller, AB, T0J 0Y0
www.bbcanada.com/pearls
E-mail pearls1@telusplanet.net

403-823-9224

Fun four Families. Two bedroom guest cottages, privately situated on third-generation grain farm 8 km to Drumheller. Relax in your comfortable "Home away from Home." Fully equipped kitchen, private bathrooms, living room with TV/VCR, books, games. Wander wildlife trails through Coulee. Enjoy playhouse, swings, basketball, horseshoes, croquet, meditate in tipi, birdwatch throughout the quaint gardens and treed pond, run quiet country roads, absorb awesome prairie sunsets. Hosts can arrange babysitting, laundry, tee times.

ROOMS Family suitesuite, Upper floor, Ground floor, Private entrance, **Baths** Private, **Beds** Queen, Twin, Single or cots, Pullout sofa, **Smoking** Outside, **OTHERS** Babysitting, Rural, Open all year, Handicapped access, **PAYMENT** Cheques accepted, Cash, Trvl's cheques, **BREAKFASTS** Continental, Home-baked, Self-catered, **AMENITIES** Central TV, Kitchen, Fridge, Hot bev. bar, Lounge, Central VCR/DVD, **THINGS TO DO** Trail nearby, Golf, Fishing, Museums, Art, Theatre, Entertainment, Attractions, Shopping, Cross-country skiing, Downhill skiing, Tennis, Swimming, Horseback riding, Beach, Birdwatching, Antiquing, **LANGUAGE** Eng., **PRICE** (2 persons) enquire **(check with hosts for pricing details)**

DRUMHELLER

Silver Fox Inn
(Dave Meeres)

104 – 2nd St W, Munson, AB, T0J 2C0
www.bbcanada.com/2089.html
E-mail meeresd@telusplanet.net

403-823-7758
TFr 1-888-823-7758

Turn-of-the-century country home with new private rooms. Deluxe rooms with private entrances, private baths/jetted tubs, fireplace, TV/VCR movies and quality queen-size beds. All-you-can-eat waffle breakfast included. Just 8 minutes from Drumheller, 5 minutes from Badlands and 15 minutes to Tyrell Dinosaur Museum and golf course. Families welcome. All rooms non-smoking.

ROOMS Family suite, Ground floor, Lower floor, Private entrance, **Baths** Ensuite, **Beds** Queen, **Air** Central, **Smoking** Outside, **In Room** Thermostat, TV, Fireplace, VCR/DVD, **OTHERS** Urban, Open all year, Pets in residence, **PAYMENT** Visa, MC, Cheques accepted, Cash, Trvl's cheques, **BREAKFASTS** Full, **AMENITIES** Central TV, Central phone, **THINGS TO DO** Golf, Museums, Attractions, **LANGUAGE** Eng., **PRICE** (2 persons) 69–99 **(check with hosts for pricing details)**

DRUMHELLER

Taste The Past
(Dennis and Denise Simon)

Box 865, 281 – 2nd St W, Drumheller, AB, T0J 0Y0
www.bbcanada.com/taste
E-mail taste@telus.net

403-823-5889

This large, beautifully restored home was originaly built by a coal baron c. 1910. Antique decor. Enjoy refreshments in the large guest sitting room with fireplace, piano, TV, library. A specialty breakfast is served in the sunny dining room. All three guest rooms are located on second floor and all have private baths. Original artwork on display throughout the home. Open year round. Deposit required – cancellation policy. CAA approved. Alberta Best Accommodation (completed Alberta Gov accommodations course). All taxes included in room rates.

Baths Private, Ensuite, **Beds** Queen, Twin, **Smoking** Outside, **OTHERS** Open all year, **PAYMENT** Visa, MC, Cheques accepted, Cash, Trvl's cheques, **BREAKFASTS** Full, Home-baked, **AMENITIES** Central TV, Central phone, Lounge, **THINGS TO DO** Trail nearby, Golf, Fishing, Museums, Art, Theatre, Entertainment, Attractions, Shopping, Downhill skiing, Tennis, Swimming, Horseback riding, Birdwatching, **LANGUAGE** Eng., **PRICE** (2 persons) 85–100 single/double **(check with hosts for pricing details)**

DRUMHELLER

The Pope Lease Pines B&B and RV Resort

(Kent and Janice Walker)

Box 1058, Drumheller, AB, T0J 0Y0
www.thepopeleasepines.com
E-mail thepines@telusplanet.net

403-823-8281
Fax 403-572-2370

Hwy 575 – 15 minutes west of downtown Drumheller. Restored 1940s two-storey English Tudor home on Soldier Settlement Land. Furnished with period antiques. Queen- and twin-size beds. Full gourmet candlelight breakfast with silver service and royal treatment. Quiet country setting, nature's paradise. Minutes from golf courses, all tourists attractions, theatre and shopping. Visit us on the prairies and experience the beautiful sunrises and sunsets for which we are famous. Stargazing at its best. Fourteen full service RV sites.

ROOMS Upper floor, **Baths** Shared with guest, **Beds** Queen, Twin, **Air** Ceiling fans, **Smoking** Outside, **OTHERS** Seasonal, **PAYMENT** Visa, MC, Direct debit, Cash, Trvl's cheques, **BREAKFASTS** Full, Home-baked, **AMENITIES** Central TV, Central phone, Lounge, Central VCR/DVD, **THINGS TO DO** Golf, Fishing, Museums, Art, Theatre, Entertainment, Attractions, Shopping, Cross-country skiing, Horseback riding, **LANGUAGE** Eng., **PRICE** (2 persons) 80 **(check with hosts for pricing details)**

EDMONTON *(central Alberta)*

A Sage Door Bed and Breakfast

(Susan and Dayl)

205 Heagle Cres, Edmonton, AB, T6R 1V2
www.bbexpo.com/sagedoor
E-mail sagebb@attglobal.net

780-479-2372
Fax 780-430-4798

We offer a west-coast atmosphere designed to relax the senses in an all-too-often hectic life. The Starboard Room with its own full private bathroom is designed with a beachhouse flair and you will appreciate a down duvet on a queen-size bed. A full gourmet breakfast, woodburning fireplace, multilevel deck, sunroom and library await you. We look forward to your visit.

ROOMS Upper floor, **Baths** Private, **Beds** Queen, **Smoking** Outside, **In Room** Phone, **OTHERS** Urban, Adult, Open all year, Additional meals, **PAYMENT** Visa, MC, Amex, Cash, Trvl's cheques, **BREAKFASTS** Full, Continental, Home-baked, **AMENITIES** Central TV, Central phone, Laundry, Fridge, Hot bev. bar, Lounge, Patio, **THINGS TO DO** Comp. bikes, Trail nearby, Golf, Museums, Art, Theatre, Entertainment, Attractions, Shopping, Cross-country skiing, Tennis, Swimming, **LANGUAGE** Eng., Fr., Ger., **PRICE** (2 persons) 79–149 **(check with hosts for pricing details)**

EDMONTON
Chickadee Hollow Bed and Breakfast
(Russ and Linda Harke)

61 – 51109 Range Rd 220, Sherwood Park, AB, T8E 1G8
www.chickadeehollow.com
E-mail info@chickadeehollow.com

780-922-2572
Fax 780-922-2587
TFr 1-866-922-2572

Nestled on 3 acres in Strathcona County, Chickadee Hollow is a welcoming, spacious guest home. Choose from three inviting rooms with private or ensuite bathroom. Relax in comfortable surroundings, browse through our collectibles and memorabilia or listen to music. Stroll through grounds, sit among the flowers in our secluded garden or try your hand at horseshoes or bocce. Near the Northern Bear Golf Course. Ideal for bird-lovers. Adult-oriented. We are proud to hold a *Canada Select* 4-star rating. Call for single rates.

ROOMS Ground floor, Lower floor, **Baths** Private, Ensuite, **Beds** Queen, **Smoking** Outside, **In Room** Thermostat, **OTHERS** Rural, Adult, Open all year, **PAYMENT** Visa, MC, Diners, Amex, Cash, Trvl's cheques, **BREAKFASTS** Full, Continental, Home-baked, **AMENITIES** Central TV, Central phone, Fridge, Lounge, Patio, Central VCR/DVD, **THINGS TO DO** Trail nearby, Golf, Museums, Art, Theatre, Entertainment, Attractions, Shopping, Cross-country skiing, Horseback riding, Birdwatching, Antiquing, **LANGUAGE** Eng., **PRICE** (2 persons) 100–115 **(check with hosts for pricing details)**

EDMONTON
Glenora Bed & Breakfast Inn
(The Freeland Family)

12327 – 102 Ave, Edmonton, AB, T5N 0L8
www.glenorabnb.com
E-mail info@glenorabnb.com

780-488-6766
Fax 780-488-5168
TFr 1-877-453-6672

Nestled among the fine shops, restaurants and art galleries on 124th St, the Glenora Bed & Breakfast Inn lies at the heart of Edmonton's historic West End. Old-world charm, together with the comforts of today, combine to create a truly memorable experience. An elegantly restored West Edmonton landmark opened in 1912, maintains the original signage. Restorations in 1995 resulted in a friendly inn with old-fashioned wallpaper and antique furniture, each Victorian bedroom unique.

ROOMS Family suitesuite, Upper floor, **Baths** Private, Shared with guest, **Beds** King, Queen, Double, Twin, Pullout sofa, **Air** In rooms, **Smoking** Outside, **In Room** Phone, TV, Fireplace, **OTHERS** Urban, Adult, Open all year, **PAYMENT** Visa, MC, Amex, Direct debit, Cash, Trvl's cheques, **BREAKFASTS** Full, **AMENITIES** Laundry, Kitchen, Fridge, Hot bev. bar, Lounge, Patio, **THINGS TO DO** Trail nearby, Golf, Museums, Art, Theatre, Attractions, Shopping, **LANGUAGE** Eng., **PRICE** (2 persons) 70–140 **(check with hosts for pricing details)**

EDMONTON
Green Acres
Bed and Breakfast
(Erwin and Brenda Chitrinia)

Site 19, Box 7, RR #1, Edmonton, AB, T6H 4N6
www.greenacresbedandbreakfast.com
E-mail info@greenacresbb.ca

780-929-7399
Fax 780-929-8005
TFr 1-888-999-7870

Come by and wake up someplace special!
Unique suites. Great hospitality. Hearty
breakfasts. Our luxury private suite
features a cozy fireplace, pool table, kitchenette, private bedroom and bath. Sleeps
four. Spacious ensuites with jet tub, com-
pact fridges, pillowtop mattress, satellite
TV/DVD, fluffy robes, hairdryers. Country
home close to all city amenities. Easy
access to West Edmonton Mall, 10 minutes to Edmonton Intl. Airport. With your
stay, receive a complimentary bottle of
our world-famous Green Acres Spice.

ROOMS Family suitesuite, Upper floor, Lower floor,
Private entrance, **Baths** Ensuite, **Beds** Queen, Pullout
sofa, **Air** Central, **Smoking** Outside, **In Room**
Thermostat, Phone, TV, **OTHERS** Rural, Adult, Open all
year, **PAYMENT** Visa, MC, Diners, Amex, Cash, Trvl's
cheques, **BREAKFASTS** Full, Continental, Home-baked,
AMENITIES Central phone, Kitchen, Fridge, Hot bev.
bar, Lounge, Patio, **THINGS TO DO** Trail nearby, Golf,
Museums, Art, Theatre, Entertainment, Attractions,
Shopping, Horseback riding, **LANGUAGE** Eng., **PRICE**
(2 persons) 80–90 **(check with hosts for pricing
details)**

EDMONTON
Kountry Komfort
Bed and Breakfast
(Kathy and Paul Champigny)

4601 – 42 St, Beaumont, AB, T4X 1H1
www.kountrykomfort.com
E-mail kountrykomfort@shaw.ca

780-929-2342
Fax 780-929-2343

Enjoy the country setting in the town of
Beaumont, just minutes from Edmonton
and the Intl. Airport. Comfortable new
home backing onto a wooded area in
quiet community with French Canadian
theme evident in architecture. Phone, fax
and computer available for guests. Hosts
are helpful with information about the
area attractions. Silver service breakfast
served in the dining room. Parking available for guests flying out of airport. Come
as strangers, leave as friends.

ROOMS Family suitesuite, Upper floor, **Baths** Shared
with guest, **Beds** Queen, Double, Single or cots, **Air**
In rooms, **Smoking** Outside, **OTHERS** Rural, Open all
year, Pets welcome, **PAYMENT** Visa, MC, Cheques
accepted, Cash, Trvl's cheques, **BREAKFASTS** Full,
AMENITIES Central TV, Swimming pool, Barbecue,
Laundry, **THINGS TO DO** Trail nearby, Golf, Fishing,
Theatre, Entertainment, Attractions, Shopping, Tennis,
Swimming, Horseback riding, Beach, **LANGUAGE** Eng.,
Fr., **PRICE** (2 persons) 65–75 **(check with hosts for
pricing details)**

EDMONTON AND DEVON

A High Rigg Retreat B&B

(Philippa and Delton Gray)

3 – 51119 RR #255, Spruce Grove, AB, T7Y 1A8
www.highriggretreat.com
E-mail highrigg@oanet.com

780-470-0462

You will enjoy your stay at this comfortable country home, which has terrific views of the river valley. Spacious, well-appointed rooms are rustic yet elegant. King or queen beds, fridge, coffee facility, TV/VCR, stereo, hairdryers, robes, etc. Patio suite has a fireplace with ensuite bathroom. River view, a private bath. Suites sleep two to five people, have private entrances and are family/pet friendly. Just 20 minutes to Intl. Airport, 10 minutes to Devon/Botanical Gardens and 15 minutes to West Edmonton Mall. Map on Web site.

ROOMS Family suitesuite, Upper floor, Ground floor, Lower floor, Private entrance, **Baths** Private, Ensuite, **Beds** King, Queen, Double, Single or cots, Pullout sofa, **Air** Central, In rooms, **Smoking** Outside, **In Room** TV, Fireplace, VCR/DVD, **OTHERS** Rural, Open all year, Pets in residence, Pets welcome, **PAYMENT** Visa, MC, Amex, Cheques accepted, Cash, Trvl's cheques, **BREAKFASTS** Full, Continental, Home-baked, Self-catered, **AMENITIES** Fridge, Hot bev. bar, Lounge, Patio, **THINGS TO DO** Trail nearby, Golf, Fishing, Entertainment, Attractions, Shopping, Cross-country skiing, Birdwatching, Antiquing, **LANGUAGE** Eng., **PRICE** (2 persons) 80–90 **(check with hosts for pricing details)**

GRANDE CACHE *(northwest of Edmonton)*

EJ'S Roost

(Edna Bryanton)

10521 – 99th Ave, Grande Cache, AB, T0E 0Y0
www.ejsroostbedbreakfast.com
E-mail ebryanto@telusplanet.net

780-827-2652
Fax 780-827-3618

Located right in the town of Grande Cache. Turn off the highway at the "Town Center" sign, directly opposite the Shell garage. This is Hoppe Ave. Go to the second set of Pedestrian lights. Turn left and you will come to a "T" intersection. Turn left again. Tall white house with a verandah. Big B&B sign in the yard.

ROOMS Upper floor, **Baths** Ensuite, Shared with guest, **Beds** Queen, Twin, **Smoking** Outside, **In Room** Phone, TV, Internet access, VCR/DVD, **OTHERS** Urban, Open all year, **PAYMENT** Cheques accepted, Cash, Trvl's cheques, **BREAKFASTS** Full, Continental, Home-baked, **AMENITIES** Central TV, Central phone, Barbecue, Fridge, **THINGS TO DO** Rental bikes, Trail nearby, Cross-country skiing, Swimming, Horseback riding, **PRICE** (2 persons) 60–75 **(check with hosts for pricing details)**

HIGH RIVER *(south of Calgary)*

Arbuthnot's B&B

(Mac and Donna Arbuthnot)

937 – 7th St SW, High River, AB, T1V 1A9
www.canadianbandbguide.ca/bb.asp?ID=3775

403-652-4056
Fax 403-601-2990

Quiet, cozy, two-bedroom self-catering cottage in older part of town. The kitchen is fully equipped, food is stocked in cupboards. Wheelchair access, barbecue and there is a great garden. We are two blocks from the river and there is good golfing nearby. It is a popular place for honeymooners. To find us, turn west off Hwy 2, follow 12th Ave to 7th St SW. Turn right and go one block.

ROOMS Ground floor, Private entrance, **Baths** Ensuite, **Smoking** Outside, **OTHERS** Urban, Handicapped access, **PAYMENT** Cash, **BREAKFASTS** Self-catered, **AMENITIES** Barbecue, Kitchen, Fridge, Hot bev. bar, Lounge, **THINGS TO DO** Golf, **LANGUAGE** Eng., **PRICE** (2 persons) 100 **(check with hosts for pricing details)**

HINTON *(north of Jasper)*

Brule Bed & Breakfast

(Wald and Lavone Olson)

Box 24, #401, Brule, AB, T0E 0C0
www.bbcanada.com/brulebb
E-mail wolson@telusplanet.net

780-865-4417
Fax 780-865-4415

Comfortable, cozy log home. Hospitality in the pristine Alberta Rocky Mountains. We are 1 hour from Jasper Town, 30 minutes to Miette Hot Springs, 15 minutes to Jasper National Park, ands Hinton Golf Course. We have scenic hiking to Orgre Canyon and the historic Brule Coral Mines. We provide guided-trail rides for our guests. To find us, take Hwy 16 west from Hinton for 5 km, turn north on Hwy 40 for 5 km, turn left at Brule sign, follow road for 9 km into Brule townsite. We are the last house on your left.

ROOMS Upper floor, **Baths** Shared with guest, **Beds** Queen, **Smoking** Outside, **In Room** VCR/DVD, **OTHERS** Rural, Open all year, Pets in residence, **PAYMENT** Cheques accepted, Cash, Trvl's cheques, **BREAKFASTS** Continental, **AMENITIES** Central TV, Central Internet access, Central VCR/DVD, **THINGS TO DO** Trail nearby, Golf, Fishing, Shopping, Cross-country skiing, Swimming, Horseback riding, Birdwatching, Antiquing, **LANGUAGE** Eng., **PRICE** (2 persons) 50–65 **(check with hosts for pricing details)**

Collinge Hill Bed and Breakfast

(Larry and Lorraine Stirrett)

440 Collinge Rd, Hinton, AB, T7V 1L1
www.bbcanada.com/7359.html
E-mail lolastirrett@shaw.ca

780-817-1940
TFr 1-888-817-1940

Collinge Hill Bed and Breakfast is nestled in the small town of Hinton. Our home was built in 1995 and is of interest in architectural design. Our suites are tastefully decorated with queen-size beds, both offering private balconies with views of the mountains. Both suites have access to a large shared/private ensuite with a Jacuzzi tub. Jasper National Park Gate is a 15-minute drive; Jasper townsite is 45 minutes. To view more pictures of our home, please visit our Web site.

ROOMS Upper floor, **Baths** Private, Ensuite, Shared with guest, **Beds** Queen, **Air** Ceiling fans, **Smoking** Outside, **In Room** TV, VCR/DVD, **OTHERS** Urban, Adult, Open all year, **PAYMENT** Visa, MC, Cash, Trvl's cheques, **BREAKFASTS** Full, Home-baked, **AMENITIES** Central TV, Fridge, Patio, Central Internet access, **THINGS TO DO** Trail nearby, Golf, Fishing, Shopping, Cross-country skiing, Swimming, Horseback riding, Beach, **LANGUAGE** Eng., **PRICE** (2 persons) 75–85 **(check with hosts for pricing details)**

McCracken Country Inn

(Kyle and Fay McCracken)

146 Brookhart St (Hwy 16 E), Hinton, AB, T7V 1Y8
www.mccrackencountryinn.com
E-mail mccrackencountryinn@shaw.ca

780-865-5662
Fax 780-865-5664
TFr 1-888-865-5662

We offer the comfort and privacy of a luxury hotel with the ambience of an old country inn. We are located in the foothills of the beautiful Canadian Rocky Mountains – you will enjoy the peace and quiet that you deserve. Luxurious guest rooms with queen-size beds decorated with antique furnishings, A/C, fireplaces, cable TV, ensuite bathrooms and wireless Internet. We also have a full-service licensed teahouse-restaurant with homemade soups and fresh baking. Family owned and operated.

ROOMS Family suitesuite, Upper floor, Ground floor, Private entrance, **Baths** Private, Ensuite, **Beds** Queen, Twin, Single or cots, Pullout sofa, **Air** In rooms, **Smoking** Outside, **In Room** Thermostat, TV, Fireplace, Internet access, VCR/DVD, **OTHERS** Open all year, Handicapped access, Pets welcome, **PAYMENT** Visa, MC, Amex, Direct debit, Cheques accepted, Cash, **BREAKFASTS** Full, Home-baked, **AMENITIES** Central TV, Whirlpool, Fridge, Lounge, Patio, Central Internet access, Central VCR/DVD, **THINGS TO DO** Trail nearby, Golf, Fishing, Museums, Attractions, Cross-country skiing, Downhill skiing, Swimming, Horseback riding, Birdwatching, Antiquing, **LANGUAGE** Eng., **PRICE** (2 persons) 99–129 **(check with hosts for pricing details)**

JASPER *(west of Edmonton)*

A Little Log House Accommodation

(Tamar and Gary Hilworth)

712 Patricia St, Jasper, AB, T0E 1E0
www.aloghousejasper.com
E-mail stay@aloghousejasper.com

780-852-4548

Located close to shops, restaurants and bus/train station, come and enjoy our one-bedroom suite. This second-floor suite is ideal for families or couples looking for a self-contained unit. Private bathroom and private entrance, small deck, living room with double sofa bed, bedroom with queen bed, kitchenette with microwave, fridge, coffee/tea, utensils, dishes for four. Sorry, we do not serve breakfast.

ROOMS Family suitesuite, Upper floor, Private entrance, **Baths** Private, **Beds** Queen, Pullout sofa, **In Room** Thermostat, TV, **OTHERS** Open all year, **PAYMENT** Cheques accepted, Cash, Trvl's cheques, **BREAKFASTS** Self-catered, **THINGS TO DO** Trail nearby, Museums, Entertainment, Attractions, Shopping, Cross-country skiing, Downhill skiing, Tennis, Swimming, Horseback riding, Birdwatching, **PRICE** (2 persons) 75–90 **(check with hosts for pricing details)**

JASPER

Cabin Creek Accommodations

(Loretta and Don Patry)

1220 Cabin Creek Dr, Jasper, AB, T0E 1E0
www.cabincreekjasper.com
E-mail comfort@cabincreekjasper.com

780-852-7230

We have two very clean, comfortable, newly renovated main floor rooms available for your comfort and relaxation. Room 1 features a double bed, reading area and large patio doors that open to our sundeck and beautifully landscaped backyard. Room 2 features a double bed and twin flip sofa. Both rooms are accessible through a private entrance and feature a private bathroom with amenities and blowdryer, TV, fridge and complimentary coffee and tea. We offer driveway parking and daily housekeeping.

ROOMS Ground floor, Private entrance, **Baths** Private, **Beds** Queen, Double, Twin, Single or cots, **Smoking** Outside, **In Room** Thermostat, TV, **OTHERS** Open all year, **PAYMENT** Visa, MC, Amex, Cash, Trvl's cheques, **BREAKFASTS** Continental, **AMENITIES** Fridge, Patio, **THINGS TO DO** Rental bikes, Trail nearby, Rental canoe or boat, Golf, Fishing, Museums, Art, Entertainment, Attractions, Wineries/Breweries, Shopping, Cross-country skiing, Tennis, Swimming, Horseback riding, Beach, **LANGUAGE** Eng., **PRICE** (2 persons) 50–90 **(check with hosts for pricing details)**

JASPER

Casa Norma

(Norma McLean)

1219 Patricia Cres, PO Box 2049, Jasper, AB, T0E 1E0
www.bbcanada.com/casanorma
E-mail casanorma@telus.net

780-852-4146
Fax 780-852-4146

Casa Norma offers you a suite with bath-room, two bedrooms that convert to three with a folding door. The kitchen is well-equipped with two-burner cooktop, microwave, refrigerator, toaster, kettle, cof-feemaker, table to seat six, dishes, cutlery, cookware. The living room is comfortable, with sofas, armchairs, TV (2-6 guests). An additonal room with bathroom is available separately or with the suite. This room has TV, microwave, refrigerator, kettle, coffeemaker, table, dishes, cutlery, (1-2 guests).

ROOMS Family suite, Lower floor, Private entrance, **Baths** Private, Ensuite, **Beds** Queen, Double, **Smoking** Outside, **In Room** TV, **OTHERS** Seasonal, **PAYMENT** Visa, Cash, Trvl's cheques, **AMENITIES** Central phone, Kitchen, Fridge, Lounge, Patio, **THINGS TO DO** Rental bikes, Trail nearby, Rental canoe or boat, Golf, Fishing, Museums, Art, Theatre, Entertainment, Attractions, Shopping, Cross-country skiing, Downhill skiing, Tennis, Swimming, Horseback riding, Beach, Birdwatching, **LANGUAGE** Eng., Fr., Sp., **PRICE** (2 per-sons) 50–150 **(check with hosts for pricing details)**

JASPER

De Rock Arch Place

(Rosina Bruni-Bossio)

823 Geikie St, Jasper, AB, T0E 1E0
www.bbcanada.com/3537.html
E-mail rosina@telusplanet.net

780-852-3616
Fax 780-852-3646

Pricing per night from $50 (low season) to $85/$95 (high). In-room tea and coffee. Private bathrooms. Prices based on dou-ble occupancy, with $10 extra for children and $20 per adult. Rooms are bright, clean and recently renovated. Microwave and fridge are provided. Room 1 sleeps three. Room 2 sleeps four. TVs in rooms.

ROOMS Ground floor, **Baths** Private, Ensuite, **Beds** Queen, Single or cots, Pullout sofa, **In Room** TV, **OTH-ERS** Urban, Open all year, **PAYMENT** Cash, Trvl's cheques, **AMENITIES** Fridge, Hot bev. bar, **THINGS TO DO** Rental bikes, Trail nearby, Golf, Fishing, Museums, Art, Theatre, Attractions, Wineries/Breweries, Shopping, Cross-country skiing, Downhill skiing, Tennis, Swimming, Horseback riding, Beach, **LAN-GUAGE** Eng., Italian, **PRICE** (2 persons) 50–90 **(check with hosts for pricing details)**

JASPER

Home Away From Home Bed and Breakfast

(Radmila and Michael Machalka)

916 Pyramid Lake Rd, Box 2114, Jasper, AB, T0E 1E0
www.jasperhome.com
E-mail info@jasperhome.com

780-852-5291
Fax 780-852-5291

We invite you to come and stay with us and experience the beauty and tranquility of the majestic Canadian Rockies. Our beautiful newly renovated cedar log house is nestled against the wilderness in a quiet area, only a short walk to downtown Jasper, the heart of Jasper National Park. Each guest room features an ensuite bathroom, TV, dining area and kitchenette. Continental breakfast, European style, in the comfort of your room. BBQ and picnic area. Tours, transportation and skiing packages available.

ROOMS Family suitesuite, Lower floor, Private entrance, **Baths** Ensuite, **Beds** Queen, Double, **Smoking** Outside, **In Room** Thermostat, TV, VCR/DVD, **OTHERS** Open all year, Handicapped access, **PAYMENT** Visa, Cheques accepted, Cash, Trvl's cheques, **BREAKFASTS** Continental, **AMENITIES** Central phone, Barbecue, Fridge, Hot bev. bar, **THINGS TO DO** Trail nearby, Golf, Fishing, Museums, Art, Theatre, Entertainment, Attractions, Shopping, Cross-country skiing, Tennis, Swimming, Horseback riding, Beach, Birdwatching, Antiquing, **LANGUAGE** Eng., Ger., Czech., **PRICE** (2 persons) 65–130 **(check with hosts for pricing details)**

JASPER

Mount Robson Mountain River Lodge

(Claudia and Curtis Pajunen)

Swift Current Creek Rd & Hwy 16, Mount Robson, AB, T0E 1E0
www.mtrobson.com
E-mail hosts@mtrobson.com

250-566-9899
Fax 250-566-9899
TFr 1-888-566-9899

Hidden below Mount Robson, the largest mountain in the Canadian Rockies. Experience unspoiled wilderness in a traditional B&B or self-catering cabins. Comfortable, affordable accommodations, a smart alternative to staying directly in Jasper. We offer our guests a tranquil setting away from the crowds of busy centres with a wide variety of activities conveniently located nearby. Just 5 minutes to Mount Robson and famous Berg Lake Trail, 1-hour drive to Jasper.

ROOMS Upper floor, **Baths** Private, **Beds** Queen, Twin, **Smoking** Outside, **OTHERS** Rural, Adult, Open all year, Additional meals, Pets in residence, Pets welcome, **PAYMENT** Visa, MC, Cash, Trvl's cheques, **BREAKFASTS** Full, **AMENITIES** Whirlpool, Fridge, Lounge, Patio, **THINGS TO DO** Rental bikes, Trail nearby, Rental canoe or boat, Golf, Fishing, Attractions, Cross-country skiing, Downhill skiing, Horseback riding, Birdwatching, **LANGUAGE** Eng., Ger., **PRICE** (2 persons) 85–135 **(check with hosts for pricing details)**

JASPER *(near Hinton)*

Old Entrance B 'n B Cabins

(Mary Luger and Carol Wray)

Bighorn Hwy 40 N, Box 6054, AB, T7V 1X4
www.oldentrance.ab.ca
E-mail oldentrance@yahoo.com

780-865-4760 TFr 1-866-817-9700

Our cozy cabins are nestled along the beautiful Athabasca River east of Jasper National Park. Our 60-acre riverside property provides quiet country vacation rental lodging or comfortable overnight accommodation. Open year round. Home-cooked breakfasts are served in our main house. From May to October we offer teepee camping and guided horseback trail riding. For guests travelling with their own horses we have overnight holding corrals (bed and bale). Swim, canoe, fish, ice skate or cross-country ski at William Switzer Provincial Park. Visit world famous Miette Hot Springs in Jasper Park a half-hour drive away and view mountain scenery and abundant wildlife.

ROOMS Family suite, Ground floor, Private entrance, **Baths** Private, **Beds** Queen, Double, Pullout sofa, **Smoking** Outside, **In Room** Thermostat, TV, Fireplace, VCR/DVD, **OTHERS** Rural, Open all year, Pets in residence, Pets welcome, **PAYMENT** Visa, MC, Cheques accepted, Cash, Trvl's cheques, **BREAKFASTS** Full, Home-baked, Self-catered, **AMENITIES** Barbecue, Kitchen, Fridge, Central Internet access, **THINGS TO DO** Trail nearby, Rental canoe or boat, Golf, Fishing, Museums, Attractions, Shopping, Cross-country skiing, Downhill skiing, Swimming, Horseback riding, Birdwatching, **LANGUAGE** Eng., **PRICE** (2 persons) 65–145 **(check with hosts for pricing details)**

JASPER

Raven House B&B

(Mair and Tony Jones)

801 Miette Ave, Box 2143, Jasper, AB, T0E 1E0
www.ravenbb.com
E-mail info@ravenbb.com

780-852-4011

Raven House B&B caters to couples seeking comfort and relaxation. Situated in a quiet residential area on a large, private corner lot surrounded by trees. A 5-minute walk from Jasper's centre (train/bus station, restaurants and shops) and hiking trails. The recently built home features very large upstairs guest suites with sitting area, ensuite bathroom and beautiful mountain views. Tastefully decorated, including local artwork, down duvets & deep soaker tubs. A healthy continental breakfast is served to the rooms.

ROOMS Upper floor, Private entrance, **Baths** Ensuite, **Beds** Queen, **OTHERS** Open all year, **PAYMENT** Cash, Trvl's cheques, **BREAKFASTS** Continental, **AMENITIES** Fridge, Central Internet access, **THINGS TO DO** Rental bikes, Trail nearby, Rental canoe or boat, Golf, Fishing, Museums, Attractions, Shopping, Cross-country skiing, Tennis, Swimming, Horseback riding, Beach, Birdwatching, **LANGUAGE** Eng., **PRICE** (2 persons) 100–140 **(check with hosts for pricing details)**

JASPER

The Rocky Mountain Retreat Bed & Breakfast

(Walter Dong)

400 Pyramid Ave, Box 354, Jasper, AB, T0E 1E0
www.bbcanada.com/rockymountainretreat
E-mail rockymr@telusplanet.net

780-852-4090

LACOMBE *(between Calgary and Edmonton)*

Rieky's Bed & Breakfast

(Harm and Rieky Stikker-Breemhaar)

RR #1, Lacombe, AB, T4L 2N1
www.countryvacation.ca
E-mail rieky@countryvacation.ca

403-782-1505
Fax 403-782-6710

A new home located in the heart of Jasper. We offer spectacular mountain views from the upper-level, cathedral-peaked ceiling rooms. A light continental breakfast is provided in our guest common room/dining area each morning. Parking is free so you can walk to and enjoy all of the town's amenities such as the Jasper Aquatic/Activity Centre across the street, hiking trails, restaurants and shops. As long-time residents of Jasper, we offer the perfect suggestions for your daily adventures in the park.

Cosy B&B on mixed farm 10 minutes from Lacombe and a 5-minute drive from Gull Lake; 20 minutes from Red Deer and Sylvan Lake. Enjoy the beautiful view from our deck and the gazebo on Gull Lake and the countryside. Nice bedrooms with queen beds and ensuite or private bathroom. Family room with TV/VCR, fridge and coffeemaker. Private guest entrance. Full Canadian breakfast with a European touch. Come and enjoy our Dutch/Canadian hospitality. You will be surprised! Closed Dec and Jan.

ROOMS Upper floor, Lower floor, Private entrance, **Baths** Private, Ensuite, **Beds** Queen, Twin, Single or cots, **Smoking** Outside, **In Room** TV, VCR/DVD, **OTHERS** Open all year, **PAYMENT** Cash, Trvl's cheques, **BREAKFASTS** Continental, **AMENITIES** Central TV, Fridge, Hot bev. bar, Patio, Central VCR/DVD, **THINGS TO DO** Rental bikes, Trail nearby, Museums, Theatre, Entertainment, Attractions, Shopping, Cross-country skiing, Downhill skiing, Tennis, Swimming, Horseback riding, **LANGUAGE** Eng., **PRICE** (2 persons) 65–90 **(check with hosts for pricing details)**

ROOMS Lower floor, Private entrance, **Baths** Private, Ensuite, **Beds** Queen, **Smoking** Outside, **OTHERS** Rural, Open all year, Pets in residence, **PAYMENT** Visa, MC, Cheques accepted, Cash, Trvl's cheques, **BREAKFASTS** Full, **AMENITIES** Central TV, Fridge, Hot bev. bar, Lounge, Central VCR/DVD, **THINGS TO DO** Fishing, Museums, Shopping, Swimming, Beach, Birdwatching, **LANGUAGE** Eng., Fr., Ger., Dutch, **PRICE** (2 persons) 90 **(check with hosts for pricing details)**

NANTON *(south of Calgary)*

HeartsEase Bed & Breakfast

(Sam and Rosemary Squire)

Box 460, Nanton, AB, T0L 1R0
www.canadianbandbguide.ca/bb.asp?ID=2399
E-mail roseptl@telusplanet.net

403-646-5789

A gracious older home on 1-1/2 acres in a small town near the Rockies, 1-1/2 hours south of Calgary on Hwy 2. Antique shops, restaurants, Lancaster Air Museum, large model railway display; summertime rodeos. Beautiful drive through mountains to Kananaskis and Banff, or through the foothills to Waterton International Park. Visit the Bar U Ranch Historical Site, Fort Macleod, Calgary, Lethbridge, Tyrrell Museum and Badlands. Christian hosts have been in the hospitality business for many years.

ROOMS Upper floor, Private entrance, **Baths** Shared with guest, **Beds** Queen, Double, Pullout sofa, **OTHERS** Urban, Open all year, **PAYMENT** Cash, Trvl's cheques, **BREAKFASTS** Full, Continental, **AMENITIES** Central TV, Central phone, Lounge, **THINGS TO DO** Golf, Fishing, Museums, Attractions, Shopping, Swimming, **LANGUAGE** Eng., **PRICE** (2 persons) 45–65 **(check with hosts for pricing details)**

PIGEON LAKE [AREA] *(southwest of Edmonton)*

Hidden Springs Retreat & Guesthouse

(Neil and Barbara White)

Box 102, Winfield, AB, T0C 2X0
www.hiddensprings.ca
E-mail neil@hiddensprings.ca

780-682-2480

Hidden Springs is a farm-based retreat and guest house located an hour southwest of Edmonton, Alberta. Hidden Springs grew out of a desire to welcome a wide variety of guests into a unique environment of refreshment and renewal – a Canadian version of the European guest house that invites city visitors and others to recapture the simpler things of life. Located 20 km west of Pigeon Lake in scenic parkland hill country just off Hwy 13 at RR #32. Follow the signs.

ROOMS Family suitesuite, Upper floor, Ground floor, Lower floor, Private entrance, **Baths** Private, **Beds** Queen, Double, Single or cots, Pullout sofa, **Air** Ceiling fans, **Smoking** Outside, **In Room** Thermostat, Fireplace, **OTHERS** Rural, Open all year, Handicapped access, **PAYMENT** Cheques accepted, Cash, Trvl's cheques, **BREAKFASTS** Continental, **AMENITIES** Sauna, Barbecue, Laundry, Kitchen, Fridge, Hot bev. bar, Lounge, Patio, **THINGS TO DO** Comp. bikes, Trail nearby, Comp. Canoe or boat, Golf, Fishing, Museums, Shopping, Cross-country skiing, Swimming, Horseback riding, Beach, Birdwatching, Antiquing, **LANGUAGE** Eng., **PRICE** (2 persons) 65–85 **(check with hosts for pricing details)**

PINE LAKE *(northeast of Calgary)*

Daisy House/Pierce Farms

(Sandra and Percy Pierce)

Box 151, Pine Lake, AB, T0M 1S0
www.canadianbandbguide.ca/bb.asp?ID=3800
E-mail prpierce@connect.ab.ca

403-886-2767
Fax 403-886-2241

Come and enjoy the peace and charm of our vintage farm home. Seperate accommodation allows you to wander the grounds or enjoy the panoramic hilltop view from the spacious deck, at your own leisure. A homemade treat and complementary refreshments await your arrival. Outside is a covered barbecue area and fire pit for your use. Also horseshoe pit and picnic tables. Camping and RV sites available as well as a self-contained cabin. Numerous recreational opportunities and golf course at nearby Pine Lake.

ROOMS Ground floor, Private entrance, **Baths** Private, Ensuite, **Beds** Queen, Twin, Pullout sofa, **Air** Central, Ceiling fans, **Smoking** Outside, **OTHERS** Rural, Open all year, Handicapped access, **PAYMENT** Cheques accepted, Cash, **BREAKFASTS** Full, **AMENITIES** Central TV, Barbecue, Fridge, Hot bev. bar, Lounge, Patio, Central VCR/DVD, **THINGS TO DO** Trail nearby, Golf, Fishing, Museums, Attractions, Cross-country skiing, Downhill skiing, Swimming, Beach, Birdwatching, **LANGUAGE** Eng., **PRICE** (2 persons) 60 **(check with hosts for pricing details)**

RAYMOND *(southeastern Alberta)*

Crystal Butterfly B&B

(Ralph and Maurine Heninger)

321 E 2nd N (Hwy 52), Raymond, AB, T0K 2S0
www.crystalbutterflybandb.com
E-mail crystalb@telusplanet.net

403-752-3781
Fax 403-752-0050
TFr 1-877-801-1553

This is a huge, modern, chalet-style home in Raymond, Alberta. It is on Hwy 52 connecting Hwys 4 and 5 and is directly across the street from the hospital. We specialize in a nutritious, country-style breakfast, featuring homemade breads, jams, etc. We provide quiet, clean, comfortable accommodations with wholesome food and conversation. This B&B is located an hour from the Montana border and is central to many Southern Alberta locations. Honeymoon/Family suite with Jacuzzi. Other rooms have shared baths with a Jacuzzi option.

ROOMS Family suitesuite, Ground floor, **Baths** Ensuite, **Beds** Queen, Twin, **Air** Central, **Smoking** Outside, **In Room** TV, **OTHERS** Open all year, Additional meals, **PAYMENT** Visa, MC, Cash, Trvl's cheques, **BREAKFASTS** Full, Home-baked, **AMENITIES** Barbecue, Patio, Central Internet access, **THINGS TO DO** Golf, Fishing, Museums, Art, Theatre, Swimming, **LANGUAGE** Eng., **PRICE** (2 persons) 80–100 **(check with hosts for pricing details)**

Red Deer *(between Calgary and Edmonton)*

Apples and Angels
(Laveryne Green)

288 Lampard Cr, Red Deer, AB, T4R 2W5
www.applesandangels.com/
E-mail stay@applesandangels.com

403-346-9394
TFr 1-877-346-9399

Apples and Angels B&B is located in the progressive city of Red Deer, known for its friendly folks and amazing trail system. Whether your travels here are for business or relaxation, Apples and Angels B&B has taken special care to accommodate your needs. The rooms are luxurious, the breakfasts lavish and on-site spa service is available. Laveryne and Brad look forward to hosting your stay.

ROOMS Ground floor, Lower floor, Private entrance, **Baths** Ensuite, **Beds** King, Queen, **Air** Central, **In Room** TV, Fireplace, Internet access, **OTHERS** Urban, Adult, Open all year, **PAYMENT** Visa, Cheques accepted, Cash, Trvl's cheques, **BREAKFASTS** Full, Home-baked, **AMENITIES** Central TV, Central phone, Laundry, Fridge, Hot bev. bar, Lounge, Patio, Central Internet access, Central VCR/DVD, **THINGS TO DO** Comp. bikes, Trail nearby, Golf, Fishing, Museums, Art, Theatre, Entertainment, Attractions, Shopping, Cross-country skiing, Tennis, Swimming, Horseback riding, Beach, **LANGUAGE** Eng., **PRICE** (2 persons) 85–149 **(check with hosts for pricing details)**

Red Deer

Dutchess Manor
(S.M. Uiterwyk)

4813 – 54 St, Red Deer, AB, T4N 2G5
www.dmanorretreat.com
E-mail dmretreat@shaw.ca

403-346-7776

Cozy 1905-built home located in old city centre. Hostess operates a full-service aesthetic salon on the premises. Spa packages available. Come to Dutchess Manor for a Dutch retreat. Coming from the south, proceed to city centre. Turn right on 55 St, right at 48th Ave and right on 54 St. From the north, take 67 St, turn off to city centre. Turn left on 55 St and proceed as above.

ROOMS Beds King, Twin, Single or cots, **Smoking** Outside, **OTHERS** Urban, Adult, Open all year, Additional meals, **PAYMENT** Visa, Cheques accepted, Cash, **BREAKFASTS** Full, Continental, **AMENITIES** Central TV, Central phone, Sauna, Barbecue, Laundry, Fridge, Hot bev. bar, Lounge, Patio, **THINGS TO DO** Comp. bikes, Trail nearby, Golf, Theatre, Entertainment, Attractions, Shopping, Cross-country skiing, Tennis, Swimming, Horseback riding, Beach, **LANGUAGE** Eng., Fr., Sp., Dutch, **PRICE** (2 persons) 80–80 **(check with hosts for pricing details)**

ROCKY MOUNTAIN HOUSE
(between Calgary and Edmonton)

Fox Ridge Bed and Breakfast

(Agnes and Del Rieder)

3814 – 53rd Ave, Rocky Mountain House, AB, T4T 1V4
www.bbalberta.com/foxridge
E-mail foxridge@telusplanet.net

403-844-4326

Nestled in the trees, 1 km from down-town, ours is a quiet, new home with comfy beds, ensuites, private entrance and social room. Enjoy a home-cooked breakfast. Relax or take part in David Thompson Country recreation – hiking, skiing, trails, swimming and Horseback riding. A national historic site. Museums. You are welcome in our safe neighbour-hood. There is a playground nearby.

ROOMS Family suitesuite, Ground floor, Lower floor, Private entrance, **Baths** Ensuite, **Beds** Queen, Double, Single or cots, **Air** Central, In rooms, **Smoking** Outside, **OTHERS** Urban, Open all year, **PAYMENT** Visa, MC, Cash, Trvl's cheques, **BREAKFASTS** Full, Continental, Home-baked, **AMENITIES** Central TV, Lounge, Central VCR/DVD, **THINGS TO DO** Comp. bikes, Trail nearby, Golf, Fishing, Museums, Theatre, Entertainment, Attractions, Shopping, Cross-country skiing, Tennis, Swimming, Horseback riding, Beach, Antiquing, **LAN-GUAGE** Eng., **PRICE** (2 persons) 65–90 **(check with hosts for pricing details)**

VILNA *(northeast of Edmonton)*

Country Garden B&B

(Yvette and Robert Lavoie)

Box 545, Vilna, AB, T0A 3L0
www.canadianbandbguide.ca/bb.asp?ID=2021

780-636-2029

Phone for directions. Full home-baked breakfast. Rural bungalow, acreage, deck, sunroom, quiet. One single, one double, two queen (main floor). Private bath, kitchen and laundry facilities, designated smoking area. French Smokey Lake (world pumpkin weigh-off in Oct), great hunting and fishing areas. Warm welcome in spa-cious log-style home. Relax in the sun-room off the kitchen or on the deck. Hostess is well known for her cooking and baking, and can usually be found in the kitchen.

ROOMS Ground floor, **Baths** Private, **Beds** Queen, Twin, Single or cots, **Smoking** Outside, **In Room** TV, **OTHERS** Rural, Open all year, **PAYMENT** Cheques accepted, Cash, **BREAKFASTS** Full, Home-baked, **AMENITIES** Central TV, Central phone, **THINGS TO DO** Attractions, **LANGUAGE** Eng., Fr., **PRICE** (2 persons) 40–65 **(check with hosts for pricing details)**

WAINWRIGHT *(southeast of Edmonton)*

Mackenzie House Bed & Breakfast

(Annette and Dan Ermel)

1018 – 4th Ave, Wainwright, AB, T9W 1H2
www.canadianbandbguide.ca/bb.asp?ID=3802
E-mail bb@mackenziehouse.ab.ca

780-842-5867
Fax 780-842-6138
TFr 1-877-842-6108

A few minutes walk from many shops and amenities, the Mackenzie House is a totally renovated 2 1/2-storey historic heritage home with a colourful history in a quiet neighbourhood, just a block off Main St. (If you are interested, we can tell you over a cup of tea or coffee in our formal sitting room.) Three spacious guest rooms upstairs, individually decorated for an atmosphere of charm and tranquility, containing all the necessary amenities to make your stay a pleasant one.

ROOMS Upper floor, **Baths** Ensuite, **Beds** King, Queen, **Air** Central, **Smoking** Outside, **In Room** Phone, TV, Internet access, VCR/DVD, **OTHERS** Urban, Adult, Open all year, **PAYMENT** Visa, MC, Cheques accepted, Cash, Trvl's cheques, **BREAKFASTS** Full, Continental, Home-baked, **AMENITIES** Fridge, Hot bev. bar, **THINGS TO DO** Trail nearby, Golf, Fishing, Museums, Theatre, Entertainment, Attractions, Shopping, Tennis, Swimming, Beach, Birdwatching, **LANGUAGE** Eng., **PRICE** (2 persons) 85–90 **(check with hosts for pricing details)**

WESTLOCK *(north of Edmonton)*

Willow Lane B&B

(Dave and Carol Sterling)

Box 6062, Westlock, AB, T7P 2P7
www.bbalberta.com/willowlane
E-mail carolsterling@west-teq.net

780-349-5797

Willow Lane B&B is located 3 km south and 1/4 km west of Westlock on Hwy 44. Come to relax and enjoy the serenity of country life. We provide old-fashioned country hospitality in a spacious new home. Self-contained suite with kitchen facilities on request. (Suite $180/night – sleeps six.) Second phone: 780-349-0205. Pets are welcome only in heated shop.

ROOMS Family suitesuite, Lower floor, Private entrance, **Baths** Private, Shared with guest, **Beds** Queen, Twin, Pullout sofa, **Air** Central, Ceiling fans, **Smoking** Outside, **OTHERS** Rural, Open all year, Pets welcome, **PAYMENT** Cheques accepted, Cash, Trvl's cheques, **BREAKFASTS** Full, Continental, Home-baked, **AMENITIES** Central TV, Central phone, Barbecue, Kitchen, Fridge, Hot bev. bar, Lounge, Patio, Central VCR/DVD, **THINGS TO DO** Trail nearby, Golf, Fishing, Museums, Entertainment, Attractions, Shopping, Cross-country skiing, Swimming, **LANGUAGE** Eng., **PRICE** (2 persons) 65–80 **(check with hosts for pricing details)**

WETASKIWIN *(south of Edmonton)*

Country Pleasures Bed & Breakfast

(Hans and Dana Ryffel)

5712 – 45 Ave, Wetaskiwin, AB, T9A 0G7
www.country-pleasures-bb.com
E-mail relax@country-pleasures-bb.com

780-352-4335

Country Pleasures Bed & Breakfast offers visitors all the quiet charm of a country home within the city limits of Wetaskiwin, a small town located in central Alberta, midway between Edmonton and Red Deer. The word is spreading that Country Pleasures B&B is the perfect place for a peaceful getaway. The beautifully decorated rooms with ensuite bath and fireplace and the natural surroundings with five acres of lush green lawn, colourful flowers and mature trees guarantee a quiet, private experience.

ROOMS Family suite, Upper floor, Ground floor, Private entrance, **Baths** Ensuite, **Beds** Queen, Single or cots, Pullout sofa, **Smoking** Outside, **In Room** Fireplace, **OTHERS** Rural, Open all year, **PAYMENT** Visa, MC, Cash, Trvl's cheques, **BREAKFASTS** Full, Home-baked, **AMENITIES** Central phone, Barbecue, Fridge, Hot bev. bar, Lounge, Patio, **THINGS TO DO** Comp. bikes, Trail nearby, Golf, Museums, Attractions, Shopping, Tennis, Swimming, **LANGUAGE** Eng., Fr., Ger., **PRICE** (2 persons) 89–134 **(check with hosts for pricing details)**

SASKATCHEWAN

CANADIAN BED AND BREAKFAST GUIDE

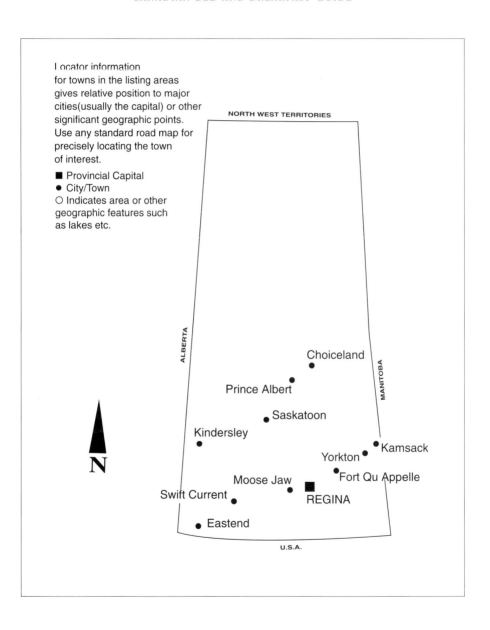

Locator information
for towns in the listing areas
gives relative position to major
cities(usually the capital) or other
significant geographic points.
Use any standard road map for
precisely locating the town
of interest.

■ Provincial Capital
● City/Town
○ Indicates area or other
geographic features such
as lakes etc.

NORTH WEST TERRITORIES

ALBERTA

MANITOBA

N

Choiceland

Prince Albert

Saskatoon

Kindersley

Kamsack

Yorkton

Fort Qu Appelle

Moose Jaw

Swift Current

REGINA

Eastend

U.S.A.

Choiceland
(northeast of Saskatoon)

Bear Paw Lodge

(Annette Smith)

Box 70, Choiceland, SK, S0J 0M0
www.bearpawlodge.ca
E-mail bearpawlodge@sasktel.net

306-428-2032

Welcome to your northern Saskatchewan getaway destination. We take pride in our deluxe accommodations and homey atmosphere. There are three rooms on the lower level of our lodge with plenty of private space for you. Take time to browse through our large yard and flowerbeds. Breakfast is served at your convenience with hearty home-cooked meals. Check out our Web site for more info. Find out why we say, "No one leaves a stranger."

ROOMS Ground floor, Private entrance, **Baths** Ensuite, Shared with guest, **Beds** Queen, Twin, **Smoking** Outside, **OTHERS** Rural, Open all year, Handicapped access, Additional meals, **PAYMENT** Cheques accepted, Cash, **BREAKFASTS** Full, Home-baked, **AMENITIES** Central TV, Central phone, Barbecue, Laundry, Kitchen, Fridge, Hot bev. bar, Lounge, Patio, Central VCR/DVD, **THINGS TO DO** Comp. bikes, Comp. Canoe or boat, Golf, Fishing, Attractions, Downhill skiing, Beach, **LANGUAGE** Eng., **PRICE** (2 persons) 60–80 **(check with hosts for pricing details)**

Eastend *(southwest of Regina)*

Northhill Cottage

(M. Fitch)

Box 425, 1 Northhill Cres, Eastend, SK, S0N 0T0
www.northhillcottage.com
E-mail northhill@sasktel.net

306-295-3536

Northhill Cottage offers a unique vacation getaway just a few minutes walk from Eastend's new T-Rex Center. Located on an acreage property above the Frenchman River Valley, under large shade trees with a panoramic view of the surrounding area, Northhill Cottage is a perfect retreat for a couple or family. The Cottage is the last house on the road to the T-Rex Center, and is within easy walking distance of local stores, the Streambank Golf Course and the Eastend swimming pool. Cell phone 306-295-7438.

ROOMS Family suite, Ground floor, Private entrance, **Baths** Private, **Beds** Queen, Double, Pullout sofa, **Smoking** Outside, **In Room** Thermostat, TV, **OTHERS** Rural, Seasonal, Pets welcome, **PAYMENT** Cash, Trvl's cheques, **BREAKFASTS** Continental, Self-catered, **AMENITIES** Central TV, Barbecue, Kitchen, Fridge, **THINGS TO DO** Comp. bikes, Trail nearby, Comp. Canoe or boat, Golf, Fishing, Museums, Art, Attractions, Swimming, Birdwatching, **LANGUAGE** Eng., **PRICE** (2 persons) 80 **(check with hosts for pricing details)**

FORT QU'APPELLE *(northeast of Regina)*

B-Say-Tah Point B&B

(Mike Maier and Eileen Lewko)

86 Grove St, Resort Village of B-Say-Tah, SK, S0G 1S0
www.canadianbandbguide.ca/bb.asp?ID=2916
E-mail eileen.lewko@sasktel.net

306-332-5988

Situated in the beautiful Qu'Appelle Valley just 20 minutes north of the #1 Hwy. B-Say-Tah Point is a resort village situated just 3 miles west of the town of Fort Qu'Appelle and 3 miles east of Echo Valley Provincial Park on Hwy 210. The entire bottom floor is reserved for guests, two bedrooms with private baths. Relax in your own sitting room. Shared kitchen. Beautiful backyard patio with hot tub and fire pit. Decorated with a nautical and garden theme. Close to beach and boat launch. Boat rides available. Evening dining may be arranged. We have a New Year's celebration special. Gift certificates available.

ROOMS Ground floor, Private entrance, **Baths** Private, **Beds** Queen, **Air** Central, **Smoking** Outside, **In Room** TV, **OTHERS** Adult, Open all year, Pets in residence, **PAYMENT** Visa, MC, Cash, Trvl's cheques, **BREAKFASTS** Full, Continental, Self-catered, **AMENITIES** Central phone, Barbecue, Kitchen, Fridge, Hot bev. bar, Lounge, Patio, **THINGS TO DO** Rental bikes, Trail nearby, Golf, Fishing, Art, Shopping, Cross-country skiing, Tennis, Swimming, Beach, **LANGUAGE** Eng., **PRICE** (2 persons) 85–110 **(check with hosts for pricing details)**

KAMSACK *(northeast of Regina)*

Border Mountain Country Bed and Breakfast

(Don and Marleen Brock)

Box 1233, Kamsack, SK, S0A 1S0
www.bbcanada.com/bordermountaincountry
E-mail donaldbrock@hotmail.com

306-542-3072
Fax 306-542-3072

From Kamsack travel 7 km east and 3 km south on Hwy 5, 5 km east on Side Rd. Quiet, secluded, scenic valley. Bird/animal viewing, hunting (big game, water fowl). Pets, farm animals including Arabian horses. Provincial park, ski areas, National Doukhobour Heritage Village, restaurants, Trans-Canada Trail. Property adjoins public accessible wildlife lands and gorgeous Duck Mountain Park (aspen forest gives way to pine). "Empty Nester" hosts, familiar with surrounding area, enjoy outdoors. In-home B&B, cabin, full-service camping.

ROOMS Family suite, Lower floor, Private entrance, **Baths** Private, Shared with guest, **Beds** King, Queen, Twin, Single or cots, **Smoking** Outside, **OTHERS** Rural, Open all year, Additional meals, Pets in residence, Pets welcome, **PAYMENT** MC, Cheques accepted, Cash, Trvl's cheques, **BREAKFASTS** Full, Continental, Home-baked, **AMENITIES** Central TV, Central phone, Barbecue, Laundry, Kitchen, Fridge, Hot bev. bar, Lounge, Patio, Central Internet access, Central VCR/DVD, **THINGS TO DO** Comp. bikes, Trail nearby, Rental canoe or boat, Golf, Fishing, Museums, Attractions, Shopping, Cross-country skiing, Downhill skiing, Tennis, Swimming, Horseback riding, Beach, Birdwatching, Antiquing, **LANGUAGE** Eng., **PRICE** (2 persons) 52–52 **(check with hosts for pricing details)**

KINDERSLEY *(southwest of Saskatoon)*

Whyley's Bed and Breakfast
(Don and Eleanor Whyley)

Box 754, Kindersley, SK, S0L 1S0
www.canadianbandbguide.ca/bb.asp?ID=3641
E-mail dewhyley@sasktel.net

306-463-4381

Cosy 50s country cottage in the heart of Saskatchewan's wheat land, overlooking the Fairmount coulee and marsh. Located 13.5 km southwest of Kindersley on the Fairmount Rd. Follow all the curves, last farm site on the right, past the old Fairmount townsite. Open May 1 to December 31. Self-contained modern cottage with kitchenette, accommodates six to eight persons on two levels. Spacious treed yard, fire pit, hiking, tipi rings, wildlife viewing, birdwatching, Horseback riding, bed and bale.

ROOMS Ground floor, Lower floor, Private entrance, **Baths** Private, **Beds** Double, Single or cots, Pullout sofa, **Air** Central, **Smoking** Outside, **In Room** Thermostat, Phone, TV, VCR/DVD, **OTHERS** Rural, Seasonal, Pets welcome, **PAYMENT** Visa, Cheques accepted, Cash, Trvl's cheques, **BREAKFASTS** Continental, Self-catered, **AMENITIES** Central TV, Central phone, Barbecue, Laundry, Kitchen, Fridge, Patio, Central VCR/DVD, **THINGS TO DO** Trail nearby, Golf, Museums, Theatre, Attractions, Shopping, Swimming, Horseback riding, Birdwatching, **LAN-GUAGE** Eng., **PRICE** (2 persons) 59–65 **(check with hosts for pricing details)**

MOOSE JAW *(west of Regina)*

Prairie Harbour Bed and Breakfast
(Laurie and Russ Lunde)

216 Cottonwood St, Caronport, SK, S0H 0S0
www.prairieharbour.ca
E-mail prairieharbour@sasktel.net

306-756-2704
Fax 306-756-2704
TFr 1-866-444-2704

Experience Prairie Harbour Bed and Breakfast, a charming "Cape Cod" home on the prairies. Located on #1 Hwy –12 minutes west of Moose Jaw halfway between Calgary and Winnipeg. Professionally prepared breakfasts by the winner of the Canadian Hospitality Foundation Culinary Excellence Award 2001. Formal dining/living room, family room with fireplace, home theatre room available to guests. Beautifully decorated bedrooms have dormers with window seats. Welcoming garden areas. Internet access. Boardroom for meetings.

ROOMS Upper floor, Lower floor, **Baths** Private, Shared with guest, **Beds** Queen, Twin, **Air** Central, **Smoking** Outside, **In Room** TV, **OTHERS** Rural, Open all year, **PAYMENT** Visa, MC, Cheques accepted, Cash, Trvl's cheques, **BREAKFASTS** Full, Continental, Home-baked, **AMENITIES** Central phone, Fridge, Hot bev. bar, Lounge, Patio, **THINGS TO DO** Comp. bikes, Golf, Museums, Art, Theatre, Entertainment, Attractions, Shopping, Tennis, Swimming, Beach, **LANGUAGE** Eng., **PRICE** (2 persons) 60–75 **(check with hosts for pricing details)**

Moose Jaw

Wakamow Heights Bed and Breakfast

(Nick and Corrie Hordyk)

690 Aldersgate St, Moose Jaw, SK, S6H 6A4
www.wakamowheights.com
E-mail wakamowheights@sasktel.net

306-693-9963

A wonderful, spacious historic home in a quiet park-like setting on the outskirts of Moose Jaw. We are close to all the attractions that Moose Jaw offers. We offer a great breakfast menu. Bathrooms have been updated and most are private.

ROOMS Family suite, Upper floor, **Baths** Private, Ensuite, Shared with guest, **Beds** Queen, Twin, Single or cots, **Air** In rooms, **In Room** TV, **OTHERS** Open all year, **PAYMENT** Visa, MC, Diners, Cash, Trvl's cheques, **BREAKFASTS** Full, Home-baked, **AMENITIES** Central phone, Whirlpool, Laundry, **THINGS TO DO** Trail nearby, Golf, Museums, Art, Attractions, **LANGUAGE** Eng., Dutch, **PRICE** (2 persons) 55–75 **(check with hosts for pricing details)**

Prince Albert *(northeast of Saskatoon)*

Hillcrest Inn

(Morris and Dalelene Yelland)

133 20th St W, Prince Albert, SK, S6V 4G1
www.hillcrestinn.ca
E-mail Info@hillcrestinn.ca

306-763-4113
Fax 306-763-4743
TFr 1-866-763-4113

Award-winning, sensibly priced elegance in a newly renovated character home. Private entrance. Five themed bedrooms. Queen beds, fresh fruit and flowers, bottled spring water. Library/guest lounge with complimentary refreshments. Balcony overlooks city. Wireless Internet. Generous breakfasts. Off-street plug-in parking. Resident cat. Bus and airport pickup. Accredited accommodation. In Prince Albert, from south, right on 20th St at crest of hill. From north, left at 22nd St lights, left at 1st Ave W, left at 20th St W.

ROOMS Upper floor, Private entrance, **Baths** Ensuite, **Beds** Queen, **Air** In rooms, **Smoking** Outside, **In Room** Phone, TV, Internet access, **OTHERS** Urban, Adult, Open all year, Pets in residence, **PAYMENT** Visa, MC, Cheques accepted, Cash, Trvl's cheques, **BREAKFASTS** Full, Home-baked, **AMENITIES** Central TV, Central phone, Fridge, Hot bev. bar, Lounge, Patio, Central Internet access, **THINGS TO DO** Trail nearby, Golf, Museums, Art, Theatre, Attractions, Shopping, Cross-country skiing, Tennis, Swimming, Birdwatching, **LANGUAGE** Eng., **PRICE** (2 persons) 69–84 **(check with hosts for pricing details)**

SASKATOON *(south-central SK)*

Meadowgreen Cottage Bed & Breakfast

(Elva Kenney and Stan Hansen)

327 Ottawa Ave S, Saskatoon, SK, S7M 3L6
www.bbcanada.com/meadowgreencottage
E-mail meadowcottage@sasktel.net

306-382-2924
Fax 306-668-8026

Charming executive-sized suite or cozy garden room. Suite offers 800 sq. ft. of totally private accommodation consisting of four lovely sunlit rooms: Queen bedroom, living room with comfortable sofa bed, private four-piece bath and full kitchen. Popular for long or short stays. Garden Room has oak day bed and optional trundle bed and shared bathroom. Air conditioned, CD players, cozy robes and slippers, plug-in parking. Immaculately clean, tastefully decorated, SCVA Accredited Accommodation.

ROOMS Family suite, Private entrance, **Baths** Ensuite, Shared with hosts, **Beds** Queen, Single or cots, Pullout sofa, **Air** Central, **In Room** Phone, TV, **OTHERS** Urban, Adult, Open all year, **PAYMENT** Visa, MC, Diners, Amex, Cash, Trvl's cheques, **BREAKFASTS** Full, Continental, Home-baked, Self-catered, **AMENITIES** Barbecue, Laundry, Kitchen, Patio, **THINGS TO DO** Golf, Museums, Art, Theatre, Entertainment, Attractions, Shopping, Tennis, Swimming, **LANGUAGE** Eng., **PRICE** (2 persons) 55–79 **(check with hosts for pricing details)**

SASKATOON

Riverview Bed and Breakfast

(Lorne and Bernadette Mysko)

1036 Spadina Cres E, Saskatoon, SK, S7K 3H7
www.bbcanada.com/7163.html
E-mail riverviewb.b@sasktel.net

306-931-0817
Fax 306-975-1186

Imagine ... country elegance combined with prairie hospitality, breakfast with a view of the South Saskatchewan River. Adjacent to Meewasin Valley trails through beautifully landscaped parks and natural areas, 15-minute walk to downtown shopping and restaurants. Furnished studio and one-bedroom suite also available. Close to the US, City Hospital, art galleries, fishing pier, Shearwater River Tours, Shakespeare on the Saskatchewan, white pelican nesting grounds and Canadian beaver habitat.

ROOMS Family suite, Upper floor, Lower floor, Private entrance, **Baths** Private, Ensuite, **Beds** Queen, Double, Single or cots, **Air** Central, **Smoking** Outside, **In Room** Thermostat, Phone, TV, Internet access, VCR/DVD, **OTHERS** Urban, Adult, Open all year, Pets in residence, **PAYMENT** Visa, MC, Cheques accepted, Cash, Trvl's cheques, **BREAKFASTS** Full, Continental, Home-baked, Self-catered, **AMENITIES** Central phone, Laundry, Kitchen, Fridge, Lounge, Patio, Central Internet access, **THINGS TO DO** Comp. bikes, Trail nearby, Golf, Fishing, Museums, Art, Theatre, Entertainment, Attractions, Shopping, Cross-country skiing, Tennis, Birdwatching, Antiquing, **LANGUAGE** Eng., **PRICE** (2 persons) 75–95 **(check with hosts for pricing details)**

SWIFT CURRENT *(West of Regina)*

Green Hectares Bed & Breakfast

(David and Esther Green)

Waker Rd (Box 2039), Swift Current, SK, S9H 4M7
www.sasktourism.com/greenhectares
E-mail greenhectares@sasktel.net

306-773-7632
Fax 306-773-7635

Friendly working cattle ranch nestled in the trees along the creek. Enjoy country life less than 10 minutes from shopping, museum, library, golf courses and biking/hiking trails, 35 minutes from Saskatchewan Landing Provincial Park. Ensuite and shared baths, A/C, no smoking or pets inside. Swift Current Petroglyph onsite. Our "Red Barn" has a wraparound deck, hot tub and fire pit. Ranch house offers sitting rooms with fireplace and TV. Enjoy ranch breakfasts and warm hospitality. On Waker Rd 0.5 km from Swift Current. From Hwy 1, take 22nd Ave NE, go north on Hwy 4 to first intersection, turn east (Saskatchewan Dr/Waker Rd) and follow signs.

ROOMS Upper floor, Ground floor, Private entrance, **Baths** Private, Ensuite, Shared with guest, **Beds** Queen, Double, Twin, Single or cots, Pullout sofa, **Air** Central, **Smoking** Outside, **OTHERS** Rural, Open all year, Pets in residence, Pets welcome, **PAYMENT** Cheques accepted, Cash, Trvl's cheques, **BREAKFASTS** Full, Continental, **AMENITIES** Central TV, Central phone, Whirlpool, Barbecue, **THINGS TO DO** Trail nearby, Golf, Fishing, Museums, Art, Attractions, Shopping, Beach, Birdwatching, **LANGUAGE** Eng., Dutch, **PRICE** (2 persons) 65–105 **(check with hosts for pricing details)**

YORKTON *(northeast of Regina)*

Patrick Place

(Gerry and Karen)

88-5th Ave N, Yorkton, SK, S3N 0Z1
www.patrickplace.com
E-mail patrickplace@sasktel.net

306-621-8656
Fax 306-786-8888

Enjoy the hospitality of Yorkton in the luxury, peace and serenity of a gracious heritage home overlooking Shaw Park and within walking distance of several restaurants. All four rooms have their own ensuite bathroom, TV/VCR, and complimentary coffee and tea. One room has a whirlpool tub. A two-room suite is available, ideal for families with children or two couples. Full breakfast is served in the dining room. Please go to our Web site for more information.

ROOMS Family suite, Upper floor, **Baths** Ensuite, **Beds** Queen, Double, Twin, **Air** In rooms, **Smoking** Outside, **In Room** Phone, TV, Internet access, VCR/DVD, **OTHERS** Urban, Open all year, **PAYMENT** Visa, MC, Cheques accepted, Cash, Trvl's cheques, **BREAKFASTS** Full, Home-baked, **AMENITIES** Central phone, Whirlpool, Lounge, Patio, **THINGS TO DO** Comp. bikes, Trail nearby, Golf, Fishing, Museums, Art, Entertainment, Attractions, Shopping, Cross-country skiing, Tennis, Swimming, Beach, Birdwatching, **LANGUAGE** Eng., **PRICE** (2 persons) 70–120 **(check with hosts for pricing details)**

Manitoba

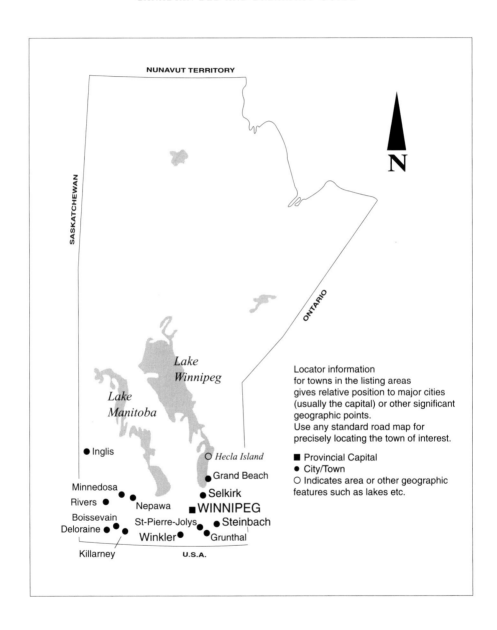

NUNAVUT TERRITORY

SASKATCHEWAN

ONTARIO

N

Lake Winnipeg

Lake Manitoba

● Inglis

○ *Hecla Island*

● Grand Beach

Minnedosa ●

Rivers ●   ● Nepawa

● Selkirk

■ WINNIPEG

Boissevain ●
Deloraine ● ●   St-Pierre-Jolys ●   ● Steinbach

Winkler ●   ● Grunthal

Killarney   U.S.A.

Locator information
for towns in the listing areas
gives relative position to major cities
(usually the capital) or other significant
geographic points.
Use any standard road map for
precisely locating the town of interest.

■ Provincial Capital
● City/Town
○ Indicates area or other geographic
features such as lakes etc.

Boissevain *(west of Winnipeg)*

Dueck's Cedar Chalet

(Henry and Hilda Dueck)

Box 370, Boissevain, MB, R0K 0E0
www.dueckscedarchalet.com
E-mail h2d@mts.net

204-534-6019
Fax 204-534-6939

A *Canada Select* 4-star B&B. Come and see how a wooden granary has been restored to an elegant "Cedar Lodge." Take the romantic getaway you've always wanted! Relax in the "Jacuzzi Suite" in the large ensuite Jacuzzi and soak your worries away. The music lovers will enjoy the ensuite piano in the "Southview Suite." You'll love the fresh air on your private deck, along with peace, tranquility and gorgeous sunsets only country living can bring. We are minutes away from major attractions.

ROOMS Family suite, Ground floor, Private entrance, **Baths** Private, Ensuite, **Beds** Queen, Twin, Single or cots, Pullout sofa, **Air** Central, **Smoking** Outside, **In Room** Thermostat, Phone, TV, Fireplace, **OTHERS** Rural, Open all year, Handicapped access, Additional meals, **PAYMENT** Visa, MC, Cheques accepted, Cash, Trvl's cheques, **BREAKFASTS** Full, Home-baked, **AMENITIES** Barbecue, Laundry, Fridge, Hot bev. bar, Patio, **THINGS TO DO** Golf, Fishing, Museums, Art, Theatre, Entertainment, Attractions, Shopping, Swimming, Beach, **LANGUAGE** Eng., Ger., **PRICE** (2 persons) 75–110 **(check with hosts for pricing details)**

Boissevain

Rowanoak Guesthouse

(Barney and Tracy Parlee)

Box 774, Boissevain, MB, R0K 0E0
www.rowanoakguesthouse.com
E-mail drydvale@mts.net

204-534-6452

According to Celtic legend, the Rowan tree symbolizes beauty, peace and a place of sanctuary. These things we offer to our guests. Located 8 miles south of Boissevain, within a 15 minute drive of the Turtle Mountain Provincial Parks, International Peace Gardens and Whitewater Lake.

ROOMS Family suite, Upper floor, Lower floor, Private entrance, **Baths** Private, **Beds** Queen, Double, Pullout sofa, **Air** Central, Ceiling fans, **Smoking** Outside, **In Room** Thermostat, VCR/DVD, **OTHERS** Rural, Open all year, Additional meals, Pets in residence, **PAYMENT** MC, Cash, Trvl's cheques, **BREAKFASTS** Home-baked, Self-catered, **AMENITIES** Whirlpool, Barbecue, Kitchen, Fridge, Patio, Central VCR/DVD, **THINGS TO DO** Trail nearby, Fishing, Museums, Art, Entertainment, Attractions, Shopping, Cross-country skiing, Swimming, Horseback riding, Birdwatching, Antiquing, **LANGUAGE** Eng., **PRICE** (2 persons) 75 **(check with hosts for pricing details)**

BOISSEVAIN

Walkinshaw Place
(Peter and Linda Albrecht)

Box 833, Boissevain, MB, R0K 0E0
www.walkinshawplace.net
E-mail walkinshawplace@mts.net

204-534-6979
Fax 204-534-3245
TFr 1-888-739-2579

We invite you to relax in a peaceful country setting in the scenic Turtle Mountains of Manitoba. Restful lodging is provided in our guesthouse, a 1907 Victorian farmhouse restored as an intriguing combination of a quaint country inn and a casual bed and breakfast, featuring four spacious guest rooms tastefully decorated with antiques and old-fashioned country charm. Nearby attractions: Turtle Mountain Provincial Park, International Peace Garden, Whitewater Lake Birding, Outdoor Murals in Boissevain.

ROOMS Family suite, Upper floor, **Baths** Private, Ensuite, **Beds** Queen, Double, Twin, Single or cots, Pullout sofa, **Air** Central, **Smoking** Outside, **In Room** TV, VCR/DVD, **OTHERS** Rural, Open all year, **PAYMENT** Visa, MC, Direct debit, Cash, **BREAKFASTS** Full, Home-baked, **AMENITIES** Central phone, Whirlpool, Hot bev. bar, Lounge, Patio, **THINGS TO DO** Trail nearby, Golf, Fishing, Museums, Art, Attractions, Shopping, Cross-country skiing, Swimming, Beach, Birdwatching, **LANGUAGE** Eng., **PRICE** (2 persons) 79 **(check with hosts for pricing details)**

DELORAINE *(west of Winnipeg)*

Country Garden Inn
(Jim and Peg Sanders)

309 Morton Ave, Box 12, Deloraine, MB, R0M 0M0
www.canadianbandbguide.ca/bb.asp?ID=3698
E-mail sandersp@mts.net

204-747-3133

Like a visit to Grandma's house when you visit our century guest home furnished with antiques. Two guest bedrooms, each with a comfy double bed and one large family room with two double beds. Two full bathrooms, central air-conditioning, TV-DVD. Hot tub and laundry facilities on request. Full breakfast each morning in our downstairs tea room. Close to hospital, stores, golf course, lake, Downhill skiing, snowmobile trails, International Peace Garden and lots of local history. Ask about our holiday packages.

ROOMS Family suite, Upper floor, Ground floor, Private entrance, **Baths** Shared with guest, **Beds** Double, Single or cots, **Air** Central, Ceiling fans, **Smoking** Outside, **OTHERS** Babysitting, Urban, Open all year, Additional meals, **PAYMENT** Visa, MC, Cash, Trvl's cheques, **BREAKFASTS** Full, Continental, Home-baked, Self-catered, **AMENITIES** Central TV, Central phone, Whirlpool, Barbecue, Laundry, Kitchen, Fridge, Hot bev. bar, Lounge, Patio, Central VCR/DVD, **THINGS TO DO** Golf, Fishing, Museums, Theatre, Shopping, Downhill skiing, Swimming, Beach, Birdwatching, Antiquing, **LANGUAGE** Eng., **PRICE** (2 persons) 65–80 **(check with hosts for pricing details)**

GRAND BEACH *(north of Winnipeg)*

Inn Among The Oaks

(Ken and Luise Avery)

Box 40, 65 Pinehurst Ave, Grand Marais, MB, R0E 0T0
www.bedandbreakfast.mb.ca
E-mail averyinn@granite.mb.ca

204-754-8109
Fax 204-754-3613

Our B&B home, built of cedar and local
pine, is located in Lake Winnipeg Cottage
Country close to Manitoba's premiere
beaches, including Grand Beach
Provincial Park. Soft white sand dunes,
hiking, nature and abundant wildlife,
cross country ski trails are yours to enjoy.
Then hide yourself "Inn" among oaks and
bushes with the heated outdoor pool,
relaxing indoor hot tub, hearty full breakfasts, and feel comfortably at home
away from home! Take Hwy 59 north of
Winnipeg and Hwy 12 to Grand Beach/
Grand Marais.

ROOMS Upper floor, Ground floor, Private entrance,
Baths Shared with guest, **Beds** Queen, Single or cots,
Air In rooms, Ceiling fans, **Smoking** Outside, **In Room**
Thermostat, **OTHERS** Rural, Open all year, **PAYMENT**
Visa, MC, Amex, Cash, Trvl's cheques, **BREAKFASTS**
Full, **AMENITIES** Central TV, Central phone, Swimming
pool, Whirlpool, Barbecue, Kitchen, Fridge, Lounge,
Patio, Central VCR/DVD, **THINGS TO DO** Comp. bikes,
Trail nearby, Rental canoe or boat, Golf, Fishing,
Entertainment, Attractions, Shopping, Cross-country
skiing, Tennis, Swimming, Beach, Birdwatching, **LAN-
GUAGE** Eng., Fr., Ger., **PRICE** (2 persons) 65–75 **(check
with hosts for pricing details)**

GRUNTHAL *(south of Winnipeg)*

Rainbow Ridge Ranch –
Bale, Bed & Breakfast

(Dan and Della Fehr)

77 Warkentine Rd, Grunthal, MB, R0A 0R0
www.rainbowridgeranch.com
E-mail info@rainbowridgeranch.com

204-434-6177
Fax 204-434-9431
TFr 1-888-305-0259

Rainbow Ridge Ranch is situated on 120
acres with 1/2 mile of property along
Joubert Creek. We have a cozy log cabin,
lots of nature walking trails and just a
peaceful, natural setting that will help
you relax, refresh and rejuvinate. From
Winnipeg go south on Hwy 59, 3 miles
south of St. Pierre. Turn left (east) on
Depape Rd and go 4 1/2 miles. Our sign
will be on your right side (South).
From Grunthal go 1 1/2 miles south and
1/2 mile west on Warkentine Rd. Our cell
number is 204-371-672.

ROOMS Ground floor, Private entrance, **Baths** Private,
Beds Queen, **Smoking** Outside, **In Room** Thermostat,
Fireplace, VCR/DVD, **OTHERS** Rural, Open all year,
Additional meals, **PAYMENT** Visa, MC, Cheques accept-
ed, Cash, Trvl's cheques, **BREAKFASTS** Full, Home-
baked, Self-catered, **AMENITIES** Central phone,
Whirlpool, Barbecue, Kitchen, Fridge, Hot bev. bar,
Lounge, Patio, Central Internet access, Central VCR/DVD,
THINGS TO DO Trail nearby, Rental canoe or boat, Golf,
Fishing, Museums, Attractions, Shopping, Cross-country
skiing, Tennis, Swimming, Horseback riding, Beach,
Birdwatching, **LANGUAGE** Eng., Ger., **PRICE** (2 persons)
65–75 **(check with hosts for pricing details)**

Hecla Island *(north of Winnipeg)*

Solmundson Gesta Hus

(Sharon and Dave Holtz)

Riverton PO Box 76, Hecla Island, MB, R0C 2R0
www.heclatourism.mb.ca/page3.html
E-mail holtz@mts.net

204-279-2088
Fax 204-279-2088

Luxurious hospitality in a comfortable
modern home located in an original
Icelandic settlement, each room is furnished with brass beds and duvets and
has a view of Lake Winnipeg. Relax on the
verandah or in the gazebo to enjoy the
tranquil and peaceful atmosphere filled
with birds and wildlife. Soak in the outdoor hot tub while gazing at the stars.
Enjoy a spa treatment using the Chi
machine, Hot-house and/or ERE, or have
your hostess treat you with Reiki or
Reflexology. Cats in-house. Meals available.

ROOMS Upper floor, Ground floor, **Baths** Ensuite,
Shared with guest, **Beds** Queen, Double, Single or
cots, **Air** Central, **Smoking** Outside, **OTHERS** Rural,
Open all year, Additional meals, Pets in residence, Pets
welcome, **PAYMENT** Visa, MC, Amex, Cheques accepted, Cash, Trvl's cheques, **BREAKFASTS** Full, Home-
baked, **AMENITIES** Central TV, Central phone,
Whirlpool, Barbecue, Kitchen, Central VCR/DVD,
THINGS TO DO Comp. bikes, Trail nearby, Rental canoe
or boat, Golf, Fishing, Museums, Attractions, Cross-
country skiing, Tennis, Swimming, Beach,
Birdwatching, **LANGUAGE** Eng., **PRICE** (2 persons)
55–80 **(check with hosts for pricing details)**

Inglis *(northwest of Winnipeg)*

Bear Creek B&B

(Darlene and Jodie Bodnariuk)

Box 167, Inglis, MB, R0J 0X0
www.bbcanada.com/4278.html

204-564-2696

Come enjoy a private country getaway in
the beautiful Asessippi Valley. Open year
round. Continental breakfast, fully
equipped kitchen, campsite, BBQ, children's play area, dog kennels, air-
conditioned, wheelchair accessible. Just
4 minutes to Asessippi ski hill, part of the
Trans-Canada Trail, minutes to Lake of The
Prairie and fly-fishing, great area for hunting, family vacations, weddings, reunions,
skidooing and cross-country skiing. Tour
Inglis Elevators Historic Site and our area
while here. Cost of $165 to rent house.

ROOMS Upper floor, Ground floor, **Baths** Shared
with guest, **Beds** Double, Single or cots, **Air** Central,
Smoking Outside, **OTHERS** Open all year,
Handicapped access, Pets welcome, **PAYMENT**
Cheques accepted, Cash, **BREAKFASTS** Continental,
AMENITIES Central TV, Central phone, Barbecue,
Kitchen, Fridge, Hot bev. bar, Patio, **THINGS TO DO**
Trail nearby, Golf, Fishing, Attractions, Shopping, Cross-
country skiing, Swimming, Beach, **LANGUAGE** Eng.,
PRICE (2 persons) 55 **(check with hosts for pricing
details)**

Killarney *(southwest of Winnipeg)*

Country Comfort B&B

(Linda and Henry Krueger)

Box 808, Killarney, MB, R0K 1G0
www.canadianbandbguide.ca/bb.asp?ID=1927
E-mail ccb2b@mts.net

204-523-8742
Fax 204-523-8511
TFr 1-877-523-8511

Enjoy the comfort and quiet of our country location. Situated off Hwy 3 between Killarney and Boissevain. Spacious accommodations include four attractive guest rooms with entertainment and recreation facilities for up to 16 guests. Workshops or retreats. Golf packages available. Area attractions include Turtle Mountain Park, International Peace Gardens, Boissevain outdoor murals, many lakes, golf courses, museums and shopping. Children welcome. Advance reservations appreciated.

ROOMS Ground floor, Lower floor, Private entrance, **Baths** Shared with guest, **Beds** Queen, Double, Twin, **Air** Central, **In Room** Thermostat, **OTHERS** Rural, Open all year, Additional meals, **PAYMENT** Cheques accepted, Cash, Trvl's cheques, **BREAKFASTS** Full, Home-baked, **AMENITIES** Central TV, Central phone, Kitchen, Fridge, Hot bev. bar, Lounge, Patio, **THINGS TO DO** Trail nearby, Golf, Fishing, Museums, Entertainment, Attractions, Shopping, Cross-country skiing, Tennis, Swimming, Beach, **LANGUAGE** Eng., **PRICE** (2 persons) 40–80 **(check with hosts for pricing details)**

Minnedosa *(west of Winnipeg)*

Fairmount Bed & Breakfast

(Susan Proven)

Box 633, Minnedosa, MB, R0J 1E0
www.bedandbreakfast.mb.ca
E-mail sproven@mts.net

204-874-2165

Restored 1914 farmhouse with stained glass windows, maple floors and furnishings. Situated on third generation working farm, on the edge of a pond, sheltered by a natural spruce grove. Relax while sheep graze on the pastures. Spend the evening around a bonfire listening to the coyotes. Watch the moon reflected in the water then sleep between sun-dried sheets under a wool duvet. Hostess loves to cook for guests, using natural farm products, like bison, rainbow trout, lamb and garden vegetables. Other phone 204-867-0792

ROOMS Family suite, Upper floor, **Baths** Private, Shared with guest, **Beds** Double, Twin, Single or cots, **Air** In rooms, **Smoking** Outside, **In Room** Phone, TV, Internet access, **OTHERS** Rural, Open all year, Additional meals, **PAYMENT** Cheques accepted, Cash, Trvl's cheques, **BREAKFASTS** Full, Continental, Home-baked, **AMENITIES** Central TV, Central phone, Barbecue, Lounge, Central Internet access, Central VCR/DVD, **THINGS TO DO** Trail nearby, Comp. Canoe or boat, Golf, Fishing, Museums, Art, Shopping, Cross-country skiing, Tennis, Swimming, Horseback riding, Beach, **LANGUAGE** Eng., Sp., **PRICE** (2 persons) 60–70 **(check with hosts for pricing details)**

Neepawa *(west of Winnipeg)*

Highland Glen B&B

(Vivian Hildebrand)

Box 2624, 353 Vivian St, Neepawa, MB, R0J 1H0
www.bedandbreakfast.mb.ca
E-mail vivonviv@mts.net

204-476-3179

A memorable experience awaits you at Highland Glen B&B. Comfortable rooms (one double, one queen), beautiful yard and view of the Whitemud River Valley – all at very affordable rates. We have three rooms, a queen ensuite on the upper floor and two on the main floor – one with a queen bed and the other with two twin beds. These two rooms share a bathroom.

ROOMS Upper floor, Ground floor, **Baths** Ensuite, Shared with guest, **Beds** Queen, Twin, **Air** Central, **Smoking** Outside, **In Room** Phone, TV, VCR/DVD, **OTHERS** Urban, Open all year, Handicapped access, Pets welcome, **PAYMENT** Visa, MC, Cheques accepted, Cash, Trvl's cheques, **BREAKFASTS** Full, Home-baked, **AMENITIES** Central TV, Central phone, Barbecue, Laundry, Kitchen, Fridge, Lounge, Patio, Central Internet access, **THINGS TO DO** Trail nearby, Golf, Fishing, Museums, Art, Theatre, Entertainment, Attractions, Shopping, Cross-country skiing, Tennis, Swimming, Birdwatching, Antiquing, **LANGUAGE** Eng., **PRICE** (2 persons) 55–65 **(check with hosts for pricing details)**

Rivers *(west of Winnipeg)*

Cozy River Inn B&B

(Jake and Lynn Kroeger)

Box 838, Rivers, MB, R0K 1X0
www.bedandbreakfast.mb.ca

204-328-4457
Fax 204-328-4457

Enjoy a taste of country living close to town in a separate guest house situated on the Little Saskatchewan River with two theme rooms, each with its own entrance and private full bath. Continental breakfast includes homemade muffins, bread, jam and in-season fruit. Lake Wahtopanah provides excellent summer and winter activities. A great hunting area. Several fine restaurants, golf course, curling, tennis court nearby. Close to Brandon, Minnesota. Smoke-free environment. Call ahead for reservations.

ROOMS Family suite, Private entrance, **Baths** Ensuite, **Beds** Queen, Pullout sofa, **Air** In rooms, **Smoking** Outside, **In Room** Thermostat, TV, **OTHERS** Open all year, **PAYMENT** MC, Cash, **BREAKFASTS** Continental, Home-baked, Self-catered, **AMENITIES** Central TV, Fridge, Patio, **THINGS TO DO** Trail nearby, Golf, Fishing, Museums, Shopping, Cross-country skiing, Tennis, Swimming, Beach, **LANGUAGE** Eng., **PRICE** (2 persons) 65–85 **(check with hosts for pricing details)**

SAINT-PIERRE-JOLYS *(south of Winnipeg)*

Château des Sages B&B

(Roger and Cecile Lesage)

327 Sabourin St N, Saint-Pierre-Jolys,
MB, R0A 1V0
www.chateaudessages.ca
E-mail info@chateaudessages.ca

204-433-3202
Fax 204-433-7585
TFr 1-866-226-2770

Relax in total privacy in our self-contained
guest suite located in a peaceful country
setting. The suite consists of a fully modern kitchen, bathroom with Jacuzzi tub
and a queen-size bed in the bedroom.
The living room has a gas fireplace and
the sofa opens to a double bed. Included
is all you need to make yourself a hearty
breakfast to enjoy at your leisure indoors
or out on your private patio. A great
country escape 30 miles south of
Winnipeg, 9 miles to St. Malo Provincial
Park and beach.

ROOMS Family suite, Ground floor, Private entrance,
Baths Private, **Beds** Queen, Pullout sofa, **Air** In rooms,
Ceiling fans, **Smoking** Outside, **In Room** Thermostat,
TV, Fireplace, Internet access, VCR/DVD, **OTHERS** Rural,
Open all year, Handicapped access, **PAYMENT** Visa,
Cash, Trvl's cheques, **BREAKFASTS** Home-baked, Self-
catered, **AMENITIES** Central phone, Barbecue,
Laundry, Kitchen, Fridge, Patio, Central Internet access,
THINGS TO DO Comp. bikes, Trail nearby, Rental canoe
or boat, Golf, Museums, Art, Attractions, Shopping,
Cross-country skiing, Swimming, Beach, Birdwatching,
Antiquing, **LANGUAGE** Eng., Fr., **PRICE** (2 persons) 75
(check with hosts for pricing details)

SAINT-PIERRE-JOLYS

Gîte de Forest B&B

(Raymond and Nicole Lavergne)

512 avenue Côté, Saint-Pierre-Jolys, MB, R0A 1V0
www.placelavergne.com
E-mail nrl@placelavergne.com

204-433-7870
Fax 204-433-7181
TFr 1-866-661-7870

Your hosts, Raymond and Nicole, are very
proud to share their Acadian and French
roots with you. Their B&B, Gîte de Forest,
offers a suite with its own bathroom,
living room complete with sofa and television and the Rivière-aux-Rats and Saint-
Pierre south rooms. The Acadian Room
also has its own bathroom. Gîte de Forest
B&B is located in Saint-Pierre-Jolys town
centre, 30 minutes south of Winnipeg and
30 minutes north of the American border
on Route 59. Alternate telephone numbers: 204-433-7758 and 204-746-4136.

ROOMS Family suite, Ground floor, Lower floor, **Baths**
Private, **Beds** Queen, Double, Twin, **Air** Central,
Smoking Outside, **OTHERS** Rural, Open all year, **PAY-
MENT** Visa, MC, Direct debit, Cash, Trvl's cheques,
BREAKFASTS Home-baked, **AMENITIES** Central TV,
Kitchen, Fridge, Lounge, Patio, **THINGS TO DO** Comp.
bikes, Trail nearby, Golf, Fishing, Museums, Art,
Shopping, Cross-country skiing, Swimming, Beach,
Antiquing, **LANGUAGE** Eng., Fr., **PRICE** (2 persons)
50–75 **(check with hosts for pricing details)**

SELKIRK *(north of Winnipeg)*

Evergreen Gate Bed and Breakfast

(Laurel and Rob Sarginson)

1138 River Rd, St. Andrews, MB, R1A 4A7
www.evergreengate.ca
E-mail evergreengate@mts.net

204-482-6248
TFr 1-877-901-0553

Explore Manitoba's Interlake from your quiet, private, comfortable room in our unique home, located in park-like surroundings 1/2 hour north of Winnipeg. On the Trans-Canada Trail high above the scenic Red River, here is the perfect location for walking, cycling and pelican watching. In minutes you can be at Lower Fort Garry National Historic Site, Oak Hammock Marsh Interpretive Centre and golf courses. The white sand beaches of Lake Winnipeg await you 1/2 hour to the north. A screened porch, lounge and kitchenette complement the guest rooms.

ROOMS Family suite, Lower floor, **Baths** Private, Ensuite, **Beds** Queen, Double, **Air** Ceiling fans, **Smoking** Outside, **In Room** Thermostat, **OTHERS** Open all year, **PAYMENT** Visa, MC, Diners, Amex, Cheques accepted, Cash, **BREAKFASTS** Full, Continental, Home-baked, Self-catered, **AMENITIES** Central TV, Central phone, Whirlpool, Kitchen, Fridge, Lounge, Patio, Central Internet access, Central VCR/DVD, **THINGS TO DO** Comp. bikes, Trail nearby, Fishing, Museums, Art, Attractions, Shopping, Cross-country skiing, Swimming, Horseback riding, Birdwatching, Antiquing, **LANGUAGE** Eng., Fr., **PRICE** (2 persons) 60–90 **(check with hosts for pricing details)**

STEINBACH *(southeast of Winnipeg)*

Chickadee Lane B&B

(Ed and Marlene Silinski)

333 Homestead Cres, Steinbach, MB, R5G 1N8
www.mystic-spirit.com/chickadeelane
E-mail mes@mts.net

204-326-3908

Relax at our country home located on a beautiful landscaped yard, 5 minutes from downtown Steinbach and less than 40 minutes from Winnipeg. Lunches and dinners available at an extra cost.

ROOMS Ground floor, **Baths** Shared with guest, **Beds** Queen, **Air** Central, **Smoking** Outside, **OTHERS** Rural, Open all year, Additional meals, **PAYMENT** Cheques accepted, Cash, **BREAKFASTS** Full, Continental, Home-baked, **AMENITIES** Central TV, Central phone, Central Internet access, Central VCR/DVD, **THINGS TO DO** Golf, Museums, Attractions, Shopping, Cross-country skiing, Swimming, Birdwatching, **PRICE** (2 persons) 50 **(check with hosts for pricing details)**

WINKLER *(south of Winnipeg)*

Siemens Bed & Breakfast

(Rudolf and Luisa Siemens)

184 Pembina Dr, Morden, MB, R6M 1H5
www.canadianbandbguide.ca/bb.asp?ID=3632

204-822-1973

Enjoy warm, welcoming hospitality at a Mennonite home in Morden. Children are welcome. We have a crib available as well as an extra sofabed. We are close to the hockey and curling arena and the hiking trail in beautiful Pembina Valley. Come for the annual Morden Apple and Corn Festival the last weekend of August. Additional meals are served on request and weekly rates are available.

ROOMS Lower floor, **Baths** Shared with guest, **Beds** Queen, Double, **Air** Central, **Smoking** Outside, **OTHERS** Urban, Open all year, Additional meals, **PAYMENT** Cash, **BREAKFASTS** Full, **AMENITIES** Central TV, Kitchen, Fridge, Hot bev. bar, Lounge, **THINGS TO DO** Trail nearby, Golf, Fishing, Museums, Art, Shopping, Cross-country skiing, Downhill skiing, Tennis, Swimming, Horseback riding, Beach, **LANGUAGE** Eng., Ger., **PRICE** (2 persons) 35 **(check with hosts for pricing details)**

WINNIPEG *(southeastern Manitoba)*

Almost Home Bed & Breakfast

(Val and Bob Friesen)

38 Zeglinski Cres, Winnipeg, MB, R2G 3S3
www.members.shaw.ca/almost_home
E-mail valfriesen1@shaw.ca

204-663-4292

Our friendly Almost Home B&B is in a large English Tudor style home, situated in the quiet neighbourhood of NE Winnipeg. Breakfast is available in the dining room, or out on the poolside deck. Downtown is 15 minutes away. Manitoba's biggest shopping/casino area is only minutes away by car. The West Wing (queen-size) is tastefully decorated and includes a wide variety of novels and magazines. The South Side has two cozy three quarter beds. Relax and feel Almost Home with Bob and Val!

ROOMS Upper floor, Private entrance, **Baths** Private, Shared with guest, **Beds** Queen, Double, **Air** Central, **Smoking** Outside, **In Room** Phone, TV, **OTHERS** Urban, Adult, Open all year, **PAYMENT** Visa, MC, Amex, Cash, Trvl's cheques, **BREAKFASTS** Full, Continental, Home-baked, **AMENITIES** Central TV, Central phone, Swimming pool, Whirlpool, Lounge, Patio, Central VCR/DVD, **THINGS TO DO** Rental bikes, Trail nearby, Golf, Museums, Art, Theatre, Entertainment, Attractions, Shopping, Tennis, Swimming, Horseback riding, Beach, **LANGUAGE** Eng., **PRICE** (2 persons) 60–75 **(check with hosts for pricing details)**

WINNIPEG
Banner Bed & Breakfast
(Diane Gourluck)

164 Harrow St, Winnipeg, MB, R3M 2Z2
www.bbcanada.com/bannerbb
E-mail gourluck@mts.net

204-256-8721

Retreat to a more genteel era in our 1906, antique-filled Victorian home in historic Crescentwood area of south-central Winnipeg. Stroll beneath the elms to trendy shops and restaurants of Corydon Village. Just a brief commute by car or bus to business and entertainment districts, hospitals, universities, shopping centres, airport, train and bus depots. Homemade jams and local products are featured in our splendid breakfasts. Internet, fax and other business services available. Special diets accommodated.

ROOMS Upper floor, **Baths** Ensuite, Shared with hosts, **Beds** Queen, Double, **In Room** Thermostat, TV, **OTHERS** Urban, Open all year, **PAYMENT** Visa, MC, Amex, Cash, Trvl's cheques, **BREAKFASTS** Full, Continental, **AMENITIES** Central TV, Central phone, **THINGS TO DO** Trail nearby, Museums, Art, Theatre, Entertainment, Attractions, Shopping, **LANGUAGE** Eng., **PRICE** (2 persons) 50–75 **(check with hosts for pricing details)**

WINNIPEG
Elsa's Place
(Werner and Elsa Neufeld)

796 Pasadena Ave, Winnipeg, MB, R3T 2T3
www.bedandbreakfast.mb.ca
E-mail klasfel7@mts.net

204-284-3176
TFr 1-866-284-3112

Enjoy a relaxed retreat within 1 km of University of Manitoba and King's Park. Shopping is nearby or take a bus to the city centre. We enjoy Travel Scrabble and quilting. Well-treed garden and deck. "Savour Vern's fabulous homemade bread." We offer a queen room with sitting area and king and twin adjacent to rec room. We speak German. We're 15 minutes to Victoria General Hospital. Go to www.destinationwinnipeg.ca for events, festivals and attractions.

ROOMS Upper floor, Lower floor, Private entrance, **Baths** Private, Shared with guest, **Beds** King, Queen, Twin, Pullout sofa, **Air** Central, In rooms, **Smoking** Outside, **In Room** Phone, Internet access, **OTHERS** Urban, Open all year, **PAYMENT** Cash, Trvl's cheques, **BREAKFASTS** Full, **AMENITIES** Central TV, Central phone, Laundry, Kitchen, Central Internet access, Central VCR/DVD, **THINGS TO DO** Trail nearby, Golf, Fishing, Museums, Art, Theatre, Entertainment, Attractions, Wineries/Breweries, Shopping, Cross-country skiing, Tennis, Swimming, Horseback riding, Beach, Birdwatching, Antiquing, **LANGUAGE** Eng., Ger., **PRICE** (2 persons) 60 **(check with hosts for pricing details)**

Winnipeg

Terry's Bed and Breakfast

(Teresa [Terry] and Jim Cannon)

130 Southwalk Bay, Winnipeg, MB, R2N 1M7
www.members.shaw.ca/terrysbb/
E-mail terrysbb@shaw.ca

204-253-8723

We are located on a quiet bay close to the Perimeter (Hwy 100) and the Trans-Canada (Hwy 1). You are a short 25 minutes from Winnipeg International Airport. Direct city bus route to downtown and the Forks, and 5 minutes to St. Vital Shopping Centre. Beautifully landscaped, large private yard with deck, patio and pond. Comfortable and newly furnished rooms with A/C. Inspected and approved. Licensed by the City of Winnipeg. High-speed internet in rooms. Laundry facilities available. Friendly, helpful hosts.

ROOMS Upper floor, **Baths** Ensuite, Shared with guest, **Beds** King, Queen, Double, **Air** Central, **Smoking** Outside, **In Room** TV, Fireplace, Internet access, **OTHERS** Urban, Open all year, **PAYMENT** Visa, MC, Amex, Cash, Trvl's cheques, **BREAKFASTS** Full, **AMENITIES** Central TV, Central phone, Laundry, Lounge, Patio, Central VCR/DVD, **THINGS TO DO** Trail nearby, Golf, Fishing, Museums, Art, Theatre, Entertainment, Attractions, Shopping, Swimming, Beach, **LANGUAGE** Eng., **PRICE** (2 persons) 85–100 **(check with hosts for pricing details)**

ONTARIO

CANADIAN BED AND BREAKFAST GUIDE

Kapuskasing
Thunder Bay
Sault Ste. Marie
Marathon
Kenora

• Sudbury

Blind River
•

Manitoulin Island

• Mindemoya

Georgian Bay

• Pointe au Baril

Lake Huron

N

ALG
F

• Parry
  Sound

Huntsville •

• Dorset

MUSKOKA

Port Carling •

• Bala

• Bracebridge

HALIBUR
HIGHLA

• Gravenhurst

• Minden

Penetanguishene •
Midland •
Lafontaine •

• Wiarton

Meaford •

• Orillia

Fenelon •

Sauble Beach •
Owen Sound •

• Thornbury
Collingwood •

Wasaga
Beach •

Chesley •

• Kimberley

• Stayner

Barrie •

• Jackson's Point

• Flesherton

Creemore •

Bethany •

Kincardine •

Aliston •

Walkerton •

• Shelburne

• Bradford West

Port H

Mildmay •

• Damascus

• Orangeville

• Whitby • Oshawa

Markham •

• Ajax

Goderich •

• Fergus

• Erin

• Elmira

• Georgetown

■ **TORONTO**

Mississauga

Bayfield •

• St. Jacobs

• Guelph

Milton •

Vineland Sta

Waterloo •

Campbellville •
• Kitchener

Oakville •

Jordan
St. Catharines •

Stratford •
Baden •

Dundas •

• Burlington
Grimsby •

• Niagara-on-the-La

• St. Marys

Hamilton •

• Niagara Falls

Paris •

Brantford •

• St. Anns

Woodstock •

• Ancaster

Welland •

• London

Cayuga •

Port Colborne •

• Fort Erie

U.S.A.

• Petrolia

• Tillsenburg

Dunnville •

Ridgeway •

• Port Dover

Windsor •

Ridgetown •

• Port Stanley
Port Burwell •

• Port Rowan

Lake Erie

• Amherstburg

N

QUEBEC

Pembroke

Plantagenet
Vancleek Hill

**ALGONQUIN
PARK**

Huntsville

Dorset

Barry's Bay

OTTAWA

Almonte

Lancaster

Palmer Rapids

Winchester

Cornwall

Maynooth

Bracebridge

HALIBURTON
HIGHLANDS

Bancroft

Rideau Ferry

Morrisburg

Gravenhurst

Minden

Prescott

U.S.A.

Kinmount

Westport

Brockville

Orillia

Fenelon Falls

Madoc

THOUSAND ISLANDS

Marmora

Gananoque

Bridgenorth

Kingston

Jackson's Point

Peterborough

Warkworth

Belleville

Bethany

ord West

Brighton

Port Hope

Prince Edward
County

Whitby   Oshawa

Wellington

Markham

Ajax

TORONTO

Lake Ontario

Vineland Sta
Jordan
St. Catharines

Niagara-on-the-Lake

Niagara Falls

lland

Colborne

Fort Erie

Ridgeway

Locator information
for towns in the listing areas
gives relative position to major cities
(usually the capital) or other significant
geographic points.
Use any standard road map for
precisely locating the town of interest.

■ Provincial Capital
● City/Town
○ Indicates area or other geographic
features such as lakes etc.

Ajax *(east of Toronto)*

Before the Mast B&B

(Greg and Rosemary Lang)

1144 Shoalpoint Rd, Ajax, ON, L1S 1E2
www.beforethemast.ca
E-mail greg@beforethemast.ca

905-683-4830

Before the Mast B&B, located on the Lake
Ontario Waterfront Trail, has two rooms
available. Both have private ensuites. Both
are equipped with satellite TV, comfort-
abe chairs, bar fridges, etc. The Captains
Quarters has two queen-size beds and its
own private deck overlooking the
Carruthers Creek Wetland. The Aft
Quarters has two single beds and overlooks the English water garden featured
on "The Secret World of Gardens" on
HGTV. Toronto is 45 minutes away.
Durham Region golf packages available.

ROOMS Upper floor, Private entrance, **Baths** Private,
Ensuite, **Beds** Queen, Twin, **Air** Central, **Smoking**
Outside, **In Room** TV, Internet access, **OTHERS** Open
all year, Additional meals, **PAYMENT** Visa, Cheques
accepted, Cash, **BREAKFASTS** Full, Continental, Home-
baked, **AMENITIES** Central TV, Central phone, Fridge,
Hot bev. bar, Lounge, Patio, **THINGS TO DO** Trail nearby, Golf, Fishing, Museums, Art, Theatre, Attractions,
Shopping, Cross-country skiing, Tennis, Swimming,
Birdwatching, Antiquing, **LANGUAGE** Eng., **PRICE** (2
persons) 90–120 **(check with hosts for pricing
details)**

Algonquin Park [Dorset]
(north of Toronto)

The Nordic Inn of Dorset

(Jane and Andre Tieman)

1019 Nordic Inn Rd, Dorset, ON, P0A 1E0
www.thenordicinn.com
E-mail info@thenordicinn.com

705-766-2343
Fax 705-766-9983

All-season gateway to Algonquin Park and
Lake-of-Bays in Muskoka, 23 km of trails for
hiking, biking, cross-country skiing and
snowshoeing to pristine Charcoal Lake,
across from Dorset lookout Tower with
560 sq. km view, surrounded by lakes for
swimming, boating and canoeing – two
cottages, 10 rooms and suite with fireplace. Whirlpool tub and hot tubs available. Satellite TV, microwaves, bar fridges.
Playground, several decks, llamas, ATV and
snowmobile heaven, nearby swimming
and boat launch ramps, restaurants nearby.

ROOMS Family suite, Ground floor, **Baths** Ensuite, **Beds**
King, Queen, Double, Twin, Single or cots, Pullout sofa,
Air In rooms, Ceiling fans, **Smoking** Outside, **In Room**
Thermostat, Phone, TV, Fireplace, Internet access,
OTHERS Rural, Open all year, Handicapped access,
Additional meals, Pets welcome, **PAYMENT** Visa, MC,
Amex, Direct debit, Cash, Trvl's cheques, **BREAKFASTS**
Full, Home-baked, **AMENITIES** Central TV, Central
phone, Whirlpool, Barbecue, Kitchen, Patio, Central
Internet access, Central VCR/DVD, **THINGS TO DO** Trail
nearby, Rental canoe or boat, Golf, Fishing, Museums,
Art, Entertainment, Attractions, Shopping, Cross-coun-
try skiing, Downhill skiing, Swimming, Horseback riding, Beach, Birdwatching, Antiquing, **LANGUAGE** Eng.,
some French and Dutch, **PRICE** (2 persons) 80–150
(check with hosts for pricing details)

ALGONQUIN PARK (HUNTSVILLE)

A Gingerbread B&B
(Tini, Will and Jag Gepkens)

882 Riverlea Rd, Huntsville, ON, P1H 1X5
www.bbcanada.com/gingerbread
E-mail agingerbreadbb@sympatico.ca

705-788-9119

Enjoy a peaceful retreat on the Muskoka River. Canoes and pedalboat are free to use, and the clean, sandy shore invites you to swim or fish here. We serve a country breakfast with organic/local products in the sunny dining room overlooking the water. We can help you plan your day visiting Muskoka, Algonquin Park and Arrowhead Park. From Huntsville's Main street, go south on Brunel Rd 2.5 km, right onto North Mary Lake Rd. Our signs will then direct you to us, another 2.5 km. Welcome!

ROOMS Upper floor, **Baths** Private, Shared with guest, **Beds** Queen, **Air** Ceiling fans, **Smoking** Outside, **OTHERS** Rural, Adult, Open all year, Pets in residence, **PAYMENT** Visa, MC, Cheques accepted, Cash, Trvl's cheques, **BREAKFASTS** Full, Home-baked, **AMENITIES** Central phone, Fridge, Lounge, Patio, **THINGS TO DO** Trail nearby, Rental canoe or boat, Comp. canoe or boat, Golf, Fishing, Museums, Theatre, Entertainment, Attractions, Shopping, Cross-country skiing, Downhill skiing, Tennis, Swimming, Horseback riding, Beach, Birdwatching, Antiquing, **LANGUAGE** Eng., Fr., Ger., Dutch, Frisian, **PRICE** (2 persons) 85–110 **(check with hosts for pricing details)**

ALGONQUIN PARK (HUNTSVILLE)

Fairy Bay Guest House
(Robert and Dawn Rye)

228 Cookson Bay Cres, Huntsville, ON, P1H 1B2
www.fairybay.ca
E-mail hosts@fairybay.ca

705-789-1492
Fax 705-789-6922
TFr 1-888-813-1101

A charming country inn set in beautiful gardens on a quiet bay of Fairy Lake. Relax in luxurious comfort or participate in the many activities available nearby. Several canoes and other watercraft are provided to enjoy the accessible 40 km of picturesque waterways. Algonquin Park, six golf courses, hiking, skiing and snowmmobiling are among the pleasant diversions in the area. This is a wonderful holiday place, full of warmth, interest, music, art and natural beauty.

ROOMS Family suite, Upper floor, Ground floor, Lower floor, **Baths** Ensuite, **Beds** King, Queen, Single or cots, Pullout sofa, **Air** Central, **Smoking** Outside, **In Room** Thermostat, Phone, TV, VCR/DVD, **OTHERS** Rural, Open all year, **PAYMENT** Visa, MC, Cheques accepted, Cash, **BREAKFASTS** Full, Home-baked, **AMENITIES** Whirlpool, Barbecue, Fridge, Hot bev. bar, Lounge, Patio, **THINGS TO DO** Comp. bikes, Trail nearby, Comp. canoe or boat, Golf, Fishing, Museums, Art, Entertainment, Attractions, Shopping, Cross-country skiing, Downhill skiing, Tennis, Swimming, Horseback riding, Beach, Birdwatching, Antiquing, **LANGUAGE** Eng., Fr., **PRICE** (2 persons) 140–205 **(check with hosts for pricing details)**

Algonquin Park (Huntsville)

Kent House Bed & Breakfast

(Carol MacDonald and Joy Barton)

1042 Hillside Cres, Huntsville, ON, P1H 2J6
www.kenthouse-algonquin.com
E-mail kentbb@bellnet.ca

705-635-9995

Kent House B&B offers privacy and convenience in a beautiful Muskoka setting. Our guest living room has satellite TV and access to our wraparound deck, and our dining room offers a fantastic view while you tuck into your sumptuous breakfast. From Toronto go north to Hwy 11. Take Hwy 60 exit at Huntsville and continue east for approximately 12 km to Lake-of-Bays. Turn left into Limberlost Rd (#8) then the first left is Hillside Cres. Kent House is at the top of the hill on the right.

ROOMS Upper floor, **Baths** Private, Ensuite, Shared with guest, **Beds** King, Queen, Double, Single or cots, **Air** Ceiling fans, **Smoking** Outside, **OTHERS** Babysitting, Rural, Open all year, Pets in residence, **PAYMENT** Cheques accepted, Cash, Trvl's cheques, **BREAKFASTS** Full, Continental, **AMENITIES** Central TV, Kitchen, Fridge, Lounge, Patio, **THINGS TO DO** Trail nearby, Rental canoe or boat, Golf, Fishing, Attractions, Shopping, Cross-country skiing, Downhill skiing, Horseback riding, Beach, Birdwatching, **LANGUAGE** Eng., Fr., **PRICE** (2 persons) 80–110 **(check with hosts for pricing details)**

Algonquin Park (Huntsville)

Maplewood Bed & Breakfast

(Marina and Peter von der Marwitz)

60, Hillside, 1001 Golf Course Rd, RR #4, Huntsville, ON, P1H 2J6
www.maplewood-bb.ca
E-mail mar_pete@vianet.ca

705-635-1378
Fax 705-635-1378

We're 30 km from West gate of Algonquin Park; 11 km from Huntsville. Historic home. Full breakfast served. Relax in lounge with satellite TV, games, library. Specials for multi-night bookings: hikers; seniors with small families and mature well-disiplined children will enjoy Algonquin Park and other outdoor activities. Two summer cabins have been designed for short- and longer-term "home base." For trans-park-activities. We encourage bookings from/to establishments east of the Park and Ottawa.

ROOMS Family suite, Upper floor, Private entrance, **Baths** Private, Ensuite, Shared with guest, Shared with hosts, **Beds** King, Double, Twin, Single or cots, Pullout sofa, **Smoking** Outside, **In Room** Thermostat, TV, **OTHERS** Rural, Adult, Seasonal, **PAYMENT** Cheques accepted, Cash, Trvl's cheques, **BREAKFASTS** Full, Continental, Self-catered, **AMENITIES** Central TV, Central phone, Kitchen, Fridge, Lounge, Patio, **THINGS TO DO** Trail nearby, Golf, Fishing, Attractions, Shopping, Cross-country skiing, Swimming, Horseback riding, Beach, **LANGUAGE** Eng.,Ger., A smatter of Latin-based languages **PRICE** (2 persons) 70–125 **(check with hosts for pricing details)**

ALGONQUIN PARK (MADAWASKA)

Riverland Lodge & Camp
(MaryAnn and Jay McRae)

Hwy 60, Madawaska, ON, K0J 2C0
www.riverlandlodge.com
E-mail info@riverlandlodge.com

613-637-5338
Fax 613-637-2988
TFr 1-800-701-8055

Riverland Bed & Breakfast is located on
Hwy 60, (the only Hwy in Algonquin), at
the Madawaska River Bridge, 20-minute
drive to the East Gate of Algonquin Park.
Swimming, boating, fishing, sightseeing,
relaxing. We are members of the Ontario
Federation of Bed & Breakfasts and have
an Ontario Tourist License. Reservations
are reccommended and we have a 24-
hour cancellation policy. We have a family
bedroom which has a queen-size bed and
two double beds and housekeeping
rental units as well as camping.

ROOMS Upper floor, Ground floor, **Baths** Shared with
guest, **Beds** Queen, Double, Single or cots, **Air** Central,
Smoking Outside, **OTHERS** Rural, Seasonal, Additional
meals, **PAYMENT** Visa, MC, Direct debit, Cash, Trvl's
cheques, **BREAKFASTS** Full, Home-baked, **AMENITIES**
Central TV, Central phone, Barbecue, Laundry, Lounge,
Patio, **THINGS TO DO** Trail nearby, Rental canoe or
boat, Fishing, Attractions, Cross-country skiing,
Swimming, Beach, **LANGUAGE** Eng., Fr., **PRICE** (2 persons) 60–135 **(check with hosts for pricing details)**

ALLISTON *(northwest of Toronto)*

Gramma's House
(Sid and Clara Kooistra)

146 Victoria St E, Alliston, ON, L9R 1K6
www.grammashousebnb.com
E-mail star7@sympatico.ca

705-434-4632
Fax 705-434-4771

A warm welcome awaits you as you enter
this classic Victorian home with a bright
and cheerful atmosphere. Close to all
amenities. Comfortably furnished with
antiques and collectibles. Semi-retired
couple with farming background have
raised a large family and enjoy meeting
people from various backgrounds. A great
getaway where you can relax inside and
out! The coffee is always on.

ROOMS Upper floor, Private entrance, **Baths** Shared
with guest, **Beds** Queen, Twin, Single or cots, **Air**
Central, **Smoking** Outside, **In Room** TV, **OTHERS**
Urban, Open all year, **PAYMENT** Visa, Cash, Trvl's
cheques, **BREAKFASTS** Full, Home-baked, **AMENITIES**
Central phone, Laundry, Patio, Central Internet access,
Central VCR/DVD, **THINGS TO DO** Trail nearby, Rental
canoe or boat, Golf, Fishing, Museums, Art, Theatre,
Entertainment, Shopping, Cross-country skiing,
Downhill skiing, Swimming, Horseback riding, Beach,
Birdwatching, Antiquing, **LANGUAGE** Eng.,
Dutch/Frisian **PRICE** (2 persons) 55–85 **(check with
hosts for pricing details)**

ALLISTON

Stevenson Farms Historical B&B

(Stephen and Susanne Milne)

5923 King St N, Alliston, ON, L9R 1V3
www.stevensonfarms.com
E-mail info@stevensonfarms.com

705-434-0844 Fax 705-434-0064

Experience 175 years of history at the former home of T.P. Loblaw – founder of the grocery empire. Our full ensuite guest rooms offer a unique combination of rustic country charm and old-world elegance, and are filled with antiques and modern amenities to make your stay comfortable and enjoyable. Wood-burning fireplaces, scenic country vistas, outdoor hot tub and hearty breakfasts are only a few of the treats awaiting you. Consider our large banquet hall for your next wedding or special function.

ROOMS Family suite, Upper floor, Ground floor, Private entrance, **Baths** Private, Ensuite, Shared with guest, **Beds** Queen, Double, Twin, Single or cots, Pullout sofa, **Air** In rooms, **Smoking** Outside, **In Room** Phone, TV, Fireplace, Internet access, VCR/DVD, **OTHERS** Rural, Open all year, Handicapped access, Additional meals, Pets in residence, **PAYMENT** Visa, MC, Direct debit, Cheques accepted, Cash, **BREAKFASTS** Full, Continental, Home-baked, Self-catered, **AMENITIES** Central TV, Central phone, Whirlpool, Barbecue, Laundry, Kitchen, Fridge, Hot bev. bar, Lounge, Patio, Central Internet access, Central VCR/DVD, **THINGS TO DO** Trail nearby, Rental canoe or boat, Golf, Fishing, Museums, Art, Theatre, Entertainment, Attractions, Wineries/Breweries, Shopping, Cross-country skiing, Downhill skiing, Tennis, Swimming, Horseback riding, Beach, Birdwatching, Antiquing, **LANGUAGE** Eng., Ger., **PRICE** (2 persons) 60–155 **(check with hosts for pricing details)**

ALMONTE *(southwest of Ottawa)*

The Squirrels

(Patricia Matheson)

190 Parkview Dr, Almonte, ON, K0A 1A0
E-mail squirrels@superaje.com

613-256-2995

A unique home situated in 3/4-acre garden noted for its home comfort, good food. Obliquely opposite the Almonte Arena in the picturesque town of Almonte with its artists, many boutiques, museums and Mississippi waterfalls. Your host has travelled the world and enjoys swapping tales with her guests. We're 30 minutes from Ottawa, 20 minutes to Smiths Falls, 15 minutes to Arnprior.

ROOMS Ground floor, **Baths** Shared with guest, **Beds** King, Twin, Single or cots, **Air** Central, **Smoking** Outside, **OTHERS** Open all year, **PAYMENT** Cheques accepted, Cash, Trvl's cheques, **BREAKFASTS** Full, **AMENITIES** Central TV, Central phone, **THINGS TO DO** Trail nearby, Golf, Fishing, Museums, Art, Shopping, Cross-country skiing, Tennis, Swimming, **LANGUAGE** Eng., basic French, **PRICE** (2 persons) 75 **(check with hosts for pricing details)**

AMHERSTBURG *(southwestern Ontario)*

Honor's Country House Bed and Breakfast

(Robert and Debra Honor)

4441 Concession 4 S, Amherstburg, ON, N9V 2Y8
www.bbcanada.com/honorsbnb
E-mail dhonor@mnsi.net

519-736-7737
TFr 1-877-253-8594

We extend a friendly welcome to our beautiful country home, featuring warm interiors and beautiful views of the gardens and countryside. Relax in the sun porch or on the deck. Have a dip in the pool or take tea on the verandah. Our cozy and comfortable rooms are furnished with antiques. Birdwatching, hiking, bicycling, golf and nature areas are close by. Quaint shopping, restaurants and attractions are minutes away in historic Amherstburg. We enjoy genealogy, history and gardening.

ROOMS Upper floor, **Baths** Private, Ensuite, **Beds** Double, Single or cots, **Air** Central, **OTHERS** Rural, Seasonal, Pets in residence, **PAYMENT** Cheques accepted, Cash, Trvl's cheques, **BREAKFASTS** Full, **AMENITIES** Central TV, Swimming pool, Central VCR/DVD, **THINGS TO DO** Trail nearby, Golf, Museums, Art, Entertainment, Attractions, Wineries/Breweries, Shopping, Swimming, Beach, Antiquing, **LANGUAGE** Eng., Fr., **PRICE** (2 persons) 70–80 **(check with hosts for pricing details)**

ANCASTER *(east of Hamilton)*

The Fiddler's Inn

(Mark and Leah Rudolph)

558 Fiddler's Green Rd, Ancaster, ON, L9G 3L1
www.thefiddlersinn.ca
E-mail info@thefiddlersinn.ca

905-648-0045
Fax 905-648-0330

We invite you to come and experience a taste of our warm hospitality and personal attention in our c. 1860 Victorian estate. Our two suites offer a special touch of romance with your choice of a private clawfoot tub or air-jet Jacuzzi tub for two. On those chilly nights crawl up to the warmth of your own in-room coal fireplace. Lie back, relax and snuggle up under your down duvet on your spacious king-size bed. Enjoy the full amenities and let us spoil you with the Inn's historic charm.

ROOMS Upper floor, Private entrance, **Baths** Private, Ensuite, **Beds** King, **Air** Central, In rooms, **Smoking** Outside, **In Room** TV, Fireplace, **OTHERS** Urban, Rural, Adult, Open all year, Pets in residence, **PAYMENT** Visa, MC, Cheques accepted, Cash, **BREAKFASTS** Full, Continental, Home-baked, **AMENITIES** Central phone, Barbecue, Fridge, Lounge, Patio, **THINGS TO DO** Rental bikes, Trail nearby, Rental canoe or boat, Golf, Fishing, Museums, Art, Theatre, Entertainment, Attractions, Wineries/Breweries, Shopping, Cross-country skiing, Downhill skiing, Tennis, Swimming, Horseback riding, Beach, Birdwatching, Antiquing, **LANGUAGE** Eng., **PRICE** (2 persons) 110–185 **(check with hosts for pricing details)**

BADEN *(west of Hamilton)*

Willow Springs Suites B&B

(Bruce and Dale Weber)

24 Brewery St, Baden, ON, N3A 2S7
www.bbcanada.com/2212.html
E-mail willowspringsbandb@rogers.com

519-634-8652
Fax 519-634-8652
TFr 1-877-467-2083

Come and enjoy our unique and private suites. Units are located in an adjoining guest house, beside the Baden waterway. All have private entrances. Cardinal Suite is perfect for honeymooners or a special night out. The Hummingbird Unit, done in pine, is suitable for vacationers, or business people. The Country Lane Unit is wheelchair accessible, and well-suited for families. Enjoy the backyard fire-pit, fish pond, or the Olde Shanty sitting room. "Come Rest Your Wings at Willow Springs!"

ROOMS Family suite, Upper floor, Ground floor, Private entrance, **Baths** Ensuite, **Beds** Queen, **Air** In rooms, **Smoking** Outside, **In Room** Thermostat, Phone, TV, Fireplace, VCR/DVD, **OTHERS** Urban, Open all year, Handicapped access, **PAYMENT** Visa, Cheques accepted, Cash, Trvl's cheques, **BREAKFASTS** Full, Home-baked, Self-catered, **AMENITIES** Barbecue, Fridge, Patio, **THINGS TO DO** Rental canoe or boat, Golf, Fishing, Museums, Theatre, Shopping, Downhill skiing, Swimming, Horseback riding, Birdwatching, Antiquing, **LANGUAGE** Eng., **PRICE** (2 persons) 50–90 **(check with hosts for pricing details)**

BALA *(north of Toronto)*

Bellhaven Bed and Breakfast

(Mary and Bill Tannahill)

1022 Guy's Rd, Box 593, Bala, ON, P0C 1A0
www.bellhaven.ca
E-mail info@bellhaven.ca

705-762-0938
Fax 705-762-2622

Set among whispering pines, this lovely Muskoka home offers a panoramic view of Lake Muskoka from its extensive deck and great room. A separate guest sitting room with fireplace overlooks terraced gardens. Swim in the pristine waters of Lake Muskoka from our private dock. A full hearty breakfast with home-baked specialties is served on the deck (weather permitting). Minutes to Bala, Port Carling, golf and dining. Relax and refresh your spirit at Bellhaven Bed and Breakfast on beautiful Lake Muskoka.

ROOMS Upper floor, Ground floor, **Baths** Private, Ensuite, **Beds** King, Queen, Twin, **Air** Central, **Smoking** Outside, **OTHERS** Open all year, **PAYMENT** Cheques accepted, Cash, Trvl's cheques, **BREAKFASTS** Full, Home-baked, **AMENITIES** Central TV, Central phone, Fridge, Lounge, Patio, Central VCR/DVD, **THINGS TO DO** Rental bikes, Trail nearby, Rental canoe or boat, Comp. canoe or boat, Golf, Fishing, Museums, Art, Theatre, Entertainment, Attractions, Wineries/Breweries, Shopping, Cross-country skiing, Swimming, Horseback riding, **LANGUAGE** Eng., **PRICE** (2 persons) 135–150 **(check with hosts for pricing details)**

BANCROFT *(northeast of Toronto)*

Dreamer's Rock
Bed and Breakfast

(Laura Smith)

RR #4 (35556 Hwy 28 E), Bancroft, ON, K0L 1C0
www.dreamersrockbandb.com
E-mail dreamers_rock@canada.com

613-332-2350

Relax in a restful haven to the sight and sounds of moving water in an historic setting. Refresh and restore your mind, body and spirit at Dreamer's Rock Bed and Breakfast. Experience the incredibly tranquil setting where quiet can still be heard, overlooking tumbling waterfalls on the timeless Little Mississippi River. Ours is a four-seasons playground near Bancroft and Algonquin Park. Welcome to the ambience of our clean, comfortable smoke-free home and our hearty country breakfasts!

ROOMS Family suite, Upper floor, Ground floor, **Baths** Ensuite, Shared with guest, **Beds** King, Queen, Single or cots, Pullout sofa, **Air** Central, Ceiling fans, **Smoking** Outside, **In Room** VCR/DVD, **OTHERS** Open all year, Additional meals, Pets in residence, **PAYMENT** Cash, **BREAKFASTS** Full, Home-baked, **AMENITIES** Central TV, Central phone, Fridge, Lounge, Patio, Central Internet access, Central VCR/DVD, **THINGS TO DO** Trail nearby, Comp. canoe or boat, Golf, Fishing, Museums, Art, Theatre, Attractions, Shopping, Swimming, Horseback riding, Beach, **LANGUAGE** Eng., **PRICE** (2 persons) 65–110 **(check with hosts for pricing details)**

BANCROFT

Maple Leaf B&B

(Ann and Albert van Dreumel)

251 McLean Rd, Box 286, Maynooth, ON, K0L 2S0
www.bbcanada.com/mapleleafbb
E-mail aaupnrth@nexicom.net

613-338-2263
Fax 613-338-2263
TFr 1-866-538-2263

We are situated in the rolling hills of the Monteagle Valley with a beautiful view from the balcony and fall scenes. Our house is a 15-year-new log home on 50 acres of wooded bush and walking trails with complete privacy and yet close to all amenities such as general store, post office, liquor store, lakes/beach, fishing, Algonquin Park, Horseback riding. Directions: Hwy 62 N to Maple Leaf, turn right on Musclow-Greenview Rd, continue 1 km south, turn left on McLean Rd and go 1 km east to 251.

ROOMS Upper floor, **Baths** Shared with guest, **Beds** Queen, Double, **Air** In rooms, **Smoking** Outside, **OTHERS** Rural, **PAYMENT** Cheques accepted, Cash, Trvl's cheques, **BREAKFASTS** Full, Home-baked, **AMENITIES** Central TV, Central phone, Barbecue, Lounge, Patio, Central VCR/DVD, **THINGS TO DO** Trail nearby, Rental canoe or boat, Golf, Fishing, Museums, Art, Theatre, Entertainment, Attractions, Shopping, Cross-country skiing, Swimming, Horseback riding, Beach, Bird-watching, Antiquing, **LANGUAGE** Eng., Dutch, **PRICE** (2 persons) 80–90 **(check with hosts for pricing details)**

Bancroft

The Gathering Place
On Golden Ponds B&B

(Al and Annette Vandendriessche)

RR #1, Coe Hill, ON, K0L 1P0
www.gatheringbb.com
E-mail relax@gatheringbb.com

613-337-5177
Fax 613-337-5250

Experience luxury for the soul in our
moderen, 16-sided stackwall home. The
Gathering Place is truly a unique experience for all seasons. Al and Annette
welcome you for a relaxing getaway in
nature's romantic setting.

ROOMS Upper floor, Ground floor, Private entrance,
Baths Private, Shared with guest, **Beds** King, Queen,
Double, Twin, **Air** Central, **Smoking** Outside, **In Room**
TV, VCR/DVD, **OTHERS** Open all year, Handicapped
access, Additional meals, **PAYMENT** Visa, Cheques
accepted, Cash, Trvl's cheques, **BREAKFASTS** Full,
Home-baked, **AMENITIES** Central TV, Central phone,
Whirlpool, Barbecue, Laundry, Kitchen, Fridge, Patio,
Central Internet access, Central VCR/DVD, **THINGS TO
DO** Rental bikes, Trail nearby, Rental canoe or boat,
Golf, Fishing, Museums, Art, Theatre, Entertainment,
Attractions, Shopping, Cross-country skiing,
Swimming, Horseback riding, Beach, Birdwatching,
Antiquing, **LANGUAGE** Eng., Fr., **PRICE** (2 persons)
85–95 **(check with hosts for pricing details)**

Barrie *(north of Toronto)*

Brookview B&B

(Charlie and Lena Simpson)

1351 Line 2 N, Shanty Bay, ON, L0L 2L0
www.bbcanada.com/brookview

705-721-0523

Brookview is situated between Barrie and
Orillia on 60 picturesque acres, a perfect
location for weddings and photographs.
We offer our guests warm hospitality with
full homecooked breakfasts. Nearby is
Downhill skiing, cross-country skiing,
mountain biking, casino, golf courses and
other attractions. Enjoy our gardens and
wildlife. Snowshoes available. To find us,
take Hwy 400 north of Barrie to Exit 111,
turn left at stop sign, go 4 km to Line 2,
turn right for 1 km to 1351.

ROOMS Family suite, Upper floor, Ground floor, Private
entrance, **Baths** Private, Shared with guest, **Beds**
Queen, Double, Pullout sofa, **Air** Central, **Smoking**
Outside, **In Room** Thermostat, Phone, TV, Fireplace,
OTHERS Rural, Open all year, **PAYMENT** Cash, **BREAK-
FASTS** Full, Home-baked, **AMENITIES** Central TV,
Central phone, Fridge, Lounge, Patio, **THINGS TO DO**
Trail nearby, Golf, Fishing, Museums, Theatre,
Entertainment, Attractions, Shopping, Cross-country
skiing, Downhill skiing, Swimming, Beach, Birdwatch-
ing, Antiquing, **LANGUAGE** Eng., **PRICE** (2 persons)
60–100 **(check with hosts for pricing details)**

BARRIE

Cozy Corner Bed and Breakfast, Barrie

(Harry and Charita Kirby)

2 Morton Cres, Barrie, ON, L4N 7T3
www.cozycornerbb.com/
E-mail cozyc@bconnex.net

705-739-0157
Fax 705-739-1946

Barrie's B&B award winner for 1999 and 2003. Find comfort and cleanliness here. Spacious suites and bedrooms, queen beds, Jacuzzi, ensuite baths, posturpedic mattresses, private TV's, central air and electronic air cleaning. Relax in the resident's lounge by the toasty fire. Wake up to Harry's (retired European Chef) Eggs Florentine, English Shirred Eggs, Eggs Benedict or various omelettes complimented with premium coffee and imported teas. Vegetarian menu with pleasure. Call re cancellation policy. 10th year.

ROOMS Family suite, Upper floor, Lower floor, **Baths** Private, Ensuite, **Beds** Queen, Twin, Single or cots, **Air** Central, **Smoking** Outside, **In Room** Phone, TV, **OTHERS** Babysitting, Urban, Open all year, **PAYMENT** Visa, Cheques accepted, Cash, Trvl's cheques, **BREAKFASTS** Full, **AMENITIES** Central TV, Central phone, Whirlpool, Laundry, Lounge, Patio, **THINGS TO DO** Golf, Fishing, Museums, Art, Theatre, Entertainment, Attractions, Shopping, Cross-country skiing, Tennis, Swimming, Horseback riding, Beach, **LANGUAGE** Eng., Sp., Ger., **PRICE** (2 persons) 65–95 **(check with hosts for pricing details)**

BARRIE

O'Kanes B&B

(Carol and Michael O'Kane)

4609 Penetanguishene Rd, Hillsdale, ON, L0L 1V0
www.okanesbb.com
E-mail carol@netrover.com

705-835-3554
Fax 705-835-3214

O'Kanes 140 year old home is in Springwater township with its lush growth of hardwood forests. Our home has been renovated – the main floor has a large dining room, a cozy den with wood stove, televison and country kitchen. Second floor has three bedrooms, central air. Bathrooms are on both floors. Off street parking on premises. We are located 15 minutes midway between Barrie and Midland, 3 kms off Hwy 400. Take exit 121 go north on Hwy 93 for 3 kms to Hillsdale on corner of Hwy 93 and Albert.

ROOMS Upper floor, **Baths** Shared with guest, **Beds** King, Queen, Twin, **Smoking** Outside, **OTHERS** Rural, Open all year, **PAYMENT** Cash, Trvl's cheques, **BREAKFASTS** Full, **AMENITIES** Central TV, Central phone, **THINGS TO DO** Comp. bikes, Theatre, Shopping, Cross-country skiing, **LANGUAGE** Eng., Sp., Portuguese, **PRICE** (2 persons) 55–65 **(check with hosts for pricing details)**

BARRIE

Richmond Manor Bed & Breakfast

(Pam and Bob Richmond)

16 Blake St, Barrie, ON, L4M 1J6
www.bbcanada.com/1145.html
E-mail richmond.manor@sympatico.ca

705-726-7103

Ivy-covered Georgian-style home (c. 1911) with traditional elegance. Situated on large forested property close to downtown, near waterfront. Delicious breakfasts served in gracious dining room. Relax on charming covered side porch and enjoy the gardens. Many hand-painted treasures abound. Come and enjoy the friendly ambience of our home.

ROOMS Upper floor, **Baths** Private, Shared with guest, **Beds** Queen, Double, Single or cots, **Air** In rooms, **Smoking** Outside, **In Room** Phone, Fireplace, **OTHERS** Urban, Adult, Open all year, **PAYMENT** Cheques accepted, Cash, Trvl's cheques, **BREAKFASTS** Full, Home-baked, **AMENITIES** Central TV, Central phone, Lounge, Patio, **THINGS TO DO** Comp. bikes, Trail nearby, Golf, Fishing, Museums, Art, Theatre, Entertainment, Attractions, Wineries/Breweries, Shopping, Cross-country skiing, Downhill skiing, Tennis, Swimming, Horseback riding, Beach, Birdwatching, Antiquing, **LANGUAGE** Eng., **PRICE** (2 persons) 85–95 **(check with hosts for pricing details)**

BARRIE

Seasons Change

(Terry Oram)

3619 Line 5 N, RR #4, Horseshoe Valley, ON, L0K 1E0
www.seasonschange.ca
E-mail seasonschange@sympatico.ca

705-835-2987
TFr 1-866-863-3330

Whether it's indulging in the lazy days of summer, winding down to a peaceful autumn, resting in the quiet tranquility of a snow-covered winter or celebrating the awakening of spring, Seasons Change has the perfect atmosphere you need to get away from it all. Nestled in picturesque Horseshoe Valley and situated on 98 acres of breathtakingly forested property, there are plenty of trails for walking/cross-country skiing. Skiers/golfers will delight in the first-class resort facilitiy just down the road.

ROOMS Upper floor, Lower floor, **Baths** Private, Ensuite, **Beds** King, Queen, Double, Twin, Single or cots, **Air** Central, **Smoking** Outside, **OTHERS** Open all year, **PAYMENT** Visa, MC, Diners, Amex, Cash, Trvl's cheques, **BREAKFASTS** Full, Home-baked, **AMENITIES** Central TV, Whirlpool, Fridge, Hot bev. bar, Lounge, Patio, Central Internet access, Central VCR/DVD, **THINGS TO DO** Trail nearby, Golf, Fishing, Museums, Art, Theatre, Entertainment, Attractions, Shopping, Cross-country skiing, Downhill skiing, Swimming, Horseback riding, Beach, Antiquing, **LANGUAGE** Eng., **PRICE** (2 persons) 90–100 **(check with hosts for pricing details)**

BARRIE

Thornton Country Gardens B&B

(Edythe Dew)

218 Barrie St, Thornton, ON, L0L 2N0
www.ThorntonCountryGardensBandB.com
E-mail info@ThorntonCountryGardensBandB.com

705-458-4650
TFr 1-888-553-4934

Whether on business or holidays, visiting the family or exploring rich cultural and natural diversity of central Ontario, you won't find a better place to stay. Strategically located within minutes of major cultural and industrial centres, Thornton still offers charm and ambience of traditional country living. Choose from three unique guest rooms, each offering privacy, relaxation and distinct character. We'll pamper you with a delicious and nourishing breakfast as well as complimentary afternoon tea.

ROOMS Family suite, Upper floor, **Baths** Private, Ensuite, **Beds** King, Queen, Twin, Single or cots, **Air** In rooms, **In Room** TV, VCR/DVD, **OTHERS** Urban, Rural, Open all year, **PAYMENT** Cheques accepted, Cash, Trvl's cheques, **BREAKFASTS** Full, **AMENITIES** Central TV, Fridge, Lounge, Patio, Central VCR/DVD, **THINGS TO DO** Trail nearby, Golf, Fishing, Museums, Art, Theatre, Entertainment, Attractions, Wineries/ Breweries, Shopping, Cross-country skiing, Downhill skiing, Tennis, Swimming, Horseback riding, Birdwatching, Antiquing, **LANGUAGE** Eng., **PRICE** (2 persons) 75–85 **(check with hosts for pricing details)**

BARRYS BAY *(east of Algonquin Park)*

Fortune's Madawaska Valley Inn

(Nancy and Warwick Fortune)

19854 Hwy 60, Barrys Bay, ON, K0J 1B0
www.madawaskavalleyinn.com
E-mail info@madawaskavalleyinn.com

613-756-9014
TFr 1-800-363-2758

Our unique Inn is nestled in the bush of the Madawaska Valley near the town of Barry's Bay. We take pride in offering our guests personal attention and service in a quiet, relaxing atmosphere. The Inn's convenient location on Hwy 60 allows easy access to the many tourist destinations and natural wonders of the Valley. It is perhaps our beautiful Dining Room with Warwick's wonderful food that really sets us apart and keeps our guests returning. Located 45 minutes east of Algonquin Park's East Gate.

ROOMS Family suite, Upper floor, Ground floor, Private entrance, **Baths** Private, Ensuite, **Beds** King, Queen, **Air** Central, **Smoking** Outside, **In Room** TV, Fireplace, Internet access, **OTHERS** Rural, Open all year, Additional meals, **PAYMENT** Visa, MC, Direct debit, Cash, Trvl's cheques, **BREAKFASTS** Full, **AMENITIES** Whirlpool, Lounge, Patio, **THINGS TO DO** Trail nearby, Rental canoe or boat, Golf, Fishing, Attractions, Shopping, Cross-country skiing, Tennis, Swimming, Beach, Birdwatching, **LANGUAGE** Eng., **PRICE** (2 persons) 95–125 **(check with hosts for pricing details)**

BAYFIELD *(west of Toronto)*

Brentwood On The Beach

(Joan & Peter Karstens)

33937 Moore Court , RR #2, Zurich, ON, N0M 2T0
www.brentwoodonthebeach.com
E-mail beachbnb@hay.net

519-236-7137
Fax 519-236-7269

Come coast awhile. Luxury nine-room B&B. Delicious breakfasts overlooking Lake Huron. Three guest sitting rooms, fireplaces, special occasion suites, indoor pool, whirlpool, sauna. Balconies, patios, screened in porch, fully equipped guest kitchen, BBQ. Walkways lead from one garden nook to the next. Blend nature with culture visit Stratford Festival, Blyth Festival and Huron Country Playhouse. Stroll the endless sandy beach, spectacular sunsets, golf courses, hiking trails nearby. Near Bayfield, Lake Huron.

ROOMS Ground floor, Lower floor, Private entrance, **Baths** Ensuite, **Beds** King, Queen, Twin, **Air** Central, **Smoking** Outside, **In Room** TV, Fireplace, **OTHERS** Rural, Adult, Open all year, **PAYMENT** Visa, MC, Direct debit, Cash, Trvl's cheques, **BREAKFASTS** Full, **AMENITIES** Central TV, Central phone, Swimming pool, Sauna, Whirlpool, Barbecue, Kitchen, Fridge, Lounge, Patio, Central Internet access, Central VCR/DVD, **THINGS TO DO** Rental bikes, Trail nearby, Rental canoe or boat, Golf, Fishing, Museums, Art, Theatre, Shopping, Cross-country skiing, Tennis, Swimming, Beach, **LANGUAGE** Eng., Fr., Ger., **PRICE** (2 persons) 115–275 **(check with hosts for pricing details)**

BAYFIELD

Lakefront Bed & Breakfast

(Jim and Dona Knight)

Lane of Pines, RR #1, Bayfield, ON, N0M 1G0
www.canadianbandbguide.ca/bb.asp?ID=3026
E-mail jdknight@wightman.ca

519-482-8591

Lakefront B&B is located on beautiful Lake Huron. Take Hwy 21 north from Bayfield 2 1/2 miles to Lane of Pines. Turn in to the lake, turn right and we are the fifth cottage on the lake. The cottage is just 17 years old. We have three rooms with five beds, all with their own thermostat. Swim in the lake, walk on the beach, watch the sunset, enjoy a campfire or relax in the family room with gas stove and TV. There is a large deck facing the lake and an upstairs private deck off the large front bedroom. Alternate telephone: 519-887-6584.

ROOMS Family suite, Upper floor, **Baths** Shared with guest, **Beds** Double, Twin, **Air** Central, In rooms, **Smoking** Outside, **In Room** Thermostat, **OTHERS** Rural, Seasonal, Pets welcome, **PAYMENT** Cheques accepted, Cash, **BREAKFASTS** Full, Home-baked, **AMENITIES** Central TV, Central phone, Hot bev. bar, Lounge, Patio, **THINGS TO DO** Comp. bikes, Trail near by, Golf, Fishing, Shopping, Swimming, Beach, Antiquing, **LANGUAGE** Eng., **PRICE** (2 persons) 60–90 **(check with hosts for pricing details)**

BAYFIELD

Magnolia Manor B&B
(Carol Pakenham)

38906 Mill Rd, Varna, ON, N0M 1G0
www.magnoliamanor.ca
E-mail info@magnoliamanor.ca

519-233-3181
Fax 519-233-3181
TFr 1-800-216-5968

Our impressive 1870 estate, in a southern plantation setting, is a haven of peace and tranquility far removed from the hustle and bustle of city living. Languish in the shade of the weeping willows, stroll the lush grounds, take a dip in the secluded outdoor swimming pool, feed the fish in the Victorian pond. Step indoors through pillared entranceway, relax in the great room, curl up by the fieldstone fireplace or read in the plant-filled, bright and breezy sunroom. Only 5 minutes from Bayfield and Lake Huron.

ROOMS Upper floor, **Baths** Private, Ensuite, Shared with guest, Shared with hosts, **Beds** King, Queen, Double, Twin, **Air** Central, **Smoking** Outside, **OTHERS** Rural, Adult, Open all year, Pets in residence, **PAYMENT** Visa, MC, Cash, Trvl's cheques, **BREAKFASTS** Full, **AMENITIES** Central TV, Central phone, Swimming pool, Fridge, Hot bev. bar, Lounge, Patio, Central VCR/DVD, **THINGS TO DO** Trail nearby, Golf, Fishing, Museums, Art, Theatre, Entertainment, Attractions, Shopping, Cross-country skiing, Swimming, Horseback riding, Beach, Birdwatching, Antiquing, **LANGUAGE** Eng., **PRICE** (2 persons) 110–130 **(check with hosts for pricing details)**

BAYFIELD

Naftel House Bed & Breakfast
(Heather and Wesley Moffatt)

78619 Bluewater Hwy, Bayfield, ON, N0M 1G0
www.naftelhouse.ca
E-mail info@naftelhouse.ca

519-524-1313
Fax 519-524-4343
TFr 1-800-390-8534

Historic Victorian hideaway, only a short walk to the beach. Located on Hwy 21, just north of the unique town of Bayfield. A quiet retreat once featured in *Century Home* magazine. Delicious full breakfasts. Tastefully decorated with antiques. Explore history dating back to the original construction in 1876. Four area golf courses, numerous biking/hiking trails nearby. We welcome you to enjoy the peace and tranquility of this secluded acreage. Come and marvel at our beautiful Lake Huron sunsets.

ROOMS Upper floor, **Baths** Ensuite, Shared with hosts, **Beds** Queen, Twin, **Air** In rooms, **Smoking** Outside, **In Room** Thermostat, **OTHERS** Open all year, **PAYMENT** Visa, MC, Cash, Trvl's cheques, **BREAKFASTS** Full, Home-baked, **AMENITIES** Central TV, Fridge, Hot bev. bar, Lounge, Patio, Central VCR/DVD, **THINGS TO DO** Trail nearby, Golf, Fishing, Museums, Art, Theatre, Shopping, Swimming, Beach, Birdwatching, Antiquing, **LANGUAGE** Eng., **PRICE** (2 persons) 89–115 **(check with hosts for pricing details)**

BAYFIELD

Pleasant Pheasant

(Alex and Caroline Harrett)

35389 Bayfield River Rd, Bayfield, ON, N0M 1G0
www.kent.net/recreation/PleasantPheasant.htm
E-mail pheasant@cabletv.on.ca

519-482-3036
TFr 1-866-802-3292

Pleasant Pheasant – stay in the country.
It's a natural! Relax and enjoy the simple
ambience of a country stay. Nestled comfortably on 15 acres of pastoral land in a
cozy five bedroom refurbished century
home. Let yourself unwind. Visit our animals – three horses, four miniature faint-
ing goats, exotic birds, bunnies and two
kitties who would really like to be house
cats. We are a country mile from the
shores of Lake Huron and the Village of
Bayfield. Enjoy Ontario's west coast pure
gold sunsets. The best!

ROOMS Upper floor, Ground floor, **Baths** Private, **Beds**
Queen, **Smoking** Outside, **In Room** TV, **OTHERS** Rural,
Open all year, Pets in residence, **PAYMENT** Cheques
accepted, Cash, Trvl's cheques, **BREAKFASTS** Full,
AMENITIES Central TV, Central phone, Barbecue,
Kitchen, Fridge, Lounge, Patio, **THINGS TO DO** Comp.
bikes, Trail nearby, Golf, Fishing, Museums, Art, Theatre,
Shopping, Beach, **LANGUAGE** Eng., **PRICE** (2 persons)
75–120 **(check with hosts for pricing details)**

BELLEVILLE *(east of Toronto)*

Bell Creek Heritage House

(Ralph and Katie Porter)

374 Airport Parkway W, Belleville, ON, K8N 4Z6
www.bbcanada.com/3097.html
E-mail ralph.porter1@sympatico.ca

613-968-4995
Fax 613-968-6632

Guests are our specialty. Carefully
planned breakfasts are served in a cozy
dining room. Renovations have returned
our home to the charm of its period.
Attractions include beaches, parks,
antique shops, trails, malls, colleges and
sports venues. Find us by taking Hwy 37
South at Belleville to College St East, turn
left and proceed 1 km to Airport Parkway
W on the right. Continue 2.3 km to #374.
A wishing well and arbor border the
driveway.

ROOMS Upper floor, Private entrance, **Baths** Ensuite,
Shared with guest, **Beds** Double, Twin, Single or cots,
Air Central, **In Room** TV, **OTHERS** Rural, Adult, Open all
year, **PAYMENT** Cheques accepted, Cash, Trvl's
cheques, **BREAKFASTS** Full, **AMENITIES** Central TV,
Central phone, Swimming pool, Barbecue, **THINGS TO
DO** Golf, Fishing, Museums, Art, Theatre, Entertain-
ment, Attractions, Wineries/Breweries, Shopping,
Tennis, Swimming, Beach, **LANGUAGE** Eng., **PRICE** (2
persons) 75–85 **(check with hosts for pricing details)**

BELLEVILLE

Hickory House Bed & Breakfast

(Kathryn Fellows)

38 Old Mill Park, Foxboro, ON, K0K 2B0
www.hickoryhouse.net
E-mail info@hickoryhouse.net

**613-968-4724
Fax 613-968-3133**

A spectacular riverside setting, luxurious Egyptian cotton linens, scented candles and foaming bath crystals for the Jacuzzis, superb food and distinctive hosts ... this is the Hickory House experience. Whether you're spending a few days in our area, travelling through, or yearning for a special getaway, allow us to pamper you with our unique form of hospitality. We're in the city limits of Belleville, halfway between Toronto and Montreal, on the Moira River, 8 km north of Hwy 401 at Exit 543B.

ROOMS Upper floor, **Baths** Private, Ensuite, **Beds** King, Queen, Double, **Air** Central, **Smoking** Outside, **In Room** TV, **OTHERS** Rural, Open all year, Pets in residence, Pets welcome, **PAYMENT** Visa, MC, Cash, Trvl's cheques, **BREAKFASTS** Full, **AMENITIES** Central TV, Central phone, Swimming pool, Lounge, Patio, **THINGS TO DO** Trail nearby, Golf, Fishing, Museums, Art, Theatre, Entertainment, Attractions, Wineries/Breweries, Shopping, Cross-country skiing, Tennis, Swimming, Horseback riding, Beach, Birdwatching, Antiquing, **LANGUAGE** Eng., **PRICE** (2 persons) 85–125 **(check with hosts for pricing details)**

BELLEVILLE

Place Victoria Place

(Daniele and Gord Snodgrass)

156 Victoria Ave, Belleville, ON, K8N 2B4
www.placevictoriaplace.ca
E-mail placevictoriaplace@bellnet.ca

613-967-8560

From 401 East or West, take Hwy 62 South (becomes North Front St). Follow North Front St through town. The road bends to the left. Stay in the left lane and go over the Moira River Bridge. Proceed straight through the set of lights at the bridge. (Post Office is on the left.) At the next set of lights turn left (which is Victoria Ave). Proceed 7 blocks and turn left on Albert St. We are on the corner of Victoria Ave and Albert St. Guest parking is on Albert St.

ROOMS Upper floor, Private entrance, **Baths** Private, **Beds** Queen, **Air** In rooms, **Smoking** Outside, **In Room** TV, **OTHERS** Urban, Open all year, Pets in residence, **PAYMENT** Visa, MC, Cash, Trvl's cheques, **BREAKFASTS** Continental, **AMENITIES** Central phone, Fridge, Lounge, Central VCR/DVD, **THINGS TO DO** Trail nearby, Fishing, Theatre, Entertainment, Attractions, Wineries/Breweries, Shopping, Antiquing, **LANGUAGE** Eng., Fr., **PRICE** (2 persons) 95 **(check with hosts for pricing details)**

BELLEVILLE

Twin Oakes Bed & Breakfast
(Carole and Tom Burmaster)

310 Bleecker Ave, Belleville, ON, K8N 3V4
www.twinoakes.com
E-mail twinoakes@bellnet.ca

613-771-0107
Fax 613-771-0107

Twin Oakes B&B, in Belleville's Old East
Hill, is centred just a few hours from
either Toronto or Montreal's International
Airports – the perfect place to ensure a
relaxing start or finish to your Ontario
vacation. Reservations preferred, but not
necessarily needed.

ROOMS Upper floor, **Baths** Ensuite, **Beds** Double,
Single or cots, **Air** Central, In rooms, **Smoking** Outside,
In Room Internet access, **OTHERS** Babysitting, Urban,
Open all year, Pets in residence, Pets welcome, **PAY-
MENT** Visa, MC, Cash, Trvl's cheques, **BREAKFASTS**
Full, **AMENITIES** Central TV, Central phone, Barbecue,
Kitchen, Fridge, Hot bev. bar, Lounge, Patio, Central
Internet access, Central VCR/DVD, **THINGS TO DO** Trail
nearby, Rental canoe or boat, Golf, Fishing, Museums,
Art, Theatre, Entertainment, Attractions, Wineries/
Breweries, Shopping, Tennis, Swimming, Horseback
riding, Beach, Birdwatching, Antiquing, **LANGUAGE**
Eng., **PRICE** (2 persons) 80–85 **(check with hosts for
pricing details)**

BETHANY *(northeast of Toronto)*

Plantation House Bed & Breakfast Country Retreat
(Rose and Rex Meghie)

982 Porter Rd, Bethany, ON, L0A 1A0
www.plantationhousebb.ca
E-mail rosemeghie@sympatico.ca

705-277-9431

A dramatic change to a relaxed lifestyle
awaits you at Plantation House. The newly
renovated Spanish-Caribbean Villa is nestled on 57 acres. We offer a rare blend of
luxury and comfort. Each guest room is
beautifully appointed. Year round you can
pamper yourself in the outdoor hot tub.
Minutes from Ganaraska Trail, 4th Line
Theatre and historic downtown Peterborough. Plantation House can be your
home while exploring the Kawartha
Lakes. Welcome to Paradise in the Village
of Bethany!

ROOMS Upper floor, **Baths** Private, Shared with guest,
Beds King, Queen, **Air** Central, **Smoking** Outside, **OTH-
ERS** Open all year, **PAYMENT** Cheques accepted, Cash,
Trvl's cheques, **BREAKFASTS** Full, Home-baked,
AMENITIES Central TV, Central phone, Whirlpool,
Lounge, Patio, Central Internet access, Central
VCR/DVD, **THINGS TO DO** Trail nearby, Golf, Fishing,
Museums, Art, Theatre, Entertainment, Attractions,
Wineries/Breweries, Shopping, Cross-country skiing,
Downhill skiing, Horseback riding, Beach, Birdwatch-
ing, Antiquing, **LANGUAGE** Eng., **PRICE** (2 persons)
100–150 **(check with hosts for pricing details)**

Blind River *(northern Ontario)*

A Taste of Home

(Yvonne Bohren)

29 Fullerton St, Blind River, ON, P0R 1B0
www.bbcanada.com/989.html
E-mail ybohren@personainternet.com

705-356-7165

From the east, we are just after the lights (Hwy 17). From the west, before lights. Make your plans to stop in this very picturesque town. Enjoy our lovely 18-hole golf course, shop or take a walk around our boardwalk or to the marina at the end of the day. Warm and friendly hospitality awaits you at this old family home from the early 1900s. Close to many day trips. A perfect halfway stop when going west from Toronto or on your return.

ROOMS Family suite, Upper floor, **Baths** Shared with guest, **Beds** Queen, Double, Twin, Pullout sofa, **Air** Central, **Smoking** Outside, **OTHERS** Open all year, **PAYMENT** Visa, MC, Cheques accepted, Cash, Trvl's cheques, **BREAKFASTS** Full, **AMENITIES** Central TV, Central phone, Lounge, **THINGS TO DO** Trail nearby, Golf, Fishing, Museums, Shopping, Cross-country skiing, Tennis, Swimming, Beach, **LANGUAGE** Eng., **PRICE** (2 persons) 50–60 **(check with hosts for pricing details)**

Bracebridge *(north of Toronto)*

Country Hearts

(Lorene and Murray Ryall)

1290 Falkenburg Rd, Bracebridge, ON, P1L 1X4
www.bbmuskoka.com/countryhearts
E-mail countryhearts@on.aibn.com

705-646-1991
TFr 1-866-646-1991

Located in the "Heart of Muskoka" nestled among rocks and trees. Be amazed by the quiet atmosphere, brilliant stars and night sky. Birdwatch, stroll the gardens or just relax. Tour the area and all its attractions. Enjoy a wholesome "country" breakfast with local produce and homemade specialties. From Hwy 11 take the exit for Hwy 118 to Bracebridge. At the stoplight by Tim Horton's turn right. Next light, Manitoba/MR #4 turn left. Go 6 km to Falkenburg Rd/MR #47 and turn left. Go 4.7 km to #1290.

ROOMS Ground floor, **Baths** Ensuite, Shared with guest, **Beds** King, Queen, **Smoking** Outside, **In Room** Thermostat, **OTHERS** Rural, Adult, Open all year, **PAYMENT** Visa, MC, Cash, Trvl's cheques, **BREAKFASTS** Full, Home-baked, **AMENITIES** Central TV, Central phone, Lounge, Patio, Central VCR/DVD, **THINGS TO DO** Trail nearby, Rental canoe or boat, Golf, Fishing, Museums, Art, Theatre, Entertainment, Attractions, Wineries/Breweries, Shopping, Cross-country skiing, Downhill skiing, Tennis, Swimming, Horseback riding, Beach, Birdwatching, Antiquing, **LANGUAGE** Eng., **PRICE** (2 persons) 75–90 **(check with hosts for pricing details)**

BRACEBRIDGE

The Yellow Door B&B

(Jessica Murray and Navarro Ralph)

74 Taylor Rd, Bracebridge, ON, P1L 1J2
www.theyellowdoor.ca
E-mail reservations@theyellowdoor.ca

705-646-2504

The Yellow Door B&B offers a relaxing
environment just a moment's walk from
downtown. Our central location puts you
at arm's-length from all of the wonders
Muskoka has to offer. Take in the Falls,
shop, dine, hike, swim, golf or simply
unwind. You are also invited to relax on
the large deck or verandah and, depending on talent, our guests are always invited to play us a tune. We offer a homemade breakfast daily. Choose from our
king- or queen-size rooms.

ROOMS Upper floor, **Baths** Shared with guest, **Beds**
King, Queen, **Air** Ceiling fans, **Smoking** Outside, **In
Room** Thermostat, TV, VCR/DVD, **OTHERS** Urban, Open
all year, Pets in residence, Pets welcome, **PAYMENT**
Cash, **BREAKFASTS** Full, **AMENITIES** Barbecue,
Lounge, Patio, **THINGS TO DO** Rental bikes, Trail near-
by, Rental canoe or boat, Golf, Fishing, Museums,
Entertainment, Attractions, Wineries/Breweries,
Shopping, Cross-country skiing, Tennis, Swimming,
Horseback riding, Beach, Birdwatching, Antiquing,
PRICE (2 persons) 75–95 **(check with hosts for pricing
details)**

BRADFORD WEST GWILLIMBURY
(north of Toronto)

Blossom The Clown's B&B

(Lorne and Carol Kay)

33 Mulock Dr, Bond Head, Bradford West Gwillimbury,
ON, L3Z 2A9
www.blossomtheclownbandb.com
E-mail blossomb-b@on.aibn.com

905-775-0088
Fax 905-775-1655
TFr 1-888-627-6690

Inside our home is a handicapped-acces-
sible bungalow, with just a few front outside steps. We have three bedrooms with
two rooms sharing a bath and the other
an ensuite. You can enjoy the TV room,
reading room with organ and card
games, or go downstairs to play snooker.
Our entire main floor is B&B with *our*
living accommodations downstairs.
Smoking is allowed only outside on the
sheltered porch. We serve full breakfasts
with day access to our kitchen, coffee, tea
and sweets. Near Cookstown Mall.

ROOMS Ground floor, **Baths** Ensuite, Shared with
guest, **Beds** Queen, Twin, Single or cots, **Air** Central,
Smoking Outside, **OTHERS** Rural, Open all year,
Handicapped access, Additional meals, **PAYMENT**
Cash, Trvl's cheques, **BREAKFASTS** Full, Home-baked,
AMENITIES Central TV, Central phone, Barbecue,
Laundry, Kitchen, Fridge, Hot bev. bar, Lounge, Patio,
Central Internet access, Central VCR/DVD, **THINGS TO
DO** Trail nearby, Golf, Fishing, Art, Theatre, Attractions,
Shopping, Cross-country skiing, Tennis, Swimming,
Horseback riding, Beach, Birdwatching, Antiquing,
LANGUAGE Eng., **PRICE** (2 persons) 60–80 **(check
with hosts for pricing details)**

Brantford *(southwest of Toronto)*

The Alexandra Bed & Breakfast

(Sharon Garner)

26 William St, Brantford, ON, N3T 3K4
www.thealexandra.ca
E-mail thealexandra@brant.net

519-758-8077

A luxurious alternative to hotel accom-modations. A private hideaway with two suites, located in a stately heritage home. Upon check-in you receive a key to the front door and suite, each having a sepa-rate sitting area, private bathroom and a small amenities closet with refrigerator, microwave, toaster, kettle and service for two. A trolley with fresh fruit, pastries, tea/coffee arrives at your door when you wish. Close to bike trails, Casino, Grand River and fine dinning. Large living room may be a conference room.

ROOMS Family suite, Ground floor, Private entrance, **Baths** Private, Ensuite, **Beds** Queen, Single or cots, **Air** In rooms, **Smoking** Outside, **In Room** Thermostat, Phone, TV, Fireplace, **OTHERS** Adult, Open all year, **PAYMENT** Cheques accepted, Cash, Trvl's cheques, **BREAKFASTS** Continental, Self-catered, **AMENITIES** Central TV, Central phone, Kitchen, Fridge, Hot bev. bar, Lounge, Patio, **THINGS TO DO** Trail nearby, Rental canoe or boat, Golf, Fishing, Museums, Art, Theatre, Entertainment, Attractions, Wineries/Breweries, Shopping, Tennis, Swimming, Horseback riding, Antiquing, **LANGUAGE** Eng., **PRICE** (2 persons) 95–115 **(check with hosts for pricing details)**

Brantford

The Country Manor

(Kathy and John Chapman)

567 Paris Rd, RR #1, Paris, ON, N3L 3E1
www.thecountrymanor.com
E-mail info@thecountrymanor.com

519-442-6551

Nestled among majestic trees, a stroll away from the Grand River and biking trails, The Country Manor invites you to put up your feet, relax and enjoy the ambience of a "home away from home." Let us pamper you with king- or queen-size beds, ensuite or private bathrooms, cable TV, Internet access, guest's lounge, private entrances, A/C and in-ground pool. "Honeymoon Suite" with in-room hot tub, full ensuite. Five beautifully appointed rooms, haven for hikers and bikers. Free shuttle service.

ROOMS Upper floor, Ground floor, Private entrance, **Baths** Private, Ensuite, **Beds** King, Queen, Twin, Single or cots, **Air** Central, **Smoking** Outside, **In Room** TV, **OTHERS** Rural, Adult, Open all year, Additional meals, **PAYMENT** Visa, MC, Diners, Amex, Cash, **BREAKFASTS** Full, Continental, Home-baked, **AMENITIES** Central TV, Central phone, Swimming pool, Whirlpool, Barbecue, Laundry, Kitchen, Fridge, Hot bev. bar, Lounge, Patio, **THINGS TO DO** Rental bikes, Trail nearby, Rental canoe or boat, Golf, Fishing, Museums, Art, Theatre, Entertainment, Attractions, Shopping, Tennis, Swimming, Horseback riding, Beach, **LANGUAGE** Eng., **PRICE** (2 persons) 85–120 **(check with hosts for pricing details)**

Bridgenorth *(northeast of Toronto)*

Birch Point Bay
(Karl Erickson and Ann Bourne Erickson)

76 Birch Point Dr, Ennismore, ON, K0L 1T0
www.bbcanada.com/1134.html
E-mail cairnwest@yahoo.ca

705-292-6000
Cell phone: 705 930 5032

Quiet, smoke-free, modern home with full access to waterfront on Pigeon Lake. Relax and have fun in all seasons! Enjoy privacy, guest living room, delicious breakfasts; sunsets, paddleboat, fishing, swimming, skating; docking facilities, public boat launch; boating and relaxation on the Trent Canal System. Just north of Peterborough, and south of Buckhorn; close to Hwys 7 and 115. Chemong Lake Causeway or Yankee Line to Boundary Rd, north 3.5 km to Birch Point Dr.

ROOMS Ground floor, Lower floor, **Baths** Private, Shared with guest, **Beds** Queen, Single or cots, **Air** Central, **Smoking** Outside, **OTHERS** Rural, Adult, Open all year, Pets in residence, Pets welcome, **PAYMENT** Cash, Trvl's cheques, **BREAKFASTS** Full, Continental, **AMENITIES** Central TV, Central phone, Laundry, Fridge, Hot bev. bar, Lounge, Patio, Central Internet access, Central VCR/DVD, **THINGS TO DO** Rental bikes, Trail nearby, Rental canoe or boat, Comp. Canoe or boat, Golf, Fishing, Museums, Art, Theatre, Entertainment, Attractions, Shopping, Cross-country skiing, Swimming, Beach, Birdwatching, Antiquing, **LAN-GUAGE** Eng., **PRICE** (2 persons) 70–110 **(check with hosts for pricing details)**

Brighton *(east of Toronto)*

Apple Manor Bed & Breakfast
(Shona Clark)

96 Main St, Box 11, Brighton, ON, K0K 1H0
www.bbcanada.com/1249.html
E-mail aplmanor@reach.net

613-475-0351

From Hwy 401 take Brighton Exit 509 (Hwy 30) south to traffic lights in town. Turn right on Main St (Hwy 2) and continue for 2 blocks. Located on the Apple Route, gracious and elegant Century home (c. 1843) with warm and relaxing ambience and authentically decorated with period furniture and original artworks. Delight in specialty breakfasts. Enjoy the shady verandah, tranquil fish pond or have a swim in the small but refreshing pool. Passes for Presqu'ile Provincial Park can be arranged.

ROOMS Upper floor, **Baths** Shared with guest, **Beds** Queen, Double, Twin, **Air** Central, **Smoking** Outside, **In Room** TV, **OTHERS** Urban, Adult, Open all year, Pets in residence, **PAYMENT** Visa, MC, Cash, Trvl's cheques, **BREAKFASTS** Full, Home-baked, **AMENITIES** Swimming pool, Lounge, Patio, **THINGS TO DO** Trail nearby, Golf, Fishing, Museums, Art, Theatre, Attractions, Shopping, Cross-country skiing, Tennis, Swimming, Beach, Birdwatching, Antiquing, **LAN-GUAGE** Eng., basic French, **PRICE** (2 persons) 60–80 **(check with hosts for pricing details)**

Brighton

Butler Creek Country Inn
(Burke Friedrichkeit and Ken Bosher)

RR #7, County Rd 30–202, Brighton, ON, K0K 1H0
www.butlercreekcountryinn.com
E-mail butlerbbb@reach.net

613-475-1248
Fax 613-475-5267
TFr 1-877-477-5827

Butler Creek Country Inn offers a rare combination, Victorian elegance, convenient location and peaceful setting. Located in a pretty valley, the home overlooks 9 acres of trees, meadows, garden and Butler Creek. Start your morning with a delicious breakfast and feast yourself during our "Gourmet packages" from November to April. Theatre Packages are available in spring and fall and golf packages in summer. CAA/AAA approved.

ROOMS Upper floor, Ground floor, **Baths** Ensuite, Shared with guest, **Beds** King, Queen, Twin, Pullout sofa, **Air** Central, **OTHERS** Urban, Rural, Open all year, Pets in residence, **PAYMENT** Visa, MC, Amex, Direct debit, Cash, Trvl's cheques, **BREAKFASTS** Full, **AMENITIES** Central TV, Central phone, Lounge, **THINGS TO DO** Trail nearby, Golf, Fishing, Museums, Art, Theatre, Attractions, Wineries/ Breweries, Cross-country skiing, Tennis, Swimming, Horseback riding, Beach, Birdwatching, Antiquing, **LANGUAGE** Eng., Fr., Ger., **PRICE** (2 persons) 85–115 **(check with hosts for pricing details)**

Brighton

Harbour Haven
Bed & Breakfast
(Linda and Jim Payne)

44 Harbour St, RR #3, Brighton, ON, K0K 1H0
www.bbcanada.com/2039.html

613-475-1006

Relax by the pool at our spacious contemporary home. Guests enjoy separate queen, double or single rooms, with fine linens, quilts and duvets. There is a private sitting area or join us in our cozy family room with fireplace. We serve a full home-baked breakfast. We are close to Presqu'ile Provincial Park, fine dining, shopping and offer everything you need for a great vacation or a weekend getaway. You will find warm hospitality awaits you. For cyclists, we are located directly on the Waterfront Trail.

ROOMS Ground floor, Private entrance, **Baths** Shared with guest, **Beds** Queen, Double, Single or cots, **Air** In rooms, **Smoking** Outside, **In Room** Thermostat, **OTHERS** Rural, Adult, Open all year, **PAYMENT** Visa, MC, Cash, Trvl's cheques, **BREAKFASTS** Full, Home-baked, **AMENITIES** Central TV, Central phone, Swimming pool, Barbecue, Lounge, Patio, **THINGS TO DO** Comp. bikes, Trail nearby, Golf, Fishing, Museums, Art, Theatre, Attractions, Shopping, Cross-country skiing, Tennis, Swimming, Beach, **LANGUAGE** Eng., Fr., **PRICE** (2 persons) 65–80 **(check with hosts for pricing details)**

BROCKVILLE *(south of Ottawa)*

Edgewood Farms B&B

(Terry and David McGurrin)

7602 7th Concession Rd, RR #2, Addison, ON, K0E 1A0
www.canadianbandbguide.ca/bb.asp?ID=3087
E-mail edgewood@ripnet.com

613-345-7894
Fax 613-345-7894

Edgewood Farms is the ultimate hideaway nestled in the village of New Dublin. Our 18th century farm offers groomed, marked trails leading to an aboriginal burial site, outdoor pool, indoor hot tub and a lavish country breakfast. After strolling through our gardens and orchard, visit our Maple Museum. A fully operational Sugar Shack and Pancake House is open seasonally. Tour the 250-acre farm on horseback or on a wagon ride. At Edgewood Farms people come as strangers and leave as friends.

ROOMS Upper floor, **Baths** Shared with guest, **Beds** Queen, Double, **Smoking** Outside, **In Room** Phone, **OTHERS** Rural, Open all year, Additional meals, Pets in residence, Pets welcome, **PAYMENT** Cash, **BREAKFASTS** Full, Home-baked, **AMENITIES** Central TV, Central phone, Swimming pool, Whirlpool, Barbecue, **THINGS TO DO** Comp. bikes, Trail nearby, Golf, Fishing, Museums, Theatre, Entertainment, Attractions, Shopping, Cross-country skiing, Swimming, Horseback riding, Antiquing, **LANGUAGE** Eng., **PRICE** (2 persons) 65–65 **(check with hosts for pricing details)**

BROCKVILLE

Misty Pines B&B

(Betty Slack)

1389 Country Rd 2 W (Formerly Hwy #2), Brockville, ON, K6V 5T3
www.bbcanada.com/1704.html
www.mistypines.ca
E-mail bslack@ripnet.com

613-342-4325

Located on the "Waterfront Bike Trail" of the 1000 Islands Region. Modern, quiet home set amidst old-growth forest with private "nature walks" to St. Lawrence River. Secure storage for scuba gear and bikes. Historic downtown Brockville – restaurants, museums, boat cruises, parks, golfing, fishing, swimming, scuba, etc. Tastefully decorated rooms, full breakfast served in dining room. Living room for TV, reading, conversation. Driving times: 45 minutes to Ottawa; 2 1/2 hours to Toronto; 1 1/2 hours to Montreal.

Baths Private, Ensuite, Shared with guest, **Beds** Queen, Twin, Single or cots, **Smoking** Outside, **In Room** Thermostat, **PAYMENT** Cash, Trvl's cheques, **BREAKFASTS** Full, **AMENITIES** Central TV, Central phone, Barbecue, Fridge, Patio, Central Internet access, Central VCR/DVD, **THINGS TO DO** Comp. bikes, Rental bikes, Trail nearby, Golf, Fishing, Museums, Art, Theatre, Attractions, Shopping, Cross-country skiing, Swimming, Horseback riding, Beach, Birdwatching, Antiquing, **LANGUAGE** Eng., some French, **PRICE** (2 persons) 75–100 **(check with hosts for pricing details)**

Brockville

Pine Street

(Francine and Michael Dunn)

92 Pine St, Brockville, ON, K6V 1G9
www.1000islandsinfo.com/pinestinn
E-mail dunnwithflair@hotmail.com

613-498-3866

Graceful 1870s home. You will be fed like royalty and treated like family. Come and hear our ghostly stories – lots of royal tales. Find out about our royal connection. Chef on premises. Picnic baskets too! Open all year.

ROOMS Upper floor, **Baths** Shared with guest, **Beds** Double, Twin, **Smoking** Outside, **OTHERS** Open all year, Additional meals, Pets in residence, Pets welcome, **PAYMENT** Cash, Trvl's cheques, **BREAKFASTS** Full, **AMENITIES** Central phone, Patio, **THINGS TO DO** Golf, Fishing, Museums, Theatre, Tennis, Swimming, Beach, Antiquing, **LANGUAGE** Eng., Fr., **PRICE** (2 persons) 75–80 **(check with hosts for pricing details)**

Burlington *(west of Toronto)*

Cedarcroft

(Arlene Glatz)

3273 Myers Lane, Burlington, ON, L7N 1K6
www.canadianbandbguide.ca/bb.asp?ID=2116
E-mail cedarcroftag@cogeco.ca

905-637-2491

Warm and welcoming country-style home in the city. Enjoy breakfast in sunroom overlooking patio and yard surrounded by evergreen trees. Close to Lake Ontario, parks and shopping. Two double rooms, one with twin beds, one with queen. Extended stay rates available. Other phone: 905-637-2079.

ROOMS Upper floor, **Baths** Shared with guest, **Beds** Queen, Twin, **Air** Central, Ceiling fans, **Smoking** Outside, **In Room** TV, **OTHERS** Urban, Open all year, **PAYMENT** Cash, **BREAKFASTS** Full, **AMENITIES** Central phone, Laundry, Kitchen, **THINGS TO DO** Trail nearby, Attractions, Shopping, Antiquing, **LANGUAGE** Eng., **PRICE** (2 persons) 65–65 **(check with hosts for pricing details)**

BURLINGTON

Seville-Roe Guesthouse and Gallery

(Peter and Linda Roe)

259 Plains Rd W, Burlington, ON, L7T 1G1
www.seville-roe.com
E-mail peterlinda.roe@sympatico.ca

905-523-9251
TFr 1-866-742-4541

We invite you to stay in our restored home, a cheerful, relaxing and comfortable retreat, minutes away (on foot) from the Royal Botanical Gardens. Burlington is midway between Niagara and Toronto. Our bedrooms are bright and sunny with ensuite or private bathrooms, all with whirlpool baths and private showers, hairdryers, etc. There are also spacious lounge areas in which to relax. We offer wholesome, healthy and creative cuisine. Our guests say we are *the* place to stay in the area.

ROOMS Upper floor, **Baths** Private, Ensuite, **Beds** Queen, Twin, **Air** Central, In rooms, Ceiling fans, **Smoking** Outside, **OTHERS** Urban, Adult, Open all year, Pets in residence, **PAYMENT** Cash, Trvl's cheques, **BREAKFASTS** Full, Home-baked, **AMENITIES** Central TV, Whirlpool, Fridge, Hot bev. bar, Lounge, Patio, Central VCR/DVD, **THINGS TO DO** Trail nearby, Golf, Fishing, Museums, Art, Theatre, Entertainment, Attractions, Wineries/Breweries, Shopping, Cross-country skiing, Horseback riding, Beach, Birdwatching, Antiquing, **LANGUAGE** Eng., **PRICE** (2 persons) 95–125 **(check with hosts for pricing details)**

CAYUGA *(south of Hamilton)*

Carrousel Bed and Breakfast

(Bernadine Tompkins)

51 Winnett St N, Cayuga, ON, N0A 1E0
www.bbcanada.com/carrouselbb
E-mail carrouselbb@mountaincable.net

905-772-5348
Fax 905-772-6183

In the heart of Cayuga, Haldimand County, next to the Grand River. A beautifully decorated home offering warmth and relaxation. Two spacious private suites each with queen-size beds, cable TV sitting area, mini kitchenette and ensuite bathrooms. One suite has a gas fireplace and extra cot. The third room has a double bed, and TV, must use common bathroom. A full-course breakfast is served in the formal dining room or outside on the porch. Sit and enjoy the fish pond and flower beds. Central air.

ROOMS Upper floor, Lower floor, **Baths** Ensuite, Shared with hosts, **Beds** Queen, Double, Single or cots, **Air** Central, **Smoking** Outside, **In Room** TV, Fireplace, **OTHERS** Urban, Open all year, Handicapped access, Pets welcome, **PAYMENT** Visa, MC, Cash, Trvl's cheques, **BREAKFASTS** Full, **AMENITIES** Central phone, Laundry, Fridge, Hot bev. bar, Patio, Central Internet access, **THINGS TO DO** Golf, Fishing, Museums, Art, Theatre, Attractions, Shopping, Swimming, Horseback riding, Antiquing, **LANGUAGE** Eng., **PRICE** (2 persons) 60–75 **(check with hosts for pricing details)**

CAYUGA

River Inn B&B

(Frank and Helen Belbeck)

1459 Haldimand Rd 17, RR #1, Cayuga, ON, N0A 1E0
www.bbcanada.com/riverinn
E-mail riverinn@linetap.com

905-774-8057
TFr 1-866-824-7878

River Inn B&B is situated in a 14-acre
park-like setting on the historic Grand
River between the charming towns of
Cayuga and Dunnville in southern
Ontario. Close to Lake Erie, 1 hour from
Niagara Falls and 90 minutes from
Pearson Airport, Toronto. We feature three
suites with queen beds and satellite TV.
A three-room fully equipped guest house
with a great view of the river and swimming pool is also available for longer
term stays, special occasions, honeymooners, and can accommodate up to
four people. Inside parking, A/C.

ROOMS Family suite, Upper floor, Ground floor, **Baths**
Ensuite, **Beds** King, Queen, Twin, Single or cots, Pullout
sofa, **Air** Central, In rooms, **Smoking** Outside, **In Room**
Phone, TV, **OTHERS** Rural, Open all year, Handicapped
access, Additional meals, **PAYMENT** Visa, MC, Amex,
Cash, **BREAKFASTS** Full, Continental, Home-baked,
Self-catered, **AMENITIES** Central TV, Central phone,
Swimming pool, Barbecue, Kitchen, Fridge, Lounge,
Patio, **THINGS TO DO** Trail nearby, Golf, Fishing,
Museums, Theatre, Attractions, Wineries/Breweries,
Shopping, Swimming, Beach, **LANGUAGE** Eng., **PRICE**
(2 persons) 65–125 **(check with hosts for pricing
details)**

CHESLEY *(northwest of Toronto)*

Sconeview B&B

(Stacy Charlton)

1645 Bruce Rd, 10 RR #3, Chesley, ON, N0G 1L0
www.bbcanada.com/sconeviewbb
E-mail stacy.charlton@sympatico.ca

519-363-6992
Fax 519-363-5147

Located on 22 acres of pines, perennial
gardens, fish pond. North Saugeen runs
through property. Canoes and kayaks
available for your enjoyment. Paddle to
Chesley, walking trails, antique shop,
restaurants; fishing for trout, bass, pike,
see resident swans. Hot tub under the
stars on spacious decks. Honeymoon
suite with two person aqua massage tub
in room/ensuites or rooms with shared
bath. On snowmobile trail, lots of parking,
packages available: Romantic, Theatre,
Snowmobile, Canoe, Kayak.

ROOMS Family suite, Upper floor, Ground floor, Private
entrance, **Baths** Private, Ensuite, Shared with guest,
Beds Queen, Double, Twin, Single or cots, **Air** In
rooms, **Smoking** Outside, **In Room** TV, **OTHERS** Urban,
Rural, Open all year, **PAYMENT** Cheques accepted,
Cash, Trvl's cheques, **BREAKFASTS** Full, **AMENITIES**
Central TV, Central phone, Whirlpool, Barbecue,
Lounge, Patio, **THINGS TO DO** Trail nearby, Comp.
Canoe or boat, Golf, Fishing, Museums, Art, Theatre,
Attractions, Wineries/Breweries, Shopping, Cross-
country skiing, Swimming, Beach, Birdwatching, **LAN-
GUAGE** Eng., **PRICE** (2 persons) 65–85 **(check with
hosts for pricing details)**

COLLINGWOOD *(northwest of Toronto)*

Pedulla's Mountainside Bed & Breakfast

(Rosemarie and Vincent Pedulla)

109 Carmichael Cres, Town of The Blue Mountains, ON, L9Y 3Z2
www.bbcanada.com/1089.html
E-mail vpedulla@bconnex.net

705-445-7307
Fax 705-444-2965

Modern, charming chalet at the south base of Blue Mountain, 2 hours north of Toronto, 3-minutes walk to Intrawest Village for dining and shops. Closest B&B to the Eco Adventure, Scenic Caves and Nordic Centre, Georgian Cycle Trail, Golf, Fishing, Tennis and Bruce Hiking Trail. Across the road from The Blue Mountain Ski runs. Sumptuous breakfasts. Comfortable rooms, equipped with luxurious "feathered beds", TV, sink and terrace. Three full bathrooms. Flexible check-in and check-out times available.

ROOMS Ground floor, **Baths** Shared with guest, **Beds** Queen, Twin, **Air** Central, **Smoking** Outside, **In Room** TV, **OTHERS** Rural, Adult, Open all year, **PAYMENT** Cheques accepted, Cash, Trvl's cheques, **BREAKFASTS** Full, **AMENITIES** Central TV, Central phone, Whirlpool, Laundry, Fridge, Hot bev. bar, Lounge, Patio, Central Internet access, Central VCR/DVD, **THINGS TO DO** Comp. bikes, Rental bikes, Trail nearby, Rental canoe or boat, Golf, Fishing, Museums, Art, Theatre, Entertainment, Attractions, Shopping, Cross-country skiing, Downhill skiing, Tennis, Swimming, Horseback riding, Beach, Antiquing, **LANGUAGE** Eng., Fr., Italian, **PRICE** (2 persons) 110 **(check with hosts for pricing details)**

COLLINGWOOD

Wild Apple Hill BnB

(Carol and Jim Deffett)

795312 The Blue Mountain, Clearview TL, Nottawa, ON, L0M 1P0
www.bbcanada.com/8755.html
E-mail wildapplehillbnb@georgian.net

705-444-6501

Carved into the side of the beautiful Niagara Escarpment (UNESCO World Biosphere Reserve). Surrounded by mature forest with acres of the Pretty River Provincial Park above us. The Blue Mountain section of the world-famous Bruce Trail is only a few minutes walk from our B&B. Discounted golf times can be arranged at Duntroon, Marlwood or Cranberry during your stay at Wild Apple Hill. Enjoy the dining at Michael Stadtlander's Eigensinn Farm (transport can be arranged). This is a non-smoking B&B.

ROOMS Family suite, Upper floor, Private entrance, **Baths** Private, Ensuite, Shared with guest, **Beds** King, Queen, Double, Twin, **Air** Central, In rooms, **In Room** TV, Fireplace, **OTHERS** Rural, Adult, Open all year, **PAYMENT** Cheques accepted, Cash, Trvl's cheques, **BREAKFASTS** Full, Home-baked, **AMENITIES** Central TV, Sauna, Fridge, Lounge, Patio, Central VCR/DVD, **THINGS TO DO** Rental bikes, Trail nearby, Golf, Fishing, Museums, Art, Theatre, Entertainment, Attractions, Shopping, Cross-country skiing, Tennis, Swimming, Horseback riding, Beach, **LANGUAGE** Eng., **PRICE** (2 persons) 85–130 **(check with hosts for pricing details)**

CORNWALL *(southeast of Ottawa)*

Lighthouse Landing
(Lesley and Gerry Samson)

18177 Hwy 2, Cornwall, ON, K6H 5R5
www.lighthouse-landing.com
E-mail lighthouselanding@cogeco.ca

613-931-2508
TFr 1-877-501-2508

Lighthouse Landing is located 1 km east of Cornwall, directly on the St. Lawrence. The B&B suite is decorated in a nautical theme and offers a cozy guest lounge with fireplace, three large bedrooms, bathroom and a self-catering kitchen. An ideal spot for overnight stays or short-term lodging. Relax at our secluded riverfront property where boat docking, fishing and BBQ facilities are available. Three 18-hole courses are minutes away. A bicycle/walking path parallels the river at our front door.

ROOMS Family suite, Lower floor, Private entrance, **Baths** Private, Shared with guest, **Beds** Queen, Double, Single or cots, **OTHERS** Open all year, Pets in residence, **PAYMENT** Cash, Trvl's cheques, **BREAK-FASTS** Continental, Self-catered, **AMENITIES** Central TV, Central phone, Barbecue, Laundry, Kitchen, Fridge, Hot bev. bar, Lounge, Patio, Central Internet access, Central VCR/DVD, **THINGS TO DO** Trail nearby, Golf, Fishing, Birdwatching, Antiquing, **LANGUAGE** Eng., Fr., **PRICE** (2 persons) 65–80 (**check with hosts for pricing details)**

CORNWALL

Mountainview B&B
(Trish and Peter Baugh)

19263 County Rd 2, Summerstown, ON, K0C 2E0
www.mountainviewbb.ca
E-mail trishbaugh2003@yahoo.ca

613-931-9686

Summerstown is located 15 minutes east of Cornwall on picturesque County Rd 2 on the St. Lawrence River. Ideally located about one hour from Ottawa or Montreal and virtually on the border of New York State. Delectable homecooked breakfasts, self-serve or in the dining room. Our rooms, each with a river view, have a private entrance and private or ensuite baths.

ROOMS Family suite, Ground floor, Private entrance, **Baths** Private, Ensuite, **Beds** Queen, Double, Twin, **Air** Central, **Smoking** Outside, **OTHERS** Rural, Open all year, Pets in residence, Pets welcome, **PAYMENT** Cash, Trvl's cheques, **BREAKFASTS** Full, Continental, Home-baked, Self-catered, **AMENITIES** Central TV, Central phone, Barbecue, Laundry, Kitchen, Fridge, Lounge, Patio, Central Internet access, Central VCR/DVD, **THINGS TO DO** Trail nearby, Rental canoe or boat, Golf, Fishing, Museums, Art, Attractions, Shopping, Cross-country skiing, Tennis, Swimming, Horseback riding, Beach, **LANGUAGE** Eng., **PRICE** (2 persons) 80–90 (**check with hosts for pricing details)**

CORNWALL

T's By The Green
Bed & Breakfast
(Linda and Laurier Tranchemontagne)

18233 County Rd 2, RR #1, Cornwall, ON, K6H 5R5
www.bbcanada.com/tsbythegreen
E-mail tsbythegreen@sympatico.ca

613-931-2576
Fax 613-931-0441

Relax in the comforts of our uniquely decorated home, observe the ocean-going
ships from our private dock as they travel
through the St. Lawrence Seaway or
embrace the serenity of the St. Lawrence
River. From the back garden arbour and
sitting areas, be entertained by a variety of
golf shots and golf swings from our local
golf experts! Or play a round yourself.
Located along the St. Lawrence River, 5
minutes from Cornwall, 1 hour from
Ottawa or Montreal. Bicycle path access
off our driveway.

ROOMS Upper floor, **Baths** Shared with guest, **Beds**
Queen, Double, **Air** In rooms, **Smoking** Outside, **In**
Room Thermostat, **OTHERS** Rural, **PAYMENT** Cheques
accepted, Cash, **BREAKFASTS** Self-catered, **AMENITIES**
Central TV, Central phone, Fridge, Lounge, Patio,
Central Internet access, **THINGS TO DO** Trail nearby,
Golf, Museums, Art, Theatre, Entertainment, Shopping,
Cross-country skiing, Swimming, Horseback riding,
Beach, **LANGUAGE** Eng., Fr., **PRICE** (2 persons) 50–60
(check with hosts for pricing details)

CORNWALL

Winook Farm B&B
(Norma and Jan Peachey)

16997 Valade Rd, St Andrews West, ON, K0C 2A0
www.bbcanada.com/2475.html
E-mail aw575@glen-net.ca

613-932-1161
Fax 613-932-7801

1823 stone farmhouse on 150 acres minutes from Cornwall, tastefully restored.
Easy access from 401. Take Brookdale
exit, go north to the end. Pick up Hwy
138 north to St. Andrews West village.
Go through lights, turn west on Valade
Rd for 2 km. We are full-time honey pro-
ducers, labrador dog lovers, and sheep
roam the property. Upper Canada Village
nearby, Maxville Highland Games (Aug)
St. Lawrence Parks, nature trails and
bike paths. Ottawa 1 hour. Enroute to
Montreal or Toronto. Church, pub and
restaurant nearby.

ROOMS Upper floor, Private entrance, **Baths** Shared
with guest, Shared with hosts, **Beds** Double, Single or
cots, **Air** Central, **Smoking** Outside, **In Room OTHERS**
Rural, Open all year, **PAYMENT** Cheques accepted,
Cash, Trvl's cheques, **BREAKFASTS** Full, **AMENITIES**
Central TV, Central phone, Swimming pool, Lounge,
Patio, **THINGS TO DO** Trail nearby, Comp. Canoe or
boat, Museums, Attractions, Shopping, Swimming,
LANGUAGE Eng., Fr., **PRICE** (2 persons) 65–70 **(check
with hosts for pricing details)**

CREEMORE *(northwest of Toronto)*
Blacksmith House B&B
(Jean and John Smart)

7 Caroline St W, Creemore, ON, L0M 1G0
www.blacksmithhouse.ca
E-mail enquiries@blacksmithhouse.ca

705-466-2885
Fax 705-466-2886

Victorian home (c.1895) located in a picturesque village nestled in the valley of the Mad and Noisy Rivers. Relax and enjoy afternoon tea in the cozy sunporch or on the deck/patio overlooking a lovely private garden. Guest rooms are attractively decorated and delightfully furnished to very high standards. Comfortable beds and a delicious cooked breakfast await our guests. Well-informed hosts will provide information/maps/brochures to enhance your enjoyment of Creemore and the surrounding area.

ROOMS Upper floor, **Baths** Shared with guest, **Beds** Queen, **Air** Central, **In Room** Thermostat, **OTHERS** Adult, Open all year, **PAYMENT** Visa, Cheques accepted, Cash, Trvl's cheques, **BREAKFASTS** Full, **AMENITIES** Central TV, Lounge, Patio, **THINGS TO DO** Comp. bikes, Trail nearby, Golf, Fishing, Theatre, Wineries/Breweries, Shopping, Cross-country skiing, Downhill skiing, Horseback riding, Antiquing, **LANGUAGE** Eng., **PRICE** (2 persons) 75–115 **(check with hosts for pricing details)**

DAMASCUS *(near Arthur, northwest of Toronto)*
The Pritty Place
(Cyril and Margaret (Meg) Pritty)

8924 Wellington Rd 16, Damascus, RR #4, Kenilworth, ON, N0G 2E0
www.bbcanada.com/3092.html
E-mail prittyplace@golden.net

519-848-3598

Very cozy and comfortable restored 1860 log home on original site, 2 acres landscaped grounds with some bush, adjacent to Damascus Lake. Perfect for quiet relaxation. We're 15 minutes to Luther Marsh Conservation and Wildlife area, 30-minutes drive to Fergus, Elora, Mount Forest and Orangeville, 45 minutes to Guelph and Elmira. Comprehensive breakfast menu, flexible mealtime. Located at south end of village of Damascus on Wellington Rd 16. North of Hwy 109, east of Arthur or south of Hwy 89, east of Mount Forest.

ROOMS Family suite, Upper floor, **Baths** Shared with guest, **Beds** Queen, Double, Twin, Pullout sofa, **Air** Central, **Smoking** Outside, **In Room** Thermostat, **OTHERS** Rural, Open all year, Handicapped access, Additional meals, Pets welcome, **PAYMENT** Cheques accepted, Cash, Trvl's cheques, **BREAKFASTS** Full, Continental, Home-baked, **AMENITIES** Central TV, Central phone, Barbecue, Laundry, Lounge, Central Internet access, Central VCR/DVD, **THINGS TO DO** Trail nearby, Golf, Museums, Theatre, Entertainment, Attractions, Shopping, Cross-country skiing, Downhill skiing, Swimming, Birdwatching, Antiquing, **LANGUAGE** Eng., **PRICE** (2 persons) 75–95 **(check with hosts for pricing details)**

Dunnville *(south of Hamilton)*
Century Home
(Joyce Cormier)

310 Helena St, Dunnville, ON, N1A 2S8
www.bbcanada.com/5376.html
E-mail centuryhome@mountaincable.net

905-774-5724

This Tudor-style home is tastefully decorated and furnished with antiques. Guests
have their choice of a queen-size bed or
twin beds. Relax in a cozy sitting room
with TV and stereo, or sit in a large sun
porch or a spacious backyard. There is
central air-conditioning for your ultimate
comfort. A full breakfast is served in the
dining room with homemade jams and
muffins.

ROOMS Upper floor, **Baths** Shared with guest, **Beds**
Queen, Twin, **Air** Central, **Smoking** Outside, **OTHERS**
Open all year, Pets in residence, **PAYMENT** Cheques
accepted, Cash, **BREAKFASTS** Full, **AMENITIES** Central
TV, Central phone, Lounge, Central VCR/DVD, **THINGS
TO DO** Antiquing, **LANGUAGE** Eng., **PRICE** (2 persons)
50–65 **(check with hosts for pricing details)**

Elmira *(west of Toronto)*
Glenna Guest House
(Wilhelmina Visscher)

RR #2, Wallenstein, ON, N0B 2S0
www.bbcanada.com/3132.html E-mail

519-638-2470
Fax 519-638-5886

Bungalow home with fireplaces and large
yard with gardens and patio. Located
near antique shops, Festival theatres, lake
and Mennonite country. Three guest
rooms plus one suite room with private
entrance, fireplace, sitting area with satellite TV and VCR, and private bath. Well
equipped for children of all ages. Located
near St. Jacobs, Drayton, Elmira, Elora and
Stratford. English and Dutch spoken.
Open all year.

ROOMS Family suite, Ground floor, Lower floor, Private
entrance, **Baths** Private, Ensuite, **Beds** Queen, Double,
Single or cots, **Air** Ceiling fans, **Smoking** Outside, **In
Room** Thermostat, Phone, TV, Fireplace, **OTHERS** Open
all year, **PAYMENT** Cheques accepted, Cash, Trvl's
cheques, **BREAKFASTS** Full, **AMENITIES** Central TV,
Central phone, Barbecue, Laundry, Kitchen, Fridge, Hot
bev. bar, Lounge, Patio, Central VCR/DVD, **THINGS TO
DO** Comp. bikes, Trail nearby, Golf, Fishing, Theatre,
Entertainment, Attractions, Shopping, Swimming,
Horseback riding, Beach, **LANGUAGE** Eng., Dutch,
PRICE (2 persons) 60–80 **(check with hosts for pricing
details)**

Elmira

The Evergreens B&B
(Doris and Rodger Milliken)

470 Sandy Hills Dr, RR #1, Elmira, ON, N3B 2Z1
www.bbcanada.com/85.html

519-669-2471

A quiet B&B nestled among the evergreens. Enjoy long walks through the
forest, swimming in the pool or cross-
country skiing in winter. Two comfortable
bedrooms with two bathrooms and
breakfast with homemade baking. In
Mennonite country with Elmira, St. Jacobs
and Elora nearby. North of Elmira, east of
Arthur St north on Sandy Hills Dr.

ROOMS Upper floor, **Baths** Private, Shared with guest,
Beds Queen, Double, Single or cots, **Smoking** Outside,
OTHERS Rural, Open all year, Pets in residence, Pets
welcome, **PAYMENT** Cheques accepted, Cash, Trvl's
cheques, **BREAKFASTS** Full, Home-baked, **AMENITIES**
Central TV, Central phone, Swim-ming pool, Barbecue,
Laundry, Fridge, Patio, **THINGS TO DO** Comp. bikes,
Trail nearby, Comp. canoe or boat, Golf, Fishing,
Museums, Art, Theatre, Entertainment, Attractions,
Wineries/Breweries, Shopping, Cross-country skiing,
Swimming, Horseback riding, **LANGUAGE** Eng., **PRICE**
(2 persons) 40–70 **(check with hosts for pricing
details)**

Erin *(west of Toronto)*

Devonshire Guest House
(Audrey and Jim Devonshire)

3 Union St, PO Box 683, Erin, ON, N0B 1T0
www.thehillsofheadwaters.com/minervasspa
E-mail devonshireguesthouse@sympatico.ca

519-833-2187
Fax 519-833-2409

Stately Victorian home nestled in an historic village on an acre of picturesque
gardens. Experience the gracious ambience of this beautifully restored heritage
home. Enjoy a luxurious night's sleep in
one of our two spacious guest rooms. The
Burgundy Room and The Green Room.
Start your day with a full English breakfast and then explore the quaint shops
and dining of Erin village, a 2-minute walk
away. A soak in the clawfoot tub will
bring a relaxing finale to your day.

ROOMS Upper floor, **Baths** Shared with guest, **Beds**
Double, **Smoking** Outside, **In Room** Thermostat, **OTH-
ERS** Rural, Open all year, Pets in residence, **PAYMENT**
Visa, MC, Cash, Trvl's cheques, **BREAKFASTS** Full,
AMENITIES Laundry, Lounge, Patio, **THINGS TO DO**
Trail nearby, Golf, Fishing, Museums, Art, Theatre,
Entertainment, Attractions, Shopping, Cross-country
skiing, Downhill skiing, Tennis, Horseback riding,
Birdwatching, Antiquing, **LANGUAGE** Eng., **PRICE** (2
persons) 90–90 **(check with hosts for pricing details)**

ERIN

Stonecroft Country Guest House

(Lynn and Ed Sholomicki)

5331 Wellington Rd 24, Erin, ON, N0B 1T0
www.stonecroft.net
E-mail info@angelfoodcatering.ca

519-833-0778
Fax 519-833-0809

Whether you are looking for an overnight stay for the business traveller, for a quiet weekend in the country, we would be more than happy to accommodate you. Nestled among 98 acres of rollings hills, just 1 hour west of Toronto taking Hwy 401 to the Trafalgar Rd exit. North on Trafalgar Rd to Hwy 7 interesection. Left on Hwy 7 for 3 km. Right onto Trafalgar Rd N, through Ballinafad.

ROOMS Family suite, Upper floor, Ground floor, Private entrance, **Baths** Ensuite, **Beds** Queen, Double, Twin, Single or cots, **Air** Central, In rooms, Ceiling fans, **Smoking** Outside, **In Room** Thermostat, Fireplace, VCR/DVD, **OTHERS** Rural, Open all year, Handicapped access, Additional meals, Pets in residence, **PAYMENT** Visa, MC, Direct debit, Cheques accepted, Cash, Trvl's cheques, **BREAKFASTS** Full, Home-baked, **AMENITIES** Central phone, Swimming pool, Whirlpool, Laundry, Hot bev. bar, Lounge, Patio, **THINGS TO DO** Trail nearby, Golf, Fishing, Theatre, Entertainment, Attractions, Shopping, Cross-country skiing, Downhill skiing, Swimming, Horseback riding, Antiquing, **LANGUAGE** Eng., **PRICE** (2 persons) 115–150 **(check with hosts for pricing details)**

FENELON FALLS *(northeast of Toronto)*

Owl's Landing B&B

(Joan Barnett)

RR #2, 1277 Cty Rd 121, Fenelon Falls, ON, K0M 1N0
www.bbcanada.com/owlslanding.html
E-mail owlslanding@bellnet.ca

705-887-9889
Fax 705-887-9889

Enjoy a relaxing time in the country. Our 19th-century Gothic-style home offers complete privacy for our guests in a quiet atmosphere of rural charm. After a sound sleep in our beautifully decorated rooms, enjoy a delicious breakfast in our large dining room, which is pleasantly decorated. Your day will be started on a happy note! Satellite TV in each room.

ROOMS Upper floor, **Baths** Ensuite, Shared with guest, **Beds** Queen, Twin, Single or cots, **Air** Central, **Smoking** Outside, **OTHERS** Babysitting, Rural, Open all year, Additional meals, **PAYMENT** Visa, MC, Diners, Amex, Cheques accepted, Cash, **BREAKFASTS** Full, Home-baked, **AMENITIES** Barbecue, Laundry, Lounge, Patio, **THINGS TO DO** Trail nearby, Rental canoe or boat, Golf, Fishing, Museums, Art, Theatre, Entertainment, Attractions, Shopping, Cross-country skiing, Tennis, Swimming, Horseback riding, Beach, **LANGUAGE** Eng., **PRICE** (2 persons) 75–95 **(check with hosts for pricing details)**

FERGUS *(west of Toronto)*

Dream Corners B&B

(Arlie and Verna Hunt)

498 St. David St N, Fergus, ON, N1M 2K2
www.dreamcorners.com
E-mail dreamcorners@sympatico.ca

519-787-7737
Fax 519-787-2152

Our century home is located in the heart of Fergus. Come enjoy our down east homey hospitality. This picturesque town and area has many unique attractions: Elora Gorge, Templen Gardens, Farmer's Market, Mennonite communities and numerous festivals taking place throughout the year. Locally, we have canoeing, fly-fishing, cycling, golf, pubs and fine dining. To find us, take Hwy 401 to Hwy 6 north through Guelph to Fergus. Our home is one block north of downtown area on the right side before the lights of Garafraxa St.

ROOMS Family suite, Upper floor, Ground floor, Private entrance, **Baths** Private, Ensuite, Shared with hosts, **Beds** Queen, Double, Twin, Single or cots, Pullout sofa, **Air** Central, Ceiling fans, **Smoking** Outside, **In Room** TV, Fireplace, Internet access, VCR/DVD, **OTHERS** Urban, Open all year, Handicapped access, **PAYMENT** Visa, MC, Cash, **BREAKFASTS** Full, Continental, Home-baked, **AMENITIES** Central TV, Barbecue, Laundry, Kitchen, Fridge, Lounge, Patio, Central Internet access, Central VCR/DVD, **THINGS TO DO** Rental bikes, Trail nearby, Rental canoe or boat, Golf, Fishing, Museums, Art, Theatre, Entertainment, Attractions, Wineries/Breweries, Shopping, Cross-country skiing, Tennis, Horseback riding, Antiquing, **LANGUAGE** Eng., **PRICE** (2 persons) 70–120 **(check with hosts for pricing details)**

FERGUS

Fergus Fly-in Bed & Breakfast

(Helen and Chris Juergensen)

RR #1, 6868 Beatty Line, Fergus, ON, N1M 2W3
www.fergusflyinbandb.com
E-mail christel.juergensen@sympatico.ca

519-843-1487
Fax 519-843-1487

Semi-retired farmer, new farmhouse with large guestrooms, TV, balcony, guest bath, central air, indoor heated pool and large sundeck. An ideal place for relaxation. Visit the Fergus weekend market, fish the Grand River, antique Elora, Mennonite country, St. Jacobs and its huge farmer's market. Hosts offer day tours in their private airplane wherever guests desire to go (at hourly rate). Country supper on request. Weekly rate on request.

ROOMS Family suite, Upper floor, Private entrance, **Baths** Private, Shared with guest, **Beds** Queen, Twin, Single or cots, Pullout sofa, **Air** Central, **Smoking** Outside, **In Room** TV, **OTHERS** Rural, Adult, Seasonal, Additional meals, **PAYMENT** Cheques accepted, Cash, Trvl's cheques, **BREAKFASTS** Full, Home-baked, **AMENITIES** Swimming pool, Barbecue, Fridge, Patio, **THINGS TO DO** Comp. bikes, Trail nearby, Fishing, Museums, Theatre, Attractions, Wineries/Breweries, Shopping, Cross-country skiing, Swimming, **LANGUAGE** Eng., Ger., **PRICE** (2 persons) 65–90 **(check with hosts for pricing details)**

Fergus

Riverwood

(Bert and Marilyn Peel)

6885 Fifth Line RR #1, Belwood, ON, N0B 1J0
www.bbcanada.com/5331.html
E-mail riverwood@sympatico.ca

519-843-9982
Fax 519-843-9967

Welcome to Riverwood: A country retreat.
Enjoy the peace and tranquility of our
new air-conditioned country home.
Riverwood is surrounded by beautiful
perennial gardens and nestled in 12 acres
of woods with the Irvine River meandering through the back of the property.
Each room is furnished with Canadian
pine furniture and decorated around a
unique theme. We are minutes to Fergus,
home of the Highland Games and Elora's
antique and artisan shops. St. Jacob's is a
35-minute drive. Enjoy tubing in the Elora
Gorge, fishing, cycling, golf, country fairs,
snowmobiling and much more.

ROOMS Lower floor, Private entrance, **Baths** Ensuite,
Beds Double, **Air** Central, **Smoking** Outside, **OTHERS**
Rural, Adult, Open all year, Pets in residence, **PAYMENT**
Cheques accepted, Cash, Trvl's cheques, **BREAKFASTS**
Full, Home-baked, **AMENITIES** Central TV, Fridge, Hot
bev. bar, Lounge, Patio, **THINGS TO DO** Trail nearby,
Golf, Fishing, Museums, Art, Theatre, Wineries/
Breweries, Shopping, Swimming, Horseback riding,
LANGUAGE Eng., **PRICE** (2 persons) 85–125 (+ tax)
(check with hosts for pricing details)

Flesherton *(northwest of Toronto)*

Toad Hall

(Jill Smith-Brodie and David Brodie)

545413 Sideroad 4A, Box 23, Markdale, ON, N0C 1H0
www.bbcanada.com/7792.html

519-270-0076

Toad Hall is a unique nature lover's retreat
just minutes from the Bruce Trail, the
Beaver Valley and Talisman Ski Resorts.
Our log home is solar powered and is
complimented by perennial gardens, a
view over two spring-fed ponds and has
2,000 feet of frontage on the Rocky
Saugeen River. Our 85-acre property
abounds with wildlife. You can swim in
our pond in summer or skate in winter. In
the evening, enjoy a campfire by the
water. We have trails for walking or snowshoeing and a telescope for stargazing.

ROOMS Family suite, Lower floor, Private entrance,
Baths Ensuite, **Beds** Queen, Twin, **OTHERS** Rural, Open
all year, Handicapped access, Pets in residence,
PAYMENT Cheques accepted, Cash, Trvl's cheques,
BREAKFASTS Full, Continental, Home-baked, **AMENI-
TIES** Central TV, Central phone, Barbecue, Lounge,
Patio, Central VCR/DVD, **THINGS TO DO** Trail nearby,
Comp. Canoe or boat, Golf, Fishing, Museums, Art,
Theatre, Attractions, Shopping, Cross-country skiing,
Swimming, Horseback riding, Birdwatching,
Antiquing, **LANGUAGE** Eng., Fr., **PRICE** (2 persons)
90–120 **(check with hosts for pricing details)**

FORT ERIE [RIDGEWAY]
(southeast of Niagara Falls)

Split Rock Farms
Bed and Breakfast
(Glen and Lynda Finbow)

1652 Ridge Rd N, Ridgeway, ON, L0S 1N0
www.splitrockfarmsbb.com
E-mail splitrockfarmsbb@aol.com

905-382-7777
Fax 905-382-7778

A unique and luxurious country retreat located in the historic village of Ridgeway, minutes from all Niagara offerings. Recently written up in *The Best Places to Bed and Breakfast in Ontario* at bbontario.com, there are 60 acres of award-winning gardens and an alpaca ranch, too! Richly decorated in antiques with eclectic touches, three sumptuous guest rooms await you. Breakfasts are full and delectable, ensuring a perfect start to your Niagara visit. Come – indulge yourselves – let the pampering begin.

ROOMS Family suite, Upper floor, Lower floor, Private entrance, **Baths** Private, Ensuite, Shared with guest, **Beds** King, Queen, Double, Single or cots, **Air** Central, **Smoking** Outside, **In Room** Fireplace, VCR/DVD, **OTHERS** Rural, Open all year, Pets in residence, **PAYMENT** Cheques accepted, Cash, Trvl's cheques, **BREAKFASTS** Full, **AMENITIES** Central phone, Lounge, Patio, **THINGS TO DO** Trail nearby, Golf, Fishing, Museums, Theatre, Entertainment, Attractions, Wineries/Breweries, Shopping, Cross-country skiing, Swimming, Horseback riding, Beach, Birdwatching, Antiquing, **PRICE** (2 persons) 115–125 **(check with hosts for pricing details)**

GANANOQUE *(south of Ottawa)*

Manse Lane Bed & Breakfast
(Jocelyn and George Bounds)

465 Stone St S, Gananoque, ON, K7G 2A7
www.manselane.com

613-382-8642
TFr 1-888-565-6379

Casual elegance abounds in this century brick home, operated as a B&B since 1989. Breakfast in the sunroom during the warm seasons, and beside the fire in our guest lounge in the colder season. Ideally situated, only five houses to the Thousand Islands boat cruises, three short blocks to the 1000 Island Playhouse, and four short blocks to downtown. Park your car in our off-street parking area. You can walk to major attractions. Attraction ticket agents. Reservations highly recommended. *Parlons un peu de Francais.*

ROOMS Upper floor, **Baths** Private, Ensuite, Shared with guest, **Beds** Queen, Twin, Single or cots, **Air** In rooms, **Smoking** Outside, **In Room** TV, **OTHERS** Urban, Adult, Open all year, **PAYMENT** Visa, MC, Diners, Amex, Cash, Trvl's cheques, **BREAKFASTS** Full, **AMENITIES** Central TV, Swimming pool, Lounge, Patio, **THINGS TO DO** Rental bikes, Trail nearby, Rental canoe or boat, Golf, Fishing, Museums, Art, Theatre, Attractions, Shopping, Swimming, Horseback riding, Beach, **LANGUAGE** Eng., Fr., **PRICE** (2 persons) 65–160 **(check with hosts for pricing details)**

Gananoque

Sleepy Hollow
Bed & Breakfast

(Marion and Don Matthews)

95 King St W, Gananoque, ON, K7G 2G2
www.sleepyhollowbb.ca
E-mail greetings@sleepyhollowbb.ca

613-382-4377
TFr 1-866-426-7422

Discover Gananoque's Sleepy Hollow B&B, nestled amidst the Thousand Islands between Kingston and Brockville. Built in 1905, our quiet three-storey Victorian mansion with stained glass windows has been restored to its original classic splendor, accented with collections of vintage memorabilia. Breakfast options range from the health-conscious to the decadent, each made to order, and every room has its own unique charm, with options including full ensuite bathrooms, two with hot tubs, one with a whirlpool tub.

ROOMS Family suite, Upper floor, **Baths** Private, Ensuite, Shared with guest, **Beds** King, Queen, Twin, **Air** Central, **OTHERS** Urban, Open all year, **PAYMENT** Visa, MC, Diners, Amex, Direct debit, Cash, Trvl's cheques, **BREAKFASTS** Full, Home-baked, **AMENITIES** Central TV, Central phone, Whirlpool, Hot bev. bar, Lounge, Central Internet access, Central VCR/DVD, **THINGS TO DO** Rental bikes, Trail nearby, Rental canoe or boat, Golf, Fishing, Museums, Art, Theatre, Entertainment, Attractions, Shopping, Cross-country skiing, Tennis, Horseback riding, Beach, **LANGUAGE** Eng., Fr., **PRICE** (2 persons) 75 Winter, 170 Summer **(check with hosts for pricing details)**

Gananoque

Tea & Crumpets
Bed & Breakfast

(Ina and Reuben Rumbolt)

260 King St W, Gananoque, ON, K7G 2G6
www.teaandcrumpetsbb.com
E-mail sleep@teaandcrumpetsbb.com

613-382-2683
TFr 1-800-335-8801

A warm welcome awaits you at our charming Victorian B&B situated on an acre, surrounded by tall trees in a park-like setting. Relax in one of four tastefully decorated bedrooms with Jacuzzi ensuites or Family suites. Enjoy the whimsically decorated living room, the verandah or our spacious backyard. We serve full delicious breakfasts in an elegant setting and are within walking distance of most attractions – Thousand Island cruises, playhouse, bicycle path, casino, shopping, golf and fine dining.

ROOMS Family suite, Upper floor, **Baths** Ensuite, Shared with guest, **Beds** King, Queen, Double, Twin, Single or cots, **Air** In rooms, **Smoking** Outside, **In Room** TV, VCR/DVD, **OTHERS** Open all year, **PAYMENT** Visa, MC, Cash, Trvl's cheques, **BREAKFASTS** Full, Home-baked, **AMENITIES** Barbecue, Lounge, **THINGS TO DO** Trail nearby, Fishing, Theatre, Attractions, Shopping, Tennis, Swimming, Horseback riding, Beach, Birdwatching, Antiquing, **LANGUAGE** Eng., **PRICE** (2 persons) 75–160 **(check with hosts for pricing details)**

GANANOQUE

The Victoria Rose Inn

(Susanne Richter and Bernard Latremouille)

279 King St West, Gananoque, ON, K7G 2G7
www.victoriaroseinn.com
E-mail info@victoriaroseinn.com

613-382-3368
Fax 613-382-8803
TFr 1-888-246-2893

A magnificent, restored Victorian mansion, set on 2 acres of award-winning gardens. Whirlpool baths, fireplaces, and beautiful bedrooms decorated in period style. All rooms have ensuite baths and air-conditioned. Secluded, yet only steps from the marina, boat tours, kayaking, Thousand Islands Playhouse, art galleries and shopping.

ROOMS Family suite, Upper floor, Ground floor, Private entrance, **Baths** Private, Ensuite, **Beds** King, Queen, Double, Twin, Single or cots, Pullout sofa, **Air** Central, In rooms, **Smoking** Outside, **In Room** TV, Fireplace, Internet access, **OTHERS** Urban, Rural, Adult, Open all year, Handicapped access, Seasonal, **PAYMENT** Visa, MC, Diners, Amex, Direct debit, Cash, Trvl's cheques, **BREAKFASTS** Continental, **AMENITIES** Central TV, Central phone, Whirlpool, Fridge, Hot bev. bar, Lounge, Patio, Central Internet access, Central VCR/DVD, **THINGS TO DO** Rental bikes, Trail nearby, Rental canoe or boat, Golf, Fishing, Museums, Art, Theatre, Entertainment, Attractions, Shopping, Swimming, Horseback riding, Beach, Birdwatching, Antiquing, **LANGUAGE** Eng., Fr., Ger., **PRICE** (2 persons) 145–285 **(check with hosts for pricing details)**

GEORGETOWN *(west of Toronto)*

L'Auberge

(Pauline Marin and Everitt Ashton)

115 King St, Terra Cotta (Caledon), ON, L7C 1P2
www.canadianbandbguide.ca/bb.asp?ID=3846
E-mail ashtonmarin@sympatico.ca

905-877-1350

Along the Credit River – beautifully renovated home with three nicely decorated bedrooms with sinks. Shared toilet and shower. Walking distance to fine restaurants. Close to Bruce Trail, conservation park, 20 km north of Hwy 401, 40 minutes to Pearson Airport. We have hosted people from most countries with many repeat visitors. Enjoyable location from spring's first bloom to the golden leaves of fall and the fairylike white of winter. Country setting attracting tourists all year. Our home is your home. Welcome!

ROOMS Upper floor, **Baths** Shared with guest, **Beds** Queen, **Air** Central, Ceiling fans, **Smoking** Outside, **In Room** TV, **OTHERS** Rural, Open all year, **PAYMENT** Cash, Trvl's cheques, **BREAKFASTS** Full, Home-baked, **AMENITIES** Patio, **THINGS TO DO** Trail nearby, Golf, Fishing, Art, Theatre, Horseback riding, Birdwatching, **LANGUAGE** Eng., Fr., **PRICE** (2 persons) 75–85 **(check with hosts for pricing details)**

Georgetown

Victorian Rose
Bed and Breakfast

(Ruth and Wayne Singleton)

34 Cindebarke Terrace, Georgetown, ON, L7G 4S5
www.victorianrose.ca
E-mail victorianrose@sympatico.ca

905-702-0166

Located on a quiet cul de sac with 10 acres of meadow, bush and stream. Lovely hamlets to explore, close to Bruce Trail. A traditional home tastefully decorated with antiques and heirlooms. Enjoy gourmet breakfasts each morning. Afternoon tea is served on verandah or hot chocolate by the fireplace. Relax under the stars in a wonderful hot tub. Ten minutes from Hwy 401, 30 minutes from the airport. Easy to find. A warm welcome awaits you.

ROOMS Upper floor, **Baths** Private, Ensuite, **Beds** King, Queen, **Air** Central, **Smoking** Outside, **In Room** Phone, **OTHERS** Urban, Open all year, Additional meals, Pets in residence, Pets welcome, **PAYMENT** Cheques accepted, Cash, Trvl's cheques, **BREAKFASTS** Full, Home-baked, **AMENITIES** Central phone, Whirlpool, Barbecue, Laundry, Fridge, Hot bev. bar, Lounge, Patio, **THINGS TO DO** Comp. bikes, Trail nearby, Golf, Fishing, Museums, Art, Theatre, Shopping, Cross-country skiing, Downhill skiing, Birdwatching, Antiquing, **LANGUAGE** Eng., Fr., **PRICE** (2 persons) 75–95 **(check with hosts for pricing details)**

Goderich *(west of Toronto)*

Astoria Bed & Breakfast

(Kevin Soehner and Garry LaRose)

69 Britannia Rd W, Goderich, ON, N7A 2B2
www.astoria-bed-n-breakfast.com/
E-mail astoria_83@sympatico.ca

519-440-0861
TFr 1-877-943-6969

Elegant, Edwardian home nestled in the heart of Goderich. Close to town square and beach. Spacious well-appointed rooms. two kings – one with fireplace, and double with private bath. Enjoy meals in our charming dining room or on the verandah in the summer. Continental or full breakfast. Guest capacity: six. Open year round. Reservations preferred. Smoking – outdoors only. No pets. Children 15-plus welcome.

ROOMS Upper floor, **Baths** Private, Ensuite, Shared with guest, Shared with hosts, **Beds** King, Queen, Double, Single or cots, **Air** Central, **Smoking** Outside, **In Room** TV, Fireplace, **OTHERS** Adult, Open all year, Pets in residence, **PAYMENT** Visa, MC, Cheques accepted, Cash, Trvl's cheques, **BREAKFASTS** Full, Home-baked, **AMENITIES** Central TV, **THINGS TO DO** Comp. bikes, Trail nearby, Golf, Fishing, Museums, Art, Theatre, Entertainment, Shopping, Cross-country skiing, Tennis, Swimming, Beach, **LANGUAGE** Eng., **PRICE** (2 persons) 85–110 **(check with hosts for pricing details)**

Goderich

Copper Beach Bed & Breakfast

(Sandi Davidson)

148 Victoria St N, Goderich, ON, N7A 2S6
www.copperbeech.ca
E-mail sandra.davidson@sympatico.ca

519-524-8522
Fax 519-524-8522

Heritage home of Samuel Platt, founder
of the salt industry in Canada. Easily located at the corner of Anglesea and Victoria
St N (Hwy #21N), in the port of Goderich,
Canada's prettiest town. Walking distance
to fine dining, downtown, hiking trails
and fishing. Minutes by car to beaches,
magnificent sunsets, golfing and boating.
Theatres in nearby towns. Bicycle storage
and packed lunches on request. Inquire
regarding bringing pets. Cross-country
skiing in the area.

ROOMS Upper floor, **Baths** Shared with guest, **Beds**
King, Queen, Twin, Single or cots, **Air** Central, **Smoking**
Outside, **In Room** TV, VCR/DVD, **OTHERS** Urban, Adult,
Open all year, Additional meals, Pets welcome, **PAY-**
MENT Visa, Cheques accepted, Cash, **BREAKFASTS**
Full, Home-baked, **AMENITIES** Central TV, Central
phone, Laundry, Fridge, Hot bev. bar, Lounge, Patio,
THINGS TO DO Rental bikes, Trail nearby, Rental canoe
or boat, Golf, Fishing, Museums, Art, Theatre, Attrac-
tions, Shopping, Cross-country skiing, Tennis,
Swimming, Horseback riding, Beach, Antiquing, **LAN-**
GUAGE Eng., **PRICE** (2 persons) 65–70 **(check with**
hosts for pricing details)

Goderich

Twin Porches B&B

(Argelyn Strote)

55 Nelson St E, Goderich, ON, N7A 1R7
www.bbcanada.com/3694.html
E-mail astrote@hurontel.on.ca

519-524-5505

Located on Nelson St across from the
Tourist Information Centre, this 1890
Victorian home, designated as the
"Asheson House" is decorated with
antiques, with some collectibles for sale.
It has three bedrooms, two with queen
beds and one with double bed. Shared
bath, air-conditioned, large, well-groomed
garden, listed in the *Best Places to B&B in*
Ontario. Expanded continental breakfast.
Open May to October. Reservations pre-
ferred. Walk to beaches and town square.
Rates $60 Double; $50 Single.

ROOMS Upper floor, **Baths** Shared with guest, **Beds**
Queen, Double, **Air** Central, **Smoking** Outside, **OTH-**
ERS Urban, Adult, Seasonal, **PAYMENT** Cheques
accepted, Cash, **BREAKFASTS** Full, Continental, Home-
baked, Self-catered, **AMENITIES** Central TV, Central
phone, Fridge, Lounge, Patio, **THINGS TO DO** Trail
nearby, Golf, Fishing, Museums, Art, Theatre,
Entertainment, Attractions, Shopping, Tennis,
Swimming, Horseback riding, Beach, **LANGUAGE** Eng.,
PRICE (2 persons) 60 **(check with hosts for pricing**
details)

GRAVENHURST *(north of Toronto)*

Eden Place
(Ethyl C Whyte-Coussey)

701 Austin St N, Gravenhurst, ON, P1P 1E3
www.edenplacebb.com
E-mail ecwc@bconnex.net

705-687-4980
TFr 1-877-656-6076

Eden Place B&B is a charming century
home near Lake Muskoka. We offer swimming, museums, farmer's market, Segwuin
and Wenonah II cruises. Full breakfast.
Children welcome.

ROOMS Upper floor, Ground floor, **Baths** Private,
Ensuite, Shared with guest, **Beds** Queen, Double, Twin,
In Room Thermostat, TV, **OTHERS** Urban, Seasonal,
PAYMENT Cash, **BREAKFASTS** Full, **AMENITIES** Central
TV, Central phone, Fridge, Lounge, Patio, **THINGS TO
DO** Rental bikes, Trail nearby, Rental canoe or boat,
Golf, Fishing, Museums, Art, Theatre, Entertainment,
Shopping, Tennis, Swimming, Beach, **LANGUAGE** Eng.,
Fr., **PRICE** (2 persons) 50–90 **(check with hosts for
pricing details)**

GRIMSBY *(east of Hamilton)*

Vinifera – The Inn on Winery Row
(Barb Van Pelt)

245 Main St E, Grimsby, ON, L3M 1P5
www.viniferainn.ca
E-mail barbatviniferainn@yahoo.ca

905-309-8873

An 1846 "Historically Designated"
Italianate home on 1 1/2 acres on the
West Niagara Wine Route. Enjoy a complimentary glass of wine on our porch
swings after checking in. Relax in our parlour or in the library by the fire where you
can enjoy a game of billiards. A four-
course gourmet breakfast is served in our
formal dining room. A swim in our
inground pool will refresh you before
going to one of the "Winery Restaurants"
for dinner. One hour to Toronto, 45 minutes to the border.

Baths Ensuite, **Beds** King, Queen, **Air** Central, **In Room**
TV, VCR/DVD, **PAYMENT** Visa, MC, Direct debit, Cash,
Trvl's cheques, **BREAKFASTS** Full, **AMENITIES**
Swimming pool, **THINGS TO DO** Comp. bikes, Golf,
Museums, Art, Theatre, Entertainment, Attractions,
Wineries/Breweries, Shopping, Swimming, Antiquing,
LANGUAGE Eng., **PRICE** (2 persons) 139–169 **(check
with hosts for pricing details)**

GUELPH *(northwest of Hamilton)*

Sugarbush Bed and Breakfast

(Ann and George Israel)

2 Sugarbush Place, Guelph, ON, N1H 7Z3
www.sugarbushbb.com
E-mail sugarbushbb@rogers.com

519-760-4103
Fax 519-836-3262

A "newer," open-concept home offering
privacy for each room and private baths
for each. Central heating/air-conditioning;
full breakfast with options for special
dietary needs; large, comfortable rooms
with either queen beds or single beds;
comfy duvets and fibrebed mattress top-
pers. TV/VCR, wireless Internet. Hot tub
outdoors in gazebo. Easily accessed, 10
minute drive to UofG. From Toronto:
Hwy 401 to Exit 295 and north to
Speedvale Ave, left on Imperial Rd, first
left on Sugarbush Pl, first house on left.

ROOMS Upper floor, Ground floor, **Baths** Private,
Ensuite, **Beds** Queen, Single or cots, **Air** Central,
Smoking Outside, **OTHERS** Urban, Open all year, **PAY-
MENT** Visa, MC, Diners, Amex, Cheques accepted,
Cash, Trvl's cheques, **BREAKFASTS** Full, **AMENITIES**
Central phone, Whirlpool, Fridge, Lounge, Central
Internet access, **THINGS TO DO** Trail nearby, Museums,
Art, Theatre, Entertainment, Attractions,
Wineries/Breweries, Horseback riding, **LANGUAGE**
Eng., Ger., **PRICE** (2 persons) 55–90 **(check with hosts
for pricing details)**

HALIBURTON HIGHLANDS
(south of Alginquin Park)

Sunny Rock Bed & Breakfast

(Sally Moore and Jan Clarke)

RR #1, 1144 Scott's Dam Rd, Minden, ON, K0M 2K0
www.sunnyrock.on.ca
E-mail info@sunnyrock.on.ca

705-286-4922
Fax 705-286-3081
TFr 1-888-786-6976

Historic Finnish log estate 2 1/2 hours
north of Toronto. River and falls view suites
guaranteed to pamper. Breathtaking, year-
round sights and sounds of moving water.
Fireplaces, steam showers, Jacuzzi. Sip a
deckside beverage while enjoying nature's
peace and quiet. Unforgettable seasonal
natural whirlpool! Web site has pictures,
programs, packages, area attractions hyper-
links. Hiking, biking, skiing. Artisan studios
and heritage tours. Perfect for groups of
2–12 adults, weddings and romantic getaways. Gift certificates available.

ROOMS Upper floor, Ground floor, **Baths** Private,
Ensuite, Shared with guest, **Beds** King, Queen, Double,
Twin, Single or cots, Pullout sofa, **Smoking** Outside, **In
Room** Thermostat, Fireplace, VCR/DVD, **OTHERS** Rural,
Adult, Open all year, Additional meals, Pets in residence,
PAYMENT Visa, Cheques accepted, Cash, Trvl's cheques,
BREAKFASTS Full, **AMENITIES** Central TV, Central
phone, Whirlpool, Barbecue, Kitchen, Fridge, Hot bev.
bar, Lounge, Patio, Central Internet access, Central
VCR/DVD, **THINGS TO DO** Trail nearby, Comp. Canoe or
boat, Golf, Fishing, Museums, Art, Theatre, Entertainment, Attractions, Wineries/Breweries, Shopping, Cross-
country skiing, Downhill skiing, Swimming, Birdwatching, Antiquing, **LANGUAGE** Eng., **PRICE** (2 persons)
125–250 **(check with hosts for pricing details)**

HAMILTON *(west of Toronto)*

Galivants Rest
Bed & Breakfast

(Anne and Gary May)

121 Dragoon Dr, Hamilton, ON, L9B 2C9
www.bbcanada.com/449.html
E-mail galivant@idirect.com

905-575-5095

From Hwy 403 take the Lincoln Alexander
Pwy to Upper James St S. At Stonechurch
Rd turn left and proceed to Upper
Wellington. Turn right. At Dragoon Dr turn
left. If coming from Hwy 53 turn north on
Upper Wellington then turn right at
Dragoon Dr. Easy to find hospitals, downtown, Hamilton Place, Dundurn Castle,
Copps Colliseum, restaurants, shopping
malls, airport, Bruce Trail. Large home
located in the heart of Hamilton's mountain or upper city. Hosts enjoy travel, birdwatching and theatre.

ROOMS Upper floor, **Baths** Shared with guest, **Beds**
Queen, Double, Single or cots, **Air** Central, Ceiling fans,
OTHERS Urban, Adult, Open all year, **PAYMENT** Cash,
Trvl's cheques, **BREAKFASTS** Full, Continental, **AMENI-
TIES** Central TV, Central phone, **THINGS TO DO** Trail
nearby, Golf, Museums, Art, Theatre, Entertainment,
Attractions, Wineries/Breweries, Shopping, Antiquing,
LANGUAGE Eng., **PRICE** (2 persons) 80 **(check with
hosts for pricing details)**

HAMILTON

Heritage House 1914

(Bert and Gale Roossien)

202 St Clair Blvd, Hamilton, ON, L8M 2P1
www.heritagehouse1914bedandbreakfast.com
E-mail beans@idirect.com

905-549-5247
Fax 905-549-6031

This Edwardian Square home, built in
1914, is furnished with antiques and has
been designated by the city as a Heritage
Home. This home is situated on a beautiful mature treed Blvd in the centre of
downtown Hamilton and is close to all
that the city has to offer. We are within an
hour's drive of either Toronto or Niagara
Falls and one block away from the local
bus system. You will find it hard to believe
you are in the centre of the city as you
enjoy the peace and quiet of this beautiful home.

ROOMS Upper floor, **Baths** Shared with guest, **Beds**
Queen, Double, **Air** In rooms, **Smoking** Outside, **OTH-
ERS** Urban, Open all year, Pets in residence, **PAYMENT**
Visa, Cash, **BREAKFASTS** Full, Continental, **AMENITIES**
Central TV, Central phone, Fridge, Lounge, Patio,
THINGS TO DO Trail nearby, Museums, Art, Theatre,
Entertainment, Attractions, Shopping, **LANGUAGE**
Eng., **PRICE** (2 persons) 75 **(check with hosts for
pricing details)**

HAMILTON

Rutherford House
Bed and Breakfast

(Janis and David Topp)

293 Park St S, Hamilton, ON, L8P 3G5
www.rutherfordbb.com
E-mail david.janis.topp@sympatico.ca

905-525-2422
Fax 905-525-5236

A heritage home with Victorian ambience and modern comforts. Located downtown, an easy walk to Convention Centre, Copps Colliseum, St. Joseph's Hospital. Close to McMaster, Royal Botanical Gardens; just off the Bruce Trail. Both rooms have ensuite, TV/VCR, small fridge, coffee/tea, and wonderful beds! The full breakfast is meant to spoil you. Fully air-conditioned and smoke-free for your comfort. From Hwy 403 exit at Aberdeen, turn left at Queen, turn right at Herkimer, turn right at Park St S, last house on left.

ROOMS Upper floor, **Baths** Ensuite, **Beds** King, Queen, Twin, **Air** Central, **In Room** TV, VCR/DVD, **OTHERS** Urban, Adult, Open all year, **PAYMENT** Visa, MC, Cash, Trvl's cheques, **BREAKFASTS** Full, **AMENITIES** Central phone, Fridge, Patio, **THINGS TO DO** Trail nearby, Golf, Museums, Art, Theatre, Entertainment, Attractions, Wineries/Breweries, Shopping, Cross-country skiing, Tennis, Swimming, **LANGUAGE** Eng., **PRICE** (2 persons) 110 **(check with hosts for pricing details)**

HAMILTON (DUNDAS)

Glenwood B&B

(Peter and Nancy Mascarin)

42 Osler Dr, Dundas, ON, L9H 4B1
www.glenwoodbb.ca
E-mail info@glenwoodbb.ca

905-628-8104
TFr 1-800-792-8765

Built in 1827, Glenwood B&B is conveniently located 5 minutes west of McMaster University and Hospital. Dundas is situated west of Hamilton between Toronto and Niagara Falls. Downtown Hamilton is a 10-minute drive away. The 5-minute walk to downtown Dundas will be especially appealing to those interested in arts, crafts, dining, shopping and nature. We offer you warm hospitality with fulfilling homemade breakfasts that will not leave you hungry. We look forward to your visit with us!

ROOMS Upper floor, **Baths** Private, Ensuite, Shared with guest, **Beds** King, Queen, Double, Twin, Single or cots, **Air** In rooms, **Smoking** Outside, **In Room** TV, **OTHERS** Urban, Open all year, Pets in residence, **PAYMENT** Visa, MC, Direct debit, Cash, Trvl's cheques, **BREAKFASTS** Full, Home-baked, **AMENITIES** Central phone, Fridge, Hot bev. bar, Lounge, Patio, **THINGS TO DO** Comp. bikes, Trail nearby, Golf, Fishing, Museums, Art, Theatre, Entertainment, Attractions, Wineries/Breweries, Shopping, Birdwatching, Antiquing, **LANGUAGE** Eng., **PRICE** (2 persons) 90 **(check with hosts for pricing details)**

HAMILTON (ANCASTER)

A Tranquility Base Bed and Breakfast

(Larry and Shirley Woods)

110 Abbey Close, Ancaster (Hamilton), ON, L9G 4K7
www.tranquilitybase.on.ca
E-mail tranquility@cogeco.ca

905-648-1506
Fax 905-648-0092
TFr 1-877-649-9290

Warm welcome and friendly hospitality in comfortable, large modern brick home located on a quiet cul-de-sac. Well travelled hosts have been collecting Victorian Cranberry, crystal, dolls, art and other antiques for more than 25 years and these are displayed throughout the house. Located in the heart of Ancaster. Walking distance to walking or cycling trails in a picturesque valley for nature lovers, or to the centre of town with plenty of shops. We want your stay to be as relaxing and pleasurable as possible.

ROOMS Upper floor, **Baths** Private, Ensuite, **Beds** King, Queen, Twin, **Air** Central, **Smoking** Outside, **In Room OTHERS** Urban, Adult, Open all year, Additional meals, Pets in residence, **PAYMENT** Visa, MC, Diners, Cheques accepted, Cash, Trvl's cheques, **BREAKFASTS** Full, **AMENITIES** Central TV, Central phone, Laundry, Fridge, Lounge, Patio, **THINGS TO DO** Trail nearby, Golf, Museums, Art, Theatre, Entertainment, Shopping, Cross-country skiing, Swimming, Horseback riding, **LANGUAGE** Eng., Fr., **PRICE** (2 persons) 75–90 **(check with hosts for pricing details)**

HAMILTON (ANCASTER)

Duck Tail Inn B&B

(Dorothy and Dan Wentworth)

1573 Butter Rd W, Ancaster (Hamilton), ON, L9G 3L1
www.ducktail.net
E-mail dwentworth@sympatico.ca

905-648-3596

From Hwy 403, take Hwy 52 (Copetown) Exit. Turn south on Hwy 52. Travel over three crossroads. Turn right unto Butter Rd, one concession. Look for duck mailbox. A modern air-conditioned one-floor home on 44 acres. Two large guest rooms. Twin bedroom with ensuite bath, queen bed with private bath with Jacuzzi tub. Full breakfast. A sunroom with wicker furnishings faces pond with ducks. We have a private museum of early Canadian artifacts. Free tours. Cat in residence. Near Hamilton Airport, Warplane Museum.

ROOMS Ground floor, Private entrance, **Baths** Private, Ensuite, **Beds** Queen, Twin, Single or cots, **Air** Central, **In Room** Phone, **OTHERS** Rural, Open all year, Handicapped access, Pets in residence, **PAYMENT** Cheques accepted, Cash, Trvl's cheques, **BREAKFASTS** Full, Home-baked, **AMENITIES** Central TV, Central phone, Fridge, Lounge, Patio, **THINGS TO DO** Trail nearby, Golf, Museums, Entertainment, Attractions, Shopping, Horseback riding, **LANGUAGE** Eng., Fr., **PRICE** (2 persons) 75–85 **(check with hosts for pricing details)**

Huntsville *(west of Algonquin Park)*

Morgan House Bed & Breakfast

(Pam Carnochan and Jamie Honderich)

83 Morgans Rd, Huntsville, ON, P1H 1A2
www.bbcanada.com/morganbb
E-mail morganbb@vianet.on.ca

705-789-1727

Our century-old stone house offers the casual comforts of country living. The 80 acres of trails and ponds invite you to explore, while the gardens and fireplace entice you to relax. The farm pets welcome attention and treats. Pam's wool studio inspires creativity and workshops are available. We are enroute to Algonquin Park and can help plan your time there. Breakfasts are hearty and feature fresh food and home baking. Families are welcome with fun for kids of all ages. Open year round.

ROOMS Upper floor, **Baths** Shared with guest, **Beds** King, Queen, Twin, **Smoking** Outside, OTHERS Rural, Open all year, PAYMENT Cheques accepted, Cash, **BREAKFASTS** Full, Home-baked, **AMENITIES** Central TV, Central phone, Barbecue, Patio, **THINGS TO DO** Trail nearby, Rental canoe or boat, Comp. Canoe or boat, Golf, Fishing, Museums, Art, Attractions, Shopping, Cross-country skiing, Tennis, Swimming, Horseback riding, Beach, **LANGUAGE** Eng., **PRICE** (2 persons) 50–80 (**check with hosts for pricing details**)

Huntsville

Muskoka Moments B&B and Cottage Court

(Joan and Rob Robertson)

57 Rowan Dr, RR #1, Huntsville, ON, P1H 2J2
www.muskokamoments.on.ca
E-mail relax@muskokamoments.on.ca

705-788-7125
Fax 705-788-7264
TFr 1-866-788-7125

The perfect setting to relax and reflect on Lake Vernon. In our year round B&B, we offer three rooms, each with queen-size bed/shared washroom/sitting room with TV/VCR, hot tub in our sunroom. We also have four fully equipped cottages onsite from May to October for your family getaway. Summer activities include swimming, boat rentals, fishing, campfires, hiking trails at nearby Algonquin Park. Winter attractions include snowmobiling, skiing, snowshoeing, tubing, dog-sledding. No pets. No smoking.

ROOMS Upper floor, **Baths** Shared with guest, **Beds** Queen, **OTHERS** Open all year, Pets in residence, **PAYMENT** Visa, MC, Diners, Amex, Direct debit, Cheques accepted, Cash, Trvl's cheques, **BREAKFASTS** Full, **AMENITIES** Central TV, Fridge, Hot bev. bar, Lounge, Central VCR/DVD, **THINGS TO DO** Trail nearby, Rental canoe or boat, Golf, Fishing, Art, Entertainment, Attractions, Shopping, Cross-country skiing, Downhill skiing, Swimming, Horseback riding, Beach, **LANGUAGE** Eng., **PRICE** (2 persons) 99–120 (**check with hosts for pricing details**)

JACKSONS POINT *(north of Toronto)*

Jackson's Landing Bed & Breakfast

(John and Lynn Gilbank)

56 Malone Rd, Jacksons Point, ON, L0E 1L0
www.jacksonslandingbb.com
E-mail jgilbank@rogers.com

905-722-7752
Fax 905-722-6651
TFr 1-866-606-6005

An elegant and storied lakeside mansion of the 1920s built on the scenic homestead of one of Canada's earliest political reformers and the home port of Stephen Leacock's legendary "Mariposa Belle". Located at the very tip of Jackson's Point, you can explore our meandering waterfront trails, take a dip in the lake or just relax on a waterside deck or private terrace and watch the boats round the Point to the harbour. Our year-round conservatory and landscaped gardens invite peaceful retreats.

ROOMS Upper floor, Ground floor, Private entrance, **Baths** Private, Ensuite, **Beds** King, Queen, Twin, **Air** In rooms, **Smoking** Outside, **In Room** Thermostat, Fireplace, Internet access, **OTHERS** Adult, Open all year, Additional meals, Pets in residence, **PAYMENT** Visa, MC, Diners, Amex, Cheques accepted, Cash, **BREAKFASTS** Full, Home-baked, **AMENITIES** Central TV, Central phone, Fridge, Lounge, Patio, Central VCR/DVD, **THINGS TO DO** Trail nearby, Rental canoe or boat, Golf, Fishing, Art, Theatre, Shopping, Swimming, Horseback riding, Beach, **LANGUAGE** Eng., **PRICE** (2 persons) 140–195 **(check with hosts for pricing details)**

JORDAN AND VINELAND
(west of Niagara Falls)

Bonnybank Bed and Breakfast

(Carla Carlson)

RR #1, Vineland Station, ON, L0R 2E0
www.bbcanada.com/4241.html
E-mail info@niagaranaturetours.ca

905-562-3746
TFr 1-888-889-8296

Our 1919 stone Tudor Revival home is nestled on the bank of the Twenty Mile Creek ANSI with Carolinian woodland trails; ponds and singing frogs; tennis court; campfire site; kayaks; star-gazing and organic gardens. Watch the moon sail by from the stone terrace and listen to the surrounding calls of owls or hear a coyote lullaby. Niagara nature wine and garden tours; weddings; private/ corporate events; tours; workshops and storytelling/musical houseparties. Nearby Inn on the Twenty Spa.

ROOMS Upper floor, **Baths** Ensuite, Shared with guest, **Beds** King, Queen, Twin, Pullout sofa, **Air** Central, **Smoking** Outside, **In Room** TV, **OTHERS** Babysitting, Rural, Open all year, Additional meals, Pets in residence, Pets welcome, **PAYMENT** Cheques accepted, Cash, Trvl's cheques, **BREAKFASTS** Full, Home-baked, **AMENITIES** Central TV, Central phone, Barbecue, Kitchen, Fridge, Hot bev. bar, Lounge, Patio, Central Internet access, Central VCR/DVD, **THINGS TO DO** Trail nearby, Comp. Canoe or boat, Golf, Fishing, Museums, Art, Theatre, Entertainment, Attractions, Wineries/Breweries, Shopping, Cross-country skiing, Tennis, Beach, Birdwatching, Antiquing, **LANGUAGE** Eng., **PRICE** (2 persons) 90–120 **(check with hosts for pricing details)**

JORDAN AND VINELAND

Traveller's Home
(Janet and Bert Dunnink)

3333 Spring Creek Rd, Jordan, ON, L0R 1S0
www.travellershome.ca
E-mail info@travellershome.ca

905-562-5656
Fax 905-562-5656

Vineland/Jordan area. Location: From
QEW Exit 57, turn south on Victoria Ave.
Travel through traffic lights, past Balls
Falls and left on Spring Creek Rd E. New
home with ensuite rooms, private
entrance, inside and outside sitting area
and mini kitchen. In Niagara wine country
with lots of fruit in season. Niagara Falls,
Bruce Trail, Jordan Antiques, Shaw
Festival, golf, wineries and the quaint
town of Niagara-on-the-Lake are not far
away. We offer warm Dutch hospitality
with the best of breakfasts.

ROOMS Family suite, Ground floor, Lower floor, Private
entrance, **Baths** Ensuite, **Beds** Queen, Single or cots,
Pullout sofa, **Air** Central, **Smoking** Outside, **In Room**
OTHERS Rural, Open all year, **PAYMENT** Cheques
accepted, Cash, Trvl's cheques, **BREAKFASTS** Full,
Home-baked, **AMENITIES** Central TV, Central phone,
Kitchen, Fridge, Patio, **THINGS TO DO** Rental bikes,
Trail nearby, Golf, Fishing, Museums, Art, Theatre,
Attractions, Wineries/Breweries, Shopping, Swimming,
Horseback riding, Beach, Antiquing, **LANGUAGE** Eng.,
Dutch **PRICE** (2 persons) 60–80 **(check with hosts for**
pricing details)

JORDAN VILLAGE

Jordan Village Guest Manor B&B
(Sheldon and Judy Kofsky)

3864 Main St, Jordan Village, ON, L0R 1S0
www.jmaks.ca
E-mail jordanbandb@jmaks.ca

905-562-8269
TFr 1-888-562-8269

We have what you want – Jordan Village
is a secret jewel in the Niagara area. We
have world renowned wineries and
restaurants within steps of our B&B. We
are a short distance from Buffalo, NY,
Toronto and all Niagara attractions. View
our Web site for additional information
and please call us with any questions. We
will be pleased to host you, your family
and friends at our B&B. Come and stay to
have a wonderful day!

ROOMS Family suite, Upper floor, Ground floor, Private
entrance, **Baths** Ensuite, Shared with guest, **Beds** King,
Double, Twin, Single or cots, Pullout sofa, **Air** Central,
Smoking Outside, **In Room** TV, **OTHERS** Babysitting,
Rural, Open all year, **PAYMENT** Visa, MC, Direct debit,
Cash, **BREAKFASTS** Continental, Self-catered, **AMENI-**
TIES Kitchen, Fridge, Hot bev. bar, Patio, **THINGS TO**
DO Rental bikes, Trail nearby, Golf, Fishing, Museums,
Art, Theatre, Entertainment, Attractions, Wineries/
Breweries, Shopping, Cross-country skiing, Swimming,
Horseback riding, **LANGUAGE** Eng., **PRICE** (2 persons)
85–249 **(check with hosts for pricing details)**

KAPUSKASING *(northern Ontario)*

Grandma Jean's B&B

(Jean Belanger)

35 Cite Des Jeunes Blvd, Kapuskasing, ON, P5N 2Z5
www.canadianbandbguide.ca/bb.asp?ID=3704
E-mail eujean@onlink.net

705-335-4968
Fax 705-335-4968

We welcome you to a warm and friendly atmosphere with a cup of your favourite brew. Our breakfast hours are flexible and we serve five great hot meals, including fresh fruits, juices, yogurts, cereals and hot-from-the-oven homemade muffins. Summer visitors can relax in the shade of our maple trees with a good cup of tea or coffee. Hwy 11 from North Bay, right at first light on Brunelle, then left on Cite Des Jeunes Blvd, Second on the right. Cell phone 705-367-6109.

ROOMS Family suite, Upper floor, Lower floor, **Baths** Private, Shared with guest, **Beds** Queen, Double, Twin, Single or cots, **Air** In rooms, **Smoking** Outside, **In Room** TV, Internet access, **OTHERS** Urban, Open all year, **PAYMENT** Visa, MC, Cash, Trvl's cheques, **BREAKFASTS** Full, Home-baked, **AMENITIES** Fridge, **THINGS TO DO** Trail nearby, Golf, Fishing, Museums, Theatre, Attractions, Shopping, Cross-country skiing, Downhill skiing, Beach, **LANGUAGE** Eng., Fr., **PRICE** (2 persons) 60–75 **(check with hosts for pricing details)**

KENORA *(northwestern Ontario)*

Northwoods Bed and Breakfast

(Joanne and Craig Forster)

817 St. Clair St, Keewatin, ON, P0X 1C0
www.northwoodsbedandbreakfast.ca
E-mail info@northwoodsbedandbreakfast.ca

807-547-2992
Fax 807-547-2993
TFr 1-888-303-4833

Northwoods Bed and Breakfast is located west of Kenora in the town of Keewatin. On the south side of Hwy 1 with a southern exposure of Lake of the Woods – a 5-minute walk to Keewatin Beach and other attractions. The building is a square-log cabin built in a Swiss Chalet style. We have two self-contained light housekeeping suites with gas BBQs and two loft bedrooms, which share the main bathroom. Directions from both the east and west are available on the rates page of our Web site.

ROOMS Family suite, Upper floor, Lower floor, Private entrance, **Baths** Ensuite, Shared with guest, Shared with hosts, **Beds** Queen, Double, Pullout sofa, **Air** Central, **Smoking** Outside, **In Room** Thermostat, TV, Fireplace, **OTHERS** Open all year, Pets in residence, **PAYMENT** Visa, MC, Amex, Cash, Trvl's cheques, **BREAKFASTS** Full, Continental, **AMENITIES** Barbecue, Kitchen, Fridge, Patio, **THINGS TO DO** Rental bikes, Trail nearby, Rental canoe or boat, Golf, Fishing, Museums, Art, Theatre, Entertainment, Attractions, Shopping, Cross-country skiing, Downhill skiing, Swimming, Horseback riding, Beach, Birdwatching, Antiquing, **LANGUAGE** Eng., **PRICE** (2 persons) 80–100 **(check with hosts for pricing details)**

KIMBERLEY *(northwest of Toronto)*

Jasper Stuart House
(Sue Barbour and Kerry Baskey)

235299 Grey Rd, 13, Kimberley, ON, N0C 1G0
www.bbcanada.com/jasperstuarthouse
E-mail jasperstuarthouse@cablerocket.com

519-599-1166
Fax 519-599-1176
TFr 1-888-268-5094

Nestled in the heart of the Beaver Valley, one of the world's designated biospheres. Our fully renovated Victorian home offers the perfect location from which to enjoy some of Ontario's finest theatre, golfing, hiking on the Bruce Trail, fishing, bicycling, skiing and other activities. Located approximately 15 minutes from Flesherton, Meaford and Thornbury, and approximately 2 hours from Toronto. For those located in Beaver Valley area, let us act as an extention to your home/chalet.

ROOMS Family suite, Upper floor, Lower floor, Private entrance, **Baths** Private, Ensuite, **Beds** Queen, Twin, Pullout sofa, **Air** Central, Ceiling fans, **In Room** Fireplace, VCR/DVD, **OTHERS** Rural, Adult, Open all year, **PAYMENT** Visa, MC, Direct debit, Cash, **BREAKFASTS** Full, Home-baked, **AMENITIES** Central TV, Central phone, Swimming pool, Lounge, Patio, Central VCR/DVD, **THINGS TO DO** Rental bikes, Trail nearby, Rental canoe or boat, Golf, Fishing, Museums, Art, Theatre, Entertainment, Attractions, Wineries/Breweries, Shopping, Cross-country skiing, Downhill skiing, Tennis, Swimming, Horseback riding, Beach, Birdwatching, **LANGUAGE** Eng., **PRICE** (2 persons) 125–125 **(check with hosts for pricing details)**

KINCARDINE *(east-central Lake Huron)*

Abide In
(Mike and Gloria Murphy)

869 Mackendrick Dr, Kincardine, ON, N2Z 1L7
www.home.tnt21.com/~abidein
E-mail abidein@tnt21.com

519-396-3912
Fax 519-396-3912

Welcome to our quiet B&B. We have pleasantly decorated bedrooms you will love. Delicous full breakfasts included. See our elegant main suite with king bed, Jacuzzi and ensuite, plus two rooms with queen beds, one room with twin beds, two other rooms with ensuite. We are a smoke-free home four blocks from the beach. TV and VCR in each room. Bridal suite available.

ROOMS Upper floor, Ground floor, Lower floor, **Baths** Ensuite, Shared with guest, Shared with hosts, **Beds** King, Queen, Twin, Single or cots, **Air** Central, **In Room** TV, **OTHERS** Urban, Open all year, Additional meals, **PAYMENT** Cheques accepted, Cash, Trvl's cheques, **BREAKFASTS** Full, Home-baked, **AMENITIES** Barbecue, Laundry, Lounge, Patio, **THINGS TO DO** Rental bikes, Trail nearby, Rental canoe or boat, Golf, Fishing, Museums, Art, Theatre, Attractions, Wineries/Breweries, Shopping, Swimming, Beach, **LANGUAGE** Eng., **PRICE** (2 persons) 59–109 **(check with hosts for pricing details)**

Kingston

Frontenac Club Inn

(Beare Weatherup and Susan Shaw)

225 King St E, Kingston, ON, K7L 3A7
www.frontenacclub.com
E-mail stay@frontenacclub.com

613-547-6167
Fax 613-549-4766

The Frontenac Club Inn is located in the heart of Kingston's historic downtown and is within walking distance of the waterfront, excellent restaurants, great shopping and Queen's University. The heritage limestone building (1845), recently renovated, offers comfortable guest rooms, some with gas fireplaces and Jacuzzis "which subscribe to a smart, unfussy sensibility", *Toronto Life*, *Getaway Guide 2001*, *2002* and *2003*. Start your day with a delicious breakfast and then go out and discover Kingston's historic charm.

ROOMS Upper floor, Ground floor, Private entrance, **Baths** Ensuite, **Beds** King, Queen, **Air** In rooms, Ceiling fans, **In Room** Phone, TV, Fireplace, **OTHERS** Urban, Open all year, **PAYMENT** Visa, MC, Amex, Direct debit, Cash, Trvl's cheques, **BREAKFASTS** Full, Home-baked, **AMENITIES** Central TV, Fridge, Lounge, Patio, Central Internet access, Central VCR/DVD, **THINGS TO DO** Golf, Museums, Art, Theatre, Entertainment, Attractions, Shopping, **LANGUAGE** Eng., **PRICE** (2 persons) 129–199 **(check with hosts for pricing details)**

Kingston

Green Woods Inn

(Nigel and Tessa Dearsley)

1368 Hwy 15, Kingston, ON, K7L 5H6
www.greenwoods-inn.ca
E-mail info@greenwoods-inn.ca

613-544-1922
TFr 1-866-878-1884

Green Woods Inn (Bed & Breakfast) is a beautifully appointed Victorian country home located on Hwy 15, just 1 mile south of Hwy 401. Situated in 2 acres, away from the hustle and bustle of the city, yet only 5 minutes from downtown Kingston. The Inn provides a centralized location for exploring Kingston, the Thousand Islands and Gananoque. An ideal midpoint. Surrounded by beautiful lakes, rivers and countryside in an area steeped in Ontario's history.

ROOMS Upper floor, **Baths** Ensuite, **Beds** Queen, Double, Twin, **Air** Central, **PAYMENT** Visa, MC, Cheques accepted, Cash, Trvl's cheques, **BREAKFASTS** Full, **AMENITIES** Hot bev. bar, Patio, Central Internet access, **THINGS TO DO** Trail nearby, Golf, Fishing, Museums, Art, Theatre, Entertainment, Attractions, Shopping, Swimming, Horseback riding, Beach, **LANGUAGE** Eng., **PRICE** (2 persons) 95–159 **(check with hosts for pricing details)**

KINGSTON

Painted Lady Inn

(Carol Franks)

181 William St, Kingston, ON, K7L 2E1
www.paintedladyinn.on.ca
E-mail cfranks@cogeco.ca

613-545-0422

Ideally placed in historic downtown, this 1872 Victorian beauty offers seven spacious guest rooms with ensuite baths, central air and antiques. Luxury rooms boast Jacuzzis and fireplaces. Executive rooms have private telephones and TV. Everyone enjoys the whimsical verandah, balcony and Victorian parlour. Full hot breakfast served – waffles, omelettes and souffles. Two self-catering suites available for long-stay guests. Free parking. Near Queen's, restaurants, farmer's market and Thousand Island cruises.

ROOMS Upper floor, Ground floor, Private entrance, **Baths** Ensuite, **Beds** King, Queen, Twin, **Air** Central, **In Room** Phone, TV, Fireplace, **OTHERS** Urban, Adult, Open all year, **PAYMENT** Visa, MC, Amex, Cash, Trvl's cheques, **BREAKFASTS** Full, **AMENITIES** Hot bev. bar, Lounge, Patio, **THINGS TO DO** Rental bikes, Trail nearby, Rental canoe or boat, Golf, Fishing, Museums, Art, Theatre, Entertainment, Attractions, Shopping, Tennis, **LANGUAGE** Eng., **PRICE** (2 persons) 99–165 **(check with hosts for pricing details)**

KINGSTON

The Secret Garden B&B Inn

(Gary Patterson and Warren Bennett)

73 Sydenham St S, Kingston, ON, K7L 3H3
www.the-secret-garden.com
E-mail innkeeper@the-secret-garden.com

613-531-9884
Fax 613-531-9502
TFr 1-877-723-1888

Our 1888 historically designated home offers seven guest suites with king or queen beds, private bathrooms, and most rooms with fireplaces. The original character has been maintained, including stained glass windows and doors, hardwood floors, detailed plaster mouldings and, of course, the traditional inviting front porch and Secret Garden side patio. To enhance your stay we offer a full gourmet breakfast each morning.

ROOMS Upper floor, Ground floor, **Baths** Private, Ensuite, **Beds** King, Queen, Twin, **Air** Central, In rooms, Ceiling fans, **OTHERS** Adult, Open all year, Pets in residence, **PAYMENT** Visa, MC, Amex, Direct debit, Cash, Trvl's cheques, **BREAKFASTS** Full, Home-baked, **AMENITIES** Central TV, Central phone, Lounge, Patio, Central Internet access, **THINGS TO DO** Rental bikes, Trail nearby, Rental canoe or boat, Golf, Fishing, Museums, Art, Theatre, Entertainment, Attractions, Wineries/Breweries, Shopping, Cross-country skiing, Tennis, Swimming, Beach, Antiquing, **LANGUAGE** Eng., **PRICE** (2 persons) 139–169 **(check with hosts for pricing details)**

Kingston

The Tymparon Inn

(Don Timperon and Zoe Piliero)

1403 Hwy 15, Kingston, ON, K7L 5H6
www.TymparonInn.com
E-mail email@tymparoninn.com

613-545-3663
Fax 613-545-3663
TFr 1-866-293-3997

The Tymparon Inn is a restored 1865 country farmhouse. Our three guest suites are impeccably decorated, featuring luxurious beds, linens and private bathrooms, two of which are ensuite. A full hot gourmet breakfast is served on Lenox china, Waterford crystal and Towle sterling silver. Hot tub, bicycles, bocce ball, horseshoes and croquet are included as amenities. Ideally situated for Thousands Islands visitors as Inn is 1 mile from Hwy 401 on Hwy 15, yet only 5 minutes from downtown Kingston and Lake Ontario.

ROOMS Upper floor, **Baths** Private, Ensuite, **Beds** King, Queen, Double, Twin, **Air** Central, **Smoking** Outside, **In Room** Internet access, **OTHERS** Rural, Adult, Open all year, Pets in residence, **PAYMENT** Visa, MC, Direct debit, Cash, Trvl's cheques, **BREAKFASTS** Full, Home-baked, **AMENITIES** Central TV, Central phone, Whirlpool, Lounge, Patio, **THINGS TO DO** Comp. bikes, Trail nearby, Rental canoe or boat, Golf, Fishing, Museums, Art, Theatre, Entertainment, Attractions, Wineries/ Breweries, Shopping, Cross-country skiing, Tennis, Swimming, Horseback riding, Beach, Birdwatching, Antiquing, **LANGUAGE** Eng., Fr., **PRICE** (2 persons) 90–130 **(check with hosts for pricing details)**

Kingsville

The Old Farmhouse Bed & Breakfast

(Barbara and John Hungler)

1389 Seacliff Dr, Kingsville, ON, N9Y 2M4
www.oldfarmhouse.com
E-mail info@oldfarmhouse.com

519-733-9660

Enjoy the full restoration of our 1870 farmhouse situated on 10 acres of apple orchard on the beautiful shores of Lake Erie. Each room has been thematically decorated with vintage furniture and accessories to celebrate the heritage of both the farmhouse and Essex County. Located near Point Pelee National Park and the ferry service to Pelee Island, the Old Farmhouse offers a peaceful retreat to nightly or longer term guests. Local amenities in either Leamington or Kingsville are just minutes away.

ROOMS Family suite, Upper floor, Ground floor, **Baths** Private, **Beds** King, Queen, Twin, Single or cots, **Air** Central, **Smoking** Outside, **In Room** Internet access, **OTHERS** Adult, Open all year, Additional meals, **PAYMENT** Visa, MC, Cheques accepted, Cash, Trvl's cheques, **BREAKFASTS** Full, Home-baked, Self-catered, **AMENITIES** Central TV, Central phone, Laundry, Kitchen, Fridge, Lounge, Patio, Central Internet access, Central VCR/DVD, **THINGS TO DO** Trail nearby, Golf, Fishing, Museums, Art, Attractions, Wineries/Breweries, Shopping, Cross-country skiing, Swimming, Birdwatching, **LANGUAGE** Eng., Ger., **PRICE** (2 persons) 85–125 **(check with hosts for pricing details)**

KINMOUNT *(northeast of Toronto)*

Kinmount House B&B
(Patrick Healey)

6 Cluxton St, Kinmount, ON, K0M 2A0
www.bbcanada.com/2253.html
E-mail healey_patrick@hotmail.com

705-488-2421
TFr 1-800-511-0211

A century home, offering an informal atmosphere. Access to rail bed for hiking, biking, walking and canoeing. Within walking distance to world famous Highland Theatre. Dinners and picnic lunches on request. Home of the Kinmount Fall Fair. Corner of Hwy 121 and Hwy 45 E. Pricing per night from $45 single, $75 double, $95 family room.

Baths Shared with guest, **Beds** Double, Twin, Single or cots, **OTHERS** Open all year, Pets in residence, **PAYMENT** Cash, **BREAKFASTS** Full, **THINGS TO DO** Trail nearby, Shopping, **LANGUAGE** Eng., **PRICE** (2 persons) 75–95 **(check with hosts for pricing details)**

KITCHENER *(west of Hamilton)*

Roses And Blessings
(Marg and Norm Warren)

112 High Acres Cres, Kitchener, ON, N2N 2Z9
www.rosesandblessings.com
E-mail nmwarren@golden.net

519-742-1280
Fax 519-742-8428
TFr 1-866-811-1280

We enjoy pampering our guests in our Christian home. Warm hospitality, home-baking and comfort are our specialties. Hospitality Award recipients. Enjoy our renowned sumptuous gourmet breakfasts – featuring fresh baking, fresh fruits and hot entrees. Enjoy evening dessert snacks and awaken to morning coffee served at your bedroom door. Excursion planning, theatre and restaurant reservations can be provided. Attraction and theatre packages are available. Extended stay discount. Many extras provided.

ROOMS Upper floor, Lower floor, **Baths** Private, **Beds** Queen, Double, Single or cots, Pullout sofa, **Air** Central, **Smoking** Outside, **In Room** TV, **OTHERS** Urban, Open all year, **PAYMENT** Visa, MC, Amex, Cash, Trvl's cheques, **BREAKFASTS** Full, Home-baked, **AMENITIES** Central TV, Central phone, Whirlpool, Barbecue, Lounge, **THINGS TO DO** Comp. bikes, Trail nearby, Golf, Museums, Art, Theatre, Entertainment, Attractions, Wineries/Breweries, Shopping, Cross-country skiing, Tennis, Swimming, Horseback riding, **LANGUAGE** Eng., basic French, **PRICE** (2 persons) 65–80 **(check with hosts for pricing details)**

LAFONTAINE *(northwest of Toronto)*

Chez-Vous Chez-Nous Couette et Cafe

(Karen and Larry Yaguchi)

160 Lafontaine Rd W, RR #3, Penetanguishene,
ON, L9M 1R3
www.chezvouscheznous.com
E-mail chez_vouse@bellnet.ca

705-533-2237
Fax 705-533-2237
TFr 1-877-533-2237

Located in Lafontaine, near Penetanguishene. From Toronto, Hwy 400 past Barrie, Elmvale to Lafontaine, Conc 16 (west of Hwy 400) or Lafontaine Rd W. Farmhouse with new extension built for guests, situated in an historic Southern Ontario rural environment, located in the heart of Huronia. Seven beautiful spacious guest rooms for families, groups or singles. Three shared baths. Full delicious breakfast. Enjoy many indoor/outdoor activities and our friendly hospitality with picturesque views from all smoke-free rooms.

ROOMS Ground floor, Lower floor, Private entrance, **Baths** Shared with guest, **Beds** Queen, Double, Twin, Single or cots, **Smoking** Outside, **In Room** Thermostat, **OTHERS** Rural, Open all year, Additional meals, **PAYMENT** Cheques accepted, Cash, Trvl's cheques, **BREAKFASTS** Full, Home-baked, **AMENITIES** Fridge, Patio, **THINGS TO DO** Trail nearby, Golf, Fishing, Museums, Theatre, Shopping, Cross-country skiing, Beach, **LANGUAGE** Eng., **PRICE** (2 persons) 70–100 **(check with hosts for pricing details)**

LANCASTER *(east of Ottawa)*

MacPine Farm's Bed & Breakfast

(Guelda and Robert MacRae)

Box 51- 20476 Service Rd, Lancaster, ON, K0C 1N0
www.bbcanada.com/688.html
E-mail macpine@glen-net.ca

613-347-2003
Fax 613-347-2814

We welcome you to stay at our modernized century dairy farm home, shaded with pine trees, on the shores of the St. Lawrence River. Exit 814 off Hwy 401 at Lancaster, 1 mile on South Service R. A quiet getaway. Full breakfast served in sunroom. Take a shortwalk to the river. Canoe, fish or relax and watch the ocean boats go by. Area attractions: golf, fishing, nature walk and birdwatching, bike path, craft and antique shop, china outlets, Upper Canada Village. Visit Ottawa, Montreal, Cornwall. Ceiling fans in rooms.

ROOMS Family suite, Upper floor, Private entrance, **Baths** Shared with guest, Shared with hosts, **Beds** Queen, Twin, Single or cots, **Air** Central, Ceiling fans, **Smoking** Outside, **In Room** Thermostat, Phone, TV, VCR/DVD, **OTHERS** Rural, Adult, Open all year, **PAYMENT** Cheques accepted, Cash, **BREAKFASTS** Full, Home-baked, **AMENITIES** Central TV, Central phone, Barbecue, Laundry, Fridge, Lounge, Patio, **THINGS TO DO** Comp. bikes, Trail nearby, Comp. Canoe or boat, Golf, Fishing, Museums, Art, Theatre, Attractions, Shopping, Cross-country skiing, Swimming, Beach, Birdwatching, Antiquing, **LANGUAGE** Eng., **PRICE** (2 persons) 65–65 **(check with hosts for pricing details)**

LEAMINGTON *(southwestern Ontario)*

B&B's Bed and Breakfast

(Bea and Bruce Patterson)

216 Erie St S, Box 98, Wheatley, ON, N0P 2P0
www.mnsi.net/~brucep
E-mail brucep@mnsi.net

519-825-8008
Fax 519-825-7737
TFr 1-800-851-3406

An historic Victorian home built in 1905. Rooms have private ensuite bathrooms with deep "soaker" tubs/showers. Guests receive a key for their room and entrance door. Country-style breakfast includes homemade breads and jams. Close to Point Pelee National Park, excellent areas for birding. Common entertainment area, pool table, satellite TV. Lovely private yard, old trees, Carolinian forest. Located in Wheatley five blocks south of lights, at 216 Erie St S.

ROOMS Ground floor, Private entrance, **Baths** Private, Ensuite, **Beds** Queen, Twin, **Air** Central, **Smoking** Outside, **In Room OTHERS** Rural, Open all year, Pets in residence, **PAYMENT** Visa, MC, Cheques accepted, **BREAKFASTS** Full, Home-baked, **AMENITIES** Central TV, Central phone, Swimming pool, Fridge, Lounge, **THINGS TO DO** Trail nearby, Golf, Fishing, Museums, Art, Theatre, Entertainment, Attractions, Wineries/Breweries, Shopping, Swimming, Beach, **LANGUAGE** Eng., Fr., Ger., **PRICE** (2 persons) 90–109 **(check with hosts for pricing details)**

LONDON *(west of Hamilton)*

Belle Vie's guest cottage

(Maria & Wouter Eshuis)

21475 Denfield Rd, RR #41, London, ON, N6H 5L2
www.bellevie.ca
E-mail maria@bellevie.ca

519-666-0998
Fax 519-666-0963
TFr 1-877-242-3366

Belle Vie's cottage is a beautiful 160-year-old guesthouse in the middle of a garden next to a swimming pool. It is lovingly restored and has all modern conveniences. The country French interior offers you one or two bedrooms to use and a four-piece bathroom with clawfoot tub and a luxurious shower. The living room is complete with satellite TV and wood burning fireplace. There is an aga cooker in the kitchen. The guesthouse will be just for you and your party and will not be shared by other guests.

ROOMS Upper floor, Ground floor, Private entrance, **Baths** Private, **Beds** Queen, Twin, **Air** Central, **Smoking** Outside, **In Room** Thermostat, Phone, TV, Fireplace, Internet access, VCR/DVD, **OTHERS** Babysitting, Rural, Open all year, **PAYMENT** Visa, MC, Cash, **BREAKFASTS** Full, Home-baked, **AMENITIES** Central TV, Central phone, Swimming pool, Barbecue, Kitchen, Fridge, Lounge, Patio, Central Internet access, Central VCR/DVD, **THINGS TO DO** Trail nearby, Golf, Museums, Art, Theatre, Entertainment, Attractions, Wineries/Breweries, Shopping, Cross-country skiing, Swimming, Horseback riding, Birdwatching, Antiquing, **LANGUAGE** Eng., Dutch, **PRICE** (2 persons) 180–180 **(check with hosts for pricing details)**

London

Charlton, Eve's Place Bed and Breakfast

(Eve Charlton)

4842 Dundas St, Thorndale, ON, N0M 2P0
www.dcharlton.on.ca
E-mail charlton@london.com

519-268-3714

Quiet and restful modern country home centered on 12 acres. Safe water. Close to city of London, airport and Hwy 401. Spacious rooms. Full country breakfast. Farm-fresh eggs, fresh roasted and ground coffee beans. Home grown organic vegetables in season. Pickup at airport, bus or train station. No Alcohol or pets. Adults preferred. "Arrive as strangers, leave as friends."

ROOMS Ground floor, **Baths** Private, Ensuite, **Beds** Queen, Double, **Air** Central, Ceiling fans, **Smoking** Outside, **OTHERS** Rural, Adult, Open all year, **PAYMENT** Visa, MC, Amex, Cash, **BREAKFASTS** Full, **AMENITIES** Central TV, **THINGS TO DO** Golf, Fishing, Museums, Art, Theatre, Entertainment, Attractions, Wineries/ Breweries, Shopping, Cross-country skiing, Downhill skiing, Birdwatching, **LANGUAGE** Eng., **PRICE** (2 persons) 45–75 **(check with hosts for pricing details)**

London

Companys' Coming

(Barb Huffman)

1015 Farnham Rd, London, ON, N6K 1S3
www.canadianbandbguide.ca/bb.asp?ID=3585
E-mail bhuffman0114@rogers.com

519-473-0005

Welcome to Companys' Coming! A quiet little upscale B&B in southwest London. Minutes from Hwys 401 and 402, 1 1/2 hours from Pearson International Airport in Toronto and 1 hour from the Bluewater Bridge in Sarnia. Easy access to University of Western Ontario, downtown London, beautiful Springbank Park and many fabulous restaurants. I look forward to meeting you ... Be my guest ... Cell phone number: 519-520-1502.

ROOMS Upper floor, **Baths** Private, Shared with guest, **Beds** Queen, Double, **Air** Central, **Smoking** Outside, **In Room** TV, **OTHERS** Urban, Adult, Open all year, Additional meals, Pets in residence, **PAYMENT** Cash, **BREAKFASTS** Full, Continental, Home-baked, **AMENITIES** Central TV, Central phone, Barbecue, Central Internet access, Central VCR/DVD, **THINGS TO DO** Golf, Museums, Art, Theatre, Entertainment, Attractions, Wineries/Breweries, Shopping, Cross-country skiing, Downhill skiing, Horseback riding, Beach, Antiquing, **LANGUAGE** Eng., **PRICE** (2 persons) 75–85 **(check with hosts for pricing details)**

MADOC *(southeast of Ottawa)*

Spotted Dog B and B

(Rob Price and Scott Williams)

RR #1, 301 St. Lawrence St W, Madoc, ON, K0K 2K0
www.spotteddogbandb.ca
E-mail info@spotteddogbandb.ca

613-473-2131
Fax 613-473-0760
TFr 1-866-776-8364

Spotted Dog is located at the west end of Madoc Village just off Hwy 7. Quiet country getaway with over 2 acres of land. Lots of private space indoors. Sunny breakfast room, large deck and pool in summer. Antiques, Moira Lake, Trail of Two Lakes, all nearby. Steeped in history, Hastings County makes a perfect choice for peace and quiet or that adventure-filled day trip. Dogs are welcome with prior arrangements. From the south, take Hwy 62 north from the 401. Proceed to Madoc and turn left on St. Lawrence St to 301. From Hwy 7, exit south to St. Lawrence West.

ROOMS Upper floor, **Baths** Shared with guest, **Beds** Queen, Twin, **Smoking** Outside, **OTHERS** Rural, Open all year, Pets in residence, Pets welcome, **PAYMENT** Visa, MC, Diners, Amex, Cheques accepted, Cash, **BREAKFASTS** Full, **AMENITIES** Central TV, Swimming pool, Barbecue, Kitchen, Fridge, Hot bev. bar, Lounge, Patio, **THINGS TO DO** Comp. bikes, Trail nearby, Golf, Fishing, **LANGUAGE** Eng., **PRICE** (2 persons) 60–80 **(check with hosts for pricing details)**

MANITOULIN ISLAND *(northwest of Toronto)*

Mindemoya Lakeview Farm B&B

(Harold and Sally Williamson)

619A Lakeshore Rd, Mindemoya, ON, P0P 1S0
www.canadianbandbguide.ca/bb.asp?ID=2928

705-377-5714

Beautiful sunrise and sunsets. Fishing, hiking, beach nearby. Auction sales, garage sales. Manitoulin Island, known as "God's Country." Home of the Great Spirit Manitou. Art galleries, M'chigeng Native Foundation.

ROOMS Upper floor, **Baths** Shared with guest, Shared with hosts, **Beds** Queen, Double, **Air** In rooms, **Smoking** Outside, **OTHERS** Rural, Open all year, **PAYMENT** Cheques accepted, Cash, Trvl's cheques, **BREAKFASTS** Full, **AMENITIES** Central TV, Central phone, Lounge, Patio, **THINGS TO DO** Trail nearby, Golf, Fishing, Museums, Art, Theatre, Shopping, Swimming, Horseback riding, Beach, **LANGUAGE** Eng., **PRICE** (2 persons) 45–50 **(check with hosts for pricing details)**

MANITOULIN ISLAND

Westview B&B

(Wayne and Denise Rutledge)

466 White's Point Rd, Little Current, ON, P0P 1K0
www.westviewwaterfront.com
E-mail wdpoint@personainternet.com

705-368-1577
Fax 705-368-1577

Waterfront location with scenic view, on private beach with clear water. Just minutes from Little Current. Located in a quiet neighbourhood, nestled in the woods on a beautiful peninsula. Watch the sunsets. Enjoy a deicious full breakfast. Watch the sailboats on Georgian Bay. Located 2 km southeast of Little Current on Hwy 6, left on White's Point Rd to 466. Rates: One person per room per night, $50 (no tax); two persons per room per night $70 (no tax).

ROOMS Upper floor, Ground floor, Private entrance, **Baths** Private, Ensuite, **Beds** Queen, Single or cots, **Smoking** Outside, **In Room** Thermostat, **OTHERS** Seasonal, **PAYMENT** Cash, Trvl's cheques, **BREAKFASTS** Full, **AMENITIES** Central TV, Lounge, Patio, **THINGS TO DO** Trail nearby, Rental canoe or boat, Golf, Fishing, Museums, Attractions, Shopping, Tennis, Swimming, Horseback riding, Beach, Birdwatching, **LANGUAGE** Eng., Fr., **PRICE** (2 persons) 50–70 **(check with hosts for pricing details)**

MARATHON *(northwestern Ontario)*

Lakeview Manor Bed and Breakfast

(Ray and Sherri Boudreau)

24 Drake St, Marathon, ON, P0T 2E0
www.bbcanada.com/3917.htlm
E-mail lakeviewmanor@shaw.ca

807-229-2248
Fax 807-229-9358

Our beautiful home offers a spectacular view of Lake Superior. Enjoy the sunsets in our large living room. Relax by the fireplace in the library and living room. We have five guest rooms with queen-size beds for your comfort. Indulge in a continental or full breakfast in our dining room with seating for eight. We are close to two provincial parks which provide breathtaking views. We are situated on 1.4 acres of town property which offers a quiet and private stay. Arrive as a guest ... leave as a friend!

ROOMS Upper floor, **Baths** Private, Ensuite, Shared with guest, **Beds** Queen, **Air** Ceiling fans, **Smoking** Outside, **In Room** TV, **OTHERS** Adult, Open all year, Additional meals, Pets in residence, Pets welcome, **PAYMENT** Visa, MC, Cash, Trvl's cheques, **BREAKFASTS** Full, Continental, Home-baked, **AMENITIES** Central TV, Central phone, Barbecue, Laundry, Kitchen, Lounge, Patio, Central Internet access, Central VCR/DVD, **THINGS TO DO** Trail nearby, Golf, Fishing, Theatre, Shopping, Cross-country skiing, Tennis, Swimming, Beach, Birdwatching, **LANGUAGE** Eng., **PRICE** (2 persons) 65–100 **(check with hosts for pricing details)**

MARKHAM *(north of Toronto)*

Valley View House 109 B&B
(Teil Hall)

109 Robinson St, Markham, ON, L3P 1P2
www.bbcanada.com/684.html
E-mail hall@cybrnet.net

905-472-3163
Fax 905-471-0643
TFr 1-866-472-3163

Suburban bungalow with lower area built into a hill on a large secluded, quiet and private lot in town centre. Shaded area with a small stream. Off-street parking to private patio, entrance to guest living room facilities to make tea/coffee, use fridge or microwave. One room with queen and ensuite, second room with twin and private ensuite. Close to Markham, Unionville shops and restaurants and hospital. Buttonville and Pearson Airports nearby. Breakfast is served on the deck or in Canadiana dining room.

ROOMS Family suite, Lower floor, Private entrance, **Baths** Private, Ensuite, **Beds** Queen, Twin, Single or cots, Pullout sofa, **Air** Central, **Smoking** Outside, **OTHERS** Open all year, **PAYMENT** Cash, Trvl's cheques, **BREAKFASTS** Continental, Home-baked, **AMENITIES** Central TV, Central phone, Fridge, Hot bev. bar, Lounge, Patio, **THINGS TO DO** Golf, Museums, Art, Theatre, Entertainment, Attractions, Shopping, Tennis, **LANGUAGE** Eng., **PRICE** (2 persons) 65–75 (**check with hosts for pricing details**)

MARMORA *(southeast of Ottawa)*

Marmora Inn
(Jan Rejcha)

29 Bursthall St, Marmora, ON, K0K 2M0
www.marmorainn.com
E-mail aberlee@bellnet.ca

613-472-6887
Fax 613-472-2562

Great place for recreation, relaxation or just fun – year round. Charming Victorian house with indoor swimming pool, hot tub, mini-library (books, VCR, DVD, Internet), outside area for picnic and BBQ. Excellent place for vacation or just a short getaway. Great spot for parties, celebrations, business or social gatherings. Short walking distance to river, tennis court, waterfront parks, eating and shopping. Nearby – lake, golf courses, many local attractions. Easy driving distance to provincial parks.

ROOMS Upper floor, Ground floor, **Baths** Private, Ensuite, **Beds** King, Queen, Double, Single or cots, **Air** Ceiling fans, **Smoking** Outside, **In Room** TV, VCR/DVD, **OTHERS** Open all year, **PAYMENT** Visa, MC, Direct debit, Cash, Trvl's cheques, **BREAKFASTS** Full, Continental, **AMENITIES** Central TV, Central phone, Swimming pool, Whirlpool, Barbecue, Kitchen, Lounge, Patio, Central Internet access, Central VCR/DVD, **THINGS TO DO** Comp. bikes, Trail nearby, Rental canoe or boat, Golf, Fishing, Museums, Theatre, Entertainment, Attractions, Shopping, Cross-country skiing, Tennis, Swimming, Horseback riding, Beach, Birdwatching, **LANGUAGE** Eng., **PRICE** (2 persons) 80–110 (**check with hosts for pricing details**)

Maynooth
(southeast of Algonquin Park)
Ironwood Hill Inn B&B
(Bill Exton)

PO Box 178, Maynooth, ON, K0L 2S0
www.canadianbandbguide.ca/bb.asp?ID=2387

613-338-2032

Large rustic log cabin located at the "height of land" and providing an expansive view of rolling forest hills, where shadow and light play, especially in the fall with a tapestry of colours as far as the eye can see (four seasons of natural splendor). Active host enjoys camping, hiking, canoeing. Located 3.2 km south of Maynooth on the east side of Hwy 62. Inquire regarding pets. Heated by wood stove. Extra person in ensuite $20.

ROOMS Upper floor, Ground floor, Private entrance, **Baths** Private, Ensuite, Shared with guest, **Beds** Queen, Double, Single or cots, **Smoking** Outside, **OTHERS** Rural, Open all year, Pets in residence, **PAYMENT** Cheques accepted, Cash, Trvl's cheques, **BREAKFASTS** Full, **AMENITIES** Central phone, Laundry, Kitchen, Lounge, **THINGS TO DO** Trail nearby, Fishing, Museums, Art, Theatre, Entertainment, Attractions, Shopping, Cross-country skiing, Swimming, Horseback riding, Beach, Birdwatching, Antiquing, **LANGUAGE** Eng., **PRICE** (2 persons) 50–80 **(check with hosts for pricing details)**

Meaford *(northwest of Toronto)*
Bridge Street Harbour Landing Bed and Breakfast
(Sarah Milne and Matt Pearson)

52 Bridge St, Meaford, ON, N4L 1B9
www.harbourlanding.com
E-mail semilne@aol.com

519-538-0155
Fax 519-538-0155

Newly renovated and decorated with period antiques and modern decor, lovely gardens and view of the harbour. This century home is located in Meaford's downtown waterfront community. Air-conditioned, private ensuite and shared baths, guest private living area, second floor outdoor patio and coffee room with fridge, microwave and kettle. Fresh home-baked goods daily, full breakfast with seasonal fruit and hot dish. Year-round access to Blue Mountain, Talisman, Georgian Trail and Bruce Trail.

ROOMS Family suite, Upper floor, **Baths** Private, Ensuite, Shared with guest, **Beds** Queen, Twin, Single or cots, **Air** Central, In rooms, **In Room** Thermostat, TV, VCR/DVD, **OTHERS** Urban, Rural, Open all year, Additional meals, Pets in residence, **PAYMENT** Cheques accepted, Cash, Trvl's cheques, **BREAKFASTS** Full, **AMENITIES** Central TV, Central phone, Whirlpool, Fridge, Hot bev. bar, Lounge, Patio, Central VCR/DVD, **THINGS TO DO** Comp. bikes, Rental bikes, Trail nearby, Rental canoe or boat, Comp. Canoe or boat, Golf, Fishing, Museums, Art, Theatre, Entertainment, Attractions, Shopping, Cross-country skiing, Downhill skiing, Tennis, Swimming, Horseback riding, Beach, Birdwatching, Antiquing, **LANGUAGE** Eng., **PRICE** (2 persons) 85–115 **(check with hosts for pricing details)**

Meaford
Holly Cottage B&B
(David and Norma Collis)

618185 Grey Rd 18, Owen Sound, ON, N4K 5W4
www.hollycottage.ca
E-mail info@hollycottage.ca

519-371-7178

Built in 1878 with a new addition added in 2000, our Stone Farm House offers the charm of yesteryear with the conveniences of today. Winner of the Meaford Chamber of Commerce Accommodation of the year Award 2002, our home features three bedrooms, two with queen-size beds and private bathrooms, one with a four-poster double bed and ensuite washroom. Our Fireplace Bedroom offers a romantic getaway for any special occasion. We offer 20 varieties of herbal teas, fair trades coffee, guest living room with satellite TV and guest fridge. Complimentary snowshoes/cross-country skis.

ROOMS Family suite, Upper floor, Private entrance, **Baths** Private, Ensuite, **Beds** Queen, Double, Single or cots, Pullout sofa, **Air** Central, Ceiling fans, **Smoking** Outside, **In Room** Phone, TV, Fireplace, Internet access, VCR/DVD, **OTHERS** Babysitting, Rural, Open all year, Pets in residence, **PAYMENT** Visa, MC, Amex, Cheques accepted, Cash, Trvl's cheques, **BREAKFASTS** Full, Home-baked, **AMENITIES** Central TV, Barbecue, Fridge, Lounge, Patio, Central Internet access, Central VCR/DVD, **THINGS TO DO** Trail nearby, Golf, Fishing, Museums, Art, Theatre, Entertainment, Attractions, Shopping, Cross-country skiing, Swimming, Horseback riding, Beach, Birdwatching, Antiquing, **LANGUAGE** Eng., **PRICE** (2 persons) 80–90 **(check with hosts for pricing details)**

Meaford
Irish Mountain B&B
(John Avery)

RR #1, Meaford, ON, N4L 1W5
www.irishmountain.net
E-mail info@irishmountain.net

519-538-2803
Fax 519-538-2467

Romantic B&B situated on cliff overlooking Georgian Bay and Blue Mountain. All private suites with fireplaces and king-size beds and private baths, satellite TVs, fridges. All suites and cabin loft in the woods have private decks with two-person hot tubs. Air-conditioned, swimming pool, sunbathing on large deck or relax by our waterfall. Gourmet breakfast served in sunroom with bay views. Host Bruce Trail hiking guide and ski patroller and keen sailor who loves to take guests out in his 29-foot yacht.

ROOMS Upper floor, Ground floor, Private entrance, **Baths** Ensuite, **Beds** King, **Air** Central, In rooms, **Smoking** Outside, **In Room** Thermostat, TV, Fireplace, VCR/DVD, **OTHERS** Rural, Adult, Open all year, Handicapped access, Pets in residence, Pets welcome, **PAYMENT** Cheques accepted, Cash, **BREAKFASTS** Full, Home-baked, **AMENITIES** Central TV, Central phone, Swimming pool, Whirlpool, Barbecue, Fridge, Hot bev. bar, Lounge, Patio, **THINGS TO DO** Comp. bikes, Trail nearby, Golf, Fishing, Museums, Art, Theatre, Entertainment, Attractions, Shopping, Cross-country skiing, Swimming, Horseback riding, Beach, **LANGUAGE** Eng., **PRICE** (2 persons) 115–159 **(check with hosts for pricing details)**

MEAFORD

Riverside Bed & Breakfast

(Diane and Paul Ratcliff)

157696 7th Line, RR #2, Meaford, ON, N4L 1W6
www.bbcanada.com/6582.html
E-mail riversidebb@bmts.com

519-538-4376
Fax 519-538-5462

Riverside B&B is situated in beautiful rolling forest and farmland with the Big Head River flowing through it. We offer our guests year round interests and gracious accommodation. Our century farmhouse has been completely renovated and offers guests comfortable rooms with private bathrooms. A full breakfast is served in the guest lounge. Featured in *The Greenwood Guide to Canada*. Special handpicked accommodation. Walk, cross-country ski or snowshoe on 10 km of trails through our 160 acres by the river.

ROOMS Family suite, Upper floor, **Baths** Private, Ensuite, **Beds** King, Queen, Twin, Single or cots, **Air** Ceiling fans, **Smoking** Outside, **In Room** Thermostat, **OTHERS** Rural, Open all year, Pets in residence, **PAYMENT** Cheques accepted, Cash, **BREAKFASTS** Full, **AMENITIES** Central TV, Lounge, Patio, Central VCR/DVD, **THINGS TO DO** Trail nearby, Golf, Fishing, Museums, Art, Theatre, Attractions, Shopping, Cross-country skiing, Tennis, Swimming, Beach, Antiquing, **LANGUAGE** Eng., **PRICE** (2 persons) 85–95 **(check with hosts for pricing details)**

MIDLAND *(north of Toronto)*

1875 A Charters Inn B&B

(Gerry and Val Lesperance)

290 Second St, Midland, ON, L4R 3R1
www.chartersinn.com
E-mail gerry@chartersinn.com

705-527-1572 TFr 1-800-724-2979

Built in 1875, steps to downtown and Midland Bay waters, this historic Victorian home boasts many amenities and floral gardens, as well as a great patio to the rear and a wraparound deck at front, where a great gourmet breakfast can be served. King, queen and single beds available, some with private and ensuite baths, private balcony, fireplaces, mini-fridge, table and chair, TVs, DVD, and access to most of the home's extras, like library room, formal dining room. Fine linens, cleanliness and friendly service.

ROOMS Upper floor, Ground floor, Private entrance, **Baths** Private, Ensuite, Shared with guest, Shared with hosts, **Beds** King, Queen, Twin, Single or cots, **Air** In rooms, **Smoking** Outside, **In Room** Thermostat, Phone, TV, Fireplace, Internet access, VCR/DVD, **OTHERS** Urban, Rural, Adult, Open all year, Additional meals, Pets in residence, **PAYMENT** Cash, Trvl's cheques, **BREAKFASTS** Full, Continental, Home-baked, Self-catered, **AMENITIES** Central TV, Central phone, Fridge, Hot bev. bar, Lounge, Patio, Central Internet access, Central VCR/DVD, **THINGS TO DO** Rental bikes, Trail nearby, Rental canoe or boat, Golf, Fishing, Museums, Art, Theatre, Entertainment, Attractions, Shopping, Cross-country skiing, Downhill skiing, Tennis, Swimming, Horseback riding, Beach, Birdwatching, Antiquing, **LANGUAGE** Eng., Fr., Sp., **PRICE** (2 persons) 65–165 **(check with hosts for pricing details)**

MIDLAND

Little Lake Inn
Bed & Breakfast

(Jennifer Hart and Milton Haynes)

669 Yonge St, Midland, ON, L4R 2E1
www.littlelakeinn.com
E-mail info@littlelakeinn.com

705-526-2750 Fax 705-526-9005
TFr 1-888-297-6130

CAA/AAA approved and rated 3 Diamonds. This unique one-storey home in the heart of Midland overlooks Little Lake and offers rooms with ensuite baths, Jacuzzis, fireplaces, TV/VCRs, movies, fridges and private entrances. Walk to fine restaurants, shops, boat cruise, Huronia Museum and Indian Village. Minutes to Martyr's Shrine, Sainte-Marie-Among-the-Hurons, Wye Marsh Wildlife Centre, Discovery Harbour. Enjoy our casual, friendly atmosphere and healthy, home-baked breakfast. Take Hwy 400 to Hwy 93 N to Yonge St.

ROOMS Family suite, Ground floor, Private entrance, **Baths** Ensuite, **Beds** Queen, Single or cots, Pullout sofa, **Air** Central, **Smoking** Outside, **In Room** Thermostat, Phone, TV, Fireplace, Internet access, VCR/DVD, **OTHERS** Urban, Open all year, Handicapped access, Pets in residence, **PAYMENT** Visa, MC, Diners, Amex, Cash, Trvl's cheques, **BREAKFASTS** Full, Home-baked, **AMENITIES** Central phone, Whirlpool, Kitchen, Fridge, Hot bev. bar, Lounge, Patio, Central Internet access, **THINGS TO DO** Trail nearby, Rental canoe or boat, Golf, Fishing, Museums, Art, Theatre, Entertainment, Attractions, Shopping, Cross-country skiing, Downhill skiing, Tennis, Swimming, Horseback riding, Beach, Birdwatching, Antiquing, **LANGUAGE** Eng., **PRICE** (2 persons) 119–149 **(check with hosts for pricing details)**

MILDMAY *(northwest of Toronto)*

Whispering Brook
Bed & Breakfast

(George and Shirley Culbert)

7 Jane St S, Mildmay, ON, N0G 2J0
www.bbcanada.com/1049.html
E-mail culbert@bmts.com

519-367-2565
Fax 519-367-5434

Warm welcome in comfortable sunny cedar home in a park-like setting. In small and friendly village. Interesting little shops and local crafts. Stocked trout pond, swans and deer on property. Hike an abandoned CN rail line, cross-country ski or snowmobile. Close to Lake Huron beaches, Blyth Theatre and Mennonite country. Sit on the lawn swing and relax. Breakfast served in a country kitchen, on a large deck or in the dining room. Evening coffee or tea. Children welcome.

ROOMS Upper floor, Private entrance, **Baths** Shared with guest, **Beds** Queen, Single or cots, **Smoking** Outside, **In Room** Thermostat, Phone, TV, **OTHERS** Rural, Open all year, Additional meals, **PAYMENT** Cash, **BREAKFASTS** Continental, Home-baked, **AMENITIES** Central TV, Central phone, Barbecue, Lounge, Patio, **THINGS TO DO** Comp. bikes, Trail nearby, Rental canoe or boat, Golf, Fishing, Theatre, Wineries/Breweries, Shopping, Cross-country skiing, Tennis, Swimming, Beach, **LANGUAGE** Eng., **PRICE** (2 persons) 60 **(check with hosts for pricing details)**

MILTON *(west of Toronto)*

Applewood Guest House

(Jan and Ernest Murdoch)

83 Tremaine Rd, Milton, ON, L9T 2W8
www.bbcanada.com/applewood
E-mail chief@globalserve.net

905-878-4016
Fax 905-878-1992

Passive solar home, minutes from Hwy
401, in the heart of the Niagara
Escarpment. Nature and recreation at
your door-step, yet minutes to the centre
of town. Central to all your favourite
activities; touring, hiking, biking, golf and
skiing/snowboarding. Near Mohawk
Raceway and conservation parks. Safe
parking available for motorcycles along
with washing and maintenance facilities
(heated drying room for wet clothes).

ROOMS Upper floor, **Baths** Shared with guest, **Beds**
Queen, Double, **Air** Central, In rooms, Ceiling fans,
Smoking Outside, **In Room** TV, VCR/DVD, **OTHERS**
Rural, Adult, Seasonal, **PAYMENT** Cheques accepted,
Cash, **BREAKFASTS** Full, **AMENITIES** Central phone,
Swimming pool, Whirlpool, Laundry, Hot bev. bar,
THINGS TO DO Trail nearby, Golf, Museums,
Attractions, Shopping, Downhill skiing, Swimming,
Birdwatching, Antiquing, **LANGUAGE** Eng., **PRICE** (2
persons) 80 **(check with hosts for pricing details)**

MILTON

Willowbrook Bed and Breakfast

(Ron and Karen Hudson)

10545 Nass/Esq Town Line, RR #1, Acton, ON, L7J 2L7
www.willowbrk.on.ca
E-mail comfort@willowbrk.on.ca

905-876-1318

A nature lover's retreat on the Niagara
Escarpment. Two smoke-free rooms with
private ensuite washrooms. We feature
gourmet breakfast from a varied menu.
Our natural setting includes bountiful
wildlife, excellent birding, onsite hiking
trails, ponds and a cold water trout
stream. We are close to many outdoor
pursuits including skiing, hiking, horseback riding, "pick your own" farms and
antiquing in nearby Campbellville. Relax
at the end of the day in our outdoor hot
tub overlooking our waterfall.

ROOMS Ground floor, **Baths** Private, Ensuite, **Beds**
Queen, Twin, **Air** Central, Ceiling fans, **Smoking**
Outside, **In Room** Phone, TV, VCR/DVD, **OTHERS** Rural,
Adult, Open all year, **PAYMENT** Cheques accepted,
Cash, Trvl's cheques, **BREAKFASTS** Full, **AMENITIES**
Whirlpool, Fridge, Lounge, Patio, **THINGS TO DO** Trail
nearby, Golf, Fishing, Museums, Art, Attractions,
Wineries/Breweries, Shopping, Cross-country skiing,
Downhill skiing, Tennis, Swimming, Horseback riding,
Beach, Birdwatching, Antiquing, **LANGUAGE** Eng.,
PRICE (2 persons) 70–80 **(check with hosts for pricing
details)**

MINDEN *(south of Algonquin Park)*

Stouffer Mill
Bed & Breakfast Getaway

(Don and Jessie Pflug)

RR #2, Halls Lake, Minden, ON, K0M 2K0
www.stouffermill.com
E-mail info@stouffermill.com

705-489-3024
Fax 705-489-3024
TFr 1-888-593-8888

A unique 12-sided post-and-beam circular home with suspended rooms, a rooftop solarium with hot tub and furnished with Canadiana antiques. Our 136-acre estate with 4.5 km of walking/snowshoe trails offers you the ultimate in peace, quiet and harmony with nature. The three guest rooms all have sliding doors to their own private deck and all have ensuite or private baths. Guest gathering room, fireplace TV, DVD and panoramic lake view. Unforgettable breakfasts. Featured in Summer 2005 issue of *Canadian Homes and Cottages*.

ROOMS Upper floor, Private entrance, **Baths** Private, Ensuite, **Beds** King, Queen, Twin, Pullout sofa, **Smoking** Outside, **In Room** Thermostat, **OTHERS** Rural, Adult, Open all year, Additional meals, Pets in residence, Pets welcome, **PAYMENT** Visa, MC, Diners, Direct debit, Cheques accepted, Cash, Trvl's cheques, **BREAKFASTS** Full, **AMENITIES** Central TV, Central phone, Swimming pool, Whirlpool, Barbecue, Fridge, Lounge, Patio, Central Internet access, Central VCR/DVD, **THINGS TO DO** Comp. bikes, Trail nearby, Comp. Canoe or boat, Golf, Fishing, Museums, Art, Theatre, Attractions, Cross-country skiing, Downhill skiing, Tennis, Swimming, Horseback riding, Beach, Birdwatching, Antiquing, **LANGUAGE** Eng., Fr., **PRICE** (2 persons) 112–125 **(check with hosts for pricing details)**

MINDEN

Wild Swan
Bed and Breakfast Inn

(Bob Baynton-Smith)

65 Invergardon, Box 119, Minden, ON, K0M 2K0
www.haliburton-couples-getaway.com/
E-mail info@wildswanbb.com

705-286-3020
TFr 1-877-959-0991

Featured in the prestigious *Best Places to Bed & Breakfast in Ontario* as a luxury romantic country getaway, Wild Swan Bed & Breakfast Inn is a riverfront heritage B&B accommodation perfect for romantic couples who need a break from the pressures of a fast-paced city lifestyle. We provide a perfect base from which to explore the Haliburton area. Directions to Wild Swan: Minden is located about 2 hours northeast of Toronto on Hwy 35, about 78 km north of Lindsay and about 37 km north of Coboconk.

ROOMS Upper floor, **Baths** Private, **Beds** Queen, **Air** Central, **Smoking** Outside, **OTHERS** Rural, Adult, **PAYMENT** Visa, MC, Cash, Trvl's cheques, **BREAKFASTS** Full, Home-baked, **AMENITIES** Barbecue, Fridge, Hot bev. bar, Lounge, Patio, **THINGS TO DO** Comp. bikes, Trail nearby, Comp. Canoe or boat, Golf, Fishing, Museums, Art, Entertainment, Shopping, Cross-country skiing, Downhill skiing, Swimming, Horseback riding, Beach, Birdwatching, Antiquing, **LANGUAGE** Eng., **PRICE** (2 persons) 128–162 **(check with hosts for pricing details)**

MISSISSAUGA *(west of Toronto)*

Applewood Bed and Breakfast

(John and Pat Kavanagh)

1208 Greening Ave, Mississauga, ON, L4Y 1H5
www.bbcanada.com/3910.html
E-mail jpkavanagh@rogers.com

905-277-2696

We extend to you a warm welcome in a beautiful comfortable home. Knowledge-able, long-time hosts will be happy to help you with itineraries. We are located less than 15 minutes from Pearson (Toronto) Airport and less than 20 minutes from downtown Toronto. To find us, from QEW take Cawthra Rd north (Exit 134), then turn right (east) on North Service Rd to Stanfield Rd (first light). Turn left (north) and proceed two blocks to Greening Ave, turn right.

ROOMS Upper floor, Ground floor, Private entrance, **Baths** Private, Shared with guest, **Beds** Queen, Twin, **Air** In rooms, **Smoking** Outside, **In Room** Thermostat, TV, Internet access, **OTHERS** Open all year, **PAYMENT** Cheques accepted, Cash, Trvl's cheques, **BREAKFASTS** Full, **AMENITIES** Central TV, Swimming pool, Lounge, Central Internet access, **THINGS TO DO** Theatre, Entertainment, Attractions, Shopping, **LANGUAGE** Eng., **PRICE** (2 persons) 55–85 **(check with hosts for pricing details)**

MISSISSAUGA

Dallimore's "Just Your Cup of Tea"

(Rob Dallimore)

2110 Varency Dr, Mississauga, ON, L5K 1C3
www.canadianbandbguide.ca/bb.asp?ID=2128

905-822-3540
Fax 905-823-5212

English-style hospitality in large, modern home located on large-treed property. Well-travelled hosts enjoy discussing mutual adventures from all over the world. Special rates for 7 days or more. Airport pickup with minimum 3-day stay. Close to large shopping centre, good restaurants, excellent local bus service to city centre. By car, visit Lake Ontario shoreline and parks, downtown Toronto, "Go" commuter train to Toronto (free parking at station), Niagara Falls. Minimum two night stay required. Phone before faxing.

ROOMS Upper floor, **Baths** Shared with guest, **Beds** Queen, Twin, **Air** Central, In rooms, Ceiling fans, **Smoking** Outside, **OTHERS** Urban, Adult, Open all year, Pets in residence, **PAYMENT** Cheques accepted, Cash, Trvl's cheques, **BREAKFASTS** Full, **AMENITIES** Central TV, Central phone, Barbecue, Laundry, Lounge, Patio, Central Internet access, Central VCR/DVD, **THINGS TO DO** Comp. bikes, Trail nearby, Museums, Theatre, Entertainment, Attractions, Shopping, Swimming, Birdwatching, Antiquing, **LANGUAGE** Eng., **PRICE** (2 persons) 40–60 **(check with hosts for pricing details)**

MORRISBURG *(south of Ottawa)*

The Village Antiques & Tea Room ~ Bed & Breakfast

(Victor Dupuis and Marcel Allard)

4326 County Rd #31/Bank St S, Williamsburg, ON, K0C 2H0
www.bbtearoom.com
E-mail info@bbtearoom.com

613-535-2463
TFr 1-877-264-3281

Halfway between Toronto and Quebec City our combination antique shop and inn is located in the heart of Eastern Ontario. Equi-distance to Ottawa, Brockville and Cornwall. Minutes to historic Upper Canada Village and 1 1/2 hours from Montreal. Intimate fine dining facilities and excellent wine list. Offering a variety of all-inclusive packages. Dinner-theatre packages/extended-stay deals/wine and dine evenings. Rural R&R in a country setting with urban flair and savoir faire. *Nous parlons français.*

ROOMS Upper floor, Ground floor, **Baths** Private, Ensuite, Shared with guest, **Beds** King, Double, Twin, **Air** Central, In rooms, **Smoking** Outside, **In Room** Thermostat, Fireplace, VCR/DVD, **OTHERS** Rural, Adult, Open all year, Additional meals, **PAYMENT** Visa, MC, Direct debit, Cash, Trvl's cheques, **BREAKFASTS** Full, Home-baked, **AMENITIES** Central TV, Central phone, Fridge, Hot bev. bar, Lounge, Patio, Central VCR/DVD, **THINGS TO DO** Rental canoe or boat, Golf, Fishing, Museums, Art, Theatre, Attractions, Wineries/Breweries, Shopping, Cross-country skiing, Swimming, Beach, Birdwatching, Antiquing, **LANGUAGE** Eng., Fr., **PRICE** (2 persons) 75–120 **(check with hosts for pricing details)**

NIAGARA FALLS *(east of Hamilton)*

Ace of Hearts

(Susie Ong)

4434 Philip St, Niagara Falls, ON, L2E 1A6
www.niagarabb.com/aceofhearts
E-mail aceofheartsbb@aol.com

905-374-8707

In a beautiful historic section of Niagara Falls, overlooking the Niagara River, only a short walk from the Falls and Casino Niagara, the perfect place to stay while exploring the Niagara Region. Built almost 100 years ago, the house retains the old-world charm of that era, boasting original hardwood floors and charming interior woodwork. Relax in the gracious living room or verandah. Rooms are fully furnished with comfortable queen beds, ample closet space and large windows. We will make your stay a pleasant and memorable one. Open all year. Reasonable prices with discounts for families and seniors. Free parking.

ROOMS Family suite, Upper floor, **Baths** Private, Ensuite, Shared with guest, Shared with hosts, **Beds** Queen, Double, **Air** In rooms, **Smoking** Outside, **In Room** TV, **OTHERS** Adult, Open all year, **PAYMENT** Cash, **BREAKFASTS** Full, Home-baked, **AMENITIES** Central TV, Lounge, Patio, **THINGS TO DO** Trail nearby, Golf, Fishing, Museums, Art, Theatre, Entertainment, Attractions, Wineries/Breweries, Shopping, Tennis, Swimming, Horseback riding, Beach, **LANGUAGE** Eng., Chinese, Malay, **PRICE** (2 persons) 75–100 **(check with hosts for pricing details)**

NIAGARA FALLS
Always Inn Bed & Breakfast
(Sharon and John Tyson)

4327 Simcoe St, Niagara Falls, ON, L2E 1T5
www.alwaysinn.ca
E-mail sharon@alwaysinn.ca

905-371-0840
TFr 1-800-700-6665

Welcome to Always Inn B&B. This beautiful 1878 Victorian is set back four houses from the Niagara River Gorge. We are conveniently located close to all area attractions, a 10- to 15-minute walk to the Falls, Casinos and the downtown Niagara tourist section, as well as the bus and train terminals. Wake up each morning to the smell of freshly baked bread, muffins and brewed coffee and await the hot daily breakfast served with full linen and silver appointments by the fireside. We look forward to your stay!

ROOMS Family suite, Upper floor, **Baths** Private, Ensuite, **Beds** Queen, Twin, **Air** Central, In rooms, Ceiling fans, **Smoking** Outside, **In Room** TV, Fireplace, **OTHERS** Open all year, **PAYMENT** Visa, MC, Cash, Trvl's cheques, **BREAKFASTS** Full, **AMENITIES** Central TV, Central phone, Fridge, Lounge, Patio, Central VCR/DVD, **THINGS TO DO** Rental bikes, Trail nearby, Golf, Fishing, Museums, Theatre, Entertainment, Attractions, Wineries/Breweries, Shopping, Horseback riding, Antiquing, **LANGUAGE** Eng., **PRICE** (2 persons) 75–275 **(check with hosts for pricing details)**

NIAGARA FALLS
Andrea's Bed and Breakfast
(Andrea Armstrong)

4286 Simcoe St, Niagara Falls, ON, L2E 1T6
www.andreasbedandbreakfast.com
E-mail andrea.bed@sympatico.ca

905-374-4776
Fax 905-356-3563

Established in 1987, an 1892 historic home in older, quieter downtown area of Niagara Falls, located one house up from River Rd between Whirlpool and Rainbow Bridges, about five blocks from bus and train stations, 20-minute walk to Falls/Casino Niagara. Niagara Parks Shuttle Bus nearby. Two bedroom/two bathroom Family suite which includes queen and king/twin beds, sitting area with fireplace, TV, fridge, private deck and entrance and two rooms with private bath for up to eight people. Three night Dinner Packages/Honeymoon Specials.

ROOMS Family suite, Upper floor, Private entrance, **Baths** Private, Ensuite, **Beds** King, Queen, Double, Twin, **Air** In rooms, **Smoking** Outside, **In Room** Thermostat, TV, Fireplace, VCR/DVD, **OTHERS** Urban, Adult, Open all year, Additional meals, **PAYMENT** Visa, MC, Diners, Amex, Direct debit, Cheques accepted, Cash, Trvl's cheques, **BREAKFASTS** Full, Continental, Home-baked, **AMENITIES** Central TV, Central phone, Fridge, Hot bev. bar, Lounge, Patio, Central Internet access, Central VCR/DVD, **THINGS TO DO** Rental bikes, Trail nearby, Golf, Fishing, Museums, Art, Theatre, Entertainment, Attractions, Wineries/Breweries, Shopping, Cross-country skiing, Tennis, Swimming, Horseback riding, Beach, Birdwatching, Antiquing, **LANGUAGE** Eng., **PRICE** (2 persons) 60–220 **(check with hosts for pricing details)**

Niagara Falls

Bed of Roses Bed & Breakfast
(Norma Lambertson)

4877 River Rd, Niagara Falls, ON, L2E 3G5
www.bedofroses.ca
E-mail bedofroses@sprint.ca

905-356-0529
Fax 905-356-3563

Bed of Roses B&B features private suites for your enjoyment. Each suite has a private entrance, bedroom, kitchenette, sitting room with fireplace and cable TV, bathroom (honeymoon suite has a Jacuzzi tub) and we bring a full, hot breakfast to your door in the morning. Coffeemaker and teapot ready for you. We are located on the beautiful River Rd about a 3-minute drive from the Falls, about a 20-minute walk. Close to attractions, bus and trains. Come and relax in total privacy. You'll love Niagara Falls.

ROOMS Family suite, Upper floor, Private entrance, **Baths** Ensuite, **Beds** Queen, Double, Pullout sofa, **Air** In rooms, **In Room** Thermostat, Phone, TV, Fireplace, **PAYMENT** Visa, MC, Cash, Trvl's cheques, **BREAKFASTS** Full, Home-baked, **AMENITIES** Central TV, Barbecue, Kitchen, Fridge, **THINGS TO DO** Trail nearby, Golf, Museums, Theatre, Entertainment, Attractions, Wineries/Breweries, Shopping, **PRICE** (2 persons) 135–220 **(check with hosts for pricing details)**

Niagara Falls

Cosy Inn Bed and Breakfast
(Marie and Walter Wyse)

5725 Robinson St, Niagara Falls, ON, L2G 2B3
www.infoniagara.com/bb/Niagara-Falls/cosyinn
E-mail wmkcoopers@yahoo.ca

905-354-1832
TFr 1-866-572-5725

Cosy Inn B&B offers comfortable and very clean lodgings in a very quiet and amazing location, with the new Niagara Fallsview Casino Resort and the new exciting tourist district right around the corner. Only a short walk away are many international restaurants, major attractions and the mighty Falls. Cosy Inn B&B offers free parking, is a pet-free and non-smoking environment. Children are always welcome. A short drive away is Marineland, Niagara-on-the-Lake, wineries and golf courses.

ROOMS Family suite, Upper floor, Ground floor, Private entrance, **Baths** Private, Ensuite, **Beds** Queen, **Air** Central, **Smoking** Outside, **In Room** TV, **OTHERS** Open all year, **PAYMENT** Visa, MC, Cash, Trvl's cheques, **BREAKFASTS** Full, Continental, **AMENITIES** Fridge, Hot bev. bar, Lounge, Patio, **THINGS TO DO** Rental bikes, Trail nearby, Golf, Fishing, Museums, Art, Theatre, Entertainment, Attractions, Wineries/Breweries, Shopping, Antiquing, **LANGUAGE** Eng., Ger., **PRICE** (2 persons) 65–130 **(check with hosts for pricing details)**

NIAGARA FALLS

Eastwood Lodge

(Joanne van Kleef)

5359 River Rd, Niagara Falls, ON, L2E 3G9
www.theEastwood.com
E-mail vacation@theEastwood.com

905-354-8686
Fax 905-371-1292

Established in 1961, Eastwood is Niagara's
longest-running B&B; a former estate,
winner of many prestigious awards, outstanding location on Niagara River Gorge,
5 minutes by foot to the mighty Niagara
Falls. Rooms with balconies overlooking
Gorge, ensuites, king beds, air-conditioning, cable, fireplaces, fridges in room, tele-
phones. Gardens, porches, private, onsite
parking. Full breakfast. English, Spanish,
German spoken. Hosts born and raised in
Niagara Region. Smoking indoors is pro-
hibited.

ROOMS Upper floor, Lower floor, Private entrance,
Baths Ensuite, **Beds** King, **Air** In rooms, **Smoking**
Outside, **In Room** Thermostat, Phone, TV, Fireplace,
OTHERS Adult, Open all year, Pets in residence, **PAY-
MENT** Visa, MC, Diners, Amex, Direct debit, Cash,
BREAKFASTS Full, **AMENITIES** Fridge, Patio, **THINGS
TO DO** Rental bikes, Trail nearby, Rental canoe or boat,
Golf, Fishing, Museums, Art, Theatre, Entertainment,
Attractions, Wineries/Breweries, Shopping, Cross-
country skiing, Tennis, Swimming, Horseback riding,
Beach, **LANGUAGE** Eng., Sp., Ger., **PRICE** (2 persons)
89–179 **(check with hosts for pricing details)**

NIAGARA FALLS

Grapeview Guesthouse on the Vineyard

(Vic and Nancy Lianga)

4163 Merritt Rd, Beamsville, ON, L0R 1B1
www.bbcanada.com/grapeview
E-mail grapevuw@becon.org

905-563-5077

Privacy for two in a beautiful vineyard B&B
with a Victorian Jacuzzi Suite, 1 hour from
Toronto, for $99/night. "Beautiful rooms,
beautiful vineyard, beautiful country."
Private bathrooms, large, hearty breakfast,
accessible to Bruce Trail, unique shops and
restaurants nearby in Jordan Village.
Located on cycling road. Directions: Exit
QEW at #64 Ontario St S, Beamsville. Follow
and turn left at King St, proceed 4 km and
turn left on Merritt Rd: 8 minutes from
QEW Hwy.

ROOMS Family suite, Upper floor, **Baths** Private,
Ensuite, **Beds** King, Queen, Single or cots, Pullout sofa,
Air Central, **Smoking** Outside, **In Room** Phone, TV,
Internet access, **OTHERS** Open all year, Additional
meals, **PAYMENT** Cheques accepted, Cash, Trvl's
cheques, **BREAKFASTS** Full, **AMENITIES** Whirlpool,
Fridge, **THINGS TO DO** Rental bikes, Trail nearby, Golf,
Fishing, Museums, Art, Theatre, Entertainment,
Attractions, Shopping, Tennis, Swimming, Horseback
riding, Beach, **LANGUAGE** Eng., Lithuian, **PRICE** (2 per-
sons) 85–99 **(check with hosts for pricing details)**

Niagara Falls

Lion's Head Bed & Breakfast
(Helena Harrington)

5239 River Rd, Niagara Falls, ON, L2E 3G9
www.lionsheadbb.com
E-mail lionshead@idirect.com

905-374-1681

An historic and original 1910 Edwardian-style estate overlooking the spectacular Niagara River Gorge, Lion's Head is loaded with history, character and charm. Being one of the closest B&Bs to the Falls, with only a 10-minute walk, makes this an ideal location. Queen ensuite rooms and third floor loft feature goose-down duvets, cotton linens, Persian rugs and antiques. The Innkeeper's past training in the kitchens of Europe and Canada make the full "French" gourmet breakfast a culinary experience.

ROOMS Family suite, Upper floor, Private entrance, **Baths** Private, Ensuite, **Beds** King, Queen, Double, **Air** In rooms, **Smoking** Outside, **In Room** Fireplace, **OTHERS** Adult, Open all year, **PAYMENT** Visa, MC, Amex, Direct debit, Cash, Trvl's cheques, **BREAKFASTS** Full, **AMENITIES** Central TV, Central phone, Fridge, Lounge, Patio, **THINGS TO DO** Trail nearby, Golf, Fishing, Theatre, Entertainment, Wineries/Breweries, Antiquing, **LANGUAGE** Eng., **PRICE** (2 persons) 95–195 **(check with hosts for pricing details)**

Niagara Falls

Marshall's B&B
(Janice Marshall)

6362 Maitland, Niagara Falls, ON, L2G 1R4
www.canadianbandbguide.ca/bb.asp?ID=3496
E-mail marshallbandb@sympatico.ca

905-356-4011

Restored century home 1/2 block off Lundy's Lane in the historic Drummondville area. This perfect location is a short walk to the Falls, casinos, Clifton Hill tourist area, museums and major tourist attractions. Lundy's Lane also offers a wide variety of dining establishments, outlet mall shopping and entertainment venues. We offer king or queen rooms, or two-room suites. All rooms have TV's, AC and private baths. Some include a private sunroom or deck for your enjoyment. We are smoke-free (permitted on decks).

ROOMS Family suite, Upper floor, Ground floor, Private entrance, **Baths** Private, Ensuite, **Beds** King, Queen, Double, Twin, Single or cots, Pullout sofa, **Air** Central, In rooms, Ceiling fans, **Smoking** Outside, **In Room** Thermostat, TV, VCR/DVD, **OTHERS** Urban, Seasonal, **PAYMENT** Visa, MC, Direct debit, Cash, Trvl's cheques, **BREAKFASTS** Full, Home-baked, **AMENITIES** Central TV, Barbecue, Kitchen, Fridge, Lounge, Patio, Central VCR/DVD, **THINGS TO DO** Rental bikes, Golf, Museums, Art, Theatre, Entertainment, Attractions, Wineries/Breweries, Shopping, Cross-country skiing, Tennis, Swimming, Horseback riding, Birdwatching, Antiquing, **LANGUAGE** Eng., **PRICE** (2 persons) 70–140 **(check with hosts for pricing details)**

Niagara Falls

Paradise Point Bed and Breakfast

(Dianne and Joe Chopp)

3533 Main St, Niagara Falls, ON, L2G 6A7
www.paradisepointbedandbreakfast.com
E-mail kdiannec@aol.com

905-295-4947

Paradise Point is located in a quiet, scenic, park-like setting along the banks of the Niagara River and the Welland River, yet minutes from the Falls and attractions. Our home features a beautiful view and guest rooms are large, clean (non-smoking) and private, with comfortable queen-size beds and large ensuite bathrooms. A substantial, homemade breakfast is served in our sunroom. There is also a Family suite with an extra bedroom, and a crib is also available at no charge.

ROOMS Family suite, Upper floor, **Baths** Ensuite, **Beds** Queen, Twin, **Air** Central, **Smoking** Outside, **In Room** TV, VCR/DVD, **OTHERS** Babysitting, Open all year, Pets in residence, **PAYMENT** Visa, MC, Cash, **BREAKFASTS** Full, Home-baked, **AMENITIES** Central TV, Lounge, Patio, Central VCR/DVD, **THINGS TO DO** Trail nearby, Golf, Fishing, Art, Theatre, Entertainment, Attractions, Wineries/Breweries, Shopping, Cross-country skiing, Tennis, Swimming, Birdwatching, Antiquing, **LANGUAGE** Eng., **PRICE** (2 persons) 100–150 **(check with hosts for pricing details)**

Niagara Falls

Park Place Bed & Breakfast

(Gary and Carolyn Burke)

4851 River Rd, Niagara Falls, ON, L2E 3G4
www.parkplaceniagara.com
E-mail gbburke@vaxxine.com

905-358-0279
Fax 905-358-0458

Park Place B&B, a Canadian designated heritage home and former estate of William Doran, a local 1800s entrepeneur, overlooks the Niagara Gorge. A careful balance between the romantic Victorian era and modern comforts has been kept. We offer luxury spa accomodations, king size beds, fireplaces and concierge services, with a full, enticing breakfast brought to our large suites, or candlelight breakfasts in The Oak Room.
"Our weekend was magical. The room ... breakfasts ... exquisite." – S&C, (guests from USA).

ROOMS Family suite, Upper floor, Private entrance, **Baths** Private, Ensuite, **Beds** King, Single or cots, Pullout sofa, **Air** In rooms, **Smoking** Outside, **In Room** TV, Fireplace, VCR/DVD, **OTHERS** Open all year, **PAYMENT** Visa, MC, Cheques accepted, Cash, Trvl's cheques, **BREAKFASTS** Full, Home-baked, **AMENITIES** Sauna, Whirlpool, Barbecue, Kitchen, Fridge, Lounge, Patio, **THINGS TO DO** Trail nearby, Golf, Fishing, Museums, Art, Theatre, Entertainment, Attractions, Wineries/Breweries, Shopping, **LANGUAGE** Eng., **PRICE** (2 persons) 120–175 **(check with hosts for pricing details)**

Niagara Falls

Redwood Bed and Breakfast

(Joe and Carmela Rinaldis)

5227 River Rd, Niagara Falls, ON, L2E 3G9
www.redwoodbb.ca
E-mail info@redwoodbb.ca

905-358-1990
Fax 905-374-6742
TFr 1-888-713-8495

Warm, rich colours abound and set the peaceful nostalgic flavour for comfort and style in this 1900 home. Newly remodeled to reflect old-world charm with a modern flair. Beautiful, original wood frames the foyer, extends into the dining room and staircase which, adorned with era pictures, invites you enchantingly into your room. All very spacious ensuite, air-conditioned rooms with cable/DVD/TV. Ideally located just minutes walking distance from the Falls, casino and all other major attractions.

ROOMS Upper floor, **Baths** Ensuite, **Beds** King, Queen, **Air** Central, **Smoking** Outside, **In Room** TV, Fireplace, Internet access, **PAYMENT** Visa, MC, Amex, Cash, Trvl's cheques, **BREAKFASTS** Full, **AMENITIES** Fridge, Patio, Central Internet access, **THINGS TO DO** Rental bikes, Trail nearby, Golf, Museums, Theatre, Entertainment, Attractions, Wineries/Breweries, Shopping, Antiquing, **LANGUAGE** Eng., Italian, **PRICE** (2 persons) 95–169 **(check with hosts for pricing details)**

Niagara Falls

Rose Arbor B&B

(Frank Spadafora)

4448 Ellis St, Niagara Falls, ON, L2E 1H4
www.rosearbor.ca
E-mail franks@rosearbor.ca

905-354-7206
TFr 1-888-501-3860

Located in the heart of historic Niagara Falls, we are just a short walk from the Falls, People Mover and many sites. Tour the beautiful Niagara Wine District. We're just a short drive from numerous wineries, historic sites, golf courses, nature walks, the Welland Canals, scenic parkways, etc. Make Rose Arbor your century home away from home. Two beautiful, well-appointed rooms from which to choose: The beautiful Marilyn, and the elegant Tuscan. Breakfast at Rose Arbor is always a special event.

ROOMS Upper floor, **Baths** Ensuite, **Beds** Queen, **Air** Central, In rooms, Ceiling fans, **Smoking** Outside, **OTHERS** Urban, Open all year, **PAYMENT** Visa, MC, Cash, Trvl's cheques, **BREAKFASTS** Full, **AMENITIES** Central TV, Central phone, Laundry, Kitchen, Fridge, Lounge, Patio, Central Internet access, **THINGS TO DO** Trail nearby, Golf, Fishing, Museums, Art, Theatre, Entertainment, Attractions, Wineries/Breweries, Shopping, Tennis, Birdwatching, Antiquing, **LANGUAGE** Eng., Fr., Sp., Italian, **PRICE** (2 persons) 75–125 **(check with hosts for pricing details)**

NIAGARA FALLS

Schaferhof Bed & Breakfast
(Lore and Dieter Schafer)

2746 Moyer St, RR #3, Fenwick, ON, L0S 1C0
www.schaferhofbb.com
E-mail info@schaferhofbb.com

905-562-4929
Fax 905-562-3028

Country property in the heart of Niagara's
wine region. Small hobby farm. Separate
two room guest house. Close to Niagara
Falls, golfing, the Bruce Trail. Quiet rural
area, safe for cycling and walking. Relax
and rejuvenate from everyday stress.
Full delicious breakfast with home-
baking, Niagara preserves and fresh fruit
in season.

ROOMS Ground floor, Private entrance, **Baths** Ensuite,
Shared with guest, **Beds** Queen, Double, Twin, **Air**
Central, **Smoking** Outside, **In Room** Thermostat, TV,
OTHERS Rural, Open all year, Additional meals, **PAY-
MENT** Visa, MC, Amex, Cash, Trvl's cheques, **BREAK-
FASTS** Full, Home-baked, **AMENITIES** Central TV,
Central phone, Lounge, Patio, **THINGS TO DO** Comp.
bikes, Trail nearby, Golf, Fishing, Art, Theatre,
Wineries/Breweries, Shopping, **LANGUAGE** Eng., Ger.,
PRICE (2 persons) 79–99 **(check with hosts for pricing
details)**

NIAGARA FALLS

Stamford Village
Bed and Breakfast
(George and Valerie Rowe)

3369 St. Paul Ave, Niagara Falls, ON, L2J 2M3
www.stamfordvillagebedandbreakfast.com
E-mail vrowe1@cogeco.ca

905-358-2642
TFr 1-877-900-5811

We invite you to capture the character
and charm of our newly expanded century home. The location offers ready access
to the scenic wine route, quaint town
of Niagara-on-the-Lake and the Falls
attractions. Our private guest entrance
welcomes you to the Chippawa or
Queenston rooms complete with
ensuites. The Niagara room on the second
floor is ideal for special occasions offering
a two-person Jacuzzi, king-size bed and
a romantic fireplace. Complimentary
wireless Internet access, smoke free and
air-conditioning.

ROOMS Upper floor, Ground floor, Private entrance,
Baths Ensuite, **Beds** King, Queen, Single or cots,
Pullout sofa, **Air** Central, **Smoking** Outside, **In Room**
TV, Fireplace, Internet access, VCR/DVD, **OTHERS** Open
all year, **PAYMENT** Visa, MC, Cash, Trvl's cheques,
BREAKFASTS Full, Home-baked, **AMENITIES** Central
TV, Swimming pool, Whirlpool, Fridge, Lounge, Patio,
Central Internet access, Central VCR/DVD, **THINGS TO
DO** Comp. bikes, Trail nearby, Golf, Museums, Theatre,
Wineries/Breweries, Shopping, Antiquing, **LANGUAGE**
Eng., **PRICE** (2 persons) 100–150 **(check with hosts for
pricing details)**

NIAGARA FALLS
Strathaird Bed and Breakfast
(Val and Tom Jackson)

4372 Simcoe St, Niagara Falls, ON, L2E 1T6
www.strathairdinn.com
E-mail reservations@strathairdinn.com

905-358-3421
Fax 905-358-2705

Strathaird is located on a quiet tree-lined street. Enjoy a short scenic walk along the gorge to the Falls. Close to casino and all major attractions. Enjoy genuine traditional Scottish hospitality. Within a short drive, enjoy winery tours and the Welland Canal.

ROOMS Upper floor, **Baths** Ensuite, **Beds** Queen, Double, Single or cots, **Air** Central, **Smoking** Outside, **OTHERS** Urban, Open all year, Pets in residence, **PAYMENT** Visa, MC, Diners, Amex, Direct debit, Cash, Trvl's cheques, **BREAKFASTS** Full, Continental, Home-baked, **AMENITIES** Central TV, Central phone, Fridge, Lounge, Patio, **THINGS TO DO** Rental bikes, Trail nearby, Golf, Fishing, Museums, Art, Theatre, Entertainment, Attractions, Wineries/Breweries, Shopping, Cross-country skiing, Tennis, Swimming, Horseback riding, Beach, **LANGUAGE** Eng., **PRICE** (2 persons) 65–105 **(check with hosts for pricing details)**

NIAGARA FALLS
Trillium Bed and Breakfast
(Brian and Mary Koke)

5151 River Rd, Niagara Falls, ON, L2E 3G8
www.trilliumbb.ca
E-mail info@trilliumbb.ca

905-354-3863

We look forward to sharing our special brand of hospitality and our home with you. Trillium Bed & Breakfast is conveniently located only minutes from the Falls, Casino Niagara and many of our area's wondrous attractions. We offer three beautifully appointed guests rooms, all with private bathroom facilites. After a perfect night's sleep, awaken to the aroma of fresh brewed coffee and enjoy a homestyle, full breakfast in our dining room overlooking the Niagara Gorge.

ROOMS Ground floor, **Baths** Private, Ensuite, **Beds** Queen, Twin, Single or cots, **Air** In rooms, **Smoking** Outside, **OTHERS** Open all year, **PAYMENT** Visa, MC, Cash, Trvl's cheques, **BREAKFASTS** Full, Continental, **AMENITIES** Lounge, **THINGS TO DO** Rental bikes, Trail nearby, Golf, Fishing, Theatre, Entertainment, Attractions, Wineries/Breweries, Shopping, Tennis, **LANGUAGE** Eng., **PRICE** (2 persons) 70–120 **(check with hosts for pricing details)**

NIAGARA FALLS
Victorian Charm B&B
(Anne-Marie Dubois)

6028 Culp St, Niagara Falls, ON, L2G 2B7
www.victoriancharmbb.com
E-mail victoriancharmbb@cogeco.ca

905-357-4221
Fax 905-357-9115
TFr 1-877-794-6758

Elegant turreted Victorian home with luxurious accommodations, four spacious bedrooms, ensuite private bath, Jacuzzi, fireplace, balcony, TV/VCR, A/C. Gourmet breakfast served 7a.m.–11a.m. in conservatory overlooking the large gardens, water pond and orchard. Situated in historic district, 15-minute walk to Falls, 20-minutes by car to Niagara-on-the-Lake, Shaw Theatre. One bedroom first floor, private entrance, 2 queen beds. Free pick up bus and train station and help from airports. From QEW, take 420, Drummond exit, turn right, follow to Culp, left.

ROOMS Family suite, Upper floor, Ground floor, Private entrance, **Baths** Ensuite, **Beds** King, Queen, Double, Twin, Single or cots, Pullout sofa, **Air** In rooms, **Smoking** Outside, **In Room** Thermostat, TV, Fireplace, **OTHERS** Babysitting, Urban, Open all year, **PAYMENT** Visa, MC, Diners, Direct debit, Cash, Trvl's cheques, **BREAKFASTS** Full, Home-baked, **AMENITIES** Central TV, Central phone, Whirlpool, Barbecue, Laundry, Kitchen, Fridge, Hot bev. bar, Patio, **THINGS TO DO** Rental bikes, Trail nearby, Rental canoe or boat, Golf, Fishing, Museums, Art, Theatre, Entertainment, Attractions, Wineries/Breweries, Shopping, Tennis, Swimming, Horseback riding, Beach, **LANGUAGE** Eng., Fr., Sp., **PRICE** (2 persons) 110–200 **(check with hosts for pricing details)**

NIAGARA FALLS
Villa Gardenia
Bed & Breakfast
(Tony and Anna D'Amico)

4741 Zimmerman Ave, Niagara Falls, ON, L2E 3M8
www.villagardeniabb.com
E-mail info@villagardeniabb.com

905-358-1723
Fax 905-358-1723
TFr 1-877-358-1723

Newly built B&B located in Niagara Falls, ON. Just a 20-minute walk or 2-minute drive to the Falls and most major attractions. We have four beautifully decorated, spacious guest rooms, each fully furnished with a full queen-size bed, private ensuite bathroom, colour cable TV, DVD player with movies, fireplace and sitting area. All prices include a full homemade breakfast of your choice each morning. House is completely non-smoking. Free parking on premises.

ROOMS Upper floor, Private entrance, **Baths** Private, Ensuite, **Beds** Queen, Single or cots, **Air** Central, Ceiling fans, **Smoking** Outside, **In Room** TV, Fireplace, **OTHERS** Open all year, **PAYMENT** Visa, MC, Direct debit, Cash, Trvl's cheques, **BREAKFASTS** Full, Continental, **AMENITIES** Central phone, Fridge, **THINGS TO DO** Fishing, Museums, Art, Theatre, Entertainment, Attractions, Wineries/Breweries, Shopping, Tennis, Horseback riding, Beach, Birdwatching, Antiquing, **LANGUAGE** Eng., Italian, **PRICE** (2 persons) 89–145 **(check with hosts for pricing details)**

NIAGARA REGION *(east of Hamilton)*

Heritage House B&B

(Patrica and John Wakelin)

29 Edmund St, St. Catharines, ON, L2R 2G3
www.heritagehousebandb.com
E-mail johnwakelin@on.aibn.com

905-682-1441
TFr 1-877-337-3313

We have a beautiful old home that we would love to share with you. Our Heritage Designation means that we can truly call ourselves Heritage House B&B. We are an adult only, non-smoking B&B. We have shared our beautiful home for nine years. Being in the middle of Wine Country and very close to the very busy Niagara tourist areas, you will enjoy our quiet location in an old section of St. Catharines. Our very central location puts you only minutes away from everything in the Niagara Region. Thank you.

Baths Ensuite, **Beds** King, Queen, Twin, **Air** Central, **Smoking** Outside, **In Room** TV, VCR/DVD, **OTHERS** Adult, Open all year, Pets in residence, **PAYMENT** Visa, MC, Amex, Cheques accepted, Cash, Trvl's cheques, **BREAKFASTS** Full, **AMENITIES** Central phone, Fridge, Lounge, Patio, **THINGS TO DO** Rental bikes, Trail nearby, Golf, Fishing, Museums, Theatre, Entertainment, Attractions, Wineries/Breweries, Shopping, Tennis, Swimming, Horseback riding, Beach, Birdwatching, Antiquing, **LANGUAGE** Eng., **PRICE** (2 persons) 95–150 **(check with hosts for pricing details)**

NIAGARA REGION

Maples of Grimsby Bed and Breakfast

(Barry and Georgina Staz)

3 Nelles Blvd, Grimsby, ON, L3M 3P9
www.bbcanada.com/maples
E-mail maples@sympatico.ca

905-945-5719

Come share our home with us. Your stay will be comfortable and enjoyable. Maples of Grimsby, c. 1923, is on a tree lined boulevard in the heart of town. A down-filled duvet compliments your room decor. Each day starts with a different breakfast speciality. We are steps to the Bruce Trail. Drive the Niagara Wine Route. Be in Toronto or the many Niagara Peninsula attractions in under an hour. Or stay "home." Relax on the verandah, beside the pool or the pond. Attention to detail will ensure a pleasant stay.

ROOMS Family suite, Upper floor, **Baths** Private, Ensuite, **Beds** Queen, Twin, **Air** Central, **Smoking** Outside, **In Room** TV, **OTHERS** Urban, Adult, Open all year, **PAYMENT** Cheques accepted, Cash, Trvl's cheques, **BREAKFASTS** Full, Home-baked, **AMENITIES** Central TV, Central phone, Swimming pool, Fridge, Lounge, Patio, **THINGS TO DO** Comp. bikes, Trail nearby, Golf, Museums, Art, Theatre, Entertainment, Attractions, Wineries/Breweries, Shopping, Tennis, Swimming, Birdwatching, Antiquing, **LANGUAGE** Eng., **PRICE** (2 persons) 105–145 **(check with hosts for pricing details)**

NIAGARA REGION

Rolanda's B&B

(Rolande Fushtey)

26 Martha Ct, Welland, ON, L3C 4N2
www.canadianbandbguide.ca/bb.asp?ID=3699

905-732-2853

Located in the Niagara region of Ontario,
a few minutes' drive from the honeymoon
capital, Niagara Falls. Enjoy the entertainment of Casino Niagara. Relax for tea
in our beautiful garden and enjoy the
brilliant colours of our summer flowers.
Welcome to the host's kitchen for your
choice in a full tasty breakfast with fresh
fruit. We speak English and French and
are open all year.

ROOMS Family suite, Ground floor, Lower floor, **Baths**
Private, Shared with hosts, **Beds** Double, Pullout sofa,
Air Central, **Smoking** Outside, **In Room** TV, **OTHERS**
Open all year, **PAYMENT** Cash, **BREAKFASTS** Full,
AMENITIES Central TV, Fridge, Patio, **THINGS TO DO**
Rental bikes, Trail nearby, Rental canoe or boat, Golf,
Fishing, Museums, Theatre, Wineries/Breweries,
Shopping, Tennis, Swimming, Beach, **LANGUAGE** Eng.,
Fr., **PRICE** (2 persons) 50–70 **(check with hosts for
pricing details)**

NIAGARA-ON-THE-LAKE *(east of Hamilton)*

6 Oak Haven
Bed and Breakfast

(Christine and Dennis Rizzuto)

6 Oak Dr, Box 397, Niagara-on-the-Lake, ON, L0S 1J0
www.oakhaven.ca
E-mail stay@oakhaven.ca

905-468-7361
TFr 1-866-818-1195

Located in Old Town, within walking distance of the lake, Shaw Festival, restaurants and shops. Features three charming
and well-appointed rooms with ensuites/
private bath. Delightful garden oasis with
gazebo, pond and waterfall invites you to
relax. Garden was featured in *Ontario
Gardener Magazine*. And then, of course,
there are Christines Fabulous Breakfasts!
A warm welcome awaits you from your
hosts Christine and Dennis Rizzuto. Visit
our Web site.

ROOMS Family suite, Upper floor, Ground floor, **Baths**
Private, Ensuite, **Beds** Queen, Pullout sofa, **Air** Central,
In rooms, **Smoking** Outside, **In Room** Phone, TV,
Fireplace, VCR/DVD, **OTHERS** Urban, Adult, Open all
year, Pets in residence, **PAYMENT** Visa, MC, Cheques
accepted, Cash, **BREAKFASTS** Full, Home-baked,
AMENITIES Central TV, Central phone, Fridge, Lounge,
Patio, **THINGS TO DO** Comp. bikes, Rental bikes, Trail
nearby, Golf, Fishing, Museums, Art, Theatre,
Entertainment, Attractions, Wineries/Breweries,
Shopping, Cross-country skiing, Tennis, Swimming,
Beach, Birdwatching, Antiquing, **LANGUAGE** Eng.,
PRICE (2 persons) 115–125 **(check with hosts for pric-
ing details)**

Niagara-on-the-Lake

A Breakfast With Friends
(Alison Hewitt)

1329 McNab Rd, Niagara-on-the-Lake, ON, L0S 1J0
www.bbcanada.com/3866.html
E-mail alison2@vaxxine.com

905-646-3499

Welcome to this peaceful 2-acre setting in the heart of Wine Country. In our spacious c. 1850 home, we have two king-size guest rooms. Your terrific gourmet breakfast can be served on the deck overlooking the heated pool and native treed garden, or inside a gracious dining room. Original stained glass works by the host lend character to the home. We are 400 metres to the lake and a short drive to the historic town, many of the wineries and fine dining. Nearby are Niagara Falls and the spectacular Welland Canal.

ROOMS Family suite, Ground floor, **Baths** Private, Ensuite, **Beds** King, Pullout sofa, **Air** In rooms, **Smoking** Outside, **OTHERS** Rural, Seasonal, Pets welcome, **PAYMENT** Visa, MC, Amex, Cash, Trvl's cheques, **BREAKFASTS** Full, **AMENITIES** Central TV, Central phone, Swimming pool, **THINGS TO DO** Comp. bikes, Rental bikes, Trail nearby, Golf, Fishing, Museums, Theatre, Entertainment, Attractions, Wineries/Breweries, Shopping, Tennis, Swimming, Beach, **LANGUAGE** Eng., Fr., Ger., Dutch, **PRICE** (2 persons) 115–130 **(check with hosts for pricing details)**

Niagara-on-the-Lake

A Fawlty Towers B&B
(Margaret and Gerry Seville)

308 Centre St, Box 1803, Niagara-on-the-Lake, ON, L0S 1J0
www.fawltytowersniagara.com
E-mail fawltyt@niagara.com

905-468-0480
TFr 905-329-5898

We are located 10-minute walk/2-minute drive to town. Only six steps to each guest room, with spacious ensuite. King one and queen four-poster rooms have walkout balcony where you can enjoy early morning coffee or a late night glass of wine in the moonlight. King 2 can be coverted to twin beds. All beds have luxury pillow top mattresses and 100% cotton sheets. Delicious gourmet breakfast with fresh-daily baking and Niagara fruits in season. We serve Starbucks coffee.

ROOMS Upper floor, **Baths** Ensuite, **Beds** King, Queen, Twin, **Air** Central, **Smoking** Outside, **OTHERS** Urban, Adult, Open all year, **PAYMENT** Visa, MC, Cheques accepted, Cash, Trvl's cheques, **BREAKFASTS** Full, Home-baked, **AMENITIES** Central TV, Central phone, Lounge, Patio, Central Internet access, Central VCR/DVD, **THINGS TO DO** Rental bikes, Trail nearby, Golf, Fishing, Museums, Art, Theatre, Attractions, Wineries/Breweries, Shopping, Cross-country skiing, Tennis, Swimming, **LANGUAGE** Eng., **PRICE** (2 persons) 130–140 **(check with hosts for pricing details)**

Niagara-on-the-Lake

Abacot Hall

(Pauline and Mike Hussey)

508 Mississauga St, Box 866, Niagara-on-the-Lake,
ON, L0S 1J0
www.abacothall.com
E-mail abacothall@sympatico.ca

905-468-8383

Large, gracious Georgian-style home on a
private 1/2-acre setting. Walk to everything. Guest lounge with fireplace and
high-speed Internet computer. Bedrooms
access large balcony. All rooms have
ensuite or private bath, full cable TV,
DVDs, wireless Internet. Fridge, ice and
coffee/tea making facilities on guest landing. Decorated in period style with
antiques and art. Central air. Smoke-free.
Flexible breakfast times and individual
tables. Courtesy bicycles. Private guest
entrance. Art gallery.

ROOMS Upper floor, Private entrance, **Baths** Private,
Ensuite, **Beds** King, Queen, Twin, Single or cots, **Air**
Central, **Smoking** Outside, **In Room** TV, Internet
access, **OTHERS** Urban, Adult, Open all year, Pets in
residence, Pets welcome, **PAYMENT** Visa, MC, Amex,
Cash, Trvl's cheques, **BREAKFASTS** Full, **AMENITIES**
Central phone, Fridge, Hot bev. bar, Lounge, Patio,
Central Internet access, **THINGS TO DO** Comp. bikes,
Trail nearby, Golf, Art, Theatre, Attractions, Wineries/
Breweries, Shopping, Swimming, **LANGUAGE** Eng., Sp.,
PRICE (2 persons) 100–135 **(check with hosts for pric-
ing details)**

Niagara-on-the-Lake

Abbotsford House B&B

(Margaret Currie)

305 John St, Box 1018, Niagara-on-the-Lake, ON,
L0S 1J0
www.abbotsfordbandb.com
E-mail stay@abbotsfordbandb.com

905-468-4646
Fax 905-468-2418

A wee bit of Scotland in Niagara-on-the-
Lake. High quality at a reasonable price.
Walking distance to Shaw, shops, golf and
the bike trail. Old-world charm and hospitality greet you. European antiques
abound. Read your morning paper in the
elegant living room with fireplace, before
having your three-course gourmet breakfast in the dining room, complete with
Flow Blue China and chandelier from a
bygone era. Hand-pressed Victorian
linens adorn the queen and twin beds
with ensuite bathrooms. Smoke-free. A/C.

ROOMS Upper floor, **Baths** Ensuite, **Beds** Queen, Twin,
Air Central, **In Room** Fireplace, **OTHERS** Open all year,
Pets in residence, **PAYMENT** Cash, Trvl's cheques,
BREAKFASTS Full, Home-baked, **AMENITIES** Lounge,
Patio, **THINGS TO DO** Trail nearby, Museums, Theatre,
Attractions, Wineries/Breweries, Shopping, **LAN-
GUAGE** Eng., **PRICE** (2 persons) 100–110 **(check with
hosts for pricing details)**

NIAGARA-ON-THE-LAKE

Abel Thomas House
Bed and Breakfast

(Robin and Mary Scott)

269 Regent St, Box 1884, Niagara-on-the-Lake,
ON, L0S 1J0
www.abelthomashouse.com
E-mail info@abelthomashouse.com

905-468-9625
Fax 905-468-7764

Abel Thomas House has been reviewed
and selected as one of the "Best B&Bs in
Ontario" by the renowned Canadian travel
writer Janette Higgins. Her review can
been seen at www.bbontario.com.
Located a short walk from the main
street, where there are unique shops,
theatres and restaurants. Ample parking
is provided for guests. The garden has a
patio area and garden swing for relaxing
on warm days. A fireplace, board games
and books in sitting room for cooler days.
All rooms have ensuite bathrooms.

ROOMS Upper floor, Private entrance, **Baths** Private,
Beds Queen, Twin, **Air** Central, **Smoking** Outside,
OTHERS Adult, Open all year, Pets in residence, **PAY-
MENT** Cheques accepted, Cash, Trvl's cheques,
BREAKFASTS Full, Home-baked, **AMENITIES** Central
TV, Central phone, Lounge, Patio, **THINGS TO DO**
Comp. bikes, Trail nearby, Golf, Fishing, Museums, Art,
Theatre, Entertainment, Attractions, Wineries/
Breweries, Shopping, Tennis, Swimming, Horseback
riding, Birdwatching, Antiquing, **LANGUAGE** Eng.,
PRICE (2 persons) 115–140 **(check with hosts for
pricing details)**

NIAGARA-ON-THE-LAKE

Adel House B&B

(John and Susi Janzen)

81 Adel Dr, St. Catharines, ON, L2M 3W9
www.bbcanada.com/3739.html
E-mail adelhous@niagara.com

905-934-0579

A warm welcome awaits you in our spacious home near the historic Welland
Canal. Take a front-row seat and watch
the ocean vessels, lakers glide past the
elevated observation platform and
through the eight locks of this amazing
waterway. Only minutes from Niagara-on-
the-Lake, Casino Niagara and Niagara
Falls. Enjoy the award-winning local
wineries and tour Niagara after a hot
breakfast of your choice complete with
fresh fruit, homemade jams and jellies
and a wide selection of home baking.
Alternate telephone: 905-327-5510. We
will help with navigating. City and area
maps are avaliable.

ROOMS Upper floor, **Baths** Shared with guest, **Beds**
Queen, Twin, **Air** Central, **Smoking** Outside, **OTHERS**
Urban, Open all year, **PAYMENT** Cheques accepted,
Cash, Trvl's cheques, **BREAKFASTS** Full, Home-baked,
AMENITIES Central TV, Central phone, Barbecue,
Laundry, Kitchen, Fridge, Hot bev. bar, Lounge, Patio,
Central Internet access, Central VCR/DVD, **THINGS TO
DO** Fishing, Museums, Art, Theatre,
Wineries/Breweries, Shopping, **LANGUAGE** Eng., Ger.,
PRICE (2 persons) 85–85 **(check with hosts for pricing
details)**

Niagara-on-the-Lake

Alfred's Coach House

(Cec and Rosie Patriquin)

279 Nassau St, Niagara-on-the-Lake, ON, L0S 1J0
www.alfredscoachhouse.com
E-mail cecandrosie@cogeco.ca

905-468-8181
Fax 905-468-7247
TFr 1-877-586-1212

Alfred's Coach House is a gracious Colonial-style home in the Old Town, one block from the lake and a short walk to theatre and shops. All suites have king beds, ensuite baths, cable TV, bar fridges and Wi-Fi access. Our Seabreeze suite has a seaside theme and a spacious sitting area overlooking the pool. The Country Lane with king/twin bed has a private sitting room and electric fireplace. The Lakewood includes a larger private sitting room with an electric fireplace and has a northern cottage theme.

ROOMS Upper floor, **Baths** Ensuite, **Beds** King, Twin, Single or cots, **Air** Central, **Smoking** Outside, **In Room** Phone, TV, Fireplace, Internet access, VCR/DVD, **OTHERS** Urban, Adult, **PAYMENT** Visa, MC, Direct debit, Cash, **BREAKFASTS** Full, Home-baked, **AMENITIES** Central phone, Swimming pool, Fridge, Lounge, Patio, **THINGS TO DO** Trail nearby, Golf, Fishing, Museums, Art, Theatre, Entertainment, Attractions, Wineries/Breweries, Shopping, Tennis, Swimming, Beach, Antiquing, **LANGUAGE** Eng., Ger., **PRICE** (2 persons) 135–150 **(check with hosts for pricing details)**

Niagara-on-the-Lake

Andrew Carroll House

(Leo and Roberta Labelle)

358 Gage St, Box 833, Niagara-on-the-Lake, ON, L0S 1J0
www.andrewcarrollhouseniagara.com
E-mail carrollhouse@mac.com

905-468-1018
Fax 905-468-9299
TFr 1-866-468-1020

Tastefully decorated B&B with three rooms, each with ensuite bathroom, for your comfort and privacy. Our two ground-level rooms have their own decks where you can sit and enjoy an early morning coffee. Our second floor room, a king/twin, has a comfortable adjoining sitting room with fridge and coffee pot. We serve a gourmet breakfast consisting of fresh fruit in season, various delicious egg dishes, quiches, croissants, muffins, coffee and a variety of teas of your choice.

ROOMS Upper floor, Ground floor, Private entrance, **Baths** Ensuite, **Beds** King, Queen, Twin, **Air** Central, **Smoking** Outside, **In Room** TV, Internet access, **OTHERS** Adult, Open all year, Pets in residence, **PAYMENT** Visa, Cheques accepted, Cash, Trvl's cheques, **BREAKFASTS** Full, **AMENITIES** Fridge, Patio, Central Internet access, **THINGS TO DO** Trail nearby, Golf, Fishing, Museums, Art, Theatre, Entertainment, Wineries/Breweries, Shopping, Cross-country skiing, Tennis, Swimming, Birdwatching, Antiquing, **LANGUAGE** Eng., Fr., **PRICE** (2 persons) 95–150 **(check with hosts for pricing details)**

NIAGARA-ON-THE-LAKE

Antonio Vivaldi B&B
(Susan Nyitrai)

275 Anne St, Box 1392, Niagara-on-the-Lake,
ON, L0S 1J0
www.bbvivaldi.com
E-mail pnyitra@sprint.ca

905-468-9535
Fax 905-468-9616

Our B&B is located in the old town of beautiful Niagara-on-the-Lake. It is a short distance from the Shaw Theatres, fine restaurants, historic sites, wineries, golf courses, Lake Ontario and Niagara Falls. You will find warm and wonderful Hungarian hospitality in our home. Many of our guests find our gift certificates ideal gifts for friends and family.

ROOMS Upper floor, Private entrance, **Baths** Ensuite, **Beds** Queen, **Air** Central, **Smoking** Outside, **In Room** Phone, TV, Fireplace, **OTHERS** Adult, Open all year, **PAYMENT** Visa, Cash, Trvl's cheques, **BREAKFASTS** Full, **AMENITIES** Central TV, Whirlpool, Laundry, Fridge, Hot bev. bar, Lounge, Patio, **THINGS TO DO** Rental bikes, Trail nearby, Golf, Museums, Art, Theatre, Entertainment, Attractions, Wineries/Breweries, Shopping, Cross-country skiing, Horseback riding, Birdwatching, Antiquing, **LANGUAGE** Eng., Fr., Hungarian, **PRICE** (2 persons) 99–150 **(check with hosts for pricing details)**

NIAGARA-ON-THE-LAKE

Arbour Breeze
Bed & Breakfast
(Siety Koopal)

2283 Four Mile Creek Rd, RR #3, Niagara-on-the-Lake,
ON, L0S 1J0
www.arbourbreeze.com
E-mail info@arbourbreeze.com

905-468-0505
Fax 905-468-9964

A comfortable home in a quiet country setting. A retreat to get away from your hectic life. Five minutes to Niagara-on-the-Lake (Shaw Festival Theatres, shopping, antiques, restaurants, museums) 15 minutes to Niagara Falls. Surrounded by orchards, close to wineries, golf. Great for biking and hiking. Two rooms with ensuite, one with private bath. All rooms have queen-size four-poster beds. Cozy seating area on landing with water cooler, kettle and coffeemaker. Scrumptious full course breakfast served.

ROOMS Family suite, Upper floor, **Baths** Private, Ensuite, **Beds** Queen, Single or cots, Pullout sofa, **Air** Central, In rooms, **Smoking** Outside, **In Room** TV, VCR/DVD, **OTHERS** Rural, Open all year, Pets in residence, **PAYMENT** Visa, MC, Diners, Amex, Cheques accepted, Cash, Trvl's cheques, **BREAKFASTS** Full, Home-baked, **AMENITIES** Central phone, Fridge, Hot bev. bar, Lounge, **THINGS TO DO** Rental bikes, Trail nearby, Golf, Museums, Art, Theatre, Attractions, Wineries/Breweries, Shopping, Tennis, Antiquing, **LANGUAGE** Eng., Dutch, **PRICE** (2 persons) 80–150 **(check with hosts for pricing details)**

Niagara-on-the-Lake

Bird Watchers Haven Cottage Suites

(Barbara Proven)

475 Regent St, Niagara-on-the-Lake, ON, L0S 1J0
www.birdhaven.on.ca
E-mail buchanan@birdhaven.on.ca

905-468-4639
TFr 1-800-778-7408

We are located in the Old Town area of Niagara-on-the-Lake, within walking distance of the theatres, boutiques and dining and across from the Pillar & Post Inn & Spa. There are two individual ground floor guest suites with direct entrance from the wicker furnished front verandah, where you can relax and watch the horses and carriages go by. A full breakfast is served ensuite at your leisure. We also have additional accommodation at our two adjoining, self-catered, ground floor guest cottages.

ROOMS Family suite, Ground floor, Private entrance, **Baths** Ensuite, **Beds** King, Queen, Twin, Single or cots, Pullout sofa, **Air** Central, **Smoking** Outside, **In Room** Phone, TV, VCR/DVD, **OTHERS** Urban, Open all year, Pets in residence, Pets welcome, **PAYMENT** Cheques accepted, Cash, Trvl's cheques, **BREAKFASTS** Full, **AMENITIES** Barbecue, Kitchen, Fridge, Hot bev. bar, Lounge, Patio, **THINGS TO DO** Rental bikes, Trail nearby, Golf, Fishing, Museums, Art, Theatre, Entertainment, Attractions, Wineries/Breweries, Shopping, Tennis, Swimming, Horseback riding, Birdwatching, Antiquing, **LANGUAGE** Eng., **PRICE** (2 persons) 100–125 **(check with hosts for pricing details)**

Niagara-on-the-Lake

Britaly Bed and Breakfast

(Graham Hall and Aldo Petronelli)

57 The Promenade, Niagara-on-the-Lake, ON, L0S 1J0
www.britaly.com
E-mail britaly@sympatico.ca

905-468-8778

Britaly is a very elegantly appointed home just 1.7 km (1 mile) from theatres and shops. Our flair for hospitality is reflected in our decor and attention to detail. Fresh flowers adorn practically every room in the house. Our gourmet four-course breakfasts, which have become almost legendary, are served daily in our elegantly appointed dining room. Relax in our private guest lounge or alternatively, in our beautifully landscaped gardens.

ROOMS Upper floor, **Baths** Private, Ensuite, **Beds** Queen, **Air** Central, **Smoking** Outside, **In Room** TV, Fireplace, Internet access, **OTHERS** Pets in residence, Pets welcome, **PAYMENT** Visa, MC, Cheques accepted, Cash, Trvl's cheques, **BREAKFASTS** Full, **AMENITIES** Lounge, Patio, **THINGS TO DO** Comp. bikes, Trail nearby, Golf, Museums, Art, Theatre, Entertainment, Attractions, Wineries/Breweries, Shopping, Beach, **LANGUAGE** Eng., Fr., Italian, **PRICE** (2 persons) 90–110 **(check with hosts for pricing details)**

Niagara-on-the-Lake

Brockamour Manor
(Douglas Herman)

433 King St, Niagara-on-the-Lake, ON, L0S 1J0
www.brockamour.com
E-mail brockamo@vaxxine.com

905-468-5527
Fax 905-468-5071

Take QEW to Rd 55 follow signs to Niagara-on the-Lake. In Old Town, turn right at light (Mary St) continue to last driveway at left before stop sign at King St. Look for a large white estate on corner. Quiet graceful elegance in lovely heritage Georgian home (c. 1809) with romantic, historic past and a gracious present. Situated in beautiful park-like environment with majestic old trees among natural wilderness. Short walk to theatres, restaurants and shops. You will enjoy our full and varied gourmet breakfast.

ROOMS Upper floor, Private entrance, **Baths** Private, Ensuite, **Beds** King, Queen, Twin, **Air** Central, Ceiling fans, **Smoking** Outside, **In Room** TV, Fireplace, VCR/DVD, **OTHERS** Urban, Adult, Open all year, **PAYMENT** Visa, MC, Amex, Direct debit, Cheques accepted, Cash, **BREAKFASTS** Full, Home-baked, **AMENITIES** Central phone, Fridge, Lounge, Patio, **THINGS TO DO** Rental bikes, Trail nearby, Golf, Fishing, Museums, Art, Theatre, Entertainment, Attractions, Wineries/ Breweries, Shopping, Cross-country skiing, Tennis, Swimming, **LANGUAGE** Eng., Fr., **PRICE** (2 persons) 200–250 **(check with hosts for pricing details)**

Niagara-on-the-Lake

Bullfrog Pond Guest House
(Barbara and Andy Furlanetto)

3801 Cherry Ave, Vineland, ON, L0R 2C0
www.bullfrogpond.com
E-mail bullfrogpond2@aol.com

905-562-1232
Fax 905-562-1232

Your hosts have experienced the delights of many English bed and breakfasts and hope to provide you with typical friendly English hospitality. We are located on 1 acre of manicured lawns within walking distance of many wineries and the Bruce Trail. Directions: Exit QEW at Exit 57 (Victoria Ave). South on Victoria for 5 km over Hwy 8 (King St W). First right after King W is Moyer Rd. Turn right and travel to stop sign. We are located on the right at the stop sign at Cherry and Moyer.

ROOMS Ground floor, Private entrance, **Baths** Ensuite, **Beds** Queen, **Air** Central, **Smoking** Outside, **In Room** TV, Fireplace, VCR/DVD, **OTHERS** Babysitting, Rural, Adult, Open all year, Handicapped access, **PAYMENT** Visa, MC, Cheques accepted, Cash, **BREAKFASTS** Full, Home-baked, **AMENITIES** Kitchen, Fridge, Hot bev. bar, Lounge, Patio, **THINGS TO DO** Comp. bikes, Trail nearby, Golf, Museums, Theatre, Entertainment, Attractions, Wineries/Breweries, Shopping, Swimming, Beach, Birdwatching, Antiquing, **LANGUAGE** Eng., Italian, **PRICE** (2 persons) 105–130 **(check with hosts for pricing details)**

NIAGARA-ON-THE-LAKE

Cedar Gables Bed and Breakfast

(Joan and Gus Medina)

107 Flynn St, PO Box 189, Niagara-on-the-Lake, ON, L0S 1J0
www.cedargables.ca
E-mail relax@cedargables.ca

905-468-8568
Fax 905-468-8592
TFr 1-877-513-3332

A warm welcome awaits you at Cedar Gables B&B. Located just a short stroll from the Shaw Festival theatres, fine dining and shopping, we are just minutes from several wineries, hiking and biking trails, and of course, Niagara Falls. Your hosts, Joan and Gus Medina, share your interests in music, theatre, hiking and travel. Relax in one of our three comfortable and tastefully decorated rooms. Unwind in our peaceful garden by the pond or the bright sunroom. Awake to a bountiful hot breakfast.

ROOMS Upper floor, Ground floor, **Baths** Private, Ensuite, **Beds** King, Queen, Twin, **Air** Central, **Smoking** Outside, **In Room** TV, Internet access, **OTHERS** Adult, **PAYMENT** Visa, MC, Cash, Trvl's cheques, **BREAKFASTS** Full, **AMENITIES** Fridge, Hot bev. bar, Lounge, Patio, **THINGS TO DO** Rental bikes, Trail nearby, Golf, Museums, Art, Theatre, Entertainment, Attractions, Wineries/Breweries, Shopping, Tennis, Antiquing, **LANGUAGE** Eng., Sp., **PRICE** (2 persons) 100–130 **(check with hosts for pricing details)**

NIAGARA-ON-THE-LAKE

Davy House Bed and Breakfast

(Jeff Jacques and Florence Vint)

230 Davy St, Niagara-on-the-Lake, ON, L0S 1J0
www.davyhouse.com
E-mail info@davyhouse.com

905-468-5307
Fax 905-468-7165
TFr 1-888-314-9046

An historically designated home beautifully restored with warmth and character. Located in the town centre. Steps to theatre, restaurants and shopping. Hotel-type privacy including TV/VCR, central air, patio area with large water garden, koi, outdoor hot tub, putting green, individual breakfast tables. Twin/queen/king rooms with private ensuite bathrooms. Spaniel in residence. Smoke-free.

ROOMS Upper floor, Ground floor, **Baths** Private, Ensuite, **Beds** King, Queen, Twin, **Air** Central, **Smoking** Outside, **In Room** TV, Fireplace, VCR/DVD, **OTHERS** Urban, Adult, Open all year, Pets in residence, **PAYMENT** Visa, MC, Amex, Direct debit, Cheques accepted, Cash, **BREAKFASTS** Full, Home-baked, **AMENITIES** Central TV, Central phone, Whirlpool, Fridge, Hot bev. bar, Lounge, Patio, Central Internet access, **THINGS TO DO** Rental bikes, Trail nearby, Golf, Fishing, Museums, Art, Theatre, Entertainment, Attractions, Wineries/Breweries, Shopping, Tennis, **LANGUAGE** Eng., **PRICE** (2 persons) 125–175 **(check with hosts for pricing details)**

NIAGARA-ON-THE-LAKE

Dietsch's Empty Nest

(Paul and Natasha Dietsch)

723 King St, Box 1835, Niagara-on-the-Lake,
ON, L0S 1J0
www.dietschsemptynest.com
E-mail natasha.dietsch081@sympatico.ca

905-468-3906
TFr 1-800-560-7743

We offer country charm with flowers, birds and a wraparound verandah. A full breakfast is served and all rooms are ensuite. Central air and smoke-free. Open all year. An Old Town location. All rooms are $99, with winter rates available. Member of the Niagara-on-the-Lake Bed and Breakfast Association and CAA.

ROOMS Upper floor, **Baths** Ensuite, **Beds** King, Queen, Twin, Single or cots, **Air** Central, **Smoking** Outside, **OTHERS** Open all year, **PAYMENT** Visa, MC, Cheques accepted, Cash, Trvl's cheques, **BREAKFASTS** Full, Home-baked, **AMENITIES** Lounge, Patio, **THINGS TO DO** Rental bikes, Trail nearby, Golf, Fishing, Museums, Art, Theatre, Attractions, Wineries/Breweries, Shopping, Birdwatching, Antiquing, **LANGUAGE** Eng., **PRICE** (2 persons) 99 **(check with hosts for pricing details)**

NIAGARA-ON-THE-LAKE

Dorset House

(Erika Koszegi)

10 Park Crt, PO Box 1874, Niagara-on-the-Lake,
ON, L0S 1J0
www.vaxxine.com/dorsethouse
E-mail dorset@vaxxine.com

905-468-5591

The Old Town ambience of Niagara-on-the-Lake meets modern comfort at Dorset House. Only short walk to restaurants, shops and the theatres and 20-minutes drive along the beautiful Niagara River Parkway to Niagara Falls. The park, with miles of scenic river trails for walking, bicycling and roller-blading, is only a few steps from our door.

ROOMS Upper floor, Private entrance, **Baths** Ensuite, **Beds** Queen, Twin, **Air** Central, **Smoking** Outside, **In Room** TV, **OTHERS** Adult, Open all year, Pets in residence, **PAYMENT** Cheques accepted, Cash, **BREAKFASTS** Full, **AMENITIES** Central TV, Whirlpool, Fridge, Lounge, Patio, **THINGS TO DO** Trail nearby, Golf, Museums, Art, Theatre, Entertainment, Attractions, Wineries/Breweries, Shopping, Antiquing, **LANGUAGE** Eng., Fr., Ger., **PRICE** (2 persons) 135 **(check with hosts for pricing details)**

Niagara-on-the-Lake

DownHome
Bed and Breakfast

(Sandy and James Down)

93 William St, Niagara-on-the-Lake, ON, L0S 1J0
www.downhomeniagara.ca
E-mail info@downhomeniagara.ca

905-468-3173
TFr 1-888-223-6433

Enter our gracious Georgian home that offers elegance wrapped in an air of tranquility and comfort with modern conveniences. Our home is situated in a quiet area of the Old Town, backing onto One Mile Creek. We are only four blocks from shops, theatres and fine restaurants. All three Shaw Festival theatres are within walking distance.

ROOMS Upper floor, Private entrance, **Baths** Ensuite, **Beds** Queen, **Air** Central, **In Room** Fireplace, Internet access, **OTHERS** Urban, Adult, Open all year, Pets in residence, **PAYMENT** Visa, MC, Amex, Cash, Trvl's cheques, **BREAKFASTS** Full, Home-baked, **AMENITIES** Central TV, Fridge, Hot bev. bar, Lounge, Patio, **THINGS TO DO** Rental bikes, Trail nearby, Golf, Museums, Art, Theatre, Entertainment, Attractions, Wineries/ Breweries, Shopping, Birdwatching, Antiquing, **LANGUAGE** Eng., Russian, Polish, Ukranian, **PRICE** (2 persons) 180–195 **(check with hosts for pricing details)**

Niagara-on-the-Lake

Globetrotters B&B/Gallery

(Donna and Fernando Vieira)

642 Simcoe St, Niagara-on-the-Lake, ON, L0S 1J0
www.globetrottersbb.ca
E-mail info@globetrottersbb.ca

905-468-4021
Fax 905-468-2382
TFr 1-866-835-4446

Taste the difference at Globetrotters B&B/Gallery in Niagara-on-the-Lake. Just minutes from the Shaw Festival Theatres, Queen St boutiques and restaurants, award-winning wineries, cycling paths, golf courses and the beautiful Niagara Parkway that leads to Niagara Falls. Our guests experience award-winning decor in air-conditioned comfort as well as fresh breakfasts bursting with global flavours and served daily in The Vineyards breakfast room or, weather permitting, on our covered verandah.

ROOMS Family suite, Upper floor, Ground floor, **Baths** Ensuite, **Beds** Queen, Twin, Single or cots, **Air** Central, **Smoking** Outside, **OTHERS** Urban, Open all year, **PAYMENT** Visa, MC, Amex, Cheques accepted, Cash, **BREAKFASTS** Full, Home-baked, **AMENITIES** Central TV, Central phone, Fridge, Lounge, Patio, **THINGS TO DO** Rental bikes, Trail nearby, Rental canoe or boat, Golf, Fishing, Museums, Art, Theatre, Entertainment, Attractions, Wineries/Breweries, Shopping, Tennis, Swimming, Horseback riding, **LANGUAGE** Eng., Fr., Sp., Ger., Portuguese, Italian, Dutch, **PRICE** (2 persons) 110–125 **(check with hosts for pricing details)**

Niagara-on-the-Lake

Hiebert's Guest House

(Otto and Marlene Hiebert)

275 John St W, Niagara-on-the-Lake, ON, L0S 1J0
www.v-ip.com/hieberts
E-mail hiebertsguesthouse@cogeco.ca

905-468-3687

Located in Old Town, we are within walking distance of the Shaw theatres, dining and shopping areas. Rooms on the private guest floor have a queen and a twin bed, ensuite/private bath, TV and mini-fridge. Relax under the garden arbour in the treed yard. A smoke- and pet-free home. A full and varied breakfast served in the dining room. Open all year. Come be our guest! Map available on Web site. Extra person in room: $25.

ROOMS Family suite, Lower floor, Private entrance, **Baths** Private, Ensuite, **Beds** Queen, Twin, Pullout sofa, **Air** Central, In rooms, **Smoking** Outside, **In Room** Thermostat, TV, **OTHERS** Urban, Open all year, **PAYMENT** Cheques accepted, Cash, Trvl's cheques, **BREAKFASTS** Full, Home-baked, **AMENITIES** Central phone, Fridge, Lounge, Patio, **THINGS TO DO** Comp. bikes, Rental bikes, Trail nearby, Golf, Fishing, Museums, Art, Theatre, Entertainment, Attractions, Wineries/Breweries, Shopping, Cross-country skiing, Tennis, Swimming, **LANGUAGE** Eng., Ger., **PRICE** (2 persons) 95–119 **(check with hosts for pricing details)**

Niagara-on-the-Lake

Hilltop Manor

(Karen Poynton)

344 Gage St, Niagara-on-the-Lake, ON, L0S 1J0
www.hilltop-manor.com
E-mail jpoynton@cogeco.ca

905-468-9363
TFr 1-866-486-2667

Our home is situated in a quiet area of Old Town, filled with trees and flower gardens; close enough to walk comfortably to shops, theatres and fine resturants. So near the busy downtown street, but a retreat to come back to at the end of the day. Niagara-on-the-Lake is a year-round tourist destination where visitors can enjoy a variety of activities and places of interest. Directions from Toronto or US: QEW Hwy follow Niagara-on-the-Lake signs down Hwy 55, turn left on Gage St.

ROOMS Upper floor, **Baths** Ensuite, **Beds** Queen, **Air** Central, **Smoking** Outside, **In Room** Fireplace, **OTHERS** Open all year, Pets in residence, **PAYMENT** Visa, MC, Direct debit, Cash, Trvl's cheques, **BREAKFASTS** Full, **AMENITIES** Fridge, Lounge, Patio, **THINGS TO DO** Rental bikes, Trail nearby, Golf, Art, Theatre, Entertainment, Attractions, Wineries/Breweries, Shopping, Cross-country skiing, Tennis, Swimming, Antiquing, **LANGUAGE** Eng., **PRICE** (2 persons) 100–140 **(check with hosts for pricing details)**

Niagara-on-the-Lake

Kia-Ora Bed and Breakfast
(Shona and Gary)

127 Mary St, Box 400, Niagara-on-the-Lake,
ON, L0S 1J0
www.niagarabb.com/kia ora.html
E-mail shonabradnam@cogeco.ca

905-468-1328
Fax 905-468-1862
TFr 1-888-208-2340

Circa 1843, built in the first half of the
19th century, this beautiful bed and
breakfast features salt-box architecture.
Enjoy your stay in elegantly decorated
spacious suites, all with private baths.
King/queen/twin beds. Central air, smoke-
free, large garden, ample parking and
courtesy bicycles. Fresh fruit salad and full
hot breakfast comprise the country
breakfast menu. Shaw Festival and wineries are among the area's most popular
attractions.

ROOMS Family suite, Upper floor, Ground floor, Private
entrance, **Baths** Private, Ensuite, **Beds** King, Queen,
Twin, Pullout sofa, **Air** Central, **Smoking** Outside, **In
Room** TV, Fireplace, **OTHERS** Open all year, Pets in res-
idence, Pets welcome, **PAYMENT** Visa, MC, Cash, Trvl's
cheques, **BREAKFASTS** Full, **AMENITIES** Central TV,
Central phone, Fridge, Hot bev. bar, Patio, **THINGS TO
DO** Comp. bikes, Trail nearby, Golf, Fishing, Museums,
Art, Theatre, Entertainment, Attractions, Wineries/
Breweries, Shopping, Tennis, **LANGUAGE** Eng., **PRICE**
(2 persons) 140–150 **(check with hosts for pricing
details)**

Niagara-on-the-Lake

Lakewinds Country Manor circa 1881
(Jane and Steve Locke)

328 Queen St, Niagara-on-the-Lake, ON, L0S 1J0
www.lakewinds.ca
E-mail lakewind@niagara.com

905-468-1888
TFr 1-866-338-1888

Over a century later, golf is still viewed
from the verandah of this elegantly
restored Victorian manor, offering visitors
superb lodging and famous breakfasts.
Manicured gardens, a fishpond and a
heated pool, all in an estate only a stroll
to the Shaw theatres. Highly acclaimed in
print and television, including *Best of Bed
and Breakfasts*.Only B&B in town chosen
for "First Class" and for the "Award of
Merit, one of Top Five B&Bs in Canada."
We do our best to make your stay at
Lakewinds special.

ROOMS Upper floor, **Baths** Ensuite, **Beds** King, Queen,
Twin, **Air** Central, **Smoking** Outside, **In Room**
Thermostat, TV, Fireplace, Internet access, VCR/DVD,
OTHERS Rural, Adult, Open all year, **PAYMENT** Visa,
MC, Direct debit, Cash, Trvl's cheques, **BREAKFASTS**
Full, Continental, **AMENITIES** Central TV, Central
phone, Swimming pool, Fridge, Lounge, Patio, Central
Internet access, **THINGS TO DO** Comp. bikes, Rental
bikes, Trail nearby, Golf, Fishing, Museums, Art, Theatre,
Entertainment, Attractions, Wineries/Breweries,
Shopping, Swimming, Birdwatching, Antiquing, **LAN-
GUAGE** Eng., Fr., **PRICE** (2 persons) 165–295 **(check
with hosts for pricing details)**

NIAGARA-ON-THE-LAKE

Newark Manor B&B
(Peggy and Kenn Moody)

1893 Lakeshore Rd, Niagara-on-the-Lake, ON, L0S 1J0
www.newarkmanorniagara.com
E-mail nm@niagara.com

905-468-9814
Fax 905-468-9814
TFr 1-866-639-2751

Experience gracious Niagara hospitality just a few moments from the prettiest town in Canada. Comfortable, airy rooms with queen-size beds, private ensuite baths and central A/C. Peggy's breakfasts will surprise and delight you. Let us help make your visit to Niagara-on-the-Lake one of your great memories.

ROOMS Upper floor, **Baths** Private, Ensuite, **Beds** Queen, **Air** Central, **Smoking** Outside, **In Room** TV, **OTHERS** Adult, Pets in residence, **PAYMENT** Visa, MC, Amex, Cheques accepted, Cash, Trvl's cheques, **BREAKFASTS** Full, **AMENITIES** Fridge, **THINGS TO DO** Rental bikes, Trail nearby, Golf, Museums, Art, Theatre, Entertainment, Attractions, Wineries/Breweries, Shopping, **LANGUAGE** Eng., **PRICE** (2 persons) 99–115 **(check with hosts for pricing details)**

NIAGARA-ON-THE-LAKE

Palatine Hill Bed & Breakfast
(Heather and Dennis Kennedy)

2222 Four Mile Creek Rd, RR #3, Niagara-on-the-Lake, ON, L0S 1J0
www.niagaraonthelakebb.com
E-mail palatine@vaxxine.com

905-468-3929

Secluded country retreat near Niagara-on-the-Lake and Niagara Falls, Canada. Unique passive-solar B&B in peaceful forest setting. Three queen guest rooms with ensuite bath, lovely furnishings, fireplace/stove, mini-fridge and TV. Two have private entrance and large windows overlooking the forested property. Full, delicious breakfast served, children welcome. Spacious deck, Gazebo and BBQ available. Home is air-conditioned, smoke-and pet-free. Near wineries, historic sites, Shaw Theatre, Niagara recreational trail and fruit farms.

ROOMS Lower floor, Private entrance, **Baths** Ensuite, **Beds** Queen, Single or cots, Pullout sofa, **Air** Central, **Smoking** Outside, **In Room** TV, Fireplace, **OTHERS** Rural, Open all year, **PAYMENT** Visa, MC, Cheques accepted, Cash, Trvl's cheques, **BREAKFASTS** Full, **AMENITIES** Central phone, Barbecue, Fridge, Hot bev. bar, Patio, **THINGS TO DO** Rental bikes, Trail nearby, Golf, Museums, Art, Theatre, Attractions, Wineries/Breweries, Shopping, **LANGUAGE** Eng., Ger., **PRICE** (2 persons) 75–145 **(check with hosts for pricing details)**

Niagara-on-the-Lake

Parliament Cottage B&B circa 1840

(Isabelle Parliament)

PO Box 1464 418 Gate St, Niagara-on-the-Lake, ON, L0S 1J0
www.parliamentcottage.ca
E-mail isabelle@parliamentcottage.ca

905-468-1342
TFr 1-877-660-6005

An 1840 home located within the Old Town. Main floor room is ideal for person with mobility impairments. Three beds in one room. A four-block stroll to the main shopping, theatre, and dining area. Two-minute ride to bike trails on courtesy bicycles. Bright, cheerful ambience both inside and out. Lounge, patio and gardens available to guests. Full varied breakfasts featuring local fresh fruits and home baking. Long-time resident of the area is your host. Helpful ideas to explore the local holiday area.

ROOMS Upper floor, Ground floor, **Baths** Private, Ensuite, **Beds** Queen, Double, Twin, **Air** Central, **Smoking** Outside, **In Room** Internet access, **OTHERS** Adult, Open all year, Pets in residence, **PAYMENT** Visa, MC, Cheques accepted, Cash, Trvl's cheques, **BREAKFASTS** Full, Home-baked, **AMENITIES** Central phone, Fridge, Lounge, Patio, **THINGS TO DO** Comp. bikes, Rental bikes, Trail nearby, Golf, Museums, Art, Theatre, Attractions, Wineries/Breweries, Shopping, Antiquing, **LANGUAGE** Eng., **PRICE** (2 persons) 95–120 **(check with hosts for pricing details)**

Niagara-on-the-Lake

Potter's Cottage B&B

(Susan Wintrop and Dean Levesque)

1242 Line 3, Niagara-on-the-Lake, ON, L0S 1J0
www.eastwestpottery.com
E-mail wintrop@eastwestpottery.com

905-468-1883
Fax 905-468-5038

Potter's Cottage is an oasis and is nestled in Niagara's wine country, just 5 minutes, 6.8 km by car to Old Town. We offer a beautifully furnished (queen) bedroom/ensuite and private sitting room on ground level with private entrance. There is also a swimming pool and bicycles for guests to enjoy. A continental breakfast is delivered to the suite so guests can breakfast at their leisure. Smoke-free. A/C, and TV. Adults only, no pets please.

ROOMS Ground floor, Private entrance, **Baths** Private, Ensuite, **Beds** Queen, **Air** Central, **Smoking** Outside, **In Room** TV, **OTHERS** Rural, Adult, Open all year, Pets in residence, **PAYMENT** Visa, MC, Cheques accepted, Cash, Trvl's cheques, **BREAKFASTS** Continental, Home-baked, **AMENITIES** Central TV, Swimming pool, Fridge, Hot bev. bar, Lounge, Patio, **THINGS TO DO** Comp. bikes, Trail nearby, Fishing, Museums, Art, Theatre, Entertainment, Attractions, Wineries/Breweries, Shopping, Swimming, **LANGUAGE** Eng., **PRICE** (2 persons) 125–135 **(check with hosts for pricing details)**

NIAGARA-ON-THE-LAKE

Serenity Garden B&B

(Telsie Boese and Guy Bell)

196 Creek Rd, PO Box 367, St. Davids, ON, L0S 1P0
www.bbniagaraontario.com
E-mail serenity@cogeco.ca

905-262-5183

The world is a better place because of the choices you make. When visiting Niagara Falls, Niagara-on-the-Lake, Queenston and St. Catharines, choose to stay at Serenity Garden B&B in the heart of Niagara only minutes to the above cities. Offering privacy, pampering service with full breakfast in a holistic atmosphere. Sitting on almost an acre, the property is transformed into many gardens, water pond, flower, vegetable, herb, front porch and decks. Created for memorable, relaxing stay away from the crowds.

ROOMS Ground floor, Private entrance, **Baths** Private, Ensuite, **Beds** Queen, **Air** Central, Ceiling fans, **In Room** TV, VCR/DVD, **OTHERS** Rural, Adult, Open all year, Pets in residence, **PAYMENT** Cheques accepted, Cash, Trvl's cheques, **BREAKFASTS** Full, **AMENITIES** Laundry, Fridge, Lounge, Patio, Central Internet access, **THINGS TO DO** Trail nearby, Golf, Fishing, Museums, Art, Theatre, Entertainment, Attractions, Wineries/ Breweries, Shopping, Tennis, Swimming, Horseback riding, Beach, Birdwatching, Antiquing, **LANGUAGE** Eng., **PRICE** (2 persons) 100–125 **(check with hosts for pricing details)**

NIAGARA-ON-THE-LAKE

Simcoe Manor

(John and Vera Gartner)

242 Simcoe St, Niagara-on-the-Lake, ON, L0S 1J0
www.simcoemanor.com
E-mail simcoemanor@cogeco.ca

905-468-4886
Fax 905-468-5369
TFr 1-866-468-4886

Stately Old Town residence graciously harmonizes tradition, ambience and friendliness with modern comforts. Park-like setting, steps from attractions (theatre, dining, shopping, golf). Enjoy spacious, elegantly appointed suites; most with private bath, and/or Jacuzzi and fireplace or sauna. All air-conditioned and smoke-free. Enjoy a full gourmet breakfast amidst the crystal, china and mahogany of the dining room or sit fireside in the parlour, relax on our elevated porch overlooking the garden, pool, creek.

ROOMS Family suite, Upper floor, Private entrance, **Baths** Private, Ensuite, Shared with guest, **Beds** King, Queen, Twin, Pullout sofa, **Air** Central, **Smoking** Outside, **In Room** Thermostat, Phone, TV, Fireplace, **OTHERS** Urban, Adult, Open all year, Pets in residence, **PAYMENT** Visa, MC, Cheques accepted, Cash, **BREAKFASTS** Full, **AMENITIES** Swimming pool, Sauna, Whirlpool, Barbecue, Laundry, Fridge, Lounge, Patio, **THINGS TO DO** Rental bikes, Trail nearby, Golf, Fishing, Museums, Theatre, Entertainment, Attractions, Wineries/Breweries, Shopping, Tennis, Swimming, Beach, **PRICE** (2 persons) 169–275 **(check with hosts for pricing details)**

Niagara-on-the-Lake

Somerset B&B

(Walt and Betty Andres)

111 Front St, Box 929, Niagara-on-the-Lake,
ON, L0S 1J0
www.somersetbb.info
E-mail somersetnotl@aol.com

905-468-5565
Fax 905-468-8899

Somerset Bed and Breakfast is situated
on the shores of Lake Ontario and the
Niagara River. Enjoy a breathtaking view
from any of the three suites: West Wing,
Master Suite and East Wing. All suites feature their own private balcony. You can sit
and relax on a warm summer day while
watching the activities on the water.
Enjoy early morning coffee on your balcony. Breakfast is served in the dining
room overlooking the water. Our season
extends from April 1 till Dec 31.

ROOMS Upper floor, Private entrance, **Baths** Private,
Ensuite, **Beds** Double, **Air** Central, **Smoking** Outside,
In Room TV, **PAYMENT** Visa, MC, Cash, Trvl's cheques,
BREAKFASTS Full, Home-baked, **AMENITIES** Central
phone, Lounge, Patio, **THINGS TO DO** Rental bikes,
Golf, Theatre, Wineries/Breweries, Shopping, **LAN-
GUAGE** Eng., Ger., **PRICE** (2 persons) 285–340 (**check
with hosts for pricing details**)

Niagara-on-the-Lake

The River Breeze

(Bert and Mimi Davesne)

14767 Niagara Pkwy, Niagara-on-the-Lake,
ON, L0S 1J0
www.bbcanada.com/1861.html
E-mail theriverbreeze@cogeco.ca

905-262-4046
Fax 905-262-0718
TFr 1-866-266-8249

A lovely country estate in the French traditional elegance of the Loire valley. Three
rooms overlook the breathtaking Niagara
River, the fourth the front garden. All have
queen beds, ensuite bath or private bath.
Two have balconies on the river. Our
home features central air. Enjoy the lovely
garden, the terrace and the pool. Full
gourmet breakfast, a daily surprise.
Smoke-free. Right on the bicycle trail.
Open all year; from $120.

ROOMS Upper floor, **Baths** Private, Ensuite, **Beds**
Queen, Single or cots, **Air** Central, **Smoking** Outside,
In Room Phone, **OTHERS** Rural, Adult, Open all year,
PAYMENT Visa, MC, Direct debit, Cash, **BREAKFASTS**
Full, Home-baked, **AMENITIES** Central TV, Swimming
pool, Lounge, Patio, **THINGS TO DO** Comp. bikes, Trail
nearby, Golf, Museums, Art, Theatre,
Wineries/Breweries, Shopping, **LANGUAGE** Eng., Fr.,
PRICE (2 persons) 120–150 (**check with hosts for pric-
ing details**)

Willowcreek House B&B

(Margaret and Jake Janzen)

Box 1028, 288 Dorchester St, Niagara-on-the-Lake, ON, L0S 1J0
www.niagaraonthelakebb.org
E-mail willowcreekhouse@sympatico.ca

905-468-9060
TFr 1-877-589-9001

Enjoy our elegant Georgian manor, nestled on a ravine lot with majestic weeping willows and a creek. Walk to theatres, shops, golfing, dining and the lake. All our rooms have private ensuite baths and king/twin-size beds. Bask in front of the fireplace in winter and enjoy the air-conditioning in summer. One room has a Jacuzzi and an extra sofa-bed. For allergy sufferers, we have a smoke- and pet-free environment. Enjoy our delicious breakfast. We are located in Old Town Niagara-on-the-Lake.

ROOMS Upper floor, **Baths** Private, Ensuite, **Beds** King, Twin, Pullout sofa, **Air** Central, **Smoking** Outside, **In Room** Fireplace, **OTHERS** Open all year, **PAYMENT** Visa, MC, Amex, Direct debit, Cheques accepted, Cash, **BREAKFASTS** Full, **AMENITIES** Central phone, Fridge, Lounge, Patio, Central Internet access, **THINGS TO DO** Rental bikes, Trail nearby, Golf, Museums, Art, Theatre, Attractions, Wineries/Breweries, Shopping, **LANGUAGE** Eng., Ger., **PRICE** (2 persons) 140–160 **(check with hosts for pricing details)**

Wishing Well Historical Cottage Rental

(Maria Rekrut)

156 Mary St, Niagara-on-the-Lake, ON, L0S 1J0
www.wishingwellcottage.com
E-mail info@celebritybb.com

905-468-4658
TFr 1-866-226-4730

Circa 1871 cottage rental, home of Canadian soprano Maria Rekrut. This "museum within a cottage" is filled with a private collection of art. This charming, non-smoking, two bed/two bath, fully equipped home with full kitchen, offers you all the comforts of home. Self-serve continental breakfast in the fridge. Cable TV, VCR, fireplaces, A/C, deck, patio, BBQ. Steps to theatres, shopping, restaurants, Lake Ontario, wine and bike route. Fifteen minutes to Casino Niagara and Niagara Falls.

ROOMS Ground floor, **Baths** Private, Ensuite, **Beds** King, Queen, **Air** Central, Ceiling fans, **Smoking** Outside, **In Room** Phone, TV, Fireplace, VCR/DVD, **OTHERS** Urban, Adult, Open all year, **PAYMENT** Cheques accepted, Cash, Trvl's cheques, **BREAKFASTS** Self-catered, **AMENITIES** Central TV, Barbecue, Laundry, Kitchen, Fridge, Hot bev. bar, Lounge, Patio, Central VCR/DVD, **THINGS TO DO** Rental bikes, Trail nearby, Golf, Fishing, Museums, Art, Theatre, Entertainment, Attractions, Wineries/ Breweries, Shopping, Cross-country skiing, Tennis, Swimming, Horseback riding, Beach, Birdwatching, Antiquing, **LANGUAGE** Eng., Fr., Sp., Italian, **PRICE** (2 persons) 150–200 **(check with hosts for pricing details)**

NIAGARA-ON-THE-LAKE

Yolanta's B&B

(Yolanta Drzewicki)

596 Simcoe St, Niagara-on-the-Lake, ON, L0S 1J0
www.yolantabb.com
E-mail yolanta@yolantabb.com

905-468-0630
Fax 905-468-5046
TFr 1-866-668-0630

Welcome to our newly decorated bed
and breakfast. We are a short walk from
historic downtown Niagara-on-the-Lake,
nestled in Ontario's prestigious wine
country. We have two beautifully furnished king/twin bedrooms each with
ensuite bathroom facilities for your
comfort and privacy. All rooms are air-
conditioned and are on the ground floor.
Enjoy your own private entrance, relax in
our sitting room by the fire in our smoke-
free home.

ROOMS Ground floor, Private entrance, **Baths** Ensuite,
Beds King, Twin, Single or cots, **Air** Central, **Smoking**
Outside, **In Room** Phone, TV, **OTHERS** Open all year,
PAYMENT Visa, MC, Cheques accepted, Cash, Trvl's
cheques, **BREAKFASTS** Full, Home-baked, **AMENITIES**
Central TV, Central phone, Fridge, Lounge, Patio,
Central VCR/DVD, **THINGS TO DO** Comp. bikes, Rental
bikes, Trail nearby, Golf, Fishing, Museums, Art, Theatre,
Attractions, Wineries/Breweries, Shopping, Cross-
country skiing, Tennis, Birdwatching, Antiquing, **LAN-
GUAGE** Eng., Polish, **PRICE** (2 persons) 115–125
(check with hosts for pricing details)

OAKVILLE *(west of Toronto)*

Melfort Cottage B&B

(Heather Donaldson)

155 Douglas Ave, Oakville, ON, L6J 3R7
www.canvisit.com/00039:WestofTO.2/
E-mail hdonaldson@sympatico.ca

905-849-9729

Melfort Cottage is located in the heart of
old Oakville on a quiet, tree-lined street,
with gardens featured in magazines, HGTV
and garden tours. Everything has been
done to make the rooms as comfortable as
possible; pocket coil mattresses, Egyptian
cotton linens, goose down duvets and cotton quilts. If you have allergies, I will do all
I can to accommodate your needs. I am
a member of the Federation of Ontario
Bed and Breakfast Accommodation
(www.fobba.com) and the Oakville
Chamber of Commerce. If you reserve for
more than one night you receive a reduc-
tion of $10 for each night you stay.

ROOMS Lower floor, **Baths** Private, **Beds** Queen, Twin,
Air Central, **Smoking** Outside, **OTHERS** Open all year,
Pets in residence, **PAYMENT** Visa, MC, Diners, Amex,
Cash, Trvl's cheques, **BREAKFASTS** Full, **AMENITIES**
Central TV, Central phone, Laundry, Fridge, Lounge,
Patio, **THINGS TO DO** Trail nearby, Golf, Museums, Art,
Theatre, Entertainment, Attractions, Shopping, Beach,
LANGUAGE Eng., **PRICE** (2 persons) 100 **(check with
hosts for pricing details)**

ORANGEVILLE
(northwest of Toronto)

In Tir Na Nog Bed & Breakfast
(Rainy O'Halloran and Nick Kosonic)

173510 County Rd 25 N, RR #2, Grand Valley,
ON, L0N 1G0
www.bbcanada.com/8773.html
E-mail nick@intirnanog.com

519-928-2948
Fax 519-928-5931

Our B&B is situated in a well-treed, park-like setting with a pond. Central to fine gourmet fare, fishing, hiking, birding and antiquing. Group rates and picnic lunches are available. We have small seminar facilities and spa packages – call for personal quotes or queries. In Tir Na Nog (In the Land of Eternal Youth) time can stand still.

ROOMS Upper floor, Ground floor, Private entrance, **Baths** Ensuite, Shared with guest, **Beds** Queen, Double, Single or cots, **Smoking** Outside, **In Room** Thermostat, **OTHERS** Rural, Open all year, Handicapped access, Additional meals, **PAYMENT** Cheques accepted, Cash, Trvl's cheques, **BREAKFASTS** Full, Continental, Self-catered, **AMENITIES** Central TV, Swimming pool, Kitchen, Fridge, Hot bev. bar, Lounge, Patio, **THINGS TO DO** Trail nearby, Rental canoe or boat, Golf, Fishing, Museums, Art, Theatre, Entertainment, Shopping, Cross-country skiing, Downhill skiing, Swimming, Birdwatching, Antiquing, **LANGUAGE** Eng., **PRICE** (2 persons) 85–125 **(check with hosts for pricing details)**

ORANGEVILLE

McKitrick House Inn Bed & Breakfast
(William and Sheila Kalyn)

255 Broadway, Orangeville, ON, L9W 1K6
www.mckitrickhouseinn.com
E-mail info@mckitrickhouseinn.com

519-941-0620
Fax 519-941-7966
TFr 1-877-625-4875

Welcome to historical McKitrick House Inn. This beautifully restored Victorian home of former Mayor Alexander McKitrick is furnished with fine antiques, located in Orangeville's Heritage District. Just a stroll away from a myriad of restaurants and shops. Artist studios, spas, hiking, skiing and golfing only a short drive. Relax in the parlour by the fire, curl up with a book in the upper sitting room or sip a cool drink on the cozy verandah. You will feel at home.

ROOMS Upper floor, **Baths** Private, Ensuite, Shared with guest, **Air** Central, In rooms, **Smoking** Outside, **In Room** Phone, TV, Fireplace, VCR/DVD, **OTHERS** Open all year, Pets in residence, Pets welcome, **PAYMENT** Visa, MC, Direct debit, Cash, Trvl's cheques, **BREAKFASTS** Full, Continental, Home-baked, **AMENITIES** Central TV, Central phone, Whirlpool, Barbecue, Laundry, Patio, Central Internet access, Central VCR/DVD, **THINGS TO DO** Rental bikes, Trail nearby, Rental canoe or boat, Golf, Fishing, Museums, Art, Theatre, Entertainment, Attractions, Wineries/Breweries, Shopping, Cross-country skiing, Downhill skiing, Swimming, Horseback riding, Beach, Antiquing, **LANGUAGE** Eng., Ukrainian, **PRICE** (2 persons) 70–170 **(check with hosts for pricing details)**

ORANGEVILLE

The Farm UpCountry HomeStay

(Janet and David Fayle)

2414 Concession Rd 3 Adjala, RR #1, Palgrave, ON, L0N 1P0
www.farmupcountry.com
E-mail fayle@csolve.net

905-729-2989
Fax 905-729-1028

HomeStayers are treated as family in our adaptively restored 1900 Ontario farmhouse with its added 1820/40 Georgian house. Enjoy the gardens, woodlands and trails on our 25 acres near the scenic Hockley Valley. Swim in the creek-fed pool, play unhurried golf on our own 9-hole (five greens) links or cross-country ski. We book only one party at a time so you have the choice of three intimate bedrooms in the farmhouse. Go 7 km north from Hwy 9 on Con Rd 3 Adjala, which is 4 km east of Airport Rd and 4 km west of Hwy 50.

ROOMS Upper floor, Private entrance, **Baths** Private, **Beds** Double, Twin, Single or cots, **In Room** Thermostat, **OTHERS** Rural, Adult, Open all year, Additional meals, Pets in residence, **PAYMENT** Cheques accepted, Cash, Trvl's cheques, **BREAKFASTS** Full, Home-baked, **AMENITIES** Central TV, Central phone, Swimming pool, THINGS **TO DO** Trail nearby, Golf, Fishing, Museums, Art, Entertainment, Attractions, Wineries/Breweries, Shopping, Cross-country skiing, Swimming, **LANGUAGE** Eng., **PRICE** (2 persons) 90 **(check with hosts for pricing details)**

ORILLIA *(north of Toronto)*

B&B on the Lake

(Peter and Marianne Heslin)

5556 Fawn Bay Rd, RR #6 Orillia, ON, L3V 6H6
www.bbonthelake.com
E-mail fawnbaybnb@sympatico.ca

705-326-3650
Fax 705-326-4190

Welcome to the gateway to northern Ontario. We are 90 minutes north of Toronto, on beautiful Lake Couchiching. Enjoy our small private beach or, in the winter, cross-country skiing on the lake. All rooms have their own bathroom and satellite TV. Enjoy the view of the lake while sitting in front of the log burning fireplace. For night life, you can enjoy Casino Rama (2 minutes away), as well as live theatre and a great variety of restaurants. Golf course, driving range and walking trail nearby.

ROOMS Upper floor, **Baths** Ensuite, **Beds** Queen, Twin, Pullout sofa, **Air** Ceiling fans, **Smoking** Outside, **OTHERS** Rural, Open all year, **PAYMENT** Visa, MC, Diners, Amex, Cash, Trvl's cheques, **BREAKFASTS** Full, **AMENITIES** Central TV, Central phone, Barbecue, Laundry, Kitchen, Fridge, Lounge, Patio, Central Internet access, **THINGS TO DO** Comp. bikes, Trail nearby, Comp. Canoe or boat, Golf, Fishing, Museums, Art, Theatre, Entertainment, Attractions, Shopping, Cross-country skiing, Downhill skiing, Tennis, Swimming, Beach, Birdwatching, Antiquing, **LANGUAGE** Eng., Ger., Dutch, **PRICE** (2 persons) 95–125 **(check with hosts for pricing details)**

ORILLIA

Betty and Tony's Waterfront Bed and Breakfast

(Betty and Tony Bridgens)

677 Broadview Ave, Orillia, ON, L3V 6P1
www.bandborillia.com
E-mail betty@bettyandtonys.com

705-326-1125
TFr 1-800-308-2579

Visit Betty and Tony's and enjoy outdoor dining on our waterfront! There is plenty of space and room to breathe, plus a calm harbour for your cruiser, or use our canoe and pedal boat. Unequalled breakfast menu served daily, choose from 10 different hot dishes. The home has central air and all rooms have their own bathrooms. Guests have use of three inside sitting rooms. There is always chocolate cake available when you reserve ahead. Dedicated "staff" – Betty, Tony and Bailey the Chocolate Labrador.

ROOMS Family suite, Lower floor, **Baths** Private, Ensuite, **Beds** King, Queen, Twin, **Air** Central, **Smoking** Outside, **In Room** Thermostat, TV, Internet access, VCR/DVD, **OTHERS** Urban, Pets in residence, Pets welcome, **PAYMENT** Visa, MC, Cheques accepted, Cash, Trvl's cheques, **BREAKFASTS** Full, Home-baked, **AMENITIES** Central TV, Central phone, Barbecue, Laundry, Fridge, Hot bev. bar, Lounge, Patio, Central Internet access, Central VCR/DVD, **THINGS TO DO** Comp. bikes, Trail nearby, Comp. Canoe or boat, Golf, Fishing, Museums, Art, Theatre, Entertainment, Attractions, Shopping, Cross-country skiing, Downhill skiing, Tennis, Swimming, Horseback riding, Beach, Birdwatching, Antiquing, **LANGUAGE** Eng., Fr., **PRICE** (2 persons) 99–145 **(check with hosts for pricing details)**

ORILLIA

Cavana House Bed & Breakfast

(Jennifer Watson and Rudy Pedersen)

241 Mississaga St W, Orillia, ON, L3V 3B7
www.orilliabandb.com
E-mail info@orilliabandb.com

705-327-7759
TFr 1-888-896-3611

Victorian elegance reflecting gracious living. Cavana House is a beautiful restored home, built in 1889 by Ontario Land Surveyor A.G. Cavana. It is decorated with antiques and traditional furnishings featuring modern luxury private ensuites with antique flair. Cavana House is centrally located just a short stroll from Orillia's finest stores, restaurants and waterfront. Relax and enjoy Jennifer's gourmet breakfasts, Rudy's historical touch, the parlour and courtyard and waterfall in the summer.

ROOMS Upper floor, Ground floor, **Baths** Ensuite, **Beds** King, Queen, Double, Single or cots, Pullout sofa, **Air** Central, In rooms, **Smoking** Outside, **In Room** TV, Internet access, **OTHERS** Urban, Adult, Open all year, Additional meals, **PAYMENT** Visa, MC, Direct debit, Cash, **BREAKFASTS** Full, Home-baked, **AMENITIES** Central phone, Barbecue, Fridge, Lounge, Patio, Central Internet access, **THINGS TO DO** Comp. bikes, Trail nearby, Rental canoe or boat, Golf, Fishing, Museums, Theatre, Entertainment, Attractions, Shopping, Cross-country skiing, Downhill skiing, Tennis, Swimming, Horseback riding, Beach, Birdwatching, Antiquing, **LANGUAGE** Eng., **PRICE** (2 persons) 90–129 **(check with hosts for pricing details)**

Orillia

Country Lane B&B
(Carol and Bob Templeton)

1115 Old Barrie Rd E, RR #2, Hawkestone, ON, L0L 1T0
www.countrylanebb.com
E-mail info@countrylanebb.com

705-487-5821
Fax 705-487-6097
TFr 1-877-725-0707

We are close to Hardwood Hills, Horseshoe Valley and Casino Rama, yet in a serene country farm setting. The house is ringed with 100-year-old maples, expansive lawns, orchards and pine and maple forests. The 68 acres offer many opportunities for birdwatching or nature walks. Country Lane includes a 550-sq. ft. country kitchen and is fully air-conditioned. Guests have three spacious bedrooms, one with a two-piece ensuite and two more full bathrooms (one with a Jacuzzi tub), and a guest lounge.

ROOMS Upper floor, **Baths** Ensuite, Shared with guest, **Beds** Queen, Double, Twin, **Air** Central, **Smoking** Outside, **OTHERS** Rural, Open all year, Additional meals, Pets in residence, Pets welcome, **PAYMENT** Visa, MC, Diners, Cheques accepted, Cash, Trvl's cheques, **BREAKFASTS** Full, Home-baked, **AMENITIES** Central TV, Lounge, **THINGS TO DO** Trail nearby, Golf, Theatre, Entertainment, Shopping, Cross-country skiing, Swimming, **PRICE** (2 persons) 75–85 **(check with hosts for pricing details)**

Orillia

Tisdale House Bed & Breakfast
(Bob Brown and Wendy Passmore)

63 Neywash St, Orillia, ON, L3V 1X2
www.tisdalehouse.ca
E-mail wendy.passmore@sympatico.ca

705-323-9715
TFr 1-877-556-4401

Victorian elegance – completely restored in the winter of 2002. You'll be pampered with a candlelight gourmet breakfast served in our gracious dining room. Relax in the lounge, living room, garden or on the back porch. Some book all four rooms and turret for special weekend retreats with family or friends. Once you arrive, there's no need to drive because stores, lake, theatre, antiques, art galleries, golf, hiking trail and restaurants are just a short stroll away ... Casino shuttle too. Gift certificates available.

ROOMS Upper floor, **Baths** Ensuite, **Beds** King, Queen, Twin, **Air** In rooms, **In Room** Thermostat, TV, **OTHERS** Urban, Open all year, **PAYMENT** Visa, MC, Direct debit, Cash, Trvl's cheques, **BREAKFASTS** Full, Home-baked, **AMENITIES** Central TV, Central phone, Barbecue, Kitchen, Fridge, Hot bev. bar, Lounge, Patio, **THINGS TO DO** Rental bikes, Trail nearby, Golf, Fishing, Museums, Art, Theatre, Entertainment, Attractions, Shopping, Cross-country skiing, Swimming, Beach, **LANGUAGE** Eng., **PRICE** (2 persons) 99–119 **(check with hosts for pricing details)**

ORILLIA (BARRIE)
The Verandahs
Bed & Breakfast
(Jacquie and Rolly Riopel)

4 Palm Beach Rd, Hawkestone, ON, L0L 1T0
www.verandahs.com
E-mail jacquie_rolly@rogers.com

705-487-1910
TFr 1-800-841-1019

The Verandahs B&B is waiting to welcome you. Our Victorian-style home sits amid wide lawns surrounded by flowerbeds. Numerous bird houses and feeders provide a wonderful show for our guests during breakfast (indoors or on the verandah). Delicious full breakfasts start with seasonal fruit and freshly brewed coffee. We are happy to accommodate special menu requests. Always available is Verandah's signature big breakfast. Our guest books attest to the comfortable beds in every room.

ROOMS Upper floor, **Baths** Private, Ensuite, **Beds** King, Queen, Twin, Single or cots, **Air** Central, **Smoking** Outside, **OTHERS** Rural, Open all year, Additional meals, **PAYMENT** Visa, MC, Cash, Trvl's cheques, **BREAKFASTS** Full, Home-baked, **AMENITIES** Central TV, Central phone, Fridge, Hot bev. bar, Lounge, Patio, Central Internet access, **THINGS TO DO** Comp. bikes, Trail nearby, Golf, Fishing, Museums, Art, Theatre, Entertainment, Attractions, Shopping, Cross-country skiing, Downhill skiing, Tennis, Swimming, Horseback riding, Beach, Birdwatching, Antiquing, **LANGUAGE** Eng., Fr., **PRICE** (2 persons) 100–110 **(check with hosts for pricing details)**

OSHAWA *(east of Toronto)*
Emerson Manor B&B
(Robert and Michelle Whyte)

132 Stevenson Rd N, Oshawa, ON, L1J 5M5
www.emersonmanor.com
E-mail info@emersonmanor.com

905-579-3766
TFr 1-877-696-3269

Oshawa is the major metropolitan area anchoring the eastern edge of the Greater Toronto Area. Emerson Manor is the oldest B&B in the city. We are centrally located and only minutes from the University of Ontario, VIA and GO trains, GM CHQ, art gallery, paved walking/biking trails, Ontario Power Generation (Pickering and Darlington Plants), Oshawa Airport, banquet halls, and Hwy 401, the Oshawa Generals' Arena, and the major regional shopping mall. Long-term rates available. We welcome you.

ROOMS Family suite, Upper floor, Private entrance, **Baths** Ensuite, **Beds** Queen, Double, **Air** Central, **Smoking** Outside, **In Room** Internet access, **OTHERS** Urban, Open all year, **PAYMENT** Visa, MC, Diners, Cash, Trvl's cheques, **BREAKFASTS** Continental, **AMENITIES** Central TV, Central phone, Whirlpool, Fridge, Hot bev. bar, Lounge, Central VCR/DVD, **THINGS TO DO** Trail nearby, Golf, Museums, Art, Theatre, Entertainment, Wineries/Breweries, Shopping, Cross-country skiing, Downhill skiing, Swimming, Birdwatching, Antiquing, **LANGUAGE** Eng., Polish and some French, **PRICE** (2 persons) 75–125 **(check with hosts for pricing details)**

OTTAWA *(eastern Ontario)*

A Rose on Colonel By B&B

(Ann Sharp, Jeremy Payne and Patrick Guenette)

9 Rosedale Ave, Ottawa, ON, K1S 4T2
www.rosebandb.com
E-mail asharp@cyberus.ca

613-291-7831

We are, happily for you, the only Bed and Breakfast in Ottawa that is centrally located and on the Rideau Canal! Do visit our Web site to see what we offer our invited guests – you won't be disappointed unless we're already fully booked for your dates! Cheers,

Ann, Jeremy and Patrick

ROOMS Upper floor, Private entrance, **Baths** Private, **Air** Ceiling fans, **Smoking** Outside, **In Room** TV, Internet access, **OTHERS** Urban, Open all year, Pets in residence, **PAYMENT** Visa, Amex, Direct debit, Cheques accepted, Cash, Trvl's cheques, **BREAKFASTS** Full, Home-baked, **AMENITIES** Central TV, Central phone, Fridge, Hot bev. bar, Lounge, Central Internet access, **THINGS TO DO** Trail nearby, Rental canoe or boat, Golf, Fishing, Museums, Art, Theatre, Entertainment, Attractions, Wineries/Breweries, Shopping, Cross-country skiing, Downhill skiing, Tennis, Swimming, Horseback riding, Beach, Birdwatching, Antiquing, **LANGUAGE** Eng., Fr., **PRICE** (2 persons) 95–110 **(check with hosts for pricing details)**

OTTAWA

Adele's Family Tree Bed & Breakfast

(Adele Gadde)

171 Glenora St, Ottawa, ON, K1S 1J6
www.adelesfamilytreebb.ca
E-mail awg1@rogers.com

613-237-3660
Fax 613-234-0920
TFr 1-866-233-5372

A historic family home just two blocks from Ottawa's famous Rideau Canal, a year-round attraction for boating, skating and walking. Major museums, theatres, parks, ski trails and hills are all nearby. Our home has three charming guest rooms, each with its own character. Hwy 417 East using Exit 118 (Lees/Main) will bring you to our street, which runs off Clegg St (between Main St and Colonel By Dr). Come and enjoy our ambience; you will be pleasantly surprised.

ROOMS Upper floor, **Baths** Shared with guest, Shared with hosts, **Beds** Queen, Double, Twin, Single or cots, Pullout sofa, **Air** Central, **Smoking** Outside, **In Room** TV, **OTHERS** Open all year, **PAYMENT** Visa, MC, Diners, Amex, Direct debit, Cash, Trvl's cheques, **BREAKFASTS** Full, **AMENITIES** Central TV, Central phone, Laundry, Kitchen, Fridge, Hot bev. bar, Lounge, Patio, Central Internet access, **THINGS TO DO** Rental bikes, Trail nearby, Rental canoe or boat, Golf, Fishing, Museums, Art, Theatre, Entertainment, Attractions, Wineries/Breweries, Shopping, Cross-country skiing, Downhill skiing, Tennis, Swimming, Horseback riding, Beach, Birdwatching, Antiquing, **LANGUAGE** Eng., **PRICE** (2 persons) 75–85 **(check with hosts for pricing details)**

OTTAWA
Allure Bed & Breakfast
(Erin and Anthony Evans)

103 York St, Ottawa, ON, K1N 5T4
www.allurebandb.com
E-mail info@allurebandb.com

613-244-0128
Fax 613-244-0128
TFr 1-877-339-8837

We are conveniently located in the heart of the ByWard Market downtown Ottawa. Step outside the door and you will find over 70 restaurants, bistros and bars, as well as shopping to suit any budget. Just a few steps further are all the major attractions Ottawa has to offer from world-renowned museums and galleries, the Rideau Canal and the beautiful Canadian Parliament buildings. This historic townhouse inn was built in 1882 and recently restored. All guest rooms have been luxuriously furnished including pillowtop mattresses and the finest of European linens, with a private or ensuite bath.

ROOMS Upper floor, Ground floor, **Baths** Private, Ensuite, **Beds** Queen, **Air** Central, **Smoking** Outside, **In Room** TV, Internet access, **OTHERS** Urban, Open all year, **PAYMENT** Visa, MC, Amex, Cheques accepted, Cash, Trvl's cheques, **BREAKFASTS** Full, Home-baked, **AMENITIES** Whirlpool, Fridge, Lounge, Patio, **THINGS TO DO** Rental bikes, Trail nearby, Rental canoe or boat, Golf, Fishing, Museums, Art, Theatre, Entertainment, Attractions, Shopping, Cross-country skiing, Downhill skiing, Tennis, Swimming, Beach, **LANGUAGE** Eng., **PRICE** (2 persons) 100–130 **(check with hosts for pricing details)**

OTTAWA
Ambience Bed and Breakfast
(Maria Giannakos)

330 Nepean St, Ottawa, ON, K1R 5G6
www.ambiencebandb.com
E-mail info@ambiencebandb.com

613-563-0421
TFr 1-888-366-8772

"A Downtown Home with Small Town Warmth." A Victorian home located on a quiet street in the heart of Ottawa. Only a 10-minute walk to Parliament Hill and most tourist attractions, so park your car here and walk everywhere. A private guest entrance leads to four secure bedrooms. Visit our Web site for more details and see what our guests are talking about. Hwy 417, exit Bronson Ave N. At Somerset St turn right. At Bay St turn left. At Nepean St turn right. Come experience Ottawa's ambience.

ROOMS Family suite, Upper floor, Private entrance, **Baths** Private, Ensuite, Shared with guest, **Beds** King, Queen, Twin, Single or cots, **Air** Central, **Smoking** Outside, **In Room** Internet access, **OTHERS** Urban, Open all year, Additional meals, Pets in residence, **PAYMENT** Visa, MC, Amex, Direct debit, Cash, Trvl's cheques, **BREAKFASTS** Full, Home-baked, **AMENITIES** Central TV, Central phone, Fridge, Hot bev. bar, Lounge, Patio, **THINGS TO DO** Rental bikes, Trail nearby, Museums, Art, Theatre, Entertainment, Attractions, Shopping, Cross-country skiing, Tennis, Swimming, Horseback riding, Beach, **LANGUAGE** Eng., Fr., Greek, **PRICE** (2 persons) 75–110 **(check with hosts for pricing details)**

Ottawa

Auberge McGee's Inn

(Ken, Judy, Jason and Sarah Armstrong)

185 Daly Ave, Ottawa, ON, K1N 6E8
www.mcgeesinn.com
E-mail contact@mcgeesinn.com

613-237-6089
Fax 613-237-6201
TFr 1-800-262-4337

Auberge McGee's Inn is located in downtown Ottawa. Abundant in Victorian charm, our B&B offers its travellers all the modern conveniences. Choose from one of our standard rooms each with a private bathroom, to one of our bridal suites, each with a double Jacuzzi tub and fireplace. All our rooms have A/C. Parking and full breakfast are complimentary. McGee's Inn is just steps to the Rideau Canal, the ByWard Market, the Congress Centre, the University of Ottawa and Parliament Hill.

ROOMS Family suite, Upper floor, Ground floor, Private entrance, **Baths** Private, Ensuite, **Beds** King, Queen, Double, Twin, Single or cots, Pullout sofa, **Air** In rooms, Ceiling fans, **Smoking** Outside, **In Room** Phone, TV, Fireplace, Internet access, VCR/DVD, **OTHERS** Urban, Adult, Open all year, **PAYMENT** Visa, MC, Amex, Direct debit, Cash, Trvl's cheques, **BREAKFASTS** Full, Home-baked, **AMENITIES** Whirlpool, Fridge, Lounge, Patio, **THINGS TO DO** Rental bikes, Trail nearby, Rental canoe or boat, Golf, Fishing, Museums, Art, Theatre, Entertainment, Attractions, Shopping, Cross-country skiing, Downhill skiing, Tennis, Swimming, Horseback riding, Beach, Birdwatching, Antiquing, **LANGUAGE** Eng., Fr., Sp., **PRICE** (2 persons) 100–168 **(check with hosts for pricing details)**

Ottawa

Australis Guest House

(Carol and Brian Waters)

35 Marlborough Ave, Ottawa, ON, K1N 8E6
www.australisguesthouse.com
E-mail waters@magma.ca

613-235-8461
Fax 613-235-8461

Oldest Ottawa B&B by Rideau Canal near Parliament. Period house with leaded glass windows, fireplaces, oak floors, 8-foot-high stained glass windows. Spacious rooms, hearty home-cooked breakfasts. Combined Australian, English and Canadian heritages. Off-street-parking. Owner is prize-winning cook, co-author of *Breakfast Companion* cookbook. Star of City Gold Award recipient, recommended by *Newsweek*, *National Geographic Traveller*, appearances on radio, TV and in several national newspapers. Owner is a Rotarian.

ROOMS Family suite, Upper floor, **Baths** Ensuite, Shared with guest, **Beds** Queen, Double, Twin, **OTHERS** Open all year, Pets in residence, **PAYMENT** Cash, Trvl's cheques, **BREAKFASTS** Full, **AMENITIES** Central TV, Central phone, **THINGS TO DO** Trail nearby, Museums, Art, Theatre, Entertainment, Attractions, Shopping, **LANGUAGE** Eng., **PRICE** (2 persons) 65–95 **(check with hosts for pricing details)**

OTTAWA

Benners' Bed and Breakfast
(Merina and John Benner)

541 Besserer St, Ottawa, ON, K1N 6C6
www.bennersbedandbreakfast.com
E-mail jbenner@cyberus.ca

613-789-8320
Fax 613-789-9563
TFr 1-877-891-5485

Location! Location! Location! This B&B is one of the most centrally located in the city on a quiet, beautiful, residential street. It is 1 mile (1.6 km) to the Chateau Laurier and less to the Market area, within walking distance to most major attractions. Each air-conditioned bedroom has a private or ensuite bathroom. Also, each room has cable TV, high-quality furnishings and linen. Access to high-speed wireless Internet is available. Breakfast changes daily and includes a main menu item, fresh fruits, juice and coffee/tea. We can cater to most special dietary requirements if asked in advance.

ROOMS Upper floor, **Baths** Private, Ensuite, **Beds** King, Queen, Double, **Air** Central, **Smoking** Outside, **In Room** TV, Fireplace, Internet access, **OTHERS** Urban, Open all year, Pets in residence, **PAYMENT** Visa, MC, Amex, Direct debit, Cash, Trvl's cheques, **BREAKFASTS** Full, Home-baked, **AMENITIES** Central phone, **THINGS TO DO** Trail nearby, Museums, Art, Theatre, Entertainment, Attractions, Shopping, **LANGUAGE** Eng., Fr., some Spanish, **PRICE** (2 persons) 90–125 **(check with hosts for pricing details)**

OTTAWA

By The Way
(Krystyna and Rafal Przednovek)

310 First Ave, Ottawa, ON, K1S 2G8
www.bytheway.com
E-mail bytheway@magma.ca

613-232-6840

Modern, elegant B&B, with a warm ambience, in downtown Ottawa. Close to most attractions, yet in a quiet historic part of town called Glebe. Walk to the famous Rideau Canal, museums, Carleton University and Parliament. Excellent shops and restaurants. Your stay will be both enjoyable and worthwhile. Ottawa has so much to offer to business or tourist traveller. But don't take our word for it ... come and see it for yourself.

ROOMS Family suite, Upper floor, Ground floor, Private entrance, **Baths** Private, Shared with guest, **Beds** Queen, Twin, **Air** Central, **Smoking** Outside, **In Room** Phone, TV, **OTHERS** Urban, Adult, Open all year, **PAYMENT** Visa, MC, Diners, Amex, Cash, Trvl's cheques, **BREAKFASTS** Full, **AMENITIES** Central TV, Central phone, Kitchen, Fridge, **THINGS TO DO** Trail nearby, Museums, Art, Theatre, Entertainment, Attractions, Shopping, Cross-country skiing, Tennis, Swimming, **LANGUAGE** Eng., Fr., Polish, **PRICE** (2 persons) 90–120 **(check with hosts for pricing details)**

OTTAWA

Country Lane Farm B&B

(Colleen and John Cox)

1772 Frank Kenny Rd, Cumberland, ON, K4C 1N8
www.bbcanada.com/3582.html

613-833-3333

Welcome home to the country! Our farm is home to naturally raised Scottish Highland Cattle. We offer restful surroundings, Ottawa Valley fifth generation hospitality and full country breakfasts. Minutes from downtown Parliament Hill, museums, shopping and beaches. Whether day-tripping, stargazing or front porch sitting ... what could be simpler ... what could be better! We are located in Ottawa's rural east end. Queensway (174) to Trim, then Old Montreal Rd to Frank Kenny. Reservations please.

ROOMS Upper floor, **Baths** Shared with guest, **Beds** Queen, Twin, **Air** Central, Ceiling fans, **In Room** Thermostat, **OTHERS** Rural, Pets in residence, **PAYMENT** Cheques accepted, Cash, Trvl's cheques, **BREAKFASTS** Full, **AMENITIES** Central TV, Central phone, **THINGS TO DO** Museums, Art, Theatre, Entertainment, Shopping, Tennis, Swimming, Horseback riding, Beach, Birdwatching, Antiquing, **LANGUAGE** Eng., **PRICE** (2 persons) 100 **(check with hosts for pricing details)**

OTTAWA

Gasthaus Switzerland Inn

(Sabina and Josef Sauter)

89 Daly Ave, Ottawa, ON, K1N 6E6
www.ottawainn.com
E-mail info@ottawainn.com

613-237-0335
Fax 613-594-3327
TFr 1-888-663-0000

"A touch of Switzerland in Downtown Ottawa." Offering warm, cozy and intimate accommodations from standard to luxuriously appointed rooms and honeymoon suites with all modern amenities. This 22-room upscale B&B/inn has been welcoming guests since 1985, offering a unique combination of friendly, traditional Swiss hospitality with privacy and personal charm. On historic Daly Ave; only two blocks from the University of Ottawa, Ottawa Congress Centre, ByWard Market. Walk to all major attractions. Free Wi-fi Internet.

ROOMS Upper floor, Ground floor, Lower floor, Private entrance, **Baths** Private, Ensuite, **Beds** King, Queen, Double, Twin, **Air** Central, In rooms, **Smoking** Outside, **In Room** Thermostat, Phone, TV, Fireplace, Internet access, **OTHERS** Open all year, **PAYMENT** Visa, MC, Diners, Amex, Cash, Trvl's cheques, **BREAKFASTS** Full, Home-baked, **AMENITIES** Laundry, Lounge, Patio, Central Internet access, **THINGS TO DO** Rental bikes, Trail nearby, Golf, Museums, Art, Theatre, Entertainment, Attractions, Shopping, Cross-country skiing, Downhill skiing, Tennis, Swimming, Horseback riding, Beach, Birdwatching, Antiquing, **LANGUAGE** Eng., Fr., Sp., Ger., **PRICE** (2 persons) 108–248 **(check with hosts for pricing details)**

OTTAWA

L'Auberge du Marché
(Nicole Faubert and JJ Charlebois)

87 Guigues St, Ottawa, ON, K1N 5H8
www.aubergedumarche.ca
E-mail info@aubergedumarche.ca

613-241-6610
TFr 1-800-465-0079

Located in the heart of scenic downtown Ottawa, in the historic area known as the ByWard Market. Here you have it all. No need to drive. We are 10 minutes to the Parliament Buildings, the National Arts Centre and the 300-store shopping mall, the Rideau Centre. Directions: take Nicholas St exit from the Queensway (Hwy 417), keep left and take Dalhousie, turn left on St. Patrick. At next light turn right on Parent, then turn right on Guigues, the next street.

ROOMS Family suite, Upper floor, Ground floor, Private entrance, **Baths** Ensuite, Shared with guest, **Beds** Queen, Double, **Air** Central, **Smoking** Outside, **OTHERS** Urban, Open all year, **PAYMENT** Visa, MC, Direct debit, Cash, Trvl's cheques, **BREAKFASTS** Full, Home-baked, **AMENITIES THINGS TO DO** Rental bikes, Trail nearby, Rental canoe or boat, Golf, Fishing, Museums, Art, Theatre, Entertainment, Attractions, Shopping, Cross-country skiing, Downhill skiing, Tennis, **LANGUAGE** Eng., Fr., **PRICE** (2 persons) 80–119 **(check with hosts for pricing details)**

OTTAWA

Rideau Inn
(Laura Depper)

177 Frank St, Ottawa, ON, K2P 0X4
www.rideauinn.ca
E-mail 2005@rogers.com

613-688-2753
TFr 1-877-580-5015

A charming 1916 Edwardian B&B in the heart of the nation's vibrant capital. We offer seven guestrooms, two with private ensuite baths, five others sharing four baths, guest parlour and fireplace, dining room, equipped kitchen, verandah and roof deck. Enjoy free local calls, cable, TV/VCR, video library, daily newspaper, all-you-can-enjoy breakfast buffet, laundry service, no-smoking, adults only, no pets, e-mail access, bike and skate rental, parking and more. Close to busy Elgin St restaurants and attractions. Toronto phone number: 416-351-1503.

ROOMS Upper floor, Private entrance, **Baths** Private, Ensuite, Shared with guest, **Beds** King, Queen, Double, Twin, Single or cots, **Air** Central, **Smoking** Outside, **In Room** TV, Fireplace, **OTHERS** Urban, Adult, Open all year, **PAYMENT** Visa, MC, Diners, Cash, Trvl's cheques, **BREAKFASTS** Full, Home-baked, **AMENITIES** Central TV, Barbecue, Laundry, Kitchen, Fridge, Lounge, Patio, **THINGS TO DO** Rental bikes, Trail nearby, Museums, Art, Theatre, Entertainment, Attractions, Shopping, Tennis, Swimming, **LANGUAGE** Eng., Fr., **PRICE** (2 persons) 70–110 **(check with hosts for pricing details)**

Owen Sound *(northwest of Toronto)*

B & C Moses Sunset Country Bed & Breakfast

(Cecilie and Bill Moses)

398139 28th Ave E, RR #6, Owen Sound,
ON, N4K 5N8
www.bmts.com/~moses
E-mail moses@bmts.com

519-371-4559

Ours is the longest established B&B in the Owen Sound area. Guests enjoy sleeping in, casual breakfasts and relaxing at our picturesque 40-acre property. Easily found, we are 1.5 km south of the 8th St E and 28th Ave E intersection; 2.4 km south of Hwy 26 on 28th Ave E; from Hwy 10, turn east on 8th St E, then right (south) on 28th Ave E and proceed 1.4 km. We are on the east side of the road, fire number 398139. Our cell phone is 519-387-4559.

ROOMS Family suite, Ground floor, Private entrance, **Baths** Private, Ensuite, Shared with guest, **Beds** King, Double, Twin, Single or cots, Pullout sofa, **Air** In rooms, Ceiling fans, **Smoking** Outside, **In Room** Thermostat, Phone, TV, Fireplace, VCR/DVD, **OTHERS** Rural, Open all year, **PAYMENT** Cash, Trvl's cheques, **BREAKFASTS** Full, Home-baked, Self-catered, **AMENITIES** Central TV, Central phone, Barbecue, Kitchen, Fridge, Hot bev. bar, Lounge, Patio, Central VCR/DVD, **THINGS TO DO** Trail nearby, Rental canoe or boat, Golf, Fishing, Museums, Art, Theatre, Entertainment, Attractions, Shopping, Cross-country skiing, Downhill skiing, Tennis, Swimming, Beach, Birdwatching, Antiquing, **LANGUAGE** Eng., **PRICE** (2 persons) 55–95 **(check with hosts for pricing details)**

Owen Sound

The Highland Manor Grand Victorian B&B

(Linda Bradford and Paul Neville)

867 4th Ave A W, Owen Sound, ON, N4K 6L5
www.highlandmanor.ca
E-mail info@highlandmanor.ca

519-372-2699
TFr 1-877-372-2699

Our 7,500-sq. ft. Victorian mansion, built in 1872, is an oasis of calm, providing an elegant yet relaxed setting for adults in search of a tranquil getaway. The house sits majestically atop the west hill of Owen Sound, Ontario, overlooking Georgian Bay and the historic city below. The second floor, for guests only, provides spacious rooms with queen beds, ensuite baths and fireplaces. A full breakfast is served in the opulent style of the formal estate dining room. A warm welcome awaits you!

ROOMS Upper floor, **Baths** Ensuite, **Beds** Queen, **In Room** Fireplace, **OTHERS** Urban, Adult, Open all year, **PAYMENT** Visa, MC, Amex, Cash, Trvl's cheques, **BREAKFASTS** Full, Home-baked, **AMENITIES** Central TV, Central phone, Fridge, Lounge, Patio, Central Internet access, Central VCR/DVD, **THINGS TO DO** Trail nearby, Golf, Fishing, Museums, Art, Theatre, Entertainment, Attractions, Shopping, Cross-country skiing, Tennis, Swimming, Horseback riding, Beach, Birdwatching, Antiquing, **LANGUAGE** Eng., **PRICE** (2 persons) 120–160 **(check with hosts for pricing details)**

PALMER RAPIDS *(east of Algonquin Park)*

Wingle Inn
(Luciana and Tino Costa)

261 Wingle Rd, Palmer Rapids, ON, K0J 2E0
www.wingleinn.com
E-mail wingleinn@mv.igs.net

613-758-2072
Fax 613-758-9925
TFr 1-866-339-9909

The triple-gabled Wingle Inn, made famous in a painting by A.J.Casson, one of Canada's Group of Seven, is a 140-year-old stone farmhouse located in the beautiful Madawaska Valley. A small establishment, we offer bed and breakfast accommodations as well as evening meals featuring Italian cuisine – fine dining in a rustic setting. The view is breathtaking and the serenity is palpable – a little piece of heaven on earth. Take Hwy 28 to 514 past Schutt, turn right at Cedar Grove Rd, then left on Wingle.

ROOMS Upper floor, Ground floor, Private entrance, **Baths** Ensuite, Shared with guest, **Beds** King, Queen, Double, Twin, Pullout sofa, **Smoking** Outside, **OTHERS** Rural, Open all year, Additional meals, Pets in residence, **PAYMENT** Visa, MC, Direct debit, Cash, Trvl's cheques, **BREAKFASTS** Full, **AMENITIES** Fridge, **THINGS TO DO** Rental bikes, Trail nearby, Rental canoe or boat, Golf, Fishing, Museums, Art, Shopping, Cross-country skiing, Swimming, Horseback riding, Beach, **LANGUAGE** Eng., Fr., Ger., Italian, **PRICE** (2 persons) 75–125 **(check with hosts for pricing details)**

PARIS *(west of Hamilton)*

Domes on the Grand
(Ted and Debbie Whitelaw)

272 West River Rd, Paris, ON, N3L 3E2
www.domesonthegrand.ca
E-mail debbie@domesonthegrand.ca

519-442-5641

Domes on the Grand offers you country living at its best. You can enjoy the many attractions and activities offered around the area. Canoeing, kayaking, biking and hiking. If you love shopping, we have the best little shops in Paris.

ROOMS Family suite, Upper floor, Ground floor, Private entrance, **Baths** Private, Ensuite, **Beds** King, Ceiling fans, Twin, **Air** Central, Ceiling fans, **Smoking** Outside, **OTHERS** Rural, Open all year, Pets in residence, **PAYMENT** Visa, MC, Amex, Direct debit, Cheques accepted, Cash, Trvl's cheques, **BREAKFASTS** Full, Continental, Home-baked, Self-catered, **AMENITIES** Central TV, Central phone, Kitchen, Fridge, Hot bev. bar, Lounge, Patio, **THINGS TO DO** Comp. bikes, Trail nearby, Comp. canoe or boat, Golf, Fishing, Theatre, Entertainment, Attractions, Shopping, Cross-country skiing, Downhill skiing, Tennis, Swimming, Horseback riding, Birdwatching, Antiquing, **LANGUAGE** Eng., **PRICE** (2 persons) 130 **(check with hosts for pricing details)**

Paris

River Ridge Bed and Breakfast
(Paul and Cathy Dawson)

232 West River Rd, RR #2, Paris, ON, N3L 3E2
www.riverridgeretreat.com
E-mail rrbedandbreakfast@bellnet.ca

519-442-0996
Fax 519-442-1909
TFr 1-866-286-7722

We like sharing our 150-year-old farm-house with others who enjoy the feel of rural days gone by that is enhanced by our antique furnishings. Yet each room offers luxurious comfort – pillowtop mattresses, A/C and satellite TV. Our 11-acre property offers a view of horse paddocks and a backdrop of Carolinian forest. Take a stroll on the marked trail (bring your rubber boots) down to our boardwalk on the west bank of the heritage Grand River. Please visit our Web site or give us a call to learn more!

ROOMS Family suite, Upper floor, Ground floor, **Baths** Private, Ensuite, Shared with guest, **Beds** Queen, Double, Twin, Single or cots, Pullout sofa, **Air** In rooms, Ceiling fans, **Smoking** Outside, **In Room** Thermostat, TV, Fireplace, VCR/DVD, **OTHERS** Babysitting, Rural, Open all year, Pets in residence, **PAYMENT** Visa, MC, Cheques accepted, Cash, Trvl's cheques, **BREAKFASTS** Full, Continental, Home-baked, **AMENITIES** Central phone, Swimming pool, Whirlpool, Kitchen, Fridge, Hot bev. bar, Lounge, Patio, Central Internet access, **THINGS TO DO** Rental bikes, Trail nearby, Rental canoe or boat, Golf, Fishing, Museums, Art, Theatre, Attractions, Shopping, Cross-country skiing, Downhill skiing, Tennis, Swimming, Horseback riding, Birdwatching, Antiquing, **LANGUAGE** Eng., Fr., **PRICE** (2 persons) 60–125 **(check with hosts for pricing details)**

Parry Sound [Pointe au Baril]
(north of Toronto)

Eye of the Eagle Retreat and B&B/Spa
(Ann and Rod Kelly)

Box 13, Hwy 529A #160, Pointe au Baril, ON, P0G 1K0
www.eyeoftheeagle.net
E-mail Website@eyeoftheeagle.net

705-366-5666
Fax 705-366-2603
TFr 1-866-366-3245

Eye of the Eagle is an intimate and a cozy getaway that pampers you in every way, from our exclusive deluxe bedrooms with private ensuites, to our delectable meals and spa services. We offer all-inclusive packages which include accommodations, meals, spa services, outdoor spa/hot tub, hiking/snowshoeing trails and beautiful gardens. Book our Couples Signature Hot Stone Massage that allows you to relax and rekindle the flame. Located a short distance north of Parry Sound.

ROOMS Upper floor, **Baths** Ensuite, **Beds** King, Queen, Twin, Single or cots, **Air** Central, **Smoking** Outside, **In Room** Thermostat, TV, VCR/DVD, **OTHERS** Rural, Adult, Open all year, Additional meals, Pets in residence, **PAYMENT** Visa, MC, Cash, Trvl's cheques, **BREAKFASTS** Full, **AMENITIES** Central TV, Central phone, Whirlpool, Barbecue, Lounge, **THINGS TO DO** Comp. bikes, Trail nearby, Rental canoe or boat, Golf, Fishing, Theatre, Attractions, Cross-country skiing, Swimming, Horseback riding, Beach, Birdwatching, **LANGUAGE** Eng., **PRICE** (2 persons) 99–129 **(check with hosts for pricing details)**

PELEE ISLAND *(southwestern Ontario)*

It's Home
(Madonna Gemus)

1431 East Shore Rd, Pelee Island, ON, N0R 1M0
www.itshome.net
E-mail welcome@itshome.net

519-737-6038

Adults are warmly welcomed to It's Home
B&B on Pelee Island by hosts Madonna
and Butch Gemus. You'll find beautifully
appointed bedrooms, guest sitting room
and screened-in porch that leads to the
patio just steps from Lake Erie's sandy
beach. Full breakfast is served with every
attention to detail in a convivial atmosphere. With your vehicle, visit historic
sites, restaurants, the winery and then
return to rest or stroll the beach. Whatever the weather, you'll like the climate
at It's Home. Alternate telephone: 519-
724-2328.

ROOMS Ground floor, Private entrance, **Baths** Shared
with guest, **Beds** King, Double, Twin, Single or cots, **Air**
Ceiling fans, **Smoking** Outside, **In Room** TV, Fireplace,
OTHERS Adult, Handicapped access, Seasonal, **PAY-
MENT** Cheques accepted, Cash, Trvl's cheques,
BREAKFASTS Full, Home-baked, **AMENITIES** Central
TV, Fridge, Hot bev. bar, Lounge, Patio, Central Internet
access, **THINGS TO DO** Comp. bikes, Trail nearby, Art,
Wineries/Breweries, Swimming, Beach, Birdwatching,
LANGUAGE Eng., Fr., **PRICE** (2 persons) 69–75 **(check
with hosts for pricing details)**

PELEE ISLAND

Twin Oaks Retreat
Bed and Breakfast
(Gail and Jim)

751 East West Rd, Pelee Island, ON, N0R 1M0
www.peleeisland.net
E-mail twinoaks@peleeisland.net

519-724-2434
TFr 1-877-735-3366

A spacious century farmhouse situated
on 14 acres, with a variety of trees including the rare Chinquapin Oaks. Spend time
on our large enclosed verandah; listen to
the sounds of nature and enjoy Gail's
famous homemade biscuits and our full
breakfast (self-catered on some days).
Rooms with private baths and our deluxe
Jacuzzi suite available. Our suite includes
a fridge, TV/VCR, separate entrance with
balcony and air-conditioning. Groups,
retreats and family reunions welcome.

ROOMS Family suite, Upper floor, Ground floor, Private
entrance, **Baths** Private, Ensuite, Shared with guest,
Beds King, Queen, Double, Single or cots, **Air** In
rooms, **Smoking** Outside, **In Room** Thermostat, TV,
OTHERS Rural, Seasonal, **PAYMENT** Visa, MC, Amex,
Cash, Trvl's cheques, **BREAKFASTS** Full, Home-baked,
Self-catered, **AMENITIES** Central phone, Whirlpool,
Fridge, Lounge, Patio, **THINGS TO DO** Rental bikes,
Trail nearby, Rental canoe or boat, Fishing, Museums,
Wineries/Breweries, Swimming, Beach, **LANGUAGE**
Eng., **PRICE** (2 persons) 85–170 **(check with hosts for
pricing details)**

PEMBROKE *(northwest of Ottawa)*

Booth House Inn
(Wendy Webster)

272 Pembroke St E, Pembroke, ON, K8A 3K1
www.bbcanada.com/5564.html
E-mail boothhouseinn@hotmail.com

613-735-1151
Fax 613-735-8000

Majestic Victorian century home, in centre town. Walk to marina, restaurants, shops. Close to Algonquin Park. In the heart of whitewater country; 150 km from Ottawa. Escape back in time surrounded by original period furniture, stroll the spacious grounds, relax by the fire. See the spectacular fall colours. Skiing and snowmobiling nearby. Enjoy the magnificent Ottawa River. Perfect setting for weddings, photo shoots, family gatherings. Perfect weekend getaway. Quiet and peaceful atmosphere.

ROOMS Family suite, Upper floor, **Baths** Private, Shared with guest, **Beds** Queen, Double, Twin, Single or cots, Pullout sofa, **Air** In rooms, **Smoking** Outside, **In Room** Thermostat, Phone, TV, **OTHERS** Urban, Open all year, **PAYMENT** Cheques accepted, Cash, Trvl's cheques, **BREAKFASTS** Continental, **AMENITIES** Central TV, Central phone, Laundry, Lounge, Patio, **THINGS TO DO** Trail nearby, Rental canoe or boat, Golf, Fishing, Museums, Art, Theatre, Attractions, Shopping, Cross-country skiing, Tennis, Swimming, Horseback riding, Beach, **LANGUAGE** Eng., **PRICE** (2 persons) 70–90 **(check with hosts for pricing details)**

PENETANGUISHENE *(north of Toronto)*

Toanche Cove B&B
(Shirley Sears and Paul Finucan)

604 Champlain Rd, RR #2, Penetanguishene, ON, L9M 1R2
www.toanchecove.com
E-mail toanchecove@sympatico.ca

705-549-6994
Fax 705-549-9738
TFr 1-866-705-0093

Our B&B is located on beautiful Penetanguishene Bay, gateway to the 30, 000 Islands of Georgian Bay, and has a lovely view over the Bay to Discovery Harbour. The B&B part of the house is upstairs, with charming decor and private from our living area downstairs. There is a great room with a breakfast area, sitting area and a walkout to the balcony for the enjoyment of our guests. Boating, snowmobiling and cross-country skiing at our doorstep. Guest comments: "A wonderful, cosy, elegant place to spend a few days".

ROOMS Upper floor, Private entrance, **Baths** Ensuite, Shared with guest, **Beds** King, Queen, Double, Single or cots, **Air** In rooms, **Smoking** Outside, **In Room** TV, VCR/DVD, **OTHERS** Rural, Pets in residence, **PAYMENT** Cheques accepted, Cash, Trvl's cheques, **BREAKFASTS** Full, Self-catered, **AMENITIES** Central phone, Fridge, Patio, **THINGS TO DO** Trail nearby, Rental canoe or boat, Golf, Fishing, Museums, Art, Theatre, Entertainment, Attractions, Shopping, Cross-country skiing, Downhill skiing, Swimming, Beach, Birdwatching, Antiquing, **LANGUAGE** Eng., **PRICE** (2 persons) 75–99 **(check with hosts for pricing details)**

PETERBOROUGH *(northeast of Toronto)*

Golden Pathways Retreat and B&B

(Cora and David Whittington)

RR #11, 3075 Wallace Pt Rd, Peterborough, ON, K9J 6Y3
www.goldenpathways.ca
E-mail cw@goldenpathways.ca

705-745-4006
Fax 705-745-0807
TFr 1-866-287-2317

Just minutes from Peterborough and you feel you are world away. Peaceful and calming, situated on 195 picturesque acres near the Otonabee River. Warm hospitality and homecooked breakfast with amazing scenic views. Enjoy cozy bedrooms, kitchen, cafe and gathering room. Take pleasure in the inviting porch, swing, sunsets, private patio, cascading water garden, pristine meadows, forests and walking paths. Ideal for getaways, retreats and meetings, or personal rest and rejuvenation.

ROOMS Ground floor, Private entrance, **Baths** Private, Shared with guest, **Beds** King, Queen, Double, Twin, Pullout sofa, **Air** Central, **Smoking** Outside, **In Room** Phone, **OTHERS** Rural, Open all year, Additional meals, **PAYMENT** Visa, Direct debit, Cheques accepted, Cash, Trvl's cheques, **BREAKFASTS** Full, **AMENITIES** Central TV, Central phone, Barbecue, Kitchen, Hot bev. bar, Lounge, Patio, **THINGS TO DO** Trail nearby, Comp. Canoe or boat, Golf, Fishing, Museums, Art, Theatre, Entertainment, Attractions, Shopping, Cross-country skiing, Swimming, Beach, **LANGUAGE** Eng., **PRICE** (2 persons) 85–110 **(check with hosts for pricing details)**

PETERBOROUGH

Hunter Farm B&B

(Ruth and Terry Hunter)

RR #9, 2590 Hwy 28 (formerly Hwy 134), Peterborough, ON, K9J 6Y1
www.whockey.com/hunterfarm
E-mail hunterfarm@peterboro.net

705-295-6253 Fax 705-295-6253

Charming Victorian farmhouse with antiques, verandahs, sunroom, family room and fireplace. Choice of shared baths or ensuites. Private setting on 245 picturesque acres with farm animals, ponds, canoeing, wildlife sanctuary, hiking and biking trails, winter skiing, skating and sleighing. A warm welcome with a hearty farm breakfast. The Kawartha Lakes Vacation Area has Indian crafts and petroglyphs, a pioneer village and a canoe museum. Location: 150 km east of Toronto, 8 km east of Peterborough and 2 km north on Hwy 28 (formerly Hwy 134).

ROOMS Family suite, Upper floor, Private entrance, **Baths** Ensuite, Shared with guest, Shared with hosts, **Beds** King, Queen, Double, Twin, Single or cots, Pullout sofa, **Smoking** Outside, **In Room** Thermostat, TV, **OTHERS** Rural, Open all year, Additional meals, Pets welcome, **PAYMENT** Cheques accepted, Cash, Trvl's cheques, **BREAKFASTS** Full, Home-baked, **AMENITIES** Central TV, Central phone, Whirlpool, Laundry, Kitchen, Fridge, Lounge, Patio, Central Internet access, Central VCR/DVD, **THINGS TO DO** Comp. bikes, Rental bikes, Trail nearby, Rental canoe or boat, Comp. Canoe or boat, Golf, Fishing, Museums, Art, Theatre, Entertainment, Attractions, Shopping, Cross-country skiing, Downhill skiing, Tennis, Swimming, Horseback riding, Beach, Birdwatching, Antiquing, **LANGUAGE** Eng., **PRICE** (2 persons) 70–125 **(check with hosts for pricing details)**

Peterborough

King Bethune House Guest House & Spa

(Marlis Lindsay)

270 King St, Peterborough, ON, K9J 2S2
www.kingbethunehouse.com
E-mail marlis@sympatico.ca

705-743-4101
TFr 1-800-574-3664

Spacious century home on a quiet street in downtown. Built in 1890s, warmed by generous use of woods, lovingly restored with ensuite baths in keyed rooms with king and queen beds, European duvets, Aveda toiletries and better amenities than most first-class hotels. Tranquil garden. Summer fireside evenings, afternoon in the hammock. Choose the Spa Suite and after a massage go to bed or relax in your private hot tub, sauna or steam room, all private to your suite. Massage by appointment. CAA/AAA. Day spa.

ROOMS Family suite, Upper floor, Lower floor, Private entrance, **Baths** Ensuite, **Beds** King, Queen, **Air** Central, **Smoking** Outside, **In Room** Phone, TV, VCR/DVD, **OTHERS** Urban, Open all year, Additional meals, Pets welcome, **PAYMENT** Visa, MC, Amex, Cheques accepted, Cash, Trvl's cheques, **BREAKFASTS** Full, **AMENITIES** Sauna, Whirlpool, Fridge, Hot bev. bar, Lounge, Patio, **THINGS TO DO** Comp. bikes, Rental bikes, Trail nearby, Rental canoe or boat, Comp. canoe or boat, Golf, Fishing, Museums, Art, Theatre, Entertainment, Attractions, Wineries/Breweries, Shopping, Cross-country skiing, Downhill skiing, Tennis, Swimming, Horseback riding, Beach, Birdwatching, Antiquing, **LANGUAGE** Eng., Fr., **PRICE** (2 persons) 94–220 **(check with hosts for pricing details)**

Peterborough

Liftlock Bed and Breakfast

(Doreen Davies)

810 Canal Rd, Peterborough, ON, K9L 1A1
www.liftlock-bed-and-breakfast.com
E-mail liftlock-bb@cogeco.ca

705-742-0110
TFr 1-866-717-7707

Located on the water (Trent Canal) within walking distance of downtown Peterborough, 6 acres of serene privacy. This luxurious lodging has ground floor, outside keyed entrances. Each suite boasts ensuite bath, A/C, cable TV, pillowtop beds, table/chairs, Living room furnishings. Pet-friendly. Wheelchair accessible. Swimming, boating/fishing onsite. In winter, skating below the liftlocks, snowbobiling or skiing on the canal. Special zoning lets us include two sika deer and German shepherd dogs as pets.

ROOMS Family suite, Ground floor, Private entrance, **Baths** Ensuite, **Beds** King, Queen, Twin, Single or cots, Pullout sofa, **Air** In rooms, **Smoking** Outside, **In Room** Thermostat, TV, Fireplace, Internet access, **OTHERS** Urban, Rural, Open all year, Handicapped access, Pets in residence, Pets welcome, **PAYMENT** Visa, MC, Cheques accepted, Cash, Trvl's cheques, **BREAKFASTS** Full, Self-catered, **AMENITIES** Swimming pool, Patio, **THINGS TO DO** Trail nearby, Rental canoe or boat, Comp. canoe or boat, Golf, Fishing, Museums, Art, Theatre, Entertainment, Attractions, Shopping, Cross-country skiing, Swimming, **LANGUAGE** Eng., **PRICE** (2 persons) 115–150 **(check with hosts for pricing details)**

PETERBOROUGH

McLeod House

(Anna Jean Buchanan)

486 Albertus Ave, Peterborough, ON, K9J 6A2
www.bbcanada.com/4795.html
E-mail mcleodhouse@hotmail.com

705-742-5330

Gracious older home in Peterborough's
Old West End, tastefully decorated with
antiques, on a quiet street with three
guest rooms. You can walk to downtown,
to the Regional Hospital and to the Trans-
Canada Trail. Other attractions include
Trent University, Fleming College, Canoe
Museum, Liftlocks, Saturday farmer's market and good golf courses. We are near a
city bus route. Pickup transportation can
be arranged from the bus station and airport. Phone for directions.

ROOMS Upper floor, **Baths** Shared with guest, Shared
with hosts, **Beds** Double, Twin, Single or cots, **Air**
Central, **Smoking** Outside, **In Room** Phone, **OTHERS**
Urban, Adult, Open all year, Pets welcome, **PAYMENT**
Cheques accepted, Cash, Trvl's cheques, **BREAKFASTS**
Full, **AMENITIES** Central TV, Central phone, Lounge,
Patio, **THINGS TO DO** Trail nearby, Golf, Fishing,
Museums, Art, Theatre, Shopping, Cross-country ski-
ing, Swimming, **LANGUAGE** Eng., **PRICE** (2 persons)
50–70 **(check with hosts for pricing details)**

PETERBOROUGH

Resonance Bed & Breakfast and Spa

(Anna and Bob Keating)

1125 Division Rd, RR #1, Douro, ON, K0L 1S0
www.resonance-retreat.ca
E-mail resonance@sympatico.ca

705-742-6885 Fax 705-742-6388

At Resonance you will discover a luxurious
nest of privacy, comfort, grace, humour and
love awaiting you. Stay in the Serenity Suite
– your very own charming, private log
cabin built in the early 1800s and refurbished to luxurious standards is located
across the laneway from the main house
and has all the amenities you will need.
Snuggle by the fire. Relax in the private spa.
Enjoy unhurried, delectable breakfasts.
Walk in our pastoral 79-acre retreat. Enjoy
our peaceful and restorative country location. Only 12 minutes east of Peterborough
or 12 minutes south of Lakefield. We
request a minimum two-night booking.

ROOMS Ground floor, Private entrance, **Baths** Private,
Ensuite, **Beds** King, **Air** Central, **Smoking** Outside, **In
Room** Thermostat, Phone, TV, Fireplace, Internet
access, VCR/DVD, **OTHERS** Rural, Adult, Open all year,
PAYMENT Visa, MC, Diners, Amex, Cheques accepted,
Cash, **BREAKFASTS** Full, **AMENITIES** Swimming pool,
Whirlpool, Barbecue, Kitchen, Fridge, Hot bev. bar,
Patio, **THINGS TO DO** Comp. bikes, Trail nearby, Comp.
canoe or boat, Golf, Fishing, Museums, Art, Theatre,
Entertainment, Attractions, Shopping, Cross-country
skiing, Downhill skiing, Tennis, Swimming, Horseback
riding, Beach, Birdwatching, Antiquing, **LANGUAGE**
Eng., Fr., Sp., Italian, Serbian, **PRICE** (2 persons)
150–175 **(check with hosts for pricing details)**

Peterborough
Shining Waters
Bed &Breakfast & Spa
(Susan Castle)

1364 3rd Line Rd, RR #2, Lakefield, ON, K0L 2H0
www.shiningwatersbb.com
E-mail ssncastle@yahoo.com

705-652-1057
Fax 705-652-1057

Our 55 scenic acres overlooking the Indian River inspire tranquility at this 170-year-old Georgian stone house with a log addition. Victorian decor is accented by antiques. Romantic queen suites feature down-filled duvets, Jacuzzis, wood stoves and TV. A full, delicious breakfast is served in the dining room or on the terrace. A kennel is available to those travelling with pets. Spa treatments available onsite. There are 3 km of trails for skiing, walking or birdwatching, and kayaking packages are also popular.

ROOMS Family suite, Upper floor, Ground floor, **Baths** Private, Ensuite, Shared with guest, **Beds** Queen, Twin, **Air** Central, In rooms, **Smoking** Outside, **In Room** TV, Fireplace, **OTHERS** Rural, Open all year, Additional meals, Pets in residence, **PAYMENT** Visa, MC, Direct debit, Cash, Trvl's cheques, **BREAKFASTS** Full, Home-baked, **AMENITIES** Central TV, Central phone, Whirlpool, Fridge, Hot bev. bar, Lounge, Patio, Central Internet access, Central VCR/DVD, **THINGS TO DO** Trail nearby, Comp. canoe or boat, Golf, Fishing, Museums, Art, Theatre, Attractions, Wineries/Breweries, Shopping, Cross-country skiing, Swimming, Horseback riding, Beach, **LANGUAGE** Eng., **PRICE** (2 persons) 60–160 **(check with hosts for pricing details)**

Peterborough
Summit Bed and Breakfast
(Eleanor Hayne)

1167 Summit Dr, Peterborough, ON, K9J 8A8
www.summitbedandbreakfast.ca
E-mail dhayne@cogeco.ca

705-743-2777
TFr 1-800-297-6105

Summit Bed & Breakfast offers: Newly renovated self contained ground level apartment, two bedrooms, a large family room, TV, gas fireplace and kitchenette. A large bed sitting room with TV, large bathroom with over size tub. Two guest rooms, one with single bed and the other with a double. We overlook the Kawartha Golf and Country club and are surrounded by English gardens. All rooms are air-conditioned. We offer a full breakfast. Smoke- and pet-free environment. Minutes to downtown and hospital.

ROOMS Family suite, Upper floor, Ground floor, Private entrance, **Baths** Private, Ensuite, Shared with guest, **Beds** Queen, Double, Twin, Single or cots, **Air** Central, **In Room** Thermostat, Phone, TV, Fireplace, **OTHERS** Open all year, **PAYMENT** Cheques accepted, Cash, Trvl's cheques, **BREAKFASTS** Full, Home-baked, **AMENITIES** Central TV, Central phone, Kitchen, Fridge, Lounge, Patio, **THINGS TO DO** Rental bikes, Trail nearby, Rental canoe or boat, Golf, Fishing, Museums, Art, Theatre, Entertainment, Attractions, Shopping, Cross-country skiing, Swimming, Beach, **LANGUAGE** Eng., **PRICE** (2 persons) 100–135 **(check with hosts for pricing details)**

PETERBOROUGH

The Moffat House
(Olive Bailey)

597 Weller St, Peterborough, ON, K9H 2N9
www.moffathouse.ca
E-mail relax@moffathouse.ca

705-743-7228
TFr 1-877-415-1646

Nestled in gracious Old West End
Peterborough, The Moffat House Bed &
Breakfast offers historic beauty with all
the comforts of home. The Moffat House
B&B is an ideal destination for visitors and
corporate travellers. Check our Web site
for room availability and take an exciting
video tour of the entire house.

ROOMS Family suite, Upper floor, **Baths** Ensuite, **Beds**
King, Queen, **Air** Central, In rooms, **Smoking** Outside,
In Room Phone, TV, Fireplace, Internet access, **OTHERS**
Adult, Open all year, Pets in residence, **PAYMENT** Visa,
MC, Direct debit, Cheques accepted, Cash, Trvl's
cheques, **BREAKFASTS** Full, **AMENITIES** Central TV,
Central phone, Whirlpool, Barbecue, Laundry, Lounge,
Patio, Central Internet access, **THINGS TO DO** Golf,
Fishing, Museums, Art, Theatre, Entertainment,
Attractions, Shopping, Cross-country skiing, Beach,
LANGUAGE Eng., **PRICE** (2 persons) 80–95 **(check
with hosts for pricing details)**

PETERBOROUGH

Wisteria Bed & Breakfast
(Sandie and Steve Wilson)

580 Gilmour St, Peterborough, ON, K9H 2K2
www.bbcanada.com/3840.html
E-mail swilson345@cogeco.ca

705-749-5714
TFr 1-888-871-1115

Warm welcome and friendly hospitality in
luxurious 130-year-old Victorian Lady. We
are in Old West End among many large
prestigious homes. Awaken to freshly
brewed coffee; and muffins, breads, coffee
cakes, scones or croissant. Fresh juice, fruit
cup and an entree of the day are served
in the formal dining room (during winter).
If you choose, breakfast may be served
pool-side or on upper verandah overlooking the gardens. Restaurants, entertainment and shopping are within walking
distance. Boat tours, museums, art galleries are a sample of what Peterborough
has to offer. From downtown go west on
Charlotte, right on Monaghan and right
on Gilmour.

ROOMS Upper floor, **Baths** Ensuite, **Beds** King, Queen,
Single or cots, **Air** In rooms, **In Room** TV, Fireplace,
OTHERS Urban, Open all year, **PAYMENT** Cheques
accepted, Cash, Trvl's cheques, **BREAKFASTS** Full,
Home-baked, **AMENITIES** Central TV, Central phone,
Swimming pool, Hot bev. bar, Lounge, Patio, **THINGS
TO DO** Rental bikes, Trail nearby, Rental canoe or boat,
Golf, Fishing, Museums, Art, Theatre, Entertain-ment,
Attractions, Shopping, Cross-country skiing,
Swimming, Horseback riding, Beach, Antiquing, **LAN-
GUAGE** Eng., **PRICE** (2 persons) 100–110 **(check with
hosts for pricing details)**

Petrolia (southwestern Ontario)

Away Inn a Manger Bed & Breakfast

(Julie and Perry Pearce)

3131 Shiloh Line, Petrolia, ON, N0N 1R0
www.awayinnamanger-bnb.ca
E-mail awaybnb@mnsi.net

519-864-4706
Fax 519-864-4706
TFr 1-888-212-7322

Come to the farm and relax in our comfy farmhouse and literally "count sheep to sleep". B&B is centrally located between Petrolia, Brigden and Sarnia on a 100-acre working sheep farm. Local attractions include history/oil museums, golf courses, theatres, waterparks, Lake Huron and St. Clair River, shopping malls, fall fairs, casinos, horse racetrack, antiquing, Bluewater Bridge to Port Huron, Michigan, etc. Enjoy the scenery with a walk to our 25-acre bush and let us be your home away from home.

ROOMS Upper floor, **Baths** Shared with guest, **Beds** Double, Single or cots, Pullout sofa, **Air** Ceiling fans, **Smoking** Outside, **In Room** Phone, TV, Internet access, **OTHERS** Babysitting, Rural, Open all year, **PAYMENT** Cash, **BREAKFASTS** Full, **AMENITIES** Central TV, Central phone, Barbecue, Laundry, Kitchen, Fridge, Patio, Central Internet access, Central VCR/DVD, **THINGS TO DO** Trail nearby, Golf, Fishing, Museums, Art, Theatre, Entertainment, Attractions, Shopping, Cross-country skiing, Swimming, Beach, Antiquing, **LANGUAGE** Eng., Fr., **PRICE** (2 persons) 65–85 **(check with hosts for pricing details)**

Petrolia

Currah's Wander Inn B&B

(Edgar and Carol Currah)

4107 Catherine St, Petrolia, ON, N0N 1R0
www.bbcanada.com/656.html
E-mail wanderinnbb@ebtech.net

519-882-1849
TFr 1-888-892-6337

Down home hospitality awaits your visit in our comfortable home filled with antiques, rustic crafts and Victorian pieces. Watch TV in our family room or relax on our verandah with a coffee or cold beverage. A full homecooked breakfast is served in our dining room. A perfect place for relaxing and enjoying your holiday.

ROOMS Family suite, Upper floor, **Baths** Shared with guest, **Beds** Double, **Air** Central, **Smoking** Outside, **OTHERS** Open all year, Pets in residence, **PAYMENT** Cheques accepted, Cash, **BREAKFASTS** Full, Homebaked, **AMENITIES** Central TV, Central phone, Whirlpool, **THINGS TO DO** Golf, Museums, Theatre, Shopping, **LANGUAGE** Eng., **PRICE** (2 persons) 50–60 **(check with hosts for pricing details)**

PLANTAGENET *(east of Ottawa)*

Catstone Farm B&B

(The Steffens Family)

6625 County Rd 17, Plantagenet, ON, K0B 1L0
www.bbcanada.com/catstonefarm.html
E-mail info@tourprescott-russell.com

613-673-5817
Fax 613-673-2783

Catstone Farm B&B welcomes you! Located next to Jessup's Falls Conservation area on the South Nation River at the end of a mapped-out 63-km canoe route. We offer old-fashioned country hospitality, cozy rooms, heated gazebo with hot tub, holiday packages with Horseback riding, craft courses, group rates. Special needs guests and diets welcome! Please call before faxing.

ROOMS Ground floor, **Baths** Shared with guest, **Beds** Double, Twin, **Smoking** Outside, **OTHERS** Rural, Open all year, Additional meals, Pets in residence, **PAYMENT** Cash, Trvl's cheques, **BREAKFASTS** Full, Continental, Home-baked, **AMENITIES** Central TV, Central phone, Whirlpool, Barbecue, Lounge, Patio, **THINGS TO DO** Trail nearby, Golf, Fishing, Museums, Art, Attractions, Shopping, Cross-country skiing, Swimming, Horseback riding, **LANGUAGE** Eng., Fr., Ger., **PRICE** (2 persons) 40–70 **(check with hosts for pricing details)**

PORT BURWELL *(southwest of Hamilton)*

Grey Gables
Bed and Breakfast

(Jim and Mary Beth Hevenor)

22 Erieus St, PO Box 297, Port Burwell, ON, N0J 1T0
www.bbcanada.com/3912.html
E-mail greygabl@amtelecom.net

519-874-4644

A carefully restored 1860s house located beside our home. Situated midway between Buffalo and Detroit on Lake Erie, Grey Gables is close to great beaches, museums, an old lighthouse, the Trans-Canada Trail, a provincial park and fine restaurants. Fishing, boating, birdwatching, cycling, hiking and swimming are popular local activities. The city stresses disappear as you adapt to the slower pace of this small lake port. Consider Grey Gables your home at the lake. Take Hwy19 from Hwy 401 to Lake Erie.

ROOMS Family suite, Upper floor, Ground floor, Private entrance, **Baths** Private, Ensuite, **Beds** King, Queen, Twin, **OTHERS** Rural, Open all year, **PAYMENT** Visa, Cheques accepted, Cash, Trvl's cheques, **BREAKFASTS** Home-baked, **AMENITIES** Central TV, Kitchen, Fridge, Lounge, **THINGS TO DO** Trail nearby, Rental canoe or boat, Fishing, Museums, Wineries/Breweries, Swimming, Beach, Antiquing, **LANGUAGE** Eng., **PRICE** (2 persons) 75 **(check with hosts for pricing details)**

"Ingleside" - Port Colborne

PORT CARLING *(north of Toronto)*

The Manse Bed and Breakfast
(Linda and Bill McAuley)

Box 337 – 12 Bailey St, Port Carling, ON, P0B 1J0
www.themansemuskoka.com
E-mail themanse@vianet.ca

705-765-1117
Fax 705-765-3902

We are centrally located on 12 Bailey Street, a residential street in the beautiful resort town of Port Carling, in the heart of the Muskoka region. Directions: From Bracebridge take Hwy 118 west about 20 minutes, to Port Carling, turn left on Bailey St, we're halfway down the block on the right #12.

ROOMS Upper floor, **Baths** Ensuite, **Beds** Queen, Ceiling fans, **Air** Central, Ceiling fans, **Smoking** Outside, **In Room** Fireplace, **OTHERS** Babysitting, Open all year, Pets in residence, Pets welcome, **PAYMENT** Direct debit, Cheques accepted, Cash, Trvl's cheques, **BREAKFASTS** Full, Home-baked, **AMENITIES** Central TV, Central phone, Barbecue, Laundry, Kitchen, Fridge, Hot bev. bar, Lounge, Patio, Central Internet access, Central VCR/DVD, **THINGS TO DO** Trail nearby, Rental canoe or boat, Golf, Fishing, Museums, Art, Theatre, Attractions, Wineries/Breweries, Shopping, Cross-country skiing, Swimming, Horseback riding, Beach, Antiquing, **LANGUAGE** Eng., **PRICE** (2 persons) 60–145 **(check with hosts for pricing details)**

PORT COLBORNE *(southeast of Hamilton)*

Ingleside Bed & Breakfast
(Sandi Paterson)

322 King St, Port Colborne, ON, L3K 4H3
www.inglesidebedandbreakfast.com
E-mail sandi@computan.on.ca

905-835-5062

Ingleside B&B is an award-winning historical home located in the very heart of Port Colborne. Stepping through the wrought iron gate into one of Niagara's most distinctive B&Bs; you are immediately transported to a bygone era of tranquillity. All five rooms with private baths and A/C are filled with antiques plus Victorian memorabilia. Many of the collections can be purchased. Come sit by our pond and enjoy a glass of Niagara wine while reading a book. Reservations are necessary to ensure availability.

ROOMS Family suite, Upper floor, **Baths** Private, Ensuite, **Beds** Double, Twin, **Air** Central, In rooms, **Smoking** Outside, **In Room** Thermostat, **OTHERS** Urban, Open all year, Pets in residence, **PAYMENT** Visa, MC, Cheques accepted, Cash, **BREAKFASTS** Full, Home-baked, **AMENITIES** Central TV, Central phone, Laundry, Kitchen, Lounge, Patio, **THINGS TO DO** Trail nearby, Rental canoe or boat, Golf, Fishing, Museums, Art, Theatre, Wineries/Breweries, Shopping, Swimming, Horseback riding, Beach, Antiquing, **LANGUAGE** Eng., **PRICE** (2 persons) 100 **(check with hosts for pricing details)**

PORT COLBORNE

Kent House B&B

(Fran and Carl Hymers)

115 Kent St, Port Colborne, ON, L3K 2Z6
www.kenthousebandb.com
E-mail info@kenthousebandb.com

905-834-1206

Guests can relax and enjoy "at home" quiet comfort and hospitality at Kent House Bed & Breakfast for an overnight stay in Port Colborne or while visiting other nearby Niagara Region attractions. Please view our Web site for full description of what Kent House B&B offers, including a vitual tour of the early 1900 B&B home environment.

ROOMS Upper floor, **Baths** Private, Ensuite, Shared with guest, **Beds** Queen, Double, Twin, Single or cots, **Air** Central, **Smoking** Outside, **OTHERS** Urban, Adult, Open all year, **PAYMENT** Visa, MC, Amex, Cheques accepted, Cash, Trvl's cheques, **BREAKFASTS** Full, **AMENITIES** Central TV, Central phone, Fridge, Lounge, Patio, **THINGS TO DO** Rental bikes, Trail nearby, Rental canoe or boat, Golf, Fishing, Museums, Art, Theatre, Entertainment, Attractions, Wineries/Breweries, Shopping, Tennis, Swimming, Horseback riding, Beach, Birdwatching, Antiquing, **LANGUAGE** Eng., **PRICE** (2 persons) 60–90 **(check with hosts for pricing details)**

PORT DOVER *(southwest of Hamilton)*

Bed & Breakfast By The Lake

(Christine and John Ivey-Baker)

30 Elm Park, Port Dover, ON, N0A 1N0
www.bbcanada.com/bbbylake
E-mail plivey@yahoo.com

519-583-1010

B&B By The Lake is a bright, open, airy ranch-style home, warmly furnished with antiques and art. From the attractive brick patio and garden, there is a lovely view of Lake Erie. Full breakfast, homemade muffins and fresh fruit. Quiet residential area in a private park overlooking Lake Erie. Access to beautiful sandy beach 100 yards from the house. Two blocks from Lighthouse Theatre. A good base for exploring Long Point, Lynn Valley Walking Trail, bicycling, golfing, scenic Port Dover Harbour. Second phone: 519-428-6028.

ROOMS Ground floor, **Baths** Private, Ensuite, **Beds** Queen, **Air** Central, **Smoking** Outside, **In Room** TV, **OTHERS** Urban, Adult, **PAYMENT** Visa, Cash, **BREAKFASTS** Full, **THINGS TO DO** Trail nearby, Golf, Fishing, Theatre, Shopping, Beach, **LANGUAGE** Eng., **PRICE** (2 persons) 65–85 **(check with hosts for pricing details)**

PORT DOVER

Clonmel Estate
Bed and Breakfast

(Robert and Connie Lawton)

11 Mill Rd, Port Dover, ON, N0A 1N1
www.kwic.com/~clonmel
E-mail clonmel@kwic.com

519-583-0519

Historic, gracious and memorable – a beautiful Georgian Revival-style mansion with Victorian interior offers the ambience of a Grand Hotel. Seven tastefully decorated rooms with private bath and air-conditioning. Full breakfast. Elegant great room for guests to relax with grand piano and original Casavant pipe organ. Overlooking the Lynn River, Lynn Valley hiking trail at the front door, seven golf courses within minutes, professional theatre, boat excursions, diving, close to beach, shopping and restaurants.

ROOMS Upper floor, **Baths** Ensuite, Shared with guest, **Beds** Queen, **Air** In rooms, **OTHERS** Adult, Open all year, **PAYMENT** Visa, MC, Diners, Amex, Cheques accepted, Cash, **BREAKFASTS** Full, **AMENITIES** Fridge, Lounge, Patio, **THINGS TO DO** Comp. bikes, Trail nearby, Golf, Fishing, Museums, Art, Theatre, Attractions, Wineries/Breweries, Shopping, Tennis, Swimming, Horseback riding, Beach, **LANGUAGE** Eng., **PRICE** (2 persons) 89–125 **(check with hosts for pricing details)**

PORT DOVER

Heritage Homestead B&B

(Don and Pat Mickle)

1615 Concession 13 Townsend, RR #4, Simcoe, ON, N3Y 4K3
www.bbontario.com/heritagehomestead.cfm
E-mail heritage@kwic.com

519-443-6745
Fax 519-443-6745

A beautifully restored heritage designated home (c. 1872). Furnished with antiques, situated in the country close to Port Dover and the charming ports along Lake Erie's north shore. Two large queen rooms, one twin, ensuite baths. Guests have exclusive use of parlour, library and up-stairs drawing room. A full country breakfast is served in the dining room. (Don loves to cook!) Featured in the *Best Places to B&B in Ontario*. Located 10 minutes north of Port Dover, 10 minutes east of Simcoe. Obtain directions when booking.

ROOMS Upper floor, Private entrance, **Baths** Ensuite, **Beds** Queen, Twin, **Air** Central, **Smoking** Outside, **OTHERS** Rural, Adult, Seasonal, Pets in residence, **PAYMENT** Cheques accepted, Cash, Trvl's cheques, **BREAKFASTS** Full, Home-baked, **AMENITIES** Fridge, Lounge, Patio, **THINGS TO DO** Comp. bikes, Trail nearby, Rental canoe or boat, Golf, Fishing, Museums, Art, Theatre, Attractions, Wineries/Breweries, Shopping, Swimming, Horseback riding, Beach, **LANGUAGE** Eng., Fr., **PRICE** (2 persons) 75–85 **(check with hosts for pricing details)**

PORT ROWAN *(southwest of Hamilton)*

Marsh Landing
(Barry and Marilyn Foster)

1014 Hwy #59, RR #3, Port Rowan, ON, N0E 1M0
www.canadianbandbguide.ca/bb.asp?ID=3795
E-mail mfoster7@aol.com

519-586-7777

Marilyn and Barry warmly welcome you to our Florida-style home. We offer a panoramic view of beautiful Long Point Bay and marshlands. Home of many species of birds, great boating, fishing, swimming, hiking and birdwatching. Long Point Beach, Backus Conservation Park and Port Rowan shopping are only 5 minutes away.

ROOMS Family suite, Upper floor, Lower floor, Private entrance, **Baths** Private, Ensuite, Shared with guest, **Beds** Queen, Twin, Pullout sofa, **Air** Central, Ceiling fans, **Smoking** Outside, **In Room** TV, Fireplace, VCR/DVD, **OTHERS** Rural, Adult, Seasonal, Pets in residence, **PAYMENT** Cheques accepted, Cash, **BREAKFASTS** Full, **AMENITIES** Central TV, Swimming pool, Whirlpool, Fridge, Central VCR/DVD, **THINGS TO DO** Trail nearby, Golf, Fishing, Shopping, Cross-country skiing, Swimming, Beach, Birdwatching, **LANGUAGE** Eng., **PRICE** (2 persons) 75–120 **(check with hosts for pricing details)**

PORT ROWAN

The Bay House Bed and Breakfast
(Robert and Linda Rapai)

14 Archibald Dr, Box 375, Port Rowan, ON, N0E 1M0
www.thebayhousebb.com
E-mail info@thebayhousebb.com

519-586-3337

Located on the shore of Long Point, a designated World Biosphere and home of Bird Studies Canada, the beautifully restored turn-of-the-century home is ideally situated on 1 3/4 acres of waterfront property. Driving directions from Toronto: Hwy 403 to Brantford, exit Hwy 24 South Rest Acres Rd to Hwy 59, turn south towards Long Point. Turn east on 42 and turn right (south) on Archibald Dr. Last house on right. From Windsor: Hwy 401 exit Hwy 19 south to Hwy 59 towards Long Point, east on 42.

ROOMS Upper floor, **Baths** Private, Ensuite, Shared with guest, **Beds** Queen, Double, **Air** Central, **Smoking** Outside, **OTHERS** Adult, Open all year, Pets in residence, **PAYMENT** Cash, **BREAKFASTS** Full, **AMENITIES** Central TV, Lounge, Patio, Central VCR/DVD, **THINGS TO DO** Rental canoe or boat, Golf, Fishing, Museums, Art, Theatre, Attractions, Wineries/Breweries, Shopping, Cross-country skiing, Swimming, Beach, Birdwatching, Antiquing, **LANGUAGE** Eng., **PRICE** (2 persons) 100–125 **(check with hosts for pricing details)**

PORT STANLEY *(southwest of Hamilton)*

Mulberry Lane B&B
(Yvonne and John Lunshof)

6324 Stone Church Rd, Union, ON, N0L 2L0
www.bbcanada.com/mulberrylane
E-mail mulberrylanebb@rogers.com

519-637-4499

Retreat to Mulberry Lane and enjoy our spacious reproduction saltbox home nestled in a captivatingly peaceful setting. Enjoy warm hospitality, comfortable principal and guest rooms, and a delicious breakfast. Relax out on the deck or in the ravined gardens. Hike, bike, boat, drive or take the historic train to explore the beauty and attractions of Elgin County. You can find us on Hwy 4 at the north end of the village of Union, 4 minutes north of picturesque Port Stanley. We'd love to meet you!

ROOMS Family suite, Upper floor, Private entrance, **Baths** Private, Ensuite, Shared with guest, **Beds** Queen, Double, Twin, **Air** Central, In rooms, **Smoking** Outside, **In Room** TV, **OTHERS** Rural, Open all year, **PAYMENT** Visa, MC, Cheques accepted, Cash, Trvl's cheques, **BREAKFASTS** Full, Home-baked, **AMENITIES** Central TV, Central phone, Laundry, Kitchen, Lounge, Patio, Central Internet access, Central VCR/DVD, **THINGS TO DO** Comp. bikes, Trail nearby, Rental canoe or boat, Comp. canoe or boat, Golf, Fishing, Museums, Art, Theatre, Entertainment, Attractions, Wineries/ Breweries, Shopping, Cross-country skiing, Swimming, Horseback riding, Beach, Birdwatching, Antiquing, **LANGUAGE** Eng., Ger., Dutch, **PRICE** (2 persons) 70–85 **(check with hosts for pricing details)**

PRESCOTT *(south of Ottawa)*

Connell Rose
Bed and Breakfast
(J.P. and Ily Connell)

2223 Ventnor Rd, RR #3, Spencerville, ON, K0E 1X0
www.bbcanada.com/connellrose
E-mail jpec@ripnet.com

613-658-2279
Fax 613-658-2607

Quiet country setting on wooded acreage close to everything that matters. Explore Prescott's Fort Wellington, Morrisburg's Upper Canada Village and the Ferguson Forest Centre in Kemptville, known for scenic nature trails. Other outdoor activities include snowmobiling in winter, golfing and fishing in summer. The St. Lawrence River provides some of the best dive sites in the world. Shop in historic towns like Merrickville and Brockville. Ottawa, only 45 minutes away, makes a perfect day trip. Call for directions.

ROOMS Upper floor, **Baths** Shared with guest, **Beds** Queen, **Air** Central, **Smoking** Outside, **In Room** Thermostat, **OTHERS** Rural, Adult, Open all year, Pets in residence, **PAYMENT** Cash, Trvl's cheques, **BREAKFASTS** Full, Home-baked, **AMENITIES** Central TV, Swimming pool, Sauna, Lounge, Patio, **THINGS TO DO** Trail nearby, Golf, Fishing, Museums, Art, Entertainment, Attractions, Shopping, Cross-country skiing, Tennis, Swimming, Beach, **LANGUAGE** Eng., **PRICE** (2 persons) 65–75 **(check with hosts for pricing details)**

PRINCE EDWARD COUNTY *(east of Toronto)*

Oeno Gallery & Guesthouse
(Carlyn Moulton and Barbara Basille)

320 Old Orchard Rd, RR #1, Carrying Place,
ON, K0K 1L0
www.oenogallery.com
E-mail info@oenogallery.com

613-394-2216
Fax 613-394-6806

Our guest house is located on the beautiful Bay of Quinte in Prince Edward County. It is a two bedroom house with laundry facilities, kitchen, dining, living room with fireplace and hot tub. You will enjoy stunning sunsets in this private setting. Our location is 1 1/2 hours east of Toronto at Exit 522 on Hwy 401. Follow Wooler Rd south to Hwy 33, south to Rednersville Rd, then turn left for 3.5 km to Old Orchard Rd. The Guesthouse is rented by the week or month with a two night minimum.

ROOMS Ground floor, Private entrance, **Baths** Private, **Beds** Queen, Double, **Smoking** Outside, **In Room** Thermostat, Fireplace, **OTHERS** Rural, Open all year, Pets in residence, **PAYMENT** Visa, MC, Cheques accepted, Cash, **BREAKFASTS** Self-catered, **AMENITIES** Central TV, Whirlpool, Barbecue, Laundry, Kitchen, Fridge, Patio, **THINGS TO DO** Rental bikes, Trail nearby, Comp. Canoe or boat, Golf, Fishing, Art, Theatre, Entertainment, Attractions, Wineries/Breweries, Shopping, Cross-country skiing, Swimming, Horseback riding, Beach, Birdwatching, Antiquing, **LANGUAGE** Eng., **PRICE** (2 persons) 150–225 **(check with hosts for pricing details)**

PRINCE EDWARD COUNTY

Wellington On The Bay Waterfront B&B
(Deb and Steve Izumi)

12 Carla Crt, Wellington, Prince Edward County,
ON, K0K 3L0
www.bbcanada.com/wellingtononthebay
E-mail wellingtononthebay@bellnet.ca

613-399-1021
Fax 613-399-1021

Located in the heart of Ontario's newest wine region, Prince Edward County. Nestled on the edge of a great lake, this upscale, contemporary, immaculate home, with vaulted ceilings, features all of today's most up-to-date amenities. Our fabulous lake view, seen from two large decks, is second to none. Shallow bay waters along an interesting pebble beach for your pleasure. We are an adult retreat welcoming your dog- and people-friendly pooch too, with special dog amenities. Open year-round.

ROOMS Ground floor, **Baths** Ensuite, **Beds** King, Twin, Pullout sofa, **Air** Central, Ceiling fans, **Smoking** Outside, **In Room** TV, **OTHERS** Urban, Adult, Open all year, **PAYMENT** Visa, MC, Amex, Direct debit, Cash, Trvl's cheques, **BREAKFASTS** Full, Home-baked, **AMENITIES** Central TV, Central phone, Fridge, Hot bev. bar, Lounge, Patio, Central VCR/DVD, **THINGS TO DO** Rental bikes, Trail nearby, Rental canoe or boat, Golf, Fishing, Museums, Art, Theatre, Entertainment, Attractions, Wineries/Breweries, Shopping, Cross-country skiing, Horseback riding, Beach, Birdwatching, Antiquing, **LANGUAGE** Eng., **PRICE** (2 persons) 115–150 **(check with hosts for pricing details)**

RIDEAU FERRY (southwest of Ottawa)

Loon Lodge Bed & Breakfast

(Bob, Sue and Devin Van Slooten)

RR #1, #18 R-13, Lombardy, ON, K0G 1L0
www.loonlodgebandb.com
E-mail loonlodge@igs.net

613-284-1053
TFr 1-888-814-7404

Loon Lodge is a lovely country home with beautiful sand beach on Big Rideau Lake, where we serve delicious home-cooked breakfasts and freshly ground coffee. Relax by the fireplace, surrounded by antiques. Be warmly greeted by our dog, Hartlin. Enjoy hiking, birding, fishing, swimming; docking. Antique shops and golf nearby. Visit Perth for shopping and dining or Smiths Falls for Hershey Chocolate and museums. We are 1 hour from Ottawa. Rideau Ferry is 10 minutes for gas, bait/tackle, dining, general store.

ROOMS Upper floor, **Baths** Private, Shared with guest, **Beds** Queen, Single or cots, **OTHERS** Rural, Open all year, Additional meals, Pets in residence, **PAYMENT** Visa, Direct debit, Cash, Trvl's cheques, **BREAKFASTS** Full, **AMENITIES** Barbecue, Fridge, Patio, **THINGS TO DO** Trail nearby, Rental canoe or boat, Comp. canoe or boat, Golf, Fishing, Museums, Art, Theatre, Attractions, Shopping, Swimming, Beach, **LANGUAGE** Eng., Sp., some Italian, **PRICE** (2 persons) 75–85 **(check with hosts for pricing details)**

RIDEAU LAKES (southwest of Ottawa)

Denaut Mansion Country Inn

(Deborah and David Peets)

5 Mathew St, Delta, ON, K0E 1G0
www.denautmansion.com
E-mail goodtimes@denautmansion.com

613-928-2588
TFr 1-877-788-0388

An 1849 mansion now transformed into a fully air-conditioned boutique inn on its own 11 wooded acres in a charming heritage village setting in the Rideau Lakes Thousand Islands. Savour an imaginatively presented three-course set menu dinner, and our commitment to local, organic, seasonal ingredients. Lovely small wine list. What to do? Plunge into the heated pool, wander our private forest path, discover the tranquil bays of the lake in our canoe, cycle our loop routes, hike, golf, or … nothing at all.

ROOMS Family suite, Upper floor, Ground floor, **Baths** Private, Ensuite, **Beds** Queen, Double, Twin, **Air** Central, **Smoking** Outside, **OTHERS** Rural, Open all year, Additional meals, **PAYMENT** Visa, MC, Direct debit, Cash, Trvl's cheques, **BREAKFASTS** Full, **AMENITIES** Swimming pool, Lounge, Patio, **THINGS TO DO** Trail nearby, Comp. canoe or boat, Golf, Fishing, Museums, Art, Theatre, Entertainment, Attractions, Cross-country skiing, Swimming, Horseback riding, Beach, Birdwatching, Antiquing, **LANGUAGE** Eng., **PRICE** (2 persons) 125–175 **(check with hosts for pricing details)**

RIDGETOWN *(southwestern Ontario)*

Ridge Farm B&B

(Anneke and Rikus Huisman)

12061 Front Line, Ridgetown, ON, N0P 1A0
www.canadianbandbguide.ca/bb.asp?ID=2380
E-mail rhuisman@MNSi.net

519-674-5934
Fax 519-674-3847

Warm welcome on cash crop farm in the rolling farmland on the "ridge" near Ridgetown. Guests are welcome to stroll the garden, relax on the deck or enjoy the gas barbecue. Breakfast is served in the guest breakfast room. Located between Exits 101/109 on Hwy 401. Take Kent Rd 15 to Lake Erie and proceed left in Troy. Ranch-style farm with view from guest rooms. Guest quarters are separate. Drive to London, Windsor, Rondeau Park, Uncle Tom's Cabin, Greenview Aviaries & Zoo, Lake Erie and beaches, Point Pelee.

ROOMS Family suite, Private entrance, **Baths** Shared with guest, **Beds** Queen, Double, **Air** Central, **OTHERS** Rural, Open all year, **PAYMENT** Cash, **AMENITIES** Central TV, Kitchen, **THINGS TO DO** Trail nearby, Golf, Fishing, Museums, Attractions, Beach, Birdwatching, Antiquing, **LANGUAGE** Eng., Ger., Dutch, **PRICE** (2 persons) 65 **(check with hosts for pricing details)**

ROCKVILLE *(Manitoulin Island)*

Rockville Inn

(Ron and Carol Sheppard)

RR #1, S-5 C-2, Mindemoya, ON, P0P 1S0
www.manitoulin-island.com/rockvilleinn
E-mail caroll@amtelecom.net

705-377-4923

The Inn is nestled on the shores of Lake Manitou with decks overlooking the lake or a verandah view the sunset. Lake Manitou is the largest freshwater, inland lake, on an island, in the world. We have been told we own a piece of paradise. Come and enjoy a stay at our inn and enjoy the sunrise from the dock or gazebo. If you can't leave the office behind, we have high-speed Internet service.

ROOMS Family suite, Upper floor, Ground floor, Private entrance, **Baths** Private, **Beds** Queen, **Air** Central, **PAYMENT** Cheques accepted, Cash, Trvl's cheques, **BREAKFASTS** Full, Home-baked, **AMENITIES** Barbecue, Kitchen, Fridge, Central Internet access, **THINGS TO DO** Trail nearby, Comp. canoe or boat, Golf, Fishing, Museums, Art, Theatre, Attractions, Shopping, Swimming, Horseback riding, Beach, Birdwatching, **LANGUAGE** Eng., **PRICE** (2 persons) 85–145 **(check with hosts for pricing details)**

Sauble Beach *(northwest of Toronto)*

Sauble Falls
Bed and Breakfast

(Brian and Gloria Currie)

6 Rankin Bridge Rd, RR #3, Wiarton, ON, N0H 2T0
www.saublefallsbb.com
E-mail info@saublefallsbb.com

519-422-3304

A special country experience awaits you at Sauble Falls B&B, just minutes from the white sands of Sauble Beach. Enjoy the tranquility of a riverside setting. The deck and campfire area afford a wonderful view of the river below. Wildlife abounds: birds, chipmunks, an occasional deer in the woods nearby. Guests love the soothing sound of the falls just yards away. Sauble Falls offers a wonderful place for that peaceful getaway, during the quieter times of the year, snowshoeing, cross-country skiing, snowmobiling, or a quiet hike on one of the area trails. Full gourmet breakfasts and warm hospitality.

ROOMS Upper floor, Private entrance, **Baths** Ensuite, **Beds** Queen, Double, Twin, **Smoking** Outside, **In Room** Thermostat, **OTHERS** Rural, Open all year, Pets in residence, **PAYMENT** Visa, MC, Cash, **BREAKFASTS** Full, Home-baked, **AMENITIES** Barbecue, Fridge, Hot bev. bar, Lounge, Patio, **THINGS TO DO** Trail nearby, Golf, Fishing, Museums, Art, Theatre, Attractions, Shopping, Cross-country skiing, Tennis, Swimming, Horseback riding, Beach, Birdwatching, Antiquing, **LANGUAGE** Eng., **PRICE** (2 persons) 80–110 **(check with hosts for pricing details)**

Sault Ste. Marie *(northern Ontario)*

Brockwell Chambers

(Maria Sutton)

183 Brock St, Sault Ste. Marie, ON, P6A 3B8
www.brockwell.biz
E-mail bedssm@sympatico.ca

705-949-1076
Fax 705-949-1076

Comfortably spacious and elegant, fully modernized, Brockwell Chambers is handily located downtown close to most major attractions, including Canadian Bushplane Museum, Agawa Canyon Tour Train. Relax in the cosy sitting room by the fireplace. All rooms ensuite. Rooms individually air-conditioned. Separate tables in the dining room; enjoy a delicious breakfast at a time of your choosing. For other meals, three fine restaurants within a stone's throw. Ample free parking onsite.

ROOMS Upper floor, Private entrance, **Baths** Ensuite, **Beds** King, Double, Twin, Single or cots, **Air** In rooms, **Smoking** Outside, **In Room** Thermostat, Phone, TV, **OTHERS** Urban, Adult, Open all year, **PAYMENT** Cheques accepted, Cash, Trvl's cheques, **BREAKFASTS** Full, **AMENITIES** Central TV, Central phone, Whirlpool, Lounge, Patio, **THINGS TO DO** Trail nearby, Fishing, Museums, Art, Theatre, Entertainment, Attractions, Shopping, Cross-country skiing, Tennis, Swimming, Horseback riding, Beach, **LANGUAGE** Eng., Ger., Dutch, **PRICE** (2 persons) 75–115 **(check with hosts for pricing details)**

SAULT STE. MARIE

Eastbourne Manor B&B
(Linda and Richard Smith)

1048 Queen St, Sault Ste. Marie, ON, P6A 2C7
www3.sympatico.ca/eastbourne/main.htm
E-mail eastbournemanor@yahoo.com

705-942-3648
TFr 1-888-431-5469

Warm welcome to our designated heritage home (c. 1903), fully restored in its
Victorian era and centrally located. Enjoy
the comfortable and friendly hospitality,
and reside in a piece of Ontario's history.
Breakfast is served in the formal Victorian
dining room. Relax with coffee in the back
garden terrace or on the front verandah
with panoramic view of St. Mary's River
through a hedge-trimmed walkway. The
rear garden fountain and waterfall are
both illuminated for evening enjoyment.
Mineou is our resident cat.

ROOMS Baths Private, Ensuite, **Beds** King, Queen,
Double, Twin, Single or cots, **Air** In rooms, **Smoking**
Outside, **In Room** VCR/DVD, **OTHERS** Adult, Open all
year, Pets in residence, **PAYMENT** Cheques accepted,
Cash, Trvl's cheques, **BREAKFASTS** Full, **AMENITIES**
Central TV, Central phone, Laundry, Central Internet
access, Central VCR/DVD, **THINGS TO DO** Golf, Fishing,
Museums, Theatre, Entertainment, Attractions,
Shopping, Cross-country skiing, Tennis, **LANGUAGE**
PRICE (2 persons) 85–95 **(check with hosts for pricing**
details)

SAULT STE. MARIE

Mountain View
Bed and Breakfast
(E. Jane Mundy)

RR #3, Thessalon, ON, P0R 1L0
www.bbcanada.com/mundys
E-mail ejmundy@sympatico.ca

705-841-1140
Fax 705-841-1365

Awarded Best in Canada by *Arrington's*
Bed & Breakfast Journal – Top 15 B&B/
Country Inns 2003 Book of Lists. Hidden
in the heart of Algoma, Mountain View
Bed and Breakfast is a perfect year-round
retreat – photographers and artist paradise. Dozens of lakes, rivers, waterfalls,
natural Jacuzzis and mountains waiting
to be explored. Enjoy a stay in the
Mississagi River Valley in a timber-frame
home overlooking Cumming Lake and
Rock Candy Mountain. Guest house available for private rental.

ROOMS Family suite, Ground floor, **Baths** Ensuite,
Shared with guest, **Beds** Queen, Double, Twin, Single
or cots, Pullout sofa, **Smoking** Outside, **In Room**
Thermostat, Phone, **OTHERS** Rural, Open all year,
Handicapped access, Additional meals, Pets welcome,
PAYMENT Visa, MC, Cheques accepted, Cash, Trvl's
cheques, **BREAKFASTS** Full, **AMENITIES** Central TV,
Central phone, Sauna, Barbecue, Laundry, Kitchen,
Patio, **THINGS TO DO** Comp. bikes, Trail nearby, Comp.
canoe or boat, Golf, Fishing, Museums, Art, Shopping,
Cross-country skiing, Swimming, Horseback riding,
Beach, **LANGUAGE** Eng., **PRICE** (2 persons) 65–75
(check with hosts for pricing details)

SHELBURNE *(northwest of Toronto)*

Anderson's Hilltop B&B

(Robert and Eleanor Anderson)

595438 Blind Line, RR #1, Shelburne, ON, L0N 1S5
www.andersonshilltopfarmbandb.com
E-mail andersonrw@sympatico.ca

519-925-5129
Fax 519-925-2073

Large, modern red brick home on 100-acre farm with a scenic country view, situated on a quiet gravel road. Relax and enjoy the rural atmosphere. Special arrangements can be made for transportation and vehicle placement for Bruce Trail hiking. Ski resorts in area. Weekly bookings.

ROOMS Upper floor, Ground floor, Private entrance, **Baths** Private, Shared with guest, **Beds** Queen, Twin, **Smoking** Outside, **OTHERS** Rural, Open all year, Handicapped access, Additional meals, **PAYMENT** Visa, Cheques accepted, Cash, **BREAKFASTS** Full, **AMENITIES** Central TV, Central phone, Laundry, Kitchen, Fridge, Lounge, **THINGS TO DO** Trail nearby, Golf, Fishing, Museums, Art, Attractions, Cross-country skiing, Horseback riding, **LANGUAGE** Eng., Fr., **PRICE** (2 persons) 55–75 **(check with hosts for pricing details)**

ST. ANNS *(southeast of Hamilton)*

Hatorp Vacation B&B

(Paul and Agnete Hatorp)

4171 Reg Rd 69, St. Anns, ON, L0R 1Y0
www.canadianbandbguide.ca/bb.asp?ID=2238
E-mail hagu@sprint.ca

905-562-4016
Fax 905-562-6479

From QEW, take Exit 57, Victoria Ave, Reg Rd 24 to Vineland. Continue south to Reg Rd 69. Turn right and proceed 3 km from B&B #4171. Located 45 km to Niagara Falls, 15 km from St. Catharines, 45 km from Hamilton. Breakfast is served in a separate guest breakfast room. Warm welcome in large farm home situated in a very convenient location. Hostess is interested in holistic medicine and organic gardening. Relax by the pond, enjoy the peaceful atmosphere and the ducks and geese.

ROOMS Ground floor, Lower floor, **Baths** Private, Ensuite, Shared with guest, Shared with hosts, **Beds** King, Double, Twin, Pullout sofa, **Smoking** Outside, **In Room** Thermostat, Phone, TV, **OTHERS** Babysitting, Rural, Open all year, Additional meals, **PAYMENT** Cheques accepted, Cash, **BREAKFASTS** Full, **AMENITIES** Laundry, Kitchen, Patio, **THINGS TO DO** Trail nearby, Comp. Canoe or boat, Golf, Museums, Theatre, Attractions, Wineries/Breweries, Shopping, Horseback riding, **LANGUAGE** Eng., Danish, **PRICE** (2 persons) 50–75 **(check with hosts for pricing details)**

ST. CATHARINES *(west of Niagara Falls)*

Bala Place B&B

(Jacqueline and Keith Curwen)

6 Bala Pl, St. Catharines, ON, L2N 5Z9
www.balaplace.com
E-mail bala-place@cogeco.ca

905-938-1873
Fax 905-938-9973

A contemporary home, Bala Place B&B is located in a quiet neighbourhood with well-maintained gardens. St. Catharines is the centre of North Niagara Region, just minutes to Niagara Falls (Casino Niagara), Niagara-on-the-Lake, 40 wineries, Welland Canal, Shaw Festival theatres and the Butterfly Conservatory. We are just 1 mile from Old Port Dalhousie. Take QEW to St. Catharines (Exit 47 Ontario St). Go north; then right on Linwell Rd. Second street on your right is Centennial Dr. First left is Bala Place.

ROOMS Ground floor, **Baths** Ensuite, Shared with guest, **Beds** King, Queen, Double, Twin, Single or cots, **Air** Central, **Smoking** Outside, **OTHERS** Rural, Open all year, **PAYMENT** Visa, MC, Amex, Direct debit, Cash, Trvl's cheques, **BREAKFASTS** Full, Continental, Home-baked, **AMENITIES** Central TV, Swimming pool, Barbecue, Lounge, Patio, **THINGS TO DO** Golf, Fishing, Museums, Theatre, Entertainment, Attractions, Wineries/Breweries, Shopping, Tennis, Swimming, Beach, **LANGUAGE** Eng., Fr., **PRICE** (2 persons) 85–99 **(check with hosts for pricing details)**

ST. CATHARINES

Omi's Haus

(Rudy and Hilda Braun)

1931 3rd St. Louth, St. Catharines, ON, L2R 6P9
www.omishaus.com
E-mail hbraun@sympatico.ca

905-684-1236

This is a century-old former farmhouse on the western outskirts of St. Catharines. The yard is beautifully landscaped with flowerbeds and a pond teaming with goldfish. A hot tub and a swimming pool are provided for your pleasure. All rooms have ensuite baths and are individually air-conditioned. Further information and prices are listed in our Web site. Please refer to it to submit your inquiry and/or reservation.

ROOMS Upper floor, Ground floor, Lower floor, **Baths** Ensuite, **Beds** Queen, Single or cots, **Air** In rooms, **Smoking** Outside, **In Room** Internet access, **PAYMENT** Visa, MC, Direct debit, Cash, Trvl's cheques, **BREAKFASTS** Full, Home-baked, **AMENITIES** Swimming pool, Hot bev. bar, Lounge, Patio, **THINGS TO DO** Rental bikes, Trail nearby, Golf, Fishing, Museums, Art, Theatre, Entertainment, Attractions, Wineries/Breweries, Shopping, Swimming, Beach, Antiquing, **LANGUAGE** Eng., Ger., **PRICE** (2 persons) 95–110 **(check with hosts for pricing details)**

St. Catharines

Ridley Gate Manor

(Peter and Teresa Kellett)

37 Henrietta St, St. Catharines, ON, L2S 2M7
www.bbcanada.com/ridleygatemanor
E-mail ridleygatemanorbb@sympatico.ca

905-323-9719
Fax 905-323-9719

Selected by Janette Higgins as "One of the best places to B&B in Ontario." The Manor is the historic former Ridley College headmaster's house. Elegant Victorian furnishings with modern comforts and convenience. Intimate award-winning private gardens and pool area all located within a safe and mature residential area of quiet, tree-lined streets. All of this within a 15-minute walk from downtown and a major shopping area. A relaxed gourmet breakfast and fresh home baking will start your day.

ROOMS Upper floor, **Baths** Private, Ensuite, **Beds** King, Queen, Twin, Single or cots, **Air** Central, **Smoking** Outside, **In Room** TV, Fireplace, VCR/DVD, **OTHERS** Open all year, **PAYMENT** Visa, MC, Direct debit, Cheques accepted, Cash, Trvl's cheques, **BREAKFASTS** Full, Home-baked, **AMENITIES** Central phone, Swimming pool, Barbecue, Lounge, Patio, Central Internet access, **THINGS TO DO** Trail nearby, Art, Entertainment, Wineries/Breweries, Shopping, **LANGUAGE** Eng., **PRICE** (2 persons) 99–150 **(check with hosts for pricing details)**

St. Jacobs *(west of Toronto)*

Beyond the Front Door

(Lynne and Earl Feick)

16 Abner's Lane, St. Jacobs, ON, N0B 2N0
www.bbcanada.com/349.html

519-664-2622

Beyond the Front Door you will be greeted by spacious accommodations and cheerfully decorated rooms: two double, one twin, a large sitting area or gardens to sit, relaxing to water rippling over rocks into the fish pond. In the morning, a full breakfast awaits you, where we always have time for friendly conversation and stories of the area. A hundred shops, fine dining, farmer's market. Take Hwy 401 to 8 W, 86 N, RR 15 exit to St. Jacobs.

ROOMS Baths Shared with guest, **Beds** Double, Twin, **Air** Central, **Smoking** Outside, **In Room** VCR/DVD, **OTHERS** Adult, Open all year, **PAYMENT** Cash, **BREAKFASTS** Full, **AMENITIES** Central TV, Lounge, Patio, Central VCR/DVD, **THINGS TO DO** Trail nearby, Golf, Museums, Art, Theatre, Entertainment, Attractions, Shopping, Cross-country skiing, Horseback riding, **LANGUAGE** Eng., Ger., **PRICE** (2 persons) 80 **(check with hosts for pricing details)**

Sᴛ. Mᴀʀʏs *(west of Hamilton)*

A Special Happening – Serendip B&B

(Ray and Eloise Hagerman)

282 Elgin St W, St. Marys, ON, N4X 1A2
www.serendip.ca
E-mail serendipbb@rogers.com

519-284-3612
Fax 519-284-3612

Serendip is located in a quiet residential neighbourhood, a short distance from shopping, restaurants, historic sites, walking trails, Canadian Baseball Hall of Fame. We offer warm "Maritime" hospitality, central air, home-baked, health-conscious breakfasts, smoke-free. Three guest bedrooms with queen or twin beds; two full bathrooms for guests. Stratford Festival is a 20-minute drive away. Serendip has a resident cat (usually outside). We issue a warm welcome to come and enjoy the hospitality of our home!

ROOMS Upper floor, **Baths** Shared with guest, **Beds** Queen, Twin, **Air** Central, **Smoking** Outside, **OTHERS** Open all year, Pets in residence, **PAYMENT** Visa, MC, Diners, Amex, Cheques accepted, Cash, **BREAKFASTS** Full, Home-baked, **THINGS TO DO** Trail nearby, Theatre, Attractions, **LANGUAGE** Eng., **PRICE** (2 persons) 68-78 **(check with hosts for pricing details)**

Sᴛ. Mᴀʀʏs

Green Arbour B&B

(Aileen and Harold Burgin)

5894 Perth Line 8, RR #1, St. Marys, ON, N4X 1C4
www.greenarbourbnb.on.ca
E-mail aburgin@greenarbourbnb.on.ca

519-229-6671
Fax 519-229-8572

Gracious 1885 Victorian farmhouse with verandah; restored and furnished with family and acquired heirlooms. Breakfast specialty is sourdough waffles with our own maple syrup. Book the luxury ensuite for a special "Country Squire" experience. Llamas can be hired to accompany you through the woodlot and farmlands or for "Llama 101". Centrally located just east of Kirkton (Hwy 23) on Perth Line 8. Only 30 minutes from Stratford and London, 12 minutes from St. Marys, Mitchell and Exeter.

ROOMS Upper floor, **Baths** Private, Ensuite, Shared with guest, **Beds** King, Queen, Twin, Single or cots, **Air** Central, **Smoking** Outside, **OTHERS** Rural, Open all year, **PAYMENT** Visa, Diners, Cheques accepted, Cash, Trvl's cheques, **BREAKFASTS** Full, Continental, Home-baked, **AMENITIES** Patio, **THINGS TO DO** Trail nearby, Golf, Museums, Theatre, Attractions, Shopping, Tennis, Birdwatching, Antiquing, **LANGUAGE** Eng., **PRICE** (2 persons) 70–110 **(check with hosts for pricing details)**

STAYNER *(northwest of Toronto)*

Donet Bed & Breakfast
(Betty Gibson)

221 Louisa St, Stayner, ON, L0M 1S0
www.canadianbandbguide.ca/bb.asp?ID=2245

705-428-3812

A warm welcome awaits you in the quiet town of Stayner. Located between Barrie and Collingwood. Warm yourself by the fireplace or relax on the patio of my taste-fully decorated bungalow, which includes fireplace, patio, TV, air-conditioning and hydro-thermo massage tub. After a hearty breakfast, set out for a fun-filled day of windsurfing, boating, fishing, swimming or shopping at Wasaga Beach, just 10 minutes away, or spend the day in beauti-ful Collingwood browsing through the antique shops at Blue Mountain. Home baking and a warm welcome.

Baths Shared with guest, **Beds** Queen, **Air** In rooms, **Smoking** Outside, **OTHERS** Open all year, Additional meals, **PAYMENT** Visa, Cheques accepted, Cash, **BREAKFASTS** Full, Home-baked, **AMENITIES** Central TV, Central phone, Kitchen, Patio, Central VCR/DVD, **THINGS TO DO** Trail nearby, Golf, Theatre, Shopping, Cross-country skiing, Downhill skiing, Swimming, Beach, **LANGUAGE** Eng., **PRICE** (2 persons) 60–80 **(check with hosts for pricing details)**

STRATFORD *(southwest of Toronto)*

At Rosita Lane
Bed and Breakfast
(Michael and Rosie Lane)

240 Jordan Cres, Mitchell, ON, N0K 1N0
www.ezlink.on.ca/~atrositalane/
E-mail rmlane@ezlink.on.ca

519-348-0423
Fax 519-384-0172

Welcome to our modern, no-smoking, quiet, comfortable home 15 minutes west of Stratford. Full breakfast, home-baking. Central air. Guest sitting room, leather sofa, fireplace, cable TV, fridge, micro-wave. Queen and double beds. Ensuite bath. Golf, horseback riding and more. Close to Amish/Mennonite, Blyth, Drayton, Bayfield, Lake Huron, etc. Parking onsite. From $70 to $90. Extra person is $20 for adults, $15 for child, day or weeks. Please call for discounts.

ROOMS Family suite, Upper floor, Lower floor, **Baths** Private, Ensuite, **Beds** Queen, Double, **Air** Central, In rooms, Ceiling fans, **Smoking** Outside, **In Room** TV, VCR/DVD, **OTHERS** Open all year, **PAYMENT** Visa, Cheques accepted, Cash, Trvl's cheques, **BREAKFASTS** Full, Continental, Home-baked, **AMENITIES** Central TV, Fridge, Hot bev. bar, Lounge, Patio, **THINGS TO DO** Trail nearby, Rental canoe or boat, Golf, Fishing, Museums, Art, Theatre, Entertainment, Attractions, Shopping, Tennis, Swimming, Horseback riding, Beach, Antiquing, **LANGUAGE** Eng., Sp., **PRICE** (2 persons) 70–90 **(check with hosts for pricing details)**

STRATFORD

Avon and John

(Ray and Leonora Hopkins)

72 Avon St, Stratford, ON, N5A 5N4
www.cyg.net/~avonjohn
E-mail avonjohn@cyg.net

519-275-2954
Fax 519-275-2956
TFr 1-877-275-2954

Come and enjoy the warm hospitality and comfort of our beautiful century home, the magnificent full English breakfast, the wonderful award-winning gardens; all providing a memorable Stratford experience. Three guest rooms each have private bath, central air, fridge, coffeemaker and bathrobes. Located in a quiet park-like setting; walk to downtown, parks and the theatres. We offer all the amenities for today's discerning traveller, together with the warmth and good fellowship of an earlier era.

ROOMS Upper floor, **Baths** Private, Ensuite, **Beds** Queen, Twin, **Air** Central, **Smoking** Outside, **OTHERS** Urban, Adult, Open all year, **PAYMENT** Visa, MC, Amex, Cheques accepted, Cash, Trvl's cheques, **BREAKFASTS** Full, **AMENITIES** Central TV, Central phone, Whirlpool, Fridge, Hot bev. bar, Lounge, Patio, Central VCR/DVD, **THINGS TO DO** Trail nearby, Rental canoe or boat, Golf, Museums, Art, Theatre, Entertain-ment, Attractions, Shopping, Antiquing, **LANGUAGE** Eng., Fr., Ger., Dutch, **PRICE** (2 persons) 105–120 **(check with hosts for pricing details)**

STRATFORD

Double CC Farm

(Roger and Elaine Cook)

4335 Rd 110, RR #1, Stratford, ON, N5A 6S2
www.bbcanada.com/1674.html

519-271-1978

Let nature nourish your spirit on our 200-acre farm, 5 minutes NE of Stratford. Hosts are very interested in the environment and have planted over 10,000 trees. Enjoy birdwatching, hiking forest, field and pondside trails. This working farm has a fully operational historic circular sawmill and a woodworking shop. Relax in the screened-in porch in our 1867 heritage home or sit by the pond at Duck Inn. Open year-round, our main floor spacious queen ensuite with woodstove makes a charming getaway. Fridge in room.

ROOMS Upper floor, Ground floor, Private entrance, **Baths** Ensuite, Shared with hosts, **Beds** Queen, Twin, Pullout sofa, **Air** Ceiling fans, **Smoking** Outside, **In Room** Fireplace, **OTHERS** Rural, Open all year, Additional meals, **PAYMENT** Cheques accepted, Cash, **BREAKFASTS** Full, Home-baked, **AMENITIES** Central TV, Central phone, Fridge, Hot bev. bar, Lounge, Patio, Central VCR/DVD, **THINGS TO DO** Comp. bikes, Trail nearby, Rental canoe or boat, Golf, Museums, Art, Theatre, Entertainment, Attractions, Shopping, Cross-country skiing, Tennis, Swimming, Birdwatching, **LANGUAGE** Eng., **PRICE** (2 persons) 60–90 **(check with hosts for pricing details)**

STRATFORD

Dunn-Drae

(Verna Dunn)

278 Mornington St, Stratford, ON, N5A 5G6
www.canadianbandbguide.ca/bb.asp?ID=2269

519-273-0619

A warm welcome awaits you at our new home nestled in the pines. Central air, lounge, patio, queen, twin/king, twin, ensuite baths. Three rooms have balconies. Extended continental breakfast. Fireplace in lounge. No smoking. Parking.

ROOMS Upper floor, Private entrance, **Baths** Private, Ensuite, **Beds** King, Queen, Twin, **Air** Central, **Smoking** Outside, **In Room** TV, **OTHERS** Adult, Open all year, **PAYMENT** Visa, MC, Cheques accepted, Cash, **BREAKFASTS** Continental, **AMENITIES** Central TV, Lounge, Patio, **THINGS TO DO** Rental bikes, Trail nearby, Rental canoe or boat, Golf, Museums, Art, Theatre, Shopping, Tennis, Swimming, **LANGUAGE** Eng., **PRICE** (2 persons) 85–120 **(check with hosts for pricing details)**

STRATFORD

Harmony House

(Karen Zwakenberg)

RR #2, Stratford, ON, N5A 6S3
www.auracom.com/harmonyhouse
E-mail harmonyhouse@mail.auracom.com

519-273-6791

The emphasis is on privacy in this relaxing retreat just 5 minutes from Stratford. Enjoy the panoramic view from your private deck or from a lounge chair by the huge in-ground pool. Private entrance, breakfast facilities, full ensuite bath, continental breakfast and many "extras." The large, airy queen suite also adapts easily for three or even four guests! Children are welcome and pets will be considered. Please try us! We know you will be delighted.

ROOMS Family suite, Ground floor, Private entrance, **Baths** Private, Ensuite, **Beds** Queen, Single or cots, **Air** Ceiling fans, **Smoking** Outside, **In Room** Thermostat, Phone, TV, Internet access, VCR/DVD, **OTHERS** Babysitting, Rural, Seasonal, Pets in residence, Pets welcome, **PAYMENT** Cheques accepted, Cash, **BREAKFASTS** Continental, **AMENITIES** Swimming pool, Barbecue, Fridge, Patio, Central Internet access, **THINGS TO DO** Comp. bikes, Trail nearby, Golf, Fishing, Museums, Art, Theatre, Entertainment, Attractions, Wineries/Breweries, Shopping, Tennis, Swimming, Beach, Birdwatching, Antiquing, **LANGUAGE** Eng., Fr., **PRICE** (2 persons) 95 **(check with hosts for pricing details)**

Harrington House

(Kate MacRitchie)

25 Water St, Stratford, ON, N5A 3B9
www.theharringtonhouse.ca
E-mail theharringtonhouse@sympatico.ca

519-273-1898
TFr 1-888-273-1898

Just park and walk. Theatres and down-town within easy walking distance from our lovely home overlooking the Avon River. Warm hospitality, healthy gourmet breakfasts, guest TV, lounge, wireless high-speed, newspaper, front sitting porch, central air and on-site parking. Our well-appointed rooms feature king-size beds with ensuite or private baths. We also offer main floor twins. All major credit cards accepted. For full details, visit our Web site.

ROOMS Upper floor, Ground floor, Private entrance, **Baths** Private, Ensuite, **Beds** King, Twin, **Air** Central, **Smoking** Outside, **In Room** Internet access, **OTHERS** Open all year, **PAYMENT** Visa, MC, Amex, Direct debit, Cheques accepted, Cash, Trvl's cheques, **BREAKFASTS** Full, Home-baked, **AMENITIES** Central TV, Central phone, Lounge, Patio, Central Internet access, **THINGS TO DO** Trail nearby, Rental canoe or boat, Museums, Art, Theatre, Entertainment, Attractions, Shopping, Tennis, Antiquing, **LANGUAGE** Eng., **PRICE** (2 persons) 85–135 **(check with hosts for pricing details)**

Stone Maiden Inn

(Jim and Elaine Spencer)

123 Church St, Stratford, ON, N5A 2R3
www.StoneMaidenInn.com
E-mail smaiden@execulink.com

519-271-7129
Fax 519-271-4615
TFr 1-866-612-3385

Relax in the warmth and charm of our 1872 Victorian B&B Inn, located in a quiet residential area. Fourteen unique gue-strooms, all with ensuite bathrooms, tele-phones and cable TV. Rooms individually air-conditioned. Full breakfast included – served 8:30 to 10:00 a.m. Non-smoking. Fully equipped suites available at Classic House Suites (across the street from the Stone Maiden Inn, at 102–104 Church St, www.classic-house-suites.com). Easy walk to downtown and theatres.

ROOMS Family suite, Upper floor, Ground floor, Lower floor, **Baths** Ensuite, **Beds** King, Queen, Double, Twin, **Air** Central, In rooms, Ceiling fans, **Smoking** Outside, **In Room** Phone, TV, Fireplace, Internet access, VCR/DVD, **OTHERS** Urban, Open all year, **PAYMENT** Visa, MC, Cheques accepted, Cash, Trvl's cheques, **BREAKFASTS** Full, Home-baked, **AMENITIES** Central TV, Whirlpool, Fridge, Hot bev. bar, Lounge, Patio, Central Internet access, Central VCR/DVD, **THINGS TO DO** Comp. bikes, Rental canoe or boat, Golf, Museums, Art, Theatre, Entertainment, Shopping, Cross-country skiing, Tennis, Swimming, Horseback riding, Bird-watching, Antiquing, **LANGUAGE** Eng., **PRICE** (2 per-sons) 100–275 **(check with hosts for pricing details)**

SUDBURY *(northern Ontario)*

Auberge-sur-lac B&B

(Carmel Girouard)

1672 South Lane Rd, Sudbury, ON, P3G 1N8
www.cyberbeach.net/asl
E-mail tommyt@cyberbeach.net

705-522-5010
Fax 705-522-5010
TFr 1-888-535-6727

Beautiful and serene lakefront estate, breathtaking vistas from private Jacuzzi, breakfast nook, hilltop swing, upper and lower decks. Pick blueberries on the grounds, fish, swim, boat, birdwatch, picnic, hike or snowshoe on trails, and relax in front of the fireplace or in the foyer with cathedral ceiling, grand piano, cello and books. Access to Internet, fully equipped office and entertainment centre. Inquire about Romantic Evening packages. Honeymooners, families and business travellers are welcome all year.

ROOMS Ground floor, **Baths** Private, Ensuite, Shared with guest, **Beds** Queen, Double, Single or cots, **Air** Smoking Outside, **In Room** Phone, **OTHERS** Babysitting, Urban, Rural, Open all year, Additional meals, Pets welcome, **PAYMENT** Visa, MC, Diners, Amex, Cheques accepted, Cash, Trvl's cheques, **BREAKFASTS** Full, Home-baked, **AMENITIES** Central TV, Central phone, Barbecue, Laundry, Lounge, Patio, Central Internet access, Central VCR/DVD, **THINGS TO DO** Comp. bikes, Trail nearby, Rental canoe or boat, Comp. Canoe or boat, Golf, Fishing, Museums, Art, Theatre, Entertainment, Attractions, Shopping, Cross-country skiing, Tennis, Swimming, Horseback riding, Beach, Birdwatching, **LANGUAGE** Eng., Fr., **PRICE** (2 persons) 110–215 **(check with hosts for pricing details)**

SUDBURY

By-the-Lake

(Phyllis and Les Davison)

65 Nepahwin Ave, Sudbury, ON, P3E 2H5
www.bbcanada.com/5799.html

705-522-3803

In the heart of Sudbury, on the shore of Lake Nipahwin, we offer a spot of tranquility. Enjoy the garden, a summer swim or relax in our guest lounge to watch TV, read a book, or do a puzzle. We are 1 km west of Science North, close to hospital, university, conservation area, Imax, restaurants and shops. Full breakfast and onsite parking. No pets, no smoking. From Hwys 17, 69, 144, follow signs to Science North, Paris St to Nepahwin.

ROOMS Upper floor, **Baths** Shared with guest, **Beds** Queen, Twin, Single or cots, **Air** In rooms, **OTHERS** Urban, Adult, Open all year, **PAYMENT** Cheques accepted, Cash, **BREAKFASTS** Full, **AMENITIES** Central TV, Fridge, Hot bev. bar, Lounge, **THINGS TO DO** Golf, Fishing, Museums, Art, Theatre, Attractions, Shopping, Swimming, Beach, **LANGUAGE** Eng., **PRICE** (2 persons) 35–50 **(check with hosts for pricing details)**

SUDBURY

Millwood Bed & Breakfast

(Janet and David Maskery)

1808 Millwood Cr, Sudbury, ON, P3E 2T1
www.bbcanada.com/5353.html
E-mail millwoodbb@sympatico.ca

705-522-1441
TFr 1-866-307-7702

Lovely home close to Hwys 69 and 17. Beautifully decorated rooms with queen and hand-painted twin beds. Water Garden Room has ensuite jet bath, four-poster and fireplace. Our Family suite offers two bedrooms and ensuite bath. All rooms have TV and ceiling fans. Lounge with fireplace and library. Water Garden, hot tub and verandahs await you. Two cats and Westie in house. From Hwy 69 – RR #46 (Regent St), turn onto Loach's Rd at Pizza Hut, 2nd left onto Windle St, 1st left onto Millwood Cr. We are on the right-hand side.

ROOMS Family suite, Ground floor, Private entrance, **Baths** Private, Ensuite, **Beds** Queen, Twin, Single or cots, **Smoking** Outside, **In Room** Thermostat, TV, Fireplace, VCR/DVD, **OTHERS** Urban, Open all year, Pets in residence, Pets welcome, **PAYMENT** Visa, MC, Amex, Cheques accepted, Cash, Trvl's cheques, **BREAKFASTS** Full, Continental, Home-baked, **AMENITIES** Central phone, Whirlpool, Laundry, Fridge, Hot bev. bar, Lounge, Patio, Central Internet access, **THINGS TO DO** Trail nearby, Golf, Fishing, Museums, Art, Theatre, Entertainment, Attractions, Shopping, Cross-country skiing, Tennis, Swimming, Horseback riding, Beach, **LANGUAGE** Eng., **PRICE** (2 persons) 55–90 **(check with hosts for pricing details)**

THORNBURY *(northwest of Toronto)*

Hillside Bed & Breakfast

(Karen and Norm Stewart)

Box 72 , 110 Brook St, Clarksburg, ON, N0H 2P0
www.bbcanada.com/hillsidebb
E-mail stewart5923@rogers.com

519-599-5523

Welcome to Hillside, overlooking the village of Clarksburg in the beautiful Beaver Valley. Our stately 1880 Victorian home is situated on 3 1/2 acres of treed and terraced lawns, and features spacious rooms with period furnishings, deep wood trims, chandeliers and fireplaces. We are just minutes from Blue Mountain and Talisman Ski Resorts, Bruce and Georgian Trails, golf courses and Georgian Bay. Fine dining, antique shops and other stores in nearby Thornbury and Collingwood. Open year-round.

ROOMS Upper floor, **Baths** Shared with guest, **Beds** Queen, Double, Twin, Single or cots, **OTHERS** Urban, Adult, Open all year, **PAYMENT** Visa, Cheques accepted, Cash, Trvl's cheques, **BREAKFASTS** Full, Home-baked, **AMENITIES** Central TV, Central phone, Lounge, **THINGS TO DO** Rental bikes, Trail nearby, Rental canoe or boat, Golf, Fishing, Museums, Art, Theatre, Entertainment, Attractions, Wineries/ Breweries, Shopping, Cross-country skiing, Downhill skiing, Tennis, Swimming, Horseback riding, Beach, Birdwatching, Antiquing, **LANGUAGE** Eng., **PRICE** (2 persons) 95 **(check with hosts for pricing details)**

THUNDER BAY *(northwestern Ontario)*

Afton Court
Bed and Breakfast
(Walter and Christine Scott)

181 Belview Rd, Thunder Bay, ON, P7G 1L6
www.petfriendly.ca/property/114.html
E-mail aftoncourt@norlink.net

807-767-4845
Fax 807-767-4845

Ranch-style bungalow set in 5 semi-rural acres with trout pond in garden. Close to Hwy 102 and Hwy 11/17. There is an antique piano for guests use. Local attractions are Old Fort William Historical Park, Kakabeka Falls, Sleeping Giant Provincial Park, Terry Fox Lookout and Ouimet Canyon.

ROOMS Ground floor, **Baths** Ensuite, Shared with guest, **Beds** Double, Twin, **OTHERS** Rural, Open all year, Handicapped access, Pets in residence, Pets welcome, **PAYMENT** Visa, MC, Cash, Trvl's cheques, **BREAKFASTS** Full, **AMENITIES** Central TV, Central phone, Barbecue, Laundry, Kitchen, **THINGS TO DO** Golf, Fishing, Museums, Art, Theatre, Attractions, Shopping, Cross-country skiing, Tennis, Swimming, Horseback riding, **LANGUAGE** Eng., **PRICE** (2 persons) 50–70 **(check with hosts for pricing details)**

TILLSONBURG *(southwest of Hamilton)*

Rosewood House B&B
(Chick McKenzie)

7 Hyman St, Tillsonburg, ON, N4G 2C3
www.bbcanada.com/rosewoodhouse
E-mail chick_rosewood@sympatico.ca

519-842-8664
Fax 519-842-7631

A country setting in the heart of town, offering a full breakfast, Rosewood House is centrally located in a mature and quiet residential neighbourhood, close to all amenities and across from historic Annandale House. Relax in our heated pool and gardens or enjoy the many activities our community offers (golf, theatre, curling and sports complex). Go sightseeing, visit Lake Lisgar and Annandale House, shop in the boutiques or relax and enjoy the local cuisine in a fine restaurant. Located 1 hour from Stratford, 2 hours to Toronto.

ROOMS Upper floor, **Baths** Private, Ensuite, **Beds** Queen, Double, **Air** Central, **Smoking** Outside, **In Room** TV, **OTHERS** Open all year, **PAYMENT** Visa, MC, Direct debit, Cash, **BREAKFASTS** Full, **AMENITIES** Central TV, Central phone, Swimming pool, Barbecue, Lounge, **THINGS TO DO** Golf, Museums, Art, Attractions, Shopping, Swimming, **LANGUAGE** Eng., **PRICE** (2 persons) 75–90 **(check with hosts for pricing details)**

TORONTO

213 Carlton – The Toronto Townhouse

(Frank Aaron and Tan Wah)

213 Carlton St, Toronto, ON, M5A 2K9
www.toronto-townhouse.com
E-mail houseboy@toronto-townhouse.com

416-323-8898
TFr 1-877-500-0466

Toronto Tourism Award Winners for Accommodation 1999 and 2000! Luxury suites and large rooms in the heart of downtown Toronto. Just three blocks to College and Yonge Subway. Close to Eaton Centre, theatres, CN Tower, Skydome, ACC Centre. Walking distance to the new Yonge/Dundas Square (Times Square). Fantastic breakfasts and free parking are included. We're in Cabbagetown: a safe, vibrant and diverse neighbourhood.

ROOMS Upper floor, Ground floor, Private entrance, **Baths** Ensuite, Shared with guest, **Beds** King, Queen, Double, **Air** Central, **Smoking** Outside, **In Room** Phone, TV, **OTHERS** Urban, Open all year, **PAYMENT** Visa, MC, Diners, Amex, Cash, Trvl's cheques, **BREAKFASTS** Full, **AMENITIES** Central phone, **THINGS TO DO** Rental bikes, Trail nearby, Museums, Art, Theatre, Entertainment, Attractions, Wineries/Breweries, Shopping, Tennis, Swimming, Beach, **LANGUAGE** Eng., **PRICE** (2 persons) 99–175 **(check with hosts for pricing details)**

TORONTO

312 Seaton, a Toronto Bed & Breakfast

(Ted Bates and Nick Franjic)

312 Seaton St, Toronto, ON, M5A 2T7
www.312seaton.com
E-mail info@312seaton.com

416-968-0775
Fax 416-924-8656
TFr 1-866 968-0775

312 Seaton, a detached Victorian home on a quiet, tree-lined street in downtown Toronto's historical "Cabbagetown". From here you are close to many of Toronto's major tourist attractions, the downtown business district and financial area as well as hundreds of restaurants and clubs that offer a variety of dining and entertainment experiences for all tastes and budgets. Check out our latest edition of the one-bedroom furnished apartment.

ROOMS Upper floor, Ground floor, Lower floor, Private entrance, **Baths** Private, Ensuite, Shared with guest, **Beds** Queen, Double, Twin, **Air** In rooms, **Smoking** Outside, **In Room** TV, Internet access, **OTHERS** Open all year, Pets in residence, **PAYMENT** Visa, MC, Amex, Direct debit, Cash, Trvl's cheques, **BREAKFASTS** Full, **AMENITIES** Fridge, Lounge, Patio, Central Internet access, **THINGS TO DO** Museums, Art, Theatre, Entertainment, Attractions, Shopping, Swimming, Beach, Antiquing, **LANGUAGE** Eng., **PRICE** (2 persons) 85–125 **(check with hosts for pricing details)**

TORONTO

A Bed and Breakfast Assoc of Downtown Toronto

(Linda Lippa)

PO Box 190 Station B, Toronto, ON, M4R 1H5
www.Torontobedandbreakfast.com
E-mail info@torontobedandbreakfast.com

416-410-3938
Fax 416-483-8822
TFr 1-888-559-5515

Established in 1980, The Downtown Toronto Association of Bed & Breakfasts is a free registry service specializing in finding you the most suitable and satisfying B&B accomodation. We match your needs to available B&Bs. Each privately owned B&B has been independently inspected and approved. We personally know your hosts and provide a comfortable alternative to hotels, with a variety of accommodations in many of downtown Toronto's most interesting neighbourhoods. Please call for pricing and amenities.

ROOMS Upper floor, Ground floor, Lower floor, Private entrance, **Baths** Private, Ensuite, Shared with guest, **Beds** King, Queen, Twin, Pullout sofa, **Air** Central, In rooms, **In Room** Phone, TV, **OTHERS** Open all year, **PAYMENT** Visa, MC, Trvl's cheques, **BREAKFASTS** Full, Continental, Home-baked, **AMENITIES** Central TV, Central phone, Kitchen, Fridge, Lounge, Patio, **THINGS TO DO** Trail nearby, Golf, Museums, Art, Theatre, Entertainment, Attractions, Shopping, Beach, **LANGUAGE** Eng., Sp., Ger., **PRICE** (2 persons) 55–195 **(check with hosts for pricing details)**

TORONTO

Alan Gardens Bed and Breakfast

(Nadia Geith)

106A Pembroke St, Toronto, ON, M5A 2N8
www.alan-gardens-bandb-toronto.ca
E-mail info@alan-gardens-bandb-toronto.ca

416-967-9614
TFr 1-800-215-1937

We welcome you to our distinctive downtown residence in historic Cabbagetown, close to the beautiful Allan Gardens Conservatory and park. Centrally located, minutes to public transport, 10-minute walk to Eaton Centre, theatres and fabulous restaurants. Antiques, modern art and many books fill the spacious rooms. Art from local artists for sale. Full warm breakfasts and gourmet specialties served on weekend by candlelight and classical music. Friendly dog and cat on premises.

Baths Ensuite, Shared with guest, **Beds** Queen, Double, Single or cots, **Air** Central, Ceiling fans, **In Room** Internet access, **OTHERS** Open all year, Pets in residence, **PAYMENT** Visa, MC, Amex, Cash, Trvl's cheques, **BREAKFASTS** Full, **AMENITIES** Central phone, Lounge, **THINGS TO DO** Museums, Art, Theatre, Entertainment, Attractions, Shopping, Antiquing, **LANGUAGE** Eng., Fr., Ger., Dutch, **PRICE** (2 persons) 110–140 **(check with hosts for pricing details)**

TORONTO
Allenby Bed & Breakfast
(Doug Shaw)

351 Wolverleigh Blvd, Toronto, ON, M4C 1S7
www.theallenby.com
E-mail etmshaw@aol.com

416-461-7095

A lovely home with private, separate quarters for the guests. Private bath starts at $85 per night single, and shared bath starts at $55 per night single. Extra person is $10. Walk to subway, restaurants, banks, shopping. TV in room, satellite TV in salon. Free local telephone use. Free parking a minute's walk away!

ROOMS Upper floor, **Baths** Shared with guest, **Beds** Double, Single or cots, **Air** In rooms, **Smoking** Outside, **In Room** TV, **OTHERS** Urban, Adult, Open all year, **PAYMENT** Visa, MC, Cash, Trvl's cheques, **BREAKFASTS** Continental, Self-catered, **AMENITIES** Central TV, Central phone, Kitchen, Fridge, Hot bev. bar, Lounge, Patio, **THINGS TO DO** Rental bikes, Trail nearby, Golf, Museums, Art, Theatre, Entertainment, Attractions, Shopping, Tennis, Swimming, Beach, **LANGUAGE** Eng., **PRICE** (2 persons) 55–85 **(check with hosts for pricing details)**

TORONTO
Annex Quest House
(Henry Lotin)

83 Spadina Rd, Toronto, ON, M5R 2T1
www.annexquesthouse.com
E-mail info@annexquesthouse.com

416-922-1934
Fax 416-922-6366

Downtown near Spadina and Bloor in the Annex neighbourhood, Annex Quest House is a short walk to U of Toronto, Royal Ontario Museum and Yorkville shops. Bedrooms with private bathrooms are designed to increase the well-being of guests through the use of vastu, India's ancient design science. Each bedroom is dedicated to one of the four basic elements: earth, air, fire or water. We also offer customary amenities: private bath, air-conditioning, high-speed Internet access, bar fridge, cable TV, phone, smoke-free environment and parking.

ROOMS Upper floor, Ground floor, Lower floor, Private entrance, **Baths** Private, Ensuite, **Beds** Double, **Air** In rooms, **In Room** Thermostat, Phone, TV, Internet access, **OTHERS** Urban, Open all year, **PAYMENT** Visa, MC, Amex, Direct debit, Cash, Trvl's cheques, **AMENITIES** Barbecue, Laundry, Fridge, Patio, **THINGS TO DO** Museums, Art, Theatre, Entertainment, Attractions, Shopping, **LANGUAGE** Eng., Mandarin, Cantonese, **PRICE** (2 persons) 89–109 **(check with hosts for pricing details)**

Toronto

B&B in the Annex
(Philomena and Dave Vallance)

31 Dalton Rd, Toronto, ON, M5R 2Y8
www.canadianbandbguide.ca/bb.asp?ID=3153
E-mail valladp@echo-on.net

416-962-2786
Fax 416-964-8837

Our turn-of-the-century home is in downtown central Toronto, two blocks from
both subway lines. Guests remark on the
stained glass, original oak and, most
importantly, how comfortable the beds
are. Our quiet street leads into a cosmo-
politan shopping district with a wide
selection of restaurants that cover the
world. Many attractions including the
museum, Yorkville, Casa Loma, the
University of Toronto and others are
within easy walking distance. Two rooms
share a bath. Guests have use of kitchenette.

ROOMS Upper floor, **Baths** Shared with guest, **Beds**
Queen, Twin, **Air** Central, **Smoking** Outside, **OTHERS**
Open all year, Pets in residence, **PAYMENT** Cash, Trvl's
cheques, **BREAKFASTS** Full, **AMENITIES** Central TV,
Central phone, Kitchen, Fridge, Patio, **LANGUAGE** Eng.,
Ger., **PRICE** (2 persons) 60–80 **(check with hosts for
pricing details)**

Toronto

Cottage in the City
(Ron and Mardelle Kish)

52 Helena Ave, Toronto, ON, M6G 2H2
www.cottageinthecity.com
E-mail mardy46ca@yahoo.ca

416-654-9105

Welcome to a restored turn-of-the-century
home in the heart of Toronto. Close to all
public transportation, attractions and a
scant 30 minutes from the airport. Inside
you will find Persian carpets, a private collection of artwork; modern, folk, and aboriginal pieces collected by a globe-trot-
ting journalist. Relax in a stress-free environment featuring rooms with heritage
colours, an antique clawfoot tub and an
old-fashioned verandah. Breakfasts
include sumptuous organic specialties.

ROOMS Upper floor, **Baths** Shared with guest, **Beds**
Queen, Double, **Air** Central, **Smoking** Outside, **OTH-
ERS** Urban, Adult, Open all year, **PAYMENT** Cash, Trvl's
cheques, **BREAKFASTS** Full, **AMENITIES** Central
phone, Lounge, Patio, **THINGS TO DO** Trail nearby,
Museums, Art, Theatre, Entertainment, Attractions,
Wineries/Breweries, Shopping, **LANGUAGE** Eng.,
PRICE (2 persons) 90–110 **(check with hosts for pric-
ing details)**

TORONTO
Feathers
(May and Max Jarvie)

132 Wells St, Toronto, ON, M5R 1P4
www.bbcanada.com/1115.html
E-mail feathersbb@hotmail.com

416-534-1923
Fax 416-534-1587

Charming Victorian family home situated in a super downtown location called the Annex. Antique furniture, oriental tapestries and original artwork lend a unique atmosphere to interesting and beautifully renovated house. Steps away from the subway and a delightful area of affordably priced restaurants and cafes. Self-contained suite great for longer stays. Walk to Casa Loma and several other major attractions, shopping and theatres. Chosen for "Best places to B&B". Located two blocks north of Bloor near Bathurst.

ROOMS Family suite, Upper floor, **Baths** Ensuite, Shared with hosts, **Beds** King, Twin, Single or cots, **Air** Central, **Smoking** Outside, **In Room** TV, OTHERS Urban, Open all year, **PAYMENT** Cash, Trvl's cheques, BREAKFASTS Continental, **AMENITIES** Central phone, Fridge, Lounge, **THINGS TO DO** Museums, Art, Theatre, Entertainment, Attractions, Shopping, LANGUAGE Eng., Fr., Ger., Dutch, **PRICE** (2 persons) 75–105 **(check with hosts for pricing details)**

TORONTO
House on McGill
(Dave Perks)

110 McGill St, Toronto, ON, M5B 1H6
www.mcgillbb.ca
E-mail mcgillbb@interlog.com

416-351-1503
TFr 1-877-580-5015

A cozy Victorian B&B, c. 1894, in the heart of exciting, vibrant Toronto, just steps to shopping, restaurants and clubs. Restored and updated with modern conveniences while retaining high ceilings, cornice moldings, antiques and charm of a bygone era. We offer six unique bedrooms, one with ensuite, two other baths, guest living room, equipped kitchen, deck and garden. Enjoy free local calls, cableTV/VCR, video library, A/C, laundry, breakfast buffet, e-mail, bike rental, airport transfer, discounts and more.

ROOMS Upper floor, Ground floor, Lower floor, **Baths** Private, Ensuite, Shared with guest, **Beds** King, Queen, Double, Twin, Single or cots, **Air** In rooms, **Smoking** Outside, **In Room** TV, OTHERS Urban, Adult, Open all year, **PAYMENT** Visa, MC, Diners, Cash, Trvl's cheques, BREAKFASTS Full, Home-baked, **AMENITIES** Central phone, Laundry, Kitchen, Fridge, Hot bev. bar, Lounge, Patio, **THINGS TO DO** Rental bikes, Trail nearby, Museums, Art, Theatre, Entertainment, Attractions, Shopping, Tennis, Swimming, LANGUAGE Eng., Fr., **PRICE** (2 persons) 50–110 **(check with hosts for pricing details)**

TORONTO
Lowtherhouse
Bed and Breakfast
(Linda Lilge)

72 Lowther Ave, Toronto, ON, M5R 1C8
www.lowtherhouse.ca
E-mail linda@lowtherhouse.ca

416-323-1589
Fax 416-961-9322
TFr 1-800-265-4158

Lowtherhouse is a three-storey, 1890 Victorian mansion. Guests at Lowtherhouse will experience an urban environment as well as a quiet community as we are located just two blocks from the vibrant Bloor and Avenue Rd area and the well established Annex neighbourhood. The St. George subway station is two blocks away and a friendly family park is just across the street. All rooms have private bathrooms. A full English-style breakfast is served every morning in the formal dining room.

ROOMS Upper floor, **Baths** Ensuite, **Beds** King, Queen, Double, Twin, **Air** Central, **Smoking** Outside, **In Room** Phone, TV, **OTHERS** Urban, Open all year, Pets in residence, **PAYMENT** Visa, MC, Amex, Cash, Trvl's cheques, **BREAKFASTS** Full, **THINGS TO DO** Museums, Art, Theatre, Entertainment, Attractions, Shopping, **LANGUAGE** Eng., Fr., **PRICE** (2 persons) 95–175 **(check with hosts for pricing details)**

TORONTO
The Red Door Bed & Breakfast
(Jean and Paul Pedersen)

301 Indian Rd, Toronto, ON, M6R 2X7
www.reddoorbb.com
E-mail info@reddoorbb.com

416-604-0544

The Red Door is an elegant 1912 home on a quiet, tree-lined residential street. Our large, beautifully furnished bedrooms have queen-size beds, private bathrooms, air-conditioning, TV, clock-radio and comfortable chairs. We are a 5-minute walk from the subway, which will take you to the centre of downtown Toronto in 15 minutes. To find us, from Hwy 401 take Hwy 427 south to Gardiner Expressway, exit to Lakeshore, then to Parkside, go to Bloor St, right two blocks to Indian Rd, right again to #301.

ROOMS Family suite, Upper floor, **Baths** Private, Ensuite, **Beds** Queen, Single or cots, Pullout sofa, **Air** In rooms, **Smoking** Outside, **In Room** TV, Fireplace, Internet access, **OTHERS** Urban, Open all year, **PAYMENT** Visa, MC, Cheques accepted, Cash, Trvl's cheques, **BREAKFASTS** Full, **AMENITIES** Central phone, **THINGS TO DO** Trail nearby, Museums, Art, Theatre, Entertainment, Attractions, Shopping, Tennis, Swimming, **LANGUAGE** Eng., Fr., **PRICE** (2 persons) 135–155 **(check with hosts for pricing details)**

TORONTO

Vanderkooy Bed & Breakfast

(Joan Vanderkooy)

53 Walker Ave, Toronto, ON, M4V 1G3
www.bbht.ca/Homes/Vanderkooy.html
E-mail j.vanderkooy@sympatico.ca

416-925-8765
Fax 416-925-8557

Built in 1910, this immaculate and cozy
home has retained many of its original
decorative touches, including excellent
examples of Edwardian stained-glass windows, antiques and a collection of original watercolours. A full breakfast is served
on an antique oak table surrounded by
fragrant plants and overlooking a colourful garden and miniature waterfall. Start
your morning with a jog through one of
the city's quietest downtown neighbourhoods, or take a nature hike through
Balfour Park. Free parking.

ROOMS Upper floor, **Baths** Ensuite, Shared with
guest, **Beds** King, Double, Twin, **Air** Central, **OTHERS**
Open all year, Pets in residence, **PAYMENT** Cheques
accepted, Cash, Trvl's cheques, **BREAKFASTS** Full,
Home-baked, **AMENITIES** Central TV, Central phone,
Lounge, Patio, Central Internet access, Central
VCR/DVD, **THINGS TO DO** Trail nearby, Museums, Art,
Theatre, Entertainment, Attractions, Wineries/
Breweries, Shopping, Antiquing, **LANGUAGE** Eng.,
PRICE (2 persons) 75–100 **(check with hosts for pric-
ing details)**

TORONTO

Victoria's Mansion

(Jayne Miles)

68 Gloucester St, Toronto, ON, M4Y 1L8
www.victoriasmansion.com
E-mail info@victoriasmansion.com

416-921-4625
Fax 416-944-1092

This charming alternative to higher
priced accomodations in Toronto is walking distance to Bloor and Yonge – *the*
place to shop and dine in Toronto.
Breakfast is served at Java Jive, around
the corner, and guests enjoy a free meal
after their third purchase (approx
$6/breakfast – with the *greatest* coffee
around!). Walk everywhere downtown
from our safe street and enjoy the exciting neighbourhood that surrounds us.

ROOMS Family suite, Upper floor, Ground floor, Lower
floor, **Baths** Private, Ensuite, **Beds** King, Queen,
Double, Twin, Single or cots, Pullout sofa, **Air** In rooms,
Smoking Outside, In rooms, **In Room** Phone, TV,
Internet access, **OTHERS** Babysitting, Urban, Open all
year, Pets welcome, **PAYMENT** Visa, MC, Direct debit,
Cash, **BREAKFASTS** Self-catered, **AMENITIES** Central
TV, Central phone, Laundry, Kitchen, Fridge, Hot bev.
bar, Central Internet access, **THINGS TO DO** Museums,
Art, Theatre, Entertainment, Attractions,
Wineries/Breweries, Shopping, Antiquing, **LANGUAGE**
Eng., Fr., Sp., **PRICE** (2 persons) 92–145 **(check with
hosts for pricing details)**

Vankleek Hill *(east of Ottawa)*

Cliftondale B&B
(Lorrie Clare)

270 Cty Rd #20, Vankleek Hill, ON, K0B 1R0
www.hawk.igs.net/~cliftond
E-mail cliftond@hawk.igs.net

613-678-6651
Fax 613-678-3908

Cliftondale is located 4 km west of Vankleek Hill, the Gingerbread Capital of Ontario. Historic 1893 Victorian family home. Home cooking is our specialty. Relax in our hot tub year round. Enjoy crafts, antiques, art galleries, flea markets, Maxville Highland Games, relax at our peaceful country getaway on the patio, or enjoy natural beauty of the area. Only 50 minutes from Ottawa, Montreal, US border. Families welcome. Package rates available. At-home hospitality. Inspection welcome. Something for everyone here.

ROOMS Upper floor, Private entrance, **Baths** Shared with guest, **Beds** Queen, Double, Twin, Single or cots, **Air** Central, Ceiling fans, **Smoking** Outside, **OTHERS** Rural, Open all year, **PAYMENT** Cheques accepted, Cash, Trvl's cheques, **BREAKFASTS** Full, Home-baked, **AMENITIES** Central TV, Central phone, Whirlpool, Lounge, Patio, **THINGS TO DO** Trail nearby, Golf, Fishing, Art, Attractions, Shopping, Cross-country skiing, Swimming, Birdwatching, Antiquing, **LANGUAGE** Eng., **PRICE** (2 persons) 75 **(check with hosts for pricing details)**

Vankleek Hill

Dreamland on the Ridge
(Ab Kastor and Monique Moulard)

5870 County Rd 10, RR #1, Fournier, ON, K0B 1G0
www.theridge.itgo.com
E-mail ambb@sprint.ca

613-524-3749

A cottage-style home on a 16-acre pine forest in the scenic lower Ottawa Valley. Come and relax by the pool, the wood-stove and hot tub. Watch birds at our feeders and rest in our peaceful country setting while enjoying our English gardens. Our rooms are cozy and beautifully decorated with a theme and view. Wake up to the smell of bread baking for breakfast. That is our specialty. French specials are served in our sunroom, special diets welcome, meals on request. Visit our craft and rustic furniture showroom.

ROOMS Family suite, Upper floor, Ground floor, Lower floor, Private entrance, **Baths** Private, Ensuite, Shared with guest, **Beds** Queen, Double, Twin, Pullout sofa, **Air** Ceiling fans, **Smoking** Outside, **In Room** Thermostat, Internet access, **OTHERS** Rural, Open all year, Additional meals, Pets welcome, **PAYMENT** Cheques accepted, Cash, Trvl's cheques, **BREAKFASTS** Full, Home-baked, **AMENITIES** Central TV, Central phone, Swimming pool, Whirlpool, Barbecue, Fridge, Lounge, Patio, Central Internet access, **THINGS TO DO** Comp. bikes, Trail nearby, Golf, Cross-country skiing, Swimming, Birdwatching, Antiquing, **LANGUAGE** Eng., Fr., **PRICE** (2 persons) 50–80 **(check with hosts for pricing details)**

VINELAND STATION *(west of Niagara Falls)*

The Occasional Rumour Guest House
(Geoff Bowden)

4340 Victoria Ave, Vineland Station, ON, L0R 2E0
www.occasionalrumour.ca
E-mail info@occasionalrumour.ca

905-562-8164
Fax 905-562-8245

An informal, comfortable, one-of-a-kind character home in the heart of the Niagara wine region, close to all major attractions. A quiet retreat ideal for writers, artists and anyone seeking a peaceful ambience that transports guests back to a simpler time. A place for storytellers to meet and share stories. There are three comfortably appointed bedrooms, and a living room where guests can relax after a day filled with activity. The emphasis is on home-style comfort and friendly hospitality.

ROOMS Ground floor, **Baths** Shared with guest, **Beds** Queen, Double, Twin, **Air** Central, **OTHERS** Urban, Adult, Open all year, Pets in residence, **PAYMENT** Visa, MC, Cash, **BREAKFASTS** Full, Continental, Home-baked, **AMENITIES** Central phone, Lounge, **THINGS TO DO** Trail nearby, Golf, Museums, Art, Theatre, Entertainment, Attractions, Wineries/Breweries, Shopping, **LANGUAGE** Eng., **PRICE** (2 persons) 89 **(check with hosts for pricing details)**

WALKERTON *(northwest of Toronto)*

Silver Creek B&B
(Ruby Huygen)

17 Yonge St S, Box 957, Walkerton, ON, N0G 2V0
www.canadianbandbguide.ca/bb.asp?ID=1986

519-881-0252
Fax 519-881-0252

Comfortable, country-style home. Spacious lawns. Flower gardens. Silver Creek in yard. One block from Saugeen River fishing and canoeing. Hearty country-style breakfast. Enjoy Victorian ambience, quiet relaxing, seasonal attractions of Saugeen country.

ROOMS Upper floor, **Baths** Ensuite, Shared with guest, Shared with hosts, **Beds** Queen, Double, Single or cots, **Air** In rooms, Ceiling fans, **Smoking** Outside, **OTHERS** Urban, Open all year, Pets in residence, Pets welcome, **PAYMENT** Cheques accepted, Cash, Trvl's cheques, **BREAKFASTS** Full, Home-baked, **AMENITIES** Central TV, Central phone, Barbecue, Central VCR/DVD, **THINGS TO DO** Trail nearby, Golf, Fishing, Museums, Wineries/Breweries, Shopping, Cross-country skiing, Tennis, Swimming, Birdwatching, Antiquing, **LANGUAGE** Eng., **PRICE** (2 persons) 55–70 **(check with hosts for pricing details)**

WARKWORTH *(east of Toronto)*

Humphrey House

(Arlene Mann)

122 Church St, Warkworth, ON, K0L 1Z0
www.humphreyhouse.com
E-mail humphreyhouse@sympatico.ca

705-924-1520
Fax 705-924-1520

Humphrey House was built in the 1850s by Israel Humphreys, a wealthy English merchant. Our 6,000 sq. ft., three-storey Victorian home is truly a heritage treasure. Nestled in the rolling hills of Northumberland, Humphrey House has been completely restored to its former glory and offers a unique experience for travellers to the area. A great place for family and friends to stay. Warkworth is a quiet village surrounded by seven hills, the site of a thriving arts community.

ROOMS Family suite, Upper floor, Ground floor, **Baths** Ensuite, Shared with guest, **Beds** Queen, Double, Twin, Single or cots, **Air** Central, Ceiling fans, **Smoking** Outside, **PAYMENT** Visa, Cheques accepted, Cash, Trvl's cheques, **BREAKFASTS** Full, Home-baked, **AMENITIES** Central TV, Central phone, Barbecue, Laundry, Lounge, Patio, Central VCR/DVD, **THINGS TO DO** Trail nearby, Golf, Fishing, Art, Theatre, Entertainment, Attractions, Shopping, Birdwatching, Antiquing, **LANGUAGE** Eng., **PRICE** (2 persons) 85–110 **(check with hosts for pricing details)**

WARKWORTH

Thornton Inn

(Ruth and Jerry Wojtiuk)

44 Main St, Warkworth, ON, K0K 3K0
www.thorntoninn.com
E-mail thornton_inn@yahoo.ca

705-924-3980

Nestled among the beautiful Northumberland Hills, 90 minutes from Toronto, the Thornton Inn is a luxury bed and breakfast located in the picturesque village of Warkworth. This newly renovated 1890 Victorian-style home is convenient to Main St boutiques, gallerys, Presqu'ile Provincial Park, three golf courses, nature trails, antique shops, wineries, restaurants and local theatres. Complete your get away with one of our home cooked full gourmet breakfasts capturing the taste of the season.

ROOMS Upper floor, **Baths** Private, Ensuite, **Beds** King, Queen, Twin, **Air** Central, **Smoking** Outside, **OTHERS** Rural, Open all year, **PAYMENT** Visa, MC, Cash, **BREAKFASTS** Full, Home-baked, **AMENITIES** Central phone, Fridge, Hot bev. bar, Lounge, Patio, **THINGS TO DO** Trail nearby, Golf, Fishing, Museums, Art, Theatre, Attractions, Wineries/Breweries, Shopping, Cross-country skiing, Swimming, Horseback riding, Beach, **LANGUAGE** Eng., **PRICE** (2 persons) 90–100 **(check with hosts for pricing details)**

WASAGA BEACH *(northwest of Toronto)*

At the Sandpiper
(Rosemarie and Bert Hoferichter)

53 – 60th St N, Wasaga Beach, ON, L0L 2P0
www.bbcanada.com/sandpiper
E-mail sandpiperbb@sympatico.ca

705-429-2746

Our tastefully decorated home is located 300 feet from the beach. We are on Georgian Bay on Hwy 26 on a 10-mile-long sand beach. We feature fine accommodations, three private rooms: two queen-size bedrooms with private ensuite, and one bedroom with two single beds. Our home has A/C. Close to Blue Mountain and Blueberry trails for cross-country/downhill skiing. Complimentary bikes, beach umbrellas and chairs. Ask us about our famous weekend special with dinner. See our Web site.

ROOMS Family suite, Upper floor, **Baths** Private, Ensuite, **Beds** Queen, Twin, **Air** Central, **Smoking** Outside, **In Room** Thermostat, Fireplace, **OTHERS** Rural, Adult, Open all year, Pets in residence, **PAYMENT** Visa, Cash, Trvl's cheques, **BREAKFASTS** Full, Home-baked, **AMENITIES** Central TV, Central phone, Barbecue, Fridge, Lounge, Patio, **THINGS TO DO** Comp. bikes, Trail nearby, Golf, Fishing, Museums, Theatre, Entertainment, Attractions, Wineries/Breweries, Shopping, Cross-country skiing, Tennis, Swimming, Horseback riding, Beach, **LANGUAGE** Eng., Ger., **PRICE** (2 persons) 75–95 **(check with hosts for pricing details)**

WASAGA BEACH

Cherry House
(Ed and Susan Mezger)

216 Cherry St, Box 1633, Stayner, ON, L0M 1S0
www.bbcanada.com/cherryhouse
E-mail edmezger@rogers.com

705-428-5549

This beautiful century home is located in Stayner, a friendly, quiet little town of about 3,000 people. Cherry House has been renovated to include three spacious guest rooms, each with its own ensuite. It is close to Wasaga Beach and Collingwood and all the area has to offer, summer and winter. Come and enjoy our small-town ambience or be on the beach or at the mountain in just a few minutes. Breakfast is always a happy event and features hearty house specialties that will delight and satisfy.

ROOMS Ground floor, Private entrance, **Baths** Ensuite, **Beds** Queen, **Air** Central, **Smoking** Outside, **In Room** Thermostat, TV, VCR/DVD, **OTHERS** Open all year, Additional meals, **PAYMENT** Visa, MC, Direct debit, Cash, Trvl's cheques, **BREAKFASTS** Full, **AMENITIES** Central phone, Fridge, **THINGS TO DO** Trail nearby, Golf, Fishing, Museums, Art, Entertainment, Attractions, Wineries/Breweries, Shopping, Cross-country skiing, Downhill skiing, Swimming, Horseback riding, Beach, Birdwatching, Antiquing, **LANGUAGE** Eng., **PRICE** (2 persons) 75–95 **(check with hosts for pricing details)**

WATERLOO *(west of Hamilton)*

Banbury Farm B&B

(Sarah Banbury)

1942 Wilby Rd, Baden, ON, N3A 3M9
www.banburyfarm.com
E-mail sbanbury@porchlight.ca

519-634-5451
TFr 1-888-892-0666

Experience the quiet, space, comfort and hospitality at Banbury Farm. Enjoy the lovely rural landscape. Relax on our screened porch. Visit the horses and emus. Daisy, our dog, loves attention. The generous breakfast features home-baking and homemade preserves. English riding lessons are available. Play golf, visit St. Jacobs, Stratford, Mennonite country, farmer's markets, universities. Farm is located 10 minutes west of Waterloo.

ROOMS Upper floor, **Baths** Shared with guest, **Beds** Double, Twin, Single or cots, **Smoking** Outside, **In Room** Thermostat, **OTHERS** Rural, Adult, Open all year, Additional meals, Pets in residence, **PAYMENT** Cash, Trvl's cheques, **BREAKFASTS** Home-baked, **AMENITIES** Central TV, Central phone, Kitchen, Lounge, Patio, **THINGS TO DO** Golf, Art, Theatre, Attractions, Shopping, **LANGUAGE** Eng., Fr., **PRICE** (2 persons) 75 **(check with hosts for pricing details)**

WESTPORT *(southwest of Ottawa)*

A Bit of Gingerbread B&B

(Anne and Robert Bradley)

27 Bedford St, Box 183, Westport, ON, K0G 1X0
www.westportrideaulakes.on.ca

613-273-7848

Victorian home in centre of picturesque village. Gourmet breakfasts. TV, library and parlour for guests. Ideal place for exploring the Rideau Lakes area. Restaurants nearby. Nature centres, walking tours, beaches, Rideau Waterway, Rideau District Museum and Foley Mountain. Centre for hiking, cycling, canoeing, antiques and shopping. Transportaion to Rideau and Trans-Canada trails, harbour and airfield. Accredited Ontario SuperHost and recipient of 1999 Tourism Award. Directions: CR 10 from Ottawa or Kingston. No pets.

ROOMS Upper floor, **Baths** Ensuite, Shared with guest, **Beds** Queen, Twin, Single or cots, **Air** In rooms, **OTHERS** Urban, Open all year, Additional meals, **PAYMENT** Cheques accepted, Cash, Trvl's cheques, **BREAKFASTS** Full, Home-baked, **AMENITIES** Central TV, Central phone, Lounge, Patio, **THINGS TO DO** Trail nearby, Rental canoe or boat, Golf, Fishing, Museums, Theatre, Attractions, Shopping, Cross-country skiing, Tennis, Swimming, Beach, Birdwatching, Antiquing, **LANGUAGE** Eng., Fr., **PRICE** (2 persons) 65–95 **(check with hosts for pricing details)**

WESTPORT

The Cove Country Inn
(Mary and Terry Cowan)

2 Bedford St, Westport, ON, K0G 1X0
www.coveinn.com
E-mail info@coveinn.com

613-273-3636
Fax 613-273-3466
TFr 1-888-268-3466

Our century B&B Inn is conveniently nestled on the harbour in the quaint resort town of Westport-on-the-Rideau, close to great shopping, boating, fishing, cross-country skiing, hiking, golf, swimming and biking. Our all-season Inn includes 15 suites, some with Jacuzzi and/or fireplaces, pool, hot tub and sauna, canoes, licensed dining rooms with patio overlooking the water, pub/piano lounge, full spa facilities adjacent (guest discount), packages and small conference facilities.

ROOMS Family suite, Upper floor, Ground floor, **Baths** Private, Ensuite, **Beds** Queen, Double, Twin, Pullout sofa, **Air** Central, In rooms, **In Room** Thermostat, Fireplace, **OTHERS** Babysitting, Rural, Open all year, Handicapped access, Additional meals, **PAYMENT** Visa, MC, Diners, Amex, Direct debit, Cheques accepted, Cash, Trvl's cheques, **BREAKFASTS** Full, **AMENITIES** Central TV, Central phone, Swimming pool, Sauna, Whirlpool, Barbecue, Laundry, Fridge, Lounge, Patio, **THINGS TO DO** Trail nearby, Rental canoe or boat, Comp. canoe or boat, Golf, Fishing, Museums, Art, Entertainment, Attractions, Wineries/Breweries, Shopping, Cross-country skiing, Tennis, Swimming, Horseback riding, Beach, Birdwatching, Antiquing, **LANGUAGE** Eng., **PRICE** (2 persons) 80–145 **(check with hosts for pricing details)**

WHITBY *(east of Toronto)*

Heritage House
(Ron and Janet Lusted)

9560 Mud Lake Rd, Myrtel Station/Ashburn, ON, L0B 1A0
www.bbcanada.com/5313.html
E-mail heritage9560@sympatico.ca

905-655-3563

Heritage House situated in the hamlet of Myrtle Station in the town of Whitby. Built by a Scottish bricklayer in 1872, we offer the charm of a century Victorian farmhouse on 80 acres. We have a complete private guest house with its own entrance and deck and private bathroom and fireplace plus private Victorian rooms with private bathroom, own entrance. We offer great hospitality and warm atmosphere. Trails and many attractions are in the area. Take Hwy 401 east to Brock St, Whitby, north on Hwy 12 to Myrtle.

ROOMS Family suite, Upper floor, Ground floor, Private entrance, **Baths** Private, Shared with hosts, **Beds** Queen, Double, Twin, **Smoking** Outside, **In Room** Thermostat, TV, Fireplace, **OTHERS** Rural, Open all year, Pets in residence, Pets welcome, **PAYMENT** Cheques accepted, Cash, Trvl's cheques, **BREAKFASTS** Full, Continental, Home-baked, Self-catered, **AMENITIES** Central TV, Central phone, Swimming pool, Barbecue, Kitchen, Fridge, Hot bev. bar, Lounge, Patio, **THINGS TO DO** Trail nearby, Golf, Fishing, Museums, Art, Theatre, Entertainment, Attractions, Wineries/Breweries, Shopping, Cross-country skiing, Tennis, Swimming, Horseback riding, **LANGUAGE** Eng., **PRICE** (2 persons) 90–110 **(check with hosts for pricing details)**

WIARTON *(northwest of Toronto)*

Down A Country Lane
(Gord and Ellie Cox)

RR #3, Wiarton, ON, N0H 2T0
www.downacountrylane.com
E-mail info@downacountrylane.com

519-534-3170
Fax 519-534-1211

A picturesque setting north of Sauble Beach on Bruce Rd 13 midway between Sauble Beach and Wiarton. Ideal for hikers, birders, cyclists, snowmobilers, skiers, canoeists and photographers, with some of the best rated sunsets in the world. Enjoy all of the activities of all four seasons. Full home-baked breakfasts, tastefully decorated rooms with queen beds, each with its own bathroom. Only an hour's drive from Tobermory, 10 minutes from Wiarton and Sauble Beach.

ROOMS Upper floor, Private entrance, **Baths** Ensuite, **Beds** Queen, Single or cots, **Air Smoking** Outside, **In Room** Thermostat, **OTHERS** Rural, Open all year, Additional meals, Pets in residence, **PAYMENT** Visa, Cheques accepted, Cash, Trvl's cheques, **BREAKFASTS** Full, Home-baked, **AMENITIES** Central TV, Barbecue, Fridge, Lounge, Patio, **THINGS TO DO** Trail nearby, Golf, Fishing, Museums, Art, Theatre, Attractions, Shopping, Cross-country skiing, Tennis, Swimming, Horseback riding, Beach, Birdwatching, Antiquing, **LANGUAGE** Eng., **PRICE** (2 persons) 75–90 **(check with hosts for pricing details)**

WINCHESTER *(southeast of Ottawa)*

The Other Place
Bed & Breakfast
(Eunice and Don Johnston)

11719 County Rd, 43W, Winchester, ON, K0C 2K0
www.theotherplace.ca
E-mail eunice@theotherplace.ca

613-774-5063
Fax 613-774-5966

Relaxed, informal country setting centrally located between Ottawa and Morrisburg. Small herd of registered miniature horses. Guest sitting room with fridge, microwave and TV. Directions: From Hwy 401, take Hwy 416 north to Exit 34. Travel 20-minutes east on Country Rd 43 or take 31 north to Winchester. Go west on 43 toward Kemptville.

ROOMS Upper floor, Ground floor, Private entrance, **Baths** Ensuite, Shared with guest, **Beds** Queen, Pullout sofa, **Air** Central, **Smoking** Outside, **OTHERS** Rural, Open all year, **PAYMENT** Cash, Trvl's cheques, **BREAKFASTS** Full, **AMENITIES** Central TV, Central phone, Fridge, Lounge, **THINGS TO DO** Theatre, **LANGUAGE** Eng., **PRICE** (2 persons) 65–90 **(check with hosts for pricing details)**

WINDSOR *(southwestern Ontario)*

Woodslee Bed & Breakfast

(Jackson and Mila Baldwin)

2510 County Rd 27, Woodslee, ON, N0R 1V0
www.woodsleebb.com
E-mail mila@mnsi.net

519-975-2591

Woodslee B&B is centrally located in Essex County, 25 minutes from Windsor and Detroit. Our home is a modern, open-concept ranch with guest rooms on the main floor. Nearby amenities include two golf courses, Fort Malden, Heritage Village, Point Pelee National Park (popular with birders), two marinas and the town of Essex. We are 5 minutes from Hwy 401 Exit 34. Turn left onto County Rd 27 (Belle River Rd) and look for our sign at number 2510.

ROOMS Ground floor, **Baths** Ensuite, Shared with guest, **Beds** Queen, Double, Twin, **Air** Central, **Smoking** Outside, **In Room** TV, Fireplace, **OTHERS** Rural, Open all year, Additional meals, Pets in residence, **PAYMENT** Visa, Cheques accepted, Cash, Trvl's cheques, **BREAKFASTS** Full, Home-baked, **AMENITIES** Central TV, Central phone, Fridge, Lounge, Patio, **THINGS TO DO** Trail nearby, Golf, Fishing, Museums, Shopping, Swimming, Beach, **LANGUAGE** Eng., **PRICE** (2 persons) 65–75 **(check with hosts for pricing details)**

WOODSTOCK *(west of Hamilton)*

Lil' Bit Country Guest Suite

(Nico and Alice Jukema)

583546 Hamilton Rd, Ingersoll, ON, N5C 3J7
www.lilbitcountry.ca
E-mail guestsuite@lilbitcountry.ca

519-485-2101
Fax 519-485-2103
TFr 1-877-454-5248

Welcome! Reduced rates for stay of three or more nights. Air-conditioned suite with full kitchenette on lower level, with a three-piece private bath on main floor level. Fluffy white towels and monogrammed robes. *Canada Select* 4 1/2-stars. Ideal if driving Hwys 401, 402, 403 or day tripping. Full breakfast in dining room at 8:30 or 'early bird' breakfast in your suite. Curl up by the gas fireplace, enjoy the stocked entertainment centre and satellite TV, or join us in the evening in our sitting room. Take a stroll over the backyard bridge. Telephone, fax, free high-speed Internet, washer, dryer, iron and ironing board, laundry service available (nomininal fee).

ROOMS Family suite, Lower floor, Private entrance, **Baths** Private, **Beds** Queen, Single or cots, Pullout sofa, **Air** Central, **Smoking** Outside, **In Room** Thermostat, Phone, TV, Fireplace, **OTHERS** Rural, Open all year, **PAYMENT** Visa, MC, Amex, Cash, Trvl's cheques, **BREAKFASTS** Full, Continental, Home-baked, Self-catered, **AMENITIES** Central TV, Central phone, Barbecue, Laundry, Kitchen, Fridge, Lounge, Patio, **THINGS TO DO** Golf, Fishing, Museums, Art, Theatre, Attractions, Wineries/Breweries, Shopping, Cross-country skiing, Swimming, **LANGUAGE** Eng., Dutch and Friesian, **PRICE** (2 persons) 75–95 **(check with hosts for pricing details)**

Woodstock

Zeelandia B&B

(Ben and Elly Veld)

405229 Beaconsfield Rd, Burgessville, ON, N0J 1C0
www.ocbba.ca/ZeelandiaBB.htm
E-mail benveld@execulink.com

519-424-9586
Fax 519-424-9589
TFr 1-866-424-3944

Our Cape Cod home is on a country road.
Enjoy peace and quiet after a day of travelling. Walk in woods, relax on verandah.
Drinks served. Crib available. Fireplace in
recreation room, games, TV, videos. Stay a
couple of days and do some day-tripping
or play golf. Close to Woodstock, Norwich,
Otterville, Tilsonburg, Paris, Ingersoll,
London and Stratford. Airport bus pickup
available at Woodstock. Go 8 km south on
59 Hwy at Exit 232 of 401 at Woodstock,
past a horse farm turn left, we are 405229
Beaconsfield Rd.

ROOMS Upper floor, Lower floor, Private entrance,
Baths Ensuite, Shared with guest, **Beds** King, Queen,
Ceiling fans, Twin, Single or cots, Pullout sofa, **Air**
Central, Ceiling fans, **Smoking** Outside, **OTHERS** Rural,
Open all year, **PAYMENT** Visa, MC, Diners, Amex, Cash,
Trvl's cheques, **BREAKFASTS** Full, Home-baked,
AMENITIES Laundry, Kitchen, Fridge, Lounge, Patio,
Central Internet access, Central VCR/DVD, **THINGS TO
DO** Trail nearby, Golf, Museums, Art, Theatre,
Attractions, Wineries/Breweries, Shopping, Bird-
watching, Antiquing, **LANGUAGE** Eng., Sp., Ger., Dutch,
PRICE (2 persons) 85 **(check with hosts for pricing
details)**

QUEBEC

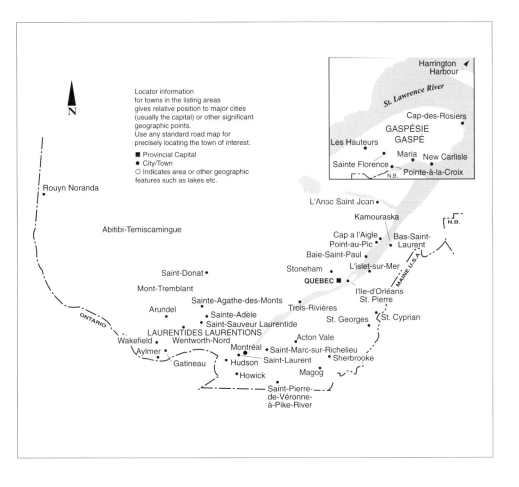

N

Locator information
for towns in the listing areas
gives relative position to major cities
(usually the capital) or other significant
geographic points.
Use any standard road map for
precisely locating the town of interest.

■ Provincial Capital
● City/Town
○ Indicates area or other geographic
features such as lakes etc.

Harrington Harbour

St. Lawrence River

Cap-des-Rosiers

GASPÉSIE
GASPÉ

Les Hauteurs

Maria New Carlisle

Sainte Florence

Pointe-à-la-Croix

N.B.

Rouyn Noranda

L'Anse Saint Jean ●

Kamouraska

Abitibi-Temiscamingue

N.B.

Cap a l'Aigle ● Bas-Saint-
Point-au-Pic ● ● Laurent

Baie-Saint-Paul ●

Saint-Donat ●

Stoneham ● L'islet-sur-Mer ●

QUEBEC ■

Mont-Tremblant

I'lle-d'Orléans
St. Pierre

Sainte-Agathe-des-Monts

Arundel ● Sainte-Adèle Trois-Rivières

St. Georges ● St. Cyprian

● Saint-Sauveur Laurentide

LAURENTIDES LAURENTIONS

Wakefield ● Wentworth-Nord

Acton Vale

Aylmer ● Montréal ● ● Saint-Marc-sur-Richelieu

Gatineau ● Hudson Saint-Laurent ● Sherbrooke

● Howick Magog ●

Saint-Pierre-
de-Véronne-
à-Pike-River

ONTARIO

MAINE U.S.A.

Abitibi-Temiscamingue
(northwestern QC)

Auberge Le Passant B&B, gite

(Michel Bellehumeur)

489 Perreault St E, Rouyn-Noranda, QC, J9X 3C7
www.lepassant.com
E-mail info@lepassant.com

819-762-9827
Fax 819-762-3820

Welcome to our home in the heart of the vast spaces of Abitibi-Temiscamingue, located in the mining centre of Quebec known as the national copper capital. This lush region is known for its quality of life. Your visit will be tranquil and peaceful as you relax in one of our large, warmly decorated rooms, or indulge in the luxury of our suite with panoramic view. Enjoy a breathtaking view of the lake, nearby hunting, fishing, cycle track, golfing, hiking, alpine skiing and snowmobiling. See you all at breakfast.

ROOMS Upper floor, Ground floor, **Baths** Ensuite, Shared with guest, **Beds** Queen, Double, **Air** Central, In rooms, **Smoking** Outside, **In Room** Thermostat, TV, **OTHERS** Urban, Open all year, **PAYMENT** Visa, Diners, Cheques accepted, Cash, **BREAKFASTS** Full, **AMENITIES** Barbecue, Laundry, Kitchen, Fridge, Patio, **THINGS TO DO** Comp. bikes, Trail nearby, Golf, Fishing, Museums, Art, Theatre, Cross-country skiing, Tennis, Swimming, **LANGUAGE** Eng., Fr., **PRICE** (2 persons) 65–80 **(check with hosts for pricing details)**

Acton Vale *(east of Montreal)*

Aux bras de Morphée

(Diane Duguay and Alain Lavoie)

514 Rang 1 E, Ste-Christine, QC, J0H 1H0
www.canadianbandbguide.ca/bb.asp?ID=3306
E-mail tirbichon@hotmail.com

819-858-2022
Fax 819-858-2577

Our guests always comment on the peaceful atmosphere of the house and appreciate the quiet outside. We are in a farming village, about 1 hour from Montreal, 2 hours from Quebec City and about 35–40 minutes from Drummond-ville, Ste-Hyacinthe, Granby and Sherbrooke. Breakfast is comprised of a fresh fruit plate served with croissants and homemade jams, followed by either waffles or pancakes with maple syrup or quiche. We are ecologically minded and we serve organic food.

ROOMS Upper floor, **Baths** Shared with guest, Shared with hosts, **Beds** Double, Twin, Single or cots, **Air** In rooms, **Smoking** Outside, **In Room** Thermostat, **OTHERS** Rural, Open all year, Pets in residence, **PAYMENT** Cash, **BREAKFASTS** Full, **AMENITIES** Central TV, Central phone, Fridge, Lounge, **THINGS TO DO** Trail nearby, Golf, Museums, Theatre, Entertainment, Attractions, Cross-country skiing, Tennis, Horseback riding, Birdwatching, Antiquing, **LANGUAGE** Eng., Fr., **PRICE** (2 persons) 60 **(check with hosts for pricing details)**

Arundel *(northeast of Montreal)*
Julia's B&B
(Julia Stuart)

73 Ch de la Rouge, Arundel, QC, J0T 1A0
www.canadianbandbguide.ca/bb.asp?ID=3170
E-mail juliamstuart@yahoo.ca

819-687-2382

Julia's B&B, at Saga Turung Farm, promises a healthy, relaxing, and inspiring retreat for individuals and groups. In the scenic Rouge River Valley, surrounded by streams and rolling pastures, we provide cozy, spacious and beautiful accommodations, with wholesome breakfasts to meet all tastes. Other meals can be arranged. We border a bike/skidoo trail, are close to golf, tennis, water sports, skiing, skating, dog-sledding. We offer courses in stainglass and sessions in alternative healing. We are non-smoking.

ROOMS Upper floor, Ground floor, Private entrance, **Baths** Ensuite, Shared with guest, **Beds** Queen, Double, Twin, **Air** In rooms, **Smoking** Outside, **In Room** Thermostat, Fireplace, **OTHERS** Rural, Open all year, Additional meals, **PAYMENT** Cheques accepted, Cash, **BREAKFASTS** Full, Home-baked, Self-catered, **AMENITIES** Central phone, Hot bev. bar, Lounge, Patio, **THINGS TO DO** Trail nearby, Golf, Fishing, Art, Attractions, Shopping, Cross-country skiing, Downhill skiing, Tennis, Swimming, Horseback riding, Beach, Birdwatching, Antiquing, **LANGUAGE** Eng., Fr., **PRICE** (2 persons) 75–90 **(check with hosts for pricing details)**

Baie St-Paul *(northeast of Quebec City)*
Noble Quêteux
(Marielou Jacques)

8 Côte du Quêteux, Baie St-Paul, QC, G3C 2C7
www.Charlevoix.qc.ca/noblequeteux
E-mail noblequeteux@charlevoix.qc.ca

418-240-2352
Fax 418-240-2377
TFr 1-866-744-2352

You'll fall in love with this ancestral house and the warmth of its interior decoration of yesteryear known at the time for offering shelter to travellers, particularly the neighbourhood beggars. A heavenly site on a hillside with view of the River and L'Isle-aux-Coudres. Magnificent view right from your bedroom window. The bright colours of fall and the intense cold of winter will sustain conversation around the fireplace. You have a selection of five bedrooms, all with queen bed and view of the St. Lawrence.

ROOMS Family suite, **Baths** Private, Shared with guest, **Beds** Queen, Single or cots, **Smoking** Outside, **OTHERS** Open all year, Pets in residence, **PAYMENT** Visa, MC, Cash, **BREAKFASTS** Full, **AMENITIES** Central Internet access, Central VCR/DVD, **THINGS TO DO** Golf, Cross-country skiing, Horseback riding, Birdwatching, Antiquing, **LANGUAGE** Eng., Fr., **PRICE** (2 persons) 80–95 **(check with hosts for pricing details)**

GASPE [CAP-DES-ROSIERS] *(eastern Gaspé)*

La Rose des Vents

(Jeanne A.B. O'Connor)

1228 boul, Cap-des-Rosiers, Cap-des-Rosiers (Gaspe),
QC, G4X 6H1
www.bbcanada.com/larosedesvents
E-mail larosedesvents@gosympatico.ca

418-892-5241
Fax 418-892-5108

Our B&B is in the first village on the south
shore of the St. Lawrence River, 1 km from
Forillon National Park and Canada's tallest
lighthouse. Peaceful and comfortable,
most rooms face the sea. Hearty breakfasts, hostess is well informed about the
area's natural, cultural and historic highlights. The breathtaking area offers
wildlife observation (seabirds, seals,
whales, land mammals), a diversity of
habitats (beaches, seacliffs, forests,
salmon rivers), outdoor activities (trails,
boat tours). Plan a three day stay.

ROOMS Upper floor, **Baths** Shared with guest, Shared
with hosts, **Beds** King, Queen, Single or cots, **Smoking**
Outside, **In Room** Thermostat, TV, **OTHERS** Rural, Open
all year, **PAYMENT** Visa, Cash, Trvl's cheques, **BREAK-
FASTS** Full, **AMENITIES** Central TV, Central phone,
Barbecue, Fridge, Lounge, Patio, **THINGS TO DO** Rental
bikes, Trail nearby, Rental canoe or boat, Fishing,
Museums, Art, Attractions, Shopping, Cross-country
skiing, Tennis, Swimming, Horseback riding, Beach,
LANGUAGE Eng., Fr., **PRICE** (2 persons) 55–60 **(check
with hosts for pricing details)**

GATINEAU *(west of Montreal)*

Stanyar House B&B

(John and Lucy Stanyar)

74 Stanyar Rd, Val des Monts, QC, J8N 7B6
www.stanyarhouse.com
E-mail info@stanyarhouse.com

819-671-3201
Fax 819-671-9009

A hidden treasure on 250 forested acres
in the Gatineau Hills of Quebec beside a
small private lake. Three rooms available
with ensuite baths. Very cozy, quilts,
antiques. Quiet, peaceful and tranquil,
only 30 minutes from downtown Ottawa,
Canada's capital, yet you feel as if you're a
million miles away. Wonderful breakfast
and coffee. Guests also have use of a
small private dining room and den with
fireplace. Dock, screened porch, use of
canoes, trails. Please see Web site for a
wealth of information and pictures.

ROOMS Upper floor, **Baths** Ensuite, **Beds** Queen, **Air**
Central, **In Room** Thermostat, Phone, Fireplace, **OTH-
ERS** Rural, Adult, Open all year, Pets in residence, **PAY-
MENT** Visa, Cheques accepted, **BREAKFASTS** Full,
Home-baked, **AMENITIES** Central TV, Whirlpool,
Barbecue, Fridge, Hot bev. bar, Lounge, Patio, **THINGS
TO DO** Comp. bikes, Rental bikes, Trail nearby, Comp.
canoe or boat, Golf, Fishing, Museums, Art, Theatre,
Entertainment, Attractions, Shopping, Cross-country
skiing, Downhill skiing, Swimming, Horseback riding,
Birdwatching, Antiquing, **LANGUAGE** Eng., Dutch,
PRICE (2 persons) 85–155 **(check with hosts for pric-
ing details)**

Gatineau [secteur Aylmer]
(west of Montreal)

La Maison John Ogilvie

(Claude Hallé)

36 Crt, Gatineau (secteur Aylmer), QC, J9H 4L7
www.maisonjohnogilvie.com
E-mail info@maisonjohnogilvie.com

819-682-1616
Fax 819-682-1368
TFr 1-866-682-1616

La Maison John Ogilvie, a Heritage house, is a healing centre where you will find massotherapy, personal care, physio-therapy services and alternative therapy. We have several packages: health, ski, sailing and aqua-fitness. Our B&B dining room with its special fondue, our pool, bonfire and spa will provide you with the warmest stay.

ROOMS Upper floor, **Baths** Shared with guest, **Beds** King, Double, Single or cots, **Air** In rooms, **Smoking** Outside, **OTHERS** Additional meals, **PAYMENT** Visa, MC, Direct debit, Trvl's cheques, **BREAKFASTS** Self-catered, **AMENITIES** Swimming pool, Whirlpool, Lounge, Patio, **THINGS TO DO** Trail nearby, Rental canoe or boat, Golf, Museums, Art, Theatre, Entertainment, Attractions, Cross-country skiing, Downhill skiing, Swimming, Beach, Antiquing, **LANGUAGE** Eng., Fr., **PRICE** (2 persons) 65–120 **(check with hosts for pricing details)**

Harrington Harbour *(eastern Quebec)*

Amy's Boarding House

(Amy Evans)

Box 73, Harrington Harbour, QC, G0G 1N0
www.canadianbandbguide.ca/bb.asp?ID=2327

418-795-3376
Fax 418-795-3176

Visit our island, home of the filming of *The Grand Seduction*. Enjoy serenity, stillness, fresh ocean breezes. Our colourful village is perched on a rocky picturesque island overlooking the sea. Delicious meals of local seafood, vegetables from our garden and wonderful home-baked breads. Much to do – walks on the boardwalk, whale and birdwatching, beautiful flora, fauna and boat rides, in season skidooing. A new museum shows you our history. Share our island with us as we share our hospitality with you.

ROOMS Upper floor, Ground floor, Lower floor, **Baths** Shared with guest, Shared with hosts, **Beds** Queen, Twin, Single or cots, **Air** In rooms, **Smoking** Outside, **In Room** Thermostat, TV, **OTHERS** Open all year, Additional meals, Pets welcome, **PAYMENT** Cheques accepted, Cash, Trvl's cheques, **BREAKFASTS** Full, Home-baked, **AMENITIES** Central TV, Laundry, Kitchen, Fridge, Lounge, Patio, **THINGS TO DO** Trail nearby, Rental canoe or boat, Comp. Canoe or boat, Fishing, Museums, Attractions, Wineries/Breweries, Beach, Birdwatching, **LANGUAGE** Eng., **PRICE** (2 persons) 70–90 **(check with hosts for pricing details)**

HOWICK *(south of Montreal)*

Rivers Edge Bed and Breakfast

(John and Gloria Peddie)

1987 ch Rivière des Anglais, Howick, QC, J0S 1G0
www.riversedgequebec.com
E-mail gpeddie@sympatico.ca

450-825-2390

Charming Victorian home, newly renovated, set amidst beautiful, extensive floral gardens and spacious grounds, overlooking the river. Ideal for birdwatching. The tranquil country atmosphere enhances the warm hospitality that greets you. Guests arrive as strangers and leave as friends. Enjoy hearty, home-cooked breakfasts with specialties. Other meals on request. Bedrooms are beautifully decorated with ensuite baths. Wheelchair access. Ideal for groups and cyclists. Quebec Rating: 4 Suns.

ROOMS Upper floor, Ground floor, **Baths** Ensuite, **Beds** Queen, Double, **Air** Ceiling fans, **Smoking** Outside, **In Room** Thermostat, TV, **OTHERS** Rural, Open all year, Handicapped access, Additional meals, Pets in residence, **PAYMENT** Cash, Trvl's cheques, **BREAKFASTS** Full, Home-baked, **AMENITIES** Fridge, Patio, **THINGS TO DO** Trail nearby, Golf, Fishing, Museums, Attractions, Wineries/Breweries, Birdwatching, Antiquing, **LANGUAGE** Eng., Fr., **PRICE** (2 persons) 65–85 **(check with hosts for pricing details)**

HUDSON *(southwest of Montreal)*

Victoria Bed and Breakfast

(Marilyn Funger)

93 Birch Hill, Hudson, QC, J0P 1H0
www3.sympatico.ca/victoria.bnb
E-mail victoria.bnb@sympatico.ca

450-458-7932

Relax and step back in time. Victoria B&B is an elegant home featuring beautifully decorated rooms appointed with fine antiques. Breakfasts are not to be missed, served with fine crystal and china in the formal dining room or poolside, weather permitting. This property is situated on Whitlock Golf Course with 100-year-old maple trees facing the backyard. Afternoon tea is available upon request. Victoria B&B is located minutes from the centre of Hudson Village with its quaint shops and fine restaurants. Please join me for a relaxing experience.

ROOMS Ground floor, **Baths** Private, **Beds** Queen, Double, Twin, Single or cots, **Air** Central, **Smoking** Outside, **In Room** Thermostat, TV, **OTHERS** Open all year, **PAYMENT** Visa, MC, Amex, Cash, **BREAKFASTS** Full, Home-baked, **AMENITIES** Central TV, Central phone, Swimming pool, Barbecue, Laundry, Fridge, Lounge, Patio, **THINGS TO DO** Rental bikes, Trail nearby, Golf, Fishing, Museums, Art, Theatre, Attractions, Shopping, Cross-country skiing, Swimming, Horseback riding, **LANGUAGE** Eng., Fr., **PRICE** (2 persons) 100–175 **(check with hosts for pricing details)**

ILE D'ORLEANS *(east of Quebec City)*

Auberge Le Vieux Presbytere

(Louise Lapointe and Hughes L'Heureux)

1247 Mgr D'Esgly, Saint-Pierre-Ile-d'Orleans,
QC, G0A 4E0
www.presbytere.com
E-mail presbytere@qc.aira.com

418-828-9723
Fax 418-828-2189
TFr 1-888-828-9723

Two-hundred-year-old ancestral home
near the oldest rural church in Quebec.
River-view with beautiful landscaping.
Buffalo, ostriches and elk roam the property. Restaurant open all year. Bicycles
may be rented in season. Come and enjoy
our warm and cozy atmosphere.

ROOMS Family suite, Upper floor, Ground floor, Private
entrance, **Baths** Private, Shared with guest, **Beds**
Queen, Double, Twin, Single or cots, **Air** In rooms,
Smoking Outside, **In Room** Thermostat, **OTHERS**
Rural, Open all year, Additional meals, **PAYMENT** Visa,
MC, Diners, Amex, Direct debit, Cash, **BREAKFASTS**
Full, **AMENITIES** Central TV, Central phone, **THINGS TO
DO** Rental bikes, Trail nearby, Golf, Museums, Art,
Theatre, Wineries/Breweries, Shopping, Cross-country
skiing, Tennis, Swimming, **LANGUAGE** Eng., Fr., **PRICE**
(2 persons) 70–130 **(check with hosts for pricing
details)**

ILE D'ORLEANS

B&B Au Giron de l'Isle

(Lucie and Gerard Lambert)

120 chemin des Lieges, St. Jean, QC, G0A 3W0
www.total.net/~giron
E-mail giron@total.net

418-829-0985
Fax 418-829-1059
TFr 1-888-280-6636

B&B rated 5 stars by *Hebergement Quebec*.
Grands Prix du tourisme award winner
area for 2001, 2002, 2003. Grands Prix du
tourisme national award winner "Gold
medal" for 2003. We are located 25 minutes from Old Quebec. B&B situated 400
metres from the main road and by the
St. Lawrence River with its impressive
boats and breathtaking sunrise and
moonlight. Relax on the verandah, patio
or your private balcony. Packages available. Retired hosts are knowledgeable
about the region. A home away from
home.

ROOMS Family suite, Upper floor, Ground floor, Private
entrance, **Baths** Private, **Beds** Queen, Twin, Pullout
sofa, **Air** Central, In rooms, **Smoking** Outside, **In Room**
Thermostat, TV, Fireplace, **OTHERS** Rural, Adult, Open
all year, **PAYMENT** Visa, MC, Amex, Direct debit, Cash,
Trvl's cheques, **BREAKFASTS** Full, Home-baked,
AMENITIES Central TV, Central phone, Fridge, Hot bev.
bar, Lounge, Patio, Central Internet access, **THINGS TO
DO** Rental bikes, Trail nearby, Golf, Art, Wineries/
Breweries, Shopping, Cross-country skiing, Downhill
skiing, Horseback riding, Beach, Birdwatching, **LAN-
GUAGE** Eng., Fr., **PRICE** (2 persons) 90–175 **(check
with hosts for pricing details)**

Ile d'Orleans

L'Oasis De Reves

(Lyette Chedore and Jean Tardif)

179, che Royal, St-Laurent de Ile d'Orleans,
QC, G0A 3Z0
www.oasisdereves.com
E-mail info@oasisdereves.com

418-829-3473
Fax 418-829-0053

You will be charmed by our beautiful victorian-style home located on the riverside. We offer you three splendid rooms: the Enchantress, the Romantic and the Sorceress. Our home environment is health-oriented. You will enjoy the serenity and abundance of nature with the hospitality and attention to details of your hosts Lyette and Jean. We will serve you a great breakfast while you contemplate the river. You will receive many helpful tips and tourist advice that will make your stay a memorable one.

ROOMS Upper floor, **Baths** Private, **Beds** Queen, **Air** Central, **In Room** Thermostat, TV, VCR/DVD, **OTHERS** Rural, Seasonal, **PAYMENT** Visa, MC, Cheques accepted, Cash, Trvl's cheques, **BREAKFASTS** Full, **AMENITIES** Swimming pool, Whirlpool, Fridge, Lounge, Patio, **THINGS TO DO** Rental bikes, Trail nearby, Rental canoe or boat, Golf, Fishing, Museums, Art, Theatre, Attractions, Wineries/Breweries, Shopping, Tennis, Swimming, Horseback riding, Beach, Birdwatching, Antiquing, **LANGUAGE** Eng., Fr., Sp., **PRICE** (2 persons) 115–150 **(check with hosts for pricing details)**

Ile d'Orleans (St-Pierre)
(east of Quebec City)

Gîte Bel Horizon

(Yvette and Paul-E. Vézina)

402 chemin Royal, Ile-d'Orleans (St-Pierre),
QC, G0A 4E0
www.inns-bb.com/belhorizon
E-mail belhorizon@sympatico.ca

418-828-9207
Fax 418-828-9207
TFr 1-877-828-9207

Welcome to the entrance to Ile d'Orleans! Directions: Rte 40 West (toward Ste-Anne-de-Beaupré), Exit 325 for Île d'Orléans. At the top of the island's hill, turn right, continue for 1 km. The character, river view and Montmorency Falls, the variety of restaurants, the vineyards and the island's arts and culture welcome you to a refreshing and very interesting stay. Come on over and check it out! Your hosts, Yvette and P.E. will be happy to accommodate you from February 1st to Nov 1st.

ROOMS Family suite, Upper floor, Ground floor, **Baths** Private, **Beds** Queen, Double, Twin, Single or cots, **Air** In rooms, **Smoking** Outside, **In Room** Thermostat, TV, **OTHERS** Rural, Adult, Seasonal, **PAYMENT** Visa, MC, Amex, Cash, Trvl's cheques, **BREAKFASTS** Full, **AMENITIES** Central phone, Fridge, Lounge, **THINGS TO DO** Rental bikes, Trail nearby, Golf, Fishing, Museums, Art, Theatre, Wineries/Breweries, Antiquing, **LANGUAGE** Eng., Fr., **PRICE** (2 persons) 72-84 **(check with hosts for pricing details)**

KAMOURASKA *(northeast of Quebec City)*

Gîte Chez Jean et Nicole
(Jean and Nicole Bossé)

81 ave Morel, Kamouraska, QC, G0L 1M0
www3.sympatico.ca/titesouris/gite.html

418-492-2921

This beautiful century-old house will leave you with unforgettable memories, marked by the rhythm of the wind and the tide. Comfort, cleanliness and *joie-de-vivre* await. Close to the sea, with a two kilometer-long promenade: What memories are made of! The sea air will whet your appetite for the gourmet breakfast to come ...

ROOMS Family suite, Upper floor, **Baths** Ensuite, Shared with guest, **Beds** Double, Single or cots, **Smoking** Outside, **In Room** Thermostat, **OTHERS** Rural, Open all year, Seasonal, **PAYMENT** Cash, Trvl's cheques, **BREAKFASTS** Home-baked, **AMENITIES** Central TV, Central phone, Lounge, Patio, **THINGS TO DO** Rental bikes, Trail nearby, Golf, Fishing, Museums, Art, Theatre, Entertainment, Attractions, Wineries/Breweries, Shopping, Cross-country skiing, Horseback riding, Beach, Birdwatching, Antiquing, **LANGUAGE** Eng., Fr., **PRICE** (2 persons) 70–85 **(check with hosts for pricing details)**

KAMOURASKA

La Villa Saint-Louis
(Martine and Jacques Genest)

125 ave Morel, Kamouraska, QC, G0L 1M0
www.lavillasaint-louis.com
E-mail info@lavillasaint-louis.com

418-492-7072

You will love your stay in this heritage home with a long history of welcoming travellers. Your visit will be steeped in tradition, from the fine old interior and furnishings, to the splendid lawn and gardens and the large heated swimming pool. Two large bedrooms are available, each with ensuite bathroom. Additional bedroom is available on request.

ROOMS Upper floor, **Baths** Private, **Beds** King, Queen, **In Room** Thermostat, **OTHERS** Rural, **PAYMENT** Visa, Cash, **BREAKFASTS** Full, Home-baked, **AMENITIES** Swimming pool, Central Internet access, **THINGS TO DO** Rental canoe or boat, Golf, Theatre, Wineries/Breweries, Beach, **LANGUAGE** Eng., Fr., **PRICE** (2 persons) 105 **(check with hosts for pricing details)**

L'Anse Saint-Jean
(northeast of Quebec City)

Le Globe-Trotter B&B

(André Bouchard)

131 Saint-Jean-Baptiste, L'Anse Saint-Jean,
QC, G0V 1J0
www.bbcanada.com/322.html
E-mail andreb7@hotmail.com

418-272-2353
Fax 418-272-1731
TFr 1-866-633-2353

Behind this B&B, you will find a river and a patio where you can enjoy your favourite novel, and the view on top of the mountains is simply gorgeous. Sunny, spacious and tastefully decorated residence. Excellent location if you are looking for a B&B offering top quality comfort and a diversified and hearty breakfast. Traveller's guide. Directions: From Quebec City via Saint-Siméon, Hwys 138 and 170 to l'Anse Saint-Jean. From Quebec City via Chicoutimi, Hwys 175 and 170 to l'Anse Saint-Jean.

ROOMS Upper floor, Ground floor, **Baths** Private, Shared with guest, Shared with hosts, **Beds** Double, **Smoking** Outside, **In Room** Thermostat, **OTHERS** Rural, Seasonal, **PAYMENT** Visa, MC, Cash, Trvl's cheques, **BREAKFASTS** Full, Home-baked, **AMENITIES** Central TV, Central phone, Fridge, Lounge, Patio, Central Internet access, **THINGS TO DO** Rental bikes, Trail nearby, Rental canoe or boat, Fishing, Art, Entertainment, Shopping, Tennis, Swimming, Horseback riding, Beach, **LANGUAGE** Eng., Fr., **PRICE** (2 persons) 65–75 **(check with hosts for pricing details)**

Laurentians, Wentworth-Nord
(northwest of Montreal)

Domaine de l'Étang

(Francine and Laurent)

1045 chemin du lac Louisa, Wentworth-Nord,
QC, J0T 1Y0
www.domainedeletang.com
E-mail domainedeletang@qc.aira.com

450-533-6571
Fax 450-533-5215
TFr 1-877-533-6571

Francine and Laurent will welcome you in a warm interior of wood paneling, inviting you to relax and to forget the big city life in the fast lane. Then let us drive you through this fantastic dream. The Domaine de l'Étang holds a luxurious house and a chalet that allows you to settle back peacefully. The main house includes five bedrooms, an interior swimming pool more than 30 ft. long, a spa and a sauna. What could be more relaxing!

ROOMS Family suite, Upper floor, Ground floor, Lower floor, Private entrance, **Baths** Private, **Beds** Queen, Double, **Smoking** Outside, **In Room** Thermostat, TV, Fireplace, Internet access, VCR/DVD, **OTHERS** Rural, Handicapped access, **PAYMENT** Visa, MC, Amex, Direct debit, Cash, Trvl's cheques, **BREAKFASTS** Full, **AMENITIES** Central phone, Swimming pool, Sauna, Whirlpool, Barbecue, Laundry, Fridge, Patio, **THINGS TO DO** Trail nearby, Rental canoe or boat, Golf, Fishing, Art, Attractions, Cross-country skiing, Swimming, Horseback riding, Beach, **LANGUAGE** Eng., Fr., **PRICE** (2 persons) 85–125 **(check with hosts for pricing details)**

L'ISLET-SUR-MER *(east of Quebec City)*

Auberge La Marguerite

(Johanne Martel and Luc Morrier)

88 Des Pionniers e L'Islet-sur-Mer, QC, G0R 2B0
www.aubergelamarguerite.com
E-mail marguerite100@videotron.ca

418-247-5454
Fax 418-247-7725
TFr 1-877-788-5454

Near the St. Lawrence River, an invitation to relive the history of the Côte-du-Sud in a manor dating from 1754. Very spacious old home, fully renovated, central-air-conditioning, bright large dining room, hearty breakfast. Large landscaped garden where you can walk, read or relax. Activities offered nearby: Visiting Grosse-Île, Maritime Museum, golf, cycling, theatre, cruise, health care, art galleries and more. Hwy 20, Exit 400, Rd 285 north 4 km, Rd 132 east, 1 km.

ROOMS Upper floor, Ground floor, **Baths** Private, **Beds** King, Queen, Double, Single or cots, **Air** Central, **Smoking** Outside, **In Room** Thermostat, TV, **OTHERS** Adult, Open all year, **PAYMENT** Visa, MC, Direct debit, Cash, Trvl's cheques, **BREAKFASTS** Full, **AMENITIES** Fridge, Patio, **THINGS TO DO** Golf, Museums, Art, Theatre, Cross-country skiing, Birdwatching, Antiquing, **LANGUAGE** Eng., Fr., **PRICE** (2 persons) 78–128 **(check with hosts for pricing details)**

MAGOG *(southeast of Montreal)*

Gite du Cerf Argente B&B

(Marc Hebert and Andre Trussart)

2984 che Georgeville, Magog, QC, J1X 3W4
www.cerfargente.com
E-mail info@cerfargente.com

819-847-4264
Fax 819-847-4036

Our 19th-century farmhouse is isolated in an idyllic setting surrounded by a flower-gardened park, ponds, patios, gazebos, a covered courtyard and view of Mt Orford and Lake Memphremagog. Five elegant rooms, each with its own cachette and private washroom. Some with active air-jet bath, queen-size bed and wood fire-place. Family room with two double beds, a hide-a-bed, wood fireplace and active air-jet bath. Art activities galore and many sports both summer and winter.

ROOMS Family suite, Upper floor, **Baths** Private, **Beds** Queen, Double, **Smoking** Outside, **In Room** Thermostat, Fireplace, **OTHERS** Rural, Open all year, **PAYMENT** Cheques accepted, Cash, Trvl's cheques, **BREAKFASTS** Continental, **AMENITIES** Central phone, Barbecue, Fridge, Patio, **THINGS TO DO** Rental bikes, Trail nearby, Rental canoe or boat, Golf, Fishing, Museums, Art, Theatre, Entertainment, Attractions, Wineries/Breweries, Shopping, Cross-country skiing, Tennis, Swimming, Horseback riding, Beach, **LANGUAGE** Eng., Fr., **PRICE** (2 persons) 60–115 **(check with hosts for pricing details)**

Maria *(south Gaspé)*

Gîte du Patrimoine
(Lola Pichette)

759 boul Perron, Maria, QC, G0C 1Y0
www.gitescanada.com/8354.html
E-mail gitedupatrimoine@globetrotter.net

418-759-3743

The Gîte du Patrimoine offers you the pleasure of an unforgettable stay in a heritage house, with preserved character-istics, and all the benefits of modern accommodation. The B&B is located on a lot which is more than 225 metres wide and 3.2 km deep. It is set back more than 90 metres from the road. B&B's special attraction: racehorses: 0.5 km track onsite for a casual walk while watching the horses in the centre.

ROOMS Upper floor, Ground floor, **Baths** Private, Shared with guest, Shared with hosts, **Beds** Queen, Single or cots, **Smoking** Outside, **In Room** Thermostat, **PAYMENT** Cheques accepted, Cash, Trvl's cheques, **BREAKFASTS** Full, Home-baked, **AMENITIES** Lounge, Patio, **THINGS TO DO** Trail nearby, Rental canoe or boat, Golf, Museums, Art, Theatre, Shopping, Tennis, Beach, **LANGUAGE** Eng., Fr., **PRICE** (2 persons) 65–80 **(check with hosts for pricing details)**

Mont-Tremblant *(north of Montreal)*

Auberge Tremblant Onwego
(Benoit Charette)

112 chemin Plouffe, Mont-Tremblant, QC, J8E 1J8
www.tremblantonwego.com
E-mail onwego@cgocable.ca

819-429-5522
Fax 819-429-6602
TFr 1-866-429-5522

We are located in the Old Mont-Tremblant village, 3 km from the International Resort Tremblant (shuttle at the door) and on the 91km of the bicycle path Le P'Tit Train du Nord. We offer rooms and condos (kitchen). Some of them are directly on our private beach. We look forward to greet you in our Amerindian-like auberge, with a spectacular sunset. Breakfast are delicious. Our theme-decorated bedrooms are really charming. Paddle boat, canoes, kayaks and bicycles are *free*. We welcome groups and families.

ROOMS Family suite, Upper floor, Ground floor, Private entrance, **Baths** Private, Shared with guest, **Beds** Queen, Twin, Single or cots, **Smoking** Outside, **In Room** Thermostat, TV, **PAYMENT** Visa, MC, Direct debit, Cash, Trvl's cheques, **BREAKFASTS** Full, **AMENITIES** Central TV, Fridge, Patio, **THINGS TO DO** Comp. bikes, Trail nearby, Comp. canoe or boat, Golf, Fishing, Art, Theatre, Attractions, Shopping, Cross-country skiing, Tennis, Swimming, Horseback riding, Beach, Birdwatching, Antiquing, **LANGUAGE** Eng., Fr., Sp., **PRICE** (2 persons) 110–170 **(check with hosts for pricing details)**

MONT-TREMBLANT

Crystal-Inn Mont-Tremblant

(Mario Jodoin)

100 Joseph Thibault, Mont-Tremblant, QC, J8E 2G4
www.crystal-inn.com
E-mail mfc@crystal-inn.com

819-681-7775

Located on a secluded street, very private and quiet, only 7 minutes from the Resort at Mont-Tremblant. We offer luxurious rooms and suites with homecooked breakfast, a wonderful hot tub and the possibility for massages on location.
A unique B&B with a touch of fantasy, please visit our Web site for amazing pictures and details.

ROOMS Upper floor, Ground floor, **Baths** Private, Ensuite, Shared with guest, **Beds** King, Queen, **Air** Ceiling fans, **Smoking** Outside, **In Room** Thermostat, TV, VCR/DVD, **OTHERS** Rural, Adult, Open all year, **BREAKFASTS** Full, Home-baked, **AMENITIES** Central TV, Central phone, Whirlpool, Barbecue, Fridge, Lounge, Patio, Central VCR/DVD, **THINGS TO DO** Rental bikes, Trail nearby, Rental canoe or boat, Golf, Fishing, Entertainment, Attractions, Shopping, Cross-country skiing, Downhill skiing, Tennis, Swimming, Horseback riding, Beach, Birdwatching, Antiquing, **LANGUAGE** Eng., Fr., **PRICE** (2 persons) 78–98 **(check with hosts for pricing details)**

MONTREAL *(southwestern Quebec)*

A Montreal Oasis

(Lena Blondel)

3000 De Breslay Rd, Montreal, QC, H3Y 2G7
www.rentalo.com/1034/amontreal.html
E-mail bb@aei.ca

514-935-2312
Fax 514-935-3154

Spacious home with garden in an excellent location in downtown Montreal. Walk to the Fine Arts Museum, the AMC, restaurants and shopping, the farmers' market, Mount Royal Parc. The house is decorated with African and Scandinavian art. A three-course plus, gourmet breakfast is served in the dining room. Host is world-travelled with a background in political science and studio arts.

ROOMS Upper floor, **Baths** Ensuite, Shared with guest, **Beds** King, Queen, Double, Twin, **Air** Ceiling fans, **Smoking** Outside, **In Room** Phone, Internet access, **PAYMENT** Cash, Trvl's cheques, **BREAKFASTS** Full, **AMENITIES** Central TV, Central phone, Fridge, Lounge, Patio, Central Internet access, **THINGS TO DO** Comp. bikes, Trail nearby, Museums, Art, Entertainment, Attractions, Shopping, Cross-country skiing, **LANGUAGE** Eng., Fr., Sp., Ger., Swedish, **PRICE** (2 persons) 70–120 **(check with hosts for pricing details)**

MONTREAL

Angelica Blue B&B

(Linda Michelle Hornby)

1213 Ste-Elizabeth St, Montreal, QC, H2X 3C3
www.angelicablue.com
E-mail info@angelicablue.com

514-844-5048
Fax 450-448-2114
TFr 1-800-878-5048

Come join us in our splendid Victorian row-house dating from the late 1800s. Located in the heart of downtown Montreal. Minutes walk to the Old Port, Convention Centre and Chinatown. Our "four-sunshine rating" by the Montreal Tourist Board definitely means we have one of the nicest B&Bs in Montreal, with our beautifully decorated rooms, all with original cachet, brick walls, old pine flooring and high ceilings. Rooms have a private bath and are all decorated with a different theme. Come and make our B&B your home away from home.

ROOMS Family suite, Upper floor, Ground floor, Lower floor, Private entrance, **Baths** Private, Ensuite, Shared with guest, **Beds** King, Queen, Twin, Single or cots, Pullout sofa, **Air** In rooms, **Smoking** Outside, **In Room** Thermostat, **OTHERS** Open all year, **PAYMENT** Visa, MC, Diners, Cheques accepted, Cash, **BREAKFASTS** Full, Home-baked, **AMENITIES** Laundry, Kitchen, Fridge, Patio, **THINGS TO DO** Comp. bikes, Museums, Art, Theatre, Entertainment, Attractions, Shopping, **LANGUAGE** Eng., Fr., Sp., **PRICE** (2 persons) 75–155 **(check with hosts for pricing details)**

MONTREAL

Anne ma soeur Anne Hôtel – Studio

(Hélène Duval and Louis Fraser)

4119 St-Denis, Montreal, QC, H2W 2M7
www.annemasoeuranne.com
E-mail infos@annemasoeuranne.com

514-281-3187
Fax 514-281-1601
TFr 1-877-281-3187

New! Seventeen air-conditioned rooms, studios with mini-kitchen, wallbed and private bathroom. Four private terraces, high-speed Internet in each room, cable TV. A few steps away from renowned restaurants, trendy bars and avant-garde boutiques. Nearby parking. Good value and warm athmosphere.

ROOMS Family suite, Upper floor, Private entrance, **Baths** Private, **Beds** King, Queen, Twin, Single or cots, **Air** Central, **Smoking** In rooms, **In Room** Thermostat, Phone, TV, **OTHERS** Urban, Adult, Open all year, Seasonal, **PAYMENT** Visa, MC, Diners, Amex, Direct debit, Cheques accepted, **BREAKFASTS** Continental, **AMENITIES** Laundry, Kitchen, Fridge, Hot bev. bar, Patio, **THINGS TO DO** Rental bikes, Trail nearby, Golf, Museums, Art, Theatre, Entertainment, Attractions, Wineries/Breweries, Shopping, **LANGUAGE** Eng., Fr., **PRICE** (2 persons) 80–210 **(check with hosts for pricing details)**

Montreal

Au Git'Ann

(Anne, Hugo and Nicolas Messier)

1806 St-Christophe, Montreal, QC, H2L 3W8
www.augitann.com
E-mail augite@cam.org

514-523-4494

Our B&B, located on a small and quiet street in the heart of Montreal and amidst its cultural activities, offers you the plush comfort of a friendly home, where our attention to small details and our choice menus will make yours a memorable stay. From our personalized service, our generous breakfasts, our well-equipped kitchenette and two pleasant sitting-rooms, everything has been arranged for your well-being.

ROOMS Family suite, Upper floor, Ground floor, **Baths** Private, Shared with guest, **Beds** King, Queen, Twin, Pullout sofa, **Air** Central, In rooms, **Smoking** Outside, **In Room** Thermostat, TV, Internet access, **OTHERS** Urban, Open all year, **PAYMENT** Visa, MC, Cash, Trvl's cheques, **BREAKFASTS** Full, **AMENITIES** Central TV, Central phone, Kitchen, Fridge, Lounge, Central Internet access, **THINGS TO DO** Trail nearby, Rental canoe or boat, Golf, Museums, Art, Theatre, Entertainment, Attractions, Wineries/Breweries, Shopping, Cross-country skiing, Tennis, Swimming, Beach, Antiquing, **LANGUAGE** Eng., Fr., **PRICE** (2 persons) 80–135 **(check with hosts for pricing details)**

Montreal

B A Guest B&B and Reservation Service

(Marian Kahn)

2033 St-Hubert, Montreal, QC, H2L 3Z6
www.bbmontreal.com
E-mail info@bbmontreal.com

514-738-9410
TFr 1-800-738-4338

B A Guest B&B is an example of the fine Montreal architecture of the early 1900s. This stone house on four levels features the typical staircases, stained glass, 13-foot ceilings and original hardwood floors. Your Montreal-born owner/hostess has filled it with eclectic collections, colour and comfort. Located in the popular downtown Latin Quarter sector, two blocks from the fabulous St. Denis St with its international restaurants, cafes, boutiques, parks. Walking distance of Old Montreal. Subway 5 minutes away.

ROOMS Upper floor, **Baths** Ensuite, Shared with guest, **Beds** Queen, Twin, **Air** Central, **Smoking** Outside, **OTHERS** Urban, Open all year, Pets in residence, **PAYMENT** Visa, MC, Amex, Cash, Trvl's cheques, **BREAKFASTS** Continental, **AMENITIES** Central phone, Fridge, Lounge, Central Internet access, **THINGS TO DO** Rental bikes, Trail nearby, Museums, Art, Theatre, Entertainment, Attractions, Shopping, Cross-country skiing, Tennis, Swimming, Birdwatching, Antiquing, **LANGUAGE** Eng., Fr., Ger., Portuguese, **PRICE** (2 persons) 75–125 **(check with hosts for pricing details)**

Montreal
B&B Le Cartier
(Richard Lemmetti)

1219 rue Cartier, Montreal, QC, H2K 4C4
www.bblecartier.com
E-mail bb_le_cartier@hotmail.com

514-917-1829
Fax 514-524-5120
TFr 1-877-524-0495

Situated in downtown/Village, B&B is within walking distance to main city attractions (fireworks, Old Montreal, Chinatown, universities, Mount Royal, cycling path) and surrounded by restaurants, cafes, shopping centres, night clubs, theatres, etc. Newly renovated and decorated, the 100-year-old stone house offers five stylish rooms (A/C, cable TV, private/shared bath) with nice front- and backyard balcony. Non-smoking inside. Free public parking in front/around B&B, 1-minute from subway (Metro Papineau).

ROOMS Family suite, Upper floor, Ground floor, Private entrance, **Baths** Ensuite, Shared with guest, **Beds** Queen, Double, Pullout sofa, **Air** Central, Ceiling fans, **Smoking** Outside, **In Room** TV, VCR/DVD, **OTHERS** Urban, Open all year, **PAYMENT** Visa, MC, Cash, Trvl's cheques, **BREAKFASTS** Continental, Self-catered, **AMENITIES** Central phone, Kitchen, Fridge, Patio, **THINGS TO DO** Rental bikes, Trail nearby, Rental canoe or boat, Fishing, Museums, Art, Theatre, Entertainment, Attractions, Wineries/Breweries, Shopping, Cross-country skiing, Tennis, Swimming, Beach, Antiquing, **LANGUAGE** Eng., Fr., **PRICE** (2 persons) 60–125 **(check with hosts for pricing details)**

Montreal
Boulanger-bassin B&B
(Ken Ilasz)

4293 rue de Brebeuf, Montreal, QC, H2J 3K6
www.bbassin.com
E-mail ken@bbassin.com

514-525-0854

Located on a quiet, tree-lined street in the Plateau Mont Royal near Lafontaine Park, Boulanger-bassin B&B offers personalized service with the comforts of home, but better. Three bedrooms with ensuite bathrooms. Children 12 and under, stay free!

ROOMS Family suite, Upper floor, **Baths** Private, Ensuite, **Beds** King, Queen, Double, **Air** In rooms, **Smoking** Outside, **In Room** Thermostat, Phone, TV, Internet access, **OTHERS** Babysitting, Adult, Open all year, **PAYMENT** Cash, Trvl's cheques, **BREAKFASTS** **THINGS TO DO** Rental bikes, Trail nearby, Museums, Art, Theatre, Entertainment, Attractions, Wineries/Breweries, Shopping, Cross-country skiing, Tennis, Swimming, **LANGUAGE** Eng., Fr., **PRICE** (2 persons) 85–146 **(check with hosts for pricing details)**

MONTRÉAL

D&D B&B

(Dorothy and David Languedoc)

703 ave Laporte, Montreal, QC, H4C 1H5
www.montreal-bb.com/
E-mail thedd.bedandbreakfast@sympatico.ca

514-931-4921
TFr 1-888-931-4921

Welcome to D&D's B&B. A lovingly restored 100-year-old greystone. We offer fine bed and breakfast accommodations, warm hospitality and the elegance of a bygone era. A wonderful mix of old-world charm and modern amenities to make sure your stay with us is enjoyable and relaxing. Within a 5-minute drive of the core of downtown Montreal and Old Montreal and the Notre Dame Antique alley. Spa packages, gourmet weekend package and many more specials. Visit our Web site for more information.

ROOMS Upper floor, Private entrance, **Baths** Private, Ensuite, **Beds** King, Queen, Double, **Air** In rooms, **Smoking** Outside, **In Room** Thermostat, **OTHERS** Urban, Open all year, Pets in residence, **PAYMENT** Visa, MC, Diners, Amex, Cheques accepted, Cash, **BREAKFASTS** Full, Continental, **AMENITIES** Central TV, Central phone, Kitchen, Fridge, Lounge, Patio, **THINGS TO DO** Trail nearby, Museums, Art, Theatre, Entertainment, Attractions, Shopping, **LANGUAGE** Eng., **PRICE** (2 persons) 95–160 **(check with hosts for pricing details)**

MONTRÉAL

Gite Maison Jacques

(Micheline and Fernand Jacques)

4444 rue Paiement, Pierrefonds, QC, H9H 2S7
www.maisonjacques.qc.ca
E-mail gite.maison.jacques@qc.aira.com

514-696-2450
Fax 514-696-2564

Retired teachers in air-conditioned home. Located in a peaceful suburb of "West Island" Montreal and in excellent proximity to the city and cycling, swimming, golfing, skiing areas. Enjoy the quiet seclusion, relax on the lawn swing in the backyard or the screened verandah after a day of sightseeing or travelling. Full breakfast served on patio, weather permitting. Children welcome. Come and stroll through the woods of nearby nature parks: Beach at Cap-Saint-Jacques, McDonald College farm, Morgan Arboretum.

ROOMS Family suite, Ground floor, Private entrance, **Baths** Private, Ensuite, **Beds** Queen, Double, Twin, Single or cots, **Air** Central, **Smoking** Outside, **OTHERS** Urban, **PAYMENT** Visa, MC, Amex, Cash, Trvl's cheques, **BREAKFASTS** Full, Home-baked, **AMENITIES** Lounge, Patio, Central Internet access, Central VCR/ DVD, **THINGS TO DO** Trail nearby, Rental canoe or boat, Golf, Theatre, Attractions, Shopping, Cross-country skiing, Tennis, Swimming, Horseback riding, Beach, Antiquing, **LANGUAGE** Eng., Fr., **PRICE** (2 persons) 58–87 **(check with hosts for pricing details)**

Montreal

Le Kensington
(Josée Lalonde and Reno Gabrielli)

4660 Kensington Ave, Montreal, QC, H4B 2W5
www.lekensington.com
E-mail info@lekensington.com

514-489-2027
Fax 514-489-2027
TFr 1-888-489-2027

At Le Kensington we use our combined 40 years of hospitality industry experience to give our guests the best value for their money. Our focus is on quality and service. Awarded a 4-Sun rating by *Tourism Quebec*, but the real accolades come from our guests with regards to food quality, service, comfort and convenience. We are situated halfway between Trudeau Airport and downtown, which you can reach in 18 minutes by public transport. Near all amenities, we believe we are the ideal B&B to visit Montreal.

ROOMS Family suite, Ground floor, **Baths** Private, Ensuite, **Air** In rooms, **Smoking** Outside, **OTHERS** Pets welcome, **PAYMENT** Visa, Amex, Cash, Trvl's cheques, **BREAKFASTS** Full, **AMENITIES** Central TV, Central phone, Fridge, Hot bev. bar, Lounge, Patio, Central Internet access, Central VCR/DVD, **THINGS TO DO** Golf, Museums, Art, Theatre, Entertainment, Attractions, Wineries/Breweries, Shopping, Tennis, Swimming, **LANGUAGE** Eng., Fr., **PRICE** (2 persons) 95–125 **(check with hosts for pricing details)**

Montreal

Le relais des Argoulets
(Ann Guy)

759 Willibrord, Montreal, QC, H4G 2T8
www.argoulets.com
E-mail lerelais@argoulets.com

514-767-3696
TFr 1-866-761-3696

Charming urban B&B located near the magnificent St. Lawrence River. We offer three bedrooms with double beds and air-conditioning. Beautiful restful garden. Metro located at 300 yards, 10 minutes from downtown. We provide bicycles for your pleasure. Your host Ann and her dog Toscane live in the flat above the B&B.

ROOMS Ground floor, **Baths** Shared with guest, **Beds** Double, **Air** In rooms, **Smoking** Outside, **OTHERS** Urban, Open all year, **PAYMENT** Visa, MC, Cash, Trvl's cheques, **BREAKFASTS** Full, **AMENITIES** Central phone, Fridge, Patio, Central Internet access, **THINGS TO DO** Comp. bikes, Trail nearby, Museums, Shopping, Swimming, Birdwatching, **LANGUAGE** Eng., Fr., Ger., understand Spanish, **PRICE** (2 persons) 75 **(check with hosts for pricing details)**

MONTREAL

Le Terra Nostra
(Mireille Lauzon)

277 Beatty, Montreal, QC, H4H 1X7
www.leterranostra.com
E-mail info@leterranostra.com

514-762-1223
TFr 1-866-550-5235

Located within 10-minutes of downtown
Montreal and Old Montreal, Le Terra Nostra
is the greeting land of the globetrotter.
Right by the bank of the St. Lawrence
River, this B&B houses three rooms inspired
by the styles of the world, Asia, Africa and
Europe, with queen-size bed and heated
floor ensuite bathroom. Breakfast is served
all-year-round in an art gallery-like dining
room, as well as in the Feng-Shui garden
from May to September.

ROOMS Upper floor, **Baths** Ensuite, **Beds** Queen, **Air**
In rooms, **Smoking** Outside, **OTHERS** Urban, Open all
year, **PAYMENT** Visa, MC, Cash, **BREAKFASTS**
Continental, **AMENITIES** Central TV, Central phone,
Lounge, Patio, Central Internet access, Central
VCR/DVD, **THINGS TO DO** Comp. bikes, Trail nearby,
Golf, Museums, Art, Entertainment, Attractions,
Shopping, Cross-country skiing, Tennis, Swimming,
LANGUAGE Eng., Fr., **PRICE** (2 persons) 85–115 **(check
with hosts for pricing details)**

MONTREAL

Mona's Downtown
(Mona Kaufmann)

1230 Docteur Penfield, Apt 905, Montreal,
QC, H3G 1B5
www.nucleus.com/~kaufmann/bandb/main.htm
E-mail monasdowntown@videotron.ca

514-842-3939
TFr 1-877-427-6966

I would like to welcome you to my comfortable home in downtown Montreal.
My immediate neighbours are McGill
University to the east, Concordia University to the west and centre city to the
south. Subway and bus facilities provide
easy access to all of Montreals festivals,
museums, restaurants and our very
charming "Old City". Please come and
accept my hospitality.

Baths Shared with guest, Shared with hosts, **Beds**
Queen, Double, Pullout sofa, **Air** In rooms, **In Room** TV,
OTHERS Urban, Adult, Open all year, **PAYMENT** Visa,
Cash, Trvl's cheques, **BREAKFASTS** Full, Home-baked,
Self-catered, **AMENITIES** Laundry, Kitchen, Fridge, Hot
bev. bar, **THINGS TO DO** Rental bikes, Trail nearby,
Museums, Art, Theatre, Entertainment, Shopping, **LAN-
GUAGE** Eng., Fr., **PRICE** (2 persons) 75–95 **(check with
hosts for pricing details)**

MONTREAL
Relais Montreal Hospitalité
(Martha Pearson)

3977 ave Laval, Montreal, QC, H2W 2H9
www.martha-pearson.com
E-mail pearson@videotron.ca

514-287-9635
TFr 1-800-363-9635

Located in the very heart of the famous
Plateau Mont-Royal, Relais Montreal
Hospitalité lives up to its name and will
provide you unequalled reception and
comfort, just as if you were at home. Our
B&B accommodations, including room
and breakfast, are available at reasonable
rates, with special packages for longer
stays. Our furnished and well equipped
apartments can be rented monthly, or
longer. Small inn, European-style. All our
residences offer unique charm and personalized service.

ROOMS Family suite, Upper floor, Ground floor, Lower
floor, Private entrance, **Baths** Private, Shared with
guest, Shared with hosts, **Beds** Queen, Double, **Air** In
rooms, **Smoking** Outside, **In Room** Thermostat, TV,
OTHERS Urban, Open all year, **PAYMENT** Visa, MC,
Cash, **BREAKFASTS** Full, **AMENITIES** Central phone,
Fridge, Hot bev. bar, Lounge, Patio, **THINGS TO DO**
Comp. bikes, Trail nearby, Museums, Art, Theatre,
Entertainment, Wineries/Breweries, Shopping, Cross-
country skiing, Tennis, Swimming, Horseback riding,
LANGUAGE Eng., Fr., **PRICE** (2 persons) 65–90 **(check
with hosts for pricing details)**

MONTREAL
Ste. Anne's Bed & Breakfast
(Gisela Touchburn)

27A rue Perrault, Ste. Anne de Bellevue, QC, H9X 2E1
www.bbcanada.com/376.html
E-mail touchburn@sympatico.ca

514-457-9504
Fax 514-457-9504

Come and enjoy our home with its
European flair. The town of Ste. Anne de
Bellevue with its French charm has many
fine restaurants, boardwalk along the
canal and interesting shops all within a
short walk from our home. We are near
Macdonald Campus of McGill University
and John Abbott College. From Hwy 40
take Exit 41, from Hwy 20, take Exit 39, follow Rue St. Pierre south to Rue Ste. Anne.
Turn left and proceed to Rue Perrault. By
car we are 30 minutes from downtown
Montreal.

ROOMS Upper floor, **Baths** Ensuite, Shared with
guest, **Beds** Queen, Twin, **Air** Central, **Smoking**
Outside, **OTHERS** Babysitting, Rural, Adult, Open all
year, **PAYMENT** Cheques accepted, Cash, Trvl's
cheques, **BREAKFASTS** Full, Home-baked, **AMENITIES**
Central phone, Swimming pool, Laundry, Lounge,
Patio, **THINGS TO DO** Comp. bikes, Trail nearby, Golf,
Fishing, Attractions, Shopping, Cross-country skiing,
Tennis, Swimming, Horseback riding, **LANGUAGE** Eng.,
Fr., Ger., **PRICE** (2 persons) 60–80 **(check with hosts
for pricing details)**

MONTREAL

University Bed & Breakfast

(Ian Atatekin and Pia Mia)

621-623 Prince Arthur W, Montreal, QC, H2X 1T9
www.universitybedandbreakfast.ca/index.htm
E-mail university@videotron.ca

514-842-6396
Fax 514-842-6396
.

We are located near University St, at the quiet end of Prince Arthur St, which is one of the favourite Montreal spots, full of sidewalk cafes and bring-your-wine restaurants. Train station, downtown shopping malls, Chinatown, festival sites and Montreal`s biggest green space (Mount Royal Park) are all within 10–15 minutes' walking distance. Apartment was built in 1921 with exposed brick walls and fireplace.

ROOMS Family suite, Upper floor, Ground floor, Private entrance, **Baths** Private, Shared with guest, **Beds** Queen, Double, Twin, Single or cots, Pullout sofa, **Air** In rooms, **Smoking** Outside, **In Room** Phone, TV, Fireplace, Internet access, VCR/DVD, **OTHERS** Babysitting, Urban, Open all year, **PAYMENT** Visa, MC, Diners, Amex, Direct debit, Cheques accepted, Cash, Trvl's cheques, **BREAKFASTS** Continental, **AMENITIES** Laundry, Kitchen, Lounge, **THINGS TO DO** Rental bikes, Trail nearby, Golf, Museums, Art, Theatre, Entertainment, Attractions, Wineries/Breweries, Shopping, Cross-country skiing, Tennis, Swimming, Birdwatching, Antiquing, **LANGUAGE** Eng., Fr., **PRICE** (2 persons) 59–119 **(check with hosts for pricing details)**

NEW CARLISLE *(south Gaspé)*

Bay View Manor/ Manoir Bay View

(Helen Hall Sawyer)

395 rte 132, Bonaventure E, Box 21, New Carlisle, QC, G0C 1Z0
www.canadianbandbguide.ca/bb.asp?ID=3145

418-752-2725

Comfortable home on main Hwy of ruggedly beautiful Gaspé Peninsula of Eastern Coastal Quebec, between villages of Bonaventure and New Carlisle. Across Hwy from natural beach, beside 18-hole Fauvel Golf Course. Open your window, feel the sea breeze, listen to the waves, watch fishermen tending nets, moonlight on the water. Near Acadian, Loyalist museums, archaeological caves, fossil sites, canoeing, horseback riding, tennis, Indian reserve, crafts, restaurants, nature reserves, parks. Photographers paradise. Alternate telephone: 418-752-6718.

ROOMS Upper floor, **Baths** Private, Shared with guest, **Beds** Queen, Twin, **Smoking** Outside, **In Room** Thermostat, **OTHERS** Rural, Seasonal, **PAYMENT** Cash, **BREAKFASTS** Full, Home-baked, **AMENITIES** Central TV, Central phone, Kitchen, Hot bev. bar, Lounge, Patio, **THINGS TO DO** Trail nearby, Golf, Fishing, Museums, Art, Theatre, Entertainment, Attractions, Shopping, Cross-country skiing, Tennis, Swimming, Horseback riding, Beach, **LANGUAGE** Eng., Fr., **PRICE** (2 persons) 40–50 **(check with hosts for pricing details)**

POINTE-À-LA-CROIX *(south Gaspé)*

Gîte La Maison verte du Parc Gaspésien

(Marie-Josée and André DesRochers)

216 che de la petite-rivière-du loup, Pointe-à-la-Croix, QC, G0C 1L0
www.bbcanada.com/parcgaspesien
E-mail parcgaspesien@globetrotter.net

418-788-2342 Fax 418-788-2489
TFr 1-866-788-2342

Historic American-style fishing lodge originally located on the world famous Restigouche River. It was moved to a marvellous 30-acre property in the country next to a park, where you can enjoy nature at its best year round. You'll certainly appreciate the relaxed settings in all of the two-bedroom suites, private and shared washroom bedrooms. Three cozy fireplaces, kitchenette, lake, trails etc. Located 3 km from New Brunswick border.

ROOMS Family suite, Upper floor, Ground floor, Lower floor, Private entrance, **Baths** Private, Ensuite, Shared with guest, **Beds** Queen, Double, Twin, Single or cots, Pullout sofa, **Air** In rooms, Ceiling fans, **Smoking** Outside, **In Room** Thermostat, Fireplace, **OTHERS** Rural, Open all year, Handicapped access, Additional meals, **PAYMENT** Visa, MC, Cheques accepted, Cash, Trvl's cheques, **BREAKFASTS** Full, Home-baked, **AMENITIES** Central TV, Central phone, Barbecue, Laundry, Kitchen, Fridge, Hot bev. bar, Lounge, Patio, Central VCR/DVD, **THINGS TO DO** Comp. bikes, Rental bikes, Trail nearby, Rental canoe or boat, Golf, Fishing, Museums, Art, Theatre, Entertainment, Attractions, Wineries/Breweries, Shopping, Cross-country skiing, Tennis, Swimming, Horseback riding, Beach, Birdwatching, Antiquing, **LANGUAGE** Eng., Fr., **PRICE** (2 persons) 55–90 **(check with hosts for pricing details)**

POINTE-AU-PIC *(northeast of Quebec City)*

La Maison Frizzi

(Raymonde Vermette)

55 Coteau-sur-mer, Charlevoix, La Malbaie, QC, G5A 3B6
www.inns-bb.com/maisonfrizzi

418-665-4668
Fax 418-665-1143

Come and discover our homey and comfortable Austrian-style home, away from the main road and overlooking the St. Lawrence River. Prize for excellence "special favourite regional 2000 and 1995–96." Well located at the centre of this magical region. We take great pleasure in assisting you to organize your stay. Friendly hospitality "a la Quebecoise." Delicious, varied breakfast awaits you. Quebec City Rd 138E to la Malbaie. Lecierc Bridge, Rd 362 W, 4 1/2 km. Turn left on Coteau-sur-mer.

ROOMS Upper floor, Private entrance, **Baths** Shared with guest, **Beds** King, Queen, Double, Twin, **Air** Ceiling fans, **Smoking** Outside, **In Room** Thermostat, **OTHERS** Babysitting, Rural, Adult, Open all year, **PAYMENT** Visa, MC, Cheques accepted, Cash, Trvl's cheques, **BREAKFASTS** Full, Home-baked, **AMENITIES** Central TV, Central phone, Laundry, Fridge, Lounge, Patio, **THINGS TO DO** Trail nearby, Golf, Fishing, Museums, Art, Entertainment, Attractions, Wineries/Breweries, Shopping, Cross-country skiing, Tennis, Swimming, Horseback riding, Beach, **LANGUAGE** Eng., Fr., Ger., Italian, **PRICE** (2 persons) 80–85 **(check with hosts for pricing details)**

QUEBEC CITY

Accueil Au Clair de Lune

(Jolanta Tardif de Moidrey)

26 ave Ste-Geneviève, Old Quebec City, QC, G1R 4B2
www.adorequebec.com
E-mail smag@sympatico.ca

418-694-9165
Fax 418-694-3487
TFr 1-877-299-0993

Accueil Au Clair de Lune B&B is situated in the heart of Old Quebec City, a few steps away from Frontenac castle, the Citadelle and the greenery of the Plains of Abraham. We feature superior comfortable beds, tastefully decorated rooms with brick walls and 12-foot-high ceiling, ensuite bathrooms, cable TV. All tourist taxes, full breakfast and parking are included in the price of a room.

Baths Ensuite, **Beds** Queen, Pullout sofa, **Smoking** Outside, **In Room** TV, **PAYMENT** Visa, MC, Diners, Amex, Cash, **BREAKFASTS** Full, **AMENITIES** Central phone, Fridge, **THINGS TO DO** Rental bikes, Trail nearby, Rental canoe or boat, Golf, Museums, Art, Theatre, Entertainment, Attractions, Wineries/ Breweries, Shopping, Cross-country skiing, Downhill skiing, Tennis, Swimming, Horseback riding, Beach, Birdwatching, Antiquing, **LANGUAGE** Eng., Fr., **PRICE** (2 persons) 115–145 **(check with hosts for pricing details)**

QUEBEC CITY

Appartements – Condos Le Méribel de Québec

(Lisette Émond)

393 rue de la Reine, Près du Vieux-Quebec,
QC, G1K 2R3
www.lemeribel.ca
E-mail lisette-remi@moncanoe.com

418-529-7027
Fax 418-529-7027

At the heart of the revitalized famed community of St-Roch, 5 minutes from Old Quebec, train and bus services are within walking distance. Renovated in 2005, Le Méribel is air-conditioned and tastefully but conservatively decorated. Reserve 1 room with breakfast or a private apartment (4–6 people) consisting of two rooms, dining room, living room: satellite TV, bathroom with shower, washer and dryer, complete kitchen with dishwasher, microwave, patio, backyard. Free parking. Soothing pool and separate shower.

ROOMS Upper floor, Ground floor, **Baths** Private, Shared with guest, **Beds** Queen, Pullout sofa, **Air** Central, **Smoking** Outside, **In Room** Thermostat, Phone, **OTHERS** Open all year, **PAYMENT** Visa, MC, Amex, Cash, Trvl's cheques, **BREAKFASTS** Self-catered, **AMENITIES** Central TV, Central phone, Laundry, Kitchen, Fridge, Hot bev. bar, Lounge, Patio, **THINGS TO DO** Rental bikes, Trail nearby, Rental canoe or boat, Golf, Fishing, Museums, Art, Theatre, Entertainment, Wineries/Breweries, Shopping, Cross-country skiing, Downhill skiing, Tennis, Swimming, Horseback riding, Beach, Birdwatching, Antiquing, **LANGUAGE** Eng., Fr., **PRICE** (2 persons) 60–85 **(check with hosts for pricing details)**

QUEBEC CITY
Au Gré du Vent B&B
(Michèle Fournier and John L'Heureux)

2 Fraser St, (Old Levis), Levis, QC, G6V 3R5
www.au-gre-du-vent.com
E-mail augreduvent@msn.com

418-838-9020
Fax 418-838-9074
TFr 1-866-838-9070

An authentic and charming B&B. Ideal stop between Ontario and the Maritimes at only 5 minutes from Hwy 20 and walking distance to the ferry for Old Quebec, boutiques, restaurants and major tourist attractions. English Victorian home (1890) offering one of the most stunning views of Old Quebec City, the river and Château Frontenac. Central air, inground-pool. Rated 5-stars by *Hebergement Quebec*. Grands Prix du tourisme Award Winner Area 2004. Please call for directions.

ROOMS Upper floor, Lower floor, **Baths** Ensuite, **Beds** Queen, Double, Twin, Single or cots, **Air** Central, **Smoking** Outside, **In Room** TV, Internet access, **OTHERS** Urban, Open all year, Pets in residence, **PAYMENT** Visa, MC, Amex, Direct debit, Cash, Trvl's cheques, **BREAKFASTS** Full, Home-baked, **AMENITIES** Central TV, Central phone, Swimming pool, Fridge, Patio, Central Internet access, Central VCR/DVD, **THINGS TO DO** Trail nearby, Golf, Museums, Art, Theatre, Entertainment, Attractions, Shopping, Cross-country skiing, Tennis, Swimming, Antiquing, **LANGUAGE** Eng., Fr., **PRICE** (2 persons) 105–135 **(check with hosts for pricing details)**

QUEBEC CITY
Au Petit Chateau
(Richard and Helene Daignault)

664 St-Joseph, Levis, QC, G6V 1J4
www.aupetitchateau.com
E-mail auchateau@videotron.ca

418-833-2798
Fax 418-833-5439
TFr 1-877-833-2798

A 1910 three-storey brick Victorian mansion located in an quiet location 5 minutes to the ferry to Old Quebec. This romantic getaway is lavishly furnished with antiques. All rooms have air-conditioning, plenty of windows and great views overlooking the St. Lawrence River. Luxury amenities. Our large grounds are wooded and flowerbeds are everywhere. A gourmet breakfast is served in our Victorian dining room or on the verandah with a view on the river.

ROOMS Family suite, Upper floor, Private entrance, **Baths** Private, Ensuite, Shared with guest, **Beds** Queen, Double, Single or cots, Pullout sofa, **Air** In rooms, **Smoking** Outside, **In Room** Thermostat, Phone, TV, Fireplace, **OTHERS** Open all year, **PAYMENT** Visa, MC, Amex, Cash, Trvl's cheques, **BREAKFASTS** Full, **AMENITIES** Central TV, Central phone, Barbecue, Laundry, Kitchen, Fridge, Hot bev. bar, Lounge, Patio, **THINGS TO DO** Rental bikes, Trail nearby, Golf, Museums, Art, Theatre, Entertainment, Attractions, Wineries/Breweries, Cross-country skiing, Swimming, Horseback riding, **LANGUAGE** Eng., Fr., Sp., Portuguese, **PRICE** (2 persons) 95–175 **(check with hosts for pricing details)**

QUEBEC CITY

Aux Années folles
(Jean Daoust)

5 rue des Saules E, Quebec City, QC, G1L 1R5
www.membres.lycos.fr/annfol
E-mail annfol@hotmail.com

418-260-9549

Are you looking for something a little out of the ordinary? Nonconformists and nostalgics, you are sure to love the Art Deco of the Roaring Twenties! A B&B in Limoilou (Colisée, ExpoCité and fairgrounds). Near Hwy 40 (Exit 315, 1ère Ave), 4 km from Vieux-Quebec (bike path, métrobus).

ROOMS Upper floor, **Baths** Shared with guest, **Beds** Double, Twin, **Smoking** Outside, **OTHERS** Urban, Open all year, **PAYMENT** Cash, **BREAKFASTS** Full, Home-baked, **AMENITIES** Central TV, Central phone, Lounge, Patio, Central VCR/DVD, **THINGS TO DO** Comp. bikes, Antiquing, **LANGUAGE** Eng., Fr., **PRICE** (2 persons) 55–75 **(check with hosts for pricing details)**

QUEBEC CITY

Aux Trois Balcons
(Isabelle Ouellet and Frédéric Benoit)

130 Saunders St, Quebec City, QC, G1R 2E3
www.troisbalcons.qc.ca
E-mail info@troisbalcons.qc.ca

418-525-5611
Fax 418-525-1106
TFr 1-866-525-5611

Your hosts Isabelle Ouellet and Frédéric Benoit invite you in this charming 1930s house located in the heart of Quebec's Upper Town's liveliness, offering the peaceful life of a quiet neighbourhood as well as the effervescent scene created by the numerous restaurants, pubs and boutiques on chic Cartier Ave and festive Grande-Allée St. The rich interior style of this residence invites comfort and relaxation. The two bedrooms in this non-smoking B&B have their own private facilities.

ROOMS Upper floor, Ground floor, Private entrance, **Baths** Private, Shared with guest, **Beds** Queen, Double, **Air** Ceiling fans, **Smoking** Outside, **OTHERS** Urban, Open all year, **PAYMENT** Cheques accepted, Cash, Trvl's cheques, **BREAKFASTS** Full, Home-baked, **AMENITIES** Central TV, Central phone, Fridge, Lounge, **THINGS TO DO** Trail nearby, Museums, Art, Theatre, Entertainment, Attractions, Wineries/Breweries, Shopping, Cross-country skiing, Downhill skiing, Antiquing, **LANGUAGE** Eng., Fr., Sp., **PRICE** (2 persons) 75–105 **(check with hosts for pricing details)**

B&B Centreville

(Bernard Couturier)

257 St-Vallier E, Quebec City, QC, G1K 3P4
www.bbcentreville.com
E-mail bbcentreville@hotmail.com

418-525-4741
Fax 418-525-6906
TFr 1-866-525-4741

An 1875 Heritage home, fully restored. We offer five beautiful rooms, one of which is a family room, each with private bathroom. Free parking. A variety of hearty breakfasts. Close to the fortified walls. We can accommodate groups for weddings or other. Your host, Bernard, a certified guide, will give you good advice. We are listed in the *Guide du Routard* and in *Lonely Planet*. Take advantage of our off-season rates. Visit our Web site.

ROOMS Family suite, Upper floor, Ground floor, Private entrance, **Baths** Private, **Beds** Queen, Twin, **In Room** Thermostat, **OTHERS** Urban, Open all year, **PAYMENT** Visa, MC, Cash, **BREAKFASTS** Full, Home-baked, Self-catered, **AMENITIES** Lounge, **THINGS TO DO** Rental bikes, Trail nearby, Golf, Museums, Art, Theatre, Entertainment, Wineries/Breweries, Shopping, Cross-country skiing, Downhill skiing, Tennis, Swimming, **LANGUAGE** Eng., Fr., **PRICE** (2 persons) 85–155 **(check with hosts for pricing details)**

Chez Monsieur Gilles 2

(Gilles Clavet)

1720 che de la Canardiere, Quebec City,
QC, G1J 2E3
www.chezmonsieurgilles.com/
E-mail mgilles@sympatico.ca

418-821-8778
Fax 418-821-8776

Regional prize winner "Coup de coeur" in 1999, and Regional "Grands prix du Tourisme Quebecois" winner for "Accueil et Service a la clientele. Castle-like cottage on three stories. We are located 5 minutes from the Walls of the Old City (1 mile or 1.6 km). Central air-conditioned, hot tub, pool table, free bikes, free parking, terrace. Host table on advance reservation, little store. We offer five large rooms, two with shared bathrooms and three with private bathrooms. We're the "spot" in Quebec.

ROOMS Family suite, Upper floor, **Baths** Private, Shared with guest, **Beds** Queen, Double, Single or cots, Pullout sofa, **Air** Central, **Smoking** In rooms, **In Room** Thermostat, TV, **OTHERS** Urban, Open all year, Additional meals, Pets in residence, **PAYMENT** Visa, Diners, Cheques accepted, Cash, Trvl's cheques, **BREAKFASTS** Full, **AMENITIES** Central TV, Central phone, Whirlpool, Fridge, Patio, **THINGS TO DO** Comp. bikes, Trail nearby, Golf, Fishing, Museums, Art, Theatre, Entertainment, Attractions, Wineries/Breweries, Shopping, Cross-country skiing, Tennis, Swimming, Horseback riding, Beach, **LANGUAGE** Eng., Fr., **PRICE** (2 persons) 90–125 **(check with hosts for pricing details)**

Quebec City

Fleet's Guest Home
(Stuart and Marie Paule Fleet)

1080 Holland Ave, Sillery, QC, G1S 3T3
www.canadianbandbguide.ca/bb.asp?ID=1956

418-688-0794

Famous "Plains of Abraham" citadel. See the changing guards, Old Quebec, Place Royale. Enjoy breakfast on the outside deck, in the solarium or dining room of this spacious home. Hosts have many years experience in the hotel business. Entire upper floor is for guests only.

ROOMS Upper floor, **Baths** Shared with guest, **Beds** Queen, Twin, **Air** Central, **In Room** TV, **PAYMENT** Visa, Cash, Trvl's cheques, **BREAKFASTS** Full, **AMENITIES** Patio, **THINGS TO DO** Attractions, Shopping, **LANGUAGE** Eng., Fr., **PRICE** (2 persons) 82-82 **(check with hosts for pricing details)**

Quebec City

La Maison Sous L'Orme
(Maud et Bruno Chouinard)

1 rue St-Felix, Levis, QC, G6V 5J1
www.geocities.com/sousorme/
E-mail sous.orme@qc.aira.com

418-833-0247
TFr 1-888-747-0247

Rated 5 Suns. Magnificent ancestral home dating back to 1870, situated in Old Levis. Ideal stop between Ontario and the Maritimes. Walking distance to the ferry for Old Quebec. Four bedrooms with queen-size beds and private baths, and three-room apartment on the ground floor, to be rented on a daily, weekly or monthly basis. A wholesome breakfast (full, vegetarian) is served including fresh fruit. Open year round. Free parking, bicycle storage and fridge available. Off season: 10% discount.

ROOMS Family suite, Upper floor, Ground floor, **Baths** Private, **Beds** Queen, Double, Single or cots, **Air** In rooms, **Smoking** Outside, **OTHERS** Babysitting, Urban, Open all year, **PAYMENT** Visa, MC, Direct debit, Cash, Trvl's cheques, **BREAKFASTS** Full, Home-baked, **AMENITIES** Central TV, Central phone, Kitchen, Fridge, Patio, **THINGS TO DO** Comp. bikes, Trail nearby, Golf, Museums, Art, Theatre, Entertainment, Wineries/ Breweries, Shopping, Cross-country skiing, Tennis, Swimming, **LANGUAGE** Eng., Fr., **PRICE** (2 persons) 85–95 **(check with hosts for pricing details)**

QUEBEC CITY

Lupins et lilas

(Marie Lepage)

860 Ave Belvédère, Quebec City, QC, G1S 3A9
www.lupinsetlilas.com
E-mail lupinsetlilas@videotron.ca

418-527-5909

Lupins et lilas is situated in the down-town area of Quebec City near the Plains of Abraham and Old Quebec. Discover the refinement favoured by the "International-style," the architectural expression of the house. Enjoy warmth, calm and privacy in our tastefully deco-rated rooms. Refined service, personal attention and a varied breakfast menu contribute to make your stay most pleas-ant. Private bathrooms, high-speed Internet access, cable television and free parking. Gastronomic and cultural pack-ages.

ROOMS Upper floor, **Baths** Private, Ensuite, **Beds** Queen, Double, Single or cots, Pullout sofa, **In Room** TV, Internet access, **OTHERS** Urban, Open all year, **PAY-MENT** Visa, Cash, Trvl's cheques, **BREAKFASTS** Full, Home-baked, **AMENITIES** Central phone, **THINGS TO DO** Trail nearby, Museums, Art, Theatre, Entertain-ment, Attractions, Wineries/Breweries, Shopping, Cross-country skiing, Downhill skiing, Tennis, Swimming, Antiquing, **LANGUAGE** Eng., Fr., **PRICE** (2 persons) 75–100 **(check with hosts for pricing details)**

QUEBEC

Maison Historique James Thompson

(Greg and Guitta Alexander)

47 rue Ste. Ursule, Old Quebec City, QC, G1R 4E4
www.bedandbreakfastquebec.com
E-mail gregalex@ca.inter.net

418-694-9042

Our house is a classified "Historic Monument" within the fortified walls of Old Quebec. About a 5-minute walk to the Chateau Frontenac. A 4 Sun rating from the Quebec government and rec-ommended in many travel guides includ-ing *Lonely Planet, Routard, Rough* and many others. The house was built in 1793 and is furnished with many antiques. Onsite parking. Our aim is to make your stay so enjoyable that you will return. Ideally situated on a street that runs between the two major roads in town. Fine restaurants and attractions are right outside the door. Cash, traveller's cheques and the honour system.
Visit us at www.quebecregion.com

ROOMS Upper floor, Ground floor, Lower floor, **Baths** Private, Ensuite, Shared with guest, **Beds** Queen, **Smoking** Outside, **In Room** Thermostat, **OTHERS** Babysitting, Urban, Open all year, **PAYMENT** Cash, Trvl's cheques, **BREAKFASTS** Full, Home-baked, **AMENITIES** Central TV, Central phone, Fridge, Lounge, Patio, **THINGS TO DO** Rental bikes, Trail nearby, Golf, Fishing, Museums, Art, Theatre, Entertainment, Attractions, Wineries/Breweries, Shopping, Cross-country skiing, Swimming, **LANGUAGE** Eng., Fr., **PRICE** (2 persons) 65–100 **(check with hosts for pricing details)**

QUEBEC CITY

Monique et Andre Saint-Aubin

(Monique Saint-Aubin)

3045 de la Seine, Ste-Foy, QC, G1W 1H8
www.quebecweb.com/staubin/introang.html
E-mail info@gitesaintaubin.com

418-658-0685
Fax 418-658-8466

Quebec City region Excellence prize 1994–1995. Warm atmosphere, residential neighbourhood. Near all facilities, we're 10 minutes from Old Quebec. Sightseeing tours and excursions can be arranged with pickup at the house. Central air-conditioning. From Montreal take Hwy 20 east to Quebec City and Pierre Laporte Bridge. Exit on Laurier Blvd. At 1st traffic light turn right to rue Lavigerie, and right on rue de la Seine (third street).

ROOMS Upper floor, Ground floor, **Baths** Shared with guest, Shared with hosts, **Beds** Queen, Twin, Single or cots, **Air** Central, **In Room** Thermostat, **OTHERS** Urban, Open all year, **PAYMENT** Cash, Trvl's cheques, **BREAKFASTS** Full, Home-baked, **AMENITIES** Central TV, Central phone, Lounge, Patio, **THINGS TO DO** Museums, Art, Theatre, Shopping, Cross-country skiing, Tennis, Swimming, **LANGUAGE** Eng., Fr., **PRICE** (2 persons) 65 **(check with hosts for pricing details)**

QUEBEC CITY [ILE D'ORLÉANS]
(south-central QC)

A la Dauphinelle (B&B)

(Denise Drapeau)

216, ch Bout de l'Ile, Ile d'Orleans (Ste-Petronille),
QC, G0A 4C0
www.pages.videotron.com/dauphine
E-mail aladauphinelle@videotron.ca

418-828-1487
Fax 418-828-1488
TFr 1-866-828-1487

A la Dauphinelle (B&B), one of the best B&Bs on Orleans Island. We offer high-quality lodging with ensuite bathrooms in every bedroom. This charming Victorian villa is very comfortable and furnished with stylish antiques. Come relive the great life of years past, in a superb environment, just 15 minutes away from Old Quebec City. This French capital is a corner of Europe in North America and it's in the heart of a most popular tourist region in Canada.

ROOMS Upper floor, **Baths** Private, Ensuite, **Beds** Queen, **Air** Central, **Smoking** Outside, **In Room** Thermostat, **OTHERS** Rural, Open all year, Pets in residence, **PAYMENT** Visa, Cash, Trvl's cheques, **BREAKFASTS** Full, Home-baked, **AMENITIES** Fridge, Lounge, Patio, **THINGS TO DO** Rental bikes, Trail nearby, Golf, Fishing, Museums, Art, Theatre, Entertainment, Attractions, Wineries/Breweries, Shopping, Cross-country skiing, Downhill skiing, Tennis, Horseback riding, Birdwatching, Antiquing, **LANGUAGE** Eng., Fr., **PRICE** (2 persons) 90–130 **(check with hosts for pricing details)**

Quebec City Downtown

À la Maison Tudor

(J. C. Kilfoil)

1037 ave Moncton, Québec City, QC, G1S 2Y9
www.lamaisontudor.com
E-mail ckilfoil@lamaisontudor.com

418-686-1033
Fax 418-686-6066

Discover enchantment in this cosy, turn-of-the-century, Tudor-style home, handy to national parks, the Convention Centre and Le Vieux-Quebec. Maximum discovery and visiting pleasure, ideal downtown location in quiet, Quartier Montcalm surroundings. Easy walk to rue Cartier/Grande Allée, fine and casual dining. Famous landmarks: Battlefields Park (3 minutes away), Promenade des Gouverneurs, Dufferin Terrace, Château Frontenac. Discreet, personal attention to your requirements.

ROOMS Family suite, Upper floor, Private entrance, **Baths** Private, Shared with guest, **Beds** Queen, Single or cots, **Air** Central, **Smoking** Outside, **In Room** Thermostat, Internet access, **PAYMENT** Visa, MC, Cash, Trvl's cheques, **BREAKFASTS** Full, **AMENITIES** Central TV, Central phone, Kitchen, Fridge, Lounge, Central Internet access, **THINGS TO DO** Rental bikes, Trail nearby, Golf, Museums, Art, Theatre, Entertainment, Attractions, Wineries/Breweries, Shopping, Cross-country skiing, Downhill skiing, Tennis, Birdwatching, Antiquing, **LANGUAGE** Eng., Fr., **PRICE** (2 persons) 105–115 **(check with hosts for pricing details)**

Saint-Donat *(north of Montreal)*

Auberge St-Donat

(Belinda and François Wisser)

350 rte 329, Saint-Donat, QC, J0T 2C0
www.aubergestdonat.com
E-mail info@aubergestdonat.com

819-424-7504
Fax 819-424-7504

Charming inn with 12 bedrooms, located at the entrance of the village of Saint-Donat, offers an unspoiled view of Lake Archambault and the Laurentian Mountains. This historic inn is close to many lakes, a bicycle path, a golf club and many ski centres. It is at the gates of Mont-Tremblant Park. Come and enjoy the pleasures of nature.

ROOMS Family suite, Upper floor, Lower floor, **Baths** Private, **Beds** King, Queen, Double, Pullout sofa, **Air** In rooms, **Smoking** Outside, **In Room** TV, **OTHERS** Rural, Open all year, Handicapped access, Additional meals, Pets welcome, **PAYMENT** Visa, MC, Cheques accepted, Cash, **BREAKFASTS** Full, **AMENITIES** Central TV, Central phone, Whirlpool, Barbecue, Kitchen, Hot bev. bar, Lounge, Patio, Central Internet access, Central VCR/DVD, **THINGS TO DO** Rental bikes, Trail nearby, Rental canoe or boat, Golf, Fishing, Museums, Art, Entertainment, Attractions, Shopping, Cross-country skiing, Downhill skiing, Swimming, Horseback riding, Beach, Birdwatching, Antiquing, **LANGUAGE** Eng., Fr., **PRICE** (2 persons) 70–100 **(check with hosts for pricing details)**

SAINTE-ADÈLE *(north of Montreal)*

A La Belle Idée

(Françoise and Michel Matte)

894, rue de l'Arbre Sec, Sainte-Adèle, QC, J8B 1X6
www.labelleidee.com
E-mail labelleidee@bellnet.ca

450-229-6173
Fax 450-229-6173
TFr 1-888-221-1313

A 4-Sun B&B, splendid Canadian home nestled on the edge of its forested area. Located in Sainte-Adèle in the heart of the Laurentian Mountains between Montreal and Mont-Tremblant. Close enough to the village for quick access to the many activities and far enough to enjoy peace and quiet and the services provided by your hosts. Four air-conditioned rooms with private baths, one suite featuring high-speed Internet access, await you. In-ground heated swimming pool. Complete details on our Web site.

ROOMS Family suite, Upper floor, Ground floor, **Baths** Private, **Beds** Queen, Double, Single or cots, **Air** Central, **Smoking** Outside, **In Room** Internet access, **OTHERS** Rural, Open all year, Additional meals, **PAYMENT** Visa, MC, Cash, Trvl's cheques, **BREAKFASTS** Full, Home-baked, **AMENITIES** Central TV, Central phone, Swimming pool, Whirlpool, Fridge, Lounge, Patio, Central VCR/DVD, **THINGS TO DO** Rental bikes, Trail nearby, Rental canoe or boat, Golf, Fishing, Museums, Art, Theatre, Entertainment, Attractions, Shopping, Cross-country skiing, Downhill skiing, Tennis, Swimming, Horseback riding, Beach, **LANGUAGE** Eng., Fr., Sp., **PRICE** (2 persons) 71-104 **(check with hosts for pricing details)**

SAINTE FLORENCE *(western Gaspé)*

Gîte au Bois Joli

(Esther Leblanc and Marcel Dionne)

852 rte 132, Sainte Florence, QC, G0J 2M0
www.gites-classifies.qc.ca/boijol.htm
E-mail gitesbj@globetrotter.net

418-756-5609

Located on Rte 132 but set back in the beautiful Matapedia Valley, 7 hours from Montreal or five hours from Quebec City. If you are going to the Gaspé Peninsula, New Brunswick, PEI, Nova Scotia or Magdalen Islands, stop by and you will be treated like family. Either fill up on your way there or on your way back. Hearty breakfasts. If you like fishing, the Matapedia River awaits you. This is the place you have been looking for.

ROOMS Family suite, Upper floor, Lower floor, Private entrance, **Baths** Private, Shared with guest, Shared with hosts, **Beds** Queen, Double, Twin, Pullout sofa, **Air** Ceiling fans, **Smoking** Outside, **In Room** TV, **OTHERS** Rural, Open all year, **PAYMENT** Cash, Trvl's cheques, **BREAKFASTS** Home-baked, **AMENITIES** Barbecue, Kitchen, Fridge, Hot bev. bar, Lounge, Patio, **THINGS TO DO** Trail nearby, Golf, Fishing, Museums, Entertainment, Attractions, Cross-country skiing, Downhill skiing, Birdwatching, Antiquing, **LANGUAGE** Fr., **PRICE** (2 persons) 62–72 **(check with hosts for pricing details)**

SAINTE-AGATHE-DES-MONTS
(north of Montreal)

Gîte la maison du lac

(Jocelyne Manseau and Normand Carpentier)

37 rue Saint-Aubin, Sainte-Agathe-Des-Monts,
QC, J8C 2Z7
www.lamaisondulac.com
E-mail info@lamaisondulac.com

819-323-3862
Fax 819-323-3863
TFr 1-866-321-5324

Directions: Autoroute des laurentides (15) north, Exit 83, at stop sign, turn left on Montée Alouette, at Rte 329 and "Le Patriote" theatre stop sign, turn right and continue for approximately 500 metres. In front of the sailing school turn right on Madeleine St, St.-Aubin St is the first one on your right. Continue until you get to the top, # 37 is the first road on your right, signpost B&B "La Maison du Lac" at the end of the road.

ROOMS Family suite, Ground floor, Private entrance, **Baths** Private, **Beds** Queen, **Smoking** Outside, **In Room** Thermostat, Internet access, **OTHERS** Open all year, **PAYMENT** Visa, MC, Cash, **BREAKFASTS** Full, Home-baked, **AMENITIES** Central TV, Fridge, Hot bev. bar, Lounge, Patio, Central Internet access, **THINGS TO DO** Rental bikes, Trail nearby, Golf, Fishing, Theatre, Attractions, Shopping, Cross-country skiing, Downhill skiing, Tennis, Beach, **LANGUAGE** Fr., **PRICE** (2 persons) 80–125 **(check with hosts for pricing details)**

SAINT-GEORGES *(south of Quebec City)*

Le Jardin des Mésanges

(Hélène Couture and Roger Provost)

482 rte Fortier, Saint-Cyprien-des-Etchemins,
QC, G0R 1B0
www.lejardindesmesanges.com
E-mail mesanges@sogetel.net

418-383-5777
TFr 1-877-383-5777

In the heart of a natural, bountiful environment, discover a peaceful oasis. The house has been entirely renovated for your comfort. Relaxing therapeutic bath. Get a taste of the country – birds, garden, farm and forest. A variety of packages are offered: health, biking, snowmobiling, etc. Tasty breakfast with homemade and regional products. Children are welcome. We are south of Quebec City and only 30 minutes from St.-Georges of Beauce.

ROOMS Family suite, Upper floor, Ground floor, **Baths** Private, Shared with guest, **Beds** Double, Twin, Single or cots, **Smoking** Outside, **In Room** Thermostat, **OTHERS** Rural, Open all year, Additional meals, Pets in residence, **PAYMENT** Visa, MC, Diners, Amex, Cash, Trvl's cheques, **BREAKFASTS** Full, Home-baked, **AMENITIES** Central TV, Central phone, Whirlpool, Barbecue, Laundry, Fridge, Lounge, Patio, Central Internet access, Central VCR/DVD, **THINGS TO DO** Trail nearby, Rental canoe or boat, Golf, Fishing, Museums, Art, Theatre, Entertainment, Attractions, Wineries/Breweries, Shopping, Cross-country skiing, Downhill skiing, Swimming, Horseback riding, Beach, Birdwatching, Antiquing, **LANGUAGE** Eng., Fr., **PRICE** (2 persons) 60–70 **(check with hosts for pricing details)**

SAINT-LAURENT *(west of Montreal)*

Studio Marhaba

(Assia and Ammar Sassi)

2265 Sigouin, Montreal, QC, H4R 1L6
www.pages.infinit.net/sassi/marhaba/index.htm
E-mail ammars@videotron.ca

514-335-7931
Fax 514-335-2177

We don't do breakfast but we do offer a lovely 3 1/2 studio apartment with bed-room/living room, kitchen, bathroom and laundry room. It accommodates from one to three people and can be rented short- or long-term. Special rates: week or month rental. Spacious, quiet, clean and comfortable. Fully equipped and fur-nished. Located in a residential area, close to all ameneties - Metro Côte Vertu (5 minutes), downtown Montreal (15 min-utes), Trudeau Airport (10 minutes). Free parking. An ideal place for you and your family.

ROOMS Lower floor, Private entrance, **Baths** Private, **Beds** Queen, Twin, Pullout sofa, **Air** Central, **Smoking** Outside, **In Room** Thermostat, Phone, TV, Internet access, VCR/DVD, **OTHERS** Babysitting, Urban, Open all year, Handicapped access, **PAYMENT** Cheques accept-ed, Cash, Trvl's cheques, **AMENITIES** Barbecue, Laundry, Kitchen, Fridge, **THINGS TO DO** Trail nearby, Golf, Museums, Art, Theatre, Entertain-ment, Attractions, Shopping, Cross-country skiing, Tennis, Swimming, **LANGUAGE** Eng., Fr., Ger., Arabic, **PRICE** (2 persons) 50–70 **(check with hosts for pricing details)**

SAINT-MARC-SUR-RICHELIEU
(east of Montreal)

Aux rêves d'antan

(Maryse Allard and Francois Thivierge)

595 Richelieu, Saint-Marc-sur-Richelieu, QC, J0L 2E0
www.pages.infinit.net/antan
E-mail fthivier@videotron.ca

450-584-3461

A beautiful Victorian-style, century-old house that once served as the village hotel and the MP's house. The three large and very comfortable rooms offer a view of the magnificiant Richelieu River. We have a warm welcome and lavish break-fast in store for you. Less than 30 minutes from Montreal and near gourmet restau-rants, golf courses and excursions to the village of the Vallée des Patriotes. Looking forward to receive you. Hwy 20, Exit 112, Rte 223 north. Classified 4 Suns by Quebec Tourism.

ROOMS Upper floor, **Baths** Private, Shared with guest, **Beds** King, Queen, Single or cots, **Smoking** Outside, **In Room** Internet access, **OTHERS** Rural, Open all year, **PAYMENT** Visa, Cash, **BREAKFASTS** Full, Home-baked, **AMENITIES** Barbecue, Lounge, Patio, Central Internet access, **THINGS TO DO** Golf, Fishing, Museums, Art, Theatre, Wineries/Breweries, Shopping, Cross-country skiing, Tennis, Swimming, Horseback riding, **LAN-GUAGE** Eng., Fr., **PRICE** (2 persons) 60–85 **(check with hosts for pricing details)**

SAINT-PIERRE-DE-VÉRONNE-À-PIKE-RIVER
(southeast of Montreal)

La Villa des Chenes

(Noelle Gasser)

300 che des Rivieres, Saint-Pierre-de-Véronne-à-Pike-River, QC, J0J 1P0
www.canadianbandbguide.ca/bb.asp?ID=2768
E-mail rngasser@netc.net

450-296-8848
Fax 450-296-4990

One hour from Montreal, we welcome you to a large home close to a river, and to our dairy farm. We offer quiet and comfortable rooms, full breakfasts and home-baked goods with Swiss flavour. We are a short distance from Lake Champlain in a rich agricultural area with vineyards and local historic museum, in an interesting loyalist region. Friendly and relaxed folks will welcome you to excellent restaurants, country fairs, art exhibits, vintage festivals and other attractions. Members of Agricotours.

ROOMS Upper floor, Lower floor, **Baths** Private, Shared with guest, **Beds** King, Queen, Double, Twin, Single or cots, Pullout sofa, **Air** Central, **Smoking** Outside, **OTHERS** Rural, **PAYMENT** Cheques accepted, Cash, Trvl's cheques, **BREAKFASTS** Full, **AMENITIES** Central TV, Central phone, Fridge, Lounge, Patio, **THINGS TO DO** Trail nearby, Rental canoe or boat, Golf, Museums, Art, Attractions, Wineries/Breweries, **LANGUAGE** Eng., Fr., Ger., **PRICE** (2 persons) 55–75 **(check with hosts for pricing details)**

SECTEUR CAP-A-L'AIGLE, LA MALBAIE
(northeast of Quebec City)

Gite Claire Villeneuve

(Claire Villeneuve)

215 rue St. Raphael, Secteur Cap-a-l'Aigle, La Malbaie, QC, G5A 2N6
www.quebecinformation.com/clairevilleneuve

418-665-2288

An old house full of simplicity waits for you on the north side of the St. Lawrence River. On Rd 138 at La Malbaie, cross the bridge, turn right and continue to village and to St. Raphael St on the right side. Full home-baked breakfast. Historic village, riverfront with view, quiet, TV, separate entrance. Parking. English. Please call for pricing.

ROOMS Upper floor, Private entrance, **Baths** Shared with guest, **Smoking** Outside, **OTHERS** Open all year, **PAYMENT** Cheques accepted, Cash, **BREAKFASTS** Full, Home-baked, **AMENITIES** Central TV, Central phone, **THINGS TO DO** Golf, Museums, Art, Shopping, Cross-country skiing, Horseback riding, Beach, **LANGUAGE** Eng., Fr., **PRICE** (2 persons) 51-76 **(check with hosts for pricing details)**

SHERBROOKE *(east of Montreal)*

La Canardiere B&B

(Chantal Ross)

400 River St, North Hatley, QC, J0B 2C0
www.bbcanada.com/2319.html
E-mail canardiere@aei.ca

819-842-2279
Fax 819-842-2279

The innkeepers of this turn-of-the-century home in the quaint village of North Hatley invite you to join them for a slow-paced quiet stop in time. Whether your pleasure is a hearty gourmet breakfast, a quiet afternoon sipping tea by the river, or a romantic evening for two, La Canardiere can satisfy your every whim. Our charming B&B is located in the heart of the village, where an array of activities is available, we are also close to Bishop's University. Our rooms are located on separate floors.

ROOMS Upper floor, Ground floor, Private entrance, **Baths** Private, Shared with guest, **Beds** Double, Twin, Single or cots, **Smoking** Outside, **In Room** Internet access, **OTHERS** Urban, Open all year, **PAYMENT** Cash, Trvl's cheques, **BREAKFASTS** Full, Home-baked, **AMENITIES** Central TV, Central phone, Central Internet access, Central VCR/DVD, **THINGS TO DO** Rental bikes, Trail nearby, Comp. Canoe or boat, Golf, Fishing, Museums, Art, Theatre, Entertainment, Shopping, Cross-country skiing, Downhill skiing, Tennis, Swimming, Horseback riding, Beach, Birdwatching, Antiquing, **LANGUAGE** Eng., Fr., **PRICE** (2 persons) 90–120 **(check with hosts for pricing details)**

TROIS-RIVIÈRES *(southwest of Quebec City)*

Gîte Saint-Laurent

(Yolande et René Bronsard)

4551 Notre-Dame O, Trois-Rivières, QC, G9A 4Z4
www.iquebec.com/bbsaint-laurent
E-mail rene.bronsard@sympatico.ca

819-378-3533
Fax 819-378-3533
TFr 1-866-866-3533

Spacious home located on the shore of St. Lawrence River. At our home, city facilities are combined with the charm of the country. Tranquility, cleanliness, comfort and security are the keys to our hospitality. Large green spaces, swimming pool, kitchen garden and a fireplace, all made for a warm welcome. Our cosy bedroom, personal attention and our substantial breakfast will make your visit a real pleasure. *Soyez les bienvenues à notre petit déjeuner gastronomique. Bienvenido a nuestra casa.*

ROOMS Upper floor, **Baths** Shared with hosts, **Beds** Queen, Twin, **Air** Central, **OTHERS** Urban, Open all year, **PAYMENT** Visa, Cheques accepted, Cash, Trvl's cheques, **BREAKFASTS** Home-baked, **AMENITIES** Swimming pool, Barbecue, Fridge, **THINGS TO DO** Trail nearby, Golf, Museums, Art, Theatre, Entertainment, Shopping, Tennis, Swimming, **LANGUAGE** Eng., Fr., Sp., **PRICE** (2 persons) 80 **(check with hosts for pricing details)**

WAKEFIELD *(west of Montreal)*

Les Trois Erables

(Joanne Hunter and Jim Fitzgibbons)

801 Riverside, Wakefield, QC, J0X 3G0
www.lestroiserables.com
E-mail lestroiserables@qc.aira.com

819-459-1118
TFr 1-877-337-2253

Les Trois Erables is a gorgeous Victorian
mansion located in the heart of Wakefield
village by the Gatineau River. We offer
five elegant rooms with ensuite baths.
Gracious, helpful hosts serve breakfast in
the dining room, afternoon tea by
appointment, boxed lunches on request.
Walk to restaurants, stores, galleries, steam
train, entertainment, boutiques, 5-minute
drive to Gatineau Park, 30 minutes from
Ottawa. To find us follow signs to Hull,
take Hwy 5 north (toward Maniwaki), then
105 north to Wakefield Exit.

ROOMS Family suite, Upper floor, **Baths** Ensuite, **Beds**
King, Queen, Double, Single or cots, Pullout sofa, **Air**
Central, Ceiling fans, **In Room** Thermostat, Fireplace,
OTHERS Open all year, Additional meals, Pets in resi-
dence, **PAYMENT** Visa, MC, Direct debit, Cheques
accepted, Cash, Trvl's cheques, **BREAKFASTS** Full,
Home-baked, **AMENITIES** Central TV, Central phone,
Fridge, Hot bev. bar, Lounge, Patio, Central Internet
access, Central VCR/DVD, **THINGS TO DO** Comp. bikes,
Rental bikes, Trail nearby, Rental canoe or boat, Comp.
Canoe or boat, Golf, Fishing, Museums, Art, Theatre,
Entertainment, Attractions, Shopping, Cross-country
skiing, Tennis, Swimming, Horseback riding, Beach,
Birdwatching, Antiquing, **LANGUAGE** Eng., Fr., **PRICE**
(2 persons) 95–175 **(check with hosts for pricing
details)**

NEW BRUNSWICK

QUEBEC

Nash Creek

Petit-Rocher ●

Caraquet ●
● Shippagan

Bathurst ● Inkerman

Gulf of St. Lawrence

● Grand Falls

Miramichi ●

● Hartland

MAINE U.S.A.

Bouctouche ●

Shediac ●

Moncton ●
Port Elgin ●

● Millville

Memramcook ●

Sackville ●

■ FREDERICTON

Hopewell Cape ●

Hopewell Hill ●

Alma ●

Bay of Fundy

St. John ●

Locator information
for towns in the listing areas
gives relative position to major cities
(usually the capital) or other significant
geographic points.
Use any standard road map for
precisely locating the town of interest.

● Grand Manan

■ Provincial Capital
● City/Town
○ Indicates area or other geographic
features such as lakes etc.

N

Alma *(southeastern NB)*

Captain's Inn
(John and Elsie O'Regan)

8602 Main St, Alma, NB, E4H 1N5
www.captainsinn.ca
E-mail captinn@nb.sympatico.ca

506-887-2017
Fax 506-887-2074

Beautifully situated in the quaint fishing port of Alma on the Bay of Fundy at the entrance to the world-famous Fundy National Park. A short drive to Cape Enrage, Mary's Point Western Hemispheric Shorebird Reserve and the Hopewell Rocks Exploration Site. Walk on the ocean floor for 1 km at low tide. Route 114 Fundy Coastal Drive. Two parlours and sunroom for the exclusive use of our guests. We take special care to ensure your visit will be pleasant and remain in your memory for years to come.

ROOMS Upper floor, Ground floor, **Baths** Ensuite, **Beds** Queen, **Smoking** Outside, **In Room** Thermostat, TV, VCR/DVD, **OTHERS** Rural, Open all year, **PAYMENT** Visa, MC, Direct debit, Cash, Trvl's cheques, **BREAK-FASTS** Full, **AMENITIES** Central TV, Central phone, Patio, **THINGS TO DO** Trail nearby, Golf, Attractions, Shopping, Cross-country skiing, Tennis, Swimming, Beach, **LANGUAGE** Eng., **PRICE** (2 persons) 92–105 **(check with hosts for pricing details)**

Alma

Falcon Ridge Inn
(Peter and Donna Colpitts)

24 Falcon Ridge Dr, Alma, NB, E4H 4Z3
www.falconridgeinn.nb.ca
E-mail falcon@falconridgeinn.nb.ca

506-887-1110
Fax 506-887-2376
TFr 1-888-321-9090

Hilltop location in Alma gives an unob-structed panoramic view of the high and low tides of the Bay of Fundy from all rooms and all points of the Inn. Our deluxe accommodations afford all the comforts of home including queen bed, ensuite, fireplace, whirlpool bath, mini-fridge, coffeemaker, phone, CATV/DVD/VCR. Includes a full, hot breakfast served in our spectatular 24-foot-ceiling Great Room dining room. Fundy National Park, Hopewell Rocks, Cape Enrage, Fundy Trail are nearby. Open all year. See Web site for packages.

ROOMS Upper floor, Ground floor, **Baths** Ensuite, **Beds** Queen, Single or cots, Pullout sofa, **Smoking** Outside, **In Room** Thermostat, Phone, TV, Fireplace, VCR/DVD, **OTHERS** Open all year, **PAYMENT** Visa, MC, Amex, Direct debit, Cash, Trvl's cheques, **BREAKFASTS** Full, Home-baked, **AMENITIES** Central TV, Whirlpool, Fridge, Lounge, **THINGS TO DO** Trail nearby, Rental canoe or boat, Golf, Museums, Attractions, Cross-country skiing, Tennis, Swimming, Horseback riding, Beach, Birdwatching, **LANGUAGE** Eng., **PRICE** (2 per-sons) 89–125 **(check with hosts for pricing details)**

BATHURST *(northeastern NB)*

Gîte Toutes Saisons B&B

(Phil and Barbara Thibodeau)

10 rue des oiseaux, Pointe Verte, NB, E8J 2V6
www.relaxseaside.com
E-mail info@relaxseaside.com

506-783-3122
TFr 1-877-783-3122

Experience panoramic views from every window in our oceanfront home nestled in its own woods. Main floor including porches, is fully accessible. Upstairs rooms have fireplaces, private balconies. All guests are welcome to enjoy the games room with billiards, the great room with wood fireplace, the trails and the rocks and the wild beach. Two- to four-day packages include lobster and scallops feast and thalasso spa supreme relaxation. Visit relaxseaside.com for beautiful photos and current rates.

ROOMS Upper floor, Ground floor, Lower floor, **Baths** Ensuite, **Beds** Queen, Twin, Pullout sofa, **Air** Ceiling fans, **Smoking** Outside, **In Room** Thermostat, **OTHERS** Babysitting, Rural, Open all year, Handicapped access, Additional meals, **PAYMENT** Visa, MC, Direct debit, Cheques accepted, Cash, Trvl's cheques, **BREAKFASTS** Full, Home-baked, **AMENITIES** Central TV, Barbecue, Laundry, Fridge, Lounge, Patio, Central Internet access, **THINGS TO DO** Trail nearby, Golf, Fishing, Museums, Art, Theatre, Entertainment, Attractions, Shopping, Tennis, Swimming, Beach, Birdwatching, Antiquing, **LANGUAGE** Eng., Fr., **PRICE** (2 persons) 98–138 **(check with hosts for pricing details)**

BOUCTOUCHE *(east-central NB)*

Les Pins Maritimes

(Jeanne Brideau)

320 Cote Sainte Anne Rd, Sainte Anne de Kent, NB, E4S 1M6
www.sn2000.nb.ca/comp/pins-maritimes
E-mail jea@nbnet.nb.ca

506-743-8450
Fax 506-743-8450

Exceptional site with ocean frontage and sandy beach. Local attractions are a short drive away. Deep-sea fishing, clam digging, golfing, swimming, berry picking, hiking, cycling, kayaking, canoeing, collecting beach glass, birdwatching, attending Acadian, English or Native cultural activities or just lazing on the beach at the doorstep, are possible from this comfortable century-old house. Long stays are popular at Les Pins Maritimes where scrumptious and healthy breakfasts are part of the experience.

ROOMS Family suite, Upper floor, Ground floor, Private entrance, **Baths** Private, Ensuite, **Beds** Queen, Double, Pullout sofa, **Air** In rooms, **Smoking** Outside, **OTHERS** Rural, Seasonal, **PAYMENT** Visa, Direct debit, Cash, Trvl's cheques, **BREAKFASTS** Full, Home-baked, **AMENITIES** Central TV, Central phone, Fridge, Hot bev. bar, Patio, Central Internet access, Central VCR/DVD, **THINGS TO DO** Comp. bikes, Trail nearby, Comp. Canoe or boat, Golf, Fishing, Museums, Art, Entertainment, Attractions, Wineries/Breweries, Tennis, Swimming, Beach, Birdwatching, Antiquing, **LANGUAGE** Eng., Fr., **PRICE** (2 persons) 70–90 **(check with hosts for pricing details)**

CARAQUET *(northeastern NB)*

Gîte "Le Poirier" B&B

(Roland and Martina Friolet)

98 boul St-Pierre O, Caraquet, NB, E1W 1B6
www.gitelepoirier.com
E-mail gitepoir@nbnet.nb.ca

506-727-4359
Fax 506-726-6084
TFr 1-888-748-9311

Gîte "Le Poirier" B&B, New England-style house built in 1927 by Charles C. Poirier who was schoolmaster, magistrate. "Le Poirier" homestead has been restored to its original spendour and furnished with antiques. Come and visit the region and you will not be disappointed. Caraquet (capital of modern Acadia) is facing and surrounded by the Baie des Chaleurs, which was recognized as one of the nicest bays of the world. Good restaurants, lot of cultural Acadian events.

ROOMS Upper floor, Ground floor, **Baths** Private, Ensuite, **Beds** Queen, Double, **Air** In rooms, **Smoking** Outside, **In Room** Thermostat, Phone, TV, Internet access, VCR/DVD, **OTHERS** Urban, Rural, Open all year, **PAYMENT** Visa, MC, Direct debit, Cash, Trvl's cheques, **BREAKFASTS** Full, Home-baked, **AMENITIES** Central TV, Central phone, Laundry, Lounge, Patio, Central Internet access, Central VCR/DVD, **THINGS TO DO** Comp. bikes, Trail nearby, Golf, Fishing, Museums, Art, Theatre, Entertainment, Attractions, Shopping, Cross-country skiing, Tennis, Swimming, Horseback riding, Beach, Birdwatching, **LANGUAGE** Eng., Fr., **PRICE** (2 persons) 79–98 **(check with hosts for pricing details)**

CARAQUET

Gîte "L'Isle-du-Randonneur" B&B

(Denise et Fernand Dumaresq)

539 boul St-Pierre O, Caraquet, NB, E1W 1A3
www.randonneurbb.com
E-mail islebb@nbnet.nb.ca

506-727-3877 Fax 506-727-4109
TFr 1-800-620-3877

Bienvenue à Caraquet heart of the Acadian peninsula. This warm, inviting, personal and unique 4 Star (3 Diamond CAA) B&B welcomes you to the comfort of an Acadian heritage home. After a delicious, full gourmet breakfast, why not spend the day visiting our famous Acadian historical village, marine center and ecopark. At the end of a splendid day, enjoy a beautiful sunset and a quiet moment on the beach. Offer fishing packages and Romantic Getaways. Queen-size beds, TV, balconies, ensuite bathrooms, spa. Open year-round.

ROOMS Family suite, Upper floor, Ground floor, **Baths** Ensuite, **Beds** Queen, Double, Single or cots, Pullout sofa, **Smoking** Outside, **In Room** Thermostat, Phone, TV, Fireplace, **OTHERS** Rural, Open all year, Handicapped access, Additional meals, Pets in residence, **PAYMENT** Visa, Cash, Trvl's cheques, **BREAKFASTS** Full, Home-baked, **AMENITIES** Central TV, Central phone, Whirlpool, Barbecue, Laundry, Kitchen, Fridge, Hot bev. bar, Lounge, Patio, **THINGS TO DO** Rental bikes, Trail nearby, Rental canoe or boat, Golf, Fishing, Museums, Art, Theatre, Entertainment, Attractions, Shopping, Cross-country skiing, Tennis, Swimming, Horseback riding, Beach, **LANGUAGE** Eng., Fr., **PRICE** (2 persons) 79–99 **(check with hosts for pricing details)**

CARAQUET
Hotel Paulin
(Karen Mersereau and Gerard Paulin)

143 blvd St. Pierre O, Caraquet, NB, E1W 1B6
www.hotelpaulin.com
E-mail innkeeper@hotelpaulin.com

506-727-9981
Fax 506-727-4808
TFr 1-866-727-9981

Internationally acclaimed seaside bou-
tique-hotel and Acadian historical landmark. On the Baie des Chaleurs, offering
spectacular sunsets, private beach, golf,
in-house spa services. Next to 130 km of
hiking, biking, ski-doo, cross-country trails.
Operated by third generation of Paulin's.
Critically acclaimed by *New York Times*,
Le Figaro Magazine, *Destinations Canada*,
Frommers, *Fodor's*. Recognized cuisine
offering many local delicacies: seafood,
wild mushrooms, artisan cheeses, natural
beef and lamb.

ROOMS Family suite, Upper floor, Private entrance,
Baths Ensuite, **Beds** King, Queen, Single or cots,
Pullout sofa, **OTHERS** Rural, Open all year, Additional
meals, **PAYMENT** Visa, MC, Direct debit, Trvl's cheques,
BREAKFASTS Full, Continental, Home-baked, **AMENI-
TIES** Central TV, Central phone, Whirlpool, Laundry,
Fridge, Hot bev. bar, Lounge, Patio, Central Internet
access, Central VCR/DVD, **THINGS TO DO** Rental bikes,
Trail nearby, Rental canoe or boat, Golf, Fishing,
Museums, Art, Theatre, Attractions, Cross-country ski-
ing, Tennis, Swimming, Beach, Birdwatching,
Antiquing, **LANGUAGE** Eng., Fr., **PRICE** (2 persons)
89–235 **(check with hosts for pricing details)**

FREDERICTON *(south-central NB)*
Country Lane B&B Inn
(Sheila and Jim MacIsaac)

594 rte 690, Lakeville Corner, NB, E4B 1N2
www.countrylanebbinn.com
E-mail stay@countrylanebbinn.com

506-385-2398
Fax 506-385-1999
TFr 1-866-385-2398

Add romance to your vacation. A *Savvy
Traveller* award-winner offering romantic
getaways. A quiet waterfront acreage 25
minutes from Fredericton. Guest rooms
features fireplaces, whirlpool baths,
and/or private outdoor hot tubs. We offer
breakfast choices served ensuite, in dining room or on the verandah overlooking
the lake. The perfect place for relaxation,
pampering and romance.

ROOMS Upper floor, Ground floor, **Baths** Ensuite,
Beds Queen, Double, **Air** Central, **Smoking** Outside, **In
Room** Thermostat, Phone, TV, Fireplace, VCR/DVD,
OTHERS Rural, Adult, Open all year, Additional meals,
PAYMENT Visa, MC, Diners, Amex, Direct debit, Cash,
Trvl's cheques, **BREAKFASTS** Full, Home-baked,
AMENITIES Whirlpool, Laundry, Hot bev. bar, **THINGS
TO DO** Comp. bikes, Comp. Canoe or boat, Golf,
Museums, Art, Attractions, Shopping, **LANGUAGE**
Eng., **PRICE** (2 persons) 130–160 **(check with hosts for
pricing details)**

GRAND FALLS *(northwestern NB)*

Cote's Bed & Breakfast/Inn

(Noel and Norma Coté)

575 Broadway Blvd W, Grand Falls, NB, E3Z 2L2
www.cotebb-inn.com
E-mail stay@cotebb-inn.com

506-473-1415
Fax 506-473-1952
TFr 1-877-444-2683

Relax in luxurious, quiet surroundings. We cater to the travellers, romantics and business people who want the very best. We offer luxuriously appointed rooms and suites, most with fireplaces, three with whirlpools and two access an outdoor hot tub. Inquire about our romantic packages. We are minutes from the "Falls & Gorge," golf course, NB TrailBoat rides, gift shops and restaurants. Exit 75 to Broadway, across bridge, go to 575 Broadway Blvd.

ROOMS Family suite, Upper floor, Lower floor, Private entrance, **Baths** Ensuite, **Beds** King, Queen, Pullout sofa, **Air** In rooms, **Smoking** Outside, **In Room** Thermostat, Phone, TV, Fireplace, **OTHERS** Urban, Adult, Open all year, Additional meals, **PAYMENT** Visa, MC, Amex, Direct debit, Cheques accepted, **BREAK-FASTS** Full, Home-baked, **AMENITIES** Central phone, Sauna, Whirlpool, Laundry, Fridge, Hot bev. bar, Patio, **THINGS TO DO** Trail nearby, Golf, Museums, Attractions, Shopping, Cross-country skiing, Tennis, Swimming, **LANGUAGE** Eng., Fr., **PRICE** (2 persons) 75–175 **(check with hosts for pricing details)**

GRAND MANAN *(south Bay of Fundy)*

McLaughlin's Wharf B&B

(Brenda McLaughlin)

1863 rte 776, Grand Manan, NB, E5G 3H1
www.canadianbandbguide.ca/bb.asp?ID=3008

506-662-8760
Fax 506-662-9998

A unique B&B located on an historic site renovated from the local post office and country general store. Within walking distance of beach, wharves, golf courses, tennis court, trails and various other activities such as whale watching, kayaking, etc. Full breakfast and dinner served daily in licensed dining room or on deck. Other phone: 506-662-3672.

ROOMS Upper floor, **Baths** Shared with guest, **Beds** Queen, Double, Twin, Single or cots, Pullout sofa, **Smoking** Outside, **In Room** Thermostat, **OTHERS** Rural, Handicapped access, Seasonal, **PAYMENT** Visa, MC, Amex, **BREAKFASTS** Full, Home-baked, **AMENITIES** Fridge, Lounge, Patio, **THINGS TO DO** Trail nearby, Museums, Attractions, Shopping, Tennis, Swimming, Beach, Birdwatching, **LANGUAGE** Eng., **PRICE** (2 persons) 79–89 **(check with hosts for pricing details)**

HARTLAND *(west-central NB)*

Rebecca Farm
Bed and Breakfast

(John and Betty Lou Craig)

656 Rockland Rd, Rockland, NB, E7P 1J7
www.rebeccafarm.com
E-mail rebeccafarm@hotmail.com

506-375-1699
Fax 506-375-4848

Historically renovated 1828 farmhouse situated on 124 acres. Just 7 minutes from the longest covered bridge in the world. Seven delux air-conditioned rooms with private baths. A full country breakfast with lots of homemade jams starts your day. Experience our warm hospitality and you won't want to leave. Enjoy nature while you walk, golf, four-wheel or snowmobile. There is no place like Rebecca Farm. From Rte 2 take Exit 170 at Hartland. Turn left unto Orser St and follow our signs to 656 Rockland Rd. *Canada Select* 4-star.

ROOMS Upper floor, Ground floor, **Baths** Private, Ensuite, **Beds** King, Queen, **Air** Central, **Smoking** Outside, **In Room** Thermostat, **OTHERS** Rural, Open all year, Handicapped access, **PAYMENT** Visa, MC, Diners, Amex, Direct debit, Cash, **BREAKFASTS** Full, **AMENITIES** Central TV, Central phone, Laundry, Patio, **THINGS TO DO** Trail nearby, Golf, Attractions, Shopping, **LANGUAGE** Eng., Fr., some French, **PRICE** (2 persons) 100–130 **(check with hosts for pricing details)**

HOPEWELL CAPE *(east-central NB)*

Florentine Manor B and B

(Mary and Cyril Tingley)

356 rte 915, Harvey, Albert County, NB, E4H 2M2
www.florentinemanor.com
E-mail florainn@nb.aibn.com

506-882-2271
TFr 1-800-665-2271

Nestled in the upper reaches of the Bay of Fundy we are less than 20 minutes from Hopewell Rocks and 25 minutes from Fundy National Park. Mary's Point Bird Sanctuary is nearby. Our *Canada Select* 4 1/2-star B&B is in a quiet country setting and has been serving guests for 22 years. With nine guest rooms and all-private baths we are able to cater to small groups (hikers, birders, small meetings) to 20 people. Dinner is available for our guests with prior reservation.

ROOMS Upper floor, Ground floor, **Baths** Private, Ensuite, **Beds** King, Queen, Double, Twin, Single or cots, **Smoking** Outside, **In Room** Thermostat, Fireplace, **OTHERS** Rural, Open all year, Additional meals, **PAYMENT** Visa, MC, Direct debit, Cash, Trvl's cheques, **BREAKFASTS** Full, Home-baked, **AMENITIES** Central TV, Central phone, Whirlpool, Central VCR/DVD, **THINGS TO DO** Trail nearby, Golf, Fishing, Museums, Attractions, Cross-country skiing, Horseback riding, Beach, Birdwatching, **LANGUAGE** Eng., **PRICE** (2 persons) 99–149 **(check with hosts for pricing details)**

HOPEWELL HILL *(east-central NB)*

Peck Colonial House B/B & Tearoom

(Stephen and Elaine Holmstrom)

5566 rte 114, Hopewell Hill, NB, E4H 3N5
www.peckcolonial.com
E-mail stay@peckcolonial.com

506-882-2114

Two-hundred-year old ancestral Colonial home set on 340 acres of land granted to our family in 1765, surrounded by beautiful gardens. Peaceful quiet surroundings overlooking Grindstone Island in Fundy Bay. Just 20 minutes to all activities in area, Hopewell Rocks, Fundy Park. Enjoy wonderful homecooked breakfast, best ever. Lunch and light dinners served in unique "19th Century" tea room, featuring homemade chowders, soups, breads and much more. Hosts are very knowledgeable about local history and events.

ROOMS Upper floor, **Baths** Shared with guest, **Beds** Double, Twin, Single or cots, **Air** Central, **Smoking** Outside, **OTHERS** Rural, Open all year, Additional meals, **PAYMENT** Visa, Cash, Trvl's cheques, **BREAKFASTS** Full, Home-baked, **AMENITIES** Central TV, Lounge, Central VCR/DVD, **THINGS TO DO** Trail nearby, Golf, Museums, Art, Attractions, Horseback riding, Beach, **LANGUAGE** Eng., **PRICE** (2 persons) 50–65 **(check with hosts for pricing details)**

INKERMAN [SHIPPAGAN]
(northeastern NB)

Le Gîte de l'Ardora Bed and Breakfast

(Ginette Doucet and Jean-Guy F Robichaud)

1932, chemin Four Rd, Inkerman, NB, E8P 1B1
www.ardora.ca
E-mail ardora@nbnet.nb.ca

506-336-9262

Come and enjoy an authentic Acadian experience on a century-old farm. Your hosts will be happy to share the knowledge about their oyster and blueberry productions, as well as their other daily activities. Many antiquities and great decorations help preserve the "old days" atmosphere. The name of our residence is inspired by a boat once owned by a member of our family. Come and visit where you will be at home in our home. We are awaiting your arrival.

ROOMS Upper floor, **Baths** Shared with guest, **Beds** Double, Single or cots, **Smoking** Outside, **OTHERS** Rural, Open all year, **PAYMENT** Cash, **BREAKFASTS** Continental, Home-baked, **AMENITIES** Central TV, Central phone, Barbecue, Kitchen, Central Internet access, Central VCR/DVD, **THINGS TO DO** Comp. bikes, Golf, Fishing, Museums, Theatre, Entertainment, Attractions, Cross-country skiing, Beach, Birdwatching, **LANGUAGE** Eng., Fr., **PRICE** (2 persons) 50 **(check with hosts for pricing details)**

MEMRAMCOOK *(eastern NB)*

Gîte Les 3 Moulins B&B

(Thérèse Melanson)

172 rte La Vallée, Memramcook, NB, E4K 2A6
www.bbcanada.com/6168.html
E-mail 3moulins@rogers.com

506-758-0911

Renovated historic home – Rte 106 in Memramcook, NB, known as the "Cradle of Acadia." A perfect place to learn about the history and culture of the Acadians. Photos, works of art and a collection of books reflect owner's interest and enthusiasm. Close to restaurants, 18-hole golf course, spa, nature trails and many other tourist attractions such as Monument-Lefebvre, well-known national historic site. Packages available. Inquire about special rates for groups or extended stay. Ideal for immersion-French or English.

Baths Ensuite, Shared with guest, **Beds** Queen, Double, Twin, **OTHERS** Urban, Open all year, **PAYMENT** Cash, Trvl's cheques, **BREAKFASTS** Full, **THINGS TO DO** Trail nearby, Golf, Museums, Attractions, Shopping, **LANGUAGE** Eng., Fr., **PRICE** (2 persons) 50–85 **(check with hosts for pricing details)**

MILLVILLE *(northwest of Fredericton)*

LedgeRock Bed and Breakfast

(Marguerite and Ellis Fawcett)

715 rte 585, Nortondale, NB, E6E 1N8
www.bbcanada.com/4454.html
E-mail ledgeroc@nbnet.nb.ca

506-463-0002

LedgeRock, located in Nortondale, high atop one of the rolling hills surrounding Millville, offers: private entrance, library/ games room, bedrooms large enough to accommodate families, open deck, covered verandah, outside fireplace and panoramic view. Nature provides the sunrise, sunset, stars and maybe Northern Lights. Near Kings Landing, Hartland's longest covered bridge, waterfalls, golfing and Crabbe Mountain. Take advantage of "extended stay" and "senior" discounts. Clean, friendly and great value!

ROOMS Family suite, Ground floor, Private entrance, **Baths** Ensuite, **Beds** Queen, Twin, Single or cots, **Air** Ceiling fans, **Smoking** Outside, **In Room** Thermostat, **OTHERS** Rural, Open all year, Handi-capped access, Additional meals, Pets in residence, **PAYMENT** Visa, Cash, **BREAKFASTS** Full, Home-baked, **AMENITIES** Central TV, Central phone, Laundry, Lounge, Patio, Central Internet access, Central VCR/DVD, **THINGS TO DO** Trail nearby, Golf, Attractions, Shopping, Cross-country skiing, Horseback riding, Beach, Birdwatching, Antiquing, **LANGUAGE** Eng., **PRICE** (2 persons) 70 **(check with hosts for pricing details)**

MIRAMICHI *(northeastern NB)*

Country Bed & Breakfast

(Ruth and Donald Newton)

116 N Black River Rd, Black River Bridge, NB, E1N 5S4
www.sn2000.nb.ca/comp/all-night-all-day

506-773-6252

Enjoy a quiet, comfortable night's sleep followed by a full, homecooked or continental breakfast served with homemade breads and jams. We are situated 10 minutes south of Miramichi City – 1 km off Rte 11 on North Black River Rd.

ROOMS Upper floor, Ground floor, **Baths** Ensuite, Shared with guest, **Beds** Double, Single or cots, **Smoking** Outside, **OTHERS** Rural, Handicapped access, Seasonal, **PAYMENT** Visa, MC, Direct debit, Cash, Trvl's cheques, **BREAKFASTS** Full, Continental, Home-baked, **AMENITIES** Central TV, Central phone, Swimming pool, Laundry, **THINGS TO DO** Trail nearby, Golf, Swimming, **LANGUAGE** Eng., **PRICE** (2 persons) 55–65 **(check with hosts for pricing details)**

MONCTON *(east-central NB)*

Bonaccord House

(Jeremy Martin)

250 Bonaccord St, Moncton, NB, E1C 5M6
www.canadianbandbguide.ca/bb.asp?ID=1924

506-388-1535
Fax 506-853-7191

Large yellow, three-storey, turn-of-the-century residence with a double living room, complete with fireplace and bay window, offering a convivial atmosphere in which to meet fellow travellers or just sit quietly and read. Centrally located and an ideal place from which to explore downtown Moncton and southeast New Brunswick. Located in downtown at the corner of John St. From Main St, turn north on Bonaccord St, or from Mountain Rd turn south on Bonaccord.

ROOMS Family suite, Upper floor, Ground floor, **Baths** Private, Ensuite, **Beds** Queen, Double, Twin, Single or cots, **Air** Central, **Smoking** Outside, **In Room** Phone, TV, VCR/DVD, **OTHERS** Urban, Open all year, **PAYMENT** Visa, MC, Amex, Cheques accepted, Cash, Trvl's cheques, **BREAKFASTS** Full, **AMENITIES** Central TV, Lounge, Patio, Central VCR/DVD, **THINGS TO DO** Trail nearby, Museums, Art, Theatre, Entertainment, Attractions, Shopping, Beach, **LANGUAGE** Eng., Fr., Sp., **PRICE** (2 persons) 40–75 **(check with hosts for pricing details)**

MONCTON

Gîte du voyageur Chez-Aanna
(Pierre-Édouard Landry)

30 prom Baffin, Moncton, NB, E1A 5P1
www.gitescanada.com/6017.html
E-mail aanna@nbnet.nb.ca

506-856-5961
Fax 506-383-7795
TFr 1-877-856-5961

Situated in a quiet neighbourhood, our
Canada Select 4 1/2-star B&B is 0.5 km
from Hwy 2, as well as near downtown.
Large spacious and comfortable bedrooms with TV, DVD, telephone, Internet
and private bathrooms in each room.
Family Suite and spacious Mini-Suite with
king-size bed. Pleasant, relaxing area, nice
living room and outside patios with view
of the garden. Non-smoking and central
air-conditioning. Laundry service. Bilingual.
Acadian breakfast.

ROOMS Family suite, **Baths** Private, **Beds** King, Queen,
Double, **Air** Central, Ceiling fans, **Smoking** Outside, **In
Room** Thermostat, Phone, TV, Internet access,
VCR/DVD, **OTHERS** Babysitting, Urban, Open all year,
PAYMENT Visa, MC, Direct debit, Cash, Trvl's cheques,
BREAKFASTS Full, Home-baked, **AMENITIES**
Barbecue, Laundry, Fridge, Lounge, Patio, Central
Internet access, **THINGS TO DO** Rental bikes, Trail
nearby, Rental canoe or boat, Golf, Fishing, Museums,
Art, Theatre, Entertainment, Attractions, Wineries/
Breweries, Shopping, Cross-country skiing, Tennis,
Swimming, Horseback riding, Beach, Birdwatching,
Antiquing, **LANGUAGE** Eng., Fr., **PRICE** (2 persons)
79–129 **(check with hosts for pricing details)**

MONCTON

Leah Jane's Bed and Breakfast
(Ron Collins)

146 Church St, Moncton, NB, E1C 4Z7
www.leahjanesbb.com
E-mail leahjane@nbnet.nb.ca

506-854-9207
Fax 506-389-9329
TFr 1-800-581-5324

Conveniently located in the heart of
Moncton, 7 minutes from the downtown
area, which offers a great variety of
restaurants and live entertainment. Leah-
Jane's clean and comfortable rooms provide a good night's rest. With both a bed
and breakfast and a reflex massage therapy clinic under one roof, your relaxation
needs are taken care of both efficiently
and professionally. For directions, please
see Web site.

ROOMS Family suite, Upper floor, Ground floor, **Baths**
Private, Ensuite, Shared with guest, **Beds** Queen, Twin,
Single or cots, **Air** In rooms, Ceiling fans, **Smoking**
Outside, **In Room** Phone, TV, VCR/DVD, **OTHERS**
Urban, Open all year, Additional meals, Pets welcome,
PAYMENT Visa, MC, Direct debit, Cash, Trvl's cheques,
BREAKFASTS Continental, **AMENITIES** Central phone,
Swimming pool, Barbecue, Laundry, Kitchen, Fridge,
Patio, Central Internet access, **THINGS TO DO** Trail
nearby, Golf, Museums, Theatre, Entertainment,
Attractions, Shopping, Cross-country skiing, Tennis,
Swimming, Birdwatching, Antiquing, **LANGUAGE** Eng.,
Fr., **PRICE** (2 persons) 60–80 **(check with hosts for
pricing details)**

Moncton

Lori's Bed and Breakfast

(Lori Smith)

761 Hillsborough Rd, Riverview, NB, E1B 3W1
www.lorisbedandbreakfast.com
E-mail lorisbedandbreakfast@hotmail.com

506-386-6055

Our large, clean and modernized home offers our guests the very best in hospitality. From hardwood floors to fluffy wind-dried towels, our guests can relax and unwind in any one of our many rooms. We hope you wake up hungry because our hearty breakfast is something in which Lori takes pride. The table is full of home cooking from the jams to rolls. You have choice of many dishes as well as other requests if possible.

ROOMS Upper floor, **Baths** Ensuite, Shared with guest, **Beds** Queen, Twin, **Air** Central, **OTHERS** Urban, **PAYMENT** Cash, **BREAKFASTS** Full, **AMENITIES** Central TV, Central phone, Barbecue, Laundry, Kitchen, Fridge, Lounge, Patio, Central Internet access, Central VCR/DVD, **THINGS TO DO** Trail nearby, Shopping, Cross-country skiing, Birdwatching, **LANGUAGE** Eng., **PRICE** (2 persons) 65–75 **(check with hosts for pricing details)**

Nash Creek *(north-central NB)*

Hayes House Bed & Breakfast

(Kathleen and Allan Hayes)

22 Hayes Rd, Nash Creek, NB, E8G 1A8
www.bbcanada.com/2291.html
E-mail hayesbb@nbnet.nb.ca

506-237-2252
TFr 1-866-237-5228

Hayes House, built by our Irish ancestors, welcomes you to share our spacious grounds and verandah with a view of the Bay Chaleur and mountains of Gaspé. Enjoy a superb breakfast served with freshly squeezed orange juice, fruit, homemade breads and jams. Aboriginal Gardens, Acadian Village and Chamber Music Festival, museums are part of the cultural activities of the area. Water sports, golf, fishing and beaches are nearby. We are on the Acadian Coastal Dr, Rte 134 or Rte 11, Exit 357.

ROOMS Upper floor, Ground floor, **Baths** Private, Ensuite, **Beds** Queen, Double, Twin, **Smoking** Outside, **In Room** Thermostat, **OTHERS** Rural, Seasonal, **PAYMENT** Visa, MC, Cash, Trvl's cheques, **BREAKFASTS** Full, Home-baked, **AMENITIES** Central TV, Central phone, Fridge, Lounge, **THINGS TO DO** Golf, Fishing, Museums, Art, Entertainment, Attractions, Shopping, Cross-country skiing, Swimming, Beach, **LANGUAGE** Eng., Fr., **PRICE** (2 persons) 68–92 **(check with hosts for pricing details)**

PETIT-ROCHER *(north-central NB)*

Auberge d'Anjou

(Pauline and Jean-Yves Fournier)

587 rue Principale, Petit-Rocher, NB, E8J 1H6
www.sn2000.nb.ca/comp/auberge-d'anjou
E-mail auberge.anjou@nb.aibn.com

506-783-0587
Fax 506-783-5587
TFr 1-866-783-0587

This building, built in 1917, is a 5-minutes walk to the local wharf. Renovated in 1994 to comply with actual regulations. With its verandah running along the facade and the north side, the building reflects the architectural style of the great Acadian homes of the '20s. Today, people can still admire this stately home with its antique cachet. This *Canada Select* 4-star classification bed and breakfast offers six rooms decorated with furnishings redolent of the first half of the century.

ROOMS Upper floor, Private entrance, **Baths** Private, **Beds** King, Queen, Double, Twin, Single or cots, Pullout sofa, **Air** Central, **Smoking** Outside, **In Room** Thermostat, Phone, TV, **OTHERS** Open all year, Additional meals, **PAYMENT** Visa, MC, Direct debit, Cash, Trvl's cheques, **BREAKFASTS** Full, Home-baked, **AMENITIES** Barbecue, Laundry, Fridge, Central Internet access, Central VCR/DVD, **THINGS TO DO** Comp. bikes, Rental canoe or boat, Golf, Fishing, Museums, Art, Theatre, Entertainment, Attractions, Shopping, Cross-country skiing, Tennis, Swimming, Beach, Birdwatching, Antiquing, **LANGUAGE** Eng., Fr., **PRICE** (2 persons) 68–88 **(check with hosts for pricing details)**

PORT ELGIN *(east-central NB)*

Pumpkinn Inn B&B

(Lynda Lukey)

9 Mill St, Port Elgin, NB, E4M 2E4
www.bbcanada.com/pumpkinnbb
E-mail pumpkinnbb@hotmail.com

506-538-1906
TFr 1-866-495-6450

An ocean harbour's historic peaceful village home. A comfortable Victorian home built in 1902, located on a quiet cul-de-sac within walking distance to village square. Warm sumptuous breakfast together or on enclosed porch overlooking our ocean (11-foot) tides. An eco-sanctuary of Atlantic birds and wilderness beaches ... yet, convenient to Moncton Airport and Confederation Bridge. Bicycling and canoe available next to the Trans-Canada Trail and local museum. Families most welcome.

ROOMS Family suite, Upper floor, **Baths** Private, Ensuite, Shared with guest, **Beds** Queen, Double, Twin, Single or cots, **Air** Ceiling fans, **Smoking** Outside, **OTHERS** Rural, Seasonal, Additional meals, Pets welcome, **PAYMENT** Cheques accepted, Cash, Trvl's cheques, **BREAKFASTS** Full, Home-baked, Self-catered, **AMENITIES** Central TV, Central phone, Laundry, Fridge, Hot bev. bar, Lounge, **THINGS TO DO** Rental bikes, Trail nearby, Rental canoe or boat, Golf, Fishing, Museums, Theatre, Wineries/Breweries, Horseback riding, Beach, Birdwatching, Antiquing, **LANGUAGE** Eng., Fr., **PRICE** (2 persons) 65–95 **(check with hosts for pricing details)**

Sackville *(east-central NB)*

Marshlands Inn

(Lucy and Barry Dane)

55 Bridge St, Sackville, NB, E4L 3N8
www.marshlands.nb.ca
E-mail marshlds@nbnet.nb.ca

506-536-0170
Fax 506-536-0721
TFr 1-800-561-1266

Victorian home and carriage house featuring 18 rooms with private ensuite bath, furnished with period antiques. Extensive gardens and marshlands on the 8-acre property provide ample area for walking or sitting and reading or relaxing. Licensed double parlour and front porch for refreshments, relaxation and conversation. The 80-seat licensed fine dining room offers three meals per day and specializes in seafood and local fare. Located close to downtown area and Mount Allison University.

ROOMS Family suite, Upper floor, Ground floor, Lower floor, **Baths** Private, Ensuite, **Beds** King, Queen, Double, Twin, **Air** In rooms, **Smoking** Outside, **In Room** Thermostat, Phone, TV, Internet access, **OTHERS** Open all year, Additional meals, Pets welcome, **PAYMENT** Visa, MC, Direct debit, Cash, Trvl's cheques, **BREAKFASTS** Full, Home-baked, **AMENITIES** Lounge, Patio, **THINGS TO DO** Trail nearby, Golf, Museums, Art, Theatre, Attractions, Wineries/Breweries, Birdwatching, Antiquing, **LANGUAGE** Eng., Sp., Italian, **PRICE** (2 persons) 95–175 **(check with hosts for pricing details)**

Saint John on the Bay of Fundy *(southern NB)*

Beach House Bed & Breakfast (Kingston) Inc.

(Glenise and Tony Peck)

198 rte 850, Kingston Peninsula, NB, E5N 1W4
www.beachhouse-kingston.com
E-mail info@beachhouse-kingston.com

506-832-7192
Fax 506-832-7192

A friendly English-owned countryside home offering relaxation, tranquility, spectacular scenery and great hospitality. A century-old home, carefully renovated and extended to provide our guests with all the comforts of home away from home. Leave your cares behind and explore one of New Brunswick's hidden treasures – the Loyalist area of the Kingston Peninsula which is located within a short distance of the city of Saint John. For more information, check out our Web site.

ROOMS Family suite, Upper floor, **Baths** Private, Ensuite, Shared with guest, **Beds** Queen, Double, Twin, Pullout sofa, **Air** In rooms, Ceiling fans, **Smoking** Outside, **In Room** Phone, **OTHERS** Rural, Adult, Open all year, Seasonal, Pets in residence, Pets welcome, **PAYMENT** Visa, MC, Cheques accepted, Cash, Trvl's cheques, **BREAKFASTS** Full, Home-baked, Self-catered, **AMENITIES** Central TV, Central phone, Barbecue, Laundry, Kitchen, Fridge, Lounge, Patio, Central Internet access, Central VCR/DVD, **THINGS TO DO** Trail nearby, Rental canoe or boat, Golf, Fishing, Museums, Attractions, Birdwatching, Antiquing, **LANGUAGE** Eng., **PRICE** (2 persons) 95–135 **(check with hosts for pricing details)**

Saint John on the Bay of Fundy

Homeport Historic B&B/ Inn c. 1858

(Ralph and Karen Holyoke)

80 Douglas Ave, Saint John, NB, E2K 1E4
www.homeport.nb.ca
E-mail stay@homeport.nb.ca

506-672-7255
Fax 506-672-7250
TFr 1-888-678-7678

Set high on a hill with a commanding view of the Bay of Fundy, and the historic port and skyline of Saint John, the Homeport Historic B&B/Inn c. 1858 provides the perfect setting to relax and enjoy the gracious ambience of Canada's oldest incorporated city. After a great night's sleep, Ralph and Karen want you to start the day off right with the very special and filling rise and dine breakfast. The hot main course is complimented by fresh in-season fruits and a selection of home-made pastries.

ROOMS Family suite, Upper floor, Ground floor, **Baths** Ensuite, **Beds** Queen, Twin, Single or cots, Pullout sofa, **Smoking** Outside, **In Room** Thermostat, Phone, TV, Internet access, VCR/DVD, **OTHERS** Urban, Open all year, Pets in residence, Pets welcome, **PAYMENT** Visa, MC, Cash, Trvl's cheques, **BREAKFASTS** Full, Home-baked, **THINGS TO DO** Trail nearby, Golf, Museums, Art, Theatre, Entertainment, Attractions, Wineries/ Breweries, Shopping, Swimming, Beach, Birdwatching, Antiquing, **LANGUAGE** Eng., **PRICE** (2 persons) 95–165 **(check with hosts for pricing details)**

Shediac *(east-central NB)*

Auberge, Maison Vienneau

(Marie and Norbert Vienneau)

426 Main, Shediac, NB, E4P 2G4
www.maisonvienneau.com
E-mail info@maisonvienneau.com

506-532-5412
Fax 506-532-7998
TFr 1-866-532-5412

Welcome to Maison Vienneau, a charming B&B offering you good, wholesome Maritime hospitality and, with the Shediac region, will offer cultural and sport activities to fulfill your stay. The Maison Vienneau, ideal as a romantic escape, business trip or perhaps a family reunion. A beautiful Victorian home full of cultural history on a quiet street in the heart of the peaceful village that time almost forgot. You enter our B&B into a beautiful lobby decorated with antique furniture. Free high-speed Internet.

ROOMS Upper floor, Private entrance, **Baths** Private, Ensuite, **Beds** Queen, **Air** In rooms, **Smoking** Outside, **In Room** Thermostat, Phone, TV, Fireplace, Internet access, **OTHERS** Rural, Seasonal, **PAYMENT** Visa, MC, Diners, Amex, Direct debit, Cash, Trvl's cheques, **BREAKFASTS** Full, Home-baked, **AMENITIES** Central TV, Central phone, Barbecue, Kitchen, Fridge, Patio, Central VCR/DVD, **THINGS TO DO** Comp. bikes, Trail nearby, Rental canoe or boat, Golf, Fishing, Museums, Art, Entertainment, Attractions, Wineries/Breweries, Shopping, Cross-country skiing, Swimming, Horseback riding, Beach, Birdwatching, **LANGUAGE** Eng., Fr., **PRICE** (2 persons) 79–109 **(check with hosts for pricing details)**

Prince Edward Island

CANADIAN BED AND BREAKFAST GUIDE

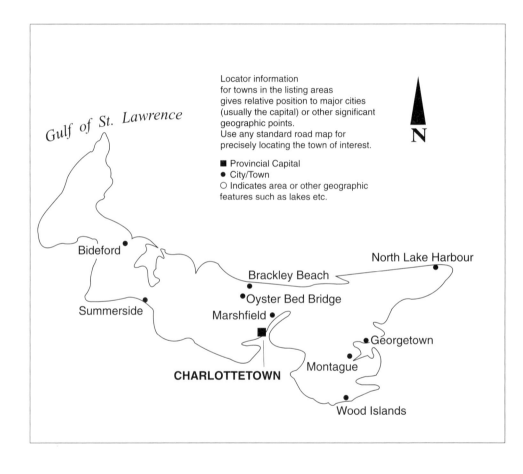

Locator information
for towns in the listing areas
gives relative position to major cities
(usually the capital) or other significant
geographic points.
Use any standard road map for
precisely locating the town of interest.

■ Provincial Capital
● City/Town
○ Indicates area or other geographic
features such as lakes etc.

N

Gulf of St. Lawrence

Bideford

North Lake Harbour

Brackley Beach

●Oyster Bed Bridge

Summerside

Marshfield ●

●Georgetown

CHARLOTTETOWN

Montague

Wood Islands

BIDEFORD *(western PEI)*

Hilltop Acres Bed & Breakfast

(Janice and Wayne Trowsdale)

694 Bideford Rd, Rte 166, Bideford, PEI, C0B 1J0
www3.pei.sympatico.ca/~wjt_hilltop
E-mail wjt_hilltop@pei.sympatico.ca

902-831-2817
Fax 902-831-2817
TFr 1-877-305-2817

Enjoy the quiet of the country in historic Bideford overlooking Malpeque Bay. Relax on second-storey balcony, garden swings, decks, screened gazebo or in our guest living room. Stroll about our spacious lawn or walk around our 60-acre property located 3 km from Confederation Trail. Queen room has private bath ensuite; two-bedroom suite for party of four has private bath. Homemade preserves. Multi-night discount. Follow Lady Slipper Dr (Rte 12) to Bideford Rd (Rte 166). Near Bideford Parsonage Museum.

ROOMS Upper floor, **Baths** Private, Ensuite, **Beds** Queen, Double, **Smoking** Outside, **OTHERS** Rural, Seasonal, **PAYMENT** Visa, MC, Direct debit, Cash, Trvl's cheques, **BREAKFASTS** Full, Home-baked, **AMENITIES** Whirlpool, Barbecue, **THINGS TO DO** Trail nearby, Museums, Art, Entertainment, Attractions, **LANGUAGE** Eng., **PRICE** (2 persons) 60–70 **(check with hosts for pricing details)**

BRACKLEY BEACH *(north-central PEI)*

Red Island Bed & Breakfast

(Em and David Zember)

4224 Portage Rd, Winsloe RR #9, Brackley Beach, PEI, C1E 1Z3
www.redisland.com
E-mail redisland@pei.sympatico.ca

902-672-2242
TFr 1-800-698-5530

Family oriented B&B. Hosts: young family (separate quarters). Educational farm experience, 8 a.m./8 p.m.: milk goats, hold bunnies, wear 1880s costumes! Shallow, natural beach, 10-minute walk. Weekly soap-making, dog demonstrations. View government-produced television show about property, 100-plus pictures, see Web site. Very clean, freshly decorated, large 1880s farmhouse, excellent condition, 13 acres. Guest convenience kitchen. National park beaches, seven restaurants, 4-minutes; Charlottetown, Cavendish, 15-minutes!

ROOMS Family suite, Upper floor, Private entrance, **Baths** Private, Ensuite, **Beds** Queen, Double, Single or cots, **Air** In rooms, **Smoking** Outside, **In Room** Thermostat, Phone, TV, **OTHERS** Rural, Open all year, Pets welcome, **PAYMENT** Visa, MC, Amex, Direct debit, Cash, Trvl's cheques, **BREAKFASTS** Continental, Self-catered, **AMENITIES** Central TV, Kitchen, Fridge, Hot bev. bar, **THINGS TO DO** Trail nearby, Theatre, Attractions, Shopping, Swimming, Horseback riding, Beach, **PRICE** (2 persons) 70–110 **(check with hosts for pricing details)**

CHARLOTTETOWN *(south-central PEI)*

Betty & Mark's 'River Winds'

(Betty and Mark Robertson)

9 Colonel Gray Dr, Charlottetown, PEI, C1A 2S4
www.canadianbandbguide.ca/bb.asp?ID=3813
E-mail mark.robertson@pei.sympatico.ca

902-892-2285
Fax 902-566-1188
TFr 1-877-892-2285

An elegant riverside home with a great
view from the bedroom, which has a
queen-size bed and ensuite bath. Plenty
of flower gardens for you to enjoy, and
two friendly Siamese cats. We serve a
breakfast of your choice.

ROOMS Upper floor, **Baths** Ensuite, **Beds** Queen, **Air**
Ceiling fans, **Smoking** Outside, **In Room** Thermostat,
TV, Internet access, VCR/DVD, **OTHERS** Urban, Adult,
Seasonal, Pets in residence, **PAYMENT** Cheques
accepted, Cash, Trvl's cheques, **BREAKFASTS** Full,
AMENITIES Laundry, Patio, **THINGS TO DO** Rental
bikes, Golf, Museums, Art, Theatre, Entertainment,
Attractions, Shopping, Tennis, Swimming, Beach, **LAN-
GUAGE** Eng., **PRICE** (2 persons) 90–90 **(check with
hosts for pricing details)**

CHARLOTTETOWN

Fairholm National Historic Inn

(Brooke MacMillan – owner
Terry O'Malley – Innkeeper)

230 Prince St, Charlottetown, PEI, C1N 4S1
www.fairholm.pe.ca
E-mail historic@fairholm.pe.ca

902-892-5022
Fax 902-894-5060
TFr 1-888-573-5022

Be swept back into time when you walk
through the doors of this 18th-century
home. Fairholm, a designated National
Historic Site, is an enchanting home that
boasts large rooms with superb architectural detail, inlaid hardwood floors, fine
stained glass and an impressive sunroom.
Seven elegantly appointed suites, with
private ensuite baths, will charm even the
most disconcerning guest. So come and
make yourself at home, allowing yourself
to be spoiled by our staff and the
grandeur of this beautiful home.

ROOMS Family suite, Upper floor, Ground floor, Lower
floor, **Baths** Ensuite, **Beds** Queen, Single or cots,
Pullout sofa, **Air** In rooms, **In Room** Thermostat,
Phone, TV, Fireplace, **OTHERS** Urban, Open all year,
Handicapped access, **PAYMENT** Visa, MC, Amex, Cash,
Trvl's cheques, **BREAKFASTS** Full, **AMENITIES** Central
TV, Central phone, Swimming pool, Sauna, Whirlpool,
Laundry, Kitchen, Fridge, **THINGS TO DO** Rental bikes,
Rental canoe or boat, Golf, Fishing, Museums, Art,
Theatre, Entertainment, Attractions, Wineries/
Breweries, Shopping, Swimming, Horseback riding,
Beach, **LANGUAGE** Eng., **PRICE** (2 persons) 125–285
(check with hosts for pricing details)

CHARLOTTETOWN

Heritage Harbour House Inn B&B

(Arie and Jinny van der Gaag)

9 Grafton St, Charlottetown, PEI, C1A 1K3
www.hhhouse.net
E-mail hhhouse@attglobal.net

902-892-6633
Fax 902-892-8420
TFr 1-800-405-0066

Located in the heart of historic Charlotte-town, in a quiet residential area, yet only two blocks from the city centre. Easy walking distance to all downtown attractions, theatre, restaurants, shops, Victoria Park and the waterfront.

ROOMS Family suite, Upper floor, Ground floor, Lower floor, **Baths** Private, Ensuite, **Beds** King, Queen, Double, Twin, Pullout sofa, **Air** In rooms, **In Room** Thermostat, Phone, TV, Internet access, **OTHERS** Urban, Open all year, Handicapped access, **PAYMENT** Visa, MC, Diners, Amex, Direct debit, Cash, Trvl's cheques, **BREAKFASTS** Full, **AMENITIES** Whirlpool, Laundry, Kitchen, Fridge, Lounge, Patio, **THINGS TO DO** Trail nearby, Museums, Art, Theatre, Attractions, Shopping, Swimming, Horseback riding, Beach, **LANGUAGE** Eng., Sp., Japanese, **PRICE** (2 persons) 80–185 **(check with hosts for pricing details)**

CHARLOTTETOWN

Shipwright Inn

(Judy and Trevor Pye)

51 Fitzroy St, Charlottetown, PEI, C1A 1R4
www.shipwrightinn.com
E-mail innkeeper@shipwrightinn.com

902-368-1905
Fax 902-628-1905
TFr 1-888-306-9966

Award-winning heritage inn: 1865 heritage home. Easy walk to historic sites, restaurants, shops, parks and waterfront, 25 golf courses nearby. Classic architecture lovingly restored, nautical theme, fireplaces, antiques, old books, secluded garden, balconies, whirlpools, ships-plank floors, Internet access (Wi-Fi). All rooms have quality beds, private baths, air-conditioning, telephones. Three luxury suites. Cable TV, VCRs some DVDs. Off-street parking, shady, quiet safe street. Open year-round.

ROOMS Family suite, Upper floor, Ground floor, Lower floor, Private entrance, **Baths** Private, Ensuite, **Beds** King, Queen, Double, Twin, Single or cots, Pullout sofa, **Air** In rooms, **Smoking** Outside, **In Room** Thermostat, Phone, TV, Fireplace, Internet access, VCR/DVD, **OTHERS** Urban, Open all year, **PAYMENT** Visa, MC, Amex, Cash, Trvl's cheques, **BREAKFASTS** Full, Home-baked, **AMENITIES** Central phone, Whirlpool, Laundry, Fridge, Hot bev. bar, Lounge, Patio, Central Internet access, **THINGS TO DO** Rental bikes, Trail nearby, Rental canoe or boat, Golf, Fishing, Museums, Art, Theatre, Entertainment, Attractions, Wineries/Breweries, Shopping, Cross-country skiing, Swimming, Horseback riding, Beach, Birdwatching, Antiquing, **LANGUAGE** Eng., Fr., **PRICE** (2 persons) 99–289 **(check with hosts for pricing details)**

CHARLOTTETOWN

The Great George
(Mike Murphy and Paul Smith)

58 Great George St, Charlottetown, PEI, C1A 4K3
www.thegreatgeorge.com
E-mail innkeeper@innsongreatgeorge.com

902-892-0606
Fax 902-628-2079
TFr 1-800-361-1118

Treat yourself to the Great George – a unique cluster of fully restored *Canada Select* 4 1/2-star heritage buildings situated within the streetscape splendor of Charlottetown's National Historic District, with 53 guest rooms sure to satisfy the senses of the most discriminating traveller. Choose from romantic Hideaway Suites, family-friendly townhouses, business-savvy suites and more. Deluxe rooms feature fireplace, Jacuzzi or clawfoot tub. *Frommers* 2004: "One of Charlottetown's very classy addresses."

ROOMS Family suite, Upper floor, Ground floor, **Baths** Private, **Beds** King, Queen, Double, Twin, **Air** Central, **In Room** Fireplace, **OTHERS** Babysitting, Open all year, Handicapped access, **PAYMENT** Visa, MC, Diners, Amex, Direct debit, Cash, **BREAKFASTS** Continental, **AMENITIES** Central TV, Central phone, Kitchen, Fridge, Hot bev. bar, Lounge, Patio, **THINGS TO DO** Rental bikes, Trail nearby, Golf, Museums, Art, Theatre, Entertainment, Attractions, Wineries/Breweries, Shopping, Beach, **LANGUAGE** Eng., Fr., **PRICE** (2 persons) 135–359 **(check with hosts for pricing details)**

CHARLOTTETOWN

The Snapdragon
Bed and Breakfast Inn
(Laura and Steve Armour)

177 Fitzroy St, Charlottetown, PEI, C1A 1S3
www.thesnapdragon.com
E-mail relax@thesnapdragon.com

902-368-8070
Fax 902-569-4217
TFr 1-866-235-7164

When you come home at the end of a perfect day, you'll be pampered in a well-appointed, modern facility that has been designed to give you the comfort of a first-class hotel while maintaining the charm and personal touch you look for in a great B&B. Features include a great downtown location, large comfortable rooms, exquisite handmade quilts, private ensuite bathrooms, whisper-quiet air-conditioners, romantic fireplaces and adjoining decks where you can just relax and enjoy the company of friends.

ROOMS Upper floor, Ground floor, **Baths** Ensuite, **Beds** King, Queen, Double, Twin, **Air** In rooms, **Smoking** Outside, **In Room** Thermostat, TV, Fireplace, **PAYMENT** Visa, MC, Diners, Amex, Direct debit, Cash, **BREAKFASTS** Full, **AMENITIES** Central phone, **THINGS TO DO** Trail nearby, Golf, Fishing, Museums, Art, Theatre, Entertainment, Attractions, Wineries/Breweries, Shopping, Cross-country skiing, Tennis, Swimming, Horseback riding, Beach, Birdwatching, Antiquing, **LANGUAGE** Eng., **PRICE** (2 persons) 95–150 **(check with hosts for pricing details)**

GEORGETOWN *(eastern PEI)*

The Georgetown Inn
(Don Taylor and Arlene Smith)

62 Richmond St, Georgetown, PEI, C0A 1L0
www.georgetowninn.org
E-mail gtowninn@isn.net

902-652-2511
Fax 902-652-2544
TFr 1-877-641-2414

Totally remodelled 1840s heritage home
one block from historic Georgetown
harbour. Tastefully decorated in Scottish
Victorian theme. Our most sought after
Ivy and Forgetmenot rooms have a deck
and harbour view. The Heather room in
White Battenburg is the prettiest on the
Scottish floor. Minutes from Confed-
erationTrail, Brudenell and Dundarave
golf courses. Kayakers, cyclists delight.
Our location is perfect for exploring all of
eastern PEI yet is only 35 minutes from
Charlottetown or the ferry.

ROOMS Upper floor, **Baths** Ensuite, **Beds** Queen, Twin,
Smoking Outside, **In Room** Thermostat, **OTHERS**
Urban, Adult, Seasonal, Additional meals, **PAYMENT**
Visa, MC, Amex, Cheques accepted, Cash, **BREAK-
FASTS** Full, **AMENITIES** Central TV, Central phone,
Laundry, Fridge, Lounge, **THINGS TO DO** Trail nearby,
Golf, Fishing, Museums, Theatre, Wineries/Breweries,
Shopping, Tennis, Swimming, Horseback riding, Beach,
LANGUAGE Eng., **PRICE** (2 persons) 90–125 **(check
with hosts for pricing details)**

MARSHFIELD *(south-central PEI)*

Woodmere B&B
(Wallace and Doris Wood)

98 Linden Rd, Marshfield, PEI, C1A 7J7
www.bbcanada.com/725.html
E-mail woodmere@pei.sympatico.ca

902-628-1783
Fax 902-628-1783
TFr 1-800-747-1783

On Rte 2 east 6 km from downtown
Charlottetown. Cleanliness and guests
comfort a priority. Standardbred horses
graze in the fields. Fragrant roses bloom
in the gardens. Spacious rooms with a
view of surrounding countryside feature
ensuite baths, fridge, individual heat,
handcrafted pine furnishings. Separate
guest entrance, two rooms with queen
bed, two rooms with two doubles.
Minutes to airport, famous golf courses,
harness racing, theatre, national parks.
An ideal location from which to explore
our island.

ROOMS Upper floor, Private entrance, **Baths** Ensuite,
Beds Queen, Double, **Smoking** Outside, **In Room**
Thermostat, TV, **OTHERS** Rural, Adult, Open all year,
PAYMENT Visa, MC, Cheques accepted, Cash, Trvl's
cheques, **BREAKFASTS** Full, Home-baked, Self-catered,
AMENITIES Central phone, Fridge, **THINGS TO DO**
Golf, Fishing, Museums, Art, Theatre, Entertainment,
Attractions, Shopping, **LANGUAGE** Eng., **PRICE** (2 per-
sons) 75–95 **(check with hosts for pricing details)**

MONTAGUE *(southeastern PEI)*

Elms at Brudenell Bed and Breakfast

(Lynn Arnold)

304 Brudenell Pt Rd, Montague, PEI, C0A 1R0
www.elmsatbrudenell.com
E-mail elms@pei.sympatico.ca

902-838-2965
Fax 902-838-2965
TFr 1-800-838-2965

Majestic elms canopy the driveway to our beautiful century home, 3 minutes to Montague's fine dining and small town appeal, 30 minutes to historic Charlotte-town. Woodland setting, adjoins Confederation Trail for hiking and biking. Enjoy a beverage on the verandah or sunny deck featuring a maze of gardens. Beaches nearby, golfer's paradise, packages to PEI Links, best rates offered. Lovely rooms, comfy beds, private bathrooms, breakfast delights the most discriminating taste-buds. Our home is your home.

ROOMS Upper floor, **Baths** Private, Ensuite, **Beds** Queen, Single or cots, **Air** Central, **Smoking** Outside, **In Room** Phone, **OTHERS** Rural, Open all year, Pets in residence, Pets welcome, **PAYMENT** Visa, MC, Cheques accepted, Cash, Trvl's cheques, **BREAKFASTS** Full, Home-baked, **AMENITIES** Central TV, Central phone, Barbecue, Laundry, Fridge, Lounge, Patio, Central Internet access, Central VCR/DVD, **THINGS TO DO** Comp. bikes, Trail nearby, Rental canoe or boat, Golf, Fishing, Museums, Art, Theatre, Entertainment, Attractions, Wineries/Breweries, Shopping, Cross-country skiing, Swimming, Horseback riding, Beach, Birdwatching, Antiquing, **LANGUAGE** Eng., **PRICE** (2 persons) 75–90 **(check with hosts for pricing details)**

NORTH LAKE HARBOUR *(northeastern PEI)*

Harbour Lights Guest House

(Bruce and Patricia Craig)

6434 North Side Rd, Elmira, PEI, C0A 1K0
www.harbourlightshouse.com
E-mail info@harbourlightshouse.com

902-357-2127
TFr 1-866-687-9949

Harbour Lights Guest House is an 1880s renovated farmhouse set amidst the rural farmfields of eastern Kings County. Overlooking North Lake Harbour, our guest house offers breathtaking views of both harbour and ocean. A full farm breakfast is included as part of your stay; other meals can also be arranged. We are located close to the Confederation Trail, pristine beaches, provincial museums and parks, as well as some of the Island's most reknowned golf courses. Visit our Web site.

ROOMS Upper floor, Ground floor, **Baths** Shared with guest, Shared with hosts, **Beds** Queen, Double, **Smoking** Outside, **OTHERS** Rural, Adult, Seasonal, Pets in residence, **PAYMENT** Visa, MC, Cheques accepted, Cash, Trvl's cheques, **BREAKFASTS** Full, **AMENITIES** Central TV, Central VCR/DVD, **THINGS TO DO** Rental bikes, Trail nearby, Rental canoe or boat, Golf, Fishing, Museums, Art, Theatre, Entertainment, Attractions, Wineries/Breweries, Swimming, Beach, Birdwatching, Antiquing, **LANGUAGE** Eng., Mandarin (survival level), **PRICE** (2 persons) 65–70 **(check with hosts for pricing details)**

Oyster Bed Bridge *(north central PEI)*

Misty Meadows
Bed & Breakfast
(Dot and Jim Campbell)

RR #10, Box 6237, Charlottetown, PEI, C1E 1Z4
www.mistymeadowspei.com
E-mail mistymeadowspei@msn.com

902-621-0820

Misty Meadows – The warmth of a B&B,
the privacy of a hotel! A lovely country
B&B situated at the end of a long, paved
lane on 10 acres of meadows and woods.
Minutes away from beaches, shopping,
theatre, golfing, lobster suppers, walking
and biking trails, and deep sea fishing!
Directions from the Confederation Bridge:
Rte 1 to Crapaud, Rte 13 to Hunter River.
Cross Rte 2 and take Rte 251 to Oyster
Bed Bridge. Look for #59 on your right.

ROOMS Ground floor, **Baths** Ensuite, **Beds** Queen, **Air**
Ceiling fans, **OTHERS** Seasonal, **PAYMENT** Visa, MC,
Amex, Trvl's cheques, **BREAKFASTS** Full, **AMENITIES**
Central TV, Barbecue, Fridge, Lounge, Patio, **THINGS
TO DO** Trail nearby, Golf, Fishing, Art, Attractions,
Shopping, Swimming, Horseback riding, Beach, **LAN-
GUAGE** Eng., **PRICE** (2 persons) 60–70 **(check with
hosts for pricing details)**

Summerside *(southwestern PEI)*

Copple Summer Home
(Peter and Jacquie Copple)

92 Summer St, Summerside, PEI, C1N 3H9
www.copplesummerholme.com/
E-mail pjcopple@pei.sympatico.ca

902-436-3100
TFr 1-866-622-3100

A cozy respite as you explore the Island.
Easy walking distance to the harbour,
restaurants, shops and local attractions.
Perfectly situated to enjoy world-famous
golf courses and beaches. Rooms have
private and ensuite bathrooms. Coffee/
tea is delivered each morning at wakeup.
Enjoy our delightful gourmet breakfast
and consider an optional gourmet picnic
or dinner by arrangement. Copple
Summer Holme, *Canada Select* 4-stars, is
ideal for the traveller with discerning
taste. Seasonal, June 1 through October
31.

ROOMS Upper floor, **Baths** Private, Ensuite, **Beds**
Queen, Twin, Single or cots, **Smoking** Outside, **OTH-
ERS** Urban, Adult, Seasonal, Additional meals, **PAY-
MENT** Visa, MC, Direct debit, Cash, Trvl's cheques,
BREAKFASTS Full, **AMENITIES** Central TV, Central
phone, Fridge, Lounge, Patio, Central Internet access,
Central VCR/DVD, **THINGS TO DO** Comp. bikes, Rental
bikes, Trail nearby, Rental canoe or boat, Golf, Fishing,
Museums, Art, Theatre, Entertainment, Attractions,
Shopping, Tennis, Swimming, Beach, Birdwatching,
Antiquing, **LANGUAGE** Eng., **PRICE** (2 persons) 90
(check with hosts for pricing details)

Summerside
Lecky's Bed & Breakfast Inn
(Allen and Dorothy Lecky)

11 Lady Slipper Dr, PO Box 273, Summerside,
PEI, C1N 4Y8
www3.pei.sympatico.ca/~lecky
E-mail lecky@pei.sympatico.ca

902-436-3216
TFr 1-888-220-4059

Experience true Island hospitality at its
very best. Lecky's Inn offers 14 spacious
theme bedrooms with their own private
baths in a beautifully renovated century
home. Sunbathe on the wraparound
verandah or view an island sunset from
the observation deck. Located minutes
from shopping, beaches, golf, museums,
bingo and the Confederation Trail,
Cavendish beach and other attractions
are just a scenic 30-km-drive away!
Request a mouthwatering lobster dinner,
then listen to enteraining stories from
your hosts.

ROOMS Family suite, Upper floor, Ground floor, Private
entrance, **Baths** Private, **Beds** Queen, Double, Single
or cots, **Smoking** Outside, **In Room** TV, Fireplace, **OTH-
ERS** Babysitting, Rural, Open all year, Additional meals,
PAYMENT Visa, MC, Cash, Trvl's cheques, **BREAKFASTS**
Full, **AMENITIES** Central TV, Central phone, Whirlpool,
Barbecue, Kitchen, Fridge, Hot bev. bar, Lounge, Patio,
THINGS TO DO Rental bikes, Trail nearby, Rental canoe
or boat, Golf, Fishing, Museums, Art, Theatre, Entertainment, Attractions, Wineries/Breweries, Shopping,
Cross-country skiing, Tennis, Swimming, Horseback
riding, Beach, **LANGUAGE** Eng., Fr., **PRICE** (2 persons)
69–129 **(check with hosts for pricing details)**

Summerside
The Raspberry Inn
(Rikki and Thomas Neukom)

1925 Mill Rd, RR #2, Lower Freetown, PEI, C0B 1L0
www.raspberryinn.ca
E-mail info@raspberryinn.ca

902-887-2935
Fax 902-887-2935
TFr 1-888-273-2525

Situated in the tranquil and scenic countryside, The Raspberry Inn specializes in
attention to quality, comfort and well-
being. Relax in one of our four luxurious
bedrooms each with its own private
ensuite. Wake up to the aromas of fresh
PEI roasted coffee and enjoy a full gourmet breakfast featuring local products
prepared by a professional chef. Stay for a
few days as The Raspberry Inn is located
only 10 minutes from Summerside and
central to most of PEI's beautiful sites and
attractions.

ROOMS Upper floor, Ground floor, Private entrance,
Baths Private, Ensuite, **Beds** Queen, Double, Single or
cots, **Air** Central, **Smoking** Outside, **OTHERS** Rural,
Open all year, Pets in residence, **PAYMENT** Visa, MC,
Cash, **BREAKFASTS** Full, Home-baked, **AMENITIES**
Central TV, Central phone, Laundry, Lounge, **THINGS
TO DO** Trail nearby, Golf, Fishing, Museums, Art,
Theatre, Entertainment, Attractions, Swimming, Beach,
LANGUAGE Eng., Fr., Ger., **PRICE** (2 persons) 100–125
(check with hosts for pricing details)

Wood Islands
(southeastern PEI)

Bayberry Cliff Inn

(Katharina Sieg)

RR #4, Little Sands, PEI, C0A 1W0
www.bayberrycliffinn.com
E-mail bayberrycliffinn@hotmail.com

902-962-3395
Fax 902-962-3082
TFr 1-800-668-3395

Come and enjoy a stay at this very unique restored post-and-beam B&B overlooking the Northumberland Strait. Our secluded inn is only 5 minutes from the Wood Islands Ferry Terminal. There are four units with rustic decor. Relax on the private decks and sitting areas overlooking the water, watching the porpoises and letting the tranquility of nature refresh and restore you at Bayberry Cliff.

ROOMS Family suite, Upper floor, Private entrance, **Baths** Private, Ensuite, **Beds** Queen, Double, Single or cots, **Smoking** Outside, **In Room** Thermostat, **OTHERS** Rural, Seasonal, Pets in residence, Pets welcome, **PAYMENT** Visa, MC, Cash, Trvl's cheques, **BREAKFASTS** Full, **AMENITIES** Central TV, Central phone, Barbecue, Fridge, Lounge, Patio, **THINGS TO DO** Trail nearby, Golf, Fishing, Theatre, Wineries/Breweries, Swimming, Horseback riding, Beach, Birdwatching, Antiquing, **LANGUAGE** Eng., Fr., Sp., Ger., **PRICE** (2 persons) 110–130 **(check with hosts for pricing details)**

NOVA SCOTIA

CANADIAN BED AND BREAKFAST GUIDE

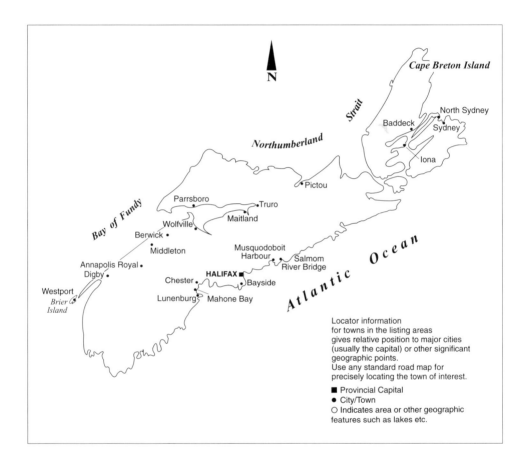

Locator information
for towns in the listing areas
gives relative position to major cities
(usually the capital) or other significant
geographic points.
Use any standard road map for
precisely locating the town of interest.

■ Provincial Capital
● City/Town
○ Indicates area or other geographic
features such as lakes etc.

ANNAPOLIS ROYAL *(southwestern NS)*

King George Inn
(Faith M. McStravick)

548 St. George St, Annapolis Royal, NS, B0S 1A0
www.kinggeorgeinn.20m.com
E-mail kinggeorgeinn@hotmail.com

902-532-5286
Fax 902-532-0144
TFr 1-888-799-5464

Grand Victorian sea captain's mansion.
Registered Heritage Property c.1868.
Eight gracious air-conditioned rooms, all
with private ensuite baths. Honeymoon
and family suites, private decks, Jacuzzis,
gift shop. Victorian elegance furnished
with period antiques. Short walk to all
major attractions. Scent- and smoke-free
inn. Open May to December.

ROOMS Family suite, Upper floor, Ground floor, Lower
floor, **Baths** Ensuite, **Beds** King, Queen, **Air** In rooms,
Smoking Outside, **In Room** Thermostat, TV, Fireplace,
Internet access, **OTHERS** Rural, Seasonal, Pets in resi-
dence, Pets welcome, **PAYMENT** Visa, MC, Cash, Trvl's
cheques, **BREAKFASTS** Full, Home-baked, **AMENITIES**
Central phone, Whirlpool, Laundry, Patio, **THINGS TO
DO** Comp. bikes, Trail nearby, Golf, Fishing, Museums,
Art, Theatre, Entertainment, Attractions, Wineries/
Breweries, Shopping, Tennis, Swimming, Beach, **LAN-
GUAGE** Eng., Fr., **PRICE** (2 persons) 80–200 **(check
with hosts for pricing details)**

ANNAPOLIS ROYAL

Reminisce Bed and Breakfast
(Cheryl Haines)

81 South Queen St, RR #3 Bridgetown, NS, B0S 1C0
www.reminisce.ca
E-mail reminiscehosts@yahoo.com

902-665-4745
TFr 1-866-665-4785

Featured in *Country Discoveries* magazine
as a B&B that is simply unforgettable,
Reminisce (rem-in-iss) is nestled between
the north and south mountains in
Bridgetown, the prettiest town in the
Annapolis Valley. Reminisce is only 20
minutes to Annapolis Royal and centrally
located for day trips. With tall, stately
trees and water fountains, the house
(c. 1860) has recently been restored to its
original grandeur. Located on 3 acres, the
house is surrounded by perennial gardens. Visit our Web site.

ROOMS Upper floor, **Baths** Private, Ensuite, **Beds** King,
Queen, Twin, **Air** Ceiling fans, **Smoking** Outside, **In
Room** Thermostat, **OTHERS** Urban, Adult, Open all
year, Pets in residence, **PAYMENT** Visa, MC, Cash, Trvl's
cheques, **BREAKFASTS** Full, **AMENITIES** Central TV,
Central phone, Barbecue, Lounge, Patio, Central
VCR/DVD, **THINGS TO DO** Trail nearby, Golf, Fishing,
Museums, Theatre, Attractions, Shopping, Swimming,
Birdwatching, Antiquing, **LANGUAGE** Eng., **PRICE** (2
persons) 75–85 **(check with hosts for pricing details)**

Baddeck *(central Cape Breton Island)*
Blue Seas Bed & Breakfast
(Erika and Alex McNeil)

776 Rte 105, Boularderie E, NS, B1X 1J4
www.blueseas.ca
E-mail reservations@blueseas.ca

902-674-0973
Fax 902-674-0938
TFr 1-800-367-5112

Blue Seas Bed & Breakfast is located on 8 acres overlooking the Great Bras D'Or Channel: the entrance from the Atlantic Ocean into Cape Breton's famous "Inland Sea." The start of the Cabot Trail, the Gaelic College and the Newfoundland Ferry Terminal are located just 20 minutes away. Baddeck, site of the Alexander Graham Bell Museum and former home is also nearby. Breathtaking views, colourful wildflowers, fresh salt air and generous hospitality will greet you at every turn.

ROOMS Upper floor, **Baths** Shared with guest, **Beds** Queen, **In Room** Thermostat, Phone, **OTHERS** Rural, Seasonal, **PAYMENT** Visa, Cash, **BREAKFASTS** Full, **AMENITIES** Central phone, Laundry, Patio, **THINGS TO DO** Trail nearby, Rental canoe or boat, Golf, Fishing, Museums, Theatre, Entertainment, Attractions, **LAN-GUAGE** Eng., Ger., **PRICE** (2 persons) 75 **(check with hosts for pricing details)**

Bayside *(south of Halifax)*
Anchors Gate B&B
(George and Nancy Pike)

4281 Prospect Rd, Bayside, NS, B3Z 1L4
www.anchorsgatebb.com
E-mail salr@accglobal.net

902-852-3906
Fax 902-852-4018

Beautiful home in "nautical theme" overlooking the ocean, 20 minutes from Halifax/Peggy's Cove. Good locale for day trips. Features three bedrooms, with oceanview, private entrance and patios, plus self-contained unit with fridge, stove, washer/dryer, patio, microwave, plus extra bed, sleeps four. Hearty breakfasts. All rooms have ensuite baths, cable TV, radios. No smoking/pets. Open year-round, ocean access, golf, crafts, boat tours, kayak, birdwatch. Restaurants in area.

ROOMS Family suite, Upper floor, Ground floor, Private entrance, **Baths** Ensuite, **Beds** Queen, Double, Twin, Pullout sofa, **Smoking** Outside, **In Room** Thermostat, TV, **PAYMENT** Visa, MC, Diners, Cash, Trvl's cheques, **BREAKFASTS** Full, Home-baked, **AMENITIES** Laundry, Fridge, Patio, **THINGS TO DO** Trail nearby, Golf, Attractions, Shopping, Swimming, Beach, **LANGUAGE** Eng., **PRICE** (2 persons) 89–110 **(check with hosts for pricing details)**

BERWICK *(west of Halifax)*

Annapolis Bed & Breakfast

(Carol Stewart and Jill Smith)

244 Commercial St, Berwick, NS, B0P 1E0
www.annapolisbedandbreakfast.ca
E-mail info@annapolisbedandbreakfast.ca

902-538-2627
Fax 902-538-3685
TFr 1-888-666-2627

Annapolis Bed & Breakfast is a distinctive Italianate Victorian home offering three themed rooms. The award-winning African Room has a two-person jet tub and queen bed with air-conditioning. Apple Blossom Room, large shower and queen bed. Country Room has a four-piece-bath and queen bed. Guest parlour and Internet hookup available. Full breakfast 8–9a.m. Check in after four, check out at noon. Artist-home with art and photography available. We're in the heart of town near shopping, restaurants and attractions.

ROOMS Upper floor, Private entrance, **Baths** Private, Ensuite, **Beds** Queen, Single or cots, **Air** In rooms, **Smoking** Outside, **OTHERS** Rural, Open all year, Pets in residence, Pets welcome, **PAYMENT** Visa, MC, Cheques accepted, Cash, Trvl's cheques, **BREAKFASTS** Full, Continental, Home-baked, **AMENITIES** Central TV, Central phone, Whirlpool, Fridge, Lounge, Patio, **THINGS TO DO** Trail nearby, Golf, Museums, Art, Theatre, Entertainment, Attractions, Wineries/ Breweries, Shopping, Horseback riding, Beach, **LANGUAGE** Eng., **PRICE** (2 persons) 95–115 **(check with hosts for pricing details)**

BERWICK

Hidden Gardens
Bed & Breakfast

(Judy and Medford Hogan)

274 Main St, Berwick, NS, B0P 1E0
www.bbcanada.com/hiddengardens
E-mail hiddengardens@ns.sympatico.ca

902-538-0813
Fax 902-690-2813
TFr 1-866-299-0813

Centrally located in the Annapolis Valley, this century-plus home is perfect for exploring this beautiful region from historic Grand Pre to Annapolis Royal, Port Royal. It offers easy access to theatre, fine dining, scenic golf courses, a local zoo (lions/rare tigers), museums, interesting architecture, local arts and crafts. We offer quiet intimacy and privacy, 20x40 pool, flower gardens, hanging vines and privacy hedges. Nestled among towering maples, Hidden Gardens B&B embodies casual country charm and comfort.

ROOMS Family suite, Upper floor, **Baths** Private, Ensuite, **Air** In rooms, **Smoking** Outside, **In Room** TV, **OTHERS** Rural, Open all year, **PAYMENT** Visa, MC, Amex, Cash, Trvl's cheques, **BREAKFASTS** Full, Continental, Home-baked, **AMENITIES** Central TV, Swimming pool, Whirlpool, Fridge, Lounge, Patio, **THINGS TO DO** Trail nearby, Golf, Museums, Art, Theatre, Entertainment, Attractions, Wineries/ Breweries, Shopping, Swimming, Horseback riding, **LANGUAGE** Eng., **PRICE** (2 persons) 95–110 **(check with hosts for pricing details)**

CHESTER
(west of Halifax)

Mecklenburgh Inn
(Suzi Fraser)

78 Queen St, Box 350, Chester, NS, B0J 1J0
www.mecklenburghinn.ca
E-mail suzi@mecklenburghinn.ca

902-275-4638

A seaside heritage property c. 1890.
Covered balconies with water views. Airy
bedrooms feature featherbeds, down
duvets, spruce floors, hooked mats, toiletries. TV/DVD and three fireplaces in
living room/dining room/kitchen. Books,
games, a hammock on the upper balcony,
and a full cookie jar. Casual atmosphere.
Innkeeper is a Cordon Bleu chef. Golf, tennis, sailing, kayaking, fishing in the area.
Live theatre, shopping and restaurants, all
within a block of the Inn.

ROOMS Upper floor, **Baths** Private, Ensuite, **Beds**
Queen, Double, Twin, Single or cots, Pullout sofa,
Smoking Outside, **In Room** Thermostat, Internet
access, **OTHERS** Rural, Adult, Seasonal, Pets in resi-
dence, **PAYMENT** Visa, MC, Cash, Trvl's cheques,
BREAKFASTS Full, **AMENITIES** Central TV, Central
phone, Fridge, Lounge, Patio, Central Internet access,
Central VCR/DVD, **THINGS TO DO** Rental bikes, Trail
nearby, Rental canoe or boat, Golf, Fishing, Museums,
Art, Theatre, Shopping, Tennis, Swimming, Beach, **LAN-
GUAGE** Eng., **PRICE** (2 persons) 85–135 **(check with
hosts for pricing details)**

DIGBY *(west of Halifax)*

Harmony Bed & Breakfast / Suites
(Heather Cookson)

111 Montague Row, Digby, NS, B0V 1A0
www.harmonybedbreakfast.ns.ca
E-mail harmony@harmonybedbreakfast.ns.ca

902-245-2817
Fax 902-245-2152
TFr 1-800-890-4637

Canada Select 4-star non-smoking property, restored lodge c. 1870. Pleasant informal atmosphere, tasteful decor, covered
private balcony with oceanview overlooking world-famous Scallop Fleet. Parking 5-
minute walk to marina and restaurants,
5-minute drive to ferry and golf course.
Cable TV, VCR, phone, clock radio, hairdryer, fridge, high-speed Internet access in
every room, three- and four-piece ensuite
baths. Whale-watching tours arranged,
and your hosts will be happy to suggest
things to see and do while in this area. .

ROOMS Family suite, Upper floor, Ground floor, Private
entrance, **Baths** Private, Ensuite, **Beds** King, Queen,
Pullout sofa, **Air** In rooms, **In Room** Thermostat,
Phone, TV, **OTHERS** Open all year, Handicapped
access, **PAYMENT** Visa, MC, Diners, Amex, Direct debit,
Cash, **BREAKFASTS** Full, Continental, **AMENITIES**
Fridge, Lounge, Patio, **THINGS TO DO** Golf, Fishing,
Museums, **LANGUAGE** Eng., **PRICE** (2 persons)
100–125 **(check with hosts for pricing details)**

DIGBY

Thistle Down Country Inn

(Mel Thomas and Don Ellis)

98 Montague Row, Digby, NS, B0V 1A0
www.thistledown.ns.ca
E-mail thstldwn@tartannet.ns.ca

902-245-4490
Fax 902-245-6717
TFr 1-800-565-8081

Lovely turn-of-the-century Edwardian home on the harbour, with breathtaking views of the Annapolis Basin, Scallop Fleet and world famous high tides. Non-smoking, 12 gracious rooms, king and queen beds, private bath, full breakfast included. Scallop omelettes – our specialty. Candlelight dinners in The Queen Alexandra Room, Fresh Digby Scallops and seafood, fine Nova Scotia wines, whale-watch, golf, harbour and fishing tours arranged. Central to many activities and scenic sites. Grand views from our restful waterside garden. Gift shop.

ROOMS Upper floor, Ground floor, Private entrance, **Baths** Private, Ensuite, **Beds** King, Queen, Double, Twin, Single or cots, **Air** In rooms, **Smoking** Outside, **In Room** Thermostat, TV, Internet access, VCR/DVD, **OTHERS** Urban, Seasonal, Additional meals, Pets in residence, Pets welcome, **PAYMENT** Visa, MC, Diners, Amex, Direct debit, Cash, Trvl's cheques, **BREAKFASTS** Full, **AMENITIES** Central TV, Central phone, Laundry, Fridge, Patio, Central Internet access, Central VCR/DVD, **THINGS TO DO** Rental bikes, Trail nearby, Golf, Fishing, Museums, Art, Attractions, Shopping, Birdwatching, Antiquing, **LANGUAGE** Eng., Fr., **PRICE** (2 persons) 85–125 **(check with hosts for pricing details)**

HALIFAX *(east-central NS)*

By the Harbour Bed & Breakfast

(Carol Gardner and Eric Boudreau)

1581 Cole Harbour Rd, Dartmouth, NS, B2Z 1B9
www3.ns.sympatico.ca/carol.gardner
E-mail carol.gardner@ns.sympatico.ca

902-433-1996
Fax 902-435-7491
TFr 1-866-218-5210

The highlight of your stay in this charming English-Tudor-style home will be the three-course gourmet breakfast served at 8 or 9 a.m. We also have a wonderful view of Cole Harbour and are only 10 minutes from beaches, birdwatching, walking trails, etc. If you prefer sightseeing and shopping, we are 15 minutes from downtown amenities. Our rooms are decorated in themes: Acadian, Oriental, Mexican and French Romantique – complete with canopy bed! We also provide hairdryers and select toiletries. Call for further pricing.

ROOMS Upper floor, **Baths** Private, Ensuite, **Beds** Queen, Twin, Single or cots, **Air** Central, **In Room** Thermostat, **OTHERS** Urban, Open all year, **PAYMENT** Visa, MC, Cash, Trvl's cheques, **BREAKFASTS** Full, Home-baked, **AMENITIES** Central TV, Central phone, Patio, **THINGS TO DO** Trail nearby, Rental canoe or boat, Golf, Fishing, Museums, Art, Theatre, Entertainment, Attractions, Wineries/Breweries, Shopping, Swimming, Beach, **LANGUAGE** Eng., Fr., **PRICE** (2 persons) 75–115 **(check with hosts for pricing details)**

Caribou Lodge Bed & Breakfast

(Anna and Bruce Ellis)

6 Armada Dr, Halifax, NS, B3M 1R7
www.cariboulodgebb.com
E-mail info@cariboulodgebb.com

902-445-5013
Fax 902-445-4303
TFr 1-877-445-5013

Secluded Armada Dr is off the Bedford Hwy near Mount St.Vincent University. This Heritage B&B is only minutes from the downtown core. Furnished in Victorian-style, our B&B offers comfort and Nova Scotia hospitality. Your hosts can suggest dining, scenic drives and special events. Music is encouraged, piano in residence! The Gallery showcases talent from across the Maritimes and features wildlife watercolours and prints by Cape Breton's A.J. Scanlan.

ROOMS Family suite, Upper floor, Ground floor, Private entrance, **Baths** Private, Ensuite, **Beds** Queen, Double, Single or cots, Pullout sofa, **Air** In rooms, **Smoking** Outside, **In Room** Phone, TV, **OTHERS** Urban, Open all year, Handicapped access, Pets in residence, Pets welcome, **PAYMENT** Visa, Amex, Cheques accepted, Cash, Trvl's cheques, **BREAKFASTS** Continental, **AMENITIES** Whirlpool, Laundry, Lounge, Patio, **THINGS TO DO** Trail nearby, Golf, Fishing, Museums, Art, Theatre, Attractions, Wineries/Breweries, Shopping, Swimming, Horseback riding, Beach, **LANGUAGE** Eng., **PRICE** (2 persons) 75–110 **(check with hosts for pricing details)**

Garden View Bed and Breakfast

(Joe Bowlby-Lalonde and Carol Sifton)

6052 Williams St, Halifax, NS, B3K 1E9
www.Interdesign.ca/gardenview
E-mail carol.sifton@ns.sympatico.ca

902-423-2943
Fax 902-423-4355
TFr 1-888-737-0778

Share our garden and Victorian-style home, complete with antiques and original art in a very quiet residential neighbourhood close to downtown and many attractions. Fantastic breakfasts! Whirpool tub, living room, fireplace, cable TV. Garden Room: Ensuite, four-piece bath with antique soaker tub, beautiful view of the garden, queen bed, TV/phone. Rose Room: queen bed, antique single daybed, antique cherry wood chest and writing table. Arbor Room: Queen bed and queen pullout sofa.

ROOMS Upper floor, **Baths** Ensuite, Shared with guest, **Beds** Queen, Twin, Pullout sofa, **Smoking** Outside, **In Room** Phone, TV, **OTHERS** Urban, Open all year, Pets in residence, **PAYMENT** Visa, MC, Cash, Trvl's cheques, **BREAKFASTS** Full, Home-baked, **AMENITIES** Central TV, Central phone, Whirlpool, Kitchen, Lounge, Patio, Central VCR/DVD, **THINGS TO DO** Rental bikes, Trail nearby, Rental canoe or boat, Golf, Fishing, Museums, Art, Theatre, Entertainment, Attractions, Wineries/Breweries, Shopping, Cross-country skiing, Tennis, Swimming, Horseback riding, Beach, **LANGUAGE** Eng., **PRICE** (2 persons) 60–120 **(check with hosts for pricing details)**

Halifax

Julie's Walk Bed and Breakfast
(Patricia Gagne)

17 Julie's Walk, Halifax, NS, B3M 2Z8
www.julieswalk.com
E-mail julieswalk@hfx.eastlink.ca

902-429-5162
Fax 902-431-4763
TFr 1-866-429-5162

Luxurious *Canada Select* 4 1/2-star B&B in Halifax with harbour views. Conveniently located 10 minutes from downtown and 20 minutes from Halifax's airport. All spacious A/C rooms (one honeymoon suite, double whirlpool) feature ensuite four- to six-piece baths. Free onsite parking and delicious full hot breakfast. Serene half-acre setting with four balconies plus a gazebo. Beautiful Peggy's Cove, historic Lunenburg and Grand Pre are all within 1-hour day commutes. A great base for your Nova Scotian visit.

ROOMS Upper floor, **Baths** Ensuite, **Beds** Queen, **Air** In rooms, **Smoking** Outside, **In Room** Thermostat, Phone, TV, Internet access, VCR/DVD, **OTHERS** Open all year, **PAYMENT** Visa, MC, Amex, Cash, Trvl's cheques, **BREAKFASTS** Full, **AMENITIES** Whirlpool, Lounge, Patio, **THINGS TO DO** Golf, Museums, Art, Theatre, Entertainment, Attractions, Shopping, Tennis, Horseback riding, **LANGUAGE** Eng., **PRICE** (2 persons) 115–199 **(check with hosts for pricing details)**

Halifax

SeaWatch Bed & Breakfast
(Elaine and Stan Hatfield)

139 Ferguson's Cove Rd, Halifax, NS, B3V 1L7
www.seawatch.ca
E-mail seawatch@eastlink.ca

902-477-1506

Two private suites, each features private entrance, deck, unique nautical decor, one queen, one double, each with ensuite, cable TV, VCR, microwave, fridge, coffeemaker, light breakfast served ensuite or on deck with panoramic view of Halifax Harbour. Oceanfront (40 feet from water), on a quiet road. Whales often seen from deck, 15 minutes from downtown Halifax, 45 minutes from Halifax airport, 5-minute walk to historic Fort York Redoubt and nature trails, 20 minutes to beach. Great romantic hideaway.

ROOMS Upper floor, Ground floor, Private entrance, **Baths** Ensuite, **Beds** Queen, Double, Pullout sofa, **Smoking** Outside, **In Room** Thermostat, TV, **OTHERS** Rural, Open all year, **PAYMENT** Cash, Trvl's cheques, **BREAKFASTS** Continental, **AMENITIES** Central phone, Fridge, Patio, **THINGS TO DO** Trail nearby, Fishing, Attractions, Shopping, Swimming, Beach, **LANGUAGE** Eng., **PRICE** (2 persons) 130–150 **(check with hosts for pricing details)**

HALIFAX

The Inn At Fishermans Cove
(Elda Naugler and Erin Naugler)

1531 Shore Rd, Eastern Passage, Halifax, NS, B3G 1M5
www.theinnatfishermanscove.com
E-mail info@theinnatfishermanscove.com

902-465-3455
Fax 902-404-3257
TFr 1-866-725-3455

Halifax's waterfront inn; located at scenic Fisherman's Cove, a 200-year-old restored fishing village within the city's boundaries. Our balcony rooms feature spectacular views of the Atlantic Ocean, Lawlor, McNabs and Devils Island, as well as the night lights of downtown Halifax shimmering off the water. Boutique shopping, seafood restaurants, boardwalks, private charters, whales, dolphins, eagles and osprey, only 20 minutes to downtown Halifax and 30 minutes to the Halifax International Airport.

ROOMS Upper floor, Private entrance, **Baths** Private, Ensuite, **Beds** Queen, Single or cots, **Smoking** Outside, **In Room** Thermostat, Phone, TV, **OTHERS** Open all year, **PAYMENT** Visa, MC, Amex, Direct debit, Cash, **BREAKFASTS** Continental, **AMENITIES** Central phone, Patio, **THINGS TO DO** Trail nearby, Rental canoe or boat, Golf, Fishing, Museums, Art, Theatre, Entertainment, Attractions, Wineries/Breweries, Shopping, Swimming, Beach, **LANGUAGE** Eng., **PRICE** (2 persons) 75–135 **(check with hosts for pricing details)**

HALIFAX

Welcome Inn Halifax Bed and Breakfast
(Angela Kidston)

1984 Connaught Ave, Halifax, NS, B3H 4E1
www.welcomeinnhalifax.com
E-mail info@welcomeinnhalifax.com

902-446-6500
Fax 902-835-3805
TFr 1-877-288-2999

Lovely Dutch Colonial situated in Halifax's presigous south end. Make this your "home away from home." Stay with us and enjoy the history and beauty of Halifax. We are a 10-minute drive from the downtown and waterfront which is always full of activity. Fine restaurants, fabulous pubs, live entertainment, art galleries and museums, boat tours and bus tours. Many things to see and do. When you have seen all you can see in a day, come home and relax in your comfortable room.

ROOMS Upper floor, Ground floor, **Baths** Private, Ensuite, **Beds** Queen, **In Room** Phone, TV, Fireplace, VCR/DVD, **OTHERS** Urban, Open all year, Pets in residence, **PAYMENT** Visa, MC, Amex, Cash, Trvl's cheques, **BREAKFASTS** Full, **AMENITIES** Fridge, Patio, Central Internet access, **THINGS TO DO** Rental bikes, Rental canoe or boat, Golf, Fishing, Museums, Art, Theatre, Entertainment, Attractions, Wineries/Breweries, Shopping, Cross-country skiing, Downhill skiing, Tennis, Swimming, Horseback riding, Beach, Birdwatching, Antiquing, **LANGUAGE** Eng., **PRICE** (2 persons) 95–175 **(check with hosts for pricing details)**

Iona *(central Cape Breton Island)*

Old Grand Narrows Hotel B&B

(Terry and Elaine Mac Neil)

11 Derby Point Rd, Grand Narrows, NS, B1T 1E1
www.grandnarrowshotel.ca
E-mail info@grandnarrowshotel.ca

902-622-1330
Fax 902-622-2743
TFr 1-888-702-3720

Heritage Property (c. 1887). Very centrally located former 15-bedroom hotel right on the water with beautiful view and stunning sunsets! Location in the middle of Cape Breton Island makes it a perfect multi-night accommodation. Quiet and relaxing with friendly hosts and satisfying breakfast of home baking, fruits, jams and more! Just 4 hours from Halifax airport and 1 hour from Newfoundland Ferry. Museum, golf, boat tours, shopping all within an hours drive. Evening meal with reservation. Exits 4 and 6 from Trans-Canada Hwy 105.

ROOMS Upper floor, **Baths** Private, Ensuite, **Beds** Queen, Single or cots, **Air** Ceiling fans, **Smoking** Outside, **In Room** Thermostat, **OTHERS** Babysitting, Rural, Open all year, Pets in residence, **PAYMENT** Visa, MC, Direct debit, Cash, Trvl's cheques, **BREAKFASTS** Full, **AMENITIES** Central TV, Central phone, Barbecue, Laundry, Lounge, Patio, Central Internet access, Central VCR/DVD, **THINGS TO DO** Comp. bikes, Trail nearby, Golf, Fishing, Museums, Art, Entertainment, Attractions, Cross-country skiing, Downhill skiing, Swimming, Beach, Birdwatching, Antiquing, **LANGUAGE** Eng., **PRICE** (2 persons) 100–125 **(check with hosts for pricing details)**

Lunenburg *(southwest of Halifax)*

1826 Maplebird House Bed & Breakfast

(Barry Chappell and Susie Scott)

36 Pelham St, Lunenburg, NS, B0J 2C0
www.maplebirdhouse.ca
E-mail barry.susie@maplebirdhouse.ca

902-634-3863
TFr 1-888-395-3863

A restored heritage home (c.1826), within the UNESCO World Heritage Site, sits in a large garden with swimming pool, veran-dah and patio overlooking Lunenburg Harbour and golf course ... once a dairy farm. Our home offers four rooms with ensuite bathrooms and is rated by *Canada Select* 4-stars. Our guests' living room has a fireplace, Internet access, TV/DVD and library. Lunenburg is a desti-nation with its historical architecture, art galleries, Fisheries Museum of the Atlantic and *Bluenose II*.

ROOMS Upper floor, Ground floor, **Baths** Ensuite, **Beds** Queen, **Smoking** Outside, **OTHERS** Urban, Open all year, **PAYMENT** Visa, MC, Cash, Trvl's cheques, **BREAKFASTS** Full, Home-baked, **AMENITIES** Central TV, Central phone, Swimming pool, Barbecue, Fridge, Lounge, Patio, Central Internet access, Central VCR/DVD, **THINGS TO DO** Rental bikes, Trail nearby, Rental canoe or boat, Golf, Fishing, Museums, Art, Theatre, Entertainment, Attractions, Wineries/Breweries, Shopping, Tennis, Swimming, Beach, Antiquing, **LANGUAGE** Eng., **PRICE** (2 persons) 85–110 **(check with hosts for pricing details)**

Lunenburg

1860 Kaulbach House Historic Inn

(Glenn Martin and Derrick MacDonald)

75 Pelham St, Lunenburg, NS, B0J 2C0
www.kaulbachhouse.com
E-mail info@kaulbachhouse.com

902-634-8818
Fax 902-640-3036
TFr 1-800-568-8818

Centrally located in the heart of the historic district, this award-winning Victorian mansion is just steps from eateries, museums and boutiques. Private offstreet parking. Inroom amenities include coffee, robes, iron and board. LCD TV, DVD and more. Upscale linens. Most rooms have harbour views. Rooms are air-conditioned and tastefully decorated. Relax in our parlour and read one of the many books of local interest. Full gourmet breakfast in the formal dining room. One day is not enough. Less than 55 minutes from Halifax.

ROOMS Upper floor, Ground floor, Lower floor, **Baths** Private, Ensuite, **Beds** King, Queen, Twin, Pullout sofa, **Air** In rooms, **Smoking** Outside, **In Room** TV, Internet access, VCR/DVD, **OTHERS** Urban, Adult, Seasonal, **PAYMENT** Visa, MC, Direct debit, Cash, Trvl's cheques, **BREAKFASTS** Full, **AMENITIES** Central phone, Fridge, Lounge, Patio, Central Internet access, Central VCR/DVD, **THINGS TO DO** Rental bikes, Trail nearby, Rental canoe or boat, Golf, Fishing, Museums, Art, Theatre, Entertainment, Attractions, Wineries/Breweries, Shopping, Cross-country skiing, Tennis, Swimming, Beach, Birdwatching, Antiquing, **LANGUAGE** Eng., **PRICE** (2 persons) 99–169 **(check with hosts for pricing details)**

Lunenburg

Atlantic Sojourn Bed and Breakfast

(Sebelle Deese and Susan Budd)

56 Victoria Rd, Lunenburg, NS, B0J 2C0
www.atlanticsojourn.com
E-mail atlanticsojournbandb@ns.aliantzinc.ca

902-634-3151
Fax 902-634-4535
TFr 1-800-550-4824

We invite you to come sojourn with us in our newly remodeled (c. 1904) home. Make Lunenburg your base for exploring Halifax, Peggy's Cove, Annapolis Royal and Kejimkujik. Lunenburg offers buggy and walking tours, fishing, whale-watching, museums, shopping, art galleries, restaurants, period architecture, birding, golf, tennis and beaches. Enjoy a quiet moment watching the koi in our garden pond. Secure bike storage. Wireless Internet. Bountiful breakfasts. Gracious hospitality. *Canada Select* 4 1/2-stars.

ROOMS Upper floor, **Baths** Private, Ensuite, **Beds** Queen, Twin, Pullout sofa, **In Room** Internet access, **OTHERS** Open all year, **PAYMENT** Visa, MC, Direct debit, Cash, Trvl's cheques, **BREAKFASTS** Full, Home-baked, **AMENITIES** Central TV, Central phone, Barbecue, Laundry, Fridge, Hot bev. bar, Lounge, Patio, Central Internet access, Central VCR/DVD, **THINGS TO DO** Trail nearby, Golf, Fishing, Museums, Art, Theatre, Entertainment, Attractions, Wineries/Breweries, Shopping, Tennis, Swimming, Beach, Birdwatching, Antiquing, **LANGUAGE** Eng., **PRICE** (2 persons) 90–125 **(check with hosts for pricing details)**

LUNENBURG

Lincoln House B&B
(Georgia and Tony Morris)

130 Lincoln St, Lunenburg, NS, B0J 2C0
www.lincolnhouse.ca
E-mail lincolnhouse@ns.aliantzinc.ca

902-634-7179
Fax 902-634-7189
TFr 1-877-634-7179

"A moment in time ..." enjoy the restored (c. 1855) Victorian elegance of ornate fireplaces, stained glass, magnificently carved woodwork and sunrooms overlooking the harbour. A *Canada Select* 4 1/2-star luxury B&B in the heart of a UNESCO world heritage site, Lincoln House is within easy walking distance of the waterfront, shops, restaurants, museums, galleries and unique architecture which makes Lunenburg such a pleasant place to visit. Exit 11 from Hwy 103, straight to Lincoln St in the Old Town.

ROOMS Upper floor, **Baths** Private, Ensuite, **Beds** Queen, Double, **Air** Ceiling fans, **Smoking** Outside, **In Room** Thermostat, **OTHERS** Seasonal, **PAYMENT** Visa, MC, Amex, Direct debit, Trvl's cheques, **BREAKFASTS** Full, Home-baked, **AMENITIES** Central TV, Central phone, Lounge, Central Internet access, **THINGS TO DO** Trail nearby, Golf, Fishing, Museums, Art, Theatre, Entertainment, Attractions, Wineries/Breweries, Shopping, Tennis, Swimming, Beach, Antiquing, **LANGUAGE** Eng., **PRICE** (2 persons) 85–125 **(check with hosts for pricing details)**

LUNENBURG AREA

The Backman House Bed and Breakfast
(Patsy and David Perkins)

235 Riverport Rd, Riverport, NS, B0J 2W0
www.thebackmanhouse.com
E-mail thebackmanhouse@eastlink.ca

902-766-4967
Fax 902-766-4967
TFr 1-866-766-4967

Located on Ritcey Cove at the mouth of the La Have River in Riverport only 15 minutes west of Lunenburg on Hwy 332. Recently restored and modernized, this century-old house combines modern comfort and convenience with early 20th-century ambience. Three comfortable rooms, a queen, a twin double or a double, all with ensuite three-piece bathrooms. There is a comfortable guest lounge with cable TV, VCR, phone, games, books, etc. Fax and Internet access available. Close to beaches and the Ovens Natural Park.

ROOMS Upper floor, **Baths** Ensuite, **Beds** Queen, Double, **Air** Ceiling fans, **Smoking** Outside, **In Room** Thermostat, **OTHERS** Rural, Open all year, Pets in residence, **PAYMENT** Visa, MC, Amex, Cash, Trvl's cheques, **BREAKFASTS** Full, **AMENITIES** Central TV, Central phone, Laundry, Lounge, Central Internet access, **THINGS TO DO** Trail nearby, Golf, Fishing, Museums, Art, Theatre, Entertainment, Attractions, Wineries/Breweries, Shopping, Swimming, Beach, Birdwatching, Antiquing, **LANGUAGE** Eng., **PRICE** (2 persons) 90–95 **(check with hosts for pricing details)**

MAHONE BAY *(southwest of Halifax)*

Mahone Bay Bed and Breakfast

(Patricia and John McHugh)

558 Main St, Mahone Bay, NS, B0J 2E0
www.bbcanada.com/4078.html
E-mail mahonebaybandb@bwr.eastlink.ca

902-624-6388
Fax 902-624-0023
TFr 1-866-239-6252

Canada Select 4 1/2-stars. Four lovely rooms each with colour cable TV and VCR, radio and hairdryer; two rooms have a queen bed and ensuite bathroom; third queen room has private bathroom, and the twin room also has private bathroom; fluffy white robes are provided; full gourmet breakfast is served in the elegant dining room. Enjoy the heirloom antiques, oil paintings and Victorian blue and white willow china. There is an extensive film and book library in the "Bump" overlooking the Three Churches.

ROOMS Upper floor, **Baths** Private, Ensuite, **Beds** Queen, Twin, **Smoking** Outside, **OTHERS** Seasonal, **PAYMENT** Visa, MC, Cash, Trvl's cheques, **BREAKFASTS** Full, **AMENITIES** Fridge, **THINGS TO DO** Trail nearby, Rental canoe or boat, Golf, Fishing, Museums, Art, Theatre, Entertainment, Wineries/Breweries, Shopping, **LANGUAGE** Eng., **PRICE** (2 persons) 65–115 **(check with hosts for pricing details)**

MAITLAND *(north of Halifax)*

Cresthaven By The Sea ... A Country Inn

(Glenn Martin and Derrick MacDonald)

19 Ferry Lane, Maitland, NS, B0N 1T0
www.cresthavenbythesea.com
E-mail innkeeper@cresthavenbythesea.com

902-261-2001
Fax 902-261-2044
TFr 1-866-870-2001

Revel in the history of this Greek-revival shipbuider's home (c. 1860) at the waters edge on Cobequid Bay and the Shubenacadie River. Licensed dining room, recognized by *Where To Eat In Canada* featuring local and international cuisine. Outdoor spa on terrace, view of Tidal Bore from our property as well as eagle watching. Walking distance to museum, artisan and an antique shops, tidal bore rafting. Four lavishly appointed suites. All have a full ensuite, and satellite TV. Full gourmet breakfast included. Pet boarding available.

ROOMS Upper floor, Ground floor, **Baths** Ensuite, **Beds** Queen, **Air** In rooms, **Smoking** Outside, **In Room** Thermostat, TV, Fireplace, VCR/DVD, **OTHERS** Rural, Adult, Seasonal, Additional meals, Pets in residence, **PAYMENT** Visa, MC, Diners, Amex, Direct debit, Cash, **BREAKFASTS** Full, Home-baked, **AMENITIES** Central phone, Whirlpool, Lounge, Patio, **THINGS TO DO** Trail nearby, Golf, Fishing, Museums, Art, Theatre, Entertainment, Attractions, Wineries/Breweries, Shopping, Swimming, Horseback riding, Beach, Birdwatching, Antiquing, **LANGUAGE** Eng., **PRICE** (2 persons) 109–149 **(check with hosts for pricing details)**

Middleton *(west of Halifax)*

Century Farm Inn (c.1886)

(Richard and Shae Griffith)

10 Main St (Rte 1), Middleton, NS, B0S 1P0
www.centuryfarminn.com
E-mail shae.griffith@ns.sympatico.ca

902-825-6989
Fax 902-825-6989
TFr 1-800-237-9896

Fully restored 1886 Victorian farmhouse furnished in period antiques to enhance its original charm. Guest rooms feature king or queen beds, ensuite private bathrooms, air-conditioning, cable TV, wireless Internet access, hairdryers. Situated on a 110-acre estate "Fairfield" on the Annapolis River. Mountain and meadow views, nature trails with abundant wildlife. Walking distance to museums, restaurants, tourist bureau, shopping. Centrally located for day trips, golf, whale-watching, historic sites.

ROOMS Upper floor, Ground floor, **Baths** Ensuite, **Beds** King, Queen, Double, Twin, **Air** In rooms, **Smoking** Outside, **In Room** Thermostat, Phone, TV, Internet access, VCR/DVD, **OTHERS** Urban, Rural, Adult, Seasonal, **PAYMENT** Visa, MC, Diners, Amex, Direct debit, Cash, Trvl's cheques, **BREAKFASTS** Full, **AMENITIES** Central phone, Laundry, Fridge, Lounge, Patio, **THINGS TO DO** Trail nearby, Golf, Fishing, Museums, Art, Theatre, Entertainment, Attractions, Wineries/Breweries, Shopping, Cross-country skiing, Tennis, Swimming, Horseback riding, Beach, Birdwatching, Antiquing, **LANGUAGE** Eng., **PRICE** (2 persons) 75–115 **(check with hosts for pricing details)**

Musquodoboit Harbour
(northeast of Halifax)

The Elephant's Nest Bed & Breakfast

(June and John Meehan)

127 Pleasant Dr, Gaetz Brook, NS, B0J 1N0
www.elephantsnestbnb.ca
E-mail info@elephantsnestbnb.ca

902-827-3891
Fax 902-827-3891
TFr 1-866-633-6378

A *Canada Select* 4 1/2-star luxury lakeside home on beautiful Lake Petpeswick, just 40 minutes from downtown Halifax and the international airport. Three tastefully decorated rooms with ensuite bathrooms (one with a hydrotherapy tub). Queen, king or twin beds (twins for multiple night stay only). Beautiful gardens, an outdoor hot tub and a sandy beach make the stay so much more fulfilling. The B&B is situated 7 km west of Musquodoboit Harbour, Hwy 7 to Pinehill Dr to Pleasant Dr.

ROOMS Upper floor, Ground floor, **Baths** Ensuite, **Beds** King, Queen, Twin, Single or cots, Pullout sofa, **Smoking** Outside, **In Room** Thermostat, Phone, TV, Fireplace, Internet access, VCR/DVD, **OTHERS** Rural, Open all year, Pets in residence, Pets welcome, **PAYMENT** Visa, MC, Cash, Trvl's cheques, **BREAKFASTS** Full, **AMENITIES** Whirlpool, Barbecue, Lounge, Patio, Central Internet access, **THINGS TO DO** Trail nearby, Comp. Canoe or boat, Golf, Fishing, Museums, Art, Entertainment, Attractions, Shopping, Swimming, Beach, Birdwatching, Antiquing, **LANGUAGE** Eng., **PRICE** (2 persons) 95–150 **(check with hosts for pricing details)**

North Sydney
(northeast Cape Breton Island)

Annfield Manor

(Mark and Lisat Teeter)

317 Church Rd, Little Bras d'Or, NS, B1Y 3A3
www.annfieldmanor.com
E-mail annfield@eastlink.ca

902-736-8770
Fax 902-544-1835
TFr 1-888-818-5028

A unique heritage country B&B located in Cape Breton, Nova Scotia. Only minutes' drive to the Newfoundland Ferries and North Sydney and to all Cape Breton Island attractions. Take a step back in time and let yourself enjoy warm, traditional hospitality and great food in this beautiful 28-room historic mansion furnished with fine antiques. Est. 1893, 15 minutes away from Sydney, 25 minutes away from Baddeck, 20 minutes away from the Cabot trail and 40 minutes from the Fortress of Louisbourg.

ROOMS Family suite, Upper floor, Lower floor, **Baths** Private, Ensuite, **Air** Ceiling fans, **Smoking** Outside, **In Room** TV, Fireplace, VCR/DVD, **OTHERS** Open all year, Additional meals, **PAYMENT** Visa, MC, Amex, Cash, Trvl's cheques, **BREAKFASTS** Full, **AMENITIES** Central phone, Fridge, Lounge, Patio, Central VCR/DVD, **THINGS TO DO** Trail nearby, Comp. Canoe or boat, Golf, Fishing, Museums, Art, Theatre, Entertainment, Attractions, Shopping, Cross-country skiing, Tennis, Swimming, Horseback riding, Beach, Birdwatching, Antiquing, **LANGUAGE** Eng., **PRICE** (2 persons) 70–109 **(check with hosts for pricing details)**

North Sydney

Gowrie House Country Inn

(Clifford Matthews and Ken Tutty)

840 Shore Rd, Sydney Mines, NS, B1V 1A6
www.gowriehouse.com
E-mail gowriehouse@ns.sympatico.ca

902-544-1050
Fax 902-736-0077
TFr 1-800-372-1115

Built c.1820 in the Georgian-style, Gowrie House has been redecorated and elegantly furnished with fine antiques and works of art. The Inn has been awarded 4 1/2-stars by *Canada Select*. Ten rooms with private ensuite baths, A/C, fireplaces and a caretaker's cottage for deluxe accommodation. Comfortable rooms, friendly people and superb food. Centrally located on beautiful Cape Breton Island, it's a great point from which to explore. Five minutes from the North Sydney Ferry to Newfoundland.

ROOMS Upper floor, Ground floor, Private entrance, **Baths** Private, Ensuite, **Beds** King, Queen, Twin, Pullout sofa, **Air** In rooms, **In Room** Thermostat, Phone, TV, Fireplace, Internet access, VCR/DVD, **OTHERS** Rural, Seasonal, Additional meals, Pets welcome, **PAYMENT** Visa, MC, Amex, Direct debit, Cash, Trvl's cheques, **BREAKFASTS** Full, Home-baked, **AMENITIES** Fridge, Lounge, Patio, Central Internet access, Central VCR/DVD, **THINGS TO DO** Trail nearby, Golf, Museums, Entertainment, Attractions, Shopping, Swimming, Horseback riding, Beach, Birdwatching, Antiquing, **LANGUAGE** Eng., **PRICE** (2 persons) 125–265 **(check with hosts for pricing details)**

PARRSBORO *(western NS)*

The Maple Inn

(Ulrike Rockenbauer and Johannes Hiesberger)

2358 Western Ave, Parrsboro, NS, B0M 1S0
www.mapleinn.ca
E-mail office@mapleinn.ca

902-254-3735
Fax 902-254-3735
TFr 1-877-627-5346

The Maple Inn is a charming bed and breakfast inn located in Parrsboro on the Fundy Shore of Nova Scotia. Two century-old houses have been renovated to provide a variety of accommodations. The Inn has eight double occupancy rooms, all with private bath. We also offer a two-bedroom suite with private whirlpool bath and king-size bed. All accommodations include full breakfast. The Inn is within walking distance of professional summer theatre, the Fundy Geological Museum, Ottawa House and the beach.

ROOMS Family suite, Upper floor, Ground floor, Private entrance, **Baths** Private, Ensuite, **Beds** King, Queen, Double, Twin, Single or cots, Pullout sofa, **Air** In rooms, **Smoking** Outside, **In Room** TV, **OTHERS** Open all year, **PAYMENT** Visa, MC, Diners, Amex, Direct debit, Cash, Trvl's cheques, **BREAKFASTS** Full, Home-baked, **AMENITIES** Central TV, Central phone, Laundry, Fridge, Lounge, Central Internet access, Central VCR/DVD, **THINGS TO DO** Trail nearby, Rental canoe or boat, Golf, Fishing, Museums, Art, Theatre, Attractions, Beach, Birdwatching, Antiquing, **LANGUAGE** Eng., Ger., **PRICE** (2 persons) 90–150 **(check with hosts for pricing details)**

PARRSBORO

The Parrsboro Mansion

(Sabine and Christian Schoene)

3916 Eastern Ave, Parrsboro, NS, B0M 1S0
www.parrsboromansion.com
E-mail sabine@parrsboromansion.com

902-254-2585
Fax 902-254-2585
TFr 1-866-354-2585

Enjoy the peaceful setting of our fine historic home. The Parrsboro Mansion is nestled on a 4-acre downtown property, set far back from daily noises. Relax in one of the elegant and spacious ground floor rooms with king, queen and twin double beds and ensuite bathrooms. Rejuvenate in our heated inground pool and pamper yourself with a German gourmet buffet breakfast in the sunny dining room. Rated 4 1/2-stars by *Canada Select* and close to all attractions. Highest tides in the world, rock and gem hunting.

ROOMS Family suite, Upper floor, Ground floor, **Baths** Private, Ensuite, **Beds** King, Queen, Double, Twin, Single or cots, Pullout sofa, **Air** In rooms, Ceiling fans, **Smoking** Outside, **In Room** Thermostat, TV, Internet access, VCR/DVD, **OTHERS** Seasonal, Pets in residence, **PAYMENT** Visa, MC, Amex, Direct debit, Cash, Trvl's cheques, **BREAKFASTS** Full, Home-baked, **AMENITIES** Central phone, Swimming pool, Sauna, Laundry, Patio, Central Internet access, **THINGS TO DO** Trail nearby, Golf, Fishing, Museums, Art, Theatre, Entertainment, Attractions, Shopping, Tennis, Swimming, Beach, Birdwatching, Antiquing, **LANGUAGE** Eng.Ger **PRICE** (2 persons) 100–150 **(check with hosts for pricing details)**

PICTOU *(northern Nova Scotia)*

Evening Sail Bed & Breakfast & Housekeeping Unit

(Michelle and Gail LeBlanc)

279 Denoon St, Box 209, Pictou, NS, B0K 1H0
www.eveningsail.ca
E-mail stay@eveningsail.ca

902-485-5069
Fax 902-485-5472

Friendly down-east hospitality in one of our restored 19th-century houses. Built around two adjacent homes nestled in the trees in historical Pictou, we offer three B&B rooms and three housekeeping units with kitchens, fireplaces, private bathrooms and furnished with antiques. Generous healthy-heart breakfast buffet served 7:30 and 8:30. Centrally located within a 10 minute walk to historic downtown shops, pubs, restaurants, waterfront, two marinas, public swimming pool, walking trails and golf. Take the water taxi or a short drive to beaches, museums, PEI Ferry. Clean comfortable beds, top quality service and satisfaction.

ROOMS Family suite, Upper floor, Ground floor, Lower floor, Private entrance, **Baths** Private, Ensuite, **Beds** Queen, Double, Single or cots, **Air** In rooms, **Smoking** Outside, **In Room** Thermostat, Phone, TV, Fireplace, Internet access, **OTHERS** Urban, Open all year, **PAYMENT** Visa, MC, Amex, Cash, Trvl's cheques, **BREAKFASTS** Full, Home-baked, **AMENITIES** Central TV, Central phone, Barbecue, Laundry, Kitchen, Fridge, Patio, **THINGS TO DO** Trail nearby, Golf, Museums, Art, Entertainment, Attractions, Wineries/Breweries, Shopping, Tennis, Swimming, Beach, **LANGUAGE** Eng., **PRICE** (2 persons) 75–125 **(check with hosts for pricing details)**

SALMON RIVER BRIDGE-JEDDORE *(northeast of Halifax)*

Salmon River House Country Inn

(Adrien Blanchette and Elisabeth Schwarzer)

9931 Hwy 7, Salmon River Bridge, Musquodoboit Harbour-Jeddore, NS, B0J 1P0
www.salmonriverhouse.com
E-mail salmonrh@ca.inter.net

902-889-3353
Fax 902-889-3653
TFr 1-800-565-3353

We're 40 minutes away from Halifax or Halifax International Airport. Hwy 7 to Musquodoboit Harbour. Arriving at the end of Hwy 107, turn right, drive through the Village of Musquodoboit Harbour. On the left side you can see the Railway Museum, stay on this road. This is the old #7; continue until Salmon River bridge, approx 15 minutes (passing the green bridge and Forest Hill Shopping Center). We are located just across the bridge on the water.

ROOMS Family suite, Upper floor, Ground floor, **Baths** Private, Ensuite, **Beds** King, Queen, Double, Twin, **Air** In rooms, **OTHERS** Handicapped access, Seasonal, **PAYMENT** Visa, MC, Diners, Amex, Direct debit, Cheques accepted, Cash, Trvl's cheques, **BREAKFASTS** Full, Continental, Home-baked, **AMENITIES** Central TV, Central phone, Kitchen, Fridge, Patio, **THINGS TO DO** Trail nearby, Comp. Canoe or boat, Golf, Museums, Art, Attractions, Swimming, Beach, Birdwatching, Antiquing, **LANGUAGE** Eng., Fr., Sp., Ger., **PRICE** (2 persons) 84–148 **(check with hosts for pricing details)**

SYDNEY *(northeast Cape Breton Island)*

A Paradise Found B&B
(Rick and Connie Bowers)

62 Milton St, Sydney, NS, B1P 4L8
www3.ns.sympatico.ca/paradisefound
E-mail paradisefound@ns.sympatico.ca

902-539-9377
Fax 902-539-9377
TFr 1-877-539-9377

Make our centrally located charming
home your peaceful retreat when visiting
beautiful Cape Breton. On a quiet, tree-
lined street in the heart of Sydney,
A Paradise Found is ideally situated for
you to explore the island by day, enjoy
the food and frolic of Sydney by night
and relax in the comfort of one of the
area's fine old homes. Sydney's first
Canada Select 4 1/2-star B&B, A Paradise
Found offers three spacious rooms, each
with private ensuite bath. Connie's full
deluxe breakfasts get rave reviews. Book
early and let us help you plan your stay
on Cape Breton Island.

ROOMS Upper floor, **Baths** Ensuite, **Beds** King, Queen,
Twin, **Air** Ceiling fans, **Smoking** Outside, **In Room** TV,
Internet access, VCR/DVD, **OTHERS** Urban, Open all
year, Pets in residence, **PAYMENT** Visa, MC, Amex,
Direct debit, Cheques accepted, Cash, **BREAKFASTS**
Full, **AMENITIES** Central phone, **THINGS TO DO** Trail
nearby, Golf, Museums, Theatre, Entertainment,
Attractions, Shopping, Cross-country skiing,
Swimming, Beach, Birdwatching, Antiquing, **LAN-
GUAGE** Eng., Fr., **PRICE** (2 persons) 95–110 **(check
with hosts for pricing details)**

TRURO *(north of Haliafax)*

The Udder Place
(Betty and John Blaauwendraat)

#2217 Hwy 236, Beaver Brook, NS, B2N 5A9
www.theudderplace.com
E-mail blaauwendraat@ns.sympatico.ca

902-893-7113
TFr 1-866-244-0558

Welcome to a place of quiet, mind-tran-
quility, calmness and clarity – in the midst
of a too busy world. Majestic rolling green
pastures, country meadows, along with
the meandering Beaver Brook, give you a
true feeling of peacefulness. Take a relaxing stroll down our shaded lane that
leads to the farm where our cows, horses,
goats and hens are eager to greet you.
Our air-conditioned ranch-style house is
ideally located to give you an amazing
bucolic setting of our operating dairy
farm. Full country breakfast with farm-
fresh eggs.

ROOMS Family suite, Ground floor, **Baths** Private,
Beds Queen, Twin, **Air** Central, Ceiling fans, **Smoking**
Outside, **OTHERS** Rural, Open all year, **PAYMENT** Visa,
MC, Amex, Direct debit, Cash, Trvl's cheques, **BREAK-
FASTS** Full, Home-baked, **AMENITIES** Central TV,
Central phone, Whirlpool, Fridge, Hot bev. bar, Lounge,
Patio, **THINGS TO DO** Comp. bikes, Trail nearby, Golf,
Fishing, Museums, Theatre, Entertain-ment,
Attractions, Wineries/Breweries, Shopping, Cross-
country skiing, Downhill skiing, Tennis, Swimming,
Beach, Birdwatching, Antiquing, **LANGUAGE** Eng.,
PRICE (2 persons) 85–135 **(check with hosts for pric-
ing details)**

TRURO

Tulips and Thistle Bed & Breakfast

(Ann and Larry MacCormack)

913 Pictou Rd, Truro, NS, B2N 5B1
www.bbcanada.com/tulipsthistle
E-mail tulipsthistle@tru.eastlink.ca

902-895-6141
Fax 902-895-6089
TFr 1-866-724-7796

Tulips and Thistle B&B is a *Canada Select* 4-star property offering guests a quiet, park-like setting among mature trees and manicured gardens. Located in the heartland of Nova Scotia, Tulips and Thistle B&B is the perfect base for exploring central Nova Scotia. Enjoy Tidal Bore rafting, walks on the ocean bottom, sea kayaking, hiking, fossil and mineral hunting, swimming or golfing, to name but a few activities. Let us make you welcome and allow us to make your stay a memorable experience.

ROOMS Family suite, Upper floor, **Baths** Private, Ensuite, **Beds** Queen, Twin, Single or cots, Pullout sofa, **Air** Ceiling fans, **Smoking** Outside, **In Room** Thermostat, TV, Internet access, VCR/DVD, **OTHERS** Open all year, **PAYMENT** Visa, MC, Direct debit, Cash, Trvl's cheques, **BREAKFASTS** Full, Continental, Home-baked, **AMENITIES** Central TV, Central phone, Barbecue, Laundry, Fridge, Lounge, Patio, Central Internet access, Central VCR/DVD, **THINGS TO DO** Golf, Museums, Art, Theatre, Entertainment, Attractions, Wineries/Breweries, Shopping, Cross-country skiing, Downhill skiing, Swimming, Beach, Birdwatching, Antiquing, **LANGUAGE** Eng., Fr., Sp., Dutch, **PRICE** (2 persons) 75–115 **(check with hosts for pricing details)**

WESTPORT, BRIER ISLAND
(Brier Island Bay of Fundy)

Bay of Fundy Inn

(Penny and Roy Graham)

137 Second St, Westport, Brier Island, NS, B0V 1H0
www.novascotiawhalewatching.ca/guesthouse.php
E-mail info@novascotiawhalewatching.ca

902-839-2346
Fax 902-839-2070
TFr 1-800-239-2189

The Bay of Fundy Inn, a restored historical home (c.1830) overlooking Grand Passage, provides a comfortable overnight stay for travellers after an exciting day of whale watching, hiking and sightseeing. The Inn is located within walking distance of all amenities, nature hiking trails, lighthouses, seals and shorebird watching. Relax in one of three comfortable rooms, 2 queen and 1 double, one 3-piece and one 4-piece shared baths. Whale watching and accommodation packages available. No Smoking or pets please.

ROOMS Upper floor, **Baths** Shared with guest, **Beds** Queen, Double, Single or cots, **Air** Ceiling fans, **Smoking** Outside, **PAYMENT** Visa, MC, Amex, Direct debit, Cash, Trvl's cheques, **BREAKFASTS** Continental, **AMENITIES** Central TV, Central VCR/DVD, **THINGS TO DO** Trail nearby, Fishing, Attractions, Beach, Birdwatching, **LANGUAGE** Eng., **PRICE** (2 persons) 67–75 **(check with hosts for pricing details)**

WOLFVILLE *(northwest of Halifax)*

The Farmhouse Inn

(Julie Kelly and Andrea Kelly)

9757 Main St, PO Box 38, Canning, NS, B0P 1H0
www.farmhouseinn.ns.ca
E-mail farmhous@ns.sympatico.ca

902-582-7900
TFr 1-800-928-4346

Renovated c. 1840 farmhouse in a picturesque village surrounded by the world's highest tides! Deluxe accommodation with ensuite bathrooms, A/C, phones, fireplaces, two-person whirlpool tubs. *Canada Select* 4 1/2-stars, CAA/AAA 3-Diamonds. Professional theatre, world-class dining, beaches, hiking, the Lookoff, Blomidon Provincial Park, wineries are all minutes from our door. Full, hot breakfast and afternoon tea along with coffee, tea or juice at your door an hour before breakfast.

ROOMS Family suite, Upper floor, Ground floor, Private entrance, **Baths** Ensuite, **Beds** King, Queen, Twin, Pullout sofa, **Air** In rooms, **In Room** Thermostat, Phone, TV, Fireplace, **OTHERS** Rural, Open all year, **PAYMENT** Visa, MC, Amex, Trvl's cheques, **BREAKFASTS** Full, **AMENITIES** Whirlpool, Laundry, Lounge, **THINGS TO DO** Trail nearby, Golf, Museums, Art, Theatre, Attractions, Wineries/Breweries, Shopping, Horseback riding, Beach, **LANGUAGE** Eng., **PRICE** (2 persons) 89–155 **(check with hosts for pricing details)**

WOLFVILLE

Tides In Guest Suites

(Dick Killiam and Madonna Spinazola)

4079, Hwy 359 RR #3 Centreville, Hall's Harbour,
NS, B0P 1J0
www.tidesinhallsharbour.com
E-mail tidesinhallsharbour@xcountry.tv

902-679-1949
Fax 902-679-0975
TFr 1-866-808-9622

Your hosts, photographic artist Dick Killam and Madonna, hope you come to experience Nova Scotia, and in particular Hall's Harbour. They live in a powerful yet peaceful community, and if a quaint working fishing village filled with hospitality, good food, the best-tasting lobsters, great sunsets and exceptional views, as well as being home to the "Highest Tides in the World," is to your liking, you will love your stay here! Each suite has private entrance with Jacuzzi, king bed, balcony and more! *Canada Select* 4 1/2-stars

ROOMS Family suite, Upper floor, Ground floor, Private entrance, **Baths** Ensuite, **Beds** King, Pullout sofa, **Smoking** Outside, **In Room** Thermostat, Phone, TV, **OTHERS** Rural, Open all year, **PAYMENT** Visa, MC, Cheques accepted, Cash, Trvl's cheques, **BREAKFASTS** Continental, Self-catered, **AMENITIES** Whirlpool, Barbecue, Laundry, Kitchen, Fridge, Hot bev. bar, Patio, **THINGS TO DO** Trail nearby, Rental canoe or boat, Golf, Fishing, Museums, Art, Theatre, Entertainment, Attractions, Wineries/Breweries, Shopping, Cross-country skiing, Swimming, Horseback riding, Beach, **LANGUAGE** Eng., **PRICE** (2 persons) 150–175 **(check with hosts for pricing details)**

Wolfville Area
Brownings Bed & Breakfast
(Orval and Gerri Browning)

8358 Hwy 221, Centreville, Kings County, NS, B0P 1J0
www3.ns.sympatico.ca/brownings
E-mail brownings@ns.sympatico.ca

902-582-7062
Fax 902-582-7869

Canada Select 4-stars. Centrally located on Evangeline Trail between Wolfville and Kentville, surrounded by acres of natural beauty, 5 minutes to golf, close to Halls Harbour, hiking trails and 1 hour by car will take you to many notable locations. Royal Suite offers king-size bed, Jacuzzi and fridge. West wing guest house is spacious, with private entrance and full kitchen. Wake up to the birds singing. Refreshments. Exit 13 off 101, to Kentville to Rte 359 to Centreville, to 221 E. Turn left go 2 km.

ROOMS Family suite, Lower floor, Private entrance, **Baths** Private, **Beds** King, Queen, Twin, Single or cots, Pullout sofa, **Smoking** Outside, **In Room** Phone, TV, **OTHERS** Rural, Seasonal, **PAYMENT** Visa, MC, Diners, Cheques accepted, Cash, Trvl's cheques, **BREAKFASTS** Full, Home-baked, **AMENITIES** Central phone, Barbecue, Laundry, Kitchen, Fridge, Lounge, Patio, Central Internet access, Central VCR/DVD, **THINGS TO DO** Trail nearby, Golf, Fishing, Museums, Attractions, Wineries/Breweries, **LANGUAGE** Eng., **PRICE** (2 persons) 99–149 **(check with hosts for pricing details)**

Newfoundland and Labrador

CANADIAN BED AND BREAKFAST GUIDE

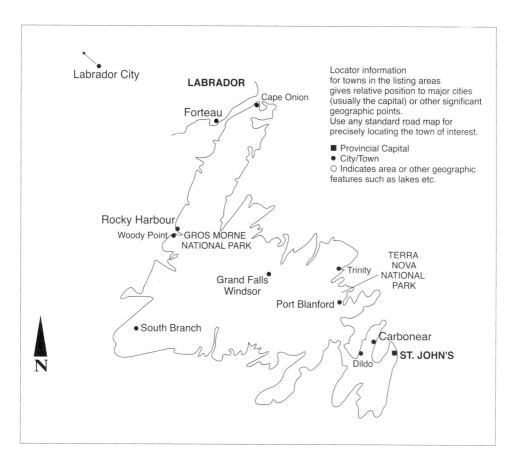

Labrador City

LABRADOR

Cape Onion

Forteau

Locator information
for towns in the listing areas
gives relative position to major cities
(usually the capital) or other significant
geographic points.
Use any standard road map for
precisely locating the town of interest.

■ Provincial Capital
● City/Town
○ Indicates area or other geographic
features such as lakes etc.

Rocky Harbour

Woody Point GROS MORNE
NATIONAL PARK

TERRA
NOVA
Trinity NATIONAL
PARK

Grand Falls
Windsor

Port Blanford

South Branch

Carbonear

■ ST. JOHN'S

Dildo

N

CAPE ONION *(northern NFLD)*

Tickle Inn at Cape Onion

(David and Barbara Adams, Sophia Bessey)

RR #1, Box 62, Cape Onion, NFLD, A0K 4J0
www.tickleinn.net
E-mail adams@nl.rogers.com

709-452-4321
Fax 709-452-4321
TFr 1-866-814-8567

Experience "top of the rock" hospitality at the Tickle Inn, an attractively restored Registered Heritage Home. The ocean is at the doorstep in Cape Onion, a pictur-esque cove surrounded by meadows and hills. Enjoy liesurely walks and challeng-ing hikes. Join us for dinner in our licensed dining room (*Where to Eat in Canada*), followed by a cultural experi-ence in the parlour during July and Aug. The Tickle Inn has received several tourism awards and strives to maintain a high standard for its guests.

ROOMS Upper floor, **Baths** Shared with guest, **Beds** Queen, Double, Twin, **Smoking** Outside, **In Room** Thermostat, **OTHERS** Rural, Seasonal, Additional meals, **PAYMENT** Visa, MC, Cheques accepted, Cash, Trvl's cheques, **BREAKFASTS** Full, Continental, Home-baked, **AMENITIES** Central TV, Central phone, Lounge, Central Internet access, Central VCR/DVD, **THINGS TO DO** Trail nearby, Museums, Theatre, Entertainment, Attractions, Shopping, Beach, Birdwatching, **LAN-GUAGE** Eng., **PRICE** (2 persons) 60–70 **(check with hosts for pricing details)**

CARBONEAR *(northwest of St. John's)*

Sophia's Fine Dining & Bed and Breakfast

(Jennifer and Dennis Davis)

150 Water St, Carbonear, NFLD, A1Y 1B7
www.sophiasmanor.com
E-mail sophias@warp.nfld.net

709-596-3400
Fax 709-596-3088
TFr 1-866-596-3088

Nestled in the waterfront Heritage District of historic Carbonear, Sophia's is the former 1890s home of the mercantile Duff family. Elegantly restored, Sophia's has four tastefully appointed guest rooms and a fine dining restaurant. King- and queen-size beds, in-room whirlpools, antique furniture, down duvets, luxurious linens, fireplaces and warm hospitality. Enjoy a light lunch or gourmet dinner prepared with only the finest local ingre-dients by our trained chef. Open daily and fully licensed. *Canada Select* 4-stars.

ROOMS Upper floor, **Baths** Ensuite, **Beds** King, Queen, **Air** In rooms, Ceiling fans, **Smoking** Outside, **In Room** Thermostat, TV, Internet access, VCR/DVD, **OTHERS** Open all year, Additional meals, **PAYMENT** Visa, MC, Amex, Direct debit, Cash, Trvl's cheques, **BREAKFASTS** Full, Home-baked, **AMENITIES** Central phone, Whirlpool, Laundry, **THINGS TO DO** Trail nearby, Golf, Museums, Theatre, Entertainment, Wineries/Breweries, Shopping, Cross-country skiing, Swimming, Horseback riding, Beach, Birdwatching, Antiquing, **LANGUAGE** Eng., **PRICE** (2 persons) 89–129 **(check with hosts for pricing details)**

CORNER BROOK *(southwestern NFLD)*

The Doctors House
(Geri Wheaton)

435 Curling St, Corner Brook, NFLD, A2H 5K3
www.thedoctorshousebandb.ca
E-mail gwheaton@thedoctorshousebandb.ca

709-785-2230
Fax 709-785-2235

The Doctor's House, built in the early
1900s by a sea merchant in the community then known as Birchy Cove, is now
called Curling in the city of Corner Brook.
Overlooking beautiful Bay of Islands on
the scenic west coast of Newfoundland
and Labrador. Initially known as the Barry
House, it was then owned for many years
by Dr. Murray. This B&B still offers the
charm, history and beautiful architecture
of years gone by. Huge library and reading room overlooking Bay of Islands.
Check in after 3p.m., out by 11a.m.
Canada Select 3 1/2-stars.

ROOMS Upper floor, Ground floor, Lower floor, **Baths**
Private, Ensuite, **Beds** King, Queen, Twin, **Smoking**
Outside, **In Room** Phone, **OTHERS** Open all year,
Additional meals, Pets welcome, **PAYMENT** Visa, MC,
Direct debit, Cash, **BREAKFASTS** Full, **AMENITIES**
Central TV, Barbecue, Laundry, Lounge, Central
Internet access, Central VCR/DVD, **THINGS TO DO** Trail
nearby, Rental canoe or boat, Golf, Fishing, Museums,
Art, Theatre, Entertainment, Attractions, Shopping,
Cross-country skiing, Downhill skiing, Swimming,
Beach, **LANGUAGE** Eng., **PRICE** (2 persons) 70–80
(check with hosts for pricing details)

DILDO *(west of St. John's)*

Inn By The Bay
(Todd Warren)

78-80 Front Rd, Dildo, NFLD, A0B 1P0
www.innbythebaydildo.com
E-mail info@innbythebaydildo.com

709-582-3170
Fax 709-582-3175
TFr 1-888-339-7829

Perched by the bay in Dildo, an ancient
fishing village on Trinity Bay, our historic
bayside inn accented with antiques, offers
exceptional accommodations and an
incredible scenic experience. George
House c. 1885 and Rowe House c. 1888,
offering evening dinner with ocean views,
inviting guestrooms, delicious breakfast
while watching the whales, seabirds and
fishing boats, all with service to remember. Come and enjoy the inn on the ocean
front. *Canada Select* 4 1/2-stars. CAA/AAA
3 Diamonds.

ROOMS Family suite, Upper floor, Ground floor, **Baths**
Ensuite, **Beds** Queen, Double, Twin, Single or cots, **Air**
In rooms, **Smoking** Outside, **In Room** Thermostat,
Phone, TV, Internet access, VCR/DVD, **OTHERS**
Babysitting, Rural, Seasonal, Additional meals, **PAY-
MENT** Visa, MC, Diners, Amex, Direct debit, Cheques
accepted, Cash, Trvl's cheques, **BREAKFASTS** Full,
AMENITIES Central TV, Central phone, Laundry,
Lounge, Patio, Central Internet access, Central
VCR/DVD, **THINGS TO DO** Rental bikes, Trail nearby,
Rental canoe or boat, Golf, Fishing, Museums, Art,
Theatre, Entertainment, Attractions, Wineries/
Breweries, Shopping, Swimming, Horseback riding,
Beach, Birdwatching, Antiquing, **LANGUAGE** Eng., Fr.,
PRICE (2 persons) 89–199 **(check with hosts for pric-
ing details)**

FORTEAU *(southeastern Labrador)*

Grenfell Louie A Hall Bed & Breakfast

(Peggy Hancock)

3 Willow Ave, Box 137, Forteau, NFLD, A0K 2P0
www3.nf.sympatico.ca/peggy.hancock
E-mail peggy.hancock@nf.sympatico.ca

709-931-2916
Fax 709-931-2189
TFr 1-877-931-2916

An historic bed and breakfast which was originally a Grenfell Nursing Station built in 1946. In operation as a hospital until 1983. Now privately owned as a B&B. Owners were born in the building when it was a hospital. Located near Basque Whaling Site, Point Amour Lighthouse Museum, Maritime Archaic Site, falls, Salmon River, sandy beaches, trails, dinner theatre, documentaries of Grenfell and Labrador. Near new Trans-Labrador Hwy. Enjoy one of the world's last adventure sites filled with natural beauty.

ROOMS Upper floor, **Baths** Shared with guest, **Beds** Double, Twin, Pullout sofa, **Air** In rooms, **In Room** Thermostat, **OTHERS** Rural, Open all year, Pets in residence, **PAYMENT** Visa, Cheques accepted, Cash, Trvl's cheques, **BREAKFASTS** Continental, **AMENITIES** Central TV, Central phone, Barbecue, Lounge, Patio, **THINGS TO DO** Trail nearby, Fishing, Museums, Art, Theatre, Entertainment, Attractions, Wineries/Breweries, Shopping, Swimming, Beach, **LANGUAGE** Eng., **PRICE** (2 persons) 45–60 **(check with hosts for pricing details)**

GRAND FALLS-WINDSOR *(central NFLD)*

Carriage House Inn

(Regina Robinson)

181 Grenfell Heights, Grand Falls-Windsor, NFLD, A2A 2J2
www.carriagehouseinn.ca
E-mail togina@nf.sympatico.ca

709-489-7185
Fax 709-489-1990
TFr 1-800-563-7133

Located in the beautiful Exploits Valley. Quiet, exceptionally clean, with a very cozy decor. Lots of space to relax. The Carriage House Inn has well-appointed rooms, library, large air-conditioned sitting room and verandah complete with porch swing. The patio deck captures the afternoon sun and sunsets. We offer quality accommodations and hospitality at its finest. To find us, take exit 20 off the Trans-Canada Hwy and turn right on Grenfell Heights to our sign.

ROOMS Family suite, Upper floor, Ground floor, **Baths** Private, Ensuite, **Beds** King, Queen, Double, Twin, **Air** In rooms, **Smoking** Outside, **In Room** Thermostat, Phone, TV, Internet access, VCR/DVD, **OTHERS** Urban, Open all year, Pets welcome, **PAYMENT** Visa, MC, Amex, Direct debit, Cash, Trvl's cheques, **BREAKFASTS** Full, Self-catered, **AMENITIES** Central phone, Whirlpool, Barbecue, Laundry, Fridge, Lounge, Patio, **THINGS TO DO** Trail nearby, Rental canoe or boat, Golf, Fishing, Museums, Theatre, Entertainment, Attractions, Shopping, Cross-country skiing, Tennis, Swimming, Horseback riding, Birdwatching, **LANGUAGE** Eng., **PRICE** (2 persons) 59–109 **(check with hosts for pricing details)**

GRAND FALLS-WINDSOR

Hill Road Manor

(Elizabeth Wyatt and Brett Beech)

1 Hill Rd, Grand Falls-Windsor, NFLD, A2A 1G9
www.hillroadmanor.com
E-mail info@hillroadmanor.com

709-489-5451
Fax 709-489-5431
TFr 1-866-489-5451

A distinctive, older home boasting original leaded-glass windows, French doors
and curved mouldings as lovely as they
were 65 years ago. *Canada Select* 4-star
rating, the Manor is set on mature-treed
grounds surrounded by a stone wall.
Deluxe beds and linens are standard in
large, comfortable rooms with private
bathrooms. Located in the scenic Exploits
River Valley, salmon fishing, hiking and
birdwatching are a must. An ideal base
for day trips to view icebergs or whales,
sea kayaking and white-water rafting.

ROOMS Upper floor, **Baths** Private, Ensuite, **Beds** King,
Queen, Twin, Single or cots, **Smoking** Outside, **In
Room** TV, Internet access, VCR/DVD, **OTHERS** Urban,
Open all year, Pets in residence, **PAYMENT** Visa, MC,
Amex, Cash, Trvl's cheques, **BREAKFASTS** Full, Home-
baked, **AMENITIES** Barbecue, Laundry, Patio, **THINGS
TO DO** Trail nearby, Golf, Fishing, Museums, Art,
Theatre, Attractions, Shopping, Tennis, Swimming,
Horseback riding, Birdwatching, **LANGUAGE** Eng.,
PRICE (2 persons) 69–120 **(check with hosts for pric-
ing details)**

GROS MORNE NATIONAL PARK
[WOODY POINT] *(west-central NFLD)*

Aunt Jane's Place B&B

(Jenny and Stan Parsons)

1 Water St, Woody Point, Gros Morne National Park,
NFLD, A0K 1P0
www.grosmorne.com/victorianmanor
E-mail vmanor.grosmorne@nf.sympatico.ca

709-453-2485
Fax 709-453-2485
TFr 1-866-453-2485

Aunt Jane's Place is rich in Newfoundland
history and culture. It is located on the
waterfront of scenic Woody Point, in Gros
Morne National Park. It is a great find for
the outdoor enthusiast! We offer our
guests the finest in Newfoundland hospitality! We offer five B&B rooms that simply
take you back to yesteryear! Nearby, kms
of hiking trails that allow you to explore
the natural wonders of Gros Morne. To
find us, take Rte 430 at Deer Lake, drive to
Wiltondale. From there take Rte 431 to
Woody Point.

ROOMS Upper floor, **Baths** Private, Shared with guest,
Beds Queen, Double, **In Room** Thermostat, **OTHERS**
Rural, Seasonal, **PAYMENT** Visa, MC, Direct debit, Cash,
Trvl's cheques, **BREAKFASTS** Continental, **AMENITIES**
Central TV, Central phone, Laundry, Fridge, **THINGS TO
DO** Trail nearby, Rental canoe or boat, Fishing, Theatre,
Attractions, Beach, **LANGUAGE** Eng., **PRICE** (2 per-
sons) 50–70 **(check with hosts for pricing details)**

GROS MORNE NATIONAL PARK
(ROCKY HARBOUR)

Wildflowers B&B

(Rod and Lerley Bryenton)

Main St N, Rocky Harbour, NFLD, A0K 4N0
www.wildflowerscountryinn.com
E-mail wildflowers@nf.aibn.com

709-458-3000
TFr 1-888-811-7378

Our *Canada Select* 4-star rated 70-year-old home is surrounded by trees and wild-flowers overlooking the ocean, situated in the centre of Gros Morne National Park. Watch the sunset from our upstairs sitting room or from our wraparound porch. All rooms have queen or king beds, private bathrooms and cable TV. Full breakfast is included in the price of the room. Whole house smoke-free. Boat tours nearby. Restaurants a few minutes away.

ROOMS Upper floor, Ground floor, Private entrance, **Baths** Private, Ensuite, **Beds** King, Queen, **Smoking** Outside, **In Room** Thermostat, TV, **OTHERS** Open all year, **PAYMENT** Visa, MC, Cash, Trvl's cheques, **BREAKFASTS** Full, Home-baked, **AMENITIES** Central phone, Fridge, Lounge, Patio, Central Internet access, **THINGS TO DO** Trail nearby, Fishing, Theatre, Entertainment, Attractions, Cross-country skiing, Swimming, **LANGUAGE** Eng., **PRICE** (2 persons) 89–119 **(check with hosts for pricing details)**

LABRADOR CITY
(southwestern Labrador)

Tamarack Bed & Breakfast

(Rose and Don Dinn)

852 Tamarack Dr, Labrador City, NFLD, A2V 2V6
http://home.crrstv.net/rdinn
E-mail rdinn@crrstv.net

709-944-6002
Fax 709-944-3090
TFr 1-866-944-6002

We provide clean, comfortable, spacious rooms at a quality price. We are located in a very quiet neighbourhood. We provide a guest lounge with TV, VCR/DVD and a large selection of books about Newfoundland and Labrador. Your home away from home. Come and taste our home-made jams made from local wild berries and experience Newfoundland hospitality at its best.

ROOMS Upper floor, **Baths** Private, Shared with guest, **Beds** Double, Twin, Single or cots, **Smoking** Outside, **In Room** Thermostat, **OTHERS** Open all year, Pets in residence, **PAYMENT** Visa, MC, Amex, Direct debit, Cash, Trvl's cheques, **BREAKFASTS** Continental, **AMENITIES** Central TV, Central phone, Barbecue, Central Internet access, Central VCR/DVD, **THINGS TO DO** Trail nearby, Golf, Fishing, Shopping, Cross-country skiing, Swimming, **LANGUAGE** Eng., **PRICE** (2 persons) 40–55 **(check with hosts for pricing details)**

PORT BLANDFORD *(eastern NFLD)*

Terra Nova
(Rhoda Parsons)

Box 111, Port Blandford, NFLD, A0C 2G0
www.terranova.nfld.net
E-mail terranovahosp@nf.aibn.com

709-543-2260
Fax 709-543-2241
TFr 1-888-267-2333

Located on the Trans-Canada Hwy in the Town of Port Blandford, Newfoundland and Labrador, in beautiful Bonavista Bay, we are proud to offer something special for absolutely everybody, no matter what your needs may be. From private cottages with all the amenities of home, to conference facilities, winter and summer outdoor adventure and recreational activities and even weddings and family reunions. Let's not forget the relaxation in our beautiful, peaceful surroundings!

ROOMS Family suite, Upper floor, Ground floor, Private entrance, **Baths** Ensuite, **Beds** Double, **Air** Ceiling fans, **Smoking** Outside, **In Room** TV, **OTHERS** Rural, Open all year, Additional meals, **PAYMENT** Visa, MC, Diners, Amex, Direct debit, Cheques accepted, Cash, Trvl's cheques, **BREAKFASTS** Full, Home-baked, **AMENITIES** Central TV, Central phone, Barbecue, Laundry, Kitchen, Fridge, Hot bev. bar, Lounge, Patio, Central Internet access, Central VCR/DVD, **THINGS TO DO** Trail nearby, Rental canoe or boat, Golf, Fishing, Art, Theatre, Attractions, Wineries/Breweries, Shopping, Cross-country skiing, Downhill skiing, Tennis, Swimming, Beach, Birdwatching, **LANGUAGE** Eng., **PRICE** (2 persons) 55–125 **(check with hosts for pricing details)**

SOUTH BRANCH *(southwestern NFLD)*

Granada House
(Marcel and Julianne Muise)

General Delivery, South Branch, NFLD, A0N 2B0
www.canadianbandbguide.ca/bb.asp?ID=3053
E-mail granadahouse@nf.sympatico.ca

709-955-3334

A modern two-storey home in a beautiful rural area. Very quiet area on the Trans-Canada Hwy Rte 1, 35 miles from Port Aux Basques Ferry Terminal. Situated on a good salmon river in season, and guides are available. Hiking trails nearby, as well as canoe and boat rentals. Close to an internationally recognized wetlands area with a great variety of waterfowl in season. Other points of interest within driving distance are Grand Codroy Wildlife Museum and Cape Anquille Lighthouse.

ROOMS Upper floor, **Baths** Ensuite, Shared with guest, **Beds** Queen, Double, Single or cots, Pullout sofa, **Smoking** Outside, **In Room** TV, **OTHERS** Rural, Open all year, **PAYMENT** Cash, Trvl's cheques, **BREAKFASTS** Continental, **AMENITIES** Central TV, Central phone, Whirlpool, Laundry, Kitchen, Lounge, Patio, **THINGS TO DO** Trail nearby, Rental canoe or boat, Golf, Fishing, Horseback riding, **LANGUAGE** Eng., **PRICE** (2 persons) 50–70 **(check with hosts for pricing details)**

St. John's *(eastern NFLD)*

Angel House Heritage Inn
(Patricia Pin and Russell Floren)

146 Hamilton Ave, St. John's, NFLD, A1E 1J3
www.angelhousebb.com
E-mail info@heritageislands.com

709-739-4223
Fax 709-576-3367
TFr 1-866-719-4223

Angel House Heritage Inn was built in
1879 for the Angel family of St. John's.
Today, the Inn is managed by Heritage
Islands Inc., a company committed to
antiquities, history and storytelling. The Inn
is set back from the road on an acre of
beautifully landscaped grounds, with a formal garden, extensive lawns, herb and vegetable gardens, stone retaining walls,
mature trees and flowering shrubs. All four
ensuite guest rooms have all of the modern day amenities of a 5-star hotel, yet with
the privacy and comfort befitting a country home within the heart of St. John's.

ROOMS Upper floor, **Baths** Ensuite, **Beds** Queen,
Single or cots, **In Room** Thermostat, Phone, TV,
Fireplace, Internet access, VCR/DVD, **OTHERS** Open all
year, **PAYMENT** Visa, MC, Diners, Amex, Cash, Trvl's
cheques, **BREAKFASTS** Full, **AMENITIES** Central TV,
Central phone, Whirlpool, Laundry, Kitchen, Lounge,
Patio, Central Internet access, Central VCR/DVD,
THINGS TO DO Trail nearby, Golf, Fishing, Museums,
Art, Theatre, Entertainment, Attractions, Shopping,
Birdwatching, Antiquing, **LANGUAGE** Eng., Italian,
PRICE (2 persons) 89–299 **(check with hosts for pric-
ing details)**

St. John's

At Wit's Inn
(Tanya and Mike O'Neil)

3 Gower St, St. John's, NFLD, A1C 1M9
www.atwitsinn.ca
E-mail info@atwitsinn.ca

709-739-7420
TFr 1-877-739-7420

At Wit's Inn has been restored to preserve
its original features, fireplaces, hardwood
floors and tall ceilings. We are located in
the heart of downtown, only minutes'
walking to shops, restaurants, night-life,
historic sites and attractions. Our spacious
rooms have private bath, luxury beds
with down-filled duvets, colour TV/VCR
and working fireplaces. We also offer
homemade hot breakfast or continental
breakfast.

Baths Private, **Beds** Queen, Twin, **Air** In rooms, **In
Room** Thermostat, TV, Fireplace, **OTHERS** Urban, Open
all year, **PAYMENT** Visa, MC, Amex, Direct debit, Cash,
Trvl's cheques, **BREAKFASTS** Full, Continental, Home-
baked, Self-catered, **AMENITIES** Central phone, Fridge,
THINGS TO DO Rental bikes, Trail nearby, Rental canoe
or boat, Golf, Fishing, Museums, Art, Theatre,
Entertainment, Attractions, Wineries/Breweries,
Shopping, **LANGUAGE** Eng., **PRICE** (2 persons) 79–129
(check with hosts for pricing details)

St. John's

Bonne Esperance House Bed & Breakfast

(Regina Anthony)

20 Gower St, St. John's, NFLD, A1C 1N1
www.BonneEsperanceHouse.ca
E-mail Regina@BonneEsperanceHouse.ca

709-726-3835
Fax 709-739-0496
TFr 1-888-726-3835

Located in the heart of downtown St. John's, we are a collection of Victorian heritage houses built in the late 1890s, with a *Canada Select* 4-star rating. We offer a variety of furnished rooms and luxury suites, which include a traditional focus of antique furnishings with a modern flair, hardwood floors, 12-foot ceilings decorative mouldings and original stained glass.

ROOMS Family suite, Upper floor, Ground floor, Lower floor, Private entrance, **Baths** Private, Ensuite, **Beds** Queen, Double, Twin, Single or cots, Pullout sofa, **Smoking** Outside, **In Room** Phone, TV, Fireplace, Internet access, VCR/DVD, **OTHERS** Open all year, **PAYMENT** Visa, MC, Amex, Direct debit, Cash, Trvl's cheques, **BREAKFASTS** Full, Home-baked, **AMENITIES** Central TV, Central phone, Barbecue, Laundry, Kitchen, Fridge, Patio, Central Internet access, Central VCR/DVD, **THINGS TO DO** Rental bikes, Trail nearby, Golf, Museums, Art, Theatre, Entertainment, Attractions, Shopping, Antiquing, **LANGUAGE** Eng., **PRICE** (2 persons) 95–225 **(check with hosts for pricing details)**

St. John's

Compton House Heritage Inn

(Bob and Cindy Holden)

26 Waterford Bridge Rd, St. John's, NFLD, A1E 1C6
www3.nf.sympatico.ca/comptonhouse
E-mail comptonhouse@nf.sympatico.ca

709-739-5789
Fax 709-738-1770

Designated a heritage property, this elegant Victorian mansion is set in a large garden and has been beautifully restored and furnished with period furniture. Full homecooked breakfasts are elegantly served in the formal dining room. We offer beautifully appointed guest rooms, Jacuzzi suites and efficiency units. We are situated in a fine old residential neighbourhood a 15-minute walk or short bus ride from downtown. Hosts and staff are very knowledgeable about local history and welcome inquiries.

ROOMS Upper floor, Ground floor, Private entrance, **Baths** Private, Ensuite, **Beds** Queen, Double, Pullout sofa, **Air** In rooms, **Smoking** Outside, **In Room** Thermostat, Phone, TV, Fireplace, Internet access, VCR/DVD, **OTHERS** Urban, Adult, Open all year, **PAYMENT** Visa, MC, Diners, Amex, Cash, Trvl's cheques, **BREAKFASTS** Full, **AMENITIES** Whirlpool, Barbecue, Laundry, Fridge, Hot bev. bar, Lounge, Patio, Central Internet access, **THINGS TO DO** Trail nearby, Golf, Fishing, Museums, Art, Theatre, Entertainment, Attractions, Wineries/Breweries, Shopping, Cross-country skiing, Tennis, Swimming, **LANGUAGE** Eng., **PRICE** (2 persons) 69–199 **(check with hosts for pricing details)**

St. John's

Waterford Manor Heritage Inn

(David Badrudin)

185 Waterford Bridge Rd, St. John's, NFLD, A1E 1C7
www.waterfordmanor.com
E-mail info@waterfordmanor.nf.ca

709-754-4139
Fax 709-754-4155
TFr 1-888-488-4170

The Waterford Manor Heritage Inn provides an authentic example of a turn-of-the-century riverside mansion. Featuring three honeymoon suites and four tastefully decorated guest rooms, the accommodation is complimented by a gourmet breakfast as well as a 24-hour self-serve snack bar. Located minutes from downtown St. John's and walking distance of the City's Bowering Park, the Manor is a haven of elegance for any celebration, business meeting or corporate retreat. The Web site says it all; please take a tour.

ROOMS Upper floor, **Baths** Ensuite, **Beds** King, Queen, Double, Single or cots, **Air** In rooms, **Smoking** Outside, **In Room** Thermostat, Phone, TV, Fireplace, **OTHERS** Urban, Adult, Open all year, Handicapped access, Additional meals, **PAYMENT** Visa, MC, Diners, Amex, Direct debit, Cash, **BREAKFASTS** Full, Self-catered, **AMENITIES** Central phone, Whirlpool, Barbecue, Fridge, Hot bev. bar, Lounge, Patio, **THINGS TO DO** Trail nearby, Golf, Museums, Art, Theatre, Entertainment, Attractions, Shopping, **LANGUAGE** Eng., **PRICE** (2 persons) 95–215 **(check with hosts for pricing details)**

St. John's

Winterholme Heritage Inn

(Dick, Ruby and Lisa Cook)

79 Rennies Mill Rd, St. John's, NFLD, A1C 3R1
www.winterholme.com
E-mail info@winterholme.com

709-739-7979
Fax 709-753-9411
TFr 1-800-599-7829

Winterholme is an outstanding example of Queen Anne-revival-style architecture, centrally located in the city's Heritage District. Influenced by British and American models, Winterholme has eclectic historical motifs, picturesque design and distinctive windows. Built in 1905–1907, Winterholme has a splendid opulent interior, featuring decorative plaster and elaborate woodwork. The house is a key landmark in this historic district.

ROOMS Family suite, Upper floor, Ground floor, **Baths** Ensuite, **Beds** King, Queen, **Smoking** Outside, **In Room** Phone, TV, Fireplace, Internet access, VCR/DVD, **OTHERS** Open all year, **PAYMENT** Visa, MC, Diners, Amex, Direct debit, Cheques accepted, **BREAKFASTS** Full, **AMENITIES** Whirlpool, Laundry, Fridge, Patio, **THINGS TO DO** Trail nearby, Golf, Museums, Art, Theatre, Entertainment, Attractions, Wineries/Breweries, Shopping, Tennis, Swimming, Horseback riding, **LANGUAGE** Eng., **PRICE** (2 persons) 129–199 **(check with hosts for pricing details)**

TERRA NOVA NATIONAL PARK *(eastern NFLD)*

The Serendipity B and B & Cottage

(Elsie and Gerald Davis)

110 Main St, Port Blandford, NFLD, A0C 2G0
www.serendipitybandb.com
E-mail gdavis@nf.sympatico.ca

709-543-2555
Fax 709-543-2555

The Serendipity B and B & Cottage, "Where Lifelong Friendships are Formed," overlooking beautiful Clode Sound, is located on the Eastern Gateway to Terra Nova National Park off Rte 1. We are home to two scenic golf courses – 9-hole Eagle Creek and 18-hole Twin Rivers. Rate for the cottage is $110/night; for other rates, see below.

ROOMS Upper floor, Lower floor, **Baths** Ensuite, **Beds** **Air** In rooms, **Smoking** Outside, **In Room** Thermostat, TV, **OTHERS** Babysitting, Open all year, Handicapped access, **PAYMENT** Visa, MC, Amex, Direct debit, Cash, Trvl's cheques, **BREAKFASTS** Full, Continental, Home-baked, **AMENITIES** Central TV, Central phone, Barbecue, Laundry, Kitchen, Fridge, Hot bev. bar, Lounge, Patio, Central Internet access, Central VCR/DVD, **THINGS TO DO** Rental bikes, Rental canoe or boat, Golf, Fishing, Museums, Art, Theatre, Entertainment, Attractions, Shopping, Cross-country skiing, Downhill skiing, Swimming, Beach, **LANGUAGE** Eng., **PRICE** (2 persons) 60–110 **(check with hosts for pricing details)**

TRINITY *(eastern NFLD)*

Artisan Inn

(Tineke Gow)

High St, Trinity, NFLD, A0C 2S0
www.trinityvacations.com
E-mail tgow@trinityvacations.com

709-464-3377
TFr 1-877-464-7700

Escape from the city to a quiet, historic coastal village. With breathtaking views of the sea all around, this peaceful setting provides a tranquil contrast to everyday routine. Relax, breathe the fresh air, stroll the hills and meadows or explore the town ... the choice is yours. Take the Trans-Canada Hwy to Clarenville. Turn onto Rte 230A, Discovery Trail, direction Bonavista and drive for approximately 70 km. Take Rte 239 to Trinity.

ROOMS Family suite, Upper floor, Ground floor, Private entrance, **Baths** Ensuite, **Beds** Queen, Single or cots, Pullout sofa, **Air** In rooms, **Smoking** Outside, **In Room** Thermostat, Phone, TV, Internet access, VCR/DVD, **OTHERS** Rural, Handicapped access, Seasonal, Additional meals, **PAYMENT** Visa, MC, Diners, Amex, Direct debit, Cash, Trvl's cheques, **BREAKFASTS** Full, **AMENITIES** Barbecue, Laundry, Kitchen, Lounge, Patio, **THINGS TO DO** Trail nearby, Golf, Museums, Art, Theatre, Entertainment, Shopping, Birdwatching, **LANGUAGE** Eng., Dutch, **PRICE** (2 persons) 115–135 **(check with hosts for pricing details)**

FRENCH LISTINGS

Canadian Bed and Breakfast Guide

CALGARY *(sud de l'Alberta)*

A B&B at Calgary Lions Park

(Dori Wood)

1331-15 St NW, Calgary, AB, T2N 2B7
www.lionsparkbb.com
Adresse électronique info@lionsparkbb.com

403-282-2728
No de téléc. 403-289-3485
No d'appel sans frais 1-800-475-7262

Centre de Calgary-1911, résidence ancestrale
de la 1re bibliothécaire en chef de Calgary. Près
du centre-ville, Université de Calgary. Cinq minutes à pied de: Institut de technologie du Sud
de l'Alberta, Auditorium Jubilee, Alberta
College of Art & Design. Quartier Kensington,
20 minutes de l'aéroport. Deux rues au sud de
la route transcanadienne. Petits déjeuners
nutritifs. Voyageurs d'affaires ou d'agrément,
relaxez et conversez avec des visiteurs du
monde entier. Spa thérapeutique/piscine d'eau
salée.

CHAMBRES Suite familiale, Étage supérieur, Entrée
privée, **Salles de bains** Privée, Chambres communi-
cantes, **Lits** Très grand lit, Grand lit, Lits jumeaux,
Climatisation Climatiseur central, Dans les chambres,
Dans la chambre Téléphone, TV, Accès Internet,
AUTRES Urbain, Toutes saisons, **PAIEMENT** Visa, MC,
Amex, Débit électronique, En espèces, Chèques de
voyage, **PETITS DÉJEUNERS** Complet, Fait à la maison,
COMMODITÉS TV centrale, Téléphone central, Piscine,
Blanchisserie, Réfrigérateur, Service de boissons
chaudes, Salon pour invités, Patio pour invités, Accès
Internet central, Magnétoscope central, **CHOSES À
FAIRE** Bicyclettes à titre gracieux, Location de bicy-
clettes, Sentier à proximité, Golf, Pêche, Musées,
Galeries d'art, Théâtre, Divertissement, Attractions,
Vineries/Brasseries, Magasinage, Ski de fond, Tennis,
Natation, Équitation, Antiquités, **LANGUES** Ang., Fr.,
PRIX (2 personnes) 85–150 **(vérifiez avec les hôtes les
details des prix)**

CALGARY

Calgary Westways
Guest House

(Jonathon Lloyd et Graham McKay)

216 - 25 Ave SW, Calgary, AB, T2S 0L1
www.westways.ab.ca
Adresse électronique calgary@westways.ab.ca

403-229-1758
No d'appel sans frais 1-866-846-7038

Maison historique artisanale de 1912 au caractère anglais. Soyez détendu, confortable, et
naturel, disent Jonathon et Graham. Située
dans le district Mission (votée la communauté
idéale de Calgary). Le centre-ville n'est qu'à 20
minutes de marche et le Stampede de Calgary
à 10 minutes. Le seul gîte trois diamond
CAA/AAA de Calgary. Venez profiter de notre
expérience de Calgary, de notre hospitalité, de
nos petits déjeuners consistants, préparés par
votre hôte/chef primé Jonathon. *Canada Select*
4 étoiles. Merci.

CHAMBRES Étage supérieur, **Salles de bains**
Chambres communicantes, **Lits** Très grand lit, Grand
lit, Lits à une place ou lits pliants, **Climatisation**
Climatiseur central, Dans les chambres, Ventilateurs
de plafond, **Fumeurs** À l'extérieur, **Dans la chambre**
Thermostat, Téléphone, TV, Foyer, Accès Internet,
Magnétoscope, **AUTRES** Urbain, Adulte, Animaux de
compagnie à l'intérieur, Animaux de compagnie
acceptés, **PAIEMENT** Visa, MC, Amex, Débit électron-
ique, En espèces, Chèques de voyage, **PETITS
DÉJEUNERS** Complet, **COMMODITÉS** TV centrale,
Téléphone central, Bain tourbillon, Blanchisserie,
Réfrigérateur, Service de boissons chaudes, Salon
pour invités, Patio pour invités, Accès Internet central,
Magnétoscope central, **CHOSES À FAIRE** Bicyclettes à
titre gracieux, Sentier à proximité, Golf, Pêche, Musées,
Galeries d'art, Théâtre, Divertissement, Attractions,
Magasinage, Ski de fond, Tennis, Natation,
Observation d'oiseaux, Antiquités, **LANGUES** Ang.,
PRIX (2 personnes) 69–149 **(vérifiez avec les hôtes les
details des prix)**

CANMORE *(à l'ouest de Calgary)*

Avens ReNaissance B&B

(Marie-Joëlle Driard)

252 Lady MacDonald Dr, Canmore, AB, T1W 1H8
www.bbcanmore.com/renaissance
Adresse électronique renaisbb@telusplanet.net

403-678-1875
No de téléc. 403-678-1875

Près de Banff et autres parcs nationaux et provinciaux. Charmante maison nichée aux pieds des superbes rocheuses canadiennes. Coin résidentiel ensoleilé et paisible à côté des sentiers du ruisseau/gorge Cougar. La suite luxueuse séduira vos âmes et volera vos coeurs. Entrée privée au niveau du sol, côté jardin. Déjeuner délicieux et sains. Originaire du Québec, l'hôtesse est artiste et instructrice de ski/telemark. Profitez d'un service exclusif. Sans taxes. Allez, vous le méritez bien!

CHAMBRES Suite familiale, Rez-de-chaussée, Entrée privée, **Salles de bains** Chambres communicantes, **Lits** Grand lit, Divan-lit, **Climatisation** Climatiseur central, **Fumeurs** À l'extérieur, **Dans la chambre** TV, Foyer, Accès Internet, Magnétoscope, **AUTRES** Gardiennage d'enfants, Rural, Toutes saisons, Repas additionnels, **PAIEMENT** Chèques acceptés, En espèces, Chèques de voyage, **PETITS DÉJEUNERS** Complet, Fait à la maison, **COMMODITÉS** Téléphone central, Barbeque, Blanchisserie, Réfrigérateur, Patio pour invités, **CHOSES À FAIRE** Location de bicyclettes, Sentier à proximité, Golf, Pêche, Musées, Galeries d'art, Théâtre, Divertissement, Attractions, Vineries/Brasseries, Magasinage, Ski de fond, Ski alpin, Tennis, Natation, Équitation, Plage, Observation d'oiseaux, Antiquités, **LANGUES** Ang., Fr., **PRIX** (2 personnes) 150–170 **(vérifiez avec les hôtes les details des prix)**

BANFF/CANMORE *(à l'ouest de Calgary)*

Creekside Country Inn

(Kirsty Hughes et Jen Racicot)

709 Benchlands Tr, Canmore, AB, T1W 3G9
www.creeksidecountryinn.com
Adresse électronique info@creeksidecountryinn.com

403-609-5522
No de téléc. 403-609-5599
No d'appel sans frais 1-866-609-5522

Creekside Country Inn de Canmore, Alberta, est une magnifique auberge-gîte à 12 chambres nichée dans le quartier Eagle Terrace. Loin de la voie ferrée et de l'autoroute, auberge pittoresque avec charpente en bois et ardoise, dans un décor montagneux. Idéale pour les voyageurs individuels, réunions de famille, mariages, conférences ou réunions privées. Peut héberger de 2 à 46 personnes pour la nuit et jusqu'à 85 pour un repas servi par des traiteurs dans notre salle Sunview. Visitez notre site Web!

CHAMBRES Suite familiale, Étage supérieur, Rez-de-chaussée, Sous-sol, **Salles de bains** Privée, **Lits** Très grand lit, Grand lit, Divan-lit, **Climatisation** Dans les chambres, Ventilateurs de plafond, **AUTRES** Gardiennage d'enfants, Urbain, Toutes saisons, Animaux de compagnie acceptés, **PAIEMENT** Visa, MC, Amex, En espèces, Chèques de voyage, **PETITS DÉJEUNERS** Continental, Fait à la maison, **COMMODITÉS** TV centrale, Téléphone central, Sauna, Barbeque, Cuisine disponible, Réfrigérateur, Service de boissons chaudes, Salon pour invités, Patio pour invités, Accès Internet central, Magnétoscope central, **CHOSES À FAIRE** Location de bicyclettes, Golf, Pêche, Musées, Galeries d'art, Divertissement, Attractions, Vineries/Brasseries, Magasinage, Ski de fond, Ski alpin, Natation, Équitation, Observation d'oiseaux, Antiquités, **LANGUES** Ang., Fr., **PRIX** (2 personnes) 89–199 **(vérifiez avec les hôtes les details des prix)**

KAMLOOPS *(centre-sud de la C-B)*

Sunshine Mountain Bed and Breakfast

(Carlos et Danielle Alburquenque)

1417 Sunshine Crt, Kamloops, C-B, V2E 2M3
www.sunshinemountainbnb.ca
Adresse électronique bookasuite@sunshinemountainbnb.ca

250-377-0713

Venez relaxer dans notre grande suite exclusive à 2 chambres à coucher. Un grand lit et un lit 2 places vous attendent parés de fine literie. Cette suite de 1200 pi2 inclut climatisation, entrée privée, cuisine avec frigo et four à micro-ondes, salon avec TV, VCR, téléphone, et salle de bain luxueuse avec grand bain à jets. À quelques minutes des centre d'information, centre commercial, théâtres, terrains de golf et restaurants. Massothérapeute disponible. Copieux petit déjeuner continental inclus.

CHAMBRES Suite familiale, Sous-sol, Entrée privée, **Salles de bains** Privée, **Lits** Grand lit, Lit à 2 places, Divan-lit, **Climatisation** Climatiseur central, **Dans la chambre** Téléphone, TV, Magnétoscope, **AUTRES** Urbain, Toutes saisons, Animaux de compagnie à l'intérieur, **PAIEMENT** Visa, Amex, En espèces, Chèques de voyage, **PETITS DÉJEUNERS** Continental, **COMMODITÉS** TV centrale, Téléphone central, Bain tourbillon, Cuisine disponible, Réfrigérateur, Patio pour invités, Magnétoscope central, **CHOSES À FAIRE** Sentier à proximité, Golf, Théâtre, Magasinage, Tennis, **LANGUES** Ang., Esp., **PRIX** (2 personnes) 75–140 **(vérifiez avec les hôtes les details des prix)**

KELOWNA *(centre-sud de la C-B)*

A View To Remember B&B

(Sue and Dann Willis)

1090 Trevor Dr, Kelowna, C-B, V1Z 2J8
www.KelownaBandB.com
Adresse électronique Info@KelownaBandB.com

250-769-4028
No de téléc. 250-769-6168
No d'appel sans frais 1-888-311-9555

Établi en 1982, gîte touristique original de Kelowna. Situé à Lakeview Heights parmi les vineries du côté ouest de Kelowna, vue panoramique du lac Okanagan, des montagnes, des vergers de pommiers et des vignobles exubérantes. Nos suites très spacieuses, magnifiquement décorées, avec grand lit et entrée privée, assurent non seulement un séjour reposant aux voyageurs, mais les commodités et le confort de la maison à ceux qui désirent séjourner et passer leur vacance au cœur de la vallée de l'Okanagan.

CHAMBRES Rez-de-chaussée, Entrée privée, **Salles de bains** Chambres communicantes, **Lits** Grand lit, Divan-lit, **Climatisation** Climatiseur central, **Fumeurs** À l'extérieur, **Dans la chambre** TV, Foyer, Accès Internet, Magnétoscope, **AUTRES** Rural, Toutes saisons, Animaux de compagnie à l'intérieur, Animaux de compagnie acceptés, **PAIEMENT** Visa, MC, Diners, Amex, En espèces, Chèques de voyage, **PETITS DÉJEUNERS** Complet, Fait à la maison, **COMMODITÉS** Téléphone central, Réfrigérateur, Service de boissons chaudes, Patio pour invités, **CHOSES À FAIRE** Location de bicyclettes, Sentier à proximité, Location de canoë ou de bateau, Golf, Pêche, Musées, Galeries d'art, Théâtre, Divertissement, Attractions, Vineries/Brasseries, Magasinage, Ski de fond, Ski alpin, Tennis, Natation, Équitation, Plage, Observation d'oiseaux, **LANGUES** Ang., **PRIX** (2 personnes) 89–110 **(vérifiez avec les hôtes les details des prix)**

CHEMAINUS *(au nord de Victoria)*

Ladysmith Bed and Breakfast
(Celeste Bonnet)

515 Louise Rd, Ladysmith, C-B, V9G 1W7
www.LadysmithBandB.com
Adresse électronique Book@LadysmithBandB.com

250-245-0633
No d'appel sans frais 1-866-568-4060

Composez le 1-866-568-4060 pour réserver
votre place à notre nouvelle maison avec vue
de l'océan. Vue fantastique de l'océan/la forêt,
délicieux petit déjeuner continental, chambres
de luxe avec salles de bains privées. Nous
accueillons les groupes; familles; grands-par-
ents; couples Ceux qui aiment la solitude, le
confort et la beauté. Juste 10 minutes de
Chemainus ou du lieu historique Ladysmith au
centre-ville, l'autoroute Island jusqu'au chemin
Davis, puis le chemin Louise. (Petits enfants à la
maison.)

CHAMBRES Suite familiale, Étage supérieur, Rez-de-
chaussée, Entrée privée, **Salles de bains** Privée,
Partagée avec un client, **Lits** Grand lit, Lits à une place
ou lits pliants, **Climatisation** Ventilateurs de plafond,
Fumeurs À l'extérieur, **Dans la chambre** TV, **AUTRES**
Gardiennage d'enfants, Urbain, Adulte, Toutes saisons,
Animaux de compagnie à l'intérieur, **PAIEMENT** Visa,
MC, En espèces, Chèques de voyage, **PETITS
DÉJEUNERS** Continental, Fait à la maison,
COMMODITÉS Téléphone central, Réfrigérateur,
Service de boissons chaudes, Salon pour invités, Patio
pour invités, Accès Internet central, **CHOSES À FAIRE**
Sentier à proximité, Location de canoë ou de bateau,
Golf, Pêche, Musées, Galeries d'art, Théâtre,
Divertissement, Attractions, Vineries/ Brasseries,
Magasinage, Tennis, Natation, Équitation, Plage,
Observation d'oiseaux, Antiquités, **LANGUES** Ang.,
PRIX (2 personnes) 95 **(vérifiez avec les hôtes les
details des prix)**

WEST VANCOUVER *(au nord de Vancouver)*

The Tree House
Bed & Breakfast
(Penny Nelson-Abbott et Neville Abbott)

125 Sunset Dr, Lions Bay, C-B, V0N 2E0
www.thetreehousebnb.com
Adresse électronique stay@thetreehousebnb.com

604-921-5991
No de téléc. 604-922-5290

En pleine forêt, vue spectaculaire de l'océan.
The Tree House est idéal pour les évasions esti-
vales ou hivernales. Activités extérieures
proches (golf et randonnées) en été, ski/con-
duite sur les pentes des Jeux Olympiques 2010
à Montagnes Cypress et Whistler en hiver, ou
venez vous détendre. 15 minutes de la gare
maritime Horseshoe Bay, 25 minutes du centre-
ville de Vancouver et 1 heure de Whistler. Sortie
Lions Bay de l'autoroute Sea to Sky (Autoroute
99) jusqu'à Sunset Dr. Visiter le site Web pour
les détails.

CHAMBRES Étage supérieur, **Salles de bains**
Chambres communicantes, **Lits** Grand lit, Lits
jumeaux, **Dans la chambre** Thermostat, TV, Accès
Internet, Magnétoscope, **AUTRES** Rural, Toutes
saisons, Repas additionnels, Animaux de compagnie à
l'intérieur, **PAIEMENT** Visa, MC, Débit électronique, En
espèces, Chèques de voyage, **PETITS DÉJEUNERS** Fait
à la maison, **COMMODITÉS** TV centrale, Téléphone
central, Bain tourbillon, Barbeque, Réfrigérateur,
Service de boissons chaudes, Salon pour invités, Patio
pour invités, Accès Internet central, Magnétoscope
central, **CHOSES À FAIRE** Location de bicyclettes,
Sentier à proximité, Location de canoë ou de bateau,
Golf, Pêche, Musées, Galeries d'art, Théâtre,
Attractions, Ski de fond, Ski alpin, Natation, Équitation,
Plage, Observation d'oiseaux, **LANGUES** Ang., **PRIX** (2
personnes) 135–165 **(vérifiez avec les hôtes les
details des prix)**

SIDNEY *(au nord de Victoria)*

Honeysuckle Cottage Bed & Breakfast

(Andrew Truman et Brenda LaPrairie)

1030 Clayton Rd, North Saanich, C-B, V8L 5P6
www.honeysucklecottagebb.com
Adresse électronique honeysuckle_cottage@shaw.ca

250-655-6474

Chalet de 650 pi2, éclairé, et en retrait sur un domaine tranquille à la campagne. Idéal pour vacances romantiques ou familiales. Cuve thermale à ozonateur utilisable à l'année dans un pavillon fermé. Chambre à coucher avec duvets et robes de chambre confortables, salle de bain et salon séparé avec foyer à gaz, TV et DVD. Coin repas séparé, cuisine complète, buanderie et terrasse privée avec barbeque. Accès Internet haute vitesse et appel locaux gratuits. Thé et café gratuits. Usage du tabac non permis.

CHAMBRES Suite familiale, Rez-de-chaussée, Entrée privée, **Salles de bains** Privée, Chambres communicantes, **Lits** Grand lit, Lits à une place ou lits pliants, Divan-lit, **Climatisation** Dans les chambres, **Fumeurs** À l'extérieur, **Dans la chambre** Thermostat, Téléphone, TV, Foyer, Accès Internet, Magnétoscope, **AUTRES** Rural, Toutes saisons, Accessible aux personnes handicapées, **PAIEMENT** Chèques acceptés, En espèces, Chèques de voyage, **PETITS DÉJEUNERS** Continental, Fait à la maison, Préparé soi-même, **COMMODITÉS** TV centrale, Téléphone central, Bain tourbillon, Barbeque, Blanchisserie, Cuisine disponible, Réfrigérateur, Patio pour invités, Accès Internet central, Magnétoscope central, **CHOSES À FAIRE** Location de bicyclettes, Sentier à proximité, Location de canoë ou de bateau, Golf, Pêche, Musées, Galeries d'art, Théâtre, Divertissement, Attractions, Vineries/Brasseries, Magasinage, Ski de fond, Ski alpin, Tennis, Natation, Équitation, Plage, Observation d'oiseaux, Antiquités, **LANGUES** Ang., **PRIX** (2 personnes) 100–140 (**vérifiez avec les hôtes les details des prix)**

WHITE ROCK

The Daly Bed and Bread Guest House

(Susan et John Howard)

13152 Marine Dr, Surrey, C-B, V4A 1E7
www.dalybedandbread.com
Adresse électronique reservations@dalybedand bread.com

604-531-2531 No de téléc. 604-531-2531
No d'appel sans frais 1-877-523-1399

Suites avec balcons et entrées privées, vue fantastique de l'océan et des montagnes. Frigo/micro-ondes, pour préparer le thé/café, téléphone, alarme de sécurité, accès Internet haute vitesse et TV par satellite, convient aux séjours prolongés. Petits déjeuners servis dans notre salle à manger avec vue de l'océan. Près de : autoroutes, frontière des É-U, Vancouver, aéroports. À quelques minutes de : plage White Rock, quai/promenade, plage Crescent et Blackie's Spit's World Heritage Wildlife Site.

CHAMBRES Suite familiale, Rez-de-chaussée, Sous-sol, Entrée privée, **Salles de bains** Privée, Chambres communicantes, **Lits** Grand lit, Lits à une place ou lits pliants, Divan-lit, **Climatisation** Ventilateurs de plafond, **Fumeurs** À l'extérieur, **Dans la chambre** Thermostat, Téléphone, TV, Foyer, Accès Internet, Magnétoscope, **AUTRES** Urbain, Toutes saisons, Repas additionnels, Animaux de compagnie acceptés, **PAIEMENT** Visa, MC, Diners, Amex, Chèques acceptés, En espèces, Chèques de voyage, **PETITS DÉJEUNERS** Complet, Continental, Fait à la maison, Préparé soi-même, **COMMODITÉS** Barbeque, Blanchisserie, Cuisine disponible, Réfrigérateur, Service de boissons chaudes, Salon pour invités, Patio pour invités, **CHOSES À FAIRE** Bicyclettes à titre gracieux, Sentier à proximité, Location de canoë ou de bateau, Golf, Pêche, Musées, Galeries d'art, Théâtre, Divertissement, Attractions, Vineries/Brasseries, Magasinage, Tennis, Natation, Équitation, Plage, Observation d'oiseaux, Antiquités, **LANGUES** Ang., Fr., All., **PRIX** (2 personnes) 90–150 (**vérifiez avec les hôtes les details des prix)**

Tofino *(centre-ouest de l'Île de Vancouver)*

Seafarers B&B

(Siegrun Meszaros [Ziggy])

1212 Lynn Rd, Tofino, C-B, V0R 2Z0
www.seafarersbb.com
Adresse électronique seafarer@island.net

250-725-1267
No de téléc. 250-725-1268

Le Seafarers B&B est classé 4 1/2 étoiles par
Canada Select. Situé à la magnifique plage
Chesterman, niché entre de grands conifères.
L'océan Pacifique est à 250 pieds de distance.
Nous avons 2 grandes chambres avec coin
salon, foyer, TV, magnétoscope, salle de bain
privée avec baignoire à remous. La chambre
Portside dispose d'un très grand lit et la cham-
bre Santa Fe d'un grand lit deux places et un lit
simple. Petit déjeuner complet. Cuve thermale.
Enfants plus âgés bienvenus. Visa, MC, Amex
acceptés.

CHAMBRES Suite familiale, Étage supérieur, **Salles de
bains** Privée, **Lits** Très grand lit, Grand lit, Lits à une
place ou lits pliants, **Fumeurs** À l'extérieur, **Dans la
chambre** Thermostat, TV, **AUTRES** Toutes saisons,
Animaux de compagnie acceptés, **PAIEMENT** Visa,
MC, Amex, En espèces, Chèques de voyage, **PETITS
DÉJEUNERS** Complet, Fait à la maison, Préparé soi-
même, **COMMODITÉS** TV centrale, Bain tourbillon,
Blanchisserie, Cuisine disponible, Réfrigérateur,
Service de boissons chaudes, Salon pour invités, Patio
pour invités, **CHOSES À FAIRE** Location de bicyclettes,
Sentier à proximité, Golf, Pêche, Galeries d'art,
Magasinage, Plage, **LANGUES** Ang., All., Hungarian,
PRIX (2 personnes) 140–160 **(vérifiez avec les hôtes
les détails des prix)**

Tofino

Solwood

(Janine Wood)

1298 Lynn Rd, Box 468, Tofino, C-B, V0R 2Z0
www.solwood.ca
Adresse électronique solwood@island.net

250-725-2112
No d'appel sans frais 1-866-725-2112

Maison unique de la côte Ouest nichée dans
nos arboretums de Chesterman Beach. Restez
à la maison principale et savourez un délicieux
petit déjeuner complet préparé pour vous et
les vôtres. Ou louez l'un de nos chalets confortables et préparez vos repas dans votre propre
cuisinette. Profitez de notre éventail de traite-
ments de spas thérapeutiques, nos clients
bénéficient d'un escompte de 5%. Terminez la
journée avec une promenade sur la plage au
coucher du soleil à quelques minutes de
marche seulement.

CHAMBRES Suite familiale, Étage supérieur, Rez-de-
chaussée, Entrée privée, **Salles de bains** Privée,
Chambres communicantes, Partagée avec un client,
Lits Très grand lit, Grand lit, Lit à 2 places, Lits
jumeaux, Divan-lit, **Fumeurs** À l'extérieur, **Dans la
chambre** Thermostat, Foyer, **AUTRES** Gardiennage
d'enfants, Rural, Toutes saisons, Animaux de compagnie à l'intérieur, Animaux de compagnie acceptés,
PAIEMENT Visa, MC, Chèques acceptés, En espèces,
Chèques de voyage, **PETITS DÉJEUNERS** Complet,
Préparé soi-même, **COMMODITÉS** Téléphone central,
Cuisine disponible, Réfrigérateur, Salon pour invités,
Patio pour invités, **CHOSES À FAIRE** Sentier à proximité, Golf, Pêche, Galeries d'art, Attractions, Magasinage,
Tennis, Natation, Plage, **LANGUES** Ang., Esp., **PRIX** (2
personnes) 85–225 **(vérifiez avec les hôtes les détails
des prix)**

TOFINO

Summerhill Guest House

(Melody Sadler)

Box 512, 1101 Fellowship Dr, Tofino, C-B, V0R 2Z0
www.alberni.net/summerhill
Adresse électronique summerhill@alberni.net

250-725-2447
No de téléc. 250-725-2447

Vos hôtes accueillants offrent un logement privé et confortable dans le décor serein d'une vieille forêt dense. Près des plages sablonneuses de l'océan Pacifique et de la ville de Tofino. Suites autonomes avec cuisinette privée pour les familles et couples désirant explorer le parc national Pacific Rim. Les deux suites incluent entrée privée, salle de bains et insonorisation. Activités locales: randonnées pédestres, observation de baleines, ours et oiseaux, surf, sources thermales, kayak et plongée.

CHAMBRES Suite familiale, Rez-de-chaussée, Entrée privée, **Salles de bains** Privée, Chambres communicantes, **Lits** Grand lit, Lit à 2 places, Lits jumeaux, Lits à une place ou lits pliants, Divan-lit, **Dans la chambre** Thermostat, Téléphone, TV, Magnétoscope, **AUTRES** Rural, Toutes saisons, **PAIEMENT** Chèques acceptés, En espèces, Chèques de voyage, **PETITS DÉJEUNERS** Continental, Fait à la maison, Préparé soi-même, **COMMODITÉS** Cuisine disponible, Réfrigérateur, Service de boissons chaudes, Patio pour invités, **CHOSES À FAIRE** Location de bicyclettes, Sentier à proximité, Location de canoë ou de bateau, Golf, Pêche, Musées, Galeries d'art, Attractions, Magasinage, Tennis, Natation, Plage, Observation d'oiseaux, **LANGUES** Ang., **PRIX** (2 personnes) 90–120 **(vérifiez avec les hôtes les details des prix)**

VANCOUVER *(sud-ouest de la C-B)*

AnnSarah Camilla House Bed and Breakfast

(Sarah Ma)

2538 West 13th Ave, Vancouver, C-B, V6K 2T1
www.vancouver-bb.com
Adresse électronique info@vancouver-bb.com

604-737-2687
No de télé. 604-739-3328
No d'appel sans frais 1-866-563-0051

Bienvenue! Luxe et confort vous attendent au gîte touristique AnnSarah's Camilla House, situé sur une rue bordée d'arbres au cœur de Vancouver, C-B, Canada. Camilla House vous offre ce qu'il y a de mieux en fait d'hébergement. Nous mettons l'accent sur le confort, la propreté et la présentation. Une hospitalité chaude, amicale et une ambiance luxueuse vous attendent à ce gîte élégant et traditionnel de Vancouver situé tout près d'une foule de magasins, restaurants, plages et excursions touristiques.

CHAMBRES Suite familiale, Étage supérieur, Rez-de-chaussée, Sous-sol, **Salles de bains** Privée, Chambres communicantes, Partagée avec un client, **Lits** Très grand lit, Grand lit, Lit à 2 places, Lits jumeaux, **Dans la chambre** Thermostat, Téléphone, TV, Foyer, Accès Internet, **AUTRES** Toutes saisons, **PAIEMENT** Visa, MC, En espèces, Chèques de voyage, **PETITS DÉJEUNERS** Complet, **COMMODITÉS** TV centrale, Téléphone central, Barbeque, Blan-chisserie, Cuisine disponible, Réfrigérateur, Service de boissons chaudes, Salon pour invités, Accès Internet central, **CHOSES À FAIRE** Théâtre, Attractions, Magasinage, Plage, **LANGUES** Ang., Chinoix, **PRIX** (2 personnes) 65–155 **(vérifiez avec les hôtes les details des prix)**

VANCOUVER

Chocolate Lily

(Karen Erickson et Rob Grant)

1353 Maple St, Vancouver, C-B, V6J 3S1
www.chocolatelily.com
Adresse électronique choclily@telus.net

604-731-9363
No de tél. 604-731-9363

Élégantes suites autonomes avec terrasses privées. Excellent endroit près de Kitsilano Beach, Stanley Park, centre-ville, Granville Island, UBC et transport en commun. Cuisinettes complètes avec micro-ondes, frigo, bouilloire, cafetière, grille-pain et évier. Accès Internet haute vitesse sans fil, TV, stéréo. Salles de bains magnifiquement tuilées. Stationnement couvert privé. Tout près de plusieurs cafés, boulangeries et charcuteries de choix. Grands lits confortables. Excellent lieu d'hébergement.

CHAMBRES Entrée privée, **Salles de bains** Privée, **Lits** Grand lit, **Fumeurs** Dans les chambres, **Dans la chambre** Thermostat, Téléphone, TV, Foyer, Accès Internet, **AUTRES** Urbain, Toutes saisons, **PAIEMENT** Visa, MC, Chèques acceptés, En espèces, Chèques de voyage, **PETITS DÉJEUNERS** Préparé soi-même, **CHOSES À FAIRE** Location de bicyclettes, Sentier à proximité, Location de canoë ou de bateau, Musées, Galeries d'art, Théâtre, Divertissement, Attractions, Magasinage, Tennis, Natation, Plage, **LANGUES** Ang., **PRIX** (2 personnes) 95–165 **(vérifiez avec les hôtes les details des prix)**

VICTORIA *(sud de l'Île de Vancouver)*

Cougar's Crag Extreme B&B

(Steve Schweighofer et Michel Wagner)

1155 Woodley Ghyll Dr, Victoria, C-B, V9C 4H9
www.cougarscrag.com
Adresse électronique info@cougarscrag.com

250-478-8993
No de tél. 250-478-8993
No d'appel sans frais 1-888-808-2724

Le Crag est un pavillon d'art et d'artisanat aux logements à niveaux multiples remplis de commodités. Situé sur une butte entourée de 15 âcres de nature sauvage à 30 minutes du centre ville de Victoria. Près des plus jolis parcs de l'île de Vancouver, nous aimons les animaux favoris et pouvons rendre des services spéciaux à nos clients (tel que la cueillette au traversier). Nous hébergeons mariages, réceptions et retraites – parfait pour la lune de miel. Visitez notre site Web pour plus de détails.

CHAMBRES Suite familiale, Entrée privée, **Salles de bains** Privée, **Lits** Grand lit, Divan-lit, **Climatisation** Climatiseur central, **Fumeurs** À l'extérieur, **Dans la chambre** Thermostat, TV, Foyer, Magnétoscope, **AUTRES** Rural, Toutes saisons, Repas additionnels, Animaux de compagnie à l'intérieur, Animaux de compagnie acceptés, **PAIEMENT** Visa, MC, Chèques acceptés, En espèces, Chèques de voyage, **PETITS DÉJEUNERS** Complet, Continental, Fait à la maison, **COMMODITÉS** TV centrale, Barbeque, Blanchisserie, Cuisine disponible, Réfrigérateur, Patio pour invités, Accès Internet central, **CHOSES À FAIRE** Location de bicyclettes, Sentier à proximité, Location de canoë ou de bateau, Golf, Pêche, Musées, Galeries d'art, Attractions, Vineries/Brasseries, Natation, Équitation, Plage, Observation d'oiseaux, Antiquités, **LANGUES** Ang., Fr., **PRIX** (2 personnes) 160–300 **(vérifiez avec les hôtes les details des prix)**

Whit e Rock *(à l'est de Vancouver)*

"A Beach House B&B ... on the Beach ... Naturally!"

(Marke et June Barens)

15241 Marine Dr, White Rock, C-B, V4B 1C7
www.WhiteRockBedBreakfast.ca
Adresse électronique ABeachHouse@Telus.net

604-536-5200
No de téléc. 604-536-1948

Situé au bord de l'eau, vue incomparable. Vivre sur la côte ouest! Maison de plage, simple avec terrasses océaniques, toitures-terrasses, douches thermales, cuisine d'hôte. Retraite paisible, privée ou d'affaires. Lits de plume, lingerie fine, robes veloutées, 5 minutes de la frontière É-U/Canada, 30 minutes du centre-ville de Vancouver, 2 minutes des cafés, spas d'un jour, galeries d'art, artistes. Ramassez des coquillages à pieds nus dans le sable. Voté gîte d'hébergement #1 2004/2005. Conseillers de voyage.

CHAMBRES Suite familiale, Étage supérieur, Rez-de-chaussée, **Salles de bains** Chambres communicantes, Partagée avec un client, **Lits** Très grand lit, Grand lit, Lit à 2 places, Lits jumeaux, Divan-lit, **Climatisation Fumeurs** À l'extérieur, **Dans la chambre** Thermostat, TV, Foyer, Accès Internet, Magnétoscope, **AUTRES** Gardiennage d'enfants, Urbain, Adulte, Toutes saisons, Animaux de compagnie à l'intérieur, **PAIEMENT** Visa, MC, Amex, Débit électronique, En espèces, **PETITS DÉJEUNERS** Complet, Continental, Préparé soi-même, **COMMODITÉS** Téléphone central, Barbeque, Blanchisserie, Cuisine disponible, Réfrigérateur, Salon pour invités, Patio pour invités, Accès Internet central, **CHOSES À FAIRE** Sentier à proximité, Location de canoe ou de bateau, Golf, Pêche, Musées, Galeries d'art, Théâtre, Divertissement, Attractions, Vineries/Brasseries, Magasinage, Ski de fond, Ski alpin, Tennis, Natation, Équitation, Plage, Observation d'oiseaux, Antiquités, **LANGUES** Ang., **PRIX** (2 personnes) 75–150 **(vérifiez avec les hôtes les details des prix)**

Saint Pierre-Jolys *(au sud de Winnipeg)*

Château des Sages B&B

(Roger et Cecile Lesage)

327 Sabourin St N, Saint-Pierre-Jolys, MB, R0A 1V0
www.chateaudessages.ca
Adresse électronique info@chateaudessages.ca

204-433-3202
No de téléc. 204-433-7585
No d'appel sans frais 1-866-226-2770

Relaxez en toute intimité dans notre suite d'hôte autonome sise dans un décor rural paisible. Cuisine moderne complète, salle de bains avec bain jacuzzi, grand lit dans la chambre à coucher. Le salon a un foyer à gaz et le sofa s'ouvre en lit à 2 places. Tout ce qu'il faut pour préparer un copieux petit déjeuner que vous dégusterez à l'intérieur ou sur la terrasse privée est fourni. Une évasion parfaite à 30 milles au sud de Winnipeg, 9 milles du parc provincial St. Malo et de la plage.

CHAMBRES Suite familiale, Rez-de-chaussée, Entrée privée, **Salles de bains** Privée, **Lits** Grand lit, Divan-lit, **Climatisation** Dans les chambres, Ventilateurs de plafond, **Fumeurs** À l'extérieur, **Dans la chambre** Thermostat, TV, Foyer, Accès Internet, Magnétoscope, **AUTRES** Rural, Toutes saisons, Accessible aux personnes handicapées, **PAIEMENT** Visa, En espèces, Chèques de voyage, **PETITS DÉJEUNERS** Fait à la maison, Préparé soi-même, **COMMODITÉS** Téléphone central, Barbeque, Blanchisserie, Cuisine disponible, Réfrigérateur, Patio pour invités, Accès Internet central, **CHOSES À FAIRE** Bicyclettes à titre gracieux, Sentier à proximité, Location de canoë ou de bateau, Golf, Musées, Galeries d'art, Attractions, Magasinage, Ski de fond, Natation, Plage, Observation d'oiseaux, Antiquités, **LANGUES** Ang., Fr., **PRIX** (2 personnes) 75–75 **(vérifiez avec les hôtes les details des prix)**

SAINT-PIERRE-JOLYS

Gîte de Forest B&B

(Raymond et Nicole Lavergne)

512 ave Côté, Saint-Pierre-Jolys, MB, R0A 1V0
www.placelavergne.com
Adresse électronique nrl@placelavergne.com

204-433-7870
No de téléc. 204-433-7181
No d'appel sans frais 1-866-661-7870

Les hôtes, Raymond et Nicole, sont fiers de partager leurs racines acadienne et francophone. Le Gîte deForest offre un appartement avec sa salle de bain, un salon avec divan et téléviseur avec la chambre de la Rivière-aux-Rats et la chambre Saint-Pierre sud. La chambre Acadienne a aussi sa salle de bain. Le Gîte deForest est sisi au centre du village de Saint-Pierre-Jolys, 30 min. au sud de Winnipeg et 30 min au nord de la frontière américaine sur la route 59. Numero de téléphone alternative : 204-433-7758 et 204-746-4136.

CHAMBRES Suite familiale, Rez-de-chaussée, Sous-sol, **Salles de bains** Privée, **Lits** Grand lit, Lit à 2 places, Lits jumeaux, **Climatisation** Climatiseur central, **Fumeurs** À l'extérieur, **AUTRES** Rural, Toutes saisons, **PAIEMENT** Visa, MC, Débit électronique, En espèces, Chèques de voyage, **PETITS DÉJEUNERS** Fait à la maison, **COMMODITÉS** TV centrale, Cuisine disponible, Réfrigérateur, Salon pour invités, Patio pour invités, **CHOSES À FAIRE** Bicyclettes à titre gracieux, Sentier à proximité, Golf, Pêche, Musées, Galeries d'art, Magasinage, Ski de fond, Natation, Plage, Antiquités, **LANGUES** Ang., Fr., **PRIX** (2 personnes) 50–75 **(vérifiez avec les hôtes les details des prix)**

SELKIRK *(au nord de Winnipeg)*

Evergreen Gate
Bed and Breakfast

(Laurel et Rob Sarginson)

1138 River Rd, St. Andrews, MB, R1A 4A7
www.evergreengate.ca
Adresse électronique evergreengate@mts.net

204-482-6248
No d'appel sans frais 1-877-901-0553

Admirez la région interlac du Manitoba de notre maison unique, dans un parc 1/2 heure au nord de Winnipeg. Sur le sentier transcanadien en haut de la rivière Rouge, endroit idéal pour la marche, le vélo et observer les pélicans. À quelques minutes du lieu national historique Lower Fort Garry, du centre d'interprétation du marais Oak Hammock et des terrains de golf. Les plages de sable blanc du lac Winnipeg sont à 1/2 heur au nord. Véranda grillagée, chaise longue et kitchenette complètent les chambres d'hôte.

CHAMBRES Suite familiale, Sous-sol, **Salles de bains** Privée, Chambres communicantes, **Lits** Grand lit, Lit à 2 places, **Climatisation** Ventilateurs de plafond, **Fumeurs** À l'extérieur, **Dans la chambre** Thermostat, **AUTRES** Toutes saisons, **PAIEMENT** Visa, MC, Diners, Amex, Chèques acceptés, En espèces, **PETITS DÉJEUNERS** Complet, Continental, Fait à la maison, Préparé soi-même, **COMMODITÉS** TV centrale, Téléphone central, Bain tourbillon, Cuisine disponible, Réfrigérateur, Salon pour invités, Patio pour invités, Accès Internet central, Magnétoscope central, **CHOSES À FAIRE** Bicyclettes à titre gracieux, Sentier à proximité, Pêche, Musées, Galeries d'art, Attractions, Magasinage, Ski de fond, Natation, Équitation, Observation d'oiseaux, Antiquités, **LANGUES** Ang., Fr., **PRIX** (2 personnes) 60–90 **(vérifiez avec les hôtes les details des prix)**

Alma *(sud-est du N-B)*

Captain's Inn
(John et Elsie O'Regan)

8602 Main St, Alma, N-B, E4H 1N5
www.captainsinn.ca
Adresse électronique captinn@nb.sympatico.ca

506-887-2017
No de téléc. 506-887-2074

Situé dans le charmant port de pêche d'Alma à l'entrée du parc national Fundy de la baie du même nom. À quelques minutes de Cape Enrage, de la Réserve d'oiseaux de rivage de l'hémisphère occidental à Mary's Point et du site d'exploration Hopewell Rocks. Marchez 1 km dans l'océan à marée basse. Rte 114, Rte du littoral de Fundy. Deux salons et un solarium à l'usage exclusif de nos clients. Nous faisons tout pour que votre visite soit plaisante et reste gravée dans votre mémoire pour des années à venir.

CHAMBRES Étage supérieur, Rez-de-chaussée, **Salles de bains** Chambres communicantes, **Lits** Grand lit, **Fumeurs** À l'extérieur, **Dans la chambre** Thermostat, TV, Magnétoscope, **AUTRES** Rural, Toutes saisons, **PAIEMENT** Visa, MC, Débit électronique, En espèces, Chèques de voyage, **PETITS DÉJEUNERS** Complet, **COMMODITÉS** TV centrale, Téléphone central, Patio pour invités, **CHOSES À FAIRE** Sentier à proximité, Golf, Attractions, Magasinage, Ski de fond, Tennis, Natation, Plage, **LANGUES** Ang., **PRIX** (2 personnes) 92–105 **(vérifiez avec les hôtes les details des prix)**

Alma

Falcon Ridge Inn
(Peter et Donna Colpitts)

24 Falcon Ridge Dr, Alma, N-B, E4H 4Z3
www.falconridgeinn.nb.ca
Adresse électronique falcon@falconridgeinn.nb.ca

506-887-1110
No de téléc. 506-887-2376
No d'appel sans frais 1-888-321-9090

Érigé sur une colline à Alma, vue dégagée des marées hautes et basses de la baie de Fundy de partout dans l'auberge. Hébergement de luxe incluant tout le confort de la maison, chambres communicantes avec grand lit, foyer, bain tourbillon, mini-frigo, cafetière, téléphone, CATV/DVD/VCR. Inclut un petit déjeuner chaud complet servi dans notre salle à dîner de 24 pieds de hauteur. Le parc national Fundy, Hopewell Rocks, Cape Enrage, la route Fundy sont à proximité. Voir notre site Web pour les forfaits.

CHAMBRES Étage supérieur, Rez-de-chaussée, **Salles de bains** Chambres communicantes, **Lits** Grand lit, Lits à une place ou lits pliants, Divan-lit, **Fumeurs** À l'extérieur, **Dans la chambre** Thermostat, Téléphone, TV, Foyer, Magnétoscope, **AUTRES** Toutes saisons, **PAIEMENT** Visa, MC, Amex, Débit électronique, En espèces, Chèques de voyage, **PETITS DÉJEUNERS** Complet, Fait à la maison, **COMMODITÉS** TV centrale, Bain tourbillon, Réfrigérateur, Salon pour invités, **CHOSES À FAIRE** Sentier à proximité, Location de canoë ou de bateau, Golf, Musées, Attractions, Ski de fond, Tennis, Natation, Équitation, Plage, Observation d'oiseaux, **LANGUES** Ang., **PRIX** (2 personnes) 89–125 **(vérifiez avec les hôtes les details des prix)**

CARAQUET *(nord-est du N-B)*

Gîte "Le Poirier" B&B

(Roland et Martina Friolet)

98 boul St-Pierre Ouest, Caraquet, N-B, E1W 1B6
www.gitelepoirier.com
Adresse électronique gitepoir@nbnet.nb.ca

506-727-4359
No de téléc. 506-726-6084
No d'appel sans frais 1-888-748-9311

Gîte "Le Poirier" B&B, maison de style Nouvel
Angleterre, construite en 1927 par M Charles C.
Poirier qui fût maître d'école, magistrat et juge.
Gîte "Le Poirier" B&B a été restauré dans toute
sa splendeur originale et meublé à l'ancienne.
Caraquet (Capital de l'acadie moderne) fait
face à la Baie des Chaleurs, qui est reconnue
comme une des plus belles du monde.
Caraquet vous offre de très bons restaurants, et
une culture acadienne vivante.

CHAMBRES Étage supérieur, Rez-de-chaussée, **Salles
de bains** Privée, Chambres communicantes, **Lits**
Grand lit, Lit à 2 places, **Climatisation** Dans les chambres, **Fumeurs** À l'extérieur, **Dans la chambre**
Thermostat, Téléphone, TV, Accès Internet, Magnétoscope, **AUTRES** Urbain, Rural, Toutes saisons,
PAIEMENT Visa, MC, Débit électronique, En espèces,
Chèques de voyage, **PETITS DÉJEUNERS** Complet, Fait
à la maison, **COMMODITÉS** TV centrale, Téléphone
central, Blanchisserie, Salon pour invités, Patio pour
invités, Accès Internet central, Magnétoscope central,
CHOSES À FAIRE Bicyclettes à titre gracieux, Sentier à
proximité, Golf, Pêche, Musées, Galeries d'art, Théâtre,
Divertissement, Attractions, Magasinage, Ski de fond,
Tennis, Natation, Équitation, Plage, Observation
d'oiseaux, **LANGUES** Ang., Fr., **PRIX** (2 personnes)
79–98 **(vérifiez avec les hôtes les details des prix)**

CARAQUET

Hotel Paulin

(Karen Mersereau et Gerard Paulin)

143 boul St. Pierre Ouest, Caraquet, N-B, E1W 1B6
www.hotelpaulin.com
Adresse électronique innkeeper@hotelpaulin.com

506-727-9981
No de téléc. 506-727-4808
No d'appel sans frais 1-866-727-9981

Boutique-hôtel au bord de la mer, point d'intérêt historique de renommée mondiale. Sur la
baie des Chaleurs, couchers de soleil spectacu-
laires, plage privée, golf, services de spa
internes. Près de 130 km de sentiers de
marche, vélo, motoneige, ski de fond. Exploité
par la 3e génération de Paulin. Loué par la
critique du *New York Times, Le Figaro, Destinations Canada, Frommers, Fodor*. Reconnu pour
ses délices locaux: fruits de mer, champignons
sauvages, fromages d'artisans, bœuf et agneau
naturels.

CHAMBRES Suite familiale, Étage supérieur, Entrée
privée, **Salles de bains** Chambres communicantes, **Lits**
Très grand lit, Grand lit, Lits à une place ou lits pliants,
Divan-lit, **AUTRES** Rural, Toutes saisons, Repas addi-
tionnels, **PAIEMENT** Visa, MC, Débit électronique,
Chèques de voyage, **PETITS DÉJEUNERS** Complet,
Continental, Fait à la maison, **COMMODITÉS** TV cen-
trale, Téléphone central, Bain tourbillon, Blanchisserie,
Réfrigérateur, Service de boissons chaudes, Salon pour
invités, Patio pour invités, Accès Internet central,
Magnétoscope central, **CHOSES À FAIRE** Location de
bicyclettes, Sentier à proximité, Location de canoë ou
de bateau, Golf, Pêche, Musées, Galeries d'art, Théâtre,
Attractions, Ski de fond, Tennis, Natation, Plage,
Observation d'oiseaux, Antiquités, **LANGUES** Ang., Fr.,
PRIX (2 personnes) 89–235 **(vérifiez avec les hôtes les
details des prix)**

MONCTON *(est du N-B)*

Gîte du voyageur Chez-Aanna
(Pierre-Édouard Landry)

30 prom Baffin, Moncton, N-B, E1A 5P1
www.gitescanada.com/6017.html
Adresse électronique aanna@nbnet.nb.ca

506-856-5961
No de téléc. 506-383-7795
No d'appel sans frais 1-877-856-5961

Situé dans un cartier tranquille et paisible, notre gîte 4 1/2 étoiles est à 0.5 km de la chemintrans-canadienne #2 et près du centre-ville. Chambres spacieuses et comfortables avec télévision, DVD, téléphone, Internet et salle de bain privée attenante à la chambre. Suite familiale et mini-suite spacieuse avec très grand lit (king). Aire de détente agréable: grand salon et patio extérieur avec vue sur le jardin. Environnement non-fumeur et air climatisé central. Buanderie. Bilingue. Déjeuner acadien et autre.

CHAMBRES Suite familiale, **Salles de bains** Privée, **Lits** Très grand lit, Grand lit, Lit à 2 places, **Climatisation** Climatiseur central, Ventilateurs de plafond, **Fumeurs** À l'extérieur, **Dans la chambre** Thermostat, Téléphone, TV, Accès Internet, Magnétoscope, **AUTRES** Gardiennage d'enfants, Urbain, Toutes saisons, **PAIEMENT** Visa, MC, Débit électronique, En espèces, Chèques de voyage, **PETITS DÉJEUNERS** Complet, Fait à la maison, **COMMODITÉS** Barbeque, Blanchisserie, Réfrigérateur, Salon pour invités, Patio pour invités, Accès Internet central, **CHOSES À FAIRE** Location de bicyclettes, Sentier à proximité, Location de canoë ou de bateau, Golf, Pêche, Musées, Galeries d'art, Théâtre, Divertissement, Attractions, Vineries/Brasseries, Magasinage, Ski de fond, Tennis, Natation, Équitation, Plage, Observation d'oiseaux, Antiquités, **LANGUES** Ang., Fr., **PRIX** (2 personnes) 79–129 **(vérifiez avec les hôtes les details des prix)**

MONCTON

Leah Jane's Bed and Breakfast
(Ron Collins)

146 Church St, Moncton, N-B, E1C 4Z7
www.leahjanesbb.com
Adresse électronique leahjane@nbnet.nb.ca

506-854-9207
No de téléc. 506-389-9329
No d'appel sans frais 1-800-581-5324

Convenablement situé au cœur de Moncton, à 7 minutes du centre ville, offrant une grande variété de restaurants et de spectacles sur scène. Les chambres propres et confortables de Leah-Jane's, vous assurent une bonne nuit de repos. Avec un gîte touristique et une clinique de massothérapie reflex sous un même toit, nous nous occupons efficacement et professionnellement de vos besoins de relaxation. Pour les directions, veuillez consulter notre site Web.

CHAMBRES Suite familiale, Étage supérieur, Rez-de-chaussée, **Salles de bains** Privée, Chambres communicantes, Partagée avec un client, **Lits** Grand lit, Lits jumeaux, Lits à une place ou lits pliants, **Climatisation** Dans les chambres, Ventilateurs de plafond, **Fumeurs** À l'extérieur, **Dans la chambre** Téléphone, TV, Magnétoscope, **AUTRES** Urbain, Toutes saisons, Repas additionnels, Animaux de compagnie acceptés, **PAIEMENT** Visa, MC, Débit électronique, En espèces, Chèques de voyage, **PETITS DÉJEUNERS** Continental, **COMMODITÉS** Téléphone central, Piscine, Barbeque, Blanchisserie, Cuisine disponible, Réfrigérateur, Patio pour invités, Accès Internet central, **CHOSES À FAIRE** Sentier à proximité, Golf, Musées, Théâtre, Divertissement, Attractions, Magasinage, Ski de fond, Tennis, Natation, Observation d'oiseaux, Antiquités, **LANGUES** Ang., Fr., **PRIX** (2 personnes) 60–80 **(vérifiez avec les hôtes les details des prix)**

Petit-Rocher *(nord du N-B)*

Auberge d'Anjou

(Pauline et Jean-Yves Fournier)

587 rue Principale, Petit-Rocher, N-B, E8J 1H6
www.sn2000.nb.ca/comp/auberge-d'anjou
Adresse électronique auberge.anjou@nb.aibn.com

506-783-0587
No de tél. 506-783-5587
No d'appel sans frais 1-866-783-0587

Construit en 1917, à environ 5 minutes de marche du quai local, cet édifice fut complètement renové en 1994 afin de rencontrer les normes actuelles. Ornée d'une grande véranda qui s'étend de la façade jusqu'au côté nord, il reflète l'architecture des grandes maisons acadiennes des années vingt. Cette demeure au cachet antique continue toujours d'attirer les regards. Classifié 4 étoiles par *Canada Select*, ce gîte présente 6 chambres meublées à l'image de la première moitié du siècle.

CHAMBRES Étage supérieur, Entrée privée, **Salles de bains** Privée, **Lits** Très grand lit, Grand lit, Lit à 2 places, Lits jumeaux, Lits à une place ou lits pliants, Divan-lit, **Climatisation** Climatiseur central, **Fumeurs** À l'extérieur, **Dans la chambre** Thermostat, Téléphone, TV, **AUTRES** Toutes saisons, Repas additionnels, **PAIEMENT** Visa, MC, Débit électronique, En espèces, Chèques de voyage, **PETITS DÉJEUNERS** Complet, Fait à la maison, **COMMODITÉS** Barbeque, Blanchisserie, Réfrigérateur, Accès Internet central, Magnétoscope central, **CHOSES À FAIRE** Bicyclettes à titre gracieux, Location de canoë ou de bateau, Golf, Pêche, Musées, Galeries d'art, Théâtre, Divertissement, Attractions, Magasinage, Ski de fond, Tennis, Natation, Plage, Observation d'oiseaux, Antiquités, **LANGUES** Ang., Fr., **PRIX** (2 personnes) 68–88 (**vérifiez avec les hôtes les details des prix**)

Moncton

Lori's Bed and Breakfast

(Lori Smith)

761 Hillsborough Rd, Riverview, N-B, E1B 3W1
www.lorisbedandbreakfast.com
Adresse électronique lorisbedandbreakfast @hotmail.com

506-386-6055

Dans notre grande maison propre et modernisée, nos invités jouissent de l'hospitalité à son meilleur. Des parquets en bois dur aux serviettes duveteuses séchées par le vent, vous pourrez relaxer et vous reposer dans l'une de nos nombreuses chambres. Nous espérons vous trouver en appétit au réveil car notre petit déjeuner consistant est l'orgueil de Lori. La table abonde de plats maison, des confitures aux petits pains. Choisissez parmi les mets suivants ou vos demandes spéciales si possible.

CHAMBRES Étage supérieur, **Salles de bains** Chambres communicantes, Partagée avec un client, **Lits** Grand lit, Lits jumeaux, **Climatisation** Climatiseur central, **AUTRES** Urbain, **PAIEMENT** En espèces, **PETITS DÉJEUNERS** Complet, **COMMODITÉS** TV centrale, Téléphone central, Barbeque, Blanchisserie, Cuisine disponible, Réfrigérateur, Salon pour invités, Patio pour invités, Accès Internet central, Magnétoscope central, **CHOSES À FAIRE** Sentier à proximité, Magasinage, Ski de fond, Observation d'oiseaux, **LANGUES** Ang., **PRIX** (2 personnes) 65–75 (**vérifiez avec les hôtes les details des prix**)

Sackville *(est du N-B)*

Marshlands Inn

(Lucy et Barry Dane)

55 Bridge St, Sackville, N-B, E4L 3N8
www.marshlands.nb.ca
Adresse électronique marshlds@nbnet.nb.ca

506-536-0170
No de téléc. 506-536-0721
No d'appel sans frais 1-800-561-1266

Auberge-relais victorienne de 18 chambres avec salles de bains privées et mobilier d'époque. De nombreux jardins et marais sur la propriété de 8 acres permettent de se promener ou de s'asseoir et lire ou relaxer. Salle d'accueil double/débit de boisson pour consommations, détente et conversation. Salle à dîner gastronomique de 80 places munie d'une licence servant trois repas par jour. Spécialité : poissons et fruits de mer et plats locaux. Situé près du centre ville et de l'université Mount Allison.

CHAMBRES Suite familiale, Étage supérieur, Rez-de-chaussée, Sous-sol, **Salles de bains** Privée, Chambres communicantes, **Lits** Très grand lit, Grand lit, Lit à 2 places, Lits jumeaux, **Climatisation** Dans les chambres, **Fumeurs** À l'extérieur, **Dans la chambre** Thermostat, Téléphone, TV, Accès Internet, **AUTRES** Toutes saisons, Repas additionnels, Animaux de compagnie acceptés, **PAIEMENT** Visa, MC, Débit électronique, En espèces, Chèques de voyage, **PETITS DÉJEUNERS** Complet, Fait à la maison, **COMMODITÉS** Salon pour invités, Patio pour invités, **CHOSES À FAIRE** Sentier à proximité, Golf, Musées, Galeries d'art, Théâtre, Attractions, Vineries/Brasseries, Observation d'oiseaux, Antiquités, **LANGUES** Ang., Esp., Italian, **PRIX** (2 personnes) 95–175 **(vérifiez avec les hôtes les details des prix)**

Bouctouche *(est du N-B)*

Les Pins Maritimes

(Jeanne Brideau)

320 Cote Sainte Anne Rd, Sainte Anne de Kent, N-B, E4S 1M6
www.sn2000.nb.ca/comp/pins-maritimes
Adresse électronique jea@nbnet.nb.ca

506-743-8450
No de téléc. 506-743-8450

Site enchanteur pour les amants de la nature. Maison centenaire située sur une longue plage sablonneuse. De somptueux déjeuners santé sont servis. Les séjours prolongés sont populaires. Jouïssez de votre séjour en faisant des randonnées pédestres, du vélo, du kayak, du canoë, du golfe, en participant à une excursion de pêche, en vous baignant ou simplement en vous prélassant sur la plage.

CHAMBRES Suite familiale, Étage supérieur, Rez-de-chaussée, Entrée privée, **Salles de bains** Privée, Chambres communicantes, **Lits** Grand lit, Lit à 2 places, Divan-lit, **Climatisation** Dans les chambres, **Fumeurs** À l'extérieur, **AUTRES** Rural, Saisonnier, **PAIEMENT** Visa, Débit électronique, En espèces, Chèques de voyage, **PETITS DÉJEUNERS** Complet, Fait à la maison, **COMMODITÉS** TV centrale, Téléphone central, Réfrigérateur, Service de boissons chaudes, Patio pour invités, Accès Internet central, Magnétoscope central, **CHOSES À FAIRE** Bicyclettes à titre gracieux, Sentier à proximité, Canoë ou bateau à titre gracieux, Golf, Pêche, Musées, Galeries d'art, Divertissement, Attractions, Vineries/Brasseries, Tennis, Natation, Plage, Observation d'oiseaux, Antiquités, **LANGUES** Ang., Fr., **PRIX** (2 personnes) 70–90 **(vérifiez avec les hôtes les details des prix)**

SHEDIAC *(est du N-B)*

Auberge, Maison Vienneau

(Marie et Norbert Vienneau)

426 Main, Shediac, N-B, E4P 2G4
www.maisonvienneau.com
Adresse électronique info@maisonvienneau.com

506-532-5412
No de téléc. 506-532-7998
No d'appel sans frais 1-866-532-5412

Bienvenue à la Maison Vienneau, gîte charmant offrant la bonne vieille hospitalité des maritimes et, avec la région de Shédiac, des activités culturelles et sportives pour rendre votre séjour agréable. Idéale pour les évasions romantiques, voyages d'affaires ou réunions familiales. Jolie maison victorienne pleine d'histoire culturelle sur une rue calme du village paisible presque délaissé par le temps. Hall d'entrée magnifiquement décoré avec des meubles anciens. Accès Internet à grande vitesse gratuit.

CHAMBRES Étage supérieur, Entrée privée, **Salles de bains** Privée, Chambres communicantes, **Lits** Grand lit, **Climatisation** Dans les chambres, **Fumeurs** À l'extérieur, **Dans la chambre** Thermostat, Téléphone, TV, Foyer, Accès Internet, **AUTRES** Rural, Saisonnier, **PAIEMENT** Visa, MC, Diners, Amex, Débit électronique, En espèces, Chèques de voyage, **PETITS DÉJEUNERS** Complet, Fait à la maison, **COMMODITÉS** TV centrale, Téléphone central, Barbeque, Cuisine disponible, Réfrigérateur, Patio pour invités, Magnétoscope central, **CHOSES À FAIRE** Bicyclettes à titre gracieux, Sentier à proximité, Location de canoë ou de bateau, Golf, Pêche, Musées, Galeries d'art, Divertissement, Attractions, Vineries/Brasseries, Magasinage, Ski de fond, Natation, Équitation, Plage, Observation d'oiseaux, **LANGUES** Ang., Fr., **PRIX** (2 personnes) 79–109 **(vérifiez avec les hôtes les détails des prix)**

ST. JOHN'S *(est de T-N)*

Bonne Esperance House Bed & Breakfast

(Regina Anthony)

20 Gower St, St John's, T-N, A1C 1N1
www.BonneEsperanceHouse.ca
Adresse électronique Regina@BonneEsperance House.ca

709-726-3835
No de téléc. 709-739-0496
No d'appel sans frais 1-888-726-3835

Situé au cœur du centre ville de St. John's, nous sommes une collection de maisons victoriennes historiques construites durant les années 1890, avec une classification d'hébergement *Canada Select* 4 étoiles. Nous offrons une variété de chambres meublées et de suites de luxe, qui incluent un accent traditionnel de meubles anciens avec un flair moderne, planchers en bois dur, plafonds de 12 pieds, moulures décoratives et verre coloré original.

CHAMBRES Suite familiale, Étage supérieur, Rez-de-chaussée, Sous-sol, Entrée privée, **Salles de bains** Privée, Chambres communicantes, **Lits** Grand lit, Lit à 2 places, Lits jumeaux, Lits à une place ou lits pliants, Divan-lit, **Fumeurs** À l'extérieur, **Dans la chambre** Téléphone, TV, Foyer, Accès Internet, Magnétoscope, **AUTRES** Toutes saisons, **PAIEMENT** Visa, MC, Amex, Débit électronique, En espèces, Chèques de voyage, **PETITS DÉJEUNERS** Complet, Fait à la maison, **COMMODITÉS** TV centrale, Téléphone central, Barbeque, Blanchisserie, Cuisine disponible, Réfrigérateur, Patio pour invités, Accès Internet central, Magnétoscope central, **CHOSES À FAIRE** Location de bicyclettes, Sentier à proximité, Golf, Musées, Galeries d'art, Théâtre, Divertissement, Attractions, Magasinage, Antiquités, **LANGUES** Ang., **PRIX** (2 personnes) 95–225 **(vérifiez avec les hôtes les détails des prix)**

GROS MORNE NATIONAL PARK
[WOODY POINT]*(centre-ouest de T-N)*

Aunt Jane's Place B&B

(Jenny et Stan Parsons)

1 Water St, Woody Point, Gros Morne National Park,
T-N, A0K 1P0
www.grosmorne.com/victorianmanor
Adresse électronique vmanor.grosmorne@nf
.sympatico.ca

709-453-2485
No de téléc. 709-453-2485
No d'appel sans frais 1-866-453-2485

Le gîte Aunt Jane's Place révèle l'histoire et la
culture de Terre-Neuve. Il est situé sur le
secteur riverain de Woody Point, dans le parc
national du Gros-Morne. Endroit idéal pour l'a-
mateur de plein air. Ce qu'il y a de mieux en
fait d'hospitalité terre-neuvienne! Les cinq
chambres avec petit déjeuner évoquent les
jours d'antan! Des kms de sentiers pédestres
vous permettent d'explorer les phénomènes
naturels de Gros-Morne. Rte 430 à Deer Lake,
jusqu'à Wiltondale. Puis la Rte 431 jusqu'à
Woody Point.

CHAMBRES Étage supérieur, **Salles de bains** Privée,
Partagée avec un client, **Lits** Grand lit, Lit à 2 places,
Dans la chambre Thermostat, **AUTRES** Rural,
Saisonnier, **PAIEMENT** Visa, MC, Débit électronique, En
espèces, Chèques de voyage, **PETITS DÉJEUNERS**
Continental, **COMMODITÉS** TV centrale, Téléphone
central, Blanchisserie, Réfrigérateur, **CHOSES À FAIRE**
Sentier à proximité, Location de canoe ou de bateau,
Pêche, Théâtre, Attractions, Plage, **LANGUES** Ang.,
PRIX (2 personnes) 50–70 **(vérifiez avec les hôtes les
details des prix)**

HALIFAX *(entre-est de la N-É)*

By the Harbour
Bed & Breakfast

(Carol Gardner et Eric Boudreau)

1581 Cole Harbour Rd, Dartmouth, N-É, B2Z 1B9
www3.ns.sympatico.ca/carol.gardner
Adresse électronique carol.gardner@ns.sympatico.ca

902-433-1996
No de téléc. 902-435-7491
No d'appel sans frais 1-866-218-5210

Le clou de votre visite sera le petit-déjeuner
haute cuisine de trois plats dans cette charmante maison du style Tudor qui a une vue
magnifique de Cole Harbour. Elle se trouve à
10 minutes des plages, des sentiers pédestres
et on peut aussi faire du canoë, du kayac, et du
plongée sous-marin. Si vous préférez aller
magasiner, visiter des sites historiques, nous
sommes à 15 minutes du centre-ville. Nos
chambres sont décorées en thèmes - acadienne, orientale, mexicaine et français romantique pourvu d'un baldaquin.

CHAMBRES Étage supérieur, **Salles de bains** Privée,
Chambres communicantes, **Lits** Grand lit, Lits
jumeaux, Lits à une place ou lits pliants, **Climatisation**
Climatiseur central, **Dans la chambre** Thermostat,
AUTRES Urbain, Toutes saisons, **PAIEMENT** Visa, MC,
En espèces, Chèques de voyage, **PETITS DÉJEUNERS**
Complet, Fait à la maison, **COMMODITÉS** TV centrale,
Téléphone central, Patio pour invités, **CHOSES À
FAIRE** Sentier à proximité, Location de canoë ou de
bateau, Golf, Pêche, Musées, Galeries d'art, Théâtre,
Divertissement, Attractions, Vineries/Brasseries,
Magasinage, Natation, Plage, **LANGUES** Ang., Fr., **PRIX**
(2 personnes) 75–115 **(vérifiez avec les hôtes les
details des prix)**

Salmon River Bridge-Jeddore
(au nord-est de Halifax)

Salmon River House Country Inn

(Adrien Blanchette et Elisabeth Schwarzer)

9931 Rte 7, Salmon River Bridge,
Musquodoboit Harbour-Jeddore, N-É, B0J 1P0
www.salmonriverhouse.com
Adresse électronique salmonrh@ca.inter.net

902-889-3353
No de télé. 902-889-3653
No d'appel sans frais 1-800-565-3353

À 40 minutes de distance de Halifax ou de l'aéroport de Halifax. Autoroute 7 jusqu'à Musquodoboit Harbour. Arrivés à la fin de l'autoroute 107, tournez à droite, traversez le village de Musquodoboit Harbour. À gauche vous pouvez voir le musée ferroviaire, continuez sur cette route. C'est l'ancienne Rte #7, continuez jusqu'au pont de la Rivière à saumons, environ 15 minutes, (au-delà du pont vert et du centre commercial Forest Hill). Nous sommes juste de l'autre côté du pont au bord de l'eau.

CHAMBRES Suite familiale, Étage supérieur, Rez-de-chaussée, **Salles de bains** Privée, Chambres communicantes, **Lits** Très grand lit, Grand lit, Lit à 2 places, Lits jumeaux, **Climatisation** Dans les chambres, **AUTRES** Accessible aux personnes handicapées, Saisonnier, **PAIEMENT** Visa, MC, Diners, Amex, Débit électronique, Chèques acceptés, En espèces, Chèques de voyage, **PETITS DÉJEUNERS** Complet, Continental, Fait à la maison, **COMMODITÉS** TV centrale, Téléphone central, Cuisine disponible, Réfrigérateur, Patio pour invités, **CHOSES À FAIRE** Sentier à proximité, Canoë ou bateau à titre gracieux, Golf, Musées, Galeries d'art, Attractions, Natation, Plage, Observation d'oiseaux, Antiquités, **LANGUES** Ang., Fr., Esp., All., **PRIX** (2 personnes) 84–148 **(vérifiez avec les hôtes les détails des prix)**

Parrsboro *(nord-ouest de la N-É)*

The Maple Inn

(Ulrike Rockenbauer et Johannes Hiesberger)

2358 Western Ave, Parrsboro, N-É, B0M 1S0
www.mapleinn.ca
Adresse électronique office@mapleinn.ca

902-254-3735
No de télé. 902-254-3735
No d'appel sans frais 1-877-627-5346

Le gîte Maple Inn, est une ravissante auberge située à Parrsboro sur la rive de la baie de Fundy en Nouvelle-Écosse. Deux maisons centenaires rénovées offrent une variété d'hébergements. Huit chambres pour deux personnes, toutes avec salle de bains privée. Aussi une suite à deux chambres à coucher avec bain tourbillon privé et très grands lits. Tous les forfaits incluent un petit déjeuner complet. Situé à quelques pas du théâtre d'été professionnel, Fundy Geogical Museum, Ottawa House et la plage.

CHAMBRES Suite familiale, Étage supérieur, Rez-de-chaussée, Entrée privée, **Salles de bains** Privée, Chambres communicantes, **Lits** Très grand lit, Grand lit, Lit à 2 places, Lits jumeaux, Lits à une place ou lits pliants, Divan-lit, **Climatisation** Dans les chambres, **Fumeurs** À l'extérieur, **Dans la chambre** TV, **AUTRES** Toutes saisons, **PAIEMENT** Visa, MC, Diners, Amex, Débit électronique, En espèces, Chèques de voyage, **PETITS DÉJEUNERS** Complet, Fait à la maison, **COMMODITÉS** TV centrale, Téléphone central, Blanchisserie, Réfrigérateur, Salon pour invités, Accès Internet central, Magnétoscope central, **CHOSES À FAIRE** Sentier à proximité, Location de canoë ou de bateau, Golf, Pêche, Musées, Galeries d'art, Théâtre, Attractions, Plage, Observation d'oiseaux, Antiquités, **LANGUES** Ang., All., **PRIX** (2 personnes) 90–150 **(vérifiez avec les hôtes les détails des prix)**

Parrsboro

The Parrsboro Mansion
(Sabine et Christian Schoene)

3916 Eastern Ave, Parrsboro, N-É, B0M 1S0
www.parrsboromansion.com
Adresse électronique sabine@parrsboromansion.com

902-254-2585
No de télé. 902-254-2585
No d'appel sans frais 1-866-354-2585

Appréciez le décor paisible de notre gracieuse maison ancestrale. Parrsboro Mansion est nichée sur une propriété de quatre âcres du centre ville, loin du bruit. Chambres élégantes et spacieuses au rez-de-chaussée, lits très grands, grands et lits jumeaux à 2 places, salles de bains communicantes. Piscine creusée chauffée, petit déjeuner gourmet allemand dans la salle à dîner ensoleillée. Coté 4 1/2 étoiles de *Canada Select*, près de toutes les attractions. Marées les plus hautes du monde, prospection amateur.

CHAMBRES Suite familiale, Étage supérieur, Rez-de-chaussée, **Salles de bains** Privée, Chambres communicantes, **Lits** Très grand lit, Grand lit, Lit à 2 places, Lits jumeaux, Lits à une place ou lits pliants, Divan-lit, **Climatisation** Dans les chambres, Ventilateurs de plafond, **Fumeurs** À l'extérieur, **Dans la chambre** Thermostat, TV, Accès Internet, Magnétoscope, **AUTRES** Saisonnier, Animaux de compagnie à l'intérieur, **PAIEMENT** Visa, MC, Amex, Débit électronique, En espèces, Chèques de voyage, **PETITS DÉJEUNERS** Complet, Fait à la maison, **COMMODITÉS** Téléphone central, Piscine, Sauna, Blanchisserie, Patio pour invités, Accès Internet central, **CHOSES À FAIRE** Sentier à proximité, Golf, Pêche, Musées, Galeries d'art, Théâtre, Divertissement, Attractions, Magasinage, Tennis, Natation, Plage, Observation d'oiseaux, Antiquités, **LANGUES** Ang., All., **PRIX** (2 personnes) 100–150 (**vérifiez avec les hôtes les details des prix**)

Amherstburg *(sud-ouest de l'Ontario)*

Honor's Country House Bed and Breakfast
(Robert et Debra Honor)

4441 Conc 4 S, Amherstburg, ON, N9V 2Y8
www.bbcanada.com/honorsbnb
Adresse électronique dhonor@mnsi.net

519-736-7737
No d'appel sans frais 1-877-253-8594

Nous vous invitons amicalement à notre charmante maison de campagne avec une vue magnifique des jardins et de la campagne. Relaxez au solarium ou sur la terrasse. Profitez de la piscine ou prenez le thé sur la véranda. Chambres confortables meublées à l'ancienne. Observation d'oiseaux, randonnées pédestres, vélo, golf et la nature sont tous à proximité. Magasinage, restaurants et attractions à quelques minutes dans la ville historique d'Amherstburg. Nous aimons la généalogie, l'histoire et le jardinage.

CHAMBRES Étage supérieur, **Salles de bains** Privée, Chambres communicantes, **Lits** Lit à 2 places, Lits à une place ou lits pliants, **Climatisation** central, **AUTRES** Rural, Saisonnier, Animaux de compagnie à l'intérieur, **PAIEMENT** Chèques acceptés, En espèces, Chèques de voyage, **PETITS DÉJEUNERS** Complet, **COMMODITÉS** TV centrale, Piscine, Magnétoscope central, **CHOSES À FAIRE** Sentier à proximité, Golf, Musées, Galeries d'art, Attractions, Vineries/Brasseries, Magasinage, Natation, Plage, Antiquités, **LANGUES** Ang., Fr., **PRIX** (2 personnes) 70–80 (**vérifiez avec les hôtes les details des prix**)

BELLEVILLE *(à l'est de Toronto)*

Place Victoria Place
(Daniele et Gord Snodgrass)

156 Victoria Ave, Belleville, ON, K8N 2B4
www.placevictoriaplace.ca
Adresse électronique placevictoriaplace@bellnet.ca

613-967-8560

De la 401 Est ou Ouest, prenez la route 62 Sud
(devient la rue Front Nord). Suivez la rue Front
Nord jusqu'en ville. La route tourne à gauche,
restez dans la voie de gauche et traversez le
pont de la rivière Moira. Continuez tout droit
au feu du pont. (Le bureau de poste est à
gauche). Au prochain feu tournez à gauche
(sur l'ave Victoria). Continuez pour 7 pâtés et
tournez à gauche à la rue Albert. Nous sommes
au coin de l'ave Victoria et la rue Albert.
Stationnement des clients sur la rue Albert.

CHAMBRES Étage supérieur, Entrée privée, **Salles de
bains** Privée, **Lits** Grand lit, **Climatisation** Dans les
chambres, **Fumeurs** À l'extérieur, **Dans la chambre** TV,
AUTRES Urbain, Toutes saisons, Animaux de compag-
nie à l'intérieur, **PAIEMENT** Visa, MC, En espèces,
Chèques de voyage, **PETITS DÉJEUNERS** Continental,
COMMODITÉS Téléphone central, Réfrigérateur, Salon
pour invités, Magnétoscope central, **CHOSES À FAIRE**
Sentier à proximité, Pêche, Théâtre, Divertissement,
Attractions, Vineries/Brasseries, Magasinage,
Antiquités, **LANGUES** Ang., Fr., **PRIX** (2 personnes) 95
(vérifiez avec les hôtes les details des prix)

BELLEVILLE

Twin Oakes Bed & Breakfast
(Carole et Tom Burmaster)

310 Bleecker Ave, Belleville, ON, K8N 3V4
www.twinoakes.com
Adresse électronique twinoakes@bellnet.ca

613-771-0107
No de télé. 613-771-0107

Le gîte Twin Oakes B&B situé dans le quartier
Old East Hill de Belleville, se trouve à quelques
heures seulement des aéroports interna-
tionaux de Toronto ou de Montréal – l'endroit
idéal en l'Ontario pour un début ou une fin de
vacance relaxante. Bien qu'elles soient préfér-
ables, les réservations ne sont pas nécessaire-
ment requises.

CHAMBRES Étage supérieur, **Salles de bains**
Chambres communicantes, **Lits** Lit à 2 places, Lits à
une place ou lits pliants, **Climatisation** Climatiseur
central, Dans les chambres, **Fumeurs** À l'extérieur,
Dans la chambre Accès Internet, **AUTRES**
Gardiennage d'enfants, Urbain, Toutes saisons,
Animaux de compagnie à l'intérieur, Animaux de
compagnie acceptés, **PAIEMENT** Visa, MC, En espèces,
Chèques de voyage, **PETITS DÉJEUNERS** Complet,
COMMODITÉS TV centrale, Téléphone central,
Barbeque, Cuisine disponible, Réfrigérateur, Service de
boissons chaudes, Salon pour invités, Patio pour
invités, Accès Internet central, Magnétoscope central,
CHOSES À FAIRE Sentier à proximité, Location de
canoë ou de bateau, Golf, Pêche, Musées, Galeries
d'art, Théâtre, Divertissement, Attractions,
Vineries/Brasseries, Magasinage, Tennis, Natation,
Équitation, Plage, Observation d'oiseaux, Antiquités,
LANGUES Ang., **PRIX** (2 personnes) 80–85 **(vérifiez
avec les hôtes les details des prix)**

Brighton *(à l'est de Toronto)*

Butler Creek Country Inn

(Burke Friedrichkeit et Ken Bosher)

RR #7, County Rd 30-202, Brighton, ON, K0K 1H0
www.butlercreekcountryinn.com
Adresse électronique butlerbbb@reach.net

613-475-1248
No de téléc. 613-475-5267
No d'appel sans frais 1-877-477-5827

Le gîte Butler Creek Country Inn vous propose une combinaison rare, son élégance victorienne, sa facilité d'accès et sa tranquillité. Sise dans une adorable vallée, la maison surplombe neuf âcres d'arbres, de prés, de jardins et le crique Butler Creek. Débutez votre journée avec un petit déjeuner délicieux et régalez-vous durant nos "Forfaits gastronomiques" offerts de novembre à avril. Nous offrons des "Forfaits théâtre" au printemps et à l'automne et des "Forfaits golf" à l'été. Approuvé CAA/AAA.

CHAMBRES Étage supérieur, Rez-de-chaussée, **Salles de bains** Chambres communicantes, Partagée avec un client, **Lits** Très grand lit, Grand lit, Lits jumeaux, Divan-lit, **Climatisation** Climatiseur central, **AUTRES** Urbain, Rural, Toutes saisons, Animaux de compagnie à l'intérieur, **PAIEMENT** Visa, MC, Amex, Débit électronique, En espèces, Chèques de voyage, **PETITS DÉJEUNERS** Complet, **COMMODITÉS** TV centrale, Téléphone central, Salon pour invités, **CHOSES À FAIRE** Sentier à proximité, Golf, Pêche, Musées, Galeries d'art, Théâtre, Attractions, Vineries/Brasseries, Ski de fond, Tennis, Natation, Équitation, Plage, Observation d'oiseaux, Antiquités, **LANGUES** Ang., Fr., All., **PRIX** (2 personnes) 85–115 **(vérifiez avec les hôtes les details des prix)**

Cayuga *(au sud de Hamilton)*

River Inn B&B

(Frank et Helen Belbeck)

1459 Haldimand Rd 17, RR #1, Cayuga, ON, N0A 1E0
www.bbcanada.com/riverinn
Adresse électronique riverinn@linetap.com

905-774-8057
No d'appel sans frais 1-866-824-7878

River Inn B&B, situé dans un parc de 14 âcres sur la rivière Grand entre les villes de Cayuga et Dunnville du sud de l'Ontario, près du lac Érié, à 1 heure de Niagara Falls et 90 minutes de l'aéroport Pearson de Toronto. Trois suites, grands lits, TV par satellite. Un petit hôtel de trois chambres tout à fait meublé avec vue de la rivière et une piscine est aussi offerte pour les séjours prolongés, occasions spéciales, nouveaux mariés, accueille jusqu'à quatres personnes. Stationnement intérieur, climatiseur.

CHAMBRES Suite familiale, Étage supérieur, Rez-de-chaussée, **Salles de bains** Chambres communicantes, **Lits** Très grand lit, Grand lit, Lits jumeaux, Lits à une place ou lits pliants, Divan-lit, **Climatisation** Climatiseur central, Dans les chambres, **Fumeurs** À l'extérieur, **Dans la chambre** Téléphone, TV, **AUTRES** Rural, Toutes saisons, Accessible aux personnes handicapées, Repas additionnels, **PAIEMENT** Visa, MC, Amex, En espèces, **PETITS DÉJEUNERS** Complet, Continental, Fait à la maison, Préparé soi-même, **COMMODITÉS** TV centrale, Téléphone central, Piscine, Barbeque, Cuisine disponible, Réfrigérateur, Salon pour invités, Patio pour invités, **CHOSES À FAIRE** Sentier à proximité, Golf, Pêche, Musées, Théâtre, Attractions, Vineries/Brasseries, Magasinage, Natation, Plage, **LANGUES** Ang., **PRIX** (2 personnes) 65–125 **(vérifiez avec les hôtes les details des prix)**

Gananoque *(au sud d'Ottawa)*

Manse Lane Bed & Breakfast
(Jocelyn et George Bounds)

465 Stone St South, Gananoque, ON, K7G 2A7
www.manselane.com

613-382-8642
No d'appel sans frais 1-888-565-6379

Charmante maison de brique centenaire util-isée comme gîte touristique depuis 1989. Petit déjeuner servi au solarium durant les saisons chaudes, et près du feu dans le salon privé lorsqu'il fait plus froid. À seulement cinq maisons des bateaux de croisière des 1000 Îles, trois rues du théâtre des 1000 Îles, et quatres rues du centre ville. Stationnement privé pour votre voiture. Marchez aux principales attrac-tions. Agents de billets d'attractions. Réserva-tions fortement recommandées. Parlons un peu français. Merci.

CHAMBRES Étage supérieur, **Salles de bains** Privée, Chambres communicantes, Partagée avec un client, **Lits** Grand lit, Lits jumeaux, Lits à une place ou lits pli-ants, **Climatisation** Dans les chambres, **Fumeurs** À l'extérieur, **Dans la chambre** TV, AUTRES Urbain, Adulte, Toutes saisons, **PAIEMENT** Visa, MC, Diners, Amex, En espèces, Chèques de voyage, **PETITS DÉJEUNERS** Complet, **COMMODITÉS** TV centrale, Piscine, Salon pour invités, Patio pour invités, **CHOSES À FAIRE** Location de bicyclettes, Sentier à proximité, Location de canoë ou de bateau, Golf, Pêche, Musées, Galeries d'art, Théâtre, Attractions, Magasinage, Natation, Équitation, Plage, **LANGUES** Ang., Fr., **PRIX** (2 personnes) 65–160 **(vérifiez avec les hôtes les details des prix)**

Algonquin Park [Huntsville]
(au nord de Toronto)

Fairy Bay Guest House
(Robert et Dawn Rye)

228 Cookson Bay Cres, Huntsville, ON, P1H 1B2
www.fairybay.ca
Adresse électronique hosts@fairybay.ca

705-789-1492
No de tél. 705-789-6922
No d'appel sans frais 1-888-813-1101

Charmante auberge de campagne aux jardins magnifiques située dans une baie paisible de Fairy Lake. Appréciez son confort luxueux ou participez aux nombreuses activités avoisi-nantes. Plusieurs canots/embarcations sont fournis pour accéder aux 40 kilomètres de voies d'eau pittoresques. Le Parc Algonquin, 6 terrains de golf, des randonnées pédestres, le ski, la motoneige sont parmi les divertisse-ments locaux. Merveilleux site touristique, débordant de chaleur, d'Intérêt, de musique, d'art et de beautés naturelles.

CHAMBRES Suite familiale, Étage supérieur, Rez-de-chaussée, Sous-sol, **Salles de bains** Chambres com-municantes, **Lits** Très grand lit, Grand lit, Lits à une place ou lits pliants, Divan-lit, **Climatisation** Climatiseur central, **Fumeurs** À l'extérieur, **Dans la chambre** Thermostat, Téléphone, TV, Magnétoscope, **AUTRES** Rural, Toutes saisons, **PAIEMENT** Visa, MC, Chèques acceptés, En espèces, **PETITS DÉJEUNERS** Complet, Fait à la maison, **COMMODITÉS** Bain tourbil-lon, Barbeque, Réfrigérateur, Service de boissons chaudes, Salon pour invités, Patio pour invités, **CHOSES À FAIRE** Bicyclettes à titre gracieux, Sentier à proximité, Canoe ou bateau à titre gracieux, Golf, Pêche, Musées, Galeries d'art, Divertissement, Attractions, Magasinage, Ski de fond, Ski alpin, Tennis, Natation, Équitation, Plage, Observation d'oiseaux, Antiquités, **LANGUES** Ang., Fr., **PRIX** (2 personnes) 140–205 **(vérifiez avec les hôtes les details des prix)**

KAPUSKASING *(nord de l'Ontario)*

Grandma Jean's B&B

(Jean Belanger)

35 Cite Des Jeunes Blvd, Kapuskasing, ON, P5N 2Z5
www.canadianbandbguide.ca/bb.asp?ID=3704
Adresse électronique eujean@onlink.net

705-335-4968

Nous vous attendons dans une atmosphère chaude et amicale avec une tasse de votre breuvage favori. Horaire de petit déjeuner flexible, nous servons cinq délicieux repas chauds tels que fruits frais, jus, yogourts, céréales et muffins maison. En été, relaxez à l'ombre de nos érables avec une bonne tasse de thé ou de café. Autoroute #11 de North Bay, tournez à droite au premier feu de circulation sur Brunelle, puis à gauche sur le Boulevard de la Cité des Jeunes. Deuxième à droite. Télé. cellular 705-367-6109.

CHAMBRES Suite familiale, Étage supérieur, Sous-sol, **Salles de bains** Privée, Partagée avec un client, **Lits** Grand lit, Lit à 2 places, Lits jumeaux, Lits à une place ou lits pliants, **Climatisation** Dans les chambres, **Fumeurs** À l'extérieur, **Dans la chambre** TV, Accès Internet, **AUTRES** Urbain, Toutes saisons, **PAIEMENT** Visa, MC, En espèces, Chèques de voyage, **PETITS DÉJEUNERS** Complet, Fait à la maison, **COMMODITÉS** Réfrigérateur, **CHOSES À FAIRE** Sentier à proximité, Golf, Pêche, Musées, Théâtre, Attractions, Magasinage, Ski de fond, Ski alpin, Plage, **LANGUES** Ang., Fr., **PRIX** (2 personnes) 60–75 **(vérifiez avec les hôtes les details des prix)**

MIDLAND *(au nord de Toronto)*

1875 A Charters Inn B&B

(Gerry et Val Lesperance)

290 Second St, Midland, ON, L4R 3R1
www.chartersinn.com
Adresse électronique gerry@chartersinn.com

705-527-1572
No d'appel sans frais 1-800-724-2979

Bâti en 1875, près du centre-ville et des eaux de la baie, maison victorienne historique, nombreux conforts et jardins de fleurs, magnifique patio arrière et terrasse avant, où un délicieux petit déjeuner gastronomique peut être servi. Lits très grands, grands et à une place, salle de bains privée ou communicante, balcon privé, foyer, mini-frigo, table et chaises, TV, la plupart des commodités de la maison, bibliothèque, salle à manger classique.

CHAMBRES Étage supérieur, Rez-de-chaussée, Entrée privée, **Salles de bains** Privée, Chambres communicantes, Partagée avec un client, Partagée avec les hôtes, **Lits** Très grand lit, Grand lit, Lits jumeaux, Lits à une place ou lits pliants, **Climatisation** Dans les chambres, **Fumeurs** À l'extérieur, **Dans la chambre** Thermostat, Téléphone, TV, Foyer, Accès Internet, Magnétoscope, **AUTRES** Urbain, Rural, Adulte, Toutes saisons, Repas additionnels, Animaux de compagnie à l'intérieur, **PAIEMENT** En espèces, Chèques de voyage, **PETITS DÉJEUNERS** Complet, Continental, Fait à la maison, Préparé soi-même, **COMMODITÉS** TV centrale, Téléphone central, Réfrigérateur, Service de boissons chaudes, Salon pour invités, Patio pour invités, Accès Internet central, Magnétoscope central, **CHOSES À FAIRE** Location de bicyclettes, Sentier à proximité, Location de canoë ou de bateau, Golf, Pêche, Musées, Galeries d'art, Théâtre, Divertissement, Attractions, Magasinage, Ski de fond, Ski alpin, Tennis, Natation, Équitation, Plage, Observation d'oiseaux, Antiquités, **LANGUES** Ang., Fr., Esp., **PRIX** (2 personnes) 65–165 **(vérifiez avec les hôtes les details des prix)**

Niagara Falls *(à l'est de Hamilton)*

Always Inn Bed & Breakfast
(Sharon et John Tyson)

4327 Simcoe St, Niagara Falls, ON, L2E 1T5
www.alwaysinn.ca
Adresse électronique sharon@alwaysinn.ca

905-371-0840
No d'appel sans frais 1-800-700-6665

Bienvenue au Always Inn, magnifique gîte victorien datant de 1878, situé à peine quatres
maisons de la gorge de la rivière Niagara. Nous
sommes près de toutes les attractions locales;
à 10-15 minutes de marche des chutes, du casino, et du secteur touristique du centre ville de
Niagara Falls, ainsi que du terminus d'autobus
et de la gare. Réveillez-vous tous les matins
avec l'arôme de pain, muffins et café frais tout
en attendant le petit déjeuner chaud servi
quotidiennement près du feu. Nous vous
attendons!

CHAMBRES Suite familiale, Étage supérieur, **Salles de**
bains Privée, Chambres communicantes, **Lits** Grand lit,
Ceiling Fans, Lits jumeaux, **Climatisation** Climatiseur
central, Dans les chambres, Ventilateurs de plafond,
Fumeurs À l'extérieur, **Dans la chambre** TV, Foyer,
AUTRES Toutes saisons, **PAIEMENT** Visa, MC, En
espèces, Chèques de voyage, **PETITS DÉJEUNERS**
Complet, **COMMODITÉS** TV centrale, Téléphone cen-
tral, Réfrigérateur, Salon pour invités, Patio pour
invités, Magnétoscope central, **CHOSES À FAIRE**
Location de bicyclettes, Sentier à proximité, Golf,
Pêche, Musées, Théâtre, Divertissement, Attractions,
Vineries/Brasseries, Magasinage, Équitation, Antiquités,
LANGUES Ang., **PRIX** (2 personnes) 75–275 **(vérifiez**
avec les hôtes les details des prix)

Niagara Falls

Andrea's Bed and Breakfast
(Andrea Armstrong)

4286 Simcoe St, Niagara Falls, ON, L2E 1T6
www.andreasbedandbreakfast.com
Adresse électronique andrea.bed@sympatico.ca

905-374-4776
No de téléc. 905-356-3563

Établi en 1987, maison historique de 1892 au
centre ville de Niagara Falls. Près de River Road
entre les ponts Whirlpool et Rainbow, à 5 rues
du terminus d'autobus/de la gare et 20 minutes de marche des Chutes et du Casino
Niagara. Navette de Niagara Parks tout près.
Suite familiale à deux chambres/deux plus
salles de bains avec grands/très grands lits
jumeaux, coin salon, foyer, télé, frigo, terrasse et
entrée privée deux chambres avec salle de
bains privée pour huit personnes. Forfait nup-
tial de trois nuits avec souper.

CHAMBRES Suite familiale, Étage supérieur, Entrée
privée, **Salles de bains** Privée, Chambres communi-
cantes, **Lits** Très grand lit, Grand lit, Lit à 2 places, Lits
jumeaux, **Climatisation** Dans les chambres, **Fumeurs**
À l'extérieur, **Dans la chambre** Thermostat, TV, Foyer,
Magnétoscope, **AUTRES** Urbain, Adulte, Toutes
saisons, Repas additionnels, **PAIEMENT** Visa, MC,
Diners, Amex, Débit électronique, Chèques acceptés,
En espèces, Chèques de voyage, **PETITS DÉJEUNERS**
Complet, Continental, Fait à la maison, **COMMODITÉS**
TV centrale, Téléphone central, Réfrigérateur, Service
de boissons chaudes, Salon pour invités, Patio pour
invités, Accès Internet central, Magnétoscope central,
CHOSES À FAIRE Location de bicyclettes, Sentier à
proximité, Golf, Pêche, Musées, Galeries d'art, Théâtre,
Divertissement, Attractions, Vineries/Brasseries,
Magasinage, Ski de fond, Tennis, Natation, Équitation,
Plage, Observation d'oiseaux, Antiquités, **LANGUES**
Ang., **PRIX** (2 personnes) 60–220 **(vérifiez avec les**
hôtes les details des prix)

NIAGARA FALLS

Paradise Point
Bed and Breakfast

(Dianne et Joe Chopp)

3533 Main St, Niagara Falls, ON, L2G 6A7
www.paradisepointbedandbreakfast.com
Adresse électronique kdiannec@aol.com

905-295-4947

Paradise Point est situé dans un décor paisible, pittoresque, sur les rives des rivières Niagara et Welland, mais à quelques minutes seulement des chutes et des attractions. La vue est magnifique et les chambres d'hôtes sont grandes, propres (non-fumeurs) et privées. Grands lits confortables, grandes salles de bains communicantes. Copieux petit déjeuner maison servi au solarium. Il y a aussi une suite familiale avec une chambre à coucher additionnelle, et un lit d'enfant est aussi disponible sans frais.

CHAMBRES Suite familiale, Étage supérieur, **Salles de bains** Chambres communicantes, **Lits** Grand lit, Lits jumeaux, **Climatisation** Climatiseur central, **Fumeurs** À l'extérieur, **Dans la chambre** TV, Magnétoscope, **AUTRES** Gardiennage d'enfants, Toutes saisons, Animaux de compagnie à l'intérieur, **PAIEMENT** Visa, MC, En espèces, **PETITS DÉJEUNERS** Complet, Fait à la maison, **COMMODITÉS** TV centrale, Salon pour invités, Patio pour invités, Magnétoscope central, **CHOSES À FAIRE** Sentier à proximité, Golf, Pêche, Galeries d'art, Théâtre, Divertissement, Attractions, Vineries/ Brasseries, Magasinage, Ski de fond, Tennis, Natation, Observation d'oiseaux, Antiquités, **LANGUES** Ang., **PRIX** (2 personnes) 100–150 **(vérifiez avec les hôtes les details des prix)**

NIAGARA FALLS

Park Place Bed & Breakfast

(Gary et Carolyn Burke)

4851 River Rd, Niagara Falls, ON, L2E 3G4
www.parkplaceniagara.com
Adresse électronique gbburke@vaxxine.com

905-358-0279
No de téléc. 905-358-0458

Park Place B&B, maison historique canadienne et ancien domaine de William Doran, entrepreneur local des années 1800, surplombant la gorge de Niagara. Un équilibre parfait entre l'ère romantique victorienne et le confort moderne a été conservé. Hébergement de luxe avec spa, très grands lits, foyers et conciergerie, petit déjeuner complet servi dans nos grandes suites, ou petits déjeuners à la chandelle dans la salle Oak Room. Notre weekend fut magique. Chambre … petits déjeuners … exquis. S&C, É-U.

CHAMBRES Suite familiale, Étage supérieur, Entrée privée, **Salles de bains** Privée, Chambres communicantes, **Lits** Très grand lit, Lits à une place ou lits pliants, Divan-lit, **Climatisation** Dans les chambres, **Fumeurs** À l'extérieur, **Dans la chambre** TV, Foyer, Magnétoscope, **AUTRES** Toutes saisons, **PAIEMENT** Visa, MC, Chèques acceptés, En espèces, Chèques de voyage, **PETITS DÉJEUNERS** Complet, Fait à la maison, **COMMODITÉS** Sauna, Bain tourbillon, Barbeque, Cuisine disponible, Réfrigérateur, Salon pour invités, Patio pour invités, **CHOSES À FAIRE** Sentier à proximité, Golf, Pêche, Musées, Galeries d'art, Théâtre, Divertissement, Attractions, Vineries/Brasseries, Magasinage, **LANGUES** Ang., **PRIX** (2 personnes) 120–175 **(vérifiez avec les hôtes les details des prix)**

NIAGARA FALLS

Rose Arbor B&B

(Frank Spadafora)

4448 Ellis St, Niagara Falls, ON, L2E 1H4
www.rosearbor.ca
Adresse électronique franks@rosearbor.ca

905-354-7206
No d'appel sans frais 1-888-501-3860

Au cœur de la ville historique de Niagara Falls,
près des chutes, du transport en commun, et
de nombreux sites. Visitez le splendide district
viticole de Niagara. Nous sommes à quelques
minutes seulement des vineries, sites historiques, terrains de golf, canaux de Welland,
balades, promenades, etc. Faites de Rose Arbor
votre deuxième demeure. Choix de deux magnifiques chambres bien aménagées: La splendide Marilyn, et l'élégante Tuscan. Le petit
déjeuner est toujours un événement spécial à
Rose Arbor.

CHAMBRES Étage supérieur, **Salles de bains**
Chambres communicantes, **Lits** Grand lit, **Climatisa-**
tion Climatiseur central, Dans les chambres,
Ventilateurs de plafond, **Fumeurs** À l'extérieur,
AUTRES Urbain, Toutes saisons, **PAIEMENT** Visa, MC,
En espèces, Chèques de voyage, **PETITS DÉJEUNERS**
Complet, **COMMODITÉS** TV centrale, Téléphone cen-
tral, Blanchisserie, Cuisine disponible, Réfrigérateur,
Salon pour invités, Patio pour invités, Accès Internet
central, **CHOSES À FAIRE** Sentier à proximité, Golf,
Pêche, Musées, Galeries d'art, Théâtre, Divertissement,
Attractions, Vineries/ Brasseries, Magasinage, Tennis,
Observation d'oiseaux, Antiquités, **LANGUES** Ang., Fr.,
Esp., Italian, **PRIX** (2 personnes) 75–125 **(vérifiez avec**
les hôtes les details des prix)

NIAGARA-ON-THE-LAKE
(à l'est de Hamilton)

6 Oak Haven
Bed and Breakfast

(Christine et Dennis Rizzuto)

6 Oak Dr Box 397, Niagara-on-the-Lake, ON, L0S 1J0
www.oakhaven.ca
Adresse électronique stay@oakhaven.ca

905-468-7361
No d'appel sans frais 1-866-818-1195

Situé dans le vieux quartier, marchez au lac,
Shaw Festival, restaurants et boutiques. Trois
chambres attrayantes et bien décorées avec
salle de bains communicante/privée. Le jardin
oasis enchanteur avec pavillon, étang et cascade vous invite à relaxer. Notre jardin figurait
dans le Ontario Gardener Magazine. Sans
oublier les Légendaires petits déjeuners de
Christine! Un accueil chaleureux vous attend
de la part de vos hôtes Christine et Dennis
Rizzuto. Visitez notre site Web au
www.oakhaven.ca.

CHAMBRES Suite familiale, Étage supérieur, Rez-de-
chaussée, **Salles de bains** Privée, Chambres communi-
cantes, **Lits** Grand lit, Divan-lit, **Climatisation**
Climatiseur central, Dans les chambres, **Fumeurs** À
l'extérieur, **Dans la chambre** Téléphone, TV, Foyer,
Magnétoscope, **AUTRES** Urbain, Adulte, Toutes saisons,
Animaux de compagnie à l'intérieur, **PAIEMENT** Visa,
MC, Chèques acceptés, En espèces, **PETITS**
DÉJEUNERS Complet, Fait à la maison, **COMMODITÉS**
TV centrale, Téléphone central, Réfrigérateur, Salon
pour invités, Patio pour invités, **CHOSES À FAIRE**
Bicyclettes à titre gracieux, Location de bicyclettes,
Sentier à proximité, Golf, Pêche, Musées, Galeries d'art,
Théâtre, Divertissement, Attractions, Vineries/
Brasseries, Magasinage, Ski de fond, Tennis, Natation,
Plage, Observation d'oiseaux, Antiquités, **LANGUES**
Ang., **PRIX** (2 personnes) 115–125 **(vérifiez avec les**
hôtes les details des prix)

NIAGARA-ON-THE-LAKE

Antonio Vivaldi B&B
(Susan Nyitrai)

275 Anne St, Box 1392, Niagara-on-the-Lake,
ON, L0S 1J0
www.bbvivaldi.com
Adresse électronique pnyitra@sprint.ca

905-468-9535
No de téléc. 905-468-9616

Notre gîte est situé dans la vieille partie de la magnifique ville de Niagara-on-the-Lake. Il est à proximité des théâtres Shaw, restaurants gastronomiques, sites historiques, vineries, terrains de golf, du lac Ontario et de Niagara Falls. Chez nous vous découvrirez l'hospitalité Hongroise, cordiale et merveilleuse. Plusieurs de nos clients donnent nos chèques-cadeaux à leurs parents et amis.

CHAMBRES Étage supérieur, Entrée privée, **Salles de bains** Chambres communicantes, **Lits** Grand lit, **Climatisation** Climatiseur central, **Fumeurs** À l'extérieur, **Dans la chambre** Téléphone, TV, Foyer, **AUTRES** Adulte, Toutes saisons, **PAIEMENT** Visa, En espèces, Chèques de voyage, **PETITS DÉJEUNERS** Complet, **COMMODITÉS** TV centrale, Bain tourbillon, Blanchisserie, Réfrigérateur, Service de boissons chaudes, Salon pour invités, Patio pour invités, **CHOSES À FAIRE** Location de bicyclettes, Sentier à proximité, Golf, Musées, Galeries d'art, Théâtre, Divertissement, Attractions, Vineries/Brasseries, Magasinage, Ski de fond, Équitation, Observation d'oiseaux, Antiquités, **LANGUES** Ang., Fr., Hongrois, **PRIX** (2 personnes) 99–150 **(vérifiez avec les hôtes les details des prix)**

NIAGARA-ON-THE-LAKE

Wishing Well Historical Cottage Rental
(Maria Rekrut)

156 Mary St, Niagara-on-the-Lake, ON, L0S 1J0
www.wishingwellcottage.com
Adresse électronique info@celebritybb.com

905-468-4658
No d'appel sans frais 1-866-226-4730

Chalet datant de 1871, maison de la soprano canadienne Maria Rekrut. Ce "chalet-musée" abrite une collection privée d'objets d'art. Ravissante maison pour non-fumeurs, deux chambres/deux salles de bains et cuisine complète, tous les conforts de la maison. Petit déjeuner continental libre-service au réfrigérateur. Cablotélé, magnétoscope, foyers, climatiseur, terrasse, barbecue. Près des théâtres, magasinage, restaurants, lac Ontario, route viticole/sentier pédestre. Casino Niagara et chutes Niagara à 15 minutes.

CHAMBRES Rez-de-chaussée, **Salles de bains** Privée, Chambres communicantes, **Lits** Très grand lit, Grand lit, **Climatisation** Climatiseur central, Ventilateurs de plafond, **Fumeurs** À l'extérieur, **Dans la chambre** Téléphone, TV, Foyer, Magnétoscope, **AUTRES** Urbain, Adulte, Toutes saisons, **PAIEMENT** Chèques acceptés, En espèces, Chèques de voyage, **PETITS DÉJEUNERS** Préparé soi-même, **COMMODITÉS** TV centrale, Barbeque, Blanchisserie, Cuisine disponible, Réfrigérateur, Service de boissons chaudes, Salon pour invités, Patio pour invités, Magnétoscope central, **CHOSES À FAIRE** Location de bicyclettes, Sentier à proximité, Golf, Pêche, Musées, Galeries d'art, Théâtre, Divertissement, Attractions, Vineries/Brasseries, Magasinage, Ski de fond, Tennis, Natation, Équitation, Plage, Observation d'oiseaux, Antiquités, **LANGUES** Ang., Fr., Esp., Italian, **PRIX** (2 personnes) 150–200 **(vérifiez avec les hôtes les details des prix)**

ORILLIA *(au nord de Toronto)*

Betty and Tony's Waterfront Bed and Breakfast

(Betty and Tony Bridgens)

677 Broadview Ave, Orillia, ON, L3V 6P1
www.bandborillia.com
Adresse électronique betty@bettyandtonys.com

705-326-1125
No d'appel sans frais 1-800-308-2579

Savourez vos repas en plein air au bord de l'eau chez Betty and Tony's! Site spacieux et serein, quai pour votre bateau à moteur, ou utilisez notre canoë et notre bateau à pédales. Petit déjeuner hors pair servi quotidien-nement, choix de dix plats chauds. Climatiseur central, toutes les chambres ont leur propre salle de bains. Trois petits salons intérieurs pour les clients. Il y a toujours du gâteau au chocolat si vous réservez d'avance. Personnel - Betty, Tony et Bailey le labrador brun chocolat.

CHAMBRES Suite familiale, Sous-sol, **Salles de bains** Privée, Chambres communicantes, **Lits** Très grand lit, Grand lit, Lits jumeaux, **Climatisation** Climatiseur cen-tral, **Fumeurs** À l'extérieur, **Dans la chambre** Thermostat, TV, Accès Internet, Magnétoscope, **AUTRES** Urbain, Animaux de compagnie à l'intérieur, Animaux de compagnie acceptés, **PAIEMENT** Visa, MC, Chèques acceptés, En espèces, Chèques de voy-age, **PETITS DÉJEUNERS** Complet, Fait à la maison, **COMMODITÉS** TV centrale, Téléphone central, Barbeque, Blanchisserie, Réfrigérateur, Service de boissons chaudes, Salon pour invités, Patio pour invités, Accès Internet central, Magnétoscope central, **CHOSES À FAIRE** Bicyclettes à titre gracieux, Sentier à proximité, Canoë ou bateau à titre gracieux, Golf, Pêche, Musées, Galeries d'art, Théâtre, Divertissement, Attractions, Magasinage, Ski de fond, Ski alpin, Tennis, Natation, Équitation, Plage, Observation d'oiseaux, Antiquités, **LANGUES** Ang., Fr., **PRIX** (2 personnes) 99–145 (**vérifiez avec les hôtes les details des prix**)

OTTAWA *(est de l'Ontario)*

Ambiance Bed and Breakfast

(Maria Giannakos)

330 Nepean St, Ottawa, ON, K1R 5G6
www.ambiancebandb.com
Adresse électronique info@ambiancebandb.com

613-563-0421
No d'appel sans frais 1-888-366-8772

Maison victorienne, rue calme au cœur d'Ottawa. Juste 10 minutes de marche de la Colline du Parlement et de la plupart des attractions touristiques, garez votre voiture ici et marchez partout. Entrée privée des invités vers quatres chambres sécuritaires. Visitez notre site Web pour plus de détails et voir les commentaires de nos invités. Autoroute 417, sortie ave. Bronson nord. À la rue Somerset tournez à droite. À la rue Bay tournez à gauche. À la rue Nepean tournez à droite. "Découvrez l'Ambiance d'Ottawa."

CHAMBRES Suite familiale, Étage supérieur, Entrée privée, **Salles de bains** Privée, Chambres communi-cantes, Partagée avec un client, **Lits** Très grand lit, Grand lit, Lits jumeaux, Lits à une place ou lits pliants, **Climatisation** Climatiseur central, **Fumeurs** À l'ex-térieur, **Dans la chambre** Accès Internet, **AUTRES** Urbain, Toutes saisons, Repas additionnels, Animaux de compagnie à l'intérieur, **PAIEMENT** Visa, MC, Amex, Débit électronique, En espèces, Chèques de voyage, **PETITS DÉJEUNERS** Complet, Fait à la maison, **COMMODITÉS** TV centrale, Téléphone central, Réfrigérateur, Service de boissons chaudes, Salon pour invités, Patio pour invités, **CHOSES À FAIRE** Location de bicyclettes, Sentier à proximité, Musées, Galeries d'art, Théâtre, Divertissement, Attractions, Magasinage, Ski de fond, Tennis, Natation, Équitation, Plage, **LANGUES** Ang., Fr., Grec, **PRIX** (2 personnes) 75–110 (**vérifiez avec les hôtes les details des prix**)

Ottawa

Gasthaus Switzerland Inn

(Sabina et Josef Sauter)

89 Daly Ave, Ottawa, ON, K1N 6E6
www.ottawainn.com
Adresse électronique info@ottawainn.com

613-237-0335
No de téléc. 613-594-3327
No d'appel sans frais 1-888-663-0000

"Un peu de la Suisse au centre-ville d'Ottawa."
Gîte chaleureux, confortable et intime offrant
des chambres ordinaires, de luxe et des suites
nuptiales avec tout le confort moderne. Ce
gîte/auberge prestigieux de 22 chambres dis-
crètes et charmantes accueille des clients
depuis 1985 avec une combinaison unique
d'hospitalité classique et amicale. Sur l'historique avenue Daly à deux pas de l'Université
d'Ottawa, du Centre des congrès d'Ottawa, du
marché ByWard. Marchez à toutes les principales attractions. Wi-Fi wireless.

CHAMBRES Étage supérieur, Rez-de-chaussée, Sous-
sol, Entrée privée, **Salles de bains** Privée, Chambres
communicantes, **Lits** Très grand lit, Grand lit, Lit à 2
places, Lits jumeaux, **Climatisation** Climatiseur central, Dans les chambres, **Fumeurs** À l'extérieur, **Dans la
chambre** Thermostat, Téléphone, TV, Foyer, Accès
Internet, **AUTRES** Toutes saisons, **PAIEMENT** Visa, MC,
Diners, Amex, En espèces, Chèques de voyage, **PETITS
DÉJEUNERS** Complet, Fait à la maison, **COMMODITÉS**
Blanchisserie, Salon pour invités, Patio pour invités,
Accès Internet central, **CHOSES À FAIRE** Location de
bicyclettes, Sentier à proximité, Golf, Musées, Galeries
d'art, Théâtre, Divertissement, Attractions,
Magasinage, Ski de fond, Ski alpin, Tennis, Natation,
Équitation, Plage, Observation d'oiseaux, Antiquités,
LANGUES Ang., Fr., Esp., All., **PRIX** (2 personnes)
108–248 **(vérifiez avec les hôtes les détails des prix)**

Paris *(à l'ouest de Hamilton)*

River Ridge Bed and Breakfast

(Paul et Cathy Dawson)

232 West River Rd, RR #2, Paris, ON, N3L 3E2
www.riverridgeretreat.com
Adresse électronique rrbedandbreakfast@bellnet.ca

519-442-0996
No de téléc. 519-442-1909
No d'appel sans frais 1-866-286-7722

Nous aimons partager notre maison de ferme
de 150 ans avec ceux qui apprécient l'époque
rurale d'antan accentuée par nos meubles
antiques. Chaque chambre est dotée d'un
matelas moelleux, de climatisation et de télé
par satellite. Notre site de 11 âcres, donne sur
des pâturages de chevaux avec une forêt car-
olinienne en arrière-plan. Marchez dans le sentier balisé (apportez vos bottes en caoutchouc)
jusqu'à notre promenade du côté ouest de la
rivière Grand River. Visitez notre site Web ou
téléphonez-nous!

CHAMBRES Suite familiale, Étage supérieur, Rez-de-
chaussée, **Salles de bains** Privée, Chambres communicantes, Partagée avec un client, **Lits** Grand lit, Lit à 2
places, Lits jumeaux, Lits à une place ou lits pliants,
Divan-lit, **Climatisation** Dans les chambres, Ventilateurs de plafond, **Fumeurs** À l'extérieur, **Dans la chambre** Thermostat, TV, Foyer, Magnétoscope, **AUTRES**
Gardiennage d'enfants, Rural, Toutes saisons, Animaux
de compagnie à l'intérieur, **PAIEMENT** Visa, MC,
Chèques acceptés, En espèces, Chèques de voyage,
PETITS DÉJEUNERS Complet, Continental, Fait à la maison, **COMMODITÉS** Téléphone central, Piscine, Bain
tourbillon, Cuisine disponible, Réfrigérateur, Service de
boissons chaudes, Salon pour invités, Patio pour
invités, Accès Internet central, **CHOSES À FAIRE**
Location de bicyclettes, Sentier à proximité, Location
de canoë ou de bateau, Golf, Pêche, Musées, Galeries
d'art, Théâtre, Attractions, Magasinage, Ski de fond, Ski
alpin, Tennis, Natation, Équitation, Observation d'oiseaux, Antiquités, **LANGUES** Ang., Fr., **PRIX** (2 personnes)
60–125 **(vérifiez avec les hôtes les détails des prix)**

Parry Sound [Pointe au Baril]
(au nord de Toronto)

Eye of the Eagle Retreat and B&B/Spa

(Ann et Rod Kelly)

Box 13, Hwy 529A #160, Pointe au Baril, ON, P0G 1K0
www.eyeoftheeagle.net
Adresse électronique website@eyeoftheeagle.net

705-366-5666
No de téléc. 705-366-2603
No d'appel sans frais 1-866-366-3245

Eye of the Eagle, escapade intime et confortable qui vous dorlote sous tous les aspects. De nos chambres de luxe exclusives avec salle de bains privée, à nos délicieux repas et services de spa. Forfaits tout compris avec hébergement, repas, spa extérieur/cuve thermale, sentiers de randonnée pédestre/raquette, et splendides jardins. Notre massage le plus populaire est notre massage à la pierre chaude pour le couple leur permettant de relaxer et d'attiser la flamme. Situé un peu au nord de Parry Sound.

CHAMBRES Étage supérieur, **Salles de bains** Chambres communicantes, **Lits** Très grand lit, Grand lit, Lits jumeaux, Lits à une place ou lits pliants, **Climatisation** Climatiseur central, **Fumeurs** À l'extérieur, **Dans la chambre** Thermostat, TV, Magnétoscope, **AUTRES** Rural, Adulte, Toutes saisons, Repas additionnels, Animaux de compagnie à l'intérieur, **PAIEMENT** Visa, MC, En espèces, Chèques de voyage, **PETITS DÉJEUNERS** Complet, **COMMODITÉS** TV centrale, Téléphone central, Bain tourbillon, Barbeque, Salon pour invités, **CHOSES À FAIRE** Bicyclettes à titre gracieux, Sentier à proximité, Location de canoë ou de bateau, Golf, Pêche, Théâtre, Attractions, Ski de fond, Natation, Équitation, Plage, Observation d'oiseaux, **LANGUES** Ang., **PRIX** (2 personnes) 99–129 (**vérifiez avec les hôtes les details des prix**)

Shelburne *(au nord-ouest de Toronto)*

Anderson's Hilltop B&B

(Robert et Eleanor Anderson)

595438 Blind Line, RR #1, Shelburne, ON, L0N 1S5
andersonshilltopfarmbandb.com
Adresse électronique andersonrw@sympatico.ca

519-925-5129
No de téléc. 519-925-2073

Grande maison de brique moderne érigée sur une ferme de 100 âcres offrant une vue panoramique de la campagne, le long d'une route en gravier non achalandée. Relaxez et profitez de l'ambiance rurale. Des arrangements spéciaux de transport et de placement de véhicule sont disponibles pour des randonnées pédestres le long du sentier Bruce Trail. Centres de ski dans la région. Réservations hebdomadaires.

CHAMBRES Étage supérieur, Rez-de-chaussée, Entrée privée, **Salles de bains** Privée, Partagée avec un client, **Lits** Grand lit, Lits jumeaux, **Fumeurs** À l'extérieur, **AUTRES** Rural, Toutes saisons, Accessible aux personnes handicapées, Repas additionnels, **PAIEMENT** Visa, Chèques acceptés, En espèces, **PETITS DÉJEUNERS** Complet, **COMMODITÉS** TV centrale, Téléphone central, Blanchisserie, Cuisine disponible, Réfrigérateur, Salon pour invités, **CHOSES À FAIRE** Sentier à proximité, Golf, Pêche, Musées, Galeries d'art, Attractions, Ski de fond, Équitation, **LANGUES** Ang., Fr., **PRIX** (2 personnes) 55–75 (**vérifiez avec les hôtes les details des prix**)

Stratford *(à l'ouest de Toronto)*

Avon and John

(Ray et Leonora Hopkins)

72 Avon St, Stratford, ON, N5A 5N4
www.cyg.net/~avonjohn
Adresse électronique avonjohn@cyg.net

519-275-2954
No de téléc. 519-275-2956
No d'appel sans frais 1-877-275-2954

Venez profiter de l'hospitalité et du confort chauds de notre merveilleuse maison ancestrale, le délicieux petit déjeuner complet à l'anglaise, les merveilleux jardins primés; une expérience tout à fait mémorable de Stratford. Trois chambres d'hôte avec salle de bains privée, climatiseur central, frigo, cafetière et robes de chambre, Décor paisible; marchez aux parcs et théâtres du centre ville. Toutes les commodités pour le voyageur averti d'aujourd'hui avec la chaleur et la joie de vivre de jadis.

CHAMBRES Étage supérieur, **Salles de bains** Privée, Chambres communicantes, **Lits** Grand lit, Lits jumeaux, **Climatisation** Climatiseur central, **Fumeurs** À l'extérieur, **AUTRES** Urbain, Adulte, Toutes saisons, **PAIEMENT** Visa, MC, Amex, Chèques acceptés, En espèces, Chèques de voyage, **PETITS DÉJEUNERS** Complet, **COMMODITÉS** TV centrale, Téléphone central, Bain tourbillon, Réfrigérateur, Service de boissons chaudes, Salon pour invités, Patio pour invités, Magnétoscope central, **CHOSES À FAIRE** Sentier à proximité, Location de canoë ou de bateau, Golf, Musées, Galeries d'art, Théâtre, Divertissement, Attractions, Magasinage, Antiquités, **LANGUES** Ang., Fr., All., Hollandais, **PRIX** (2 personnes) 105–120 (**vérifiez avec les hôtes les details des prix**)

Toronto *(rive nord du lac Ontario)*

Annex Quest House

(Henry Lotin)

83 Spadina Rd, Toronto, ON, M5R 2T1
www.annexquesthouse.com
Adresse électronique info@annexquesthouse.com

416-922-1934
No de téléc. 416-922-6366

Centre ville près de Spadina et Bloor, Annex Quest House est à deux pas de l'Université de Toronto, Musée royal de l'Ontario, boutiques Yorkville. Chambres avec salle de bains privée conçues pour améliorer le bien-être des clients au moyen de vastu, ancienne science de conception de l'Inde. Chaque chambre est dédiée à 1 de 4 éléments : terre, air, feu ou eau. Commodités d'usage : salle de bains privée, climatisation, accès Internet HV, frigo-bar, TV par câble, téléphone, non-fumeur, stationnement.

CHAMBRES Étage supérieur, Rez-de-chaussée, Sous-sol, Entrée privée, **Salles de bains** Privée, Chambres communicantes, **Lits** Lit à 2 places, **Climatisation** Dans les chambres, **Dans la chambre** Thermostat, Téléphone, TV, Accès Internet, **AUTRES** Urbain, Toutes saisons, **PAIEMENT** Visa, MC, Amex, Débit électronique, En espèces, Chèques de voyage, **COMMODITÉS** Barbeque, Blanchisserie, Réfrigérateur, Patio pour invités, **CHOSES À FAIRE** Musées, Galeries d'art, Théâtre, Divertissement, Attractions, Magasinage, **LANGUES** Ang., Mandarin, Cantonese, **PRIX** (2 personnes) 89–109 (**vérifiez avec les hôtes les details des prix**)

Toronto

Feathers

(May et Max Jarvie)

132 Wells St, Toronto, ON, M5R 1P4
www.bbcanada.com/1115.html
Adresse électronique feathersbb@hotmail.com

416-534-1923
No de téléc. 416-534-1587

Charmante maison familiale victorienne située dans un superbe endroit du centre-ville appelé Annex. Meubles anciens, tapisseries murales orientales, objets d'arts originaux, atmosphère unique, remarquablement rénovée. Près du métro, abondance de restaurants et de cafés à prix abordables. Suite autonome pour séjours prolongés. Marchez à Casa Loma et à plusieurs autres attractions majeures, magasins et théâtres. Choisi comme "Meilleurs gîtes où séjourner". Situé à deux rues de Bloor près de Bathurst.

CHAMBRES Suite familiale, Étage supérieur, **Salles de bains** Chambres communicantes, Partagée avec les hôtes, **Lits** Très grand lit, Lits jumeaux, Lits à une place ou lits pliants, **Climatisation** Climatiseur central, **Fumeurs** À l'extérieur, **Dans la chambre** TV, **AUTRES** Urbain, Toutes saisons, **PAIEMENT** En espèces, Chèques de voyage, **PETITS DÉJEUNERS** Continental, **COMMODITÉS** Téléphone central, Réfrigérateur, Salon pour invités, **CHOSES À FAIRE** Musées, Galeries d'art, Théâtre, Divertissement, Attractions, Magasinage, **LANGUES** Ang., Fr., All., Hollandaise, **PRIX** (2 personnes) 75–105 **(vérifiez avec les hôtes les details des prix)**

Toronto

Lowtherhouse
Bed and Breakfast

(Linda Lilge)

72 Lowther Ave, Toronto, ON, M5R 1C8
www.lowtherhouse.ca
Adresse électronique linda@lowtherhouse.ca

416-323-1589
No de téléc. 416-961-9322
No d'appel sans frais 1-800-265-4158

Lowtherhouse est un manoir victorien de 1890 à trois étages. Les clients de Lowtherhouse expérimenteront un milieu urbain ainsi qu'un quartier calme car nous sommes à deux coins de rue de Bloor et Avenue Road et du secteur bien établi de l'Annex. La station de métro St. George est tout près et il y a un parc familial accueillant de l'autre côté de la rue. Toutes les chambres ont une salle de bains privée. Petit déjeuner complet à l'anglaise servi tous les matins dans la salle à manger traditionnelle.

CHAMBRES Étage supérieur, **Salles de bains** Chambres communicantes, **Lits** Très grand lit, Grand lit, Lit à 2 places, Lits jumeaux, **Climatisation** Climatiseur central, **Fumeurs** À l'extérieur, **Dans la chambre** Téléphone, TV, **AUTRES** Urbain, Toutes saisons, Animaux de compagnie à l'intérieur, **PAIEMENT** Visa, MC, Amex, En espèces, Chèques de voyage, **PETITS DÉJEUNERS** Complet, **COMMODITÉS** **CHOSES À FAIRE** Musées, Galeries d'art, Théâtre, Divertissement, Attractions, Magasinage, **LANGUES** Ang., Fr., **PRIX** (2 personnes) 95–175 **(vérifiez avec les hôtes les details des prix)**

Wasaga Beach *(au nord de Toronto)*

At the Sandpiper

(Rosemarie et Bert Hoferichter)

53 – 60th St N, Wasaga Beach, ON, L0L 2P0
www.bbcanada.com/sandpiper
Adresse électronique sandpiperbb@sympatico.ca

705-429-2746

Maison décorée avec goût située à 300′ de la plage. Rte 26 dans la Baie Georgienne sur une plage sablonneuse de 10 milles de longueur. Hébergement de choix, trois chambres privées. Deux chambres avec grand lit et salle de bains communicante, et une chambre avec deux lits à une place. Climatisation centrale. Près des sentiers de ski de fond/alpin Blue Mountain et Blueberry. Bicyclettes, parasol et chaises de plage à titre gracieux. Fameux forfait de fin de semaine avec souper. Voir www.bbcanada .com/sandpiper.

CHAMBRES Suite familiale, Étage supérieur, **Salles de bains** Privée, Chambres communicantes, **Lits** Grand lit, Lits jumeaux, **Climatisation** Climatiseur central, **Fumeurs** À l'extérieur, **Dans la chambre** Thermostat, Foyer, **AUTRES** Rural, Adulte, Toutes saisons, Animaux de compagnie à l'intérieur, **PAIEMENT** Visa, En espèces, Chèques de voyage, **PETITS DÉJEUNERS** Complet, Fait à la maison, **COMMODITÉS** TV centrale, Téléphone central, Barbeque, Réfrigérateur, Salon pour invités, Patio pour invités, **CHOSES À FAIRE** Bicyclettes à titre gracieux, Sentier à proximité, Golf, Pêche, Musées, Théâtre, Divertissement, Attractions, Vineries/Brasseries, Magasinage, Ski de fond, Tennis, Natation, Équitation, Plage, **LANGUES** Ang., All., **PRIX** (2 personnes) 75–95 **(vérifiez avec les hôtes les details des prix)**

Niagara Region

Rolanda's B&B

(Rolande Fushtey)

26 Martha Crt, Welland, ON, L3C 4N2
www.canadianbandbguide.ca/bb.asp?ID=3699

905-732-2853

Au cœur de la région de Niagara en 'Ontario, à quelques minutes en voiture de la capitale mondiale des lunes de miel, Niagara Falls. Profitez des divertissements offerts par Casino Niagara. Détendez-vous en prenant le thé dans notre magnifique jardin et savourez les couleurs vives de nos fleurs en été. Vous êtes bienvenus à la cuisine de l'hôte pour votre choix d'un petit déjeuner complet et savoureux incluant des fruits frais. Nous parlons anglais et français et sommes ouverts à l'année.

CHAMBRES Suite familiale, Rez-de-chaussée, Sous-sol, **Salles de bains** Privée, Partagée avec les hôtes, **Lits** Lit à 2 places, Divan-lit, **Climatisation** Climatiseur central, **Fumeurs** À l'extérieur, **Dans la chambre** TV, **AUTRES** Toutes saisons, **PAIEMENT** En espèces, **PETITS DÉJEUNERS** Complet, **COMMODITÉS** TV centrale, Réfrigérateur, Patio pour invités, **CHOSES À FAIRE** Location de bicyclettes, Sentier à proximité, Location de canoë ou de bateau, Golf, Pêche, Musées, Théâtre, Vineries/Brasseries, Magasinage, Tennis, Natation, Plage, **LANGUES** Ang., Fr., **PRIX** (2 personnes) 50–70 **(vérifiez avec les hôtes les details des prix)**

Bideford *(ouest de l'Î-P-É)*

Hilltop Acres Bed & Breakfast

(Janice et Wayne Trowsdale)

694 Bideford Rd, Rte 166, Bideford, l'Î-P-É, C0B 1J0
www3.pei.sympatico.ca/~wjt_hilltop
Adresse électronique wjt_hilltop@pei.sympatico.ca

902-831-2817
No de téléc. 902-831-2817
No d'appel sans frais 1-877-305-2817

Dans la ville historique de Bideford surplombant la baie Malpeque. Balcon au 2e étage, balançoires de jardin, terrasses, pavillon grillagé, salon d'hôtes. Marchez sur le gazon ou faites le tour de notre propriété de 60 âcres à 3 km du sentier Confédération. Chambre Queen avec salle de bains communicante, suite à deux chambres pour groupe de 4 avec salle de bains privée. Conserves maison. Escompte multi-nuits. Lady Slipper Drive (Rte 12) jusqu'à Bideford Rd (Rte 166). Près du Bideford Parsonage Museum.

CHAMBRES Étage supérieur, **Salles de bains** Privée, Chambres communicantes, **Lits** Grand lit, Lit à 2 places, **Fumeurs** À l'extérieur, **AUTRES** Rural, Saisonnier, **PAIEMENT** Visa, MC, Débit électronique, En espèces, Chèques de voyage, **PETITS DÉJEUNERS** Complet, Fait à la maison, **COMMODITÉS** Bain tourbillon, Barbeque, **CHOSES À FAIRE** Sentier à proximité, Musées, Galeries d'art, Divertissement, Attractions, **LANGUES** Ang., **PRIX** (2 personnes) 60–70 (**vérifiez avec les hôtes les details des prix**)

Charlottetown *(centre-sud de l'Î-P-É)*

Shipwright Inn

(Judy et Trevor Pye)

51 Fitzroy St, Charlottetown, l'Î-P-É, C1A 1R4
www.shipwrightinn.com
Adresse électronique innkeeper@shipwrightinn.com

902-368-1905
No de téléc. 902-628-1905
No d'appel sans frais 1-888-306-9966

Auberge historique primée. Maison de 1865 près des sites historiques, restaurants, magasins, parcs et bord de l'eau, 25 terrains de golf à proximité. Architecture classique restaurée, thème nautique, foyers, antiquités, jardin, balcons, tourbillons, planchers en planches de bateaux, accès Internet (Wi-Fi). Lits de qualité, salles de bains privées, climatisation, téléphone. Trois suites de luxe. TV par câble, VCR quelques DVD. Stationnement privé, rue à l'ombre calme et sécuritaire. Ouvert à l'année.

CHAMBRES Suite familiale, Étage supérieur, Rez-de-chaussée, Sous-sol, Entrée privée, **Salles de bains** Privée, Chambres communicantes, **Lits** Très grand lit, Grand lit, Lit à 2 places, Lits jumeaux, Lits à une place ou lits pliants, Divan-lit, **Climatisation** Dans les chambres, **Fumeurs** À l'extérieur, **Dans la chambre** Thermostat, Téléphone, TV, Foyer, Accès Internet, Magnétoscope, **AUTRES** Urbain, Toutes saisons, **PAIEMENT** Visa, MC, Amex, En espèces, Chèques de voyage, **PETITS DÉJEUNERS** Complet, Fait à la maison, **COMMODITÉS** Téléphone central, Bain tourbillon, Blanchisserie, Réfrigérateur, Service de boissons chaudes, Salon pour invités, Patio pour invités, Accès Internet central, **CHOSES À FAIRE** Location de bicyclettes, Sentier à proximité, Location de canoë ou de bateau, Golf, Pêche, Musées, Galeries d'art, Théâtre, Divertissement, Attractions, Vineries/Brasseries, Magasinage, Ski de fond, Natation, Équitation, Plage, Observation d'oiseaux, Antiquités, **LANGUES** Ang., Fr., **PRIX** (2 personnes) 99–289 (**vérifiez avec les hôtes les details des prix**)

NORTH LAKE HARBOUR
(nord-est de l'Î-P-É)

Harbour Lights Guest House

(Bruce et Patricia Craig)

6434 North Side Rd, Elmira, l'Î-P-É, C0A 1K0
www.harbourlightshouse.com
Adresse électronique info@harbourlightshouse.com

902-357-2127
No d'appel sans frais 1-866-687-9949

Le gîte Harbour Lights, une maison de ferme rénovée des années 1880, est situé dans les champs de l'est du comté de Kings. Surplombant North Lake Harbour, il offre des vues sensationnelles du port et de l'océan. Petit déjeuner fermier complet inclut avec votre séjour; les autres repas peuvent aussi être fournis. Nous sommes près du sentier Confédération, des plages vierges, musés et parcs provinciaux, ainsi que les terrains de golf les plus célèbres de l'île. Visitez le www.harbourlightshouse.com.

CHAMBRES Étage supérieur, Rez-de-chaussée, **Salles de bains** Partagée avec un client, Partagée avec les hôtes, **Lits** Grand lit, Lit à 2 places, **Fumeurs** À l'extérieur, **AUTRES** Rural, Adulte, Saisonnier, Animaux de compagnie à l'intérieur, **PAIEMENT** Visa, MC, Chèques acceptés, En espèces, Chèques de voyage, **PETITS DÉJEUNERS** Complet, **COMMODITÉS** TV centrale, Magnétoscope central, **CHOSES À FAIRE** Location de bicyclettes, Sentier à proximité, Location de canoë ou de bateau, Golf, Pêche, Musées, Galeries d'art, Théâtre, Divertisse-ment, Attractions, Vineries/Brasseries, Natation, Plage, Observation d'oiseaux, Antiquités, **LANGUES** Ang., une peu de Mandarin, **PRIX** (2 personnes) 65–70 **(vérifiez avec les hôtes les details des prix)**

ARUNDEL *(nord-owest de Montréal)*

Julia's B&B

(Julia Stuart)

73 Ch de la Rouge, Arundel, QC, J0T 1A0
www.canadianbandbguide.ca/bb.asp?ID=3170
Adresse électronique juliamstuart@yahoo.ca

819-687-2382

Julia's B&B, à Saga Turung Farm offre un séjour sain, relaxant et inspirant, individu ou groupes. Dans la vallée de la rivière Rouge, entouré de ruisseaux et de pâturages vallonnés, hébergement confortable, spacieux et plaisant, avec copieux petits déjeuners pour tous les goûts. Autres repas fournis. Près de: piste de vélo/motoneige, golf, tennis, sports nautiques, ski, patinage, traîneau à chiens. Cours d'art de vitrail et sessions de médecine complémentaire. Gîte non-fumeurs.

CHAMBRES Étage supérieur, Rez-de-chaussée, Entrée privée, **Salles de bains** Chambres communicantes, Partagée avec un client, **Lits** Grand lit, Lit à 2 places, Lits jumeaux, **Climatisation** Dans les chambres, **Fumeurs** À l'extérieur, **Dans la chambre** Thermostat, Foyer, **AUTRES** Rural, Toutes saisons, Repas additionnels, **PAIEMENT** Chèques acceptés, En espèces, **PETITS DÉJEUNERS** Complet, Fait à la maison, Préparé soi-même, **COMMODITÉS** Téléphone central, Service de boissons chaudes, Salon pour invités, Patio pour invités, **CHOSES À FAIRE** Sentier à proximité, Golf, Pêche, Galeries d'art, Attractions, Magasinage, Ski de fond, Ski alpin, Tennis, Natation, Équitation, Plage, Observation d'oiseaux, Antiquités, **LANGUES** Ang., Fr., **PRIX** (2 personnes) 75–90 **(vérifiez avec les hôtes les details des prix)**

Gatineau [secteur Aylmer]
(à l'ouest de Montréal)

La Maison John Ogilvie
(Claude Hallé)

36 Crt Gatineau (secteur Aylmer), QC, J9H 4L7
www.maisonjohnogilvie.com
Adresse électronique info@maisonjohnogilvie.com

819-682-1616
No de téléc. 819-682-1368
No d'appel sans frais 1-866-682-1616

La maison John Ogilvie, maison ancestrale, se veut un centre de ressourcement ou on y retrouve des services de massothérapie, soins corporels, phythothérapie et médecine alternative. Nous avons plusieurs forfaits tels que: forfait santé, forfait ski, voile et aqua-forme. Notre couette et déjeuné, notre salle à manger avec sa spécialité fondue, notre piscine, feu de joie et SPA sera vous procurer un séjour des plus chaleureux.

CHAMBRES Étage supérieur, **Salles de bains** Partagée avec un client, **Lits** Très grand lit, Lit à 2 places, Lits à une place ou lits pliants, **Climatisation** Dans les chambres, **Fumeurs** À l'extérieur, **AUTRES** Repas additionnels, **PAIEMENT** Visa, MC, Débit électronique, Chèques de voyage, **PETITS DÉJEUNERS** Préparé soi-même, **COMMODITÉS** Piscine, Bain tourbillon, Salon pour invités, Patio pour invités, **CHOSES À FAIRE** Sentier à proximité, Location de canoë ou de bateau, Golf, Musées, Galeries d'art, Théâtre, Divertissement, Attractions, Ski de fond, Ski alpin, Natation, Plage, Antiquités, **LANGUES** Ang., Fr., **PRIX** (2 personnes) 65–120 **(vérifiez avec les hôtes les details des prix)**

Harrington Harbour *(est du Québec)*

Amy's Boarding House
(Amy Evans)

Box 73, Harrington Harbour, QC, G0G 1N0
www.canadianbandbguide.ca/bb.asp?ID=2327

418-795-3376
No de téléc. 418-795-3176

Venez visiter notre île, décor du film "The Great Seduction". Profitez de la sérénité, la tranquillité et des brises océaniques fraîches. Notre village coloré est perché sur une île rocheuse pittoresque surplombant la mer. Délicieux repas de poissons et de fruits de mer locaux, légumes de notre jardin et pain de ménage. Il y a beaucoup à faire:marcher sur la promenade, observer les oiseaux/baleines, flore, faune et tours de bateau, motoneige en saison. Un nouveau musée illustre notre histoire.

CHAMBRES Étage supérieur, Rez-de-chaussée, Sous-sol, **Salles de bains** Partagée avec un client, Partagée avec les hôtes, **Lits** Grand lit, Lits jumeaux, Lits à une place ou lits pliants, **Climatisation** Dans les chambres, **Fumeurs** À l'extérieur, **Dans la chambre** Thermostat, TV, **AUTRES** Toutes saisons, Repas additionnels, Animaux de compagnie acceptés, **PAIEMENT** Chèques acceptés, En espèces, Chèques de voyage, **PETITS DÉJEUNERS** Complet, Fait à la maison, **COMMODITÉS** TV centrale, Blanchisserie, Cuisine disponible, Réfrigérateur, Salon pour invités, Patio pour invités, **CHOSES À FAIRE** Sentier à proximité, Location de canoë ou de bateau, Canoë ou bateau à titre gracieux, Pêche, Musées, Attractions, Vineries/Brasseries, Plage, Observation d'oiseaux, **LANGUES** Ang., **PRIX** (2 personnes) 70–90 **(vérifiez avec les hôtes les details des prix)**

ILE-D'ORLÉANS (ST.-PIERRE)
(à l'est de Québec)

Gîte Bel Horizon

(Yvette et Paul-E. Vézina)

402 Ch Royal, Ile-d'Orléans (St-Pierre),
QC, G0A 4E0
www.inns-bb.com/belhorizon
Adresse électronique belhorizon@sympatico.ca

418-828-9207
No de téléc. 418-828-9207
No d'appel sans frais 1-877-828-9207

Bienvenue à l'entrée de l'île d'Orléans, au Gîte Bel Horizon! Pour vous y rendre, 40 Ouest (direction Ste-Anne de-Beaupré) sortie 325 pour I.O. En haut de la côte de l'île, tourner à droite, faites 1 km. La nature, la vue sur le fleuve et les chûtes Montmorency, les restaurants variés, les vignobles et les arts et culture de l'île invitent à un séjour reposant et plus qu' intéressant. Venez constater! Vos hôtes, Yvette et P.E. vous recevront avec plaisir dans leur demeure du 1er Février au 1er Nov.

CHAMBRES Suite familiale, Étage supérieur, Rez-de-chaussée, **Salles de bains** Privée, **Lits** Grand lit, Lit à 2 places, Lits jumeaux, Lits à une place ou lits pliants, **Climatisation** Dans les chambres, **Fumeurs** À l'extérieur, **Dans la chambre** Thermostat, TV, **AUTRES** Rural, Adulte, Saisonnier, **PAIEMENT** Visa, MC, Amex, En espèces, Chèques de voyage, **PETITS DÉJEUNERS** Complet, **COMMODITÉS** Téléphone central, Réfrigérateur, Salon pour invités, **CHOSES À FAIRE** Location de bicyclettes, Sentier à proximité, Golf, Pêche, Musées, Galeries d'art, Théâtre, Vineries/Brasseries, Antiquités, **LANGUES** Ang., Fr., **PRIX** (2 personnes) 72–84 **(vérifiez avec les hôtes les details des prix)**

POINTE-AU-PIC *(au nord-est de Québec)*

La Maison Frizzi

(Raymonde Vermette)

55 Coteau-sur-Mer, Charlevoix, La Malbaie,
QC, G5A 3B6
www.inns-bb.com/maisonfrizzi

418-665-4668
No de téléc. 418-665-1143

Venez découvrir notre maison de style autrichien intime et confortable, éloignéet de la grande route et surplombant le fleuve Saint-Laurent. Prix d'excellence "Favorite distinctive régionale" 2000 et 1995-1996. Bien située au centre de cette région magique. Nous aimons bien vous aider à organiser votre séjour. Hospitalité accueillante "à la québécoise". Un délicieux petit déjeuner varié vous attend. Rte 138 de Québec à la Malbaie. Pont Leclerc, Rte 362 ouest, 4, 4 km. Tournez à gauche à Coteau-sur-Mer.

CHAMBRES Étage supérieur, Entrée privée, **Salles de bains** Partagée avec un client, **Lits** Très grand lit, Grand lit, Lit à 2 places, Lits jumeaux, **Climatisation** Ventilateurs de plafond, **Fumeurs** À l'extérieur, **Dans la chambre** Thermostat, **AUTRES** Gardiennage d'enfants, Rural, Adulte, Toutes saisons, **PAIEMENT** Visa, MC, Chèques acceptés, En espèces, Chèques de voyage, **PETITS DÉJEUNERS** Complet, Fait à la maison, **COMMODITÉS** TV centrale, Téléphone central, Blanchisserie, Réfrigérateur, Salon pour invités, Patio pour invités, **CHOSES À FAIRE** Sentier à proximité, Golf, Pêche, Musées, Galeries d'art, Divertissement, Attractions, Vineries/Brasseries, Magasinage, Ski de fond, Tennis, Natation, Équitation, Plage, **LANGUES** Ang., Fr., All., Italian, **PRIX** (2 personnes) 80–85 **(vérifiez avec les hôtes les détails des prix)**

L'Anse Saint-Jean *(au nord-est de Québec)*

Le Globe-Trotter B&B

(André Bouchard)

131 Saint-Jean-Baptiste, l'Anse Saint-Jean,
QC, G0V 1J0
www.bbcanada.com/322.html
Adresse électronique andreb7@hotmail.com

418-272-2353
No de téléc. 418-272-1731
No d'appel sans frais 1-866-633-2353

A l'arrière du gîte, une rivière et une terrasse
où vous pourrez vous abandonner à votre
roman préféré et la vue sur les montagnes est
splendide. Logis ensoleillé, spacieux et très
bien décoré. Excellente adresse si vous
recherchez un gîte d'une qualité, d'un confort
supérieur et un petit déjeuner varié et copieux.
Le Guide du Routard. Pour s'y rendre: de
Québec via Saint Siméon, Rtes 138 et 170
jusqu'à l'Anse Saint Jean. De Québec Via
Chicoutimi, Rtes 175 et 170 jusqu'à l'Anse
Saint-Jean.

CHAMBRES Étage supérieur, Rez-de-chaussée, **Salles
de bains** Privée, Partagée avec un client, Partagée
avec les hôtes, **Lits** Lit à 2 places, **Fumeurs** À l'extérieur, **Dans la chambre** Thermostat, **AUTRES** Rural,
Saisonnier, **PAIEMENT** Visa, MC, En espèces, Chèques
de voyage, **PETITS DÉJEUNERS** Complet, Fait à la maison, **COMMODITÉS** TV centrale, Téléphone central,
Réfrigérateur, Salon pour invités, Patio pour invités,
Accès Internet central, **CHOSES À FAIRE** Location de
bicyclettes, Sentier à proximité, Location de canoë ou
de bateau, Pêche, Galeries d'art, Divertissement,
Magasinage, Tennis, Natation, Équitation, Plage,
LANGUES Ang., Fr., **PRIX** (2 personnes) 65–75 **(vérifiez
avec les hôtes les details des prix)**

Les Hauteurs *(bas-Saint-Laurent)*

Gîte Le Beau Lieu

(Josette Beaulieu et Augustin Bélanger)

102 2e-et-3e rang est, Les Hauteurs, QC, G0K 1C0
www.canadianbandbguide.ca/gitescan/bb.asp?ID=3742
Adresse électronique gitelebeaulieu@hotmail.com

418-798-4435

Pour le calme, le changement d'air et le repos.
40 minutes de Rimouski – c'est un rendez-vous
avec la nature. En hiver – raquette, ski du fond,
motoneige et ski alpin au Parc du Mont-Comi.
En été – randonnée pédeste dans le sous-bois
et bicyclette (non fournie) Situé à quelques
kilométres de la Zec du Bas-St Laurent.

CHAMBRES Étage supérieur, **Salles de bains** Partagée
avec les hôtes, **Lits** Lit à 2 places, **Fumeurs** À l'extérieur, **AUTRES** Gardiennage d'enfants, Rural, Toutes
saisons, Repas additionnels, **PAIEMENT** En espèces,
PETITS DÉJEUNERS Fait à la maison, **COMMODITÉS**
TV centrale, Téléphone central, Réfrigérateur, Accès
Internet central, **CHOSES À FAIRE** Bicyclettes à titre
gracieux, Sentier à proximité, Ski de fond, Ski alpin,
Équitation, **LANGUES** Ang., Fr., **PRIX** (2 personnes) 50
(vérifiez avec les hôtes les details des prix)

L'Islet-sur-Mer
(au nord-est de Québec)

Auberge La Marguerite

(Johanne Martel et Luc Morrier)

88 Des Pionniers est, L'Islet-sur-Mer, QC, G0R 2B0
www.aubergelamarguerite.com
Adresse électronique marguerite100@videotron.ca

418-247-5454
No de téléc. 418-247-7725
No d'appel sans frais 1-877-788-5454

Près du fleuve Saint-Laurent, venez revivre l'histoire de la Côte-du-Sud dans un manoir bâti en 1754. Ancienne maison très spacieuse complètement rénovée, climatiseur central, grande salle à manger claire, copieux petit déjeuner. Grand jardin paysagé où vous pourrez marcher, lire, relaxer. Activités offertes à proximité : visite de Grosse-Île, musée maritime, golf, vélo, théâtre, croisière, soins de santé, galeries d'art et plus encore. Autoroute 20, sortie 400, rte 285 nord, 4 km, Rte 132 est, 1 km.

CHAMBRES Étage supérieur, Rez-de-chaussée, **Salles de bains** Privée, **Lits** Très grand lit, Grand lit, Lit à 2 places, Lits à une place ou lits pliants, **Climatisation** Climatiseur central, **Fumeurs** À l'extérieur, **Dans la chambre** Thermostat, TV, **AUTRES** Adulte, Toutes saisons, **PAIEMENT** Visa, MC, Débit électronique, En espèces, Chèques de voyage, **PETITS DÉJEUNERS** Complet, **COMMODITÉS** Réfrigérateur, Patio pour invités, **CHOSES À FAIRE** Golf, Musées, Galeries d'art, Théâtre, Ski de fond, Observation d'oiseaux, Antiquités, **LANGUES** Ang., Fr., **PRIX** (2 personnes) 78–128 **(vérifiez avec les hôtes les details des prix)**

Maria *(sud de la Gaspésie)*

Gîte De Lune

(Lola Pichette)

759 boul Perron, Maria, QC, G0C 1Y0
www.gitescanada.com/8354.html
Adresse électronique gitedupatrimoine@globe
trotter.net

418-759-3743

Le gite du patrimoine vous offre le plaisir d'un séjour inoubliable dans une demeure ancestrale, au caractère préservé et avec tout l'agrément du confort moderne. Le gîte est situé sur un terrain de plus de 225 mètres de largeur et de 3.2 km de profondeur. Il est à plus de 90 mètres de la route. Attraction particulière au gite: chevaux de course. Piste de 0.5 kilomètre sur le terrain pour une marche tranquille tout en regardant les chevaux au centre.

CHAMBRES Étage supérieur, Rez-de-chaussée, **Salles de bains** Privée, Partagée avec un client, Partagée avec les hôtes, **Lits** Grand lit, Lits à une place ou lits pliants, **Fumeurs** À l'extérieur, **Dans la chambre** Thermostat, **PAIEMENT** Chèques acceptés, En espèces, Chèques de voyage, **PETITS DÉJEUNERS** Complet, Fait à la maison, **COMMODITÉS** Salon pour invités, Patio pour invités, **CHOSES À FAIRE** Sentier à proximité, Location de canoë ou de bateau, Golf, Musées, Galeries d'art, Théâtre, Magasinage, Tennis, Plage, **LANGUES** Ang., Fr., **PRIX** (2 personnes) 65–80 **(vérifiez avec les hôtes les details des prix)**

Montréal *(sud-ouest du Québec)*

Gîte touristique Le Saint-André-des-Arts

(Johanne Lacasse, Robert Derome)

1654 rue Saint-André, Montréal, QC, H2L 3T6
www.saintandredesarts.com
Adresse électronique lacasse.johanne@saint
andredesarts.com

514-527-7118
No d'appel sans frais 1-866-527-7118

Tous les services du centre-ville sur une rue résidentielle tranquille face à un parc. Maison patrimoniale de 1883 meublée d'antiquités et d'œuvres d'art. Grand appartement luxueux réservé aux clients avec leur entrée privée. Vous vous y sentirez rapidement chez vous ... Une vie de quartier à la française au coeur de l'arrondissement Ville-Marie historique et culturel sur une rue résidentielle tranquille à quelques pas du Quartier Latin et du Village gai de Montréal.

CHAMBRES Étage supérieur, Entrée privée, **Salles de bains** Partagée avec un client, **Lits** Très grand lit, Grand lit, Lits à une place ou lits pliants, Divan-lit, **Climatisation** Ventilateurs de plafond, **Fumeurs** À l'extérieur, **Dans la chambre** Thermostat, TV, Accès Internet, **AUTRES** Urbain, Toutes saisons, **PAIEMENT** Visa, MC, En espèces, **PETITS DÉJEUNERS** Complet, Fait à la maison, **COMMODITÉS** TV centrale, Téléphone central, Cuisine disponible, Réfrigérateur, Salon pour invités, Patio pour invités, Magnétoscope central, **CHOSES À FAIRE** Musées, Galeries d'art, Théâtre, Divertissement, Attractions, Vineries/Brasseries, Magasinage, Antiquités, **LANGUES** Ang., Fr., **PRIX** (2 personnes) 90–105 **(vérifiez avec les hôtes les details des prix)**

Montréal

Mona's Downtown

(Mona Kaufmann)

1230 Docteur Penfield, Apt 905, Montréal,
QC, H3G 1B5
www.nucleus.com/~kaufmann/bandb/main.htm
Adresse électronique monasdowntown@videotron.ca

514-842-3939
No d'appel sans frais 1-877-427-6966

Soyez les bienvenus à ma maison confortable du centre-ville de Montréal. Mes voisins immédiats sont l'Université McGill à l'est, l'Université Concordia à l'ouest et le centre-ville au sud. Les services de métro et d'autobus vous faciliteront l'accès à tous les festivals, musées, restaurants de Montréal, et à notre très ravissant "Vieux Montréal". Je vous invite à venir me voir et accepter mon hospitalité.

CHAMBRES Salles de bains Partagée avec un client, Partagée avec les hôtes, **Lits** Grand lit, Lit à 2 places, Divan-lit, **Climatisation** Dans les chambres, **Dans la chambre** TV, **AUTRES** Urbain, Adulte, Toutes saisons, **PAIEMENT** Visa, En espèces, Chèques de voyage, **PETITS DÉJEUNERS** Complet, Fait à la maison, Préparé soi-même, **COMMODITÉS** Blanchisserie, Cuisine disponible, Réfrigérateur, Service de boissons chaudes, **CHOSES À FAIRE** Location de bicyclettes, Sentier à proximité, Musées, Galeries d'art, Théâtre, Divertissement, Magasinage, **LANGUES** Ang., Fr., **PRIX** (2 personnes) 75–95 **(vérifiez avec les hôtes les details des prix)**

MONTRÉAL

University Bed & Breakfast

(Ian Atatekin et Pia Mia)

621- 623 Prince Arthur W, Montréal, QC, H2X 1T9
www.universitybedandbreakfast.ca/index.htm
Adresse électronique university@videotron.ca

514-842-6396
No de téléc. 514-842-6396

Nous sommes situés près de la rue University, dans un endroit tranquille de la rue Prince Arthur qui est l'un des endroits favoris de Montréal avec de nombreux cafés-terrasse et restaurants "apportez votre vin". La gare, les centres commerciaux du centre-ville, le quartier chinois, les sites de festivals et le plus grand espace vert de Montréal (le parc mont Royal) sont tous à moins de 10-15 minutes de marche. L'appartement a été construit en 1921 avec des murs et un foyer de briques apparents.

CHAMBRES Suite familiale, Étage supérieur, Rez-de-chaussée, Entrée privée, **Salles de bains** Privée, Partagée avec un client, **Lits** Grand lit, Lit à 2 places, Lits jumeaux, Lits à une place ou lits pliants, Divan-lit, **Climatisation** Dans les chambres, **Fumeurs** À l'extérieur, **Dans la chambre** Téléphone, TV, Foyer, Accès Internet, Magnétoscope, **AUTRES** Gardiennage d'enfants, Urbain, Toutes saisons, **PAIEMENT** Visa, MC, Diners, Amex, Débit électronique, Chèques acceptés, En espèces, Chèques de voyage, **PETITS DÉJEUNERS** Continental, **COMMODITÉS** Blanchisserie, Cuisine disponible, Salon pour invités, **CHOSES À FAIRE** Location de bicyclettes, Sentier à proximité, Golf, Musées, Galeries d'art, Théâtre, Divertissement, Attractions, Vineries/Brasseries, Magasinage, Ski de fond, Tennis, Natation, Observation d'oiseaux, Antiquités, **LANGUES** Ang., Fr., **PRIX** (2 personnes) 59–119 **(vérifiez avec les hôtes les details des prix)**

QUÉBEC

Accueil Au Clair De Lune

(Jolanta Tardif de Moidrey)

26 ave Ste-Geneviève, Old Québec City, QC, G1R 4B2
www.adorequebec.com
Adresse électronique smag@sympatico.ca

418-694-9165
No de téléc. 418-694-3487
No d'appel sans frais 1-877-299-0993

Le gîte Accueil Au Clair de Lune est situé au cœur du vieux Québec, à quelques pas du Château Frontenac, de la Citadelle et de la verdure des Plaines d'Abraham. Lits d'un confort supérieur, chambres décorées avec goût avec murs en briques et plafonds de 12 pied, salles de bains communicantes, TV par câble. Taxes touristiques, petit déjeuner complet et stationnement inclus dans le prix de la chambre. Pour plus d'information, ou pour réserver téléphoner.

CHAMBRES Salles de bains Chambres communicantes, **Lits** Grand lit, Divan-lit, **Fumeurs** À l'extérieur, **Dans la chambre** TV, **PAIEMENT** Visa, MC, Diners, Amex, En espèces, **PETITS DÉJEUNERS** Complet, **COMMODITÉS** Téléphone central, Réfrigérateur, **CHOSES À FAIRE** Location de bicyclettes, Sentier à proximité, Location de canoë ou de bateau, Golf, Musées, Galeries d'art, Théâtre, Divertissement, Attractions, Vineries/Brasseries, Magasinage, Ski de fond, Ski alpin, Tennis, Natation, Équitation, Plage, Observation d'oiseaux, Antiquités, **LANGUES** Ang., Fr., **PRIX** (2 personnes) 115–145 **(vérifiez avec les hôtes les details des prix)**

QUÉBEC

Appartements - Condos Le Méribel de Québec

(Lisette Émond)

393 rue de la Reine, Près du Vieux-Québec,
QC, G1K 2R3
www.lemeribel.ca
Adresse électronique lisette-remi@moncanoe.com

418-529-7027
No de téléc. 418-529-7027

Au coeur du fameux quartier revitalisé de St-Roch, à 5 minutes du Vieux-Québec, tous les services sont accessible en marchant. Gare, autobus. Rénové en 2005, Le Méribel est climatisé et décoré avec goût et sobriété. Réserver une chambre avec déjeuner ou un appartement privé (4-6 personnes) comprenant: 2 chambres, salle à manger, salon : télé satellit, salle de bain et douche, laveuse et sécheuse, cuisine équipée : lave-vaisselle, micro-onde, terrasse, cour arriére. Statiommement gratuit. Bain de détente et douche indépendante.

CHAMBRES Étage supérieur, Rez-de-chaussée, **Salles de bains** Privée, Partagée avec un client, **Lits** Grand lit, Divan-lit, **Climatisation** Climatiseur central, **Fumeurs** À l'extérieur, **Dans la chambre** Thermostat, Téléphone, **AUTRES** Toutes saisons, **PAIEMENT** Visa, MC, Amex, En espèces, Chèques de voyage, **PETITS DÉJEUNERS** Préparé soi-même, **COMMODITÉS** TV centrale, Téléphone central, Blanchisserie, Cuisine disponible, Réfrigérateur, Service de boissons chaudes, Salon pour invités, Patio pour invités, **CHOSES À FAIRE** Location de bicyclettes, Sentier à proximité, Location de canoë ou de bateau, Golf, Pêche, Musées, Galeries d'art, Théâtre, Divertissement, Vineries/Brasseries, Magasinage, Ski de fond, Ski alpin, Tennis, Natation, Équitation, Plage, Observation d'oiseaux, Antiquités, **LANGUES** Ang., Fr., **PRIX** (2 personnes) 60–85 **(vérifiez avec les hôtes les details des prix)**

QUÉBEC CITY DOWNTOWN
(centre-sud du Québec)

À la Maison Tudor

(J.C. Kilfoil)

1037 ave Moncton, Québec City, QC, G1S 2Y9
www.lamaisontudor.com
Adresse électronique ckilfoil@lamaisontudor.com

418-686-1033
No de téléc. 418-686-6066

L'enchantement est au rendez-vous: magnifique résidence bourgeoise début 1900, à l'allure élégante et au cachet unique, près des Plaines d'Abraham, du Vieux-Québec et du Centre des congrès. Toutes les pièces de la maison sont décorées avec goût et raffinement. Tout est accessible à pied : Vieux-Québec, restaurants, cinéma, musées, concerts, théâtre, Plaines d'Abraham, Promenade des Gouverneurs, Terrasse Dufferin, Château Frontenac. À deux pas: pistes cyclables, patin à roues alignées et ski de fond.

CHAMBRES Suite familiale, Étage supérieur, Entrée privée, **Salles de bains** Privée, Partagée avec un client, **Lits** Grand lit, Lits à une place ou lits pliants, **Climatisation** Climatiseur central, **Fumeurs** À l'extérieur, **Dans la chambre** Thermostat, Accès Internet, **PAIEMENT** Visa, MC, En espèces, Chèques de voyage, **PETITS DÉJEUNERS** Complet, **COMMODITÉS** TV centrale, Téléphone central, Cuisine disponible, Réfrigérateur, Salon pour invités, Accès Internet central, **CHOSES À FAIRE** Location de bicyclettes, Sentier à proximité, Golf, Musées, Galeries d'art, Théâtre, Divertissement, Attractions, Vineries/Brasseries, Magasinage, Ski de fond, Ski alpin, Tennis, Observation d'oiseaux, Antiquités, **LANGUES** Ang., Fr., **PRIX** (2 personnes) 105–115 **(vérifiez avec les hôtes les details des prix)**

Québec *(centre-sud du Québec)*

A la Roseraie, gîte

(Doris Lavoie)

865 ave Dessane, Québec City, QC, G1S 3J7
www.gitedelaroseraie.com
Adresse électronique info@gitedelaroseraie.com

418-688-5076
No de téléc. 418-688-9217

Vous serez accueillis en toute simplicité dans cette spacieuse et lumineuse demeure des années 40. Blottie dans le paisible quartier Montcalm, vous serez au centre de toutes les activités. Un vaste salon pour vous détendre des chambres confortables, ainsi qu'un copieux petit déjeuner vous feront apprécier votre séjour dans notre magnifique ville. Accès par le Boul. René Levesque, ou par le Chemin Ste-Foy.

CHAMBRES Rez-de-chaussée, **Salles de bains** Privée, Partagée avec un client, **Lits** Très grand lit, Grand lit, Lits jumeaux, **Fumeurs** À l'extérieur, **AUTRES** Toutes saisons, **PAIEMENT** Visa, MC, En espèces, Chèques de voyage, **PETITS DÉJEUNERS** Complet, **COMMODITÉS** TV centrale, Téléphone central, Bain tourbillon, Accès Internet central, **CHOSES À FAIRE** Sentier à proximité, Golf, Musées, Galeries d'art, Théâtre, Vineries/Brasseries, Magasinage, Ski de fond, **LANGUES** Ang., Fr., **PRIX** (2 personnes) 55–90 **(vérifiez avec les hôtes les details des prix)**

Québec

Aux Années folles

(Jean Daoust)

5 rue des Saules est, Québec City, QC, G1L 1R5
www.membres.lycos.fr/annfol
Adresse électronique annfol@hotmail.com

418-260-9549

Vous cherchez un endroit différent? Non-conformistes et nostalgiques des années 20, vous aimerez l'Art déco des Années folles! Un esprit, une collection, un lieu de séjour … à découvrir. Un gîte dans Limoilou (Colisée, ExpoCité). Près de l'autoroute 40 (sortie 315, 1re ave) à 4 km du Vieux-Québec piste cyclable, métrobus).

CHAMBRES Étage supérieur, **Salles de bains** Partagée avec un client, **Lits** Lit à 2 places, Lits jumeaux, **Fumeurs** À l'extérieur, **AUTRES** Urbain, Toutes saisons, **PAIEMENT** En espèces, **PETITS DÉJEUNERS** Complet, Fait à la maison, **COMMODITÉS** TV centrale, Téléphone central, Salon pour invités, Patio pour invités, Magnétoscope central, **CHOSES À FAIRE** Bicyclettes à titre gracieux, Antiquités, **LANGUES** Ang., Fr., **PRIX** (2 personnes) 55–75 **(vérifiez avec les hôtes les details des prix)**

Québec

B&B Centreville

(Bernard Couturier)

257 St-Vallier est, Québec City, QC, G1K 3P4
www.bbcentreville.com
Adresse électronique bbcentreville@hotmail.com

418-525-4741
No de téléc. 418-525-6906
No d'appel sans frais 1-866-525-4741

Maison ancestrale datant de 1875, entièrement rénovée. Nous offrons 5 magnifique chambres, dont une familiale, chacune avec salle de bain privée. Stationnement gratuit. Déjeuner copieux et variés. À proximité des Murs fortifiés. Nous pouvons accueillir des groupes pour mariages ou autres. Votre Hôte, Bernard, guide certifié, pourra bien vous conseiller. Nous sommes inscrits dans le *Guide du Routard* et dans *Lonely Planet*. Profitez de nos tarifs hors saison. Consultez notre site; bbcentreville.com.

CHAMBRES Suite familiale, Étage supérieur, Rez-de-chaussée, Entrée privée, **Salles de bains** Privée, **Lits** Grand lit, Lits jumeaux, **Dans la chambre** Thermostat, **AUTRES** Urbain, Toutes saisons, **PAIEMENT** Visa, MC, En espèces, **PETITS DÉJEUNERS** Complet, Fait à la maison, Préparé soi-même, **COMMODITÉS** Salon pour invités, **CHOSES À FAIRE** Location de bicyclettes, Sentier à proximité, Golf, Musées, Galeries d'art, Théâtre, Divertissement, Vineries/Brasseries, Magasinage, Ski de fond, Ski alpin, Tennis, Natation, **LANGUES** Ang., Fr., **PRIX** (2 personnes) 85–155 **(vérifiez avec les hôtes les details des prix)**

Québec

Chez Monsieur Gilles 2

(Gilles Clavet)

1720 che de la Canardiere, Québec City, QC, G1J 2E3
www.chezmonsieurgilles.com/
Adresse électronique mgilles@sympatico.ca

418-821-8778
No de téléc. 418-821-8776

Gagnant du Prix régional Coup de cœur en 1999. Gagnant du Prix régional Grands prix du Tourisme Québécois pour Accueil et Service à la clientèle. Chalet à trois étages genre château. Situé à 5 minutes des murs de l'ancienne cité (1 mille ou 1.6 km) Climatiseur central, cuve thermale, table de billard, vélos/stationnement gratuits, terrasse. Table d'hôte avec réservation, petit magasin. Cinq grandes chambres, deux avec salles de bains partagées et trois avec salles de bains privées. Nous sommes "la perle rare" du Québec.

CHAMBRES Suite familiale, Étage supérieur, **Salles de bains** Privée, Partagée avec un client, **Lits** Grand lit, Lit à 2 places, Lits à une place ou lits pliants, Divan-lit, **Climatisation** Climatiseur central, **Fumeurs** Dans les chambres, **Dans la chambre** Thermostat, TV, **AUTRES** Urbain, Toutes saisons, Repas additionnels, Animaux de compagnie à l'intérieur, **PAIEMENT** Visa, Diners, Chèques acceptés, En espèces, Chèques de voyage, **PETITS DÉJEUNERS** Complet, **COMMODITÉS** TV centrale, Téléphone central, Bain tourbillon, Réfrigérateur, Patio pour invités, **CHOSES À FAIRE** Bicyclettes à titre gracieux, Sentier à proximité, Golf, Pêche, Musées, Galeries d'art, Théâtre, Divertissement, Attractions, Vineries/Brasseries, Magasinage, Ski de fond, Tennis, Natation, Équitation, Plage, **LANGUES** Ang., Fr., **PRIX** (2 personnes) 90–125 **(vérifiez avec les hôtes les details des prix)**

Saint-Georges *(au sud de Québec)*

Le Jardin des Mésanges

(Hélène Couture et Roger Provost)

482 Route Fortier, Saint-Cyprien-des-Etchemins,
QC, G0R 1B0
www.lejardindesmesanges.com
Adresse électronique mesanges@sogetel.net

418-383-5777
No d'appel sans frais 1-877-383-5777

Découvrez le charme de la nature du Québec par notre jardin, ses oiseaux, la forêt et ses parcs. Chez-nous, c`est le calme de la campagne qui vous permet de refaire le plein d`énergie pour mieux profiter des nombreuses activités : vélo, marche, ski, motoneige, etc. Petite ferme pour le plaisir. Plusieurs forfaits : cabane à sucre, golf, théâtre, ... Cachet d`autrefois, confort d`aujourd`hui. Délicieux déjeuner maison avec produits régionaux. Souper familiale. Vous accueillir est un plaisir.

CHAMBRES Suite familiale, Étage supérieur, Rez-de-chaussée, **Salles de bains** Privée, Partagée avec un client, **Lits** Lit à 2 places, Lits jumeaux, Lits à une place ou lits pliants, **Fumeurs** À l'extérieur, **Dans la chambre** Thermostat, **AUTRES** Rural, Toutes saisons, Repas additionnels, Animaux de compagnie à l'intérieur, **PAIEMENT** Visa, MC, Diners, Amex, En espèces, Chèques de voyage, **PETITS DÉJEUNERS** Complet, Fait à la maison, **COMMODITÉS** TV centrale, Téléphone central, Bain tourbillon, Barbeque, Blanchisserie, Réfrigérateur, Salon pour invités, Patio pour invités, Accès Internet central, Magnétoscope central, **CHOSES À FAIRE** Sentier à proximité, Location de canoë ou de bateau, Golf, Pêche, Musées, Galeries d'art, Théâtre, Divertissement, Attractions, Vineries/Brasseries, Magasinage, Ski de fond, Ski alpin, Natation, Équitation, Plage, Observation d'oiseaux, Antiquités, **LANGUES** Ang., Fr., **PRIX** (2 personnes) 60–70 (**vérifiez avec les hôtes les details des prix**)

Saint-Donat *(au nord de Montréal)*

Auberge St-Donat

(Belinda et François Wisser)

350 Route 329, Saint-Donat, QC, J0T 2C0
www.aubergestdonat.com
Adresse électronique info@aubergestdonat.com

819-424-7504
No de téléc. 819-424-7504

Charmante auberge de 12 chambres, située à l'entrée du village de Saint-Donat, offrant une vue imprenable sur le lac Archambault et les montagnes Laurentiennes. Auberge d'époque à proximité de plusieurs lacs, d'une piste cyclable, d'un club de golf, de plusieurs centres de ski et située aux portes du parc du Mont-Tremblant. Venez goûter au plaisir au naturel.

CHAMBRES Suite familiale, Étage supérieur, Sous-sol, **Salles de bains** Privée, **Lits** Très grand lit, Grand lit, Lit à 2 places, Divan-lit, **Climatisation** Dans les chambres, **Fumeurs** À l'extérieur, **Dans la chambre** TV, **AUTRES** Rural, Toutes saisons, Accessible aux personnes handicapées, Repas additionnels, Animaux de compagnie acceptés, **PAIEMENT** Visa, MC, Chèques acceptés, En espèces, **PETITS DÉJEUNERS** Complet, **COMMODITÉS** TV centrale, Téléphone central, Bain tourbillon, Barbeque, Cuisine disponible, Service de boissons chaudes, Salon pour invités, Patio pour invités, Accès Internet central, Magnétoscope central, **CHOSES À FAIRE** Location de bicyclettes, Sentier à proximité, Location de canoë ou de bateau, Golf, Pêche, Musées, Galeries d'art, Divertissement, Attractions, Magasinage, Ski de fond, Ski alpin, Natation, Équitation, Plage, Observation d'oiseaux, Antiquités, **LANGUES** Ang., Fr., **PRIX** (2 personnes) 70–100 (**vérifiez avec les hôtes les details des prix**)

SAINTE ADÈLE *(au nord de Montréal)*

A La Belle Idée

(Françoise et Michel Matte)

894, rue de l'arbre sec, Sainte Adèle, QC, J8B 1X6
www.labelleidee.com
Adresse électronique labelleidee@bellnet.ca

450-229-6173
No de téléc. 450-229-6173
No d'appel sans frais 1-888-221-1313

Gîte 4 soleils, dans une magnifique canadienne nichée au bord de son boisé. Situé à Sainte, au coeur des Laurentides à mi-chemin entre Montréal et Mont-Tremblant. Assez proche du village pour accéder rapidement aux nombreuses activités et suffisament loin pour profiter du calme et des prestations fournies par vos hôtes. Quatres chambres climatisées avec salle de bains privée dont une suite avec accès internet haut débit vous attendent. Piscine creusée et chauffée. Tous les détails sur notre site du Web.

CHAMBRES Suite familiale, Étage supérieur, Rez-de-chaussée, **Salles de bains** Privée, **Lits** Grand lit, Lit à 2 places, Lits à une place ou lits pliants, **Climatisation** Climatiseur central, **Fumeurs** À l'extérieur, **Dans la chambre** Accès Internet, **AUTRES** Rural, Toutes saisons, Repas additionnels, **PAIEMENT** Visa, MC, En espèces, Chèques de voyage, **PETITS DÉJEUNERS** Complet, Fait à la maison, **COMMODITÉS** TV centrale, Téléphone central, Piscine, Bain tourbillon, Réfrigérateur, Salon pour invités, Patio pour invités, Magnétoscope central, **CHOSES À FAIRE** Location de bicyclettes, Sentier à proximité, Location de canoë ou de bateau, Golf, Pêche, Musées, Galeries d'art, Théâtre, Divertissement, Attractions, Magasinage, Ski de fond, Ski alpin, Tennis, Natation, Équitation, Plage, **LANGUES** Ang., Fr., Esp., **PRIX** (2 personnes) 71–104 **(vérifiez avec les hôtes les details des prix)**

SAINTE FLORENCE *(ouest de la Gaspésie)*

Gîte au Bois Joli

(Esther Leblanc et Marcel Dionne)

852 Route 132, Sainte Florence, QC, G0J 2M0
www.gites-classifies.qc.ca/boijol.htm
Adresse électronique gitesbj@globetrotter.net

418-756-5609

Le Gîte Au Bois Joli Situé sur la route 132 mais en retrait. Dans La Belle Vallée de la Matapédia. A 7 heures de Montréal ou à 5 heures de Québec direction Gaspé. Maison centenaire. Vous allez en Gaspésie, au Nouveau Brunswick. à l'Ile du PE en Nouvelle Ecosse ou au Iles de la Madeleine. Arrètez vous , vous serez reçu comme de la famille. Pour faire le plein à l'aller comme au retour. Déjeuners copieux. Vous aimez la pèche, la rivière Matapédia vous attend l'endroit rechercher c'est ici.

CHAMBRES Suite familiale, Étage supérieur, Sous-sol, Entrée privée, **Salles de bains** Privée, Partagée avec un client, Partagée avec les hôtes, **Lits** Grand lit, Lit à 2 places, Lits jumeaux, Divan-lit, **Climatisation** Ventilateurs de plafond, **Fumeurs** À l'extérieur, **Dans la chambre** TV, **AUTRES** Rural, Toutes saisons, **PAIEMENT** En espèces, Chèques de voyage, **PETITS DÉJEUNERS** Fait à la maison, **COMMODITÉS** Barbeque, Cuisine disponible, Réfrigérateur, Service de boissons chaudes, Salon pour invités, Patio pour invités, **CHOSES À FAIRE** Sentier à proximité, Golf, Pêche, Musées, Divertissement, Attractions, Ski de fond, Ski alpin, Observation d'oiseaux, Antiquités, **LANGUES** Fr., **PRIX** (2 personnes) 62-72 **(vérifiez avec les hôtes les details des prix)**

SAINTE-AGATHE-DES-MONTS
(au nord de Montréal)

Gîte la maison du lac

(Jocelyne Manseau, Normand Carpentier)

37 rue Saint-Aubin, Sainte-Agathe-Des- Monts,
QC, J8C 2Z7
www.lamaisondulac.com
Adresse électronique info@lamaisondulac.com

819-323-3862
No de téléc. 819-323-3863
No d'appel sans frais 1-866-321-5324

Itinéraire d'accès :
Autoroute des laurentides (15) nord, Sortie 83,
au stop tournez à gauche Montée Alouette,
arrivé au stop de la 329 et du théâtre "Le
Patriote" tournez à droite faire 500 mètres environ, en face de l'école de voile tournez à droite
dans la rue Madeleine, la rue St-Aubin est la
1ère sur votre droite, montez jusqu'en haut le
#37 est le premier chemin sur votre droite,
poteau indicateur B&B "La Maison du Lac" au
fond du chemin.

CHAMBRES Suite familiale, Rez-de-chaussée, Entrée
privée, **Salles de bains** Privée, **Lits** Grand lit, **Fumeurs**
À l'extérieur, **Dans la chambre** Thermostat, Accès
Internet, **AUTRES** Toutes saisons, **PAIEMENT** Visa, MC,
En espèces, **PETITS DÉJEUNERS** Complet, Fait à la
maison, **COMMODITÉS** TV centrale, Réfrigérateur,
Service de boissons chaudes, Salon pour invités, Patio
pour invités, Accès Internet central, **CHOSES À FAIRE**
Location de bicyclettes, Sentier à proximité, Golf,
Pêche, Théâtre, Attractions, Magasinage, Ski de fond,
Ski alpin, Tennis, Plage, **LANGUES** Fr., **PRIX** (2 person-
nes) 80–125 **(vérifiez avec les hôtes les details des
prix)**

BAS SAINT-LAURENT
(au nord-est de Québec)

La Ferme Paysagée

(Gabrielle et Régis Rouleau)

121 rte 293 Sud, Saint-Jean-de-Dieu, QC, G0L 3M0
www.ferme-paysagee.com
Adresse électronique rouls@globetrotter.net

418-963-3315

Une spendide ferme laitière. Petits animaux
exotiques soit llamas, paons bébés, lapins,
poules ... L'initiation de la traite des vaches. Un
petit-déjeuner copieux avec crêpes au sirop
d'érable, confiture maison, sortes de jus et café
volonte. Nous offront le repas du soir aussi.
Nous sommes situé dans le Bas St Laurent près
du Fleuve St. Laurent. Les familles sont les bienvenue. De Québec Aut 20 est, rte 293 sud
jusqu'a St. Jean De-Dieu. Faire 4 km aprè
l'église. Notre gîte a trois soleils.

CHAMBRES Étage supérieur, Entrée privée, **Salles de
bains** Partagée avec un client, Partagée avec les
hôtes, **Lits** Lit à 2 places, **Climatisation** Ventilateurs de
plafond, **Fumeurs** À l'extérieur, **Dans la chambre**
AUTRES Toutes saisons, Repas additionnels,
PAIEMENT Chèques acceptés, En espèces, Chèques de
voyage, **PETITS DÉJEUNERS** Fait à la maison,
COMMODITÉS TV centrale, Téléphone central,
Blanchisserie, Cuisine disponible, Réfrigérateur,
Service de boissons chaudes, Salon pour invités, Patio
pour invités, Accès Internet central, **CHOSES À FAIRE**
Sentier à proximité, Divertissement, **LANGUES** Fr.,
PRIX (2 personnes) 50–50 **(vérifiez avec les hôtes les
details des prix)**

Saint-Pierre-de-Véronne-à-Pike-River
(au sud-est de Montréal)

La Villa des Chenes

(Noelle Gasser)

300 che des Rivieres, Saint-Pierre-de-Véronne-à-Pike-River, QC, J0J 1P0
www.canadianbandbguide.ca/bb.asp?ID=2768
Adresse électronique rngasser@netc.net

450-296-8848
No de téléc. 450-296-4990

À une heure de Montréal, bienvenue à notre grande maison près de la rivière, sur notre ferme laitière. Chambres paisibles et confortables, petits déjeuners complets et plats familiaux d'origine suisse. Près du lac Champlain, région loyaliste séduisante, riche en agriculture, vignobles et musée historique local. Des gens aimables et sereins vous accueillent à de superbes restaurants, aux foires agricoles, expositions d'œuvres d'art, festivals des vendanges et autres attractions. Membres d'Agricotours.

CHAMBRES Étage supérieur, Sous-sol, **Salles de bains** Privée, Partagée avec un client, **Lits** Très grand lit, Grand lit, Lit à 2 places, Lits jumeaux, Lits à une place ou lits pliants, Divan-lit, **Climatisation** Climatiseur central, **Fumeurs** À l'extérieur, **AUTRES** Rural, **PAIEMENT** Chèques acceptés, En espèces, Chèques de voyage, **PETITS DÉJEUNERS** Complet, **COMMODITÉS** TV centrale, Téléphone central, Réfrigérateur, Salon pour invités, Patio pour invités, **CHOSES À FAIRE** Sentier à proximité, Location de canoë ou de bateau, Golf, Musées, Galeries d'art, Attractions, Vineries/Brasseries, **LANGUES** Ang., Fr., All., **PRIX** (2 personnes) 55–75 **(vérifiez avec les hôtes les details des prix)**

Québec

Fleet's Guest Home/Chez Stuart & Marie Paule Fleet

(Stuart et Marie Paule Fleet)

1080 Holland Ave, Sillery, QC, G1S 3T3
www.canadianbandbguide.ca/bb.asp?ID=1956

418-688-0794

Fameuse citadelle des Plaines d'Abraham. Voyez la relève de la garde, le Vieux Québec, Place Royale. Savourez votre petit déjeuner sur la terrasse extérieure, dans le solarium ou la salle à manger de cette maison spacieuse. Les hôtes ont plusieurs années d'expérience dans le domaine de l'hôtellerie. L'étage supérieur est complètement réservé aux clients.

CHAMBRES Étage supérieur, **Salles de bains** Partagée avec un client, **Lits** Grand lit, Lits jumeaux, **Climatisation** Climatiseur central, **Dans la chambre** TV, **PAIEMENT** Visa, En espèces, Chèques de voyage, **PETITS DÉJEUNERS** Complet, **COMMODITÉS** Patio pour invités, **CHOSES À FAIRE** Attractions, Magasinage, **LANGUES** Ang., Fr., **PRIX** (2 personnes) 82 **(vérifiez avec les hôtes les details des prix)**

QUÉBEC

Au Pignon Vert

(Edmond et Monique Proulx)

2631 Jean Brillant, Ste Foy Québec, QC, G1W 1E9
www.canadianbandbguide.ca/gitescan/bb.asp?I
Adresse électronique pignonvert@videotron.ca

418-651-8487

Nous sommes bien située et facile d'acces, Entrant a Ste Foy a 10 minutes du Vieux Quebec A proximité vous avez l'hopital de l'"université, a 3 minutes a pieds des centres commerciaux et 10 minutes de l'université. Nous sommes bien entouré, le village indien, les chutes Mont-morency, L"ile d'Orleans et selon la saison les jeux au village Val Cartier, les traineaux a chiens ou la cabane a sucre. Nous offrons aussi les reservation pour les baleines et plus.

CHAMBRES Rez-de-chaussée, Sous-sol, Entrée privée, **Salles de bains** Partagée avec un client, Partagée avec les hôtes, **Lits** Lit à 2 places, Lits à une place ou lits pliants, **Fumeurs** À l'extérieur, **Dans la chambre** Thermostat, Accès Internet, **AUTRES** Urbain, Adulte, Toutes saisons, **PAIEMENT** Chèques de voyage, **PETITS DÉJEUNERS** Complet, Fait à la maison, **COMMODITÉS** TV centrale, Blanchisserie, Cuisine disponible, Réfrigérateur, Salon pour invités, Accès Internet central, **CHOSES À FAIRE** Bicyclettes à titre gracieux, Sentier à proximité, Golf, Musées, Galeries d'art, Théâtre, Divertissement, Attractions, Vineries/ Brasseries, Magasinage, Ski de fond, Ski alpin, Tennis, Natation, Équitation, Plage, Observation d'oiseaux, Antiquités, **LANGUES** Ang., Fr., **PRIX** (2 personnes) 45–55 **(vérifiez avec les hôtes les details des prix)**

STONEHAM *(au nord de Québec)*

Gîte et Centre de santé des Loups

(Sylvie Cournoyer et Pierre Taschereau)

570 1e ave, Stoneham, QC, G0A 4P0
www.gitedesloups.com
Adresse électronique info@gitedesloups.com

418-848-4483
No d'appel sans frais 1-866-334-4483

Un gîte pittoresque du début du siècle vous accueille dans une ambiance traditionnelle et inspirante. 5 chambres typiques et les services d'un centre de santé où l'on prend soin de vous. Incluant le petit déjeûner Autoroute 73 nord, sortie 167, 175 sud, sortie 167. Rendez-vous au deuxième clignotant, suivez nos panneaux indicateurs.

CHAMBRES Étage supérieur, **Salles de bains** Partagée avec un client, Partagée avec les hôtes, **Lits** Grand lit, Lit à 2 places, Lits à une place ou lits pliants, **Fumeurs** À l'extérieur, **AUTRES** Rural, Toutes saisons, Animaux de compagnie à l'intérieur, Animaux de compagnie acceptés, **PAIEMENT** Chèques acceptés, En espèces, Chèques de voyage, **PETITS DÉJEUNERS** Complet, Fait à la maison, **COMMODITÉS** TV centrale, Téléphone central, Sauna, Bain tourbillon, Réfrigérateur, Salon pour invités, Patio pour invités, **CHOSES À FAIRE** Bicyclettes à titre gracieux, Location de bicyclettes, Sentier à proximité, Location de canoë ou de bateau, Golf, Pêche, Théâtre, Ski de fond, Ski alpin, Tennis, Natation, Équitation, Plage, Observation d'oiseaux, **LANGUES** Ang., Fr., Esp., **PRIX** (2 personnes) 57–92 **(vérifiez avec les hôtes les details des prix)**

Beds and Breakfasts Mentioning Bird Watching Opportunities

This varies from backyard to prime watching sites near the B&B

Prov.	Near	B&B Name
AB	Banff	A Homestead Bed & Breakfast
AB	Banff/ Canmore	Creekside Country Inn
AB	Brooks	A Lake Shore B&B
AB	Calgary	1910 Elbow River Manor Bed & Breakfast
AB	Calgary	1919@Along River Ridge Bed & Breakfast
AB	Calgary	A Hilltop Ranch B&B
AB	Calgary	Calgary Westways Guest House
AB	Calgary	Pathway Cottage Bed and Breakfast
AB	Calgary	Riverview Bed and Breakfast
AB	Canmore	Avens ReNaissance B&B
AB	Canmore	Riverview & Main B&B
AB	Cochrane	Mountview Cottage B&B
AB	Cold Lake	Hamilton House Bed and Breakfast Inn
AB	Crowsnest Pass	Blairmore Heritage House B&B, Tea & Gift Shop
AB	Drumheller	Pearl's Country Cottages
AB	Drumheller	Taste The Past
AB	Edmonton	Chickadee Hollow Bed and Breakfast
AB	Edmonton and Devon	A High Rigg Retreat B&B
AB	Hinton	Brule Bed & Breakfast
AB	Hinton	McCracken Country Inn
AB	Jasper	A Little Log House Accommodation
AB	Jasper	Casa Norma
AB	Jasper	Home Away From Home Bed and Breakfast
AB	Jasper	Mount Robson Mountain River Lodge
AB	Jasper	Old Entrance B 'n B Cabins
AB	Jasper	Raven House B&B
AB	Lacombe	Rieky's Bed & Breakfast
AB	Pigeon Lake (area)	Hidden Springs Retreat & Guesthouse
AB	Pine Lake	Daisy House/Pierce Farms
AB	Wainwright	Mackenzie House Bed & Breakfast
BC	100 Mile House	Attwood Creek Ranch Bale, Bed & Breakfast
BC	100 Mile House	Maverick Moose B&B
BC	Armstrong	A Country Haven Bed & Breakfast
BC	Bowser	Shoreline Bed and Breakfast
BC	Bridge Lake	Hawthorn Acres Bed & Breakfast
BC	Burns Lake	Nobody's Inn
BC	Chemainus	Be Delighted B&B
BC	Chemainus	Island Haven B&B
BC	Chemainus	Ladysmith Bed and Breakfast
BC	Chilliwack	Cedar Grove Bed and Breakfast
BC	Clearwater	Tanglewood
BC	Cobble Hill (Victoria)	Country Treasures B and B Guest Cottage
BC	Comox	Alpine House B&B
BC	Comox	Copes Islander Oceanfront B&B

Prov.	Near	B&B Name
BC	Comox	Singing Sands Bed & Breakfast
BC	Denman Island	Hawthorn House B&B
BC	Duncan	Sunflower Inn Bed & Breakfast
BC	Fernie	Barbara Lynn's Country Inn
BC	Gabriola Island	Island Bed & Breakfast
BC	Gibsons	A Waterfront Hideaway
BC	Gibsons	Ocean Breezes Bed & Breakfast
BC	Gibsons	Rosewood Country House
BC	Gibsons	The Maritime Cottage and Suites
BC	Golden	Blaeberry Mountain Lodge
BC	Golden	Columbia Valley Lodge, B&B
BC	Golden	Farview Bed and Breakfast
BC	Golden	Historic HG Parson House B&B
BC	Harrison Hot Springs	Harrison Heritage House & Kottages
BC	Hope	Evergreen B&B & Spa
BC	Hope	Mountainview Bed and Breakfast
BC	Invermere	Harmington House
BC	Kelowna	A Lakeview Heights Bed & Breakfast
BC	Kelowna	A View To Remember B&B
BC	Kelowna	A Mykonos
BC	Kelowna	Cozy Corner Guesthouse B&B
BC	Kelowna	Joyce House Bed & Breakfast
BC	Kelowna	Love's Lakeview Bed & Breakfast
BC	Kelowna	Magical Bliss Bed & Breakfast
BC	Kelowna	Mission Hills Vacation Suite
BC	Kelowna	Wine Country Suites Bed and Breakfast
BC	Kelowna	Yellow Rose Bed and Breakfast
BC	Kimberley	Wasa Lakeside B&B Resort
BC	Ladysmith	Hansen House Vacation Suite
BC	Lake Cowichan	Kidd's B&B
BC	Maple Ridge	Bob's B&B
BC	Mill Bay	Bluemoon Bed and Breakfast
BC	Mission	Cascade Falls Bed and Breakfast
BC	Mission	Fleur de Sel French Country Bed and Breakfast
BC	Nanaimo	Island View B&B
BC	Nanaimo	Pacific Terrace Bed & Breakfast
BC	Parksville	Arrowsmith Bed and Breakfast (House on the Corner)
BC	Peachland	Casa Serene
BC	Pemberton	Country Meadows Bed & Breakfast
BC	Pender Island	Gnome's Hollow Bed & Breakfast
BC	Penticton	Inn Paradise Bed & Breakfast
BC	Penticton	Pinetree Bed and Breakfast
BC	Penticton	Royal Bed and Breakfast
BC	Port Alberni	Alpine Springs Farm and B&B
BC	Port Hardy	Hamilton Bed and Breakfast
BC	Port McNeill	C-Shasta Bed & Breakfast
BC	Powell River	Adventure B&B
BC	Powell River	Beacon B&B and Spa

BC	Prince George	Chalet Sans Souci B&B
BC	Prince George	Rosels Bed and Breakfast
BC	Prince Rupert	Eagle Bluff B&B
BC	Qualicum Beach	A & K Oceanside Retreat
BC	Salt Spring Island	Belvedere Place
BC	Salt Spring Island	Blue Heron
BC	Salt Spring Island	Cedar Lane Bed & Breakfast
BC	Salt Spring Island	Ocean Spray Bed & Breakfast By The Sea
BC	Salt Spring Island	Quarrystone House
BC	Sechelt	A Place by the Sea Bed and Breakfast & Spa
BC	Sidney	Honeysuckle Cottage Bed & Breakfast
BC	Sidney	Inlet Beach House B&B
BC	Sidney	Lovat House B&B
BC	Sidney	Seventh Haven
BC	Smithers	Bulkley Valley Guesthouse
BC	Smithers	Glacier View
BC	Sooke	A Secluded Romantic Retreat at Sooke River Estuary
BC	Sooke	Blue Waters Bed and Breakfast
BC	Sooke	Lilac House B&B & Wisteria Honeymoon Cottage
BC	Sorrento (Shuswap Lake)	A Rover's Rest Bed & Breakfast
BC	Sorrento (Shuswap Lake)	The Roost Bed and Breakfast
BC	Squamish	Coneybeare Lodge
BC	Squamish	True North Bed and Breakfast
BC	Summerland	A Touch of English Bed & Breakfast
BC	Summerland	Grape Escape Guest House
BC	Sun Peaks	Sun Valley Bed & Breakfast
BC	Tofino	Cable Cove Inn
BC	Tofino	Clayoquot Retreat
BC	Tofino	Gull Cottage Bed & Breakfast
BC	Tofino	Summerhill Guest House
BC	Valemount	Summit River Lodge, Cabins and campsites
BC	Vancouver	A Suite @ Kitsilano Cottage
BC	Vancouver	Alida's Twin Hollies Bed & Breakfast
BC	Vancouver	Duck Inn Riverfront Cottages
BC	Vancouver	Ellison House
BC	Vancouver	Kitsilano Cottage By The Sea
BC	Vancouver	Ocean Breeze B&B and Furnished Apartments
BC	Vancouver	Pendrell Suites
BC	Vancouver	The Doorknocker Bed and Breakfast
BC	Vancouver	ThistleDown House
BC	Vancouver (S Delta)	Our House Bed and Breakfast
BC	Vancouver (Surrey)	Bed & Breakfast On the Ridge
BC	Vernon	Alpineflowers Bed and Breakfast
BC	Vernon	Castle On The Mountain
BC	Vernon	Cedar Grove B&B
BC	Vernon	Harbour Lights B&B
BC	Vernon	The Maples
BC	Victoria	Amethyst Inn at Regents Park
BC	Victoria	Arbutus Hill Bed and Breakfast
BC	Victoria	Beacon Inn at Sidney
BC	Victoria	Bender's Bed & Breakfast
BC	Victoria	Birds of a Feather Victoria Oceanfront B&B
BC	Victoria	Cordova Bay Vacations
BC	Victoria	Cougar's Crag Extreme B&B
BC	Victoria	Millstream Llama Farm Bed & Breakfast
BC	Victoria	Oceanside Gardens Retreat
BC	Victoria	Prior House B&B Inn
BC	Victoria	Wintercott Country House
BC	West Vancouver	The Tree House Bed & Breakfast
BC	Whistler	Farmhouse Bed and Breakfast
BC	Whistler	Inn at Clifftop Lane
BC	White Rock	A Beach House B&B... on the Beach...Naturally!
BC	White Rock	Bellevue House Bed and Breakfast
BC	White Rock	Kent Manor Guest House B&B
BC	White Rock	Sand & Sea B&B Guest Suites
BC	White Rock	The Daly Bed and Bread Guest House
BC	Williams Lake	Rowat's Waterside Bed & Breakfast
MB	Boissevain	Rowanoak Guesthouse
MB	Boissevain	Walkinshaw Place
MB	Deloraine	Country Garden Inn
MB	Grand Beach	Inn Among The Oaks
MB	Grunthal	Rainbow Ridge Ranch – Bale, Bed & Breakfast
MB	Hecla Island	Solmundson Gesta Hus
MB	Neepawa	Highland Glen B&B
MB	Saint-Pierre-Jolys	Château des Sages B&B
MB	Selkirk	Evergreen Gate Bed and Breakfast
MB	Steinbach	Chickadee Lane B&B
MB	Winnipeg	Elsa's Place
NB	Alma	Falcon Ridge Inn
NB	Bathurst	Gîte Toutes Saisons B&B
NB	Bouctouche	Les Pins Maritimes
NB	Caraquet	Gîte Le Poirier B&B
NB	Caraquet	Hotel Paulin
NB	Grand Manan	McLaughlin's Wharf B&B
NB	Hopewell Cape	Florentine Manor B and B
NB	Inkerman (Shippagan)	Le Gîte de l'Ardora Bed and Breakfast
NB	Millville	LedgeRocK Bed and Breakfast
NB	Moncton	Gîte du voyageur Chez-Aanna
NB	Moncton	Leah Jane's Bed and Breakfast
NB	Moncton	Lori's Bed and Breakfast
NB	Petit-Rocher	Auberge d'Anjou
NB	Port Elgin	Pumpkinn Inn B&B
NB	Sackville	Marshlands Inn
NB	Saint John on the Bay of Fundy	Beach House Bed & Breakfast Beach House Bed & Breakfast (Kingston) Inc.
NB	Saint John on the Bay of Fundy	Homeport Historic B&B/Inn c1858
NB	Shediac	Auberge, Maison Vienneau
NL	Cape Onion	Tickle Inn at Cape Onion
NL	Carbonear	Sophia's Fine Dining & Bed and Breakfast
NL	Dildo	Inn By The Bay
NL	Grand Falls-Windsor	Carriage House Inn
NL	Grand Falls-Windsor	Hill Road Manor
NL	Port Blandford	Terra Nova

NL	St John's	Angel House Heritage Inn
NL	Trinity	Artisan Inn
NS	Annapolis Royal	Reminisce Bed and Breakfast
NS	Digby	Thistle Down Country Inn
NS	Halifax	Welcome Inn Halifax Bed and Breakfast
NS	Iona	Old Grand Narrows Hotel B&B
NS	Lunenburg	1860 Kaulbach House Historic Inn
NS	Lunenburg	Atlantic Sojourn Bed and Breakfast
NS	Lunenburg area	The Backman House Bed and Breakfast
NS	Maitland	Cresthaven By The Sea...A Country Inn
NS	Middleton	Century Farm Inn (c.1886)
NS	Musquodoboit Harbour	The Elephant's Nest Bed & Breakfast
NS	North Sydney	Annfield Manor
NS	North Sydney	Gowrie House Country Inn
NS	Parrsboro	The Maple Inn
NS	Parrsboro	The Parrsboro Mansion
NS	Salmon River Bridge-Jeddore	Salmon River House Country Inn
NS	Sydney	A Paradise Found B&B
NS	Truro	The Udder Place
NS	Truro	Tulips and Thistle Bed & Breakfast
NS	Westport, Brier Island	Bay of Fundy Inn
NT	Yellowknife	Gill-Power Bed & Breakfast
ON	Ajax	Before the Mast B&B
ON	Algonquin Park (Dorset)	The Nordic Inn of Dorset
ON	Algonquin Park (Huntsville)	A Gingerbread B&B
ON	Algonquin Park (Huntsville)	Fairy Bay Guest House
ON	Algonquin Park (Huntsville)	Kent House Bed & Breakfast
ON	Alliston	Gramma's House
ON	Alliston	Stevenson Farms Historical B&B
ON	Ancaster	The Fiddler's Inn
ON	Baden	Willow Springs Suites B&B
ON	Bancroft	Maple Leaf B&B
ON	Bancroft	The Gathering Place On Golden Ponds B&B
ON	Barrie	Brookview B&B
ON	Barrie	Richmond Manor Bed & Breakfast
ON	Barrie	Thornton Country Gardens B&B
ON	Barrys Bay	Fortune's Madawaska Valley Inn
ON	Bayfield	Magnolia Manor B&B
ON	Bayfield	Naftel House Bed & Breakfast
ON	Belleville	Hickory House Bed & Breakfast
ON	Belleville	Twin Oakes Bed & Breakfast
ON	Bethany	Plantation House Bed & Breakfast Country Retreat
ON	Bracebridge	Country Hearts
ON	Bracebridge	The Yellow Door B&B
ON	Bradford West Gwillimbury	Blossom The Clown's B&B
ON	Bridgenorth	Birch Point Bay
ON	Brighton	Apple Manor Bed & Breakfast
ON	Brighton	Butler Creek Country Inn
ON	Brockville	Misty Pines B&B
ON	Burlington	Seville-Roe Guesthouse & Gallery
ON	Chesley	Sconeview B&B
ON	Cornwall	Lighthouse Landing

ON	Damascus	The Pritty Place
ON	Erin	Devonshire Guest House
ON	Flesherton	Toad Hall
ON	Fort Erie (Ridgeway)	Split Rock Farms Bed and Breakfast
ON	Gananoque	Tea & Crumpets Bed & Breakfast
ON	Gananoque	The Victoria Rose Inn
ON	Georgetown	L'Auberge
ON	Georgetown	Victorian Rose Bed and Breakfast
ON	Haliburton Highlands	Sunny Rock Bed & Breakfast
ON	Hamilton (Dundas)	Glenwood B&B
ON	Jordan and Vineland	Bonnybank Bed and Breakfast
ON	Kenora	Northwoods Bed and Breakfast
ON	Kimberley	Jasper Stuart House
ON	Kingston	The Tymparon Inn
ON	Kingsville	The Old Farmhouse Bed & Breakfast
ON	Lancaster	MacPine Farm's Bed & Breakfast
ON	London	Belle Vie's guest cottage
ON	London	Charlton, Eve's Place Bed & Breakfast
ON	Manitoulin Island	Westview B&B
ON	Marathon	Lakeview Manor Bed & Breakfast
ON	Marmora	Marmora Inn
ON	Maynooth	Ironwood Hill Inn B&B
ON	Meaford	Bridge Street Harbour Landing Bed and Breakfast
ON	Meaford	Holly Cottage B&B
ON	Midland	1875 A Charters Inn B&B
ON	Midland	Little Lake Inn Bed & Breakfast
ON	Milton	Applewood Guest House
ON	Milton	Willowbrook Bed and Breakfast
ON	Minden	Stouffer Mill Bed & Breakfast Getaway
ON	Minden	Wild Swan Bed and Breakfast Inn
ON	Mississauga	Dallimore's Just Your Cup of Tea
ON	Morrisburg	The Village Antiques & Tea Room – Bed & Breakfast
ON	Niagara Falls	Andrea's Bed and Breakfast
ON	Niagara Falls	Marshall's B&B
ON	Niagara Falls	Paradise Point Bed and Breakfast
ON	Niagara Falls	Rose Arbor B&B
ON	Niagara Falls	Villa Gardenia Bed & Breakfast
ON	Niagara Region	Heritage House B&B
ON	Niagara Region	Maples of Grimsby Bed and Breakfast
ON	Niagara-on-the-Lake	6 Oak Haven Bed and Breakfast
ON	Niagara-on-the-lake	Abel Thomas House Bed and Breakfast
ON	Niagara-on-the-Lake	Andrew Carroll House
ON	Niagara-on-the-Lake	Antonio Vivaldi B&B
ON	Niagara-on-the-Lake	Bird Watchers Haven Cottage Suites
ON	Niagara-on-the-Lake	Bullfrog Pond Guest House
ON	Niagara-on-the-Lake	Dietsch's Empty Nest
ON	Niagara-on-the-lake	DownHome Bed and Breakfast
ON	Niagara-on-the-Lake	Lakewinds Country Manor circa 1881

ON	Niagara-on-the-Lake	Serenity Garden B&B
ON	Niagara-on-the-Lake	Wishing Well Historical Cottage Rental
ON	Niagara-on-the-Lake	Yolanta's B&B
ON	Orangeville	In Tir Na Nog Bed & Breakfast
ON	Orillia	B&B on the Lake
ON	Orillia	Betty and Tony's Waterfront Bed and Breakfast
ON	Orillia	Cavana House Bed & Breakfast
ON	Orillia (Barrie)	The Verandahs Bed & Breakfast
ON	Oshawa	Emerson Manor B&B
ON	Ottawa	A Rose on Colonel By B&B
ON	Ottawa	Adele's Family Tree Bed & Breakfast
ON	Ottawa	Auberge McGee's Inn
ON	Ottawa	Country Lane Farm B&B
ON	Ottawa	Gasthaus Switzerland Inn
ON	Owen Sound	B & C Moses Sunset Country Bed & Breakfast
ON	Owen Sound	The Highland Manor Grand Victorian B&B
ON	Paris	Domes on the Grand
ON	Paris	River Ridge Bed and Breakfast
ON	Parry Sound (Pointe au Baril)	Eye of the Eagle Retreat and B&B/Spa
ON	Pelee Island	It's Home
ON	Penetanguishene	Toanche Cove B&B
ON	Peterborough	Hunter Farm B&B
ON	Peterborough	King Bethune House Guest House & Spa
ON	Peterborough	Resonance Bed & Breakfast and Spa
ON	Port Colborne	Kent House B&B
ON	Port Rowan	Marsh Landing
ON	Port Rowan	The Bay House Bed and Breakfast
ON	Port Stanley	Mulberry Lane B&B
ON	Prince Edward County	Oeno Gallery & Guesthouse
ON	Prince Edward County	Wellington On The Bay Waterfront B&B
ON	Rideau Lakes	Denaut Mansion Country Inn
ON	Ridgetown	Ridge Farm B&B
ON	Rockville	Rockville Inn
ON	Sauble Beach	Sauble Falls Bed and Breakfast
ON	St. Marys	Green Arbour B&B
ON	Stratford	Double CC Farm
ON	Stratford	Harmony House
ON	Stratford	Stone Maiden Inn
ON	Sudbury	Auberge-sur-lac B&B
ON	Thornbury	Hillside Bed & Breakfast
ON	Vankleek Hill	Cliftondale B&B
ON	Vankleek Hill	Dreamland on the Ridge
ON	Walkerton	Silver Creek B&B
ON	Warkworth	Humphrey House
ON	Wasaga Beach	Cherry House
ON	Westport	A Bit of Gingerbread B&B
ON	Westport	The Cove Country Inn
ON	Wiarton	Down A Country Lane
ON	Woodstock	Zeelandia B&B
PE	Charlottetown	Shipwright Inn
PE	Charlottetown	The Snapdragon Bed and Breakfast Inn
PE	Montague	Elms at Brudenell Bed and Breakfast
PE	North Lake Harbour	Harbour Lights Guest House
PE	Summerside	Copple Summer Home
PE	Wood Islands	Bayberry Cliff Inn
QC	Acton Vale	Aux bras de Morphée
QC	Arundel	Julia's B&B
QC	Baie St-Paul	Noble Quêteux
QC	Gatineau	Stanyar House B&B
QC	Harrington Harbour	Amy's Boarding House
QC	Howick	Rivers Edge Bed and Breakfast
QC	Ile d'Orleans	B&B Au Giron de l'Isle
QC	Ile d'Orleans	L'Oasis De Reves
QC	Kamouraska	Gîte Chez Jean et Nicole
QC	L'Islet-sur-Mer	Auberge La Marguerite
QC	Mont Tremblant	Crystal-Inn Mont Tremblant
QC	Montreal	B A Guest B&B and Reservation Service
QC	Montreal	Le relais des Argoulets
QC	Montreal	University Bed & Breakfast
QC	Mont-Tremblant	Auberge Tremblant Onwego
QC	Pointe-à-la-Croix	Gîte La Maison verte du Parc la-Croix Gaspésien
QC	Quebec	Accueil Au Clair De Lune
QC	Quebec	Appartements – Condos Le Méribel de Québec
QC	Quebec	Au Pignon Vert 3563
QC	Quebec City (Ile d'Orléans)	A la Dauphinelle (B&B)
QC	Quebec City Downtown	À la Maison Tudor
QC	Saint-Donat	Auberge St-Donat
QC	Sainte Florence	Gîte au Bois Joli
QC	Saint-Georges	Le Jardin des Mésanges
QC	Sherbrooke	La Canardiere B&B
QC	Stoneham	Gîte et Centre de santé des Loups
QC	Wakefield	Les Trois Erables
SK	Eastend	Northhill Cottage
SK	Kamsack	Border Mountain Country Bed and Breakfast
SK	Kindersley	Whyley's Bed and Beakfast
SK	Prince Albert	Hillcrest Inn
SK	Saskatoon	Riverview Bed and Breakfast
SK	Swift Current	Green Hectares Bed & Breakfast
SK	Yorkton	Patrick Place
YT	Faro	Blue B&B (Nature Friends)
YT	Whitehorse	Muktuk Guest Ranch

Beds and Breakfasts
Mentioning Internet Access

Prov.	Near	B&B Name
AB	Banff	Pension Tannenhof
AB	Banff/ Canmore	Creekside Country Inn
AB	Brooks	A Lake Shore B&B
AB	Calgary	1910 Elbow River Manor Bed & Breakfast
AB	Calgary	1919@Along River Ridge Bed & Breakfast
AB	Calgary	60 Harvest Lake Bed & Breakfast
AB	Calgary	A B&B at Calgary Lions Park
AB	Calgary	A Good Knight B&B
AB	Calgary	A Hilltop Ranch B&B
AB	Calgary	Bow River House B&B
AB	Calgary	Calgary Westways Guest House
AB	Calgary	Pathway Cottage Bed and Breakfast
AB	Calgary	Riverview Bed and Breakfast
AB	Calgary	Shangarry Bed and Breakfast
AB	Calgary	Sweet Dreams and Scones
AB	Canmore	Avens ReNaissance B&B
AB	Canmore	Riverview & Main B&B
AB	Cochrane	Mountview Cottage B&B
AB	Cold Lake	Hamilton House Bed and Breakfast Inn
AB	Crowsnest Pass	Blairmore Heritage House B&B, Tea & Gift Shop
AB	Grande Cache	EJ'S Roost
AB	Hinton	Brule Bed & Breakfast
AB	Hinton	Collinge Hill Bed and Breakfast
AB	Hinton	McCracken Country Inn
AB	Jasper	Old Entrance B 'n B Cabins
AB	Jasper	Raven House B&B
AB	Raymond	Crystal Butterfly B&B
AB	Red Deer	Apples and Angels
AB	Wainwright	Mackenzie House Bed & Breakfast
BC	Balfour	Murray Pond B&B
BC	Burns Lake	Ninth Ave Guest House
BC	Chemainus	Be Delighted B&B
BC	Chemainus	Ladysmith Bed and Breakfast
BC	Chilliwack	Cedar Grove Bed and Breakfast
BC	Comox	Copes Islander Oceanfront B&B
BC	Coquitlam	Fig Tree B&B
BC	Denman Island	Hawthorn House B&B
BC	Fernie	Barbara Lynn's Country Inn
BC	Gibsons	A Waterfront Hideaway
BC	Gibsons	Caprice Bed and Breakfast
BC	Gibsons	Ocean Breezes Bed & Breakfast
BC	Gibsons	Rosewood Country House
BC	Gibsons	The Maritimer Cottage and Suites
BC	Golden	Columbia Valley Lodge, B&B
BC	Hazelton (Kispiox River)	Poplar Park Farm & B&B
BC	Hope	Evergreen B&B & Spa
BC	Hope	Mountainview Bed and Breakfast
BC	Kamloops	Riverside Mansion Bed and Breakfast
BC	Kelowna	A Lakeview Heights Bed & Breakfast
BC	Kelowna	A View To Remember B&B
BC	Kelowna	Accounting for Taste Bed and Breakfast
BC	Kelowna	Alto Vista B&B
BC	Kelowna	A Mykonos
BC	Kelowna	An English Rose Garden
BC	Kelowna	Lakeshore Bed & Breakfast
BC	Kelowna	Magical Bliss Bed & Breakfast
BC	Kelowna	Mission Hills Vacation Suite
BC	Kelowna	The Grapevine Bed & Breakfast
BC	Kelowna	Wine Country Suites Bed and Breakfast
BC	Kelowna	Yellow Rose Bed and Breakfast
BC	Ladysmith	Hansen House Vacation Suite
BC	Mill Bay	Bluemoon Bed and Breakfast
BC	Parksville	Arrowsmith Bed and Breakfast (House on the Corner)
BC	Pemberton	Country Meadows Bed & Breakfast
BC	Penticton	Inn Paradise Bed & Breakfast
BC	Penticton	Pinetree Bed and Breakfast
BC	Penticton	Royal Bed and Breakfast
BC	Port Alberni	Alpine Springs Farm and B&B
BC	Port McNeill	C-Shasta Bed & Breakfast
BC	Powell River	Beacon B&B and Spa
BC	Prince George	Chalet Sans Souci B&B
BC	Prince George	Griffiths on Gilbert Bed and Breakfast
BC	Prince George	Rosels Bed and Breakfast
BC	Prince George	Water's Edge
BC	Prince Rupert	Eagle Bluff B&B
BC	Prince Rupert	Studio 1735 Bed & Breakfast & Art Retreat
BC	Quadra Island	Firesign Art & Design Studio and B&B
BC	Qualicum Beach	A & K Oceanside Retreat
BC	Revelstoke	Alpenrose Bed and Breakfast
BC	Salt Spring Island	Quarrystone House
BC	Savona (Kamloops)	The Rock and River Rustic Retreat
BC	Sechelt	A Place by the Sea Bed and Breakfast & Spa
BC	Sidney	Honeysuckle Cottage Bed & Breakfast
BC	Sidney	Inlet Beach House B&B
BC	Smithers	Bulkley Valley Guesthouse
BC	Sooke	Barking Crow
BC	Sooke	Lilac House B&B & Wisteria Honeymoon Cottage
BC	Sorrento (Shuswap Lake)	A Rover's Rest Bed & Breakfast
BC	Squamish	Coneybeare Lodge
BC	Squamish	True North Bed and Breakfast
BC	Summerland	A Touch of English Bed & Breakfast
BC	Surrey (Cloverdale)	Cloverdale Manor Bed & Breakfast
BC	Valemount	Summit River Lodge, Cabins and campsites
BC	Vancouver	A Harbourview Retreat B&B
BC	Vancouver	A Suite @ Kitsilano Cottage

Province	City	Name
BC	Vancouver	Alida's Twin Hollies Bed & Breakfast
BC	Vancouver	Alma Beach B&B Manor & Spa
BC	Vancouver	AnnSarah Camilla House Bed and Breakfast
BC	Vancouver	Arbutus House Bed & Breakfast
BC	Vancouver	Beachside Vancouver Bed & Breakfast
BC	Vancouver	Cassiar Figs Bed and Breakfast
BC	Vancouver	Chocolate Lily
BC	Vancouver	Corkscrew Inn
BC	Vancouver	Duck Inn Riverfront Cottages
BC	Vancouver	Greystone Bed and Breakfast
BC	Vancouver	Kitsilano Cottage By The Sea
BC	Vancouver	Mickeys Kits Beach Chalet
BC	Vancouver	'O Canada' House B&B
BC	Vancouver	Ocean Breeze B&B and Furnished Apartments
BC	Vancouver	Pendrell Suites
BC	Vancouver	The Doorknocker Bed and Breakfast
BC	Vancouver	ThistleDown House
BC	Vancouver (S Delta)	Our House Bed and Breakfast
BC	Vancouver (Surrey)	Bed & Breakfast On the Ridge
BC	Vancouver Island	Island Treasures B&B , Vacation Rental
BC	Vernon	Cedar Grove B&B
BC	Vernon	Harbour Lights B&B
BC	Victoria	A View to Sea
BC	Victoria	Amethyst Inn at Regents Park
BC	Victoria	Arbutus Hill Bed and Breakfast
BC	Victoria	Beacon Inn at Sidney
BC	Victoria	Bender's Bed & Breakfast
BC	Victoria	Birds of a Feather Victoria Oceanfront B&B
BC	Victoria	Bonavista B&B
BC	Victoria	Cordova Bay Vacations
BC	Victoria	Cougar's Crag Extreme B&B
BC	Victoria	Forgett-Me-Nott B&B
BC	Victoria	Morningside Bed and Breakfast
BC	Victoria	Prior House B&B Inn
BC	Victoria	Wintercott Country House
BC	W Vancouver	The Tree House Bed & Breakfast
BC	Whistler	Farmhouse Bed and Breakfast
BC	Whistler	Inn at Clifftop Lane
BC	White Rock	A Beach House B&B … on the Beach … Naturally!
BC	White Rock	Bellevue House Bed and Breakfast
BC	White Rock	Sand & Sea B&B Guest Suites
BC	White Rock	The Daly Bed and Bread Guest House
BC	Williams Lake	Rowat's Waterside Bed & Breakfast
MB	Grunthal	Rainbow Ridge Ranch - Bale, Bed & Breakfast
MB	Minnedosa	Fairmount Bed & Breakfast
MB	Neepawa	Highland Glen B&B
MB	Saint-Pierre-Jolys	Château des Sages B&B
MB	Selkirk	Evergreen Gate Bed and Breakfast
MB	Steinbach	Chickadee Lane B&B
MB	Winnipeg	Elsa's Place
MB	Winnipeg	Terry's Bed and Breakfast
NB	Bathurst	Gîte Toutes Saisons B&B
NB	Bouctouche	Les Pins Maritimes
NB	Caraquet	Gîte Le Poirier B&B
NB	Caraquet	Hotel Paulin
NB	Inkerman (Shippagan)	Le Gîte de l'Ardora Bed and Breakfast
NB	Millville	LedgeRock Bed and Breakfast
NB	Moncton	Gîte du voyageur Chez-Aanna
NB	Moncton	Leah Jane's Bed and Breakfast
NB	Moncton	Lori's Bed and Breakfast
NB	Petit-Rocher	Auberge d'Anjou
NB	Sackville	Marshlands Inn
NB	Saint John on the Bay of Fundy	Beach House Bed & Breakfast (Kingston) Inc.
NB	Saint John on the Bay of Fundy	Homeport Historic B&B/Inn c. 1858
NB	Shediac	Auberge, Maison Vienneau
NL	Cape Onion	Tickle Inn at Cape Onion
NL	Carbonear	Sophia's Fine Dining & Bed and Breakfast
NL	Corner Brook	The Doctors House
NL	Dildo	Inn By The Bay
NL	Grand Falls-Windsor	Carriage House Inn
NL	Grand Falls-Windsor	Hill Road Manor
NL	Gros Morne National Park (Rocky Harbour)	Wildflowers B&B
NL	Labrador City	Tamarack Bed & Breakfast
NL	Port Blandford	Terra Nova
NL	St John's	Angel House Heritage Inn
NL	St John's	Bonne Esperance House Bed & Breakfast
NL	St John's	Compton House Heritage Inn
NL	St John's	Winterholme Heritage Inn
NL	Terra Nova National Park	The Serendipity B and B & Cottage
NL	Trinity	Artisan Inn
NS	Annapolis Royal	King George Inn
NS	Chester	Mecklenburgh Inn
NS	Digby	Thistle Down Country Inn
NS	Halifax	Julie's Walk Bed and Breakfast
NS	Halifax	Welcome Inn Halifax Bed and Breakfast
NS	Iona	Old Grand Narrows Hotel B&B
NS	Lunenburg	1826 Maplebird House Bed & Breakfast
NS	Lunenburg	1860 Kaulbach House Historic Inn
NS	Lunenburg	Atlantic Sojourn Bed and Breakfast
NS	Lunenburg	Lincoln House B&B
NS	Lunenburg area	The Backman House Bed and Breakfast
NS	Middleton	Century Farm Inn (c.1886)
NS	Musquodoboit Harbour	The Elephant's Nest Bed & Breakfast
NS	North Sydney	Gowrie House Country Inn
NS	Parrsboro	The Maple In
NS	Parrsboro	The Parrsboro Mansion
NS	Pictou	Evening Sail Bed & Breakfast & Housekeeping Unit
NS	Sydney	A Paradise Found B&
NS	Truro	Tulips and Thistle Bed & Breakfast
NS	Wolfville Area	Brownings Bed & Breakfast
NT	Yellowknife	Gill-Power Bed & Breakfast
ON	Ajax	Before the Mast B&

ON	Algonquin Park (Dorset)	The Nordic Inn of Dorset
ON	Alliston	Gramma's House
ON	Alliston	Stevenson Farms Historical B&B
ON	Bancroft	Dreamer's Rock Bed and Breakfast
ON	Bancroft	The Gathering Place On Golden Ponds B&B
ON	Barrie	Seasons Change
ON	Barrys Bay	Fortune's Madawaska Valley Inn
ON	Bayfield	Brentwood On The Beach
ON	Belleville	Twin Oaks Bed & Breakfast
ON	Bethany	Plantation House Bed & Breakfast Country Retreat
ON	Bradford W Gwillimbury	Blossom The Clown's B&B
ON	Bridgenorth	Birch Point Bay
ON	Brockville	Misty Pines B&B
ON	Cayuga	Carrousel Bed and Breakfast
ON	Collingwood	Pedulla's Mountainside Bed & Breakfast
ON	Cornwall	Lighthouse Landing
ON	Cornwall	Mountainview B&B
ON	Cornwall	T's By The Green Bed & Breakfast
ON	Damascus	The Pritty Place
ON	Fergus	Dream Corners B&B
ON	Gananoque	Sleepy Hollow Bed & Breakfast
ON	Gananoque	The Victoria Rose Inn
ON	Guelph	Sugarbush Bed and Breakfast
ON	Haliburton Highlands	Sunny Rock Bed & Breakfast
ON	Jacksons Point	Jackson's Landing Bed & Breakfast
ON	Jordan and Vineland	Bonnybank Bed and Breakfast
ON	Kapuskasing	Grandma Jean's B&B
ON	Kingston	Frontenac Club Inn
ON	Kingston	Green Woods Inn
ON	Kingston	The Secret Garden B&B Inn
ON	Kingston	The Tymparon Inn
ON	Kingsville	The Old Farmhouse Bed & Breakfast
ON	London	Belle Vie's guest cottage
ON	London	Companys' Coming
ON	Marathon	Lakeview Manor Bed & Breakfast
ON	Marmora	Marmora Inn
ON	Meaford	Holly Cottage B&B
ON	Midland	1875 A Charters Inn B&B
ON	Midland	Little Lake Inn Bed & Breakfast
ON	Minden	Stouffer Mill Bed & Breakfast Getaway
ON	Mississauga	Applewood Bed and Breakfast
ON	Mississauga	Dallimore's Just Your Cup of Tea
ON	Niagara Falls	Andrea's Bed and Breakfast
ON	Niagara Falls	Grapeview Guesthouse on the Vineyard
ON	Niagara Falls	Redwood Bed and Breakfast
ON	Niagara Falls	Rose Arbor B&B
ON	Niagara Falls	Stamford Village Bed and Breakfast
ON	Niagara-on-the-Lake	A Fawlty Towers B&B
ON	Niagara-on-the-Lake	Abacot Hall
ON	Niagara-on-the-Lake	Adel House B&B
ON	Niagara-on-the-Lake	Alfred's Coach House
ON	Niagara-on-the-Lake	Andrew Carroll House
ON	Niagara-on-the-Lake	Britaly Bed and Breakfast
ON	Niagara-on-the-Lake	Cedar Gables Bed and Breakfast
ON	Niagara-on-the-Lake	Davy House Bed and Breakfast
ON	Niagara-on-the-Lake	DownHome Bed and Breakfast
ON	Niagara-on-the-Lake	Lakewinds Country Manor (circa 1881)
ON	Niagara-on-the-Lake	Parliament Cottage B&B (circa 1840)
ON	Niagara-on-the-Lake	Serenity Garden B&B
ON	Niagara-on-the-Lake	Willowcreek House B&B
ON	Orangeville	McKitrick House Inn Bed & Breakfast
ON	Orillia	B&B on the Lake
ON	Orillia	Betty and Tony's Waterfront Bed and Breakfast
ON	Orillia	Cavana House Bed & Breakfast
ON	Orillia (Barrie)	The Verandahs Bed & Breakfast
ON	Oshawa	Emerson Manor B&B
ON	Ottawa	A Rose on Colonel By B&B
ON	Ottawa	Adele's Family Tree Bed & Breakfast
ON	Ottawa	Allure Bed & Breakfast
ON	Ottawa	Ambiance Bed and Breakfast
ON	Ottawa	Auberge McGee's Inn
ON	Ottawa	Benners' Bed and Breakfast
ON	Ottawa	Gasthaus Switzerland Inn
ON	Owen Sound	The Highland Manor Grand Victorian B&B
ON	Paris	River Ridge Bed and Breakfast
ON	Pelee Island	It's Home
ON	Peterborough	Hunter Farm B&B
ON	Peterborough	Liftlock Bed and Breakfast
ON	Peterborough	Resonance Bed & Breakfast and Spa
ON	Peterborough	Shining Waters Bed &Breakfast & Spa
ON	Peterborough	The Moffat House
ON	Petrolia	Away Inn a Manger Bed & Breakfast
ON	Port Carling	The Manse Bed and Breakfast
ON	Port Stanley	Mulberry Lane B&B
ON	Rockville	Rockville Inn
ON	Sault Ste Marie	Eastbourne Manor B&B
ON	St Catharines	Omi's Haus
ON	St Catharines	Ridley Gate Manor
ON	Stratford	Harmony House
ON	Stratford	Harrington House
ON	Stratford	Stone Maiden Inn
ON	Sudbury	Auberge-sur-lac B&B
ON	Sudbury	Millwood Bed & Breakfast
ON	Toronto	312 Seaton, a Toronto Bed & Breakfast
ON	Toronto	Alan Gardens Bed and Breakfast
ON	Toronto	Annex Quest House
ON	Toronto	The Red Door Bed & Breakfast
ON	Toronto	Vanderkooy BeB&Breakfast
ON	Toronto	Victoria's Mansion
ON	Vankleek Hill	Dreamland on the Ridge
ON	Woodstock	Zeelandia B&B
PE	Charlottetown	Betty & Mark's 'River Winds'
PE	Charlottetown	Heritage Harbour House Inn B&B
PE	Charlottetown	Shipwright Inn

PE	Montague	Elms at Brudenell Bed and Breakfast
PE	Summerside	Copple Summer Home
QC	Baie St-Paul	Noble Quêteux
QC	Bas Saint-Laurent	La Ferme Paysagée
QC	Ile d'Orleans	B&B Au Giron de l'Isle
QC	Kamouraska	La Villa Saint-Louis
QC	L'Anse St.-Jean	Le Globe-Trotter B&B
QC	Laurentians, Wentworth-Nord	Domaine de l'Ötang
QC	Les Hauteurs	Gîte Le Beau Lieu
QC	Montreal	A Montréal Oasis
QC	Montreal	Au Git'Ann
QC	Montreal	B A Guest B&B and Reservation Service
QC	Montreal	Boulanger-bassin B&B
QC	Montreal	Gîte Maison Jacques
QC	Montreal	Gîte touristique Le Saint-André-des-Arts
QC	Montreal	Le Kensington
QC	Montreal	Le relais des Argoulets
QC	Montreal	Le Terra Nostra
QC	Montreal	University Bed & Breakfast
QC	Quebec	A la Roseraie, gîte
QC	Quebec	Au Pignon Vert
QC	Quebec	Au Gré du Vent B&B
QC	Quebec	Lupins et lilas
QC	Quebec City Downtown	À la Maison Tudor
QC	Saint-Donat	Auberge St-Donat
QC	Sainte-Adèle	A La Belle Idée
QC	Sainte-Agathe-Des-Monts	Gîte la maison du lac
QC	Saint-Georges	Le Jardin des Mésanges
QC	Saint-Laurent	Studio Marhaba
QC	Saint-Marc-sur-Richelieu	Aux rêves d'antan
QC	Sherbrooke	La Canardiere B&B
QC	Wakefield	Les Trois Erables
SK	Kamsack	Border Mountain Country Bed and Breakfast
SK	Prince Albert	Hillcrest Inn
SK	Saskatoon	Riverview Bed and Breakfast
SK	Yorkton	Patrick Place
YT	Whitehorse	Muktuk Guest Ranch

INFORMATION SOURCES
FOR THE TRAVELLER

The information published below is publicly available. The purpose in providing it is to facilitate and reduce time in web surfing by the traveller while trip planning or for emergency services while on the road. This information is updated for the 18th edition and was confirmed by direct test in November 2005. The traveller is cautioned that while most of this is stable information, it is not uncommon for web addresses and phone numbers to change, ongoing accuracy cannot be guaranteed."

Emergencies: Medical, Police, Fire
911 for most areas of Canada

ATM Finder	http://canadaonline.about.com/cs/atms/index.htm?terms=Automated+Teller+Machine
Atlas of Canada	www.atlas.gc.ca
Border Wait Times Times USA, Canada border	www.cbsa-asfc.gc.ca/general/times/menu-e.html
Calendars; 2004, 2005, etc.	www.timeanddate.com/calendar/index.html?year=2004&country=27
Currency Exchange	www.xe.net/ucc
Canada Customs	1-800-461-9999
From outside Canada	204-983-3500
Alternative	506-636-5064
Culture	www.culturecanada.gc.ca
Destination Canada	www.pathcom.com/%7Erobefish/TTRN/destinationcanada.htm
Diplomatic Representatives in Canada	www.arraydev.com/commerce/embassy/english/directory.htm
Americans entering Canada	www.amcits.com/entry_ca.asp
Encyclopedia of Canada	www.thecanadianencyclopedia.com
Festivals and Events	www.festivalseeker.com
GST rebate	www.cra-arc.gc.ca/tax/nonresidents/visitors
Genealogical Research	www.ingeneas.com
Highway Travel Guides	www.milebymile.com
History	www.culturecanada.gc.ca/chdt/interface/interface2.nsf/engdocBasic/8.html
History	www.pathcom.com/%7Erobefish/articles/grandtheatre.htm
Hunting and Fishing Regulations by Prov. And Terr.	http://www.outdoorcanada.ca/regs.shtml
Insurance for visitors	http://www.travelinsurance.ca/customers/visitors/index.html
Legal advice for visitors	www.canlaw.com/referrals/referralindex.htm
Library and Archives Canada	www.collectionscanada.ca/index-e.html
Medical assistance	www.iamat.org
National Historic Sites	www.pc.gc.ca/progs/lhn-nhs/index_E.asp
National Marine Conservation Areas	www.parkscanada.pch.gc.ca/amnc-nmca/list_e.asp
National Parks	www.parkscanada.pch.gc.ca/pn-np/list_alpha_e.asp
News: Canadian Broadcasting Corporation	www.cbc.ca/news
The Globe and Mail	www.theglobeandmail.com
Pets and travel	www.takeyourpet.com
Phone directory	www.canada411.ca
Time, North American	www.timeanddate.com/worldclock/custom.html?continent=namerica
Time, World	www.timeanddate.com/worldclock
Visitor Regulations for Canada	www.cic.gc.ca/english/visit/index.html
Weather Reports for Canada	www.weatheroffice.ec.gc.ca
Wines of Canada	www.canadianvintners.com
	613-782-2283

Lost credit card reporting

American express	1-800-268-9824
Alternate number	1-905-474-0870
Master card	1-800-307-7309
Visa	1-800-847-2911

Lost travellers cheques

AAA	1-866-866-8148
American express	1-800-221-7282
Master card	1-800-223-9920
Thomas Cook	1-800-223-7373
Visa	1-800-227-6811

Motorists', services for members and affiliates

CAA/AAA member automotive service
www.caa.ca/english/automotive/automotive.html#ERA
1-800-222-4357

Canadian Automobile Association & AAA
www.caa.ca
Highway Conditions
www.caa.ca/english/travel/travel%20conditions/travel%20conditions.html

Motorists', services for the general public

Canadian Tire Auto Club road side service
www.ctfs.com/english/autoclub/index.html
1-800-893-2582
Highway Conditions
www.canada.worldweb.com/LocalReports/RoadConditions/
Road Safety
www.tc.gc.ca/roadsafety/menu.htm

Northwest Territories

www.nwttravel.nt.ca
1-800-661-0788
arctic@explorenwt.com

Bird Watching — www.explorenwt.com/adventures/birding/index.asp
Festivals and Events — www.explorenwt.com/adventures/northern-festivals/index.asp
1-800-661-0788
Fishing Regulations — www.explorenwt.com/adventures/sport-fishing/regulations.asp
Northern Lights — www.explorenwt.com/adventures/northern-lights/index.asp
Genealogical Research — www.ssimicro.com/nonprofit/nwtgs
Golf — www.golfhere.com/northwestterritories.htm
Hunting Regulations — www.explorenwt.com/adventures/sport-hunting/regulations.asp
Inuvik — www.inuvikinfo.com
1-867-777-4321
Norman Wells Fossil Hunt — www.normanwells.com
1-867-587-2238
Northern Heritage Centre — http://pwnhc.learnnet.nt.ca/
1-867-873-7551
Theatres — www.theatrecanada.com/centres/theatres.shtml
Western Arctic T'ism. Assoc. — 1-867-777-4321
Western Canada Online Outdoor News — www.westcanoon.com
Yellowknife — www.yellowknife.worldweb.com

Yukon

www.touryukon.com
1-800-661-0494
vacation@gov.yk.ca

Alaska Highway — www.bellsalaska.com/alaska_highway.html
Bird Watching — www.environmentyukon.gov.yk.ca/viewing/birdwatch.html
Dawson City Tourism — www.dawsoncity.org
1-867-993-5575
Dempster Hwy. To Inuvik — www.transcanadahighway.com/Yukon
1-800-661-0788
Festivals and Events — www.explorenorth.com/library/canadafarnorth/bl-events-yt.htm
1-867-667-5340
Fishing Regulations — www.environmentyukon.gov.yk.ca/yukonfishing/regulations.html

Genealogical Research	www.genealogy.gc.ca/03/030213_e.html
Golf	www.golfhere.com/yukon.htm
Hunting Regulations	www.environmentyukon.gov.yk.ca/hunting/hunting.html
Klondike Visitors Association	www.dawsoncity.org/index.php
	1-867-993-5575
Northern Lights Space & Science	www.aurorawatching.com/?ref=cooglesirad
Theatres	www.theatrecanada.com/centres/theatres.shtml
Western Canada Online Outdoor News	www.westcanoon.com
White Pass & Yukon Rail Tour	www.whitepassrailroad.com
	1-800-343-7373
Whitehorse Tourism	www.city.whitehorse.yk.ca
	1-867-668-8687
Yukon Beringia Interp. Centre	www.beringia.com
Yukon First Nations Tourism	www.yfnta.org
Yukon Int. Story Telling Festival	www.yukonstory.com
Yukon Southern Lakes	www.yukonsouthernlakes.com

Prince Edward Island

	www.peiplay.com
	1-888-734-7529 phone
Anne of Green Gables	www.peiplay.com/Anne
Bird Watching	www.gov.pe.ca/birds/index.php3
Charlottetown	www.capitalcommission.pe.ca
	1-800-955-1864
Charlottetown Festival	www.confederationcentre.com
	1-800-565-0278
Confederation Bridge	www.confederationbridge.com/
Festivals and Events	www.gov.pe.ca/visitorsguide/events/index.php3
	1-888-734-7529
Genealogy	www.islandregister.com
Golf	www.golfpei.com
	902-566-4653
Hunting and Fishing Regulations	www.gov.pe.ca/infopei/index.php3?number=16669&lang=E
Summerside	www.city.summerside.pe.ca
	1-877-734-2382
Theatres	www.theatrecanada.com/centres/theatres.shtml

Nova Scotia

	www.exploreNS.com
	1-800-565-0000 explore@gov.ns.ca
Alexander Graham Bell	http://home.istar.ca/~tolm/ttd/bell.html
	1-902-295-2069
Annapolis Valley	www.valleyweb.com
Bird Watching	www.museum.gov.ns.ca/mnh/nature/nsbirds/b_sites.htm
Cabot Trail	www.cabottrail.com
	1-800-565-0000
Cape Breton Island	www.cbisland.com/index.php#
	902-563-4636
Evangeline Trail	www.evangelinetrail.com
	1-800-565-3882
Ferry, Nova Scotia/Maine	www.princeoffundy.com
	1-800-341-7540
Ferry, Nova Scotia/Maine	www.catferry.com
	1-888-249-7245
Ferry, Nova Scotia/Newfoundland	www.marine-atlantic.ca
	1-800-341-7981
Festivals and Events	www.explore.gov.ns.ca/whattodo/festivalsandevents/default.asp
	1-800-565-0000
Fishing Regulations	www.gov.ns.ca/nsaf/sportfishing/angling/index.htm
Genealogy	http://nsgna.ednet.ns.ca

Glooscap Trail	www.cnta.ns.ca
	1-800-565-0000
Golf	www.golfcourselistings.ca/Nova-Scotia-Golf-Courses.html
Halifax	www.halifaxinfo.com
Hiking	www.canadatrails.ca/hiking/hike_ns.html
Hunting Regulations	www.gov.ns.ca/natr/hunt/hunting.htm
Lighthouses	http://nslps.ednet.ns.ca/
	1-800-565-0000
Louisburg	www.novascotia.worldweb.com/Louisbourg/index.html
	?vid=31090885
Lunenburg	www.town.lunenburg.ns.ca
	902-634-4229
Outdoor Activities	www.2hwy.com/ns/o/outdoors.htm
Peggy's Cove	www.peggyscove.ca
Publications and Maps	www.gov.ns.ca/snsmr/consumer/publications
Sydney	www.sydneynovascotia.worldweb.com/index.html?vid=31090885
Theatres	www.theatrecanada.com/centres/theatres.shtml
Yarmouth	www.aboutyarmouth.com
	1-800-565-0000

ONTARIO

	www.ontariotravel.net
	1-800-668-2746
Algoma-Kinniwabi Travel Ass.	www.algomacountry.com
	1-800-263-2546
Almaguin-Nippissing Travel Ass.	www.ontariosnearnorth.on.ca
	1-800-387-0516
Bird Watching	www.birdsontario.org/index.html
Bruce Peninsula	www.brucepeninsula.org
	1-800-268-3838
Chi-Cheemaun ferry service	www.bmts.com/~northland/chiche/chiche.html
	1-800-265-3163
Cochrane-Temiskaming Travel	www.jamesbayfrontier.com
	1-800-461-3766
Festivals and Events	www.festivals-events-ont.com
	1-519-756-3359
Genealogy	www.ogs.on.ca
Golf	www.golfcourselistings.ca/Ontario-Golf-Courses.html
Great Lakes	www.great-lakes.net/tourism/
Heritage Foundation, Ontario	www.heritagefdn.on.ca
	416-325-5000
Hunting and Fishing Regulations	www.mnr.gov.on.ca/MNR/pubs/pubmenu.html
Kawarthas	www.city.kawarthalakes.on.ca
	705-324-9411
Kingston	www.tourism.kingstoncanada.com
Kitchener Waterloo	www.kw-visitor.on.ca
Muskoka	www.discovermuskoka.ca
	1-800-267-9700
Niagara Escarpment	www.escarpment.org
	905-877-5191
Niagara Falls	www.falls.net
Niagara Parks	www.niagaraparks.com
	1-877-642-7275
Niagara-on-the-Lake	www.niagaraonthelake.com
	905-468-1950
Niagara Region	www.tourismniagara.com
	1-800-263-2988
North Bay	www.city.north-bay.on.ca/tourism.htm
	705-474-0626
North of Supperior Tourism	www.nosta.on.ca
	1-800-265-3951

Ontario East Tourism	www.ontarioeast.com
	1-800-567-3278
Ottawa	www.ottawagetaways.ca
	1-800-465-1867
Ottawa Valley Tourist Assoc.	www.ottawavalley.org
	1-800-757-6580
Pelee Island and Point Pelee	www.pelee.com
Peterborough	www.city.peterborough.on.ca/
	1-800-461-6424
Prince Edward County	www.pec.on.ca/Welcome.html
	1-800-640-4717
Rainbow Country Travel Assoc.	www.rainbowcountry.com
	1 800 465 6655
Sarnia	www.sarnia.com
	519-344-8422
Southern Ontario Tourism	www.soto.on.ca
	1-800-267-3399
Sudbury	http://sudbury.foundlocally.com/Travel/index.htm
Sunset Country Travel Assoc.	www.ontariossunsetcountry.ca
	1-800-665-7567
Thunder Bay	www.thunderbay.ca/
	1-800-667-8386
Timmins	www.timmins.worldweb.com
Toronto	www.torontotourism.com
	1-877-848-4999
Rideau Canal	www.rideau-info.com/canal
Theatres	www.theatrecanada.com/centres/theatres.shtml
Trent Water Way	www.ftsw.com
Trip Planner	www.ontariotownandcountry.ca/
Welland Canals Centre	www.lock3.com
	1-800-305-5134
Windsor	www.citywindsor.ca/
	1-800-265-3633
Wine Council of Ontario	www.wineroute.com
	905-684-8070
Vintners Quality Alliance of Ontario VQA	www.vqaontario.com/
	416-367-2002

NEW BRUNSWICK

	www.TourismNewBrunswick.ca
	1-800-561-0123
Acadian Costal Drive	www.TourismNewBruswick.ca
	1-800-561-0123
Appalachian Range Route	www.TourismNewBrunswick.ca
	1-800-561-0123
Bay of Fundy	www.bayoffundy.com
	1-800-561-2324
Bird Watching	www.americanbirdcenter.com/abc-newbrunswick.html
Festivals and Events	www.tourismnewbrunswick.ca/Cultures/en-CA/Categories/Festival
	1-800-561-0123
Fishing Regulations	www.gnb.ca/0254/rules-e.asp
Fredericton	www.city.fredericton.nb.ca/
Fundy Coastal Drive	www.TourismNewBruswick.ca
	1-800-561-0123
Genealogy	www.bitheads.com/nbgs
Golf	www.golfcourselistings.ca/New-Brunswick-Golf-Courses.html
Hunting	www.gnb.ca/0078/fw/huntsum.pdf
Miramichi River Route	www.TourismNewBruswick.ca
	1-800-561-0123

Moncton	www.gomoncton.com/
New Brunswick Trails	www.sentiernbtrail.com
	1-800-526-7070
River Valley Scenic Drive	www.TourismNewBruswick.ca
	1-800-561-0123
Theatres	www.theatrecanada.com/centres/theatres.shtml

QUEBEC

	www.bonjourquebec.com
	1-877-266-5687
Appalachians	www.bonjourquebec.com/anglais/explorez/circuits/appalach.html
Beautiful Villages of Quebec	www.beauxvillages.qc.ca/
Bird Watching	www.americanbirdcenter.com/abc-quebec.html
Charlevoix World Biosphere	www.tourisme-charlevoix.com/en/circuits/paysages.asp
	1-800-667-2276
Cheese Route	www.routedesfromages.com/
Chicoutimi	www.saguenay.worldweb.com/Chicoutimi
Eastern Townships	www.tourisme-cantons.qc.ca
	819-820-2020
Festivals and Events	www.festivals.qc.ca
	1-800-361-7688
Fishing Regulations	www.fapaq.gouv.qc.ca/en/regulations/index.htm
Gaspé	www.infogaspesie.com/
Genealogy	www.cam.org/~qfhs
Golf	www.golfcourselistings.ca/Quebec-Golf-Courses.html
Hunting Regulations	www.mrnf.gouv.qc.ca/english/home.jsp
Le Quebec Maritime	www.quebecmaritime.qc.ca
Monteregie Tourism Association	www.quebecregion.com/e/sites.asp?View=Cat&lnLiensCatId=2
	450-674-5555
Montreal	www.tourism-montreal.org
	1-877-266-5687
Quebec City and Area	www.quebecregion.com
	1-877-266-5687
Quebec – Levis, Godbout Ferry	www.traversiers.gouv.qc.ca
St. Lawrence River	www.quebecweb.com/tourisme/fleuveang.html
Saguenay Region	www.quebecweb.com/tourisme/lacstjean/introang.html
Theatres	www.theatrecanada.com/centres/theatres.shtml

MANITOBA

	www.travelmanitoba.com
	1-800-665-0040 phone
Bird Watching	www.americanbirdcenter.com/abc-manitoba.html
Boissevain	www.boissevain.ca
	1-800497-2393
Brandon	www.brandon.com
	1-888-799-1111
Festivals and Events	www.travelmanitoba.com/events
	1-800-665-0204
Fishing Regulations	www.gov.mb.ca/conservation/fish/index.html
Genealogy	www.mts.net/~mgsi
Golf	www.golfcourselistings.ca/Manitoba-Golf-Courses.html
Hunting Regulations	www.gov.mb.ca/conservation/wildlife/huntingg/index.html
La Verendrye Trail	www.laverendryetrail.mb.ca
	1-888-637-7311
Manitoba Provincial Parks	www.manitobaparks.com
	1-800-665-0040 EX.AD1
Red River North	www.triplescfdc.mb.ca/tourism/recreation.htm
	1-800-894-2621
Red RiverMetis heritage Group	www.members.shaw.ca/rrmhg/

The Pas	www.thepasarea.com
	1-866-627-1134
Theatres	www.theatrecanada.com/centres/theatres.shtml
Trans Canada Yellohead Highway	www.transcanadayellowhead.com/content/tourism/index.htm
Western Canada Online Outdoor News	www.westcanoon.com
Winnipeg	www.destinationwinnipeg.ca/play_wti.php
	1-800-665-0204

NEWFOUNDLAND & LABRADOR

	www.gov.nf.ca./tourism
	1-800-563-6353
Regions of Newfoundland	www.newfoundlandandlabradortourism.com/where_to_go.zap
Bird Watching	www.americanbirdcenter.com/abc-newfoundland.html
Colony of Avalon	www.heritage.nf.ca/avalon
	1-877-326-5669
Far East	www.capespeardrive.com
Ferries local	www.gov.nf.ca/FerryServices
Ferry to Nova Scotia	www.marine-atlantic.ca
	1-800-341-7981
Festivals and Events	www.newfoundlandandlabradortourism.com/festivals.zap
	1-800-563-6353
Fishing Regulations	www.anywhere.ca/Newfoundland_and_Labrador/
	Recreation_and_Sports/Fishing/
Genealogy	www3.nf.sympatico.ca/nlgs
Golf	www.golfcourselistings.ca/Newfoundland-Golf-Courses.html
Grand Falls, Windsor	www.grandfallswindsor.com
	1-888-491-9453
Gross Morne National Park	www.pc.gc.ca/pn-np/nl/grosmorne/index_e.asp
Provincial Parks	www.gov.nf.ca/parks&reserves
	1-800-563-6353
Theatres	www.theatrecanada.com/centres/theatres.shtml
Viking Heritage/Lanse aux Meadows	www.manl.nf.ca/lanseauxmeadows.htm

ALBERTA

	www.travelalberta.com
	info@travelalberta.com
	1-800-661-8888
Alberta Attractions	www.discoveralberta.com/SightsAttractions
Alberta Central	www.travelalbertacentral.com
	1-888-414-4139
Alberta North	www.travelalbertanorth.com
	1-800-756-4351
Alberta Rockies	www.canadianrockiestourism.com
	1-800-661-8888
Alberta South	www.albertasouth.com
	1-800-661-1222
Banff	www.discoverbanff.com
Bird Watching	www1.travelalberta.com/content/outdoor/birding.cfm
Calgary	www.tourismcalgary.com
	1-800-661-8888
Calgary Stampede	www.calgary-stampede.com
	1-800-661-1260
Canmore	www.canmorealberta.com
	403-678-2244
Crows Nest Highway	www.highway3.ca/
	1-800-661-1222
Drumheller	www.dinosaurvalley.com
	403-823-8100

Edmonton	www.infoedmonton.com/
	1-800-463-4667
Festivals and Events	www1.travelalberta.com/content/specialevents
Fishing Regulations	www.albertaoutdoorsmen.ca/fishingregs/index.html
Genealogy	www.afhs.ab.ca/
Golf Course Listings	www.golfcourselistings.ca/Alberta-Golf-Courses.html
Hunting Regulations	www.albertaoutdoorsmen.org/huntingregs/index.html
Ice Fields Parkway	www.canadianrockies.net/icepwy.html
Jasper	www.jaspercanadianrockies.com/
	780-852-3858
Kananaskis	www.kananaskisalberta.ca/
Lake Louise	www.banfflakelouise.com/
Lethbridge	www.lethbridge.worldweb.com
Red Deer	www.reddeer.worldweb.com/
Rocky Mountains	www.canadianrockies.net/
Rocky Mountain Sightseeing by Train	www.rockymountaineer.com
	1-877-460-3200
Theatres	www.theatrecanada.com/centres/theatres.shtml
Trans Canada Yellowhead Highway	www.transcanadayellowhead.com/content/tourism/index.htm
Western Canada Online Outdoor News	www.westcanoon.com

SASKATCHEWAN

	www.sasktourism.com
	1-877-237-2273
Attractions	www.saskatchewan.worldweb.com/SightsAttractions
Bird Watching	www.americanbirdcenter.com/abc-saskatchewan.html
Canadian Cowboys Association	www.canadiancowboys.ca/
Festivals and Events	www.saskfestivals.com
Genealogy	www.saskgenealogy.com
Golf	www.golfsask.com
Hunting and Fishing Regulations	www.se.gov.sk.ca/fishwild
Lloydminster	www.lloydminsterinfo.com/tourism.htm
	1-800-825-6180
Nipawin	www.nipawin.com
	1-877-647-2946
North Region	www.sasktourism.com/north
Provincial Parks	www.saskparks.net
	1-877-237-2273
Regina	www.tourismregina.com
	1-800-661-5099
Saskachewan Course Listings	www.golfcourselistings.ca/Saskatchewan-Golf-Courses.html
Saskachewan Genealogical Society	www.saskgenealogy.com
Saskatoon	www.tourismsaskatoon.com/
	1-800-567-2444
The Battlefords	www.tourism.battlefords.com
	1-800-243-0394
Theatres	www.theatrecanada.com/centres/theatres.shtml
Trans Canada Yellowhead Highway	www.transcanadayellowhead.com/content/tourism/index.htm
Western Canada Online Outdoor News	www.westcanoon.com
Wanuskewin Heritage Park	www.wanuskewin.com
	1-800-665-4600
Yorkton	www.tourismyorkton.com/

BRITISH COLUMBIA

	www.HelloBC.com
	1-800-435-5622
Activities for all people	www.findfamilyfun.com
Alaska Highway	www.bellsalaska.com/alaska_highway.html
Art and Culture	www.art-bc.com/
Bird Watching	www.americanbirdcenter.com/abc-britishcolumbia.html

British Columbia Ferries	www.bcferries.com
	1-888-223-3779
British Columbia Historical Federation	www.bchistory.ca
British Columbia Islands	www.islands.bc.ca
	250-754-3500
Butchart Gardens	www.butchartgardens.com/
	1-866-652-4422
Caribou Chilcotin Coast	www.landwithoutlimits.com
	1-800-663-5885
Festivals and Events	www.britishcolumbia.com/attractions/?id=24
	604-739-9011
Fishing Regulations	http://laws.justice.gc.ca/en/F-14/SOR-96-137/
Garden tours, arts, culture, heritage	www.gardeninspiredtourism.org/getaways
	604-574-7772
Genealogy	www.bcgs.ca
Golf Course Listings	www.golfcourselistings.ca/British-Columbia-Golf-Courses.html
Barkerville, Heritage Site	www.britishcolumbia.com/regions/towns/?townID=3530
	250-994-3302
Hunting Regulations	wlapwww.gov.bc.ca/fw/wild/synopsis.htm
Inside Passage	www.britishcolumbia.com/regions/towns/?townID=3958
	250-949-7622
Kamloops	www.adventurekamloops.com/
	1-800-662-1994
Kelowna	www.britishcolumbia.com/regions/towns/?townID=3413
	1-800-663-4345
Kootenays	www.BCRockies.com
Nanaimo	www.nanaimobritishcolumbia.com/
	1-800-663-7337
Northern B.C.	www.NBCtourism.com
	1-800-663-8843
Oceanside and Comox Valley	www.chamber.parksville.bc.ca/
Okanagan	www.okanagan-bc.com/
Prince George	www.netbistro.com/tourism/princegeorge
	1-800-668-7646
Queen Charlotte Islands	www.qcinfo.ca/
Rocky Mountains	www.canadianrockies.net/
Rocky Mountain Sightseeing by Train	www.rockymountaineer.com
	1-877-460-3200
Shuswap	www.shuswap.bc.ca/
Stanley Park	www.seestanleypark.com/
Theatres	www.theatrecanada.com/centres/theatres.shtml
Trans Canada Yellohead Highway	www.transcanadayellowhead.com/content/tourism/index.htm
Thompson Okanagan Tourism	www.ThompsonOkanagan.com
	1-800-567-2275
Vancouver Attractions	www.vancouverattractions.com
	1-888-433-3735
Vancouver Coast and Moutains	www.coastandmountains.bc.ca
	1-800-667-3306
Victoria	www.tourismvictoria.com
	250-953-2033
Western Canada Online Outdoor News	www.westcanoon.com
Whistler Tourism	www.tourismwhistler.com
	1-800-944-7853
Whale, wildlife, adventure and eco tours	www.bc.worldweb.com/ToursActivitiesAdventures
Wine regions of British Columbia	www.canadianvintners.com/woc/bc.html

BEDS AND BREAKFASTS ACCESSIBLE TO THE PHYSICALLY CHALLENGED

Accessibility does not necessarily mean full compliance. The American Disabilities Act (ADA), which blankets all advisories, is the governing body and binding agency in Canada. Check with hosts at time of booking for degree of accessibility.

PROVINCE	NEAR CITY/TOWN	B&B NAME
AB	Abraham Lake	Aurum Lodge
AB	Calgary	Riverview Bed and Breakfast
AB	Cochrane	Mountview Cottage B&B
AB	Drumheller	Pearl's Country Cottages
AB	High River	Arbuthnot's B&B
AB	Hinton	McCracken Country Inn
AB	Jasper	Home Away From Home Bed and Breakfast
AB	Pigeon Lake (area)	Hidden Springs Retreat & Guesthouse
AB	Pine Lake	Daisy House/Pierce Farms
BC	Burns Lake	Ninth Ave Guest House
BC	Chemainus	Be Delighted B&B
BC	Chemainus	Island Haven B&B
BC	Dawson Creek	The Granaries on Bear Mountain
BC	Gabriola Island	Island Bed & Breakfast
BC	Harrison Hot Springs	Harrison Heritage House & Kottages
BC	Harrison Mills	Rowena's Inn on the River
BC	Invermere	Harmington House
BC	Kelowna	A Lakeview Heights Bed & Breakfast
BC	Kelowna	Mission Hills Vacation Suite
BC	Ladysmith	Hansen House Vacation Suite
BC	Lake Cowichan	Kidd's B&B
BC	Parksville	Arrowsmith Bed and Breakfast (House on the Corner)
BC	Powell River	Beacon B&B and Spa
BC	Prince George	Rosels Bed and Breakfast
BC	Prince Rupert	Eagle Bluff B&B
BC	Quadra Island	Firesign Art & Design Studio and B&B
BC	Salt Spring Island	Quarrystone House
BC	Sidney	Honeysuckle Cottage Bed & Breakfast
BC	Sooke	Barking Crow
BC	Sooke	Ocean Wilderness Inn and Spa
BC	Summerland	A Touch of English Bed & Breakfast
BC	Tofino	Cable Cove Inn
BC	Vancouver	Camelot Inn
BC	Victoria	Cordova Bay Vacations
BC	White Rock	Abbey Lane B&B
BC	White Rock	Sand & Sea B&B Guest Suites
MB	Boissevain	Dueck's Cedar Chalet
MB	Inglis	Bear Creek B&B
MB	Neepawa	Highland Glen B&B
MB	Saint-Pierre-Jolys	Chateau des Sages B&B
NB	Bathurst	Gîte Toutes Saisons B&B
NB	Caraquet	Gîte L'Isle-du-Randonneur B&B
NB	Grand Manan	McLaughlin's Wharf B&B
NB	Hartland	Rebecca Farm Bed and Breakfast
NB	Millville	LedgeRock Bed and Breakfast

NB	Miramichi	Country Bed & Breakfast
NL	St John's	Waterford Manor Heritage Inn
NL	Terra Nova National Park	The Serendipity B and B & Cottage
NL	Trinity	Artisan Inn
NS	Digby	Harmony Bed & Breakfast/Suites
NS	Halifax	Caribou Lodge Bed & Breakfast
NS	Salmon River Bridge-Jeddore	Salmon River House Country Inn
NT	Yellowknife	Gill-Power Bed & Breakfast
ON	Algonquin Park (Dorset)	The Nordic Inn of Dorset
ON	Alliston	Stevenson Farms Historical B&B
ON	Baden	Willow Springs Suites B&B
ON	Bancroft	The Gathering Place On Golden Ponds B&B
ON	Bradford West Gwillimbury	Blossom The Clown's B&B
ON	Cayuga	Carrousel Bed and Breakfast
ON	Cayuga	River Inn B&B
ON	Damascus	The Pritty Place
ON	Erin	Stonecroft Country Guest House
ON	Fergus	Dream Corners B&B
ON	Flesherton	Toad Hall
ON	Gananoque	The Victoria Rose Inn
ON	Hamilton (Ancaster)	Duck Tail Inn B&B
ON	Meaford	Irish Mountain B&B
ON	Midland	Little Lake Inn Bed & Breakfast
ON	Niagara-on-the-Lake	Bullfrog Pond Guest House
ON	Orangeville	In Tir Na Nog Bed & Breakfast
ON	Pelee Island	It's Home
ON	Peterborough	Liftlock Bed and Breakfast
ON	Sault Ste Marie	Mountain View Bed and Breakfast
ON	Shelburne	Anderson's Hilltop B&B
ON	Thunder Bay	Afton Court Bed and Breakfast
ON	Westport	The Cove Country Inn
PE	Charlottetown	Fairholm National Historic Inn
PE	Charlottetown	Heritage Harbour House Inn B&B
PE	Charlottetown	The Great George
QC	Howick	Rivers Edge Bed and Breakfast
QC	Laurentians,Wentworth-Nord	Domaine de l'Étang
QC	Pointe-Ö-la-Croix	Gîte La Maison verte du Parc Gaspésien
QC	Saint-Donat	Auberge St-Donat
QC	Saint-Laurent	Studio Marhaba
SK	Choiceland	Bear Paw Lodge
YT	Whitehorse	Muktuk Guest Ranch

STATUTORY HOLIDAYS
BY PROVINCE AND YEAR

NAME & PROVINCE	2006 DATE	2007 DATE	2008 DATE
New Years Day	Su 01-Jan	Mo 01-Jan	Tu 01-Jan
Family Day, Alberta,	Mo 20-Feb	Mo 19-Feb	Mo 18-Feb
St.Patrick's Day, Newfoundland	Fr 17-Mar	Sa 17-Mar	Mo 17-Mar
Good Friday	Fr 14-Apr	Fr 06-Apr	Fr 21-Mar
St. George' Day, Newfoundland	Su 23-Apr	Mo 23-Apr	We 23-Apr
Victoria Day	Mo 22-May	Mo 21-May	Mo 19-May
Discovery Day, Newfoundland	Sa 24-Jun	Su 24-Jun	Tu 24-Jun
St. John the Baptist Day, Quebec	Sa 24-Jun	Su 24-Jun	Tu 24-Jun
Canada Day	Sa 01-Jul	Su 01-Jul	Tu 01-Jul
Orangemen's Day	We 12-Jul	Th 12-Jul	Sa 12-Jul
Regatta Day, Newfoundland	This holiday occurs on different days, in different towns, normally in August.		
British Columbia Day	Tu 01-Aug	We 01-Aug	Fr 01-Aug
New Brunswick Day	Tu 01-Aug	We 01-Aug	Fr 01-Aug
Saskatchwan Day	Tu 01-Aug	We 01-Aug	Fr 01-Aug
Civic Holiday, Nova Scotia, Ontario, PEI	Tu 01-Aug	We 01-Aug	Fr 01-Aug
Discovery Day, Yukon	Mo 21-Aug	Mo 20-Aug	Mo 18-Aug
Labour Day	Mo 04-Sep	Mo 03-Sep	Mo 01-Sep
Thanksgiving Day	Mo 09-Oct	Mo 08-Oct	Mo 06-Oct
Rememberance Day	Sa 11-Nov	Su 11-Nov	Tu 11-Nov
Christmas Day	Mo 25-Dec	Tu 25-Dec	Th 25-Dec

- Some holidays such as Victoria Day, Canada Day and August 1 holidays may be celebrated on the Monday following the designated day.
- Certain Holidays such as Remembrance Day may only be recognized by governments as "days off".
- In booking accomodations, it is advised that if you are uncertain about holiday days to check with your hosts. In many cases these are busier times and booking further in advance may be necessary.
- Holidays, with no provincial designation are observed nationally.

To list your Bed and Breakfast in the Guide
Contact Marybeth Moyer at:
info@canadianbandbguide.ca
or go online to;
www.canadianbandbguide.ca
and click on "List with Us"

Calendar—Canada 2006

January 2006

Su	Mo	Tu	We	Th	Fr	Sa
1	2	3	4	5	6	7
8	9	10	11	12	13	14
15	16	17	18	19	20	21
22	23	24	25	26	27	28
29	30	31				

6:◗ 14:○ 22:◐ 29:●

February 2006

Su	Mo	Tu	We	Th	Fr	Sa
			1	2	3	4
5	6	7	8	9	10	11
12	13	14	15	16	17	18
19	20	21	22	23	24	25
26	27	28				

5:◗ 13:○ 21:◐ 28:●

March 2006

Su	Mo	Tu	We	Th	Fr	Sa
			1	2	3	4
5	6	7	8	9	10	11
12	13	14	15	16	17	18
19	20	21	22	23	24	25
26	27	28	29	30	31	

6:◗ 14:○ 22:◐ 29:●

April 2006

Su	Mo	Tu	We	Th	Fr	Sa
						1
2	3	4	5	6	7	8
9	10	11	12	13	14	15
16	17	18	19	20	21	22
23	24	25	26	27	28	29
30						

5:◗ 13:○ 21:◐ 27:●

May 2006

Su	Mo	Tu	We	Th	Fr	Sa
	1	2	3	4	5	6
7	8	9	10	11	12	13
14	15	16	17	18	19	20
21	22	23	24	25	26	27
28	29	30	31			

5:◗ 13:○ 20:◐ 27:●

June 2006

Su	Mo	Tu	We	Th	Fr	Sa
				1	2	3
4	5	6	7	8	9	10
11	12	13	14	15	16	17
18	19	20	21	22	23	24
25	26	27	28	29	30	

3:◗ 11:○ 18:◐ 25:●

July 2006

Su	Mo	Tu	We	Th	Fr	Sa
						1
2	3	4	5	6	7	8
9	10	11	12	13	14	15
16	17	18	19	20	21	22
23	24	25	26	27	28	29
30	31					

3:◗ 11:○ 17:◐ 25:●

August 2006

Su	Mo	Tu	We	Th	Fr	Sa
		1	2	3	4	5
6	7	8	9	10	11	12
13	14	15	16	17	18	19
20	21	22	23	24	25	26
27	28	29	30	31		

2:◗ 9:○ 16:◐ 23:● 31:◗

September 2006

Su	Mo	Tu	We	Th	Fr	Sa
					1	2
3	4	5	6	7	8	9
10	11	12	13	14	15	16
17	18	19	20	21	22	23
24	25	26	27	28	29	30

7:○ 14:◐ 22:● 30:◗

October 2006

Su	Mo	Tu	We	Th	Fr	Sa
1	2	3	4	5	6	7
8	9	10	11	12	13	14
15	16	17	18	19	20	21
22	23	24	25	26	27	28
29	30	31				

7:○ 14:◐ 22:● 29:◗

November 2006

Su	Mo	Tu	We	Th	Fr	Sa
			1	2	3	4
5	6	7	8	9	10	11
12	13	14	15	16	17	18
19	20	21	22	23	24	25
26	27	28	29	30		

5:○ 12:◐ 20:● 28:◗

December 2006

Su	Mo	Tu	We	Th	Fr	Sa
					1	2
3	4	5	6	7	8	9
10	11	12	13	14	15	16
17	18	19	20	21	22	23
24	25	26	27	28	29	30
31						

5:○ 12:◐ 20:● 27:◗

CALENDAR — CANADA 2007

January 2007

Su	Mo	Tu	We	Th	Fr	Sa
	1	2	3	4	5	6
7	8	9	10	11	12	13
14	15	16	17	18	19	20
21	22	23	24	25	26	27
28	29	30	31			

3:○ 11:◑ 19:● 25:◐

February 2007

Su	Mo	Tu	We	Th	Fr	Sa
				1	2	3
4	5	6	7	8	9	10
11	12	13	14	15	16	17
18	19	20	21	22	23	24
25	26	27	28			

2:○ 10:◐ 17:● 24:◐

March 2007

Su	Mo	Tu	We	Th	Fr	Sa
				1	2	3
4	5	6	7	8	9	10
11	12	13	14	15	16	17
18	19	20	21	22	23	24
25	26	27	28	29	30	31

3:○ 12:◐ 19:● 25:◐

April 2007

Su	Mo	Tu	We	Th	Fr	Sa
1	2	3	4	5	6	7
8	9	10	11	12	13	14
15	16	17	18	19	20	21
22	23	24	25	26	27	28
29	30					

2:○ 10:◐ 17:● 24:◐

May 2007

Su	Mo	Tu	We	Th	Fr	Sa
		1	2	3	4	5
6	7	8	9	10	11	12
13	14	15	16	17	18	19
20	21	22	23	24	25	26
27	28	29	30	31		

2:○ 10:◐ 16:● 23:◐

June 2007

Su	Mo	Tu	We	Th	Fr	Sa
					1	2
3	4	5	6	7	8	9
10	11	12	13	14	15	16
17	18	19	20	21	22	23
24	25	26	27	28	29	30

1:○ 8:◐ 15:● 22:◐ 30:○

July 2007

Su	Mo	Tu	We	Th	Fr	Sa
1	2	3	4	5	6	7
8	9	10	11	12	13	14
15	16	17	18	19	20	21
22	23	24	25	26	27	28
29	30	31				

7:◐ 14:● 22:◐ 30:○

August 2007

Su	Mo	Tu	We	Th	Fr	Sa
			1	2	3	4
5	6	7	8	9	10	11
12	13	14	15	16	17	18
19	20	21	22	23	24	25
26	27	28	29	30	31	

5:◐ 12:● 20:◐ 28:○

September 2007

Su	Mo	Tu	We	Th	Fr	Sa
						1
2	3	4	5	6	7	8
9	10	11	12	13	14	15
16	17	18	19	20	21	22
23	24	25	26	27	28	29
30						

4:◐ 11:● 19:◐ 26:○

October 2007

Su	Mo	Tu	We	Th	Fr	Sa
	1	2	3	4	5	6
7	8	9	10	11	12	13
14	15	16	17	18	19	20
21	22	23	24	25	26	27
28	29	30	31			

3:◐ 11:● 19:◐ 26:○

November 2007

Su	Mo	Tu	We	Th	Fr	Sa
				1	2	3
4	5	6	7	8	9	10
11	12	13	14	15	16	17
18	19	20	21	22	23	24
25	26	27	28	29	30	

1:◐ 9:● 17:◐ 24:○

December 2007

Su	Mo	Tu	We	Th	Fr	Sa
						1
2	3	4	5	6	7	8
9	10	11	12	13	14	15
16	17	18	19	20	21	22
23	24	25	26	27	28	29
30	31					

1:◐ 9:● 17:◐ 24:○ 31:◐

Calendar—Canada 2008

January 2008

Su	Mo	Tu	We	Th	Fr	Sa
		1	2	3	4	5
6	7	8	9	10	11	12
13	14	15	16	17	18	19
20	21	22	23	24	25	26
27	28	29	30	31		

8:● 15:◑ 22:○ 30:◐

February 2008

Su	Mo	Tu	We	Th	Fr	Sa
					1	2
3	4	5	6	7	8	9
10	11	12	13	14	15	16
17	18	19	20	21	22	23
24	25	26	27	28	29	

7:● 14:◑ 21:○ 29:◐

March 2008

Su	Mo	Tu	We	Th	Fr	Sa
						1
2	3	4	5	6	7	8
9	10	11	12	13	14	15
16	17	18	19	20	21	22
23	24	25	26	27	28	29
30	31					

7:● 14:◑ 21:○ 29:◐

April 2008

Su	Mo	Tu	We	Th	Fr	Sa
		1	2	3	4	5
6	7	8	9	10	11	12
13	14	15	16	17	18	19
20	21	22	23	24	25	26
27	28	29	30			

6:● 12:◑ 20:○ 28:◐

May 2008

Su	Mo	Tu	We	Th	Fr	Sa
				1	2	3
4	5	6	7	8	9	10
11	12	13	14	15	16	17
18	19	20	21	22	23	24
25	26	27	28	29	30	31

5:● 12:◑ 20:○ 28:◐

June 2008

Su	Mo	Tu	We	Th	Fr	Sa
1	2	3	4	5	6	7
8	9	10	11	12	13	14
15	16	17	18	19	20	21
22	23	24	25	26	27	28
29	30					

3:● 10:◑ 18:○ 26:◐

July 2008

Su	Mo	Tu	We	Th	Fr	Sa
		1	2	3	4	5
6	7	8	9	10	11	12
13	14	15	16	17	18	19
20	21	22	23	24	25	26
27	28	29	30	31		

3:● 10:◑ 18:○ 25:◐

August 2008

Su	Mo	Tu	We	Th	Fr	Sa
					1	2
3	4	5	6	7	8	9
10	11	12	13	14	15	16
17	18	19	20	21	22	23
24	25	26	27	28	29	30
31						

1:● 8:◑ 16:○ 24:◐ 30:●

September 2008

Su	Mo	Tu	We	Th	Fr	Sa
	1	2	3	4	5	6
7	8	9	10	11	12	13
14	15	16	17	18	19	20
21	22	23	24	25	26	27
28	29	30				

7:◑ 15:○ 22:◐ 29:●

October 2008

Su	Mo	Tu	We	Th	Fr	Sa
			1	2	3	4
5	6	7	8	9	10	11
12	13	14	15	16	17	18
19	20	21	22	23	24	25
26	27	28	29	30	31	

7:◑ 14:○ 21:◐ 28:●

November 2008

Su	Mo	Tu	We	Th	Fr	Sa
						1
2	3	4	5	6	7	8
9	10	11	12	13	14	15
16	17	18	19	20	21	22
23	24	25	26	27	28	29
30						

6:◑ 13:○ 19:◐ 27:●

December 2008

Su	Mo	Tu	We	Th	Fr	Sa
	1	2	3	4	5	6
7	8	9	10	11	12	13
14	15	16	17	18	19	20
21	22	23	24	25	26	27
28	29	30	31			

5:◑ 12:○ 19:◐ 27:●

Index